The Model of the Corporate Compliance Officer

Katrin Kanzenbach

The Model of the Corporate Compliance Officer

PETER LANG

Bibliographic Information published by the Deutsche Nationalbibliothek
The Deutsche Nationalbibliothek lists this publication in the Deutsche Nationalbibliografie; detailed bibliographic data is available online at http://dnb.d-nb.de.

Library of Congress Cataloging-in-Publication Data
A CIP catalog record for this book has been applied for at the Library of Congress.

Figure on the cover
Credits: Shutterstock/Mentari Merah Studio

ISBN 978-3-631-79821-8 (Print)
E-ISBN 978-3-631-79867-6 (E-PDF)
E-ISBN 978-3-631-79868-3 (EPUB)
E-ISBN 978-3-631-79869-0 (MOBI)
DOI 10.3726/b16011

Peter Lang – Berlin · Bern · Bruxelles · New York · Oxford · Warszawa · Wien

This publication has been peer reviewed.

www.peterlang.com

Acknowledgements

This book is dedicated to the unforgotten memory of my grandfather, who loved me the most. I am very grateful to my husband and my son for their understanding and their patience with me during the process of writing. They both were an invaluable resource of support.

Table of Contents

List of Abbreviations

ABA	American Bar Association, US
ACC	Association of Corporate Counsel, US
ADA	American with Disabilities Act, US
AIFM	Alternative Investment Funds Manager
AktG	German Stock Corporation Act
APER	Code of Practice for Approved Persons, UK
ArbGG	Labor Court Act, Germany
BAG	German Federal Labor Court
Bafin	Federal Banking Supervisory Authority, Germany
BGBI	Federal Law Gazette, Germany
BCM	Professional Association of Compliance Manager
BDCO	German Federal Association of Compliance Officers
BAG	Federal Labor Court, Germany
BGB	German Civil Code
BGH	Federal Supreme Court, Germany
BVerfG	Federal Constitutional Court, Germany
CA	Companies Act, UK
CAA	Clean Air Act, US
CCO	Chief Compliance Officer
Ch.	Chapter
CO	Compliance Officer
CECO	Chief Ethics and Compliance Officer
CEO	Chief Executive Officer
CF	Control Function
CFO	Chief Financial Officer
CFR	Code of Federal Regulations
CJA	Criminal Justice Act, UK
CJS	Corpus Juris Secundum
CLRG	Company Law Review Group, UK
COO	Chief Operation Officer
COSO	Committee of Sponsoring Organizations of the Treadway Commission, US
CMS	Compliance Management System
CRA	Civil Right Act, US
CRD	Capital Requirements Directive IV
CRR	Capital Requirements Regulation
CSJ	Corpus Juris Secundum
C-Suite	Senior executive board members
DCGK	German Corporate Governance Codex
DHHS	Department of Health and Human Services

DII	Defense Industry Initiative, US
DOJ	Department of Justice, US
DPA	Deferred Prosecution Agreement
DRiG	The German Judiciary Act
DTR	Disclosure and Transparency Rules
EBEF	European Business Ethics Forum
ECHR	European Convention of Human Rights
EO	Ethics Officer
ECOA	Ethics and Compliance Officers Association, US
ERC	Ethics Resource Center
EPA	Environmental Protection Agency, US
GC	General Counsel, US
GG	Basic Law for the Federal Republic of Germany
GVG	Courts Constitution Act, Germany
FCA	Financial Conduct Authority, UK former the FSA
FCPA	Foreign Corrupt Practices Act of 1977, US
FINRA	Financial Industry Regulatory Authority
FSA	Financial Services Authority, UK from 2000 to 2013
FSGO	Federal Sentencing Guidelines for Organizations, US
FSMA	Financial Services and Markets Act, UK
FTSE	Financial Times Stock Exchange, UK
FRCP	Federal Rules of Civil Procedure, US
HCCA	Health Care Compliance Association, US
HGB	German Commercial Code
ICA	Interstate Commerce Act, US
ICC	Interstate Commerce Commission, US
ICSA	Institute for Chartered Secretaries, UK
IDW	Institute of Public Auditors, Germany
IMRO	Investment Management Regulatory Organization Ltd., UK
JM	Justice Manual, US
KonTraG	German Corporate Control and Transparency Act
KSchG	Protection against Unfair Dismissal Act
KWG	German Banking Act
LAUTRO	Life Assurance and Unit Trust Regulatory Organization, UK
MAComp	Minimum requirements for compliance
MBCA	Model Business Corporation Act, US
NGO	Non-Government Organisation
NPA	Non-prosecution Agreement
NYSE	New York Stock Exchange
NASDAQ	National Association of Securities Dealers Automated Quotations
OCIE	Office of Compliance Inspections and Examinations
OFT	Office of Fair Trading, UK
OIG	Office of Inspector General, US
OWiG	Act on Regulatory Offences, Germany

PCAOB	Public Company Accounting Oversight Board, US
PRA	Prudential Regulation Authority, UK
REA	Rules Enabling Act, US
SCCE	Society of Corporate Compliance and Ethics
SE	Societas Europaea
SEC	US Securities and Exchange Commission, the Commission
SIB	Act to the Securities and Investments Board, UK
SFO	Serious Fraud Office, UK
SME	Small-Medium Sized Enterprise
SMF	Senior Management Function, UK
SOX	Sarbanes-Oxley Act, US
SRA	Sentencing Reform Act, US
SRA	Solicitors Regulation Authority, UK
SRO's	Self-regulatory organizations
StGB	German Criminal Code
UCC	Uniform Commercial Code, US
UK	United Kingdom
UKSC	United Kingdom Supreme Court
US	United States
USC	United State Code
USSC	United State Sentencing Commission
USSG	United State Sentencing Guidelines
Usu.	usually
QBD	Queen's Bench Division; UK
V-C	Vice-Chancellor
VerbStrG-E	Draft of a Criminal Code of Organizations, Germany
WpHG	German Securities Trading Act
WpDVerVO	German Regulations specifying Rules of Conduct and Organizational Requirements
ZPO	German Code of Civil Procedure

Table of Cases

US

Alpert v. 28 Williams St. Corp., 63 N.Y.2d 557 (N.Y. 1984), 557 (1984).
Am. Fed. of Tele. & Radio v. Storer Broadcasting (6th Cir. 1984), 745 F.2d 392.
Aronson v. Lewis, 473 A.2d 805 (1984).
Arthur Andersen LLP v. United States, 544 U.S. 696 (2005).
Barnes v. Andrews, 208 App. Div. 856 (S.D.N.Y. 1924), 208 856 (1924).
Bernstein v. Starrett City, Inc., (2d Dept. N.Y. 2003), 303 A.D.2d 530 (2003).
Bowles v. Ruppel, (3d Cir. 1946), 157 F.2d 944 (1946).
Kennedy, Burlington Industries, Inc. v. Ellerth, 123 F.3d 490 524 U.S. 742 97–569 (1998).
Carlson v. Metz, (Neb. 1995), 532 N.W.2d 631 (1995).
Cede & Co. v. Technicolor, Inc., 634 A.2d 345 (Del. 1993), 634 A.2d 345 (1993).
CTS Corp. v. Dynamics Corp. of America, (U.S. Supreme Court), 481 69 (1987).
Galdi v. Berg, (D. Del. 1973), 359 F. Supp. 698 (1973).
Gantler v. Stephens, 965 A.2d 695 (Del. 2009), 965 A.2d 695 (2009).
Graham v. Allis-Chalmers Manufacturing Company, 188 A.2d 125 (Del. 1963).
Grimes v. Donald, 673 A.2d 1207 (Del. 1996), 673 A.2d 1207 (1996).
Guth v. Loft, Inc., 5 A.2d 503 (Del 1939), A.2d 5 503 (1939).
Hampshire Group, Limited v. Kuttner, C.A. No. 3607-VCS (Del. Ch. 2010), (2010).
Highland Select Equity v. Motient Corp., (Del. Ch. 2006), 906 A.2d 156 (2006),
In re Caremark International Inc. Derivative Litigation, 698 A.2d 959 (Del. Ch. 1996).
In re Dow Chemical Company Derivative Litigation, No. 4349-CC (Del. Ch. 2010), (2010).
Neal Batson, In re Enron Corporation, et al., Case No. 01-16034 (AJG) (S.D.N.Y.),
In re John H. Gutfreund, et al. | Exchange Act Release No. 34-31554, 51 SEC 93 (1992).
In re Massey Energy Company (Del. Ch. 2011), C.A. No. 5430-VCSC.A.
In re The Goldman Sachs Group, Inc., WL 4826104 (2011).
In re Walt Disney Co. Derivative Litigation, (Del. 2006), 906 A.2d 27 (2006).
In re Walt Disney Co. Derivative Litig., (Del. Ch. 2004), (2004).
In re World Health Alternatives, Inc., 385 B.R. 576 (B.R. Del. 2008), (2008).
Ironworkers District Council of Philadelphia & Vicinity Retirement & Pension Plan v. Andreotti (Del. Ch. 2015), C.A. No. 9714-VCG (2015).
Leddy v. Standard Drywall, Inc., (2d Cir. 1989), 875 F.2d 383 (1989).
Lowell Hoit & Co. v. Detig, 50 N.E.2d (111. App. Ct. 1943), 50 N.E.2d.
Mason v. State 361 Ark. 357 S.W.3d 869 (Ark. 2005), (2005).
Marbury v. Madison, 5 U.S. 137 (1803).
Markow v. Synageva Biopharma Corp., (S.C. Del. 2016), (2016).
Mayers v. Stone Castle Partners, LLC, No. 650410/2013 (U.S. N.Y. 2014), (2014).

Meinhard v. Salmon 249 N.Y. 458, 164 N.E. 54, (1928).
Merritt-Chapman & Scott Corporation v. Wolfson, 321 A.2d 138, (Del. Super. Ct. 1974).
Morrison v. Nat'l Austl. Bank Ltd., 130 S. Ct. 2869, (2010).
Murphy v. Am. Home Prod., 58 N.Y.2d 293 (1983).
Myers & Chapman, Incorporated v. Thomas G. Evans, 374 S.E.2d 385 (N.C. 1988).
Payne v. Western & Atlantic Railroad Company, 81 Tenn. 507 (1884).
Real v. Driscoll Strawberry Associates Inc. D J, F.2d 748 603 (1979).
Safeway Stores, Inc. v. National Union Fire Insurance Company of Pittsburgh, (9th Cir. 1995), 64 F.3d 1282 (1995).
Schreiber v. Pennzoil Co., 419 A.2d 952 (Del. Ch. 1980), (1980).
SEC v. Dav.id P. Turner and Ousama M. Naaman, No. 10-cv-1309 (2010).
Secretary of Labor United States Department of Labor v. Lauritzen, F2d 1529 (1987).
Smith v. Van Gorkom, (Del. 1985), 488 A.2d 858 (1985).
Stone v. Ritter, 911 A.2d 362 (Del. 2006), 911 A.2d 362 (2006).
Sullivan v. Harnisch, 19 N.Y.3d 259, 19 N.Y.3d 259 (2012).
Tapia v. United States, 131 S. Ct. 2382, 180 L. Ed. 2d 357, (2011).
Troy Robillard v. Asahi Chem. Indus. Co., (Conn. Super. Ct. 1995), 44 Conn. Sup. 510.
United States of America v. American Radiator & Standard Sanitary Corp., (3d Cir. 1970), 433 F.2d 174 (1970).
United States v. Booker, 543 U.S. 220 (2005).
United States v. Dotterweich, 320 U.S. 277, No. 5 (1943).
United States v. Ionia Management, S.A. 537 F. Supp.2d 321 (D. Conn. 2008), (2008).
United States v. Kay, 513 F.3d 432 (5th Cir. 2007), (2007).
United States & SEC v. KPMG Siddharta Siddharta & Harsono, et al., (S.D. Tex. 2001) (2001).
United States v. LBS Bank-New York, Inc., (E.D.PA. 1990), 757 F. Supp. 496 (E.D. Pa. 1990), Crim. A. No. 88-00516-05 (1990).
United States v. Microsoft Corp., 253 F.3d 34 49 (2001).
United States before the SEC v. Pekin Singer Strauss Asset Management Inc., et al., Release No. 31688 (2015).
United States before the SEC v. SFX Financial Advisory Management Enterprises, Inc. and Eugene S. Mason, No. 3-16591 (2015).
United States v. Potter, 463 F.3d 9 (1st Cir. 2006), (2006).
United States v. Siemens Aktiengesellschaft, 08-cr-00367-RJL, (2008).
United States v. Siemens Aktiengesellschaft | Plea Agreement 15th December 2008, 08–cr–00367–RJL, (2008).
United States v. Siemens Aktiengesellschaft | Statement of Offense, 08-cr-00367-RJL, (2008).
United States v. Socony-Vacuum Oil Company, 310 U.S. 150 (1940), No. 346 150 (1940).
United States v. Trenton Potteries Company, 273 U.S. 392 (1927), No. 27 392 (1927).
United States v. Volkswagen AG, Audi AG, 16-CR-20394, (2016).
U.S. v. Microsemi Corp., No. 1:08 CV 1311, (2008).
U.S. Department of the Treasury v. Haider, No. 15-1518 (D. Minn. 2016), (2016).

Wieder v. Skala, 80 N.Y.2d 628 (1992).
Wilson v. United States (8th Cir. 1993), 989 F.2d 953 (1993).

UK

Aberdeen Railway Company v. Blakie, Brothers [1854] UKHL 1, Macqueen 461, 461 (1854).
*AG for Hong Kong v. Reid [*1993] UKPC 2, Privy Council Appeal No. 44 of 1992 (1993).
Agip (Africa) Ltd. v. Kingsley & Ors [1990] EWCA Civ 2 (1990), [1991] Ch 547, (1990).
AMG Global Nominees (Private) Ltd v. Africa Resources Ltd [2008] EWCA Civ 1262, (2008).
AMG Global Nominees (Private) Ltd v. SMM Holdings Ltd & Anor. [2008] EWHC 221 (Ch), (2008).
Anglo Petroleum Ltd & Anor v. TFB (Mortgages) Ltd [2007] EWCA Civ 456, (2007).
Armitage v. Nurse & Ors [1997] 2 All ER 705, [1998] Ch 241, [1997] EWCA Civ 1279, [1997] Pens LR 51, [1997] 3 WLR 1046, (1997).
Bairstow & Ors v. Queens Moat Houses Plc. [2001] 2 BCLC 531, [2001] EWCA Civ 712, [2002] BCC 91, (2001).
Barker v. Corus UK Ltd, [2006] 2 AC 572; [2006] 3 All ER 785; [2006] 2 WLR 1027; 89 BMLR 1(2006).
Barnett, Hoares & Co v. South London Tramways Co [1887] 18 QBD, 815 (1887).
Belmont Finance Corporation v. Williams Furniture [1980] 1 AER, 393, (1980).
Brandeaux Advisers (UK) Ltd & Ors v. Chadwick [2010] EWHC 3241 (QB), (2010).
British Racing Drivers Club Ltd v Hextall Erskine & Co, [1996] 3 All E.R. 667, [1996] B.C.C. 727, [1997] 1 B.C.L.C. 182, [1996] P.N.L.R. 523, (1996).
Burgin & Anor v Commission of Police for the Metropolis & Ors [2011] EWHC 1835, CO/5723/2010, CO/6227/2010 (2011).
Carmichael and Another v. National Power Plc [1999] UKHL 47; [1999] 1 WLR 2042; [1999] 4 All ER 897, (1999).
*Collier v. Sunday Referee Publishing Co Ltd [*1940] 2 KB 647 [1940] 4 All ER 234, (1940).
Commerzbank AG v. Keen [2006] EWCA Civ 1536, (2006).
Corporate Development Partners Llc v. E-Relationship Marketing Ltd [2007] EWHC 436 (Ch), (2007).
Cossington v. C2C Rail Ltd [2013] UKEAT 0053_13_1209, (2013).
Cox v. Cox & Anor [2006] EWHC 1077 (Ch), (2006).
Darker and Others and Chief Constable of The West Midlands Police, [2001] 1 AC 435; [2000] 4 All ER 193[2000] 3 WLR 747 (2000).
Dovey v. Cory [1901] AC 477, 70 LJ Ch 753, (1901).
Driver v. Air India Ltd. [2011] EWCA Civ 830, (2011).
Estafnous v. London & Leeds Business Centres Ltd. [2009] EWHC 1308 (Ch), (2009).

Farrow v. Wilson (1869) LR 4, CP 744,.
Ferguson v. Wilson (LJJ 1866) LR 2 Ch App 77, 36 LJ Ch 67 (1866).
Green v. Bestobell Industries Ltd [1982] WAR 1, (1982).
Gyrus Group Ltd & Anor, R v. [2014] EW Misc B57 (CC), (2014).
Hamid (t/a Hamid Properties) v. Francis Bradshaw Partnership [2013] EWCA Civ 470, (2013).
Harold Holdsworth & Co (Wakefield) Ltd v. Caddies [1955] 1 WLR 352, (1955).
HM Attorney General v. Blake [1997] EWCA Civ 3008 (16th December, 1997), (1997).
Holland v Revenue and Customs & Anor [2011] Bus LR 111, [2010] UKSC 51, [2011] 1 All ER 430, [2010] WLR 2793, [2010] 1 WLR 2793, [2011] BCC 1, [2010] STI 3074, (2010).
Howard Smith Limited v. Ampol Petroleum Limited and Others [1974] 2 WLR 689, 118 SJLB 330, [1974] AC 821, [1974] UKPC 3, [1974] 1 All ER 1126, (1974).
In re Exchange Banking Company (1882) LR 21 Ch D 519, (1882).
Johnson v. Gore Wood & Co. [2000] UKHL 65; [2001] 1 All ER 481; [2001] 2 WLR 72 (2000).
Lister v. Romford Ice and Cold Storage [1957] AC 555, (1957).
Market Investigations Ltd v. Minister of Social Security [1969] 2 QB 173, (1969).
Mattu v. The University Hospitals of Coventry and Warwickshire NHS Trust [2012] EWCA Civ 641, (2012).
McClelland v. Northern Ireland General Health Services [1957] 1 WLR 594, [1957] 2 All ER 129, (1957).
McKenzie, R v. Director of the SFO [2016] EWHC 102, CO/4888/2015 (2016).
Moore v. Garwood (1849) 4 Exch. 681, (1849).
Mothew (t/a Stapley & Co) v. Bristol & West Building Society [1996] 4 All ER 698, [1998] Ch 1[1996] EWCA Civ 533, [1997] PNLR 11, [1997] 2 WLR 436, (1996).
Panorama Developments (Guildford) Ltd v. Fidelis Furnishing Fabrics Ltd [1971] 2 QB 711, [1971] 3 All ER 16,.
Paros Plc v. Worldlink Group Plc [2012] EWHC 394 (Comm), (2012).
Percival v. Wright [1902] 2 Ch. 401, (1902).
Ranger v. Brown [1978] ICR 603, (1978).
Ravjani & Ors, R. v. [2012] EWCA Crim 2519, (2012).
Re a Company [1980] Ch 138, [1980] 2 WLR 241, (1980).
Ready Mixed Concrete (South East) Ltd v. Minister of Pensions and National Insurance [1967] EWHC QB 3, 497 (1967).
Re Barings plc (No. 5) [1999] 1 BCLC, [2000] 1 BCLC 523, 433 (1999).
Re Chez Nico Ltd., [1992] BCLC 192 (1991).
Re Elgindata Ltd [1991] BCLC 959, (1991).
Regal (Hastings) Ltd v. Gulliver [1942] 1 All ER 378, [1967] 2 AC 134, [1942] UKHL 1, (1942).
Re Sevenoaks Stationers (Retail) Ltd [1991] BCLC 325., (1991).
Robertson v. Newcastle Breweries Ltd [2000] EAT 1373 99 1804, (2000).
Romford Ice & Cold Storage Co v. Lister [1956] UKHL 6, (1956).
R v. Boal (CA 1992), [1992] QB 591, [1992] 2 WLR 890, (1992).

R v. Innospec Ltd [2010] EW Misc 7 (EWCC), (2010).
R v. Patel (Munir Yakub) [2012] EWCA Crim 1243, (2012).
Said v. Butt [1920] 3 KB 497, (1920).
Salomon v. Salomon [1896] UKHL 1, [1897] AC 22, [1897] A.C. 22-58 22 (1896).
Soma Oil And Gas Ltd, R v. Director of the SFO [2016] EWHC 2471, (2016).
Sosa v. Alvarez-Machain et al., 542 U.S. 692 (2004).
Standard Chartered Bank v. Pakistan National Shipping Corp [2002] UKHL 43, [2003] 1 AC 959, (2002).
Stevenson, Jordan and Harrison Ltd v. MacDonald and Evans [1952] 1 TLR 101, (1952).
Tchenguiz & Anor v. Director of the Serious Fraud Office [2014] EWHC 1315, (2014).
Tesco Supermarkets Ltd v. Nattrass [1971] 2 All ER 127, [1971] 2 WLR 1166, [1971] UKHL 1, 69 LGR 403, [1972] AC 153, 1 (1971).
Troutbeck SA v. White & Anor [2013] EWCA Civ 1171, (2013).
UBS AG (London Branch) & Anor v. Kommunale Wasserwerke Leipzig GMBH [2014] EWHC 3615, 2010 Folio 505 (2014).
Weatherford UK Ltd v. Forbes [2011] UKEAT 0038 11 2012, (2011).
Welton v. Saffery (HL 1897) [1897}, 299 AC 66 (1897).
West & Anor, R v. [2016] EWCA Crim 742, 201500057 B5 (2016).
Willford, R (On the Application Of) v. Financial Services Authority [2013] EWCA Civ 677, (2013).
William Hill Organisation Ltd v. Tucker [1998] EWCA Civ 615, (1998).

Germany

ArbG Berlin, 18.2.2010-38 Ca 12879/09 - Kündigung einer leitenden Compliance-Mitarbeiterin, 2010 CCZ 158–160 (2010).
BAG, 09.06.1993-5 AZR 123/92-Arbeitsrechtlicher Status eines Fernsehmitarbeiters, 1994 NZA 169–171 (1993).
BAG, 13.01.1983 - 5 AZR 156/82 Rundfunkfreiheit und freie Mitarbeiter, (1983).
BAG, 13.11.1991 - 7 AZR 31/91 - Dozentin in Schulabschlußkursen, 1992 NZA 1125–1129 (1991).
BAG, 15.02.2012-10 AZR 301/10-Arbeitnehmereigenschaft bei ergänzendem Aufbauunterricht in einer Justizvollzugs-anstalt, 2012 NZA 731 (2012).
BAG, 15.11.2012 - 8 AZR 705/11 - BGB § 611 Haftung des Arbeitnehmers No. 137, AP BGB § 611 Haftung des Arbeitnehmers No. 137 (2012).
BAG, 17.04.2013 - 10 AZR 272/12 - Arbeitnehmerstatus - Cutterin, 2013 NZA 903 (2013).
BAG, 18.1.2007 - 8 AZR 250/06 - Arbeitnehmerhaftung - Anspruch einer Bank gegen Wertpapierhändler, 2007 NZA 1230–1235 (2007).
BAG, 19.02.2002 - 1 ABR 26/01 (NZA) - Geltung einer Betriebsvereinbarung in einem Betriebsteil, (2002).
BAG, 20.03.2014 - 2 AZR 565/12, 2014 NJW 2219 (2014).

BAG, 20.11.2014 - 2 AZR 664/13, 2015 NZA 931 (2014).
BAG, 24.11.1987 - 8 AZR 524/82 - Haftung des Arbeitnehmers, 1988 NZA 579–584 (1987).
BAG GS, 27.09.1994 - GS 1/89 (A) - Haftung des Arbeitnehmers - Abkehr von der gefahrgeneigten Arbeit, 1994 NZA 1083–1086 (1994).
BGH, 6.3.2008 - 4 StR 669/07 - Werkstattleiters einer Transportbeton-spedition, NJW 1897–1899 (2008).
BGH, 6.7.1990 - 2 StR 549/89 - Strafrechtliche Produkthaftung - Lederspray-Entscheidung, NJW 2560–2569 (1990).
BGH, 6. 12. 2001 - 1 StR 215/01 - Untreue durch Zuwendungen aus dem Vermögen einer Aktiengesellschaft, NJW 1585–1589 (2001).
BGH, 7.12.2009 - II ZR 63/08 - Beschränkung der Revisionszulassung auf aktienrechtlichen Beschlussanfechtungs-grund, 2009 NZG 618–619 (2009).
BGH, 10. 7.2012 - VI ZR 341/10 - Keine Garantenpflicht von Vorstandsmitgliedern oder Geschäftsführern gegenüber Dritten zur Verhinderung von Vermögensschäden, NJW 3439–3443 (2012).
BGH, 15.7.1986 - 4 StR 301/86 - Garantenstellung eines Ordnungsamtsleiters, NJW 199 (1986).
BGH, 15.11.2001 - 1 StR 185/01 - Anhaltspunkte für strafbare Untreue eines Sparkassenvorstands bei Verletzung der nach KWG normierten Pflicht zum Verlangen nach Offenlegung der wirtschaftlichen Verhältnisse bei Kreditvergabe, 172–179 (2001).
BGH, 16.07.1993 - 2 StR 294/93 - Zumutbarkeit bei Erfolgsabwendungspflicht, NStZ 29 (1993).
BGH, 17.7.2009 - 5 StR 394/08 - Überhöhte Straßenreinigungsentgelte, 2009 NJW 3173–3177 (2009).
BGH, 20.10.2011 - 4 StR 71/11-BGH: Garantenstellung des Geschäftsherrn; Betriebsbezogenheit einer Straftat, 2012 NJW 157–160 (2011).
BGH, 21.12.2005 - 3 StR 470/04 -, BGHSt 50, 331-346 Mannesmann/Vodafone, NStZ 2006, 214.
BGH, 26.04.2006 - 2 StR 515/05 - Verurteilung eines Landrats wegen Untreue, NStZ-RR 307 (2006).
BGH, 29.8.2008 - 2 StR 587/07 - Siemens Case, Bildung verdeckter Kassen als Untreue, NStZ 95–100 (2008).
BGH, 31.1.2002 - 4 StR 289/01 - Wuppertaler Schwebebahn, NJW 1887–1889 (2002).
BVerfG, 23.6.2010 - 2 BvR 2559/08 - Verfassungsrechtliche Anforderungen an den strafrechtlichen Untreuetatbestand, 1143–1156 (2010).
KG, 27.9.2004 - 2 U 191/02 - Formale Anforderungen an fristlose Kündigung des Bankvorstands, 1165–1168 (2004).
LAG Hamm, 15. 7. 2014, 12. 2. 2014 - 7 Sa 94/14 ArbG, 3 Ca 176/13 - Abteilung der Konzernobergesellschaft, 2015 CCZ 94–96 (2014).
LAG Rheinland-Pfalz, 26.02.2016 - Aktenzeichen 1 Sa 358/15, 2016 FD-ArbR 378175 (Ls.) (2016).
LArbG Hamm, 15.07.2014 - 7 Sa 94/14, (2014).

LG Berlin, 3.7.2002 - 2 O 358/01 - Zulässige fristlose Kündigung eines Bankvorstands bei mangelhaftem Risikomanagement, 969–972 (2002).
LG Frankfurt a. M., 22.4.2015 - 5/12 Qs 1/15 - Angestellter oder Beauftragter, 2015 NStZ-RR 215–216 (2015).
LG München I, 04.10.2007 - 5 Kls 563 Js EGMR Aktenzeichen 45994/07, 2008 Beck RS 1235 (2007).
LG München I, 5.4.2007 - 5 HK O 15964/06 - Hohes Anfechtungsrisiko für Entlastungsbeschlüsse bei fehlender Doku-mentation, NZG 2008, 319 70–73 (2007).
LG München I, 10.12.2013 - 5 HK O 1387/10 - Pflichten des Vorstands einer AG, 2014 NZG 345–349 (2013).
OLG Celle, 15.3.2000 - 9 U 209/99 - GF bei nicht (wirksam) entrichteter Stammeinlage, NZG 1178–1179 (2000).
OLG Celle, 28.5.2008 - 9 U 184/07 - Pflichtverletzung des Vorstandes wegen unvertretbarem Risiko, NZG 2008, 669 (2008).
OLG Hamm, 16.07.2003 - 4 Ss (OWi) 373/03 - wistra 2003, 469 – Organisationsverschulden des Betriebsinhabers, 469 (2003).
OLG München, 23.1.2008 - 7 U 3668/07 - Folgen der Nichtabgabe einer Entsprechenserklärung nach § 161 AktG, 2008 NZG 337–339 (2008).
OLG Stuttgart, 7.9.1976 - 3 Ss 526/76 - Überwachungspflicht des Betriebsinhabers, 1977 NJW 1410 (1976).

Table of Statutes

AKTIENGESETZ (AKTG) | GERMAN STOCK CORPORATION ACT, BGBI. I, 1089 (1965).

ALLGEMEINES GLEICHBEHANDLUNGSGESETZ (AGG) | GENERAL ACT ON EQUAL TREATMENT, BGBI. I p. 1897, 1910 (2006).

AMERICANS WITH DISABILITIES ACT (ADA), 42 USC § 12101 PUB. L. 114-38 (1990).

AN ACT TO ESTABLISH THE JUDICIAL COURTS OF THE UNITED STATES, JUDICIARY ACT OF 1789 (1789).

ARBEITSGERICHTSGESETZ (ARBGG) | LABOR COURT ACT, BGB I, 1267 (1953).

ARBEITSSCHUTZGESETZ (ARBSCHG) | ACT ON THE IMPLEMENTATION OF MEASURES OF OCCUPATIONAL SAFETY AND HEALTH TO ENCOURAGE IMPROVEMENTS IN THE SAFETY AND HEALTH PROTECTION OF WORKERS AT WORK, BGBl. I, p. 1246 (1996).

ARBEITSZEITGESETZ (ARBZG) | WORKING TIME ACT, BGBI. I p. 1170, 1171 (1994).

BANKING ACT 1987 (REPEALED), c. 22 (1987).

BANKING ACT OF 1933, PUB.L. 73–66 48 Stat. 162 (1933).

BANK SECRECY ACT OF 1970, PUB. LAW 91-508, 31 USC § 1051 84 Stat. 1114-2 (1970).

BASIC LAW FOR THE FEDERAL REPUBLIC OF GERMANY (GG), BASIC LAW OF THE FEDERAL REPUBLIC OF GERMANY (1949).

BERUFSBILDUNGSGESETZ (BBIG) | VOCATIONAL TRAINING ACT, BGBI. I, p. 1112 last amended August 2015 p. 1474, 1538 (1969).

BUNDESDATENSCHUTZGESETZ | FEDERAL DATA PROTECTION ACT (BDSG), BGBI. I, 201 (1978).

BUNDES-IMMISSIONSSCHUTZGESETZ (BIMSCHG) | FEDERAL IMMISSION CONTROL ACT, BGBI. I, p. 721 (1974).

BÜRGERLICHES GESETZBUCH (BGB) | GERMAN CIVIL CODE, GERMAN CIVIL CODE (1896) Aug. 18. 1896; last amended by Article 4 para. 5 of the Act of 1 October 2013, BGBI. I p. 3719 (1900).

CALIFORNIA CORPORATION CODE (CORP), CAL. CORP. CODE (1947).

CIVIL RIGHTS ACT 1964 (CRA), PUB. L. 114-38, 42 USC §§ 2000E–17 78 Stat. 253 (1964).

CLEAN AIR ACT (1963), PUB. LAW 88-206, 42 USC 77 Stat. 392 (1963).

CLEAN WATER ACT (1972), PUB. LAW 92-500, 33 USC §§ 1251–1387 86 Stat. 816 (1972).

CODE NAPOLÉON, CODE CIVIL (FRANCE) CODE CIVIL DES FRANÇAIS (1804).

COMMISSION DIRECTIVE 2006/73/EC, ABI. 2006 L 241/26 (2006).

COMPANIES ACT 1862, 25 & 26 Vict. c. 89 (1862).

COMPANIES ACT 1948, c. 38 (1948).

COMPANIES ACT 1985, c. 6 (1985).

COMPANIES ACT 1989, c. 40 (1989).

COMPANIES ACT 2006, COMPANIES ACT 2006 c. 46 (2006).

COMPANIES (AUDIT, INVESTIGATIONS AND COMMUNITY ENTERPRISE) ACT 2004, c. 27 (2004).

Companies (Consolidation) Act 1908, c. 69 (1908).
Company Directors' Disqualifi-cation Act 1986, c. 46 (1986).
Consolidated versions of the Treaty on European Union and the Treaty on the Functioning of the European Union, OJ EC No. C 115 (2009).
Consolidated versions of the Treaty on European Union and the Treaty on the Functioning of the European Union, C326/01-C326/407 (2012).
Consumer Protection Act 1987, c. 43 (1987).
Council Directive 89/654/EEC of 30 November 1989 concerning the minimum safety and health requirements for the workplace (first individual directive within the meaning of Article 16 (1) of Directive 89/391/EEC), L393/1-393/12 (1989).
Council Directive 91/533/EEC of 14 October 1991 on an employer's obligation to inform employees of the conditions applicable to the contract or employment relationship, L 288/32 (1991).
Council Directive 93/22/EEC of 10 May 1993 on investment services in the securities field, L 141, 0027-0046 (1993).
Crime and Courts Act 2013, c. 22 (2013).
Criminal Justice Act 1987, c. 38 (1987).
Criminal Justice Act 1993, c. 36 (1993).
Delaware Code, Del. Code Ann.
Deutsches Richtergesetz (DRiG) | The German Judiciary Act BGBI. I, p. 1665 (1962).
Directive 2000/31/EC OF THE EUROPEAN PARLIAMENT AND OF THE COUNCIL- E-commerce - standard EU rules, 32000L0031 (2000).
Directive 2002/14/EC of the European Parliament and of the Council of 11 March 2002 establishing a general framework for informing and consulting employees in the European Community - Joint declaration of the European Parliament, the Council and the Commission on employee representation, L080/29-080/34 (2002).
Directive 2002/87/EC of the European Parliament and of the Council of 16 December 2002 on the supplementary supervision of credit institutions, insurance under-takings and investment firms, L 035, 0001-0027; (2003).
Directive 2003/88/EC of the European Parliament and of the Council of 4 November 2003 concerning certain aspects of the organisation of working time, OJ L 299, pp. 9–19 (2003).
Directive 2004/39/EC of the European Parliament and of the Council on markets in financial instruments amending Council Directives 85/611/EEC and 93/6/EEC and Directive 2000/12/EC (MIFID 2004), 32004L0039 L 241/1 (2006).
Directive 2006/46/EC of the European Parliament and of the Council of 14 June 2006 amending Council Directives 78/660/EEC on the annual accounts of certain types of companies, 83/349/EEC on consolidated accounts, 86/635/EEC on the annual accounts and consolidated accounts

of banks and other financial institutions and 91/674/EEC on the annual accounts and consolidated accounts of insurance undertakings, OJ L 224 (2006).
Directive 2006/54/EC of the European Parliament and of the Council of 5 July 2006 on the implementation of the principle of equal opportunities and equal treatment of men and women in matters of employment and occupation (recast), OJ L 204 23–36 (2006).
Directive 2011/61/EU of the European Parliament and of the Council on Alternative Investment Fund Managers and amending Directives 2003/41/EC and 2009/65/EC and Regulations (EC) No 1060/2009 and (EU) No 1095/201, OJ L 174 p. 1 (2011).
Directive 2013/36/EU of the European Parliament and of the Council (CRD IV Directive), ABI. 2013 L 176/338 (2013).
Directive 2014/56/EU of the European Parliament and of the Council amending Directive 2006/43/EC on statutory audits of annual accounts and consolidated accounts, L 158/196 (2014).
Directive on Investment Services 93/22/EEC, OJ 141 of 11.6.1993 (1993).
Dodd–Frank Wall Street Reform and Consumer Protection Act (2010), Pub. L. 111–203, § 929-Z, 15 USC § 78o 124 Stat. 1376, 1871 (2010).
Employee Retirement Income Security Act (ERISA), Pub. L. 114-38, 29 USC §§ 1001-1461 U.S.C. 88 Stat. 829 (1974).
Employment Act 2008, c. 28 (2009).
Employment Rights Act 1996, c.18 (1996).
Enterprise and Regulatory Reform Act 2013, c.24 (2013).
Equality Act 2010, c. 15 (2010).
Fair Labor Standards Act of 1938 (FSLA), Pub. L. 114-38, 29 USC, §§ 201-219 Chapter 8 (1938).
Financial Services Act 1986, Financial Services Act 1986 c. 60 (1986), Repealed (2001).
Financial Services and Markets Act (2000), c. 8 ff (2000).
Financial Services (Banking Reform) Act 2013, c. 33 (2013).
Florida Business Coordination Act, Fla. Stat. Ann. (2015) chap. 606.
Foreign Corrupt Practices Act 1977 (FCPA), Pub. Law 95-213, 15 U.S.C. § 78dd-1 91 Stat. 1494 (1977).
Foreign Corrupt Practices and Domestic and Foreign Investment Improved Disclosure Acts of 1977, (1977).
Fraud Act 2006, c. 35 (2006).
Gerichtsverfassungsgesetz (GVG) | Courts Constitution Act, Judicature Act (RGBl, 41) (1879).
Gesetz betreffend die Gesellschaften mit beschränkter Haftung (GmbHG) | Limited Liability Companies Act, RGBl., 477 (1892).
Gesetz gegen Wettbewerbsbes-chränkungen (GWB) | Act Against Restraints of Competition, BGBI. I p. 1081 (1958).

Gesetz über das Bundes-verfassungsgericht (BVerfGG) | Federal Constitutional Court Act, BGBl. I, p. 243 (1951).
Gesetz über das Kreditwesen (KWG) | German Banking Act, RGBl. I, p. 1203 (1935).
Gesetz über Ordnungswidrigkeiten (OWiG) | Act on Regulatory Offences, BGBl. I, 481 (1968).
Gesetz zur Kontrolle und Transparenz im Unternehmens-bereich (KonTraG) | German Corporate Control and Transparency Act, BGBl. I, 1998, p. 786 (1998).
Gesetz zur Umsetzung der Richtlinie über Märkte für Finanzinstrumente und der Durchführungsrichtlinie der Kommission (Finanzmarkt-Richtlinie-Umsetzungsgesetz - FRUG), BGBl. I p. 1330 (2007).
Gewerbeordnung (GewO) | German Industrial Code, BGBl. I, p. 3412 (2003).
Handelsgesetzbuch (HGB) | German Commercial Code, (1900).
Illinois Business Corporation Act (ILCS), 805 ILCS 5/ (1983).
Insolvency Act 1986, c. 45 (1986).
International Emergency Economic Powers Act | IEEPA, 50 USC §§ 1701-1708 (1977).
Interstate Commerce Act (ICA), 24 Stat. 379 (1887).
Investment Advisers Act of 1940, Pub. L. 112-90, 15 USC § 80b-1-80b-21 (1940).
Investment Company Act of 1940, Pub.L. 76–768, 15 USC §§ 80a-1–80a-64 (1940).
Joint Stock Companies Act 1844, 7 & 8 Vict. c.110 (1844).
Joint Stock Companies Act 1856, 19 & 20 Vict. c. 47 (1856).
Kündigungsschutzgesetz (KSchG) | Protection Against Unfair Dismissal Act, § 1 Kündigungsschutzgesetz BGBl. I, p. 499 (1951).
Limited Liability Act 1855, 18 & 19 Vict., c. 133 (1855).
Montana Code An., Montana Wrongful Discharge from Employment Act (1987).
Nachweisgesetz (NachwG) | Law of Proof of Substantial Conditions Applicable to the Employment Relationship, BGBl. I, p. 946 (1995).
National Labor Relations Act (NLRA), Pub. L. 49 Stat. 449, 29 USC §§ 151-169 ch. 372 (1935).
National Minimum Wage Act 1998, c. 39 (1998).
New York Business Corporation Law, N.Y. Bus. Corp. Law (1890).
Preussische Gewerbeordnung (PrGwO), (1845).
Prevention of Corruption Act 1906, 6 Edw.7 c.34 (1906).
Prosecution of Offences Act 1985, c. 23 (1985).
Public Interest Disclosure Act 1998, c.23 (1998).
Regulation Concretizing the Organizational Obligations of Investment Services Enterprises pursuant to Section 33 of the Securities Trading Act (WpHG) of October 25, 1999 | Federal Gazette No. 2010 of November 6, 1999, 18453 (1999).

Regulation (EU) No 537/2014 of the European Parliament and of the Council on specific requirements regarding statutory audit of public-interest entities and repealing Commission Decision 2005/909/EC, L 158/77 (2014).

Regulation (EU) No 575/2013 of the European Parliament and of the Council, OJ L 176, 2013, 1, L 321/6 (2013).

Rules Enabling Act (REA), 28 USC § 2071-2077 466 (1938).

Sarbanes-Oxley Act of 2002, H.R. 3763 Public Law 107-204, 15 USC, 18 USC 116 Stat. 745 (2002).

Securities Act of 1933, Pub. L. 73-22, 15 USC § 77a 48 Stat. 74 (1933).

Securities Exchange Act of 1934, Pub.L. 73–291, 15 USC § 78a 48 Stat. 881 (1934).

Sentencing Reform Act (1984), Pub. L. No. 98-473, 18 USC § 3551 98 Stat. 1987 (1984).

Sherman Antitrust Act, 15 USC §§ 1–7 26 Stat. 209 (1890).

Small Business, Enterprise and Employment Act 2015, c. 26 (2015).

Strafgesetzbuch (StGB) | German Criminal Code, BGBI. I, p. 3322 (1998).

Strafprozessordnung (StPO) | German German Code of Criminal Procedure, (RGBl. p. 253) (1879).

Supreme Court of Judicature Act 1891 (repealed).

Supreme Court Rules 2009, (2009).

The Bubble Act of 1720, 6 Geo, I. c. 18 (1720).

Theft Act 1968, c. 60, (1698).

The Working Time Regulations 1998, No. 1833 (1998).

Treaty on the Functioning of the European Union (TFEU).

Uniform Commercial Code (UCC), (1952).

United Kingdom Bribery Act 2010, 2010 c. 23 Bribery Act 2010 (2010).

United States Code (USC), United States Code (1926).

United States Sentencing Commission (USSC), Pub. L. 114-38, 28 USC, §§ 991-998 (1991).

US Const., The Constitution of the United States of America (1787).

Verbandsverantwortlichkeits-gesetz (VbVG) | Austrian Statute on Responsibility of Legal Entities, BGBI. I, Nr. 151/2005 (2006).

Versicherungsaufsichtsgesetz | Insurance Supervision Act (VAG), RGBl. S. 139 (1901).

Wertpapierdienstleistungs-Verhaltens- und Organisations-verordnung (WpDVerOV) | Securities Trading Implementing Provision, BGBI. I, p. 1432 (2007).

Wertpapierhandelsgesetz (WpHG) | German Securities Trading Act, BGBI. I, p. 1749 (1994).

Wettbewerbsregistergesetz (WRegG) | Act for Establishing a Competition Database, BGBI. I, 2739 (2017).

Wrongful Discharge From Employment Act 1987, Title 39. Labor Ch. 641, (1987).

Zivilprozessordnung (ZPO) | German Code of Civil Procedure, Code of Civil Procedure (RGBI. I, 83) (1879).

List of Figures

List of Tables

Introduction

In this increasingly regulated world, many private sector corporations have responded to the high-profile corporate scandals and financial crises seen in the United States (US), United Kingdom (UK), and Germany over the last fifty years by establishing a compliance function.[1] The key challenge is ensuring, on the one hand, that the job description of this function is tailored to a company's unique characteristics and, on the other that the compliance officer[2] (CO) is provided with the essential authority, expertise, resources, and tools.[3] Another major challenge facing international corporations is the establishment of appropriate measures to prevent corporate officers and employees from misconduct such as fraud, bribery or infidelity. There is also a need for methods to effectively manage corporate compliance efforts, such as preventative training or supervising risky businesses. For these reasons, the role and significance of the compliance position have increased considerably in recent years. Meanwhile, compliance officers at large companies have been fined, sanctioned by regulators and law enforcement, suspended and their employment contracts terminated. Thus, in the event of misconduct, compliance officers face two challenges: first, the short-term loss of their livelihood and, second, long-term damage to their personal reputation. Therefore, the present academic discussion[4] focuses on how the role has evolved over the last fifty years and

---

1 The term private sector in this book refers to the segment of the economy that is not controlled or owned by the government. The private sector is run by individuals and companies. The entities that operate in the private sector are business enterprises, small and medium-sized companies, as well as national, international, multinational corporations listed on stock exchanges. Examples include firms, organizations, corporations and companies. Black's Law Dictionary defines a corporation as "*an association of shareholders (or even a single shareholder) created under law and regarded as an artificial person by courts.*" *See in:* US Legal Inc., Corporate Law and Legal Definition |, https://definitions.uslegal.com/c/corporate-law/ (last visited Jul 15, 2015). *See also infra* the legal definition in the UK, *supra* note 3182 and 3184, p. 475.

2 The use of the terms compliance officer (CO), compliance manager, compliance personnel and compliance professional in this book shall also comprise the ethics officer in the US in particular. In the interest of readability, the male form is used throughout.

3 *See e.g.* Scott A. Roney & Patricia J. Harned, *Leading Corporate Integrity: Defining the Role of the Chief Ethics & Compliance Officer (CECO), in* Ethics Resource Center (ERC), 1 (2007).

4 *See e.g.* Rowan Bosworth-Davies, *An Analysis of Compliance Officer: Attitudes towards insider dealing*, 20 Crime Law Soc Change 339–357 (1993).; Deborah A. DeMott, *The Crucial but (Potentially) Precarious Position of the Chief Compliance Officer*, 8 BROOK. J. CORP. FIN. &COM. L. 56–79 (2013).; Nicole Dando et al., *The Evolving*

how the risks facing compliance officers may be mitigated by means of increased effectiveness.

In the current corporate climate and given the expanding role of regulations and regulators, the evidence highlights the dramatic changes in the position of the compliance officer. The legislation and statutory regulations put into place over the last half century have had a significant and far-reaching impact on corporate structures and on the role of the compliance officer today. As a result, new requirements for companies to comply more strictly with the law and to disclose relevant information have arisen and the scope of the tasks and responsibilities incumbent upon the compliance officer are set to increase further.

Initially, the compliance function was designed to eliminate statutory violations by the company by means of effective preventative measures and structures with relating to possible claims for compensation, regulatory penalties, and damage to the company's reputation. Such functions were necessitated *inter alia* by high-profile corporate scandals involving compliance failures at American and German companies, such as those at Enron,[5] WorldCom[6] or Siemens AG. These cases are illustrative of the significant and, in some instances, fatal effects loss of reputation can have on a company. International companies are highly aware of this and invest intensively in effective systems to detect and prevent compliance breaches. Today, compliance guidelines and their implementation are an essential tool for compliance officers involved in corporate business, training, auditing, reviews, reports, and compliance matters.[7] For this reason, the compliance officer's role has

---

Responsibilities & Liabilities of Ethics Representatives: A practical guide, in EBEF Paper One (2013).; Christoph E. Hauschka, *Zum Berufsbild des Compliance Officers*, 2014 CCZ 2014, 165 - BECK-ONLINE 165–170 (2014).; Christian Heuking, *Der Compliance Officer – Aufgaben und Anforderungen*, 65 Information - Wissenschaft & Praxis 327–330 (2014).; James Weber & Dana Fortun, *Ethics and Compliance Officer Profile: Survey, Comparison, and Recommendations*, 110 Business and Society Review 97–115 (2005).

5 US Legal Inc, ENRON – BANKRUPTCY, https://bankruptcy.uslegal.com/profilesfamousbankruptcies/enron/, last visited Aug 6, 2018) *"The Enron scandal was one of the largest corporate bankruptcies in the US history".*

6 Simon Romero & Riva D. Atlas, *WORLDCOM'S COLLAPSE: THE OVERVIEW; WORLDCOM FILES FOR BANKRUPTCY; LARGEST US CASE*, THE NEW YORK TIMES, July 22, 2002, http://www.nytimes.com/2002/07/22/us/worldcom-s-collapse-the-overview-worldcom-files-for-bankruptcy-largest-us-case.html (last visited Feb 3, 2014). *"The WORLDCOM (today MCI) scandal in 2002 was the largest accounting fraud in American history. This accounting scandal was the deciding factor behind the enactment of the Sarbanes-Oxley Act into United States federal law (enacted July 30, 2002) to protect investors by improving the accuracy and reliability of corporate disclosures." See also* Mark Tran, *WorldCom accounting scandal*, THE GUARDIAN, August 9, 2002, http://www.theguardian.com/business/2002/aug/09/corporatefraud.worldcom2 (last visited Feb 3, 2014).

7 *Id.* S. WEINSTEIN *&* C. WILD, LEGAL RISK MANAGEMENT, GOVERNANCE AND COMPLIANCE: A GUIDE TO BEST PRACTICE FROM LEADING EXPERTS (2013).

evolved into an essential and significant function within companies[8] and the post of compliance officer has gained a new importance in the corporate environment in response to these demands.[9] This has been confirmed by a number of studies and surveys over the last decade.[10] In addition, the academic debate focuses on the challenges and features facing the role of compliance officers.[11] The main issue is that the compliance officer and other compliance staff are relatively new positions within private sector companies.[12] It is clear that with the emergence of a new corporate position, one of the first – and most important - tasks is to define and classify precisely what this new role entails.

The current academic debate[13] also focuses on future developments, on a repositioning and structural reorganization of the compliance function and the expertise of compliance officers. Compliance officers are advised to consider the legal environment and take appropriate steps to establish a compliance culture within the company.[14] Another issue encountered in daily business is the discussion concerning the effectiveness of the compliance officer and the establishment of practical, flexible standards for this position within companies.[15] Furthermore,

---

8 *See* Patrick J. Gnazzo, *The Chief Ethics and Compliance Officer: A Test of Endurance*, 116 Business and Society Review 533–553, 533 (2011).

9 *See* Weinstein and Wild (2013), *supra* note 7 at 357.

10 *See e.g.* Chief Compliance Officer Data Survey - Consero Group, 2 (2012), https://consero.com/2012-chief-compliance-officer-data-survey/ (last visited Dec 5, 2014) This survey confirmed that, *"...the compliance function has never been more critical to long-term cor porate success"*; Matt Kelly, Sally Bernstein & Barbara Kipp, PwC-2012-compliance-study.pdf 7 (2012), http://www.pwc.com/us/en/risk-management/assets/pwc-2012-compliance-study.pdf (last visited Dec 5, 2014) This study evaluated the strengths, the weaknesses, and the scope of this function and found that *"...the scope of the compliance officer's purview is expanding...."*

11 *See* Michael D. Greenberg, *Perspectives of chief ethics and compliance officers on the detection and prevention of corporate misdeeds: what the policy community should know*, Preface (2009).

12 *See* Jan Christian Heller, Joseph E. Murphy & Mark E. Meaney, Guide to professional development in compliance Preface (2001).

13 *See e.g.* Michael D. Greenberg, *Transforming compliance: emerging paradigms for boards, management, compliance officers, and government*, (Rand Corporation ed., 2014); Chris Taylor, *The Evolution of Compliance*, 6 Journal of Investment Compliance 54–58 (2005); Michael R. Rosella & Domenick Pugliese, *The Investment Company Chief Compliance Officer: Three years later – an Assessment of the Evolution of the Role of the CCO*, 7 Journal of Investment Compliance 16–22 (2006).

14 *See* Michele Beardslee DeStefano, *Creating a Culture of Compliance: Why Departmentalization May Not Be the Answer*, 10 Hastings Business Law Journal 71–182, 136 (2013).

15 *See e.g.* Greenberg (2009), *supra* note 11; Heller, Murphy, and Meaney (2001), *supra* note 12; Gordon McMurray, *Standards and Qualities expected of Compliance Staff*, 5 Journal of Financial Regulation and Compliance 59–61 (1997).

there has been growing emphasis on the independence and impartiality of the compliance officer.[16] In the US, it has been proposed that the compliance function should be independent from the general counsel, due to its supervisory tasks on behalf of the board of directors. *Gnazzo* takes the stance that the compliance position should not be subject to the authority of the legal department, because the tasks of this function are clearly beyond the duties of the general counsel.[17] In addition, it has been proposed that reporting directly to the management would greatly enhance the compliance officer's independence, thereby reducing conflicts of interest.[18] Some authors even conlude that the compliance officer should seek independent outside sources to manage compliance conflicts.[19] Another aspect identified in business practice is the ability of companies to fulfil the increased responsibility of the compliance function, while affording the compliance officer needs a certain degree of political power, a defined framework within which to work, as well as standards to work to within the role.[20]

Taking into account the risks relating to the compliance officer function mentioned above, there have been a number of court decisions concerning the duties of corporate directors and officer under common law in the US. In particular, the landmark case *Caremark* laid the groundwork for other cases in the US.[21] This decision was the starting point for the definition of internal monitoring requirements and standards of the board under US State Corporation Law.[22] In addition, in 2009, the Delaware Supreme Court determined in *Gantler v. Stephens*:[23] Who is an officer and What is an officer's duty? In conclusion, the court held that officers of Delaware companies owe the same duties of care and loyalty as directors.[24] In the same year, 2009, a decision of the Federal Supreme Court (BGH)[25] in Germany outlined an

---

16 *See e.g.* Gnazzo (2011), *supra* note 8; Greenberg (2009), *supra* note 11; W. Michael Hoffman, John D. Neill & O. Scott Stovall, *An Investigation of Ethics Officer Independence*, 78 Journal of Business Ethics 87–95 (2008).

17 *Id.* Gnazzo (2011), *supra* note 8 at 548.

18 *See e.g.* Gnazzo (2011), *supra* note 8; Hoffman, Neill, and Stovall (2008), *supra* note 16; Thomas M. Majewski, *Conflicts of Interest Chief Compliance Officers face in implementing Compliance Programs for Investment Funds and Investment Advisers*, 7 Journal of Investment Compliance 23–27 (2006).

19 *Id.* Majewski (2006), *supra* note 18 at 26.

20 *See* DeStefano (2013), *supra* note 14 at 82.

21 *In re Caremark International Inc. Derivative Litigation*, 698 A.2d 959 (Del. Ch. 1996).

22 *See* Hillary A. Sale, *Monitoring Caremark's Good Faith*, 32 Delaware Journal of Corporate Law 719–755, 724, 755 (2007).

23 *Gantler v. Stephens*, 965 A.2d 695 (Del. 2009), 965 A.2d 695, 709 (2009).

24 *See* Marc J. Lane, Representing Corporate Officers, Directors, Managers, and Trustees 67 (2nd ed. 2010).

25 BGH, 17.7.2009 - 5 StR 394/08, BGHSt 54, 44; BGH NJW 2009, 3173, - Überhöhte Straßenreinigungsentgelte (Ger), 2009 NJW 3173–3177 (2009), Responsibility under criminal law on account of professional position.

obiter dictum regarding the compliance officer's responsibility within a company. Although this case dealt with the head of the legal department's monitoring obligations, it integrated the still relatively novel company function compliance into the German legal system.[26] In other words, the decision provides the reasoning behind summarizing the legal requirements for compliance within the company, as well as the tasks, authorities and legal obligations pertaining to the employees concerned. Following this decision of the Federal Supreme Court (BGH),[27] an academic discussion[28] about the duties and responsibilities relating to the compliance function in Germany has been underway. The key issue is that the scope of action within which a German compliance officer works is currently largely undefined in legal terms and implementation is not consistently standardized. Germany has no legal provisions governing the compliance function outside of the banking and insurance industry. In conclusion, in Germany, there is not yet any complete legally defined character of the compliance officer and a "*standardized legal profile*" is still missing.[29] There is little uniformity and standardization of the German compliance function. It has been recognized that a generally applicable definition of the compliance function is yet absent.[30] As such, it may be useful to examine the legal environment of the compliance function outside of the German framework and to explore the professional status and role of the corporate compliance officer in other countries, such as in the US and UK.

More recently, in Germany, both the case law and the legislature have begun to set out the first concrete explanations of the function. The legal practice of the Criminal Senate of the Federal Supreme Court (BGH) has gained influence on compliance practice in companies.[31] In this context, it is interesting to note that the draft

26 *Id.* n. 23 (1).

27 *Id.* n. 6, 19.

28 *See e.g.* Jürgen Bürkle, *Grenzen der strafrechtlichen Garantenstellung des Compliance-Officers*, 2010 CCZ 4–12 (2010); Tim Wybitul, *Strafbarkeitsrisiken für Compliance-Verantwortliche*, 2009 BB 2590–2593 (2009); *See also*, Gernot Zimmermann, *Die straf- und zivilrechtliche Verantwortlichkeit des Compliance Officers*, 2011 BB 634–637 (2011).

29 *See* Daniel Geiger, *Nemo ultra posse obligatur - Zur strafrechtlichen Haftung von Compliance-Beauftragten ohne Disziplinargewalt*, CCZ 170–174, 170 (2011).

30 *See e.g.* Bürkle (2010), *supra* note 28; Matthias Dann & Anja Mengel, *Tanz auf einem Pulverfass – oder: Wie gefährlich leben Compliance-Beauftragte?*, 2010 NJW 3265–3269 (2010); Geiger (2011), *supra* note 29; Steffen Krieger & Jens Günther, *Die arbeitsrechtliche Stellung des Compliance Officers Gestaltung einer Compliance-Organisation unter Berücksichtigung der Vorgaben im BGH-Urteil vom 17. 7. 2009*, 2010 NZA 367–373 (2010); Hans-Georg Meier, *Der Arbeitsvertrag des Compliance-Beauftragten – Rechtliche Notwendigkeiten und Möglichkeiten*, 2011 NZA 779–782 (2011); Zimmermann (2011), *supra* note 28.

31 BGH, 17.7.2009 - 5 StR 394/08, BGHSt 54, 44; BGH NJW 2009, 3173, *supra* note 25.

for the introduction of a new corporate criminal law[32] submitted by the conference of justice ministers specifically deals with compliance issues.[33] The draft provides for extensive legal consequences ranging from fines, the public announcement of convictions, exclusion from entitlement to subsidies, and the dissolution of the association.[34] Some critics[35] do not deem new legislation necessary arguing that these penalties could simply be adopted into existing law and voicing fears concerning the difficulties of interpretation or application of the requirements and the scope thereof under this draft.[36] Some opponents even contend that this proposed legislation could constitute a violation of the German Constitution.[37]

Regardless of this debate, the German legislator is currently examining the enhancement of sanctions against companies in cases of legal violations. Two possible options are, on the one hand, an extension of the Act on Regulatory Offences (OWiG) or, on the other, the creation of a new corporate criminal law.[38] The proposals put forward by the German federal government include the assertion that a compliance system could act as a preventative protection system to prevent violations.[39] Overall, with an altered legal environment could enhance compliance structures and the compliance function within companies in Germany. Ultimately, however, it remains to be seen whether this draft will make it into law.[40]

The German legal environment within which the compliance function is located has been the subject of controversial debate focusing mainly the following

---

32 Heretofore the German Criminal Code can only penalize natural persons, but not legal persons under private law such as limited liability companies (GmbH) or stock corporations (AG) - *societas delinquere non potest.*

33 GESETZESENTWURF ZUM UNTERNEHMENSSTRAFRECHT - VERBANDSSTRAFGESETZBUCH (VERBSTRG-E) | DRAFT OF A CRIMINAL CODE OF ORGANIZATIONS, (2013), https://www.justiz.nrw.de/WebPortal/JM/justizpolitik/jumiko/beschluesse/2013/herbstkonferenz13/zw3/TOP_II_5_Gesetzentwurf.pdf (last visited Dec 6, 2014).

34 *See* Hauschka (2014), *supra* note 4 at 165.

35 *See e.g.* Oliver Hein, *Verbandsstrafgesetzbuch (VerbStrG-E) – Bietet der Entwurf Anreize zur Vermeidung von Wirtschaftskriminalität in Unternehmen?*, CCZ 75–81, 75 (2014); Elisa Hoven, *Der nordrhein-westfälische Entwurf eines Verbandsstrafgesetzbuchs – Eine kritische Betrachtung von Begründungsmodell und Voraussetzungen der Straftatbestände*, ZIS 19–30 (2014); Kathleen Mittelsdorf, *Zur Reichweite individueller strafrechtlicher Verantwortung im Unternehmen für Fehlverhalten von unterstellten Mitarbeitern*, ZIS 123–128 (2011); Bernd Schünemann, *Die aktuelle Forderung eines Verbandsstrafrechts – Ein kriminalpolitischer Zombie*, ZIS 1–18 (2014) (Ger).

36 GESETZ ÜBER ORDNUNGSWIDRIGKEITEN (OWIG) | ACT ON REGULATORY OFFENCES, BGBI I, p. 481 (1968).

37 *See* Schünemann (2014), *supra* note 35 at 18; GRUNDGESETZ (GG) | BASIC LAW FOR THE FEDERAL REPUBLIC OF GERMANY, (1949) Art. 1, 2, 9, 12, 14, 20.

38 BUNDESTAG DRUCKSACHE (BT) | GERMAN PARLIAMENT DOCUMENT NO. 18/2187, 2 (2014).

39 *Id.* at 3.

40 *See also infra* pp. 415 et seq.

issues: What are the scope and the area of responsibility? Should the compliance officer be liable for failure to detect misconduct by employees? Is the compliance officer able to limit his liability? Is there any form of protection against dismissal for compliance officers? How should the compliance officer's employment contract be drafted?[41] These questions are inconsistent with the view taken by *Groß*, who counters that a separate job description for the *"full-time compliance officer"* has already been established.[42] Nevertheless, there is still no official job description. Additionally, the relevant practical debate on the compliance function within the German companies represents efforts to create a unique job description.[43] Such efforts have, however, been strongly criticized by legal scholars and the controversial debate looks set to continue.[44] It is clear that there are many questions regarding the position that have not yet been resolved. Creating a generally applicable definition and a modern and dynamic role for the German compliance officer may be one possible response.

Therefore, the purpose of this book is, first, to define a modern and dynamic role of the German corporate compliance officer. The assumption is that the role, function, and duties of this position need to be clearly defined and organized, since such definitions do not exist beyond the regulated financial sector and market in Germany. Thus, this book will attempt to outline a standardized but dynamic model of the German corporate compliance officer with a concise description and definition of the function. In so doing, the objective will entail, secondly, the description and evaluation of the responsibilities of the compliance officer, as well as an examination of their activities, and the scope of the legal risks inherent thereto. The analysis will also cover the specific legal and organizational environment in which

---

41 *See e.g.* Georg Gößwein & Olaf Hohmann, *Modelle der Compliance-Organisation in Unternehmen - Wider den Chief Compliance Officer als "Überoberverantwortungsne hmer,"* 2011 Betriebs-Berater 963–967 (2011); Marcus Kirsch, *Im Blickpunkt: Die Tätigkeitsschwerpunkte des Compliance-Officer*, 2011 BB V (2011); Martin Schulz & Hartmut Renz, *Der erfolgreiche Compliance-Beauftragte - Leitlinien eines branchenübergreifenden Berufsbildes*, 2012 Betriebs-Berater 2511–2517 (2012); Martin Wolf, *Der Compliance-Officer - Garant, hoheitlich Beauftragter oder Berater im Unternehmensinteresse zwischen Zivil-, Straf- und Aufsichtsrecht?*, 2011 BB 1353–1360 (2011); Wybitul (2009), *supra* note 28.

42 *See* Nadja Fee Viola Gross, Chief Compliance Officer: Compliance-Funktionsträger im Spannungsverhältnis zwischen wirksamer Compliance und arbeitsrechtlicher / gesellschaftsrechtlicher Kompetenzordnung 29 (1. ed. 2012).

43 *See e.g.* Professional Association of Compliance Manager | Berufsverband der Compliance Manager (BCM), http://www.bvdcm.de/ (last visited Dec 7, 2014).; German Federal Association of Compliance Officers | Bundesverband deutscher Compliance Officer (BDCO), http://bdco.de/ (last visited Dec 7, 2014).

44 *See e.g.* Hauschka (2014), *supra* note 4; Eckart Sünner, *Das Berufsbild des Compliance Officers*, 2014 CCZ 2014, 91 - beck-online 91– 6 (2014).

a compliance officer works. One-step will be to identify the presence of the responsibilities and liabilities of this position. Thirdly, the organizational and functional structure of compliance may generate consequences that could affect the liability and effectiveness of this position.[45] One study has shown that the legal requirements have led companies to focus on managing their compliance programs by developing organizational structures.[46] For example, the SOX of 2002[47] and the Federal Sentencing Guidelines (FSG),[48] both in the US, provide a standard comprising seven minimum requirements for an effective compliance and ethics program.[49] The US Sentencing Commission (USSC), an administrative agency in the judicial branch, promulgated guidelines, policy statements, and commentary pursuant to Section 994 (a) of Title 28, Chapter 58 of the United States Code (USC).[50] In its Federal Sentencing Guidelines for Organizations (FSGO), Chapter 8, the USSC provides various means by which organization[51] can reduce and eliminate criminal conduct by providing a structural foundation through an effective compliance and ethics program.[52] "*Compliance and ethics program*" means a program designed to prevent and detect criminal conduct.[53] These guidelines include, for example, *"high-level personnel of the organization"*, whose purpose is to ensure that the organization has an effective compliance and ethics program.[54] "*High-level personnel of the organization*" means an individual who has substantial control over the organization or who plays an essential role in the making of policy within the organization.[55] Since the launch of the guidelines, hundreds of new compliance programs have been implemented, and thousands of new positions for compliance personnel have been established in the US. Other countries, such as Australia, the UK, and Canada have followed suit.[56] Therefore, the discussion will include an examination and comparison of the US, UK and German corporate compliance structures, as required and

---

45 *See* DeStefano (2013), *supra* note 14 at 71.

46 *See* Henry Adobor, *Exploring the Role Performance of Corporate Ethics Officers*, 69 Journal of Business Ethics 57–75, 57 (2006).

47 Sarbanes-Oxley Act of 2002, H.R. 3763 Public Law 107-204, 15 USC, 18 USC. 116 Stat. 745 (2002).

48 Sentencing Reform Act (1984), Pub. L. No. 98-473, 18 USC § 3551 98 Stat. 1987 (1984).

49 US Sentencing Guidelines Manual USSC, § 8 B2.1 (1991) (2013), http://www.ussc.gov/guidelines-manual/2013/2013-1a1 (last visited Dec 7, 2014)[hereinafter US Sentencing Guidelines Manual].

50 United States Sentencing Commission, USSC, §§ 991-998 (1991).

51 US Sentencing Guidelines Manual USSC, § 8 A1.1. *See* Commentary *"Organization"* means *"a person other than an individual."*

52 *Id.* § 8.

53 *Id.* § 8 B2.1. *See* Commentary

54 *Id.* § 8 B2.1b (2) B.

55 *Id.* § 8 A1.2. *See* Commentary

56 *See* Heller, Murphy, and Meaney (2001), *supra* note 12 Preface.

implemented by legislation and by the compliance officer. Fourth, the professional standards, the concept and future development of the compliance function within firms will be explored as these aspects have remained largely unexamined despite the wide range of American[57] and German[58] literature dealing with the compliance function. The starting point for the problem statement discussed in this book is the legal framework and environment surrounding the emergence and functioning of the position of compliance officer in the US, the UK, and Germany.

As outlined above, this book aims to establish a modern and dynamic profile for the German compliance officer applicable to all sizes, business lines and legal forms of company, irrespective of the sector of alongside a concise description and definition of the function. This objective encompasses the description and evaluation of the responsibilities of the compliance officer, as well as an examination of their activities and the scope of the legal risks involved. To this end, the book will examine the following topics: (1) the legal and organizational framework within a compliance officer works, (2) the implications thereof in practice within companies in the common law and civil law systems, (3) the relevant case law in terms of compliance, (4) the enforcement of duties with respect to directors and officers, and (5) the scope of the compliance officer's responsibilities.

Under pressure of increasing globalization and global competition, it appears necessary to consider solutions from other legal systems, in order to optimize and to take account of solutions employed elsewhere in competitive legal and economic conditions in the home legal system. This is the main goal of comparative company law.[59] Therefore, the objectives of this book are, first, to ascertain how are the modern role and legal position of the compliance officer is defined under common law and in practice, second, to explore which aspects are transferable to the German Compliance Officer, and, third, to describe how the role of the German Compliance Officer could be more effectively enhanced in practice.

The answers to these questions will be important for the German academic discussion about civil and criminal liability relating to the compliance function in private-sector firms, both in theory and in practice. The results of this examination could

---

57 *See e.g.* DeMott (2013), *supra* note 4 at 56; DeStefano (2013), *supra* note 14; James A. Fanto, *Surveillant and Counselor: A Reorientation in Compliance for Financial Firms*, Brooklyn Law School 1–65 (2013); Edward H. Freeman, *Regulatory Compliance and the Chief Compliance Officer*, 16 Information Systems Security 357–361 (2007); Gnazzo (2011), *supra* note 8; Greenberg (2009), *supra* note 11. ...etc.

58 *See e.g.* Bürkle (2010), *supra* note 28; Dann and Mengel (2010), *supra* note 30; Geiger (2011), *supra* note 29; Christoph E. Hauschka, *Compliance, Compliance-Manager, Compliance-Programme: Eine geeignete Reaktion auf gestiegene Haftungsrisiken für Unternehmen und Management?*, 2004 NJW 257–261 (2004); Heuking (2014), *supra* note 4; Kirsch (2011), *supra* note 41; Meier (2011), *supra* note 30; Eckart Sünner (2014), *supra* note 44; Wybitul (2009), *supra* note 28; ...etc.

59 *See* Klaus J. Hopt, Comparative Company Law 37 1168 (2006).

thus provide a valuable contribution to the transformation of the German compliance function over the next few years. Furthermore, the findings could be expanded further to boost the understanding of the legal framework and environment of the compliance function in the business context. Moreover, the results could provide feasible solutions for legal interpretation and help to shape the further development of this role. However, the aim of this book is not a detailed analysis of the American, British, and German law, but of relevant statutory provisions and landmark cases. Accordingly, the objectives outlined above will be achieved through an abstract and general presentation of the most important general provisions applicable to this function. Finally, consideration will also be given to the ways in which potential solutions and approaches from the common law could be transferred into civil law. The conclusion should be helpful in providing non-binding recommendations.

It is also worth considering a comparison of the cultural and legal background, and the role and classification of the compliance position within companies in the US, the UK, and Germany. The provision of a legal comparison of the common law system and the civil law system could be an appropriate means of gaining a better understanding of the role of the compliance function within American, British, and German companies. The findings ought to reveal which aspects from the common law and practice could be transferred to the German compliance officer to strengthen the position. In some cases, limitations attributable to the cultural and legal background may also come to light.

In developing a proposed modern and dynamic profile of the compliance officer, a comparison of the legal position and the role of this function in the US, the UK, and Germany, will be provided. The investigation will focus on five aspects of the role of the compliance officer in the US, the UK, and Germany: (1) the legal framework in the respective jurisdiction pertaining to the function of compliance officers, (2) a classification of this function in the structure of the American, British and German companies, (3) aspects that could be adopted for the German compliance officer, and (4) the legal definition of this position. Hence, this book will comprise a legal analysis followed by a comparative legal examination. The findings of this analysis can be seen as the starting point for further research with the aim of developing a standardized model of the corporate compliance officer.

Building on the legal comparison, this book will provide a summary of the regulatory status of the compliance function in the common law and civil law systems. To understand the outcomes of the legal research, it will be necessary first to obtain an overview of the historical development and the sources of law in the common and civil law systems. Next, more recent legal developments, which includes cases, court rules, codes, statutes, and administrative regulations pertaining to compliance issues and the compliance officer's function, will be examined. Secondary sources of law explaining certain legal concepts or doctrines will also be explored. These sources are contained in commentaries on the law, law review articles, legal encyclopedias, and the American Law Reports, for example. This is helpful on two accounts: first, it facilitates an analysis of the differences and similarities in the legal framework with the primary sources of the two legal systems, and second, the secondary sources of law will help to identify primary sources and to understand the substance of the law. This approach will result in a categorized abstract of the legal framework of compliance and of the compliance function within companies in the common law and civil law systems.

The practice of comparing laws and legal procedures is simultaneously *"very old"* and *"very modern."*[60] *Hopt* argues that the method of comparative law is *"old"* because business has never stopped at the frontiers of countries and states. In this context, "*modern*" means comparative law has always been considered to be an enrichment of legal solutions.[61] *Djilani* adds that comparative law allows attorneys, legislators, and scholars alike to understand and learn from legal systems in foreign jurisdictions.[62] In the view of *Zweigert & Kötz*, the origin of comparative law lies in the analysis of legal problems.[63] They found that the primary objective of comparative law is recognition.[64] Their approach is first to identify the essential elements of the foreign law as described in national reports. There follows a consideration of the legal comparison and a critical discussion. In conclusion, the findings facilitate and provide interpretations of the national law.[65] In so doing, they postulate a fundamental methodological principle: *"The basic methodological principle of all comparative law is that of functionality."*[66] They take the stance that an issue is legally comparable only, if it concerns the same task and the same function.[67] Overall, the general research question should be posed on a clearly functional level without any legal terms from the researcher's national law.

Other - more critical - voices have concluded that the functional method in comparative law is an under-theorized approach with an undefined disciplinary position.[68] *Michaels* argues that, *"...the functional method is strong as a tool for understanding, comparing, and critiquing different laws, but a weak tool for evaluating and unifying laws."*[69] Thus, it appears that functionalist comparative law is not suitable for unifying or standardizing laws. However, this is not actually the aim of comparative law. It should be considered as an interpretive approach that integrates historical and cultural considerations. This allows the best aspects from the common law system to be cherry-picked to help improve the legal framework

60 Hopt (2006), *supra* note at 1162.
61 *Id.* at 1162, 1167.
62 *See* Jessica Naima Djilani, *The British Importation of American Corporate Compliance*, 76 Brooklyn Law Rev. 303–341, 303 (2011).
63 *See* Konrad Zweigert & Hein Kötz, Einführung in die Rechtsvergleichung auf dem Gebiete des Privatrechts (3. ed. 1996).
64 *Id.* at 14.
65 *Id.* at 6.
66 *Id.* at 33.
67 *Id.* at 34.
68 *See* Ralf Michaels, The Functional Method of Comparative Law 1–47 25 (2005), http://papers.ssrn.com/abstract=839826 (last visited Dec 8, 2014).
69 *Id.* at 45.

in other legal jurisdictions. Moreover, *Michaels* reflects that the difficulty is how to differentiate between *"true" ("good")* [...] and *"false" ("bad")*.[70] The nature of this problem is that it is not clear whether a foreign law is *"better"* than our own.[71] In conclusion, we instead need to recognize different solutions in order to facilitate the development of alternatives.[72]

The comparative law method adopted here is as follows: Chapter one explores the sources of law in the common law and civil law systems. It provides an overview of the fundamental characteristics of the main sources, the general structure of the court systems, the differences and similarities, and a summary of developments in both the common law and civil law systems in the period from 2014 and April 2017. As for the relevant literature, research is conducted in legal, business ethics, management, and governance databases. Chapter two then analyzes the terms compliance and compliance officer from a historical legal comparative perspective. This methodical approach of acquiring knowledge by analyzing the relevant literature most applicable to the legal roots and the cultural background of compliance in the US, the UK, and in Germany will lead to a general definition of the terms compliance and compliance officer for the purposes book. The results of this legal comparison will provide an overview of the historical legal roots of the compliance officer.

Chapters three to five then examine the main subject of this book; the corporate compliance officer under common law and civil law within the private sector. These chapters first highlight the relevant primary law and then secondary law relevant to the problem. They analyze, examine, and compare the legal framework of compliance in the areas of company law, bribery, criminal law, and employment law, as well as landmark cases involving compliance and compliance officers, additional guidelines and principles to outline the role and position of the compliance officer under common and civil law. In addition, online databases in the US, UK and Germany will be reviewed for relevant case law and additional information, materials, and documents on the issues involved. The findings of this legal comparison could be used first to establish an American and English role model of the corporate compliance officer under common law and then to build a modern and dynamic role for the German Compliance Officer. The issues discussed in chapters three to five will facilitate a clear understanding of the role and position of the corporate compliance officer.

Based on the findings of chapters three to five, chapter six then compares and summarizes the key aspects of the model of the compliance officer in the US, in the UK, and in Germany resulting in a recommendation for a modern and dynamic profile of the function. Finally, using the key aspects of the US and UK models as a

70 *Id.* at 43.
71 *Id.* at 43.
72 *Id.* at 43.

framework, a proposed model of the German compliance officer, applicable to all sizes and types of companies, will be developed and presented. A definitive definition of the German corporate compliance officer will also be put forward. In so doing, this book aims to contribute to a better understanding of the status and role of this relatively new position within German companies.

Comparison of the Common Law and Civil Law Systems

Everything is the sum of the past. Nothing is comprehensible except through its history.[73]

Abstract

Before it is possible to outline the legal framework applicable to the compliance function in the common law and the civil law, this chapter provides a brief historical comparison and presents a general overview focusing on the common law and civil law systems. To understand modern law, we must understand its history. Legal historians recently recognized that the history of law and legal comparison are closely intertwined.[74] Therefore, the first part of this chapter will discuss the common law and civil law history, by firstly defining the relevant terms and then comparing and contrasting the legal history in brief. The fundamental differences between these two legal systems will be examined, followed by a comparison of the main legal sources and the structures of the court systems in the common law system with those in the civil law system. Finally, it will provide an outlook for future developments of the law.

A. The Purpose of Comparing Law

In 1900, the first international congress on comparative law took place in Paris, marking the starting point of systematic legal comparison as a scientific discipline. Since then, legal scholars[75] and lawyers in Europe and America have begun studying and categorizing the differences in the various features of the common

---

73 Pierre Teilhard de Chardin, The future of man 1 (1. ed. Image Books, 2004).

74 Dolores Freda, *"Law Reporting" in Europe in the Early-Modern Period: Two Experiences in Comparison*, 30 The Journal of Legal History 263–278, 264 (2009).

75 *See generally* Freda (2009), *supra* note 74; Raluca Lupu, *Sources of Law - Judicial Precedent*, 5 Contemporary Readings in Law and Social Justice 375–381 (2013); Keith Stanton, *Comparative Law in the House of Lords and Supreme Court*, 42 Common Law World Review 269–296 (2013); Raoul C. Van Caenegem, Judges, Legislators and Professors: Chapters in European Legal History (1. ed. 1993). This author illustrated the distinction between the two legal systems in terms of ten main differences.

law and civil law systems.[76] As mentioned before, the key purpose of comparing law is to facilitate the further development of the law, since different countries may face the same legal issues. Additionally, an adequate understanding of the compared law cannot be achieved without the application of comparative law in court decisions. Many domestic courts acknowledge that experience gained in other jurisdictions may be helpful in explaining the nature of a legal problem or finding guidance concerning a specific legal position.[77] For this reason, judges of the court in one country can learn from the approach in another.

However, a study by *Stanton* found that while the English courts make considerable use of comparative common law, in contrast, materials from civil law jurisdictions were used less in recent years.[78] On the other hand, judges in the UK sometimes cited overseas cases to support the existence of a general principle of law[79] and to reinforce their arguments.[80] Overall, however, judges cite foreign cases and analyze international law to show the tendency in the matter of law in other countries.[81] Thus, the evidence shows that the courts use comparative materials to identify emerging trends in the common law. At times, a foreign case could even be used to overrule an existing domestic decision.[82] In a similar approach, through comparative law, the values of other legal systems may be drawn on to help resolve problematic legal issues despite fundamental differences between the common law and civil law systems.[83] While difficulties may arise in weighing and presenting the comparative arguments in a practical context,[84] comparative analysis can play an additional role in developing the law.

---

76 *See* Antoinette Dop, Introduction into legal English for Dutch law students 1 (1. ed. 2009).

77 *See e.g.* Stanton (2013), *supra* note 75 at 276.

78 *Id.* at 269.

79 *See e.g.* Lord Hutton in: *Darker and Others and Chief Constable of The West Midlands Police*, [2001] 1 AC 435; [2000] 4 All ER 193[2000] 3 WLR 747 (2000). He uses both Australian and English authority as support for a general principle.

80 *See* Stanton (2013), *supra* note 75 at 279.

81 *Id.* at 279.; *United States v. Manuel Then,* 464 56 F.3d (1995) Judge Calabresi stated: "*Since World War II, many countries have adopted forms of judicial review, which-though* different from *ours in many particulars-unmistakably draw their origin and inspiration from American constitutional theory and practice. These countries are our constitutional offspring and how they have dealt with problems analogous to ours can be very useful to us when we face difficult constitutional issues. Wise parents do not hesitate to learn from their children.*"; *See also* M. Andenas & D. Fairgrieve, Courts and Comparative Law 5 (1. ed. 2015) For examples: The European Court of Justice, or the International Court of Justice.

82 *See* Stanton (2013), *supra* note 75 at 280.

83 *See* Joseph Dainow, *The Civil Law and the Common Law: Some Points of Comparison,* 15 The American Journal of Comparative Law 419–435, 419 (1966).

84 *See* Andenas and Fairgrieve (2015), *supra* note 81 at 9.

I. A Brief Legal History of the Common Law and Civil Law Systems

As has been highlighted the importance of comparative law before, this section will provide the context for the terms civil law and common law and the origins of both systems. The term civil law is derived from the Latin words ius civile, which applied exclusively to Romans citizens.[85] In contrast, the common law is the body of law and jurisprudence originating from, developed, and formulated in England. It applies to most of the states and peoples of the Anglo-Saxon countries, and has developed case-by-case, through judicial decisions.[86] The common law is opposed to statutory law.[87] In a wider sense, the common law includes all original and judge-made case law.[88]

One theory of legal origin cites England and France as the *"mother countries"* for the common law system and the civil law system, respectively.[89] Scholars have traced the origins of the two different legal families to the 12th and 13th century.[90] However, other scholars of comparative law argue that the classification of countries by reference to legal origins is not always clear.[91] Besides the French model, two other civil law traditions developed the German and the Scandinavian.[92] Furthermore, it has been pointed out that the majority of legal systems are, in fact, hybrid.[93] For instance, due to the influence of EU legislation, the common law system in the UK has become more continental. Scotland, meanwhile, has its own, separate legal system, rooted in both the common law and civil law traditions.[94] Thus, one must conclude that the theory and discussion are not able to explain in full why a country belongs to a certain legal family.[95]

---

85 *See* Dainow (1966), *supra* note 83 at 420, *See also* George Mousourakis, Roman Law and the Origins of the Civil Law Tradition 27 (2015).

86 What is COMMON LAW? Definition of COMMON LAW (Black's Law Dictionary), , http://thelawdictionary.org/common-law/ (last visited Dec 11, 2014). The origin of the Anglo-Saxon Model is based on the ideas by Adam Smith (1723–1790), a Scottish economist and philosopher, and is practiced in English-speaking countries such as the UK, the US, and others.

87 *See* Peter Hay, US-amerikanisches Recht: ein Studienbuch 5 (5. ed. 2011) note 16.

88 *Id.* at 5 note 16.

89 *See* Rafael La Porta, Florencio Lopez-de-Silanes & Andrei Shleifer, *The Economic Consequences of Legal Origins*, 46 Journal of Economic Literature 285–332, 318 (2008).

90 *See* Mathias M. Siems, *Legal Origins: Reconciling Law & Finance and Comparative Law*, 52 McGill Law Journal 55–81, 58 (2007).

91 *See* Prabirjit Sarkar, *Common Law vs. Civil Law: Which System Provides More Protection to Shareholders and Creditors and Promotes Financial Development*, 2 Journal of Advanced Research in Law and Economics 143–161, 144 (2011).

92 *See* Siems (2007), *supra* note 90 at 59.

93 *See* Sarkar (2011), *supra* note 91 at 144.

94 *See* Stanton (2013), *supra* note 75 at 273.

95 *See* Siems (2007), *supra* note 90 at 59.

Irrespective of the academic discussion of the legal origin theory, this book will take a pragmatic approach to analyzing the legal roots of the common law and civil law systems. To generalize, there are two main, contrasting legal systems: the common law system in the majority of English-speaking countries as well in the US and the UK on the one hand, and on the other hand the civil law system, based on Roman law in the majority of countries in continental Europe, such as in France and Germany.

Until the 11th century, English and continental law both belonged to the oldest legal family - Roman law.[96] It was at that time that Roman law and procedure began to be transformed.[97] From the 11th to the 20th centuries, the source of Roman law developed with a particularly methodological approach formalized through codification from the *Codex Iustinianus.*[98] The predominance of Roman law at the universities was facilitated at the time by means of its reception in Germany, France, and Scotland in the 16th century.[99] Hence, the Roman law developed as a scholarly activity by professors. As a result, on the European continent the Corpus Juris and the Code Civil became the lawyer's bibles.[100] Additionally, in the 19th century, the majority of continental countries codified their law in statutes such as the French Civil Code[101] or German Civil Code.[102] In doing so, these countries summarized their law in a systematic manner.[103] As a result, the rules of law were rather abstract in continental Europe.

England, by contrast, evolved its own particular legal procedure. Therefore, England remained unaffected by legal scholarship because its universities had no law faculties at that time. Instead, lawyers, judges, and law students read and studied the cases at the inns of courts, leading European legal scholars to emphasize the "*insularity*" of the common law, with its "*atypical, native, and eccentric character.*"[104]

It was not until the 19th century that the universities in England and Wales began with legal scholarship and legal research.[105] The first English legal scholar

---

96 *See* Van Caenegem (1993), *supra* note 75 at 114.
97 *Id.* at 114.
98 *See* Geoffrey Samuel, A Short Introduction to the Common Law (1. ed. 2013). The Codex Iustinianus (Latin) is a part of the Corpus iuris civilis, the codification of the Roman law. The earliest statute preserved in the code was enacted by Emperor Hadrian; the latest come from Justinian himself. *See also* Codex Iustinianus, II, http://droitromain.upmf-grenoble.fr/Corpus/codjust.htm (last visited Dec 9, 2014).
99 *See* Van Caenegem (1993), *supra* note 75 at 121.
100 *Id.* at 125.
101 Code Napoléon, Code Civil (France) Code civil des Français (1804).
102 Bürgerliches Gesetzbuch (BGB) |German Civil Code (1896) Aug. 18. 1896; last amended by Art. 4 para. 5 of the Act of 1 October 2013, BGBI I page 3719 (1900).
103 *See* Dainow (1966), *supra* note 83 at 424.
104 *See* Freda (2009), *supra* note 74 at 264.
105 *See* Samuel (2013), *supra* note 98.

was William Blackstone[106] in the 18th century. He brought together all of the common law of England systematizing, the common law decisions by judges[107] over a period of many years, through his Commentaries on the laws of England.[108] He also identified the sources of the English common law:

> That ancient collection of unwritten maxims and customs, which is called the common law, however compounded or from whatever fountains derived had subsisted immorality in this kingdom...etc.[109]
>
> But, with us at present, the monuments and evidences of our legal customs are contained in the records of the several courts of justice in books of reports and judicial decisions,.[.].[110]

On that note, it could be argued that, over the centuries, the origins of the common law have developed from judicial opinion as collected in the Law Reports. Another decisive factor was that King Henry II[111] reduced the power of the courts by himself exercising jurisdiction through the establishment of the King's Court, Curia Regis. In doing so, he established a central court - royal courts, which were held at Westminster Hall. At the same time, the royal justices rode circuit around England to hear cases from the local people. For this reason, the law that developed from the decisions at the King's Court became common to all of England.[112] Since, the law was common to all free people in England, the term common law historically emerged.[113]

Moreover, the court's activities were determined and limited through the writ system.[114] Writs were issued by the

106 Blackstone, William (July 10, 1723 – February 24, 1780) was an English jurist and judge. He gave lectures at Oxford University. These lectures were published as the Commentaries on the Laws of England. *See* The Editors of The Encyclopædia Britannica, Sir William Blackstone | English jurist Encyclopedia Britannica, http://www.britannica.com/biography/William-Blackstone (last visited Dec 9, 2014).

107 *Id.*

108 *See e.g.* W. Blackstone, Commentaries on the Laws of England, Volume 1: A Facsimile of the First Edition of 1765–1769 (New ed. 1979).

109 *Id.* at I.

110 *Id.* at III b.

111 Henry II, King of England (March 5, 1133 – July 6, 1189)

112 *See* B. Sharon Byrd et al., Introduction to Anglo-American law & language: Einführung in die anglo-amerikanische Rechtssprache. Bd. 1: [...] 4 (3. ed. 2011).

113 *See* Van Caenegem (1993), *supra* note 75 at 44.

114 The "*writ*" was an order issued by a court in the name of a sovereign authority requiring the performance of a specific act. Writs began to be used in judicial matters by the Kings, who developed set formulas for them. The most important were original writs, for beginning actions. *See* writ | law, Encyclopedia Britannica, http://www.britannica.com/topic/writ (last visited Dec 10, 2014).

Chancellor[115] and included the order to commence a trial. These procedures were called forms of action. This meant there was no claim if a case could not be fitted into an existing writ.[116] Therefore, the common law system gradually became more and more specific and rigid. Thus, the King's Chancellor began asking the King for relief from this injustice. The second statute of Westminster II (1258) granted the Chancellor the authority to issue new writs in similar cases. The writ of "*trespass upon the case*"[117] enabled a broader scope.[118] Further to the writs, the equity[119] of the King (later of the Chancellor) emerged to bring a degree of justice in specific individual cases. This led to the development of a separate legal principle and pillar of the law: the principle of equity.[120] These two systems - the common law and equity - worked together with the Federal Rules of Civil Procedure as separate and complementary jurisdictions until 1873[121] in England and until as recently as 1938 in the US.[122] This meant that one and the same judge could apply both the principle of law and the principle of equity. Nowadays, however, the distinction between the two systems has disappeared entirely.[123]

---

115 The Lord Chancellor traditionally served as head of the judiciary and speaker of the House of Lords. *See* Lord Chancellor | British Official, Encyclopedia Britannica, http://www.britannica.com/topic/lord-chancellor (last visited Dec 10, 2014).

116 *See* Hay (2011), *supra* note 87 at 1 note 4.

117 Initially, "*trespass*" in law means unauthorized entry upon land. Once a trespass is proved, the trespasser is usually held liable for any damages. *See* trespass | law, Encyclopedia Britannica, http://www.britannica.com/topic/trespass-law (last visited Dec 17, 2014). "*Trepass on the case*" - It is the technical name of an action, instituted for the recovery of damages caused by an injury unaccompanied with force, or where the damages sustained are only consequential. *See* Trespass on the case, TheFreeDictionary.com, http://legal-dictionary.thefreedictionary.com/Trespass+on+the+case (last visited Dec 17, 2014).

118 *See* Hay (2011), *supra* note 87 at 1 note 4.

119 "*Equity*", in Anglo-American law, is the custom of courts outside the common law or coded law. Equity provided remedies in situations in which precedent or statutory law might not apply or be equitable. Equity | law, Encyclopedia Britannica, http://www.britannica.com/topic/equity (last visited Dec 18, 2014).

120 *See* Hay (2011), *supra* note 87 at 2 note 6.

121 Judicature Act (1873) was an act of the Parliament of the United Kingdom in 1873. It reorganized the English court system so that both systems should be used regularly by all courts. The Judicature Act of 1873 created the Supreme Court of Judicature. *See* Supreme Court of Judicature Act 1891 (repealed), http://www.legislation.gov.uk/ukpga/Vict/54-55/53/introduction (last visited Dec 10, 2014).

122 *See* Hay (2011), *supra* note 87 at 2 note 9. *See also* Rules Enabling Act (REA), 28 USC § 2071–2077 466 (1938). The Rules Enabling Act authorizes the Supreme Court to prescribe general rules of practice and procedure and rules of evidence for the federal courts. *See also* FRCP § 2 "*There is one form of action—the civil action.*"

123 *See* Byrd et al. (2011), *supra* note 112 at 34.

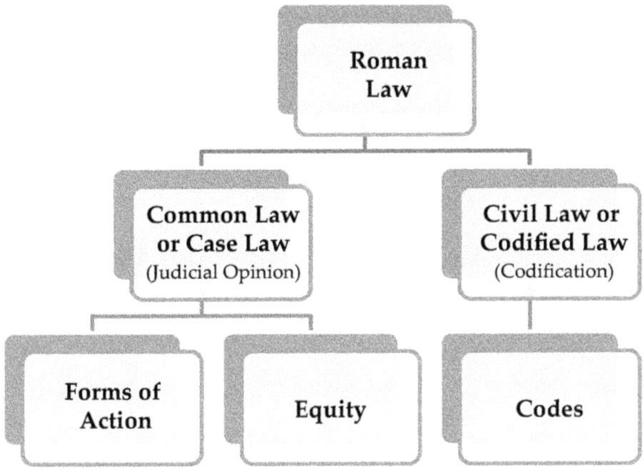

Figure 1 *The Legal Origins of the Common Law and Civil Law Systems*

The diagram summarizes the legal origins of the common law and civil law systems. It can be noted that the major distinction lies in the structure and collection of law. For instance, there are formal legal collections such *"law on the books,"* as opposed to the *"law in action"*[124] or, in other words, between "*codified law*" and "*case law.*"[125]

II. The Fundamental Differences between the Two Legal Systems

As discussed in the section above, the common law developed in England before being transferred to the US in 1607. As shown, its roots can be traced back to the English law, developed on a case-by-case basis. That is why, historically, the Anglo-American legal system belongs to the common law. Nevertheless, the US common law has been adapted to fit the specific conditions there. When the American colonies declared their independence from the British government in 1776 and passed into states, the common law became the main jurisprudence in the US.[126] Evidently, the term common law and its development in the US have also been taken into consideration in the Corpus Juris Secundum (CJS):

124 *See* Sarkar (2011), *supra* note 91 at 145.
125 *See* Freda (2009), *supra* note 74 at 267.
126 Byrd et al. (2011), *supra* note 112 at 4–5.

> The term of common law of England refers to the general system of law derived from England as opposed to the Roman law or civil law.[127]
>
> The greater part of the common law in the US is derived from the common or unwritten law of England.[128]

Furthermore, *James Kent*[129] and *Joseph Story*[130], the authors of the Commentaries on American Law[131] and Commentaries on the constitution of the United States[132], consolidated the influence of the English law.[133] There are, however, some exceptions. Louisiana, for instance, follows the French legal tradition and applies a civil code.[134] In addition, the Franco-Spanish law, particularly its matrimonial law, has influenced some western federal states in the US.[135] Nevertheless, despite these exceptions, the legal theory, legal language, and legal principles in the US are common law.[136]

It is evident from the definition and explanation of how the common law has developed and what common law comprises, that, due to the historical development, there are some significant differences between the common law and civil law systems. Legal historians assume that these differences are based on the following factors *e.g.* the history, the organization of the law, the legal sources, the legal education system, the modes of research, the styles of argumentation, and the judicial process.[137] The factor sources of law, for instances, is explained as "*the ways in which law is created or comes into being.*"[138] Other authors argue that the

> Sources of law are accepted as binding by the officials of a legal system and this collective social practice of officials provides the foundations for a legal system.[139]

---

127 Corpus Juris Secundum (CJS), 15A I. § 1.b. (1964). The CJS is an encyclopedia of US law including legal topics as developed by US federal and state cases, the primary sources of law.

128 *Id.* at II. § 3.

129 An American jurist and legal scholar, (July 31, 1763 – December 12, 1847)

130 An American lawyer and jurist, (September 18, 1779 – September 10, 1845)

131 J. Kent & G.F. Comstock, Commentaries on American Law (3. ed. 1867).

132 J. Story, Commentaries on the Constitution of the United States: With a Preliminary Review of the Constitutional History of the Colonies and States, Before the Adoption of the Constitution (1833).

133 *See* Hay (2011), *supra* note 87 at 4 note 13.

134 *See* Dainow (1966), *supra* note 83 at 420.; Hay (2011), *supra* note 87 at 4 note 14.

135 *See* Hay (2011), *supra* note 87 at 14.

136 *Id.* at 87 note 14.

137 *See e.g.* Dainow (1966), *supra* note 83 at 427. Freda (2009), *supra* note 74 at 267 note 17.; La Porta, Lopez-de-Silanes, and Shleifer (2008), *supra* note 89 at 287.; Zweigert and Kötz (1996), *supra* note 63 at 68.

138 *See* Mousourakis (2015), *supra* note 85 at 27.

139 *See* G. Lamond, *Legal Sources, the Rule of Recognition, and Customary Law*, 59 The American Journal of Jurisprudence 25–48, 25 (2014).

Thus, it can concluded that the sources of law include (1) a variety of aspects, (2) the historical development, (3) a set of rules of conduct, and (4) the relationship between people within a society.

Having identified these factors, the next section will analyze them to provide the basis for a general legal comparison. This comparison will be carried out by means of the legal sources, court systems, and the further development of the common law and civil law systems. Based on these aspects, it can be assumed that the common law and civil law systems are built on different legal sources and that there are many distinctions between the two systems.[140]

1. Comparison of the Sources of Law

All legal systems have fundamental sources of law.[141] Primary sources contain the law itself, the positive law, while secondary sources include the interpretation of the law, for example commentaries or guidelines on the law.[142] The oldest primary source of law is customary law.[143] Other major legal sources are judicial decisions and legislation. In the civil law countries, secondary sources like the treatises and commentaries of legal scholars had a great influence on the evolution of the legal system.[144] These writings analyze and classify decided cases and then evaluate the essence of those cases.[145] In contrast, the common law countries have fewer doctrinal materials, but a variety of guidelines and principles. The legal sources of the common law and the civil law system will be examined in more detail in the next sections.

a. **The Main Source of the Common Law System**

In general, it has been recognized that the essence of the common law is that it is created, developed, articulated, and applied by judges sitting in courts and deciding on disputes in individual cases. Chief Justice Jim Hannah of the Supreme Court of Arkansas highlighted this source in the case *Mason v States:*

> The common law is judicially created law that is developed on a case by case basis.[146]

According to this explanation, the decisions of the higher courts[147] played an important role as the main sources of the common law.[148] Judges developed and

---

140 *See* Carol M. Bast & Margie Hawkins, Foundations of legal research and writing / Carol M. Bast, Margie Hawkins 1 (5th ed. 2013).

141 *See* Lamond (2014), *supra* note 139 at 25.

142 *See* Bast and Hawkins (2013), *supra* note 140 at 10.

143 *See* Lupu (2013), *supra* note 75 at 376.

144 *See* Dainow (1966), *supra* note 83 at 428.

145 *Id.* at 428.

146 *Mason v. State,* 361 Ark. 357 S.W.3d 869, 368 (Ark. 2005), (2005).

147 *See e.g.* The High Court and the Court of Appeal in England, United State Supreme Court

148 *See* Freda (2009), *supra* note 74 at 275.

applied specific principles of law to resolve disputes referred to subsequently as "*binding precedent*".[149] Hence, the judges were bound by their previous decisions and were required to follow the decisions of other judges who decided similar cases previously. Thus, they follow the reasoning of the doctrine of precedent and the principle of law. This is why lawyers cite past decisions as arguments.[150] Hence, the first major source in a common law system lies in judicial decisions.

However, it is not the whole judicial decision that forms the precedent for the future. Obviously, a decision contains (1) the facts of the case; (2) the legal history of the case; (3) the issue raised on appeal, and lastly (4) the judgments in the resolution.[151] The precedent is the principle of law or more precisely known as "*stare decisis*" used to reach the judgment in a case.[152] These judicial decisions are documented in collections of case law known as the English yearbooks and reports.[153]

Finally, some rules from decisions recognized as a part of the common law originate from one or more court cases. For many authors[154] this feature is one of the main strengths of the common law. Even the judges explain new external sources in these terms, as in *Sosa v. Alvarez-Machain*:

> Now, [...] in most cases where a court is asked to state or formulate a common law principle in a new context, there is a general understanding that the law is not so much found or discovered as it is either made or created.[155]

---

149 Perell, Paul M. (1987); Also called the doctrine of precedent or of *"stare decisis"* literally translates as *"to stand by decided matters."* Is itself an abbreviation of the Latin phrase *"stare decisis et non quieta movere"* which translates as *"to stand by decisions and not to disturb settled matters." See* Paul M. Perell, STARE DECISIS AND TECHNIQUES OF LEGAL REASONING AND LEGAL ARGUMENT – BEST GUIDE TO CANADIAN LEGAL RESEARCH CANADIAN LEGAL RESEARCH BLOG (1987), http://legalresearch.org/writing-analysis/stare-decisis-techniques/ (last visited Dec 17, 2014). (Latin: *"let the decision stand")*, in Anglo-American law, principle that a question once considered by a court and answered must elicit the same response each time the same issue is brought before the courts. The principle is observed more strictly in England than in the United States. *See* stare decisis | law, ENCYCLOPEDIA BRITANNICA, http://www.britannica.com/topic/stare-decisis (last visited Dec 17, 2014).

150 *See* BYRD ET AL. (2011), *supra* note 112 at 7–8.

151 *Id.* at 15.

152 *Id.* at 15. Referred to as the "*ratio decidendi*".

153 Law report, in common law, published record of a judicial decision that is cited by lawyers and judges for their use as precedent in subsequent cases. The earliest English court reports were the yearbooks produced from the late 13th to the 16th century. *See* law report | common law, ENCYCLOPEDIA BRITANNICA, http://www.britannica.com/topic/law-report (last visited Dec 17, 2014).

154 *See e.g.* BYRD ET AL. (2011), *supra* note 112; HAY (2011), *supra* note 87; Caleb Nelson, *The Legitimacy of (Some) Federal Common Law*, 101 VIRGINIA LAW REVIEW 2–64 (2014).

155 *Sosa v. Alvarez-Machain et al.*, 542 US 692, 725 (2004).

> Whatever may be said for his [plaintiff] broad principle advances, in the present, imperfect world, it expresses an aspiration exceeding any binding customary rule with the specificity this Court requires. Creating a private cause of action to further that aspiration would go beyond any residual common law discretion we think it appropriate to exercise.[156]

In consideration of the unbroken continuity of the law, it is the fact that every case is an individual. As such, the common law system appears at times rather inflexible. American and English scholars[157] take the view that judicial decisions with the ability to shape the law on a case–by–case basis is less formalistic. In their view, this approach helps to make the law more flexible. They argue that this regulation is more adaptable to changing circumstances.[158] Additionally, *Merryman & Pérez-Perdomo* explain the difficulty with codification.[159] In their view, legislation cannot possibly foresee all potential future circumstances around a case[160] and permits judges to interpret and apply such legislation in a restrictive way only.[161]

A study by *Aron Balas et al.*[162] measures the formalism index of legal procedure for twenty common law and twenty civil law countries during the period from 1950 to 2000.[163] They found that "*formalism*"[164] is higher in civil law than in common law countries.[165] Formalism should in fact be considered in light of the impact of globalization, though globalization is most likely to affect areas of law, rather than legal procedure.[166] In conclusion, the evidence suggests that one important difference between the legal systems might be how quickly they are able to react to problems.[167] Therefore, the next section will examine the historical development of flexibility in the common law system.

---

156 *Id.* at 738 note 70.

157 *See e.g.* Sarkar (2011), *supra* note 91; Siems (2007), *supra* note 90.

158 *See e.g.* Sarkar (2011), *supra* note 91 at 144.

159 *See* J.H. Merryman *&* R. Pérez-Perdomo, The Civil Law Tradition: An Introduction to the Legal Systems of Europe and Latin America 30 (3. ed. 2007).

160 *See* La Porta, Lopez-de-Silanes, and Shleifer (2008), *supra* note 89 at 304.

161 *See* Merryman and Pérez-Perdomo (2007), *supra* note 159 at 30.

162 *See* Aron Balas et al., *The Divergence of Legal Procedures*, NATIONAL BUREAU OF ECONOMIC RESEARCH, 33 (2008) Table 1.

163 This index measures how stringently the law regulates the legal procedure itself. *See Id.* at 28.

164 The study defines *"formalism"* as the sum of seven sub-indices:(1) professionals vs. laymen; (2) written vs. oral elements; (3) legal justification; (4) statutory regulation of evidence; (5) control of superior review; (6) engagement formalities; and (7) independent procedural actions. *See Id.* at Appendix. Table 1B.

165 *See* La Porta, Lopez-de-Silanes, and Shleifer (2008), *supra* note 89 at 307.

166 *See* Balas et al (2008)., *supra* note 162 at 28.

167 *Id.* at 28.

b. Development of Equity in the English Common Law System

In the 15th century, due to the developed case law with the writ system,[168] the law in England became rigid, inflexible, and complicated. The rigid form of actions required exceptions. These were offered in the form of equity[169] with fairness in individual cases.[170] In a way, equity developed in competition with common law. In the broad sense, the term equity means fair or just, in its legal meaning the rule developed to mitigate the severity or strength of the common law. Over time, the English King, through his Chancellor, set up a special court known as the Court of Chancery.[171] This was originally the royal secretariat. The idea was to deal with the "*petitions of right*"[172] for instance claims, against the Crown that were addressed directly to the King. The Chancellor and the court clerks acted based on the facts of the case before them. In the 15th century, law and equity gradually developed as separate systems. On the one hand, the judges at the King's Court decided cases on the common law principles while on the other, the Chancellor understood the need for certainty and developed his own body of principles in the jurisprudence of the English legal system for instance equity.[173] The English distinction in trial at law and equity was also adopted in the American colonies. Today, however, the equity-courts no longer exist in the US As mentioned previously, the Federal Rules of Civil Procedure (FRCP),[174] established in 1938, determined one uniform form of action, whereas in England, the Judicature Act 1873[175] required that both systems should apply in all courts.[176] In the 19th century, this separation was seen as inconvenient and the courts were merged and nowadays, one judge applies both principles of law in the common law.[177]

---

168 Writ | law, *supra* note 153.

169 Equity | law, *supra* note 158.

170 *See* Hay (2011), *supra* note 87 at 2 note 6.

171 Court of Chancery, in England, the court of equity under the lord high chancellor that began to develop in the 15th century to provide remedies not obtainable in the courts of common law. *See* Court of Chancery | court, Encyclopedia Britannica, http://www.britannica.com/topic/Court-of-Chancery (last visited Dec 18, 2014).

172 "*Petition of right*", legal petition asserting a right against the English crown, the most notable example being the Petition of Right of 1628, which Parliament sent to Charles I complaining of a series of breaches of law. *See* petition of right | English law, Encyclopedia Britannica, http://www.britannica.com/topic/petition-of-right-English-law (last visited Dec 18, 2014).

173 Byrd et al. (2011), *supra* note 112 at 33–34.

174 *See supra* footnote 122, p. 58.

175 Supreme Court of Judicature Act 1873 passed by Parliament in 1873 and reorganized the English court system to establish the High Court and the Court of Appeal. *See* Supreme Court of Judicature Act 1891 (repealed), *supra* note 120.

176 *See* Hay (2011), *supra* note 87 at 2 note 9.

177 *See* Byrd et al. (2011), *supra* note 112 at 34.

In spite of the conjunction of these two legal sources in the common law system, the distinction between the two sources remains essential. The equity system is at once both a source of independent claims and legal remedy and pervades virtually the entire common law system. In the US, legislation promotes equity, as in the Americans with Disabilities Act (ADA) of 1990, for instance.[178]

In conclusion, both the law and equity developed from judicial decisions.[179] Sometimes, judges emphasized that the common law is flexible, since it may be changed and tailored by the courts to fit the economic and social needs. Additionally, the judges are able to amend the common law. Therefore, common law can refer to both the common law principles and the equity system as major sources.[180]

c. Legal Concepts in the Common Law

From the foregoing, it can be seen that the common law generally uses judicial decisions and equity as its primary sources of law. Other primary sources include court rules, constitutions, statutes, and administrative regulations.[181] However, there are other additional sources. Another source is called the concept of the common law. *Balganesh & Parchomovsky* define the legal concept as:

> The operational legal devices that the common law uses in doctrine to understand and compartmentalize aspects of a legal issue or dispute.[182]

If a legal principle comes to be directly embedded into a legal rule and is applied in the legal analysis, the principle becomes a legal concept.[183] In the United States, this concept is *e.g.* held in the Uniform Commercial Code (UCC),[184] which provides that

> Every contract or duty within this Act imposes an obligation of good faith in its performance or enforcement.

---

178 *See* Adobor (2006), *supra* note 46 at 66. *See also* Americans with Disabilities Act (ADA), 42 USC § 12101 Pub. L. 114-38 (1990).

179 *See also* Dainow (1966), *supra* note 83 at 423.

180 *Id.* at 423.

181 *See* Bast and Hawkins (2013), *supra* note 140 at 10.

182 *See* Shyamkrishna Balganesh & Gideon Parchomovsky, *Structure and Value in the Common Law*, 163 U. of Penn. Law. Rev. 1241–1310, 1243 (2015).

183 *Id.* at 1254.

184 Uniform Commercial Code (UCC), (1952) § 1-203; *See also* Restatement (Second) of the Law of Contracts § 205 (1979), It is a legal treatise to inform judges and lawyers about general principles of contract common law. § 205 Duty of good faith and fair dealing - Every contract imposes upon each party a duty of good faith and fair dealing in its performance and its enforcement. *See* http://www.lexinter.net/LOTWVers4/duty_of_good_faith_and_fair_dealing.htm, (last visit Dec 27, 2014)

Similar provisions are found in the codes of most civil law jurisdictions[185] such as in the German Civil Code (BGB).[186] By contrast, the English courts did not recognize an implied duty of good faith between contracting parties.[187]

However, the purpose of legal concepts is to build a balance between stability and change.[188] As opposed to rules, common law concepts take the form of legal standards.[189] Legal concepts are usually interpretive and contain a descriptive element. Hence, the legal concepts established the basis for interpretation and application of the codified law. That means that the concept could be *"modified or qualified"* depending on the relevant purpose. Today, an examination of the common law reveals legal concepts in a variety of areas *e.g.* the concepts of duty of good faith and duty of care.[190]

The existence of the duty of good faith is based on numerous judicial opinions, statutory developments, and is published in writings by professors.[191] Several reasons for the benefits of recognition and conceptualization of the duty of good faith can be found in contract law.[192] Thus, at first, this concept is a commitment of justice according to law. Second, such a doctrine or an equitable principle could be seen as a requirement of *"contractual morality"*.[193] Third, although it is only a minimum requirement, its relevance is far-reaching and plays a significant role in the common law.[194] Finally, it is a tool that judges can use to bridge gaps.[195]

In the US, legal concepts such as good faith form part of both corporate law and contract law.[196] Considering the corporate law, the duty of good faith means

---

185 *See* Christopher Braithwaite, Stephen Brown & Lee Coffey, Jones Day | Towards an Implied Duty of Good Faith Under English Law Jones Day Publications (2013), http://www.jonesday.com/towards-an-implied-duty-of-good-faith-under-english-law/ (last visited Dec 19, 2014).

186 Bürgerliches Gesetzbuch (BGB) | German Civil Code, *supra* note 102 § 242 Treu und Glauben (Ger).

187 *See* Braithwaite; Brown & Coffey (2013), *supra* note 185. *See also* Joseph Chitty *&* H. G. Beale, Chitty on contracts. Vol. 1: General principles 1-039 (31. ed. 2012)....in keeping with the principles of freedom of contract and the binding force of contract, in English contract law there is no legal principle of good faith of general application, although some authors have argued that there should be.

188 *See* Balganesh and Parchomovsky (2015), *supra* note 182 at 1243.

189 *Id.* at 1244.

190 *Id.* at 1255.

191 *See* Robert Summers, *The General Duty of Good Faith – Its Recognition and Conceptualization*, 67 Cornell Law Review 810–840, 812 (1982).

192 *Id.* at 811.

193 *Id.* at 811.

194 *Id.* at 811.

195 *Id.* at 812.

196 *See e.g.* Uniform Commercial Code (UCC), *supra* note 184. § 2-103 (2003) *Good faith* means honesty in fact and the observance of reasonable commercial standards of fair dealing.

the corporate directors' duties, which are determined primarily by members of the board of directors. In a number of recent Delaware cases,[197] it was recognized that corporate managers owe a fiduciary duty of good faith in addition to their traditional duties of care. The duty of good faith was not created by cases, but the duty has long been governed by statutory provisions *e.g.* the business judgment rule,[198] which requires directors to act in good faith.[199] It is argued that the concept of duty of good faith is instantiate of a general baseline conception comprising four elements: (1) subjective honesty, (2) non-violation of generally accepted standards of decency applicable to the conduct of business, (3) non-violation of generally accepted basic corporate norms, and (4) fidelity to office.[200] Due to these elements, the duty of good faith provides a principled basis upon which the judges in the courts can articulate new, more specific obligations in response to changes in the social and business environment.[201]

Finally, the significance of those principles lies in the further development of the law by judges.[202] If a legal concept has been accepted in the form of appropriate practices and duties, then it will also be embodied in law. In conclusion, it seems that the legal concepts used by the courts constitute a primary source of law in the common law system.[203]

d. The Major Sources in the European Civil Law System

As has been explained before, the term civil law describes the laws derived from Roman law.[204] Legal scholars and authors[205] have insisted that the accepted theory

---

197 *See infra* in detail pp. 257 et seq.; *See e.g. In re Caremark International Inc. Derivative Litigation*, 698 A.2d 959 (Del. Ch. 1996), *supra* note 20., *Stone v. Ritter*, 911 A.2d 362 (Del. 2006), 911 A.2d 362 (2006)., *Gantler v. Stephens,* 965 A.2d 695 (Del. 2009), *supra* note 23., *In re The Goldman Sachs Group, Inc.,* WL 4826104 (2011).

198 The business judgment rule is a judicially created doctrine that protects directors from personal civil liability for the decisions they make on behalf of a corporation. *See* Lori A. McMillan, *The Business Judgment Rule as an Immunity Doctrine*, 4 WM. & MARY BUS. L. REV . 521–574, 521 (2013). The role of the business judgment rule has been defined as follows: Under Delaware law, the business judgment rule is the offspring of the fundamental principle, codified in tit. 8 Del. C. § 141(a). *See Id.* at 528.

199 *See* Melvin Eisenberg, *The Duty of Good Faith in Corporate Law*, DELAWARE JOURNAL OF CORPORATE LAW 1–75, 1 (2006).

200 *See* Eisenberg (2006), *supra* note 199.

201 *Id.*

202 *See* M. AUER, MATERIALISIERUNG, FLEXIBILISIERUNG, RICHTERFREIHEIT: GENERALK LAUSELN IM SPIEGEL DER ANTINOMIEN DES PRIVATRECHTSDENKENS 198 (2005) (Ger).

203 *See* Braithwaite, Brown & Coffey (2013), *supra* note 185.

204 *See* MOUSOURAKIS (2015), *supra* note 85 at 296.

205 *See e.g.* J. GORDLEY & A.T. VON MEHREN, AN INTRODUCTION TO THE COMPARATIVE STUDY OF PRIVATE LAW: READINGS, CASES, MATERIALS (1. ed. 2009). MERRYMAN AND PÉREZ-PERDOMO (2007), *supra* note 159 at 24.

of sources of civil law recognizes only (1) statutes, (2) regulations, and (3) custom. They pointed out that this list is exclusive and appears very technical. The civil law system tends to use more abstract terms and to employ a conceptual approach to legal matters.[206] *Mousourakis* argued that the aim of the study of cases is only to show how the law works in practice. However, this theory appears too biased because there is no awareness that the sources of law could, in fact, vary.[207] In addition, the civil law sources contain both written and unwritten law, providing a considerable degree of legal certainty.

The history of the primary sources of law will be now presented. Firstly, it has been recognized that the European civil law system has its ancient origins in the Roman Republic before the beginning of the Empire, in the second century. Unlike the common law, the Roman law was based on a procedural system, not on judge-made law.[208] Despite this, there were two types of civil judges: the praetor[209] and the trial judge.[210] In general, the proceedings began with a hearing before a praetor, followed by a trial before an iudex.[211] The praetor[212] and the judges did not have much by way of legal training. Therefore, Roman justice was not professional. In contrast to the common law system, the proceedings before the iudex were free of formal controls and there was no review of the findings of the iudex. The judgments were passes orally, without reasons.[213] Hence, some authors[214] concluded that judicial decisions in the civil law system were not recognized as an important source of innovation.[215]

---

206 *See* Mousourakis (2015), *supra* note 85 at 296.

207 *Id.* at 304.

208 *See* Gordley and von Mehren (2009), *supra* note 205 at 19.

209 The praetor was one of a group of magistrates' who were elected annually. *See Id.* at 19.

210 *See* James G. Apple & Robert P. Deyling, A Primer on the Civil-Law System 4 (1995), http://www.fjc.gov/public/pdf.nsf/lookup/CivilLaw.pdf/$file/CivilLaw.pdf (last visited Dec 20, 2014).

211 *See* Gordley and von Mehren (2009), *supra* note 205 at 19. The judges were men from the upper classes of Roman society who had an interest in the law. *See also* Apple and Deyling (1995), *supra* note 210 at 4.

212 The praetor was appointed for one year only and played a limited role in the resolution of cases. *See* Apple and Deyling (1995), *supra* note 210 at 4.

213 *See* Gordley and von Mehren (2009), *supra* note 205 at 20.

214 *See* Apple and Deyling (1995), *supra* note 210; Gordley and von Mehren (2009), *supra* note 205.

215 The Roman jurist Gaius did not recognize judicial decisions as a basis of Roman law in his Institutes of Gaius, a legal textbook, written in the 2nd century AD. "*The Civil Law of the Roman people consists of statutes, plebiscites, Decrees of the Senate, Constitutions of the Emperors, the Edicts of those who have the right to promulgate them, and the opinions of jurists.*" *See* The Institutes of Gaius, http://thelatinlibrary.com/law/gaius1.html (last visited Dec 20, 2014).

In addition, as the praetorian system developed, the jurists[216] assisted the praetor in drawing up formulae with highly generalized standards. The Edict was created annually, to declare the principles of the praetor. Furthermore, the jurists provided written technical advices to judges concerning the state of the law and interpretation of textual material such as the Edict.[217] The Roman jurist Papinian[218] concluded that the law was developed by the Praetors' Edict because it was an instrument that supplemented, explained, and improved the ius civile.[219]

Secondly, in the 6th century - the next important historical era for the development of European law - the Emperor Justinian ordered the creation of a comprehensive manuscript covering all aspects of Roman law. Justinian's Institutes, the Corpus Juris Civilis,[220] included not only a refinement and adoption of Gaius' Institutes, but also the Digest,[221] the Code [early imperial legislation], and the Novels [Justinian's legislation].[222] In this legal textbook, the sources of law were divided into written[223] and unwritten law.[224] In Justinian's view, the unwritten law or local custom was a source of law, although other Roman jurists *e.g.* Papinian and Gaius, did not see the unwritten law as a legal source. For this reason, its merit was supplementing the sources of law.[225] By surveying the recent literature,[226] it has

216 Jurists in Rome had no official government powers. *See* Apple and Deyling (1995), *supra* note 210 at 4.

217 *Id.* at 4.

218 Aemilius Papinianu, (148–211)

219 The Romans called their law ius civile. This law was applied by Roman citizens to Roman citizens. *Compare* Mousourakis (2015), *supra* note 85 at 27.

220 Called the Body of Civil Law, was issued in three parts, in Latin in (529) AD. *See*, Justinian, [Corpus iuris civilis] ... commentariis Sumptibus Horatius Cardon, scholiis Contii, paratitlis Cuiacii ... novae accesserunt ad ipsum Accursium Dionysii Gothofredi, I. C. notae, ... Lugduni: Sumptibus Horatius Cardon, (1604), http://pds.lib.harvard.edu/pds/view/14856910?n=1&imagesize=1200&jp2Res=.25&printThumbnails=no (last visited Dec 20, 2014).)

221 Writings of classical jurists or Pandects, issued in (533) AD. It compiled the writings of the great Roman jurists such as Ulpian, along with current edicts. *See*, http://droitromain.upmf-grenoble.fr/Corpus/digest.htm, (last visited Dec 20, 2014)

222 *See* Apple and Deyling (1995), *supra* note 210 at 6.

223 The Institutes (535) AD, Book I, 2.3. *"The written part consists of leges (lex), plebiscita, senatusconsulta, constitutiones of emperors, edicta of magistrates, and responsa of jurisprudents [for instance jurists]." See* http://droitromain.upmf-grenoble.fr/Corpus/digest.htm, (last visited Dec 20, 2014)

224 The Institutes (535) AD, Book I, 2.9. *"The unwritten law is that which usage has established; for ancient customs, being sanctioned by the consent of those who adopt them, are like laws." See* http://droitromain.upmf-grenoble.fr/Corpus/digest.htm, (last visited Dec 20, 2014)

225 *See* Mousourakis (2015), *supra* note 85 at 28.

226 *See e.g.* Dainow (1966), *supra* note 83; Lupu (2013), *supra* note 75; Merryman and Pérez-Perdomo (2007), *supra* note 159.

been recognized that custom - as one of the oldest sources of law - is also among the primary legal sources in the civil law system.[227] In Germany, the judge can fill gaps in the written law, for example, by applying principles of customary law.[228]

The third important step in civil law history began as the civil law came to be practiced throughout Europe.[229] At this point, the role of local custom as a source of law became increasingly significant. Therefore, the European legal scholars attempted to systematize scattered and disparate written laws and local customary law and consolidated these in line with rational principles of civil law.[230] In the 16th century, the European states unified and organized their individual legal systems through codification. This process affected all European states, with the exception of England.[231] Furthermore, during the era of Humanism and Enlightenment in the 18th century, the European jurists rationalized and systematized the law in order to provide a systematic legal order. As a result of these efforts, the Codes *e.g.* Prussia's Complete Territorial Code of 1794, France's Civil Code of 1804, and the German Civil Code of 1900 were created.[232] This process is known as codification. Legal scholars[233] explain the term codification as a process of compiling and systematizing laws into a complete written body of law.[234] It can be noted that the primary written source in the civil law system is a code passed by legislation.[235] These national codes contain a highly organized collection of the entire body of law[236] and are continuously revised by the government.

Nevertheless, other authors argue that codification is not a form, but rather an attempt to understand an ideology; they base this argument on the fact that, in some civil law countries *e.g.* in Greece and Hungary, the law remained uncodified until the Second World War.[237] In spite of the codes, they argue that the influence of the source of Roman Law dominates over the ius commune in the European Codes.[238] Another aspect that they point out is that *e.g.* California has more

---

227 *See* Lupu (2013), *supra* note 75 at 376.

228 In Germany, customary law is defined as an "*actual exercise which is continually and constantly, equally and generally, and are recognized as a binding rule*" by the Federal Constitutional Court. *See* BVerfGE 22, 114 ff. (121) und 28, 21 ff. (28).

229 The Regents of the University of California, THE COMMON LAW AND CIVIL LAW TRADITIONS 2, https://www.law.berkeley.edu/library/robbins/CommonLawCivilLawTraditions.html (last visited Dec 20, 2014).

230 *Id.* at 2.

231 *See* Apple and Deyling (1995), *supra* note 210 at 14.

232 The Regents of the University of California, *supra* note 229 at 2.

233 *See e.g.* Apple and Deyling (1995), *supra* note 210; Dainow (1966), *supra* note 83; MOUSOURAKIS (2015), *supra* note 85; The Regents of the University of California, *supra* note 229.

234 Law code | law, ENCYCLOPEDIA BRITANNICA.

235 *See* BYRD ET AL. (2011), *supra* note 112 at 3.

236 *Id.* at 3.

237 *See* MERRYMAN AND PÉREZ-PERDOMO (2007), *supra* note 159 at 27.

238 *See e.g.* BYRD ET AL. (2011), *supra* note 112; MOUSOURAKIS (2015), *supra* note 85.

codes than some civil law countries.[239] Therefore, codification can also be seen as a method. Furthermore, codes can be found both in the common law and the civil law system. In contrast to the common law countries, the comprehensive and organized codes are of great significance to the interpretation and application of the law in the civil law countries. Here, judges generally interpret codes and laws very strictly.[240] Additionally, it can be noted that codes are generally annotated by legal scholars.[241]

In conclusion, the codification process and the codes have characterized and shaped the civil law system. As a result, these legislative codes became one of the major sources of law in most European countries.

e. Legislation in the European Civil Law Countries

Having explained the historical codification process in the civil law countries, this section will now examine others sources of law. As previously discussed, the codes are continuously revised trough new legislation. This process began after codification. Since then, legislation has become a separate power[242] and legislative activities have grown to modernize and adjust the legal provisions.[243] *Merryman & Pérez-Perdomo* state that, as a result, the law became synonymous with legislation in the 19th century.[244]

Additionally, legislation could delegate legal power to the executive. In the majority of civil law countries, there is a hierarchy of law. The Constitution stands at the head of the hierarchy, followed by federal codes and other statutes.[245] *O'Connor* takes the view that legislation and codification ensure a rational, logical, and systematic approach to law. Many authors[246] claim that judges generally interpret codes very strictly and consistently in compliance with the established legal order. However, the codes are updated based on research relating to socio-economic conditions and public attitutes as voiced by legal scholars.[247] Hence, in their view, the creation of new interpretations and new law is very limited.[248] Thus,

239 *See* Merryman and Pérez-Perdomo (2007), *supra* note 159 at 27.

240 *See* Vivienne O'Connor, *Common Law and Civil Law Traditions, in* PRACTITIONER'S GUIDE 1–35, 12 (2012), http://www.ssrn.com/abstract=2665675 (last visited Dec 20, 2014); *See also* BVerfG, 17.05.1960 - 2 BvL 11/59, BVerfGE 11, 126–136, (1960). In Germany, the court has to determine the objective intention of the legislature.

241 *See* Byrd et al. (2011), *supra* note 112 at 3.

242 *See* Merryman and Pérez-Perdomo (2007), *supra* note 159 at 16.

243 *See* Mousourakis (2015), *supra* note 85 at 301.

244 *See* Merryman and Pérez-Perdomo (2007), *supra* note 159.

245 *See* O'Connor (2012), *supra* note 240 at 11.

246 *See e.g.* Apple and Deyling (1995), *supra* note 210; Mousourakis (2015), *supra* note 85; O'Connor (2012), *supra* note 240.

247 *See* Apple and Deyling (1995), *supra* note 210 at 29; Mousourakis (2015), *supra* note 85 at 301.

248 *See also* Sarkar (2011), *supra* note 9 at 144.

the legislator needs to draft codes clearly and without gaps.[249] One could say that the civil law system appears rigid and inflexible; indeed, this could be the overriding assumption since recent years have seen a spate of legal reforms[250] in the European Union, and thus, in European civil law countries. As a result, national laws have adapted[251] and new laws have been passed.[252] The evidence suggets that, in light of this fact, there is also a great deal of diversity in terms of concrete responses to legal problems in the civillaw.

Despite the academic debate, legislation can be seen as a major source of law. It is responsible for the constantly updated and adjusted systematization of legal normative acts in terms of codes. *Dainow* emphasizes the importance of the law-making function of legislation in the civil law system. Even he sees legislation as the main source or basis of the law in civil law jurisdictions.[253] In addition, he points out that the comments of legal scholars and professors represent another significant feature.[254] Other authors argue that legal analysis, studies, and interpretations of legal scholars also constitute sources of law.[255] These materials were referred to as doctrine. A Romanian researcher defined this source as followed

> Doctrine is law, as conceived by theory, its scientific explanation, generalization and systematization.[256]

Prior to codification, the doctrines play an important role for judges seeking solutions in the comments of academic works. Nowadays the aim of doctrine is to facilitate the legislator in the process of creating, or law enforcement.[257] In conclusion, legal scholars view doctrine as an indirect and supporting source of law in the civil law system.

---

249 *See* MERRYMAN AND PÉREZ-PERDOMO (2007), *supra* note 159 at 30; La Porta, Lopez-de-Silanes, and Shleifer (2008), *supra* note 89 at304.

250 *See e.g.* DIRECTIVE 2000/31/EC OF THE EUROPEAN PARLIAMENT AND OF THE COUNCIL- E-COMMERCE - STANDARD EU RULES, 32000L0031 (2000).

251 BÜRGERLICHES GESETZBUCH (BGB) | GERMAN CIVIL CODE, *supra* note 102 at BGBl. I, p. 42, 2909; 2003 BGBI. I p. 738 in the version promulgated on January 2, 2002.

252 *See e.g.* ALLGEMEINES GLEICHBEHANDLUNGSGESETZ (AGG) | GENERAL ACT ON EQUAL TREATMENT, BGBl. I, p. 1897, 1910, (2006).

253 *See* Dainow (1966), *supra* note 83 at 424.

254 *Id.* at 424.

255 *See* Lupu (2013), *supra* note 75 at 377.

256 *See* Popescu. S. (2000), General theory of law, Bucharest: Lumina Lex, 159. in *Id.* at 377.

257 *Id.* at 377.

f. Customary Law in the Civil Law System

As already explained, since Justinian,[258] it has been recognized that unwritten law, or custom belongs to the sources of law. Modern authors recognized law as a social practice and in their view customary standards also comprise part of the system.[259] This initial source of law also has its origins in Roman law[260] and could be considered the oldest source of law.[261] In accordance with *Lupu*,[262] two conditions are required for a custom to become a source of law: firstly, there is a material, objective condition, namely an old and applied custom, and secondly, there is a psychological, subjective condition, according to which the specific rule is binding.

Customary law matters both in theory and in practice.[263] One important example is the development of *Bona Fides*[264] in Roman contract law. It required the contracting parties to give due consideration to the legitimate interests of the other party and to behave honestly. This custom contributed to the flexibility, informality and justice required by the community of merchants.[265]

Later, this principle found its way into the German Civil Code (BGB)[266] in the notion of "*Treu und Glauben*" as set forth in Section 157[267] and 242.[268] These paragraphs state

> Contracts shall be interpreted according to the requirement of good faith, ordinary usage being taken into consideration.[269]

At the beginning of the 19th century, the methodical academic debate on Section 242 of the German Civil Code (BGB) on the one side referred to a *"baneful plaque"* while the other side, praised it as the *"queen of rules."*[270] Nevertheless, through this principle, legislation provides an opportunity for courts to regulate a huge number

---

258 Codex Iustinianus, *supra* note 97. *See also* Klaus Luig, *Die Anfänge der Wissenschaft vom deutschen Privatrecht*, Ius Commune I, IUS COMMUNE 195–222, 200 (1967) (Ger).
259 *See e.g.* Dainow (1966), *supra* note 83; Lamond (2014), *supra* note 139 at 43; Lupu (2013), *supra* note 75 at 376.
260 *See* Reinhard Zimmermann & Simon Whittaker, *Good faith in European contract law: surveying the legal landscape, in* Good faith in European contract law 7–62, 16 (1. ed. 2000).
261 *See* Lupu (2013), *supra* note 75 at 376.
262 *Id.* at 376.
263 *See* Lamond (2014), *supra* note 139 at 27.
264 In English good faith, synonym in German Treu und Glauben (Ger), meaning literally fidelity and faith.
265 Zimmermann and Whittaker (2000), *supra* note 260 at 18.
266 Bürgerliches Gesetzbuch (BGB) | German Civil Code, *supra* note 102.
267 *Id.* § 157 „Verträge sind so auszulegen, wie Treu und Glauben mit Rücksicht auf die Verkehrssitte es erfordern (Ger)."
268 *Id.* § 242 „Der Schuldner ist verpflichtet, die Leistung so zu bewirken, wie Treu und Glauben mit Rücksicht auf die Verkehrssitte es erfordern (Ger)."
269 *See* Zimmermann and Whittaker (2000), *supra* note 260 at 18.
270 *Id.* at 20.

of different cases.[271] Hence, the legislation concedes that the judges can decide what is equitable given the circumstances of the specific case concerned. It has been shown that this legal principle could be seen as an adjustment of the rigid formalistic application of legal norms if these results in an abuse of rights.

Nonetheless, since the enactment of the German Civil Code (BGB), the courts have ruled on numerous cases concerning Section 242 of the (BGB). These cases on the general clause Section 242 of the German Civil Code (BGB) are also recorded in well-known commentaries.[272] In the meantime, legal scholars and German lawyers have attempted to categorize these countless applications into groups of cases.[273] Through these, it has been recognized that Section 242 of the German Civil Code (BGB) serves as a supplement to German civil law.[274] Finally, while custom remained a major source of law throughout the era of Roman law and the Middle Ages, its significance is preserved in the civil law system.

g. Final Comparison of the Sources of Law

To conclude, the analysis shows that the primary sources in the common law are judicial decisions and equity. The common law developed historically on a case-by-case basis, resulting in the creation of precedents, which are binding in order to ensure certainty and fairness.[275] In contrast, the primary source of law in the civil law systems is a code in the form of legislation. In addition to the primary sources, there are other sources like customary law, legal concepts, and doctrine. Overall, it can be argued that both the common law and the civil law systems contain all sources of law, as established in the comparison, but there is a different weighting and application. Thus, the essence of the comparison of the legal sources is that the main difference between the two legal systems lies in the contrast between the procedural and the theoretical origins of legal norms. A German legal historian, *Engelmann*, summarized that, due to the absence of scientific legal theory in the common law, legal practice evolved through teaching legal practice.[276]

---

271 *See e.g.* BAG, 18.07.2012 - 7 AZR 783/10, 33 (2012). *"Under German law, the court has to carry out an additional test in accordance with the requirement of good faith."*

272 *See e.g.* BÜRGERLICHES GESETZBUCH: MIT NEBENGESETZEN | COMMENTARY ON THE GERMAN CIVIL CODE, (Otto Palandt & Peter Bassenge eds., 75. ed. 2016); MÜNCHENER KOMMENTAR ZUM BÜRGERLICHEN GESETZBUCH, (Franz Jürgen Säcker & Roland Rixecker eds., 7. ed. 2015).

273 The enforcement of the claim may not oppose *"the pleading the unlawful exercise of a right such as disproportion and forfeiture" See* COMMENTARY ON THE GERMAN CIVIL CODE, *supra* note 272 § 242 note 47. *"Venire contra factum proprium." See Id.* § 242 note 55.

274 *See e.g.* COMMENTARY ON THE GERMAN CIVIL CODE, *supra* note 272 § 242 note 13.

275 *See* O'Connor (2012), *supra* note 240 at 13–14.

276 ENGELMANN, DIE WIEDERGEBURT DER RECHTSKULTUR IN ITALIEN, (1938) at 29. This note was placed in a footnote. In: GORDLEY AND VON MEHREN (2009), *supra* note 205 at 18.

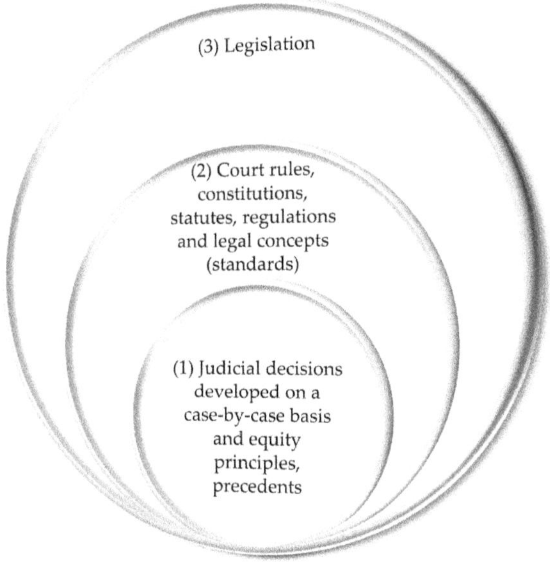

Figure 2 *The Primary and Secondary Sources of the Common Law*

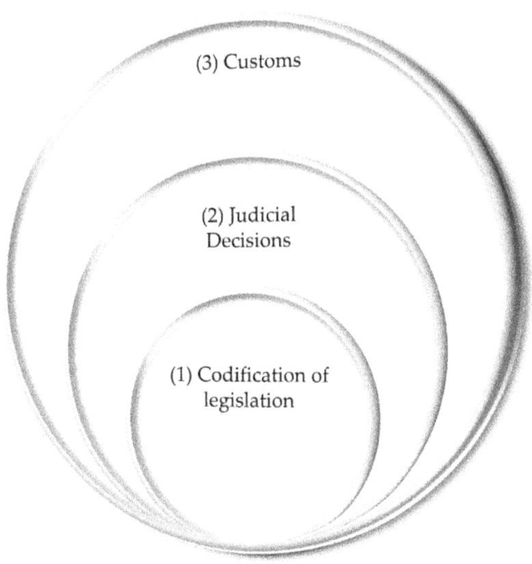

Figure 3 *The Primary and Secondary Sources of the Civil Law*

Ultimately, the foregoing figures show that each legal system possesses strong characteristic features that established its own identity.[277] However, the shared element is that all legal systems have the purpose of regulating and harmonizing social and business activities.[278] For instance, due to their parallel economic and social development, the EU Member States are required to satisfy the same social standards. Hence, they are also required to harmonize their legal development. In some cases, it seems that real differences between the civil law and the common law system will gradually disappear through the strengthening of legislation.[279]

By focusing on further legal development, many scholars have overlooked the fact that the distinctions are gradually blurring in the modern globalized world. Seemingly, the differences between the two legal systems have actually been overemphasized. Legal scholars have argued that the matter of "*mixed jurisdictions*" should also be considered. For example, *Merryman* stated that

> The two systems... are converging from different directions toward roughly equivalent mixed systems.[280]

Currently, through globalization and the trend for legal harmonization it appears this tendency is on the rise. In addition, legal comparison can also encompass an analysis of the structure of the court systems under common law and cilvil law. It is therefore vital to examine the specific structure, the role, and the organization of the court systems in the UK, US and Germany.

2. Comparison of the Structures of the Court Systems

This section will examine the different organization and practice of the courts in the common law and the civil law systems in order to substantiate the comparative analysis of law. The focus on the courts in these two legal systems can be helpful firstly in order to obtain a better insight into the use of the law in judicial decisions and, secondly, to illustrate the importance of judicial decisions for the legal framework of the compliance functions. For these reasons, this section will briefly analyze and compare the organization and practice of the court systems in the UK, in the US and in Germany. In accordance with the historical development of law, it will begin with the court system in the UK.

---

277 Dainow (1966), *supra* note 83 at 435.

278 *Id.* at 419.

279 *Id.* at 420.

280 Merryman and Pérez-Perdomo (2007), *supra* note 159 at 126.

a. The Structure of the Court System in the UK

This section presents the competences and the organizational structure of the courts in the UK.[281] The UK has an unified hierarchical court structure, referred to as a four-tier system.[282] The highest appeal court and the top level is the UK Supreme Court (UKSC).[283] The UKSC was established in 2009 by the Constitutional Reform Act 2005.[284] Section 23 (1) of this Act sets out the composition of the Supreme Court. Pursuant to Section 23 (2), the Court comprises 12 judges. According to Section 40 (1), the Supreme Court is a superior court of record and due to its establishment other jurisdiction was transferred from the House of Lords to the Supreme Court pursuant to Section 40 (4).[285] Nevertheless, it has to be considered that

> a decision of the Supreme Court on an appeal from one jurisdiction within the United Kingdom will not have effect as a binding precedent in any other such jurisdiction.[286]

The Court was designed to ensure the separation of powers between the legislature and the judiciary in accordance with the European Convention on Human Rights (ECHR). Today, the highest court plays an important role as the final interpreter of the law in the UK.[287] As a general rule, decisions can be appealed if the lower court has granted leave to appeal.[288] However, few cases ever reach this court.[289] The annual report[290] of the Supreme Court's full financial year shows a record number of hearings and judgments. The Court received

---

281 It has to be considered that the legal systems in Scotland, Northern Ireland and Wales are separate, and that there is a variety of distinctions between them. The structure of the English court system covers England and Wales. For this purpose, the tribunals system, which covers England, Wales, Northern Ireland and Scotland will not be examined.

282 *See* Byrd et al. (2011), *supra* note 112 at 186.

283 *See* Andenas and Fairgrieve (2015), *supra* note 81 at 409.

284 Constitutional Reform Act 2005, c. 4, § 5 (2005).

285 *Id.* § 40 (1); (4).

286 *Id.* at 41. Explanatory Notes 162 and 163. "*....nothing in the provisions of the Act about the Supreme Court is to affect the distinctions between the separate legal systems of the parts of the United Kingdom. This recognizes that those legal systems are separate, and that there is a variety of distinctions between them, so that, for example, Scotland differs from Northern Ireland in some ways, and in other ways from England and Wales.*"

287 *Id.* at 409.

288 *See* Andenas and Fairgrieve (2015), *supra* note 81 at 411.

289 *See* Byrd et al. (2011), *supra* note 112 at 186.

290 Supreme Court annual report and accounts: 2014 to 2015 - Publications - GOV.UK, (2015).

231 applications between 2014 and 2015, heard 89 appeals, 37 of which were ultimately allowed.[291]

The structure of the English court system, which covers England and Wales, excluding tribunals, is shown below:

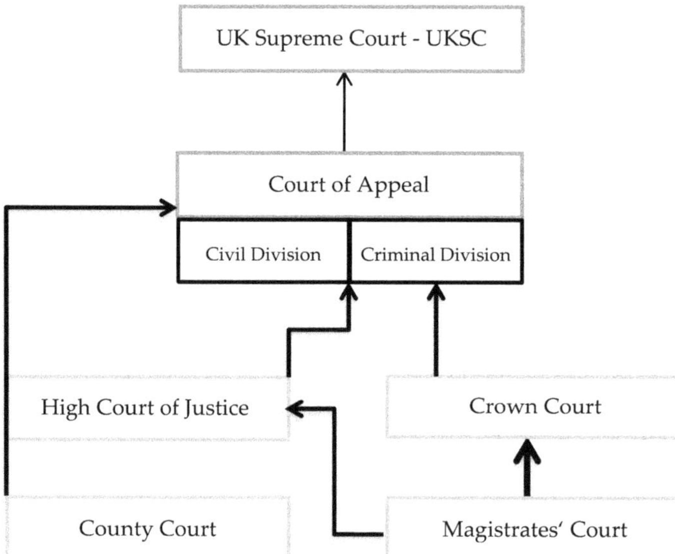

Figure 4 *The Structure of the English Court System*[292]

It can be argued that the structure of the court system in the UK is complex. Due to this complicated structure, the English justice system was cumbersome, slow and inefficient.[293] It has evolved over 1,000 years with different kinds of cases being dealt with in separate courts.[294] The first instance includes the Magistrates' Courts and the County Courts with limited jurisdiction. The Magistrates are trial courts with jurisdiction for petty criminal, family, and private law disputes, such as traffic offenses up to the value of £ 5,000.[295] The majority of judges are lay persons, but the Magistrates do have a court clerk, a lawyer who trains and advises them

291 *Id.* at 28. Sec. III.

292 *See* Byrd et al. (2011), *supra* note 112 at 188.

293 *Id.* at 406.

294 UK Judicial Press Office, Structure of the courts & tribunal system, https://www.judiciary.uk/about-the-judiciary/the-justice-system/court-structure/ (last visited Feb 13, 2016).

295 *See* Byrd et al. (2011), *supra* note 112 at 186.

on the law.[296] The County Courts are geographically limited in their jurisdiction. Conversely, the Crown Court has no geographical limitation. The County Courts deal with minor civil, contract, tort, and land law cases with a value of less than £25,000.[297] These courts help to alleviate the burden on the High Court of Justice.

The second instance comprises two courts. The first is the Crown Court, the trial court for criminal cases, and the second the High Court of Justice for private law.[298] The High Courts have three divisions: (1) the Queen's Bench Division (QBD), (2) the Family Division, and (3) the Chancery Division.[299] All three divisions hear appeals from other courts. The QDB primarily handles contract and tort cases with a value over £ 25,000; the Family Division deals with matters concerning children or families, as well as divorce cases; while the Chancery Divisions handles *e.g.* equity matters, insolvency cases, or company law cases.[300] Appeals from decisions of the County Courts proceed directly to the third instance, the Court of Appeal, whereas appeals from decisions of the Magistrates are referred to the Crown Court if the appeal has been allowed.[301]

The third instance, the Court of Appeal, has two divisions: (1) the criminal division, headed by the Lord Chief Justice, and (2) the civil division, headed by the Master of the Rolls. This Court is an exclusively appellate court similar to the Supreme Court. The final and highest court, the UK Supreme Court, is located at the top of the pyramid and hears appeals on points of law only. As already noted, it was established in 2009[302] and replaced the Law Lords as the highest Court in the UK. Today, the UKSC is located in the former Middlesex Guildhall in Parliament Square, Westminster.[303] It hears appeals on arguable points of law in both civil and criminal cases.[304]

The English court system consists of combination of traditional and new structures. Pressure has led to the introduction of various reforms.[305] In the course of these reforms, the creation of the UKSC separated the most senior level of the judiciary from the legislature and as a result of the Constitutional Reform Act 2005, the English judiciary is officially recognized as a fully separated branch of the government.[306] Since then, the judiciary has become more independent. Overall, the scope of judicial review has grown in recent years due to three influences (1) membership in the EU, (2) the expansion of the volume and scope of administrative law, and (3) as a result of parliamentary activism.[307]

296 *Id.* at 186.
297 *Id.* at 187.
298 UK Judicial Press Office, *supra* note 294.
299 *Id.*
300 *See* Byrd et al. (2011), *supra* note 112 at 187.
301 *Id.* at 187–188.
302 Supreme Court Rules 2009, 1–2 (2009). These Rules apply to civil and criminal appeals to the Court.
303 *See* Stephen R. Wilson et al., English legal system 47 (1. ed. 2014).
304 *See* M. Moran, Politics and Governance in the UK 405 (2011).
305 Supreme Court Rules 2009, *supra* note 295.
306 *See* Moran (2011), *supra* note 304 at 404.
307 *Id.* at 405.

b. The Structure of the Federal Court System in the US

The judiciary system in the US comprises two parallel systems: the federal and the state system. Each of these systems is responsible for civil and criminal cases.[308] Both the federal and state courts interpret the laws enacted by the legislature. The judiciary has the authority to review legislative and executive actions.[309] Thus, it has the capacity to tackle new social, political, or economic requirements.[310] Nevertheless, only a limited number of cases actually progress to the federal legal system, for example crimes in violation of federal law or any cases arising under US law.[311] Federal law has its origins in the US Constitution.[312] Due to its importance for criminal and corporate law, this section presents a brief overview of the federal court system in the US.

Although the common law was transferred to the American colonies, the federal court system in the US differs from the system in the UK. It is often described as a three-tiered system.[313] The US Supreme Court is the highest court and was established by the first US act, the Judiciary Act of 1789, and Article III of the US Constitution.[314] As such, the US Supreme Court has existed and worked much longer than the UKSC. Similar to the UK court system, the US system also includes trial courts and intermediate appellate courts.[315] It has evolved over more than 200 years and is built around a hierarchical structure.[316]

As discussed, the judicial system in the US is set up in accordance with Article III of the US Constitution.[317] Article III provides for one Supreme Court. The US Supreme Court consists of one Chief Justice of the US and eight associate justices.[318] Justices of the Supreme Court are appointed by the US President with the approval of the Senate. In one year, a single justice can handle and consider around 100 cases, but the court receives approximately 10,000 petitions per year.[319] The US Supreme Court as the highest Court in the US has both original jurisdiction and

---

308 THE US JUSTICE SYSTEM: AN ENCYCLOPEDIA, 1 (Steven Harmon Wilson ed., 2012).
309 *Id.* at 1.
310 *Id.* at 1.
311 *See* BYRD ET AL. (2011), *supra* note 112 at 150.
312 US CONST., THE CONSTITUTION OF THE UNITED STATES OF AMERICA (1787) Art. I, § 8. *See* THE US JUSTICE SYSTEM (2012), *supra* note 308 at 2.
313 *See* BYRD ET AL. (2011), *supra* note 112 at 147; HAY (2011), *supra* note 87 at 45–46.
314 AN ACT TO ESTABLISH THE JUDICIAL COURTS OF THE UNITED STATES, JUDICIARY ACT OF 1789 (1789); US CONST., *supra* note 312 Art. III, § 1 "*The judicial Power of the United States shall be vested in one Supreme Court, and in such inferior Courts as the Congress may* from time *to time ordain and establish.*"
315 *See* BYRD ET AL. (2011), *supra* note 112 at 147.
316 THE US JUSTICE SYSTEM (2012), *supra* note 308 at 77.
317 *See* footnote 314; US CONST., *supra* note 312 Art III, § 1.
318 28 USC, UNITED STATES CODE (1926) § 1; *See also* BYRD ET AL. (2011), *supra* note 112 at 153.
319 THE US JUSTICE SYSTEM (2012), *supra* note 308 at 89.

appellate jurisdiction according to the United States Code (USC).[320] It has exclusive jurisdiction to hear cases from the other courts.[321] In addition, it revises the decisions of the US courts of appeal.[322] To this end, the Supreme Court orders the complete record of the case from the lower courts.[323] Often, the Supreme Court decides unsettled constitutional cases or has the final say if two courts of appeal have interpreted the law differently in similar cases.[324]

The intermediate Courts of Appeal are called Circuit Courts because the country is divided into eleven geographical regions, called circuits. The circuits are named by numbers: The First Circuit, the Second Circuit, ... through the Eleventh Circuit, plus a Circuit for the District of Columbia (Washington D.C.) and the Federal Circuit (F.C.).[325] Therefore, according to the USC, the United States has a total of thirteen judicial circuits.[326] These courts hear and review the decisions of the lower courts, the US District Courts. However, in contrast to the US Supreme Court, the Appellate Courts decide in legal matters only, not on the facts of a case.[327] In general, the Courts of Appeals consist of three-judge panels,[328] which reach a decision by a simple majority.[329] The districts are within the circuits. Each judicial district has a district court.[330] Today, all districts have more than one judge who presides over the cases.[331] The US District Courts are primary trial courts, which deal with civil and criminal cases. The decisions of these courts bind the lower courts within the same circuit. The precedents remain unless the US Supreme Court overrules the decision.[332]

In addition, according to the Constitution, the Congress is authorized to enact *e.g.* "*...uniform Laws on the subject of Bankruptcies.*"[333] The bankruptcy judge is a designated judicial officer of the District Court, who deals with the matter of bankruptcy proceedings.[334]

---

320 28 USC, UNITED STATES CODE, (1926) § 1251 (a)(1948). "*The Supreme Court shall have original and exclusive jurisdiction of all controversies between two or more States.*"
321 *See* BYRD ET AL. (2011), *supra* note 112 at 153.
322 28 USC, UNITED STATES CODE, *supra* note 318 § 1254 (1948).
323 THE US JUSTICE SYSTEM (2012), *supra* note 308 at 89.
324 *Id.* at 90.
325 *See* BYRD ET AL. (2011), *supra* note 112 at 152.
326 28 USC, UNITED STATES CODE, *supra* note 318 at § 41 (1948).
327 *See* BYRD ET AL. (2011), *supra* note 112 at 46.
328 28 USC, UNITED STATES CODE, *supra* note 318 § 46 (a).
329 *See* BYRD ET AL. (2011), *supra* note 112 at 152.
330 28 USC, UNITED STATES CODE, *supra* note 318 § 132 (a).
331 THE US JUSTICE SYSTEM (2012), *supra* note 308 at 77. *See also* AN ACT TO ESTABLISH THE JUDICIAL COURTS OF THE UNITED STATES, *supra* note 313 Sess. 1, Ch. 20, 1 Stat. 73.
332 THE US JUSTICE SYSTEM (2012), *supra* note 308 at 87.
333 US CONST., *supra* note 312 Art. 1, § 8.
334 THE US JUSTICE SYSTEM (2012), *supra* note 308 at 104–105.

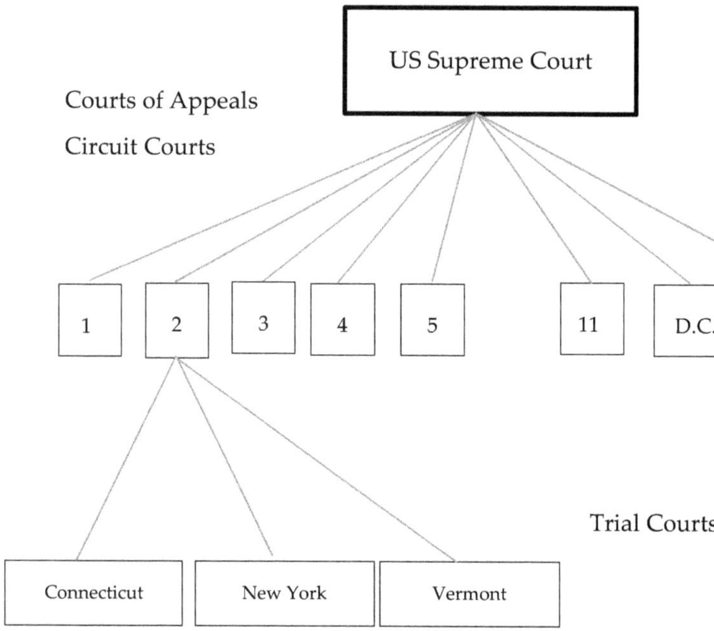

Figure 5 *The Federal US Court System*

In conclusion, *Figure 5* summarizes the general structure of the Federal United State Court system, which comprises trial courts, appellate courts and the Supreme Court. In terms of its unified hierarchical structure, the appellate system, and the name of the highest Court, the structure of the US federal court system is similar to the UK court system. The unique characteristic of the US judiciary is that it is more locally oriented. Furthermore, the structure of the US court system is very different from the court systems of the European nations, because each state in the US has its own court system, as well as a self-contained legal system.[335]

As described previously, the federal government *e.g.* the Congress possesses considerable authority over the US federal court system.[336] Although the US judiciary operates separately from the executive and legislative branches, the

335 *See* Byrd et al. (2011), *supra* note 112 at 149; Hay (2011), *supra* note 87 at 48.
336 *See* Bast and Hawkins (2013), *supra* note 140 at 7.

federal judiciary often works with both of them, as the Constitution requires.[337] Additionally, the federal legislature can establish administrative agencies[338] in order to delegate the power to promulgate administrative rules and regulations that have the force of law.[339] Therefore, the agency has the quasi-judicial power for administrative law judges. They decide disputes concerning the administrative rules and regulations.[340] Furthermore, in the US, the Judicial Conference studies caseloads, reviews staff needs, and establishes administrative guidelines for the federal judiciary.[341] In addition, unlike the Supreme Court and the district courts, the Judicial Conference reviews rules in terms of their consistency with federal law.[342] The Administrative Office, meanwhile, oversees the bureaucratic aspects of the federal judicial system.[343]

In conclusion, the American system of justice enforces and interprets the law not only through its judges but also through legislative and executive bodies and administrative agencies.[344] Over time, this characteristic of the judiciary system has developed differently to the UK judicial system and America's multifaceted judicial system is the result of its unique historical development and historic events such as the creation of the Constitution and the Declaration of the Independence from the UK.[345]

c. The Structure of the German Court System

As has been shown in the previous sections, the court systems in the common law countries are unified and organized in the form of a pyramid, with the high Supreme Court at the top.[346] Thus, the Supreme Court could, in theory, review every civil and criminal case.[347] The ultimate power to review the legality of administrative action and the constitutionality of legislative action lies with the Supreme Court.[348]

---

337 US Const., *supra* note 312 Art. III, § 2 *"..: the Supreme Court shall have appellate Jurisdiction, both as to Law and Fact, with such Exceptions, and under such Regulations as the Congress shall make."*

338 The term administrative agencies includes *e.g.* The Federal State Commission or the Environmental Protection Agency (EPA). *See* US EPA, US Environmental Protection Agency | EPA, EPA (2015), http://www3.epa.gov/ (last visited Sep 12, 2015).

339 Bast and Hawkins (2013), *supra* note 140 at 8.

340 *Id.* at 9.

341 28 USC, United States Code, *supra* note 318 § 331.

342 28 *Id.* § 331.

343 The US justice system (2012), *supra* note 308 at 109.

344 *Id.* at 7.

345 *Id.* at 8.

346 *See* Merryman and Pérez-Perdomo (2007), *supra* note 159 at 86.

347 *Id.* at 86.

348 *Id.* at 86.

Generally, the court system in civil law countries differs markedly to the unified court system of the common law countries.[349] The civil law court system is organized as a set of two or more distinct structures.[350] For example, there is a theoretical and practical distinction between public law and private law. For this reason, the court structure is more specialized and more decentralized than in the common law countries and is divided according to public law and private law cases.[351] Legal scholars refer to this system as an ordinary or regular jurisdiction, because the ordinary courts evidently influence the life of ordinary citizens.[352] The ordinary judges interpret and apply the codes. In contrast to the common law system, only the legislator has the power to make law.[353]

The German Court system evolved through the codification of German law.[354] The judiciary branch is represented by the Federal Constitutional Court (BVerfG), federal courts and state courts.[355] According to the Basic Law of the Federal Republic of Germany (GG), the judges shall be independent and are subject only to the constitution and the statutes.[356] The court system in Germany is a specialized system that encompasses trial courts and appellate courts. The German courts are, however, specialized according to subjects matter. There are five different hierarchies of courts, each with their own specific jurisdiction.[357] The German court system is structured into five independent specialized jurisdictions: (1) ordinary jurisdiction, (2) labor jurisdiction, (3) general administrative jurisdiction, (4) fiscal jurisdiction, and (5) social jurisdiction.[358] Each set of courts has its own jurisdiction, hierarchy, judiciary, and procedure.[359] According to the German Constitution, the highest Courts of Justice of the Federal Government are located at the head of each jurisdiction as the last instance.[360] These courts handle final appeals and review the decisions of the lower regional specialized courts. They have appellate jurisdiction

---

349 *See* Apple and Deyling (1995), *supra* note 210 at 24.

350 *See* Merryman and Pérez-Perdomo (2007), *supra* note 159 at 86.

351 *See* O'Connor (2012), *supra* note 240 at 15.

352 *See* Merryman and Pérez-Perdomo (2007), *supra* note 159 at 86. Nigel G. Foster & Satish Sule, German legal system & laws 82 (4. ed. 2010).

353 *See* Merryman and Pérez-Perdomo (2007), *supra* note 159 at 87.

354 *See* Foster and Sule (2010), *supra* note 352 at 80.

355 Grundgesetz (GG) | Basic Law for the Federal Republic of Germany, *supra* note 37 Art. 92.

356 *Id.* Art. 97; Gerichtsverfassungsgesetz (GVG) | Courts Constitution Act, Judicature Act (RGBl, 41) (1879) § 1.

357 *See* Foster and Sule (2010), *supra* note 352 at 81.

358 *Id.* at 82.

359 Grundgesetz (GG) | Basic Law for the Federal Republic of Germany, *supra* note 37 Art. 92.

360 *Id.* Art. 95 I.

and rule only on issues of law, not on facts.[361] An appeal on the point of law is allowed if the case is of particular or it facilitates the development of the law.[362]

The courts of first instance can also be found in smaller towns within each of the *Länder*.[363] Pursuant to Section 23 of the Courts Constitution Act (GVG), the trial courts have original jurisdiction to deal with cases with a value at dispute of up to €5,000.[364] Generally, their jurisdiction comprises civil law matters.[365] In accordance with the Courts Constitution Act, these cases are heard by a single judge, who holds a law degree.[366] The large number of courts facilitates straightforward and swift decisions. The intermediate higher regional courts have appellate and original jurisdiction. For instance, pursuant to the German Code of Civil Procedure (ZPO),[367] the appeal will be allowed if the appeal value of €600 is reached. According to the Courts Constitution Act (GVG),[368] the higher regional courts comprise both civil and criminal divisions. They handle civil cases with a value of more than € 5,000 as well as more serious criminal matters.[369] Despite this seemingly complex and highly specialized court structure, the German system is accessible and provides fast judicial decisions.[370]

It has been noted that legislative power could not be exercised by the ordinary judiciary.[371] After 1945, Germany established a rigid constitution, which provides some methods of reviewing legislative action.[372] The Federal Constitutional Court was created to review the legality of administrative action. Therefore, the separation of the legislative, judicative, and executive power works as a principle.[373] The highest and most important court is the Federal Constitutional Court (BVerfG) in

361 Zivilprozessordnung (ZPO) | German Code of Civil Procedure, RGBl, p. 83 (1879) §§ 454 (1); 546.

362 *Id.* § 543 (2).

363 The term *Länder* (Ger) should be distinguished from the term federal states (US). There are 646 towns in total. *See* http://www.bmjv.de/SharedDocs/Downloads/DE/pdfs/Anzahl_der_Gerichte_des_Bundes_und_der_Laender.html?nn=1470312, (last visit Dec 22, 2014)

364 Gerichtsverfassungsgesetz (GVG) | Courts Constitution Act, *supra* note 356 § 23 (1).

365 *Id.* § 23.

366 Deutsches Richtergesetz (DRiG), The German Judiciary Act, BGBI. I, p. 1665 (1962) § 5.

367 Zivilprozessordnung (ZPO) | German Code of Civil Procedure, *supra* note 361 § 511 a.

368 Gerichtsverfassungsgesetz (GVG) | Courts Constitution Act, *supra* note 356 § 60.

369 *See* Foster and Sule (2010), *supra* note 352 at 83–84.

370 *Id.* at 84.

371 *See* Merryman and Pérez-Perdomo (2007), *supra* note 159 at 90.

372 *Id.* at 89.; Gerichtsverfassungsgesetz (GVG) | Courts Constitution Act, *supra* note 356 § 71.

373 *See* Merryman and Pérez-Perdomo (2007), *supra* note 159 at 90.

Karlsruhe. The Federal Constitutional Court was established by the constitution in 1949 and began its work in 1951.[374] This court decides constitutional matters and cases in which compatibility of statutes with the Basic Law are under dispute.[375] The Federal Constitutional Court (BVerfG) consists of two senates with eight judges each.[376] The judges are selected to serve for twelve years and are appointed by the German Bundestag and Federal Council.[377] The first senate deals with issues concerning the basic constitutional rights pursuant to Section 13 no. 6 and 11 of the Act on the Federal Constitutional Court (BVerfGG), as set forth in the Basic Law for the Federal Republic of Germany (GG).[378] The second senate handles cases involving political actions, electoral and international law pursuant to Section 13 no. 1 to 5, 6a to 9, 11a, 12, and 14 of the Act on the Federal Constitutional Court (BVerfGG).[379] Thus, the Court's most important function is to interpret the Basic Law of the Federal Republic of Germany (GG). It decides questions of law to ensure consistency for all other courts.[380]

Generally, judges in German courts follow the rule of non-binding precedents, but judges in lower courts are aware of the decisions in the higher courts.[381] However, the rule of non-binding precedents includes one formal exception pursuant to Section 31 (1) of the Act on the Federal Constitutional Court (BVerfGG).[382] The decisions of the Federal Constitutional Court are binding on all courts, legislative and executive authorities.[383] In conclusion, the Federal Court is with competence to review whether legislation operates in accordance with the Constitution. It interprets the provisions of the German Constitution while also adapting

---

374 Grundgesetz (GG) | Basic Law for the Federal Republic of Germany, *supra* note 37 Art. 92; Gerichtsverfassungsgesetz (GVG) | Courts Constitution Act, *supra* note 356 § 1.

375 Gesetz über das Bundesverfassungsgericht (BVerfGG) | Act on the Federal Constitutional Court, BGBl. I, p. 243 (1951)§ 13 no. 1–15..

376 *See* Foster and Sule (2010), *supra* note 352 at 91; Gesetz über das Bundesverfassungsgericht (BVerfGG) | Act on the Federal Constitutional Court, *supra* note 375 § 2.

377 Gesetz über das Bundesverfassungsgericht (BVerfGG) | Act on the Federal Constitutional Court, *supra* note 375 §§ 3 (1), 5; Grundgesetz (GG) | Basic Law for the Federal Republic of Germany, *supra* note 37 Art. 93.

378 Gesetz über das Bundesverfassungsgericht (BVerfGG) | Act on the Federal Constitutional Court, *supra* note 375 § 14 (1); Grundgesetz (GG) | Basic Law for the Federal Republic of Germany, *supra* note 37 Art. 1–20.

379 Gesetz über das Bundesverfassungsgericht (BVerfGG) | Act on the Federal Constitutional Court, *supra* note 375 § 14 (2); *See also* Foster and Sule (2010), *supra* note 352 at 91.

380 *See* Foster and Sule (2010), *supra* note 352 at 91.

381 *Id.* at 54.

382 Gesetz über das Bundesverfassungsgericht (BVerfGG) | Act on the Federal Constitutional Court, *supra* note 375 § 13 (1).

383 *See* Foster and Sule (2010), *supra* note 352 at 54.

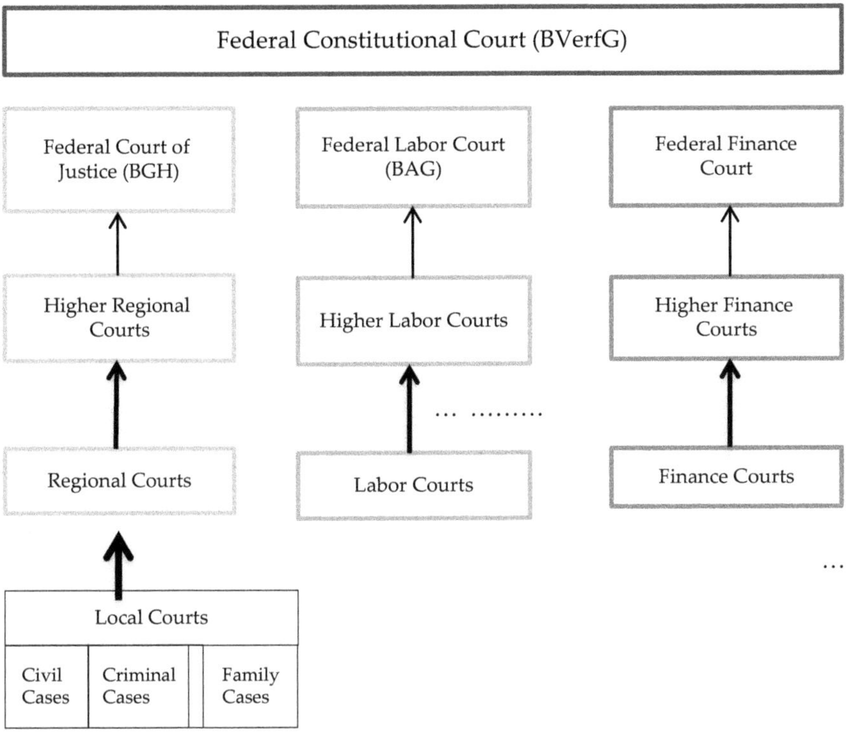

Figure 6 – *A Section of the German Court System*

the interpretation of the constitutional provisions to take account of societal developments. *Figure 6*, above, presents the ordinary and specialized structure of the German court system in brief.

d. Final Comparison of the Court Systems

This section has illustrated the key differences in the court systems in the common law and civil law countries. The common law countries have a unified hierarchical court system. As *figures 4* and *5* show, the court systems are comprised of three or four tiers.[384] The common law court system makes a general distinction between civil and criminal cases. Comparing the structure of the courts in the US and

384 *See supra* Figure 4, p. 78, Figure 5, p. 82; *See also* Bast and Hawkins (2013), *supra* note 140 at 94.

UK, the civil law countries, for example Germany, have a more specialized court system. The German court system is comprised of *e.g.* public, administrative, labor law, and other areas of the law.

Secondly, the Supreme Courts in the common law countries play a greater role than in the civil law countries. They have original and appellate jurisdiction and have the authority to review legislative and executive actions. Regardless of the number and various kinds of courts, every case could be subject to the jurisdiction of the highest court, the Supreme Court. Particularly in the US, the Supreme Court plays an important role in governing since both the executive and legislative branches of the government have a voice in the composition of this court. In Germany, the highest court, the Federal Constitution Court, is an appellate court on point of law, but holds no original jurisdiction.

Thirdly, judges in the common law countries follow the doctrine of stare decisis.[385] Judges are bound by decisions reached on similar cases in the past. The court must follow the legal principle decided by that court or a higher court in a prior similar case.[386] In the civil law system, however, judges follow the rule of non-binding precedents and are bound to the law.

In conclusion, in the common law system, the courts and judges play a greater role in the creation and development of the law, but only a small volume of cases reach the Supreme Courts. Compared with this, the civil court system with its ordinary courts seems more accessible to the citizen and the judicial process swifter than in the common law countries.

3. Development of the Law in the Two Systems

The two previous sections have explored and compared the sources of law and the structures of the court systems. This section will now compare the various aspects of the development of the law between the common law and civil law systems. It considers in brief the differences and similarities and provides perspectives on the sources and dynamism of the two systems.

a. **Development in the Common Law**

As outlined in the previous sections, the basis of common law is the establishment of judicial decisions. However, before the 20th century, there was no organized system of cases and law reports. Cases had to be analyzed orally by the lawyers and judges. Today, all major decisions are published in electronic filing systems.[387]

---

385 *See supra* footnote 149, Stare decisis | law, Latin: *"Let the decision stand." See* BAST AND HAWKINS (2013), *supra* note 140 at 2.

386 *See* BAST AND HAWKINS (2013), *supra* note 140 at 2.

387 *See* GARY SLAPPER *&* DAVID KELLY, THE ENGLISH LEGAL SYSTEM (18. ed. 2017). *See for example* The UK Supreme Court, DECIDED CASES - THE UK SUPREME COURT THE SUPREME COURT, https://www.supremecourt.uk/decided-cases/index.html (last

Thus, it is also important to note that the common law is constantly and orderly evolving.

Furthermore, legal scholars assert that the focus for the development of law in the common law has been the judge.[388] As such, he is a much more powerful figure than in the civil law. Judges were traditionally vested with the ability to create law.[389] The historical development shows that judges interpret the law on a case–by–case basis in order to shape that same law. Thus, it has been recognized that the common law was originally created and grown through judges' decisions.[390] As a result, *Sakar* asserts that this approach may help to make legal regulation more adaptable to changing circumstances and, thus, also helps fit with the generally accepted theory.[391]

In addition, the courts also exercise judicial review over federal statutes and the actions of official bodies, and determine the constitutionality of federal and national laws.[392] Through the concept of stare decisis,[393] judicial decisions in the common law can act as binding precedent for subsequent decisions. This means that, in the interest of legal certainty, the principles of law set forth in cases upon which individuals have relied should not be overruled.[394] A precedent thus helps to ensure consistency and reliability in the common law.[395]

On the other hand, in some cases it has been recognized that the common law courts have in some instances overruled rules established previously.[396] For example, the US Supreme Court and the state counterparts overruled their precedent and interpreted a new understanding of the law, which they could apply to future cases presenting the same case and legal issue.[397] The technique of overruling has made room for flexibility and permitted adjustment to these new conditions. In addition, since joining the European Union, the UK common law system has had to contend with a new source of law in the form of the *acquis communautaire*.[398]

---

visited Feb 24, 2019); USA.Gov., Electronic Filing - The US Supreme Court Supreme Court of the US, https://www.supremecourt.gov/filingandrules/electronicfiling.aspx (last visited Feb 24, 2019).

388 *See* Dainow (1966), *supra* note 83 at 425.

389 *See* O'Connor (2012), *supra* note 240 at 23.

390 *See* Merryman and Pérez-Perdomo (2007), *supra* note 159 at 34.

391 *See* Sarkar (2011), *supra* note 91.

392 *See* http://www.cec.org/lawdatabase/us01.cfm?varlan=english, (last visit Dec 2, 2015)

393 *See supra* note 189, stare decisis | law.

394 *See* Byrd et al. (2011), *supra* note 112 at 9.

395 *See* Bast and Hawkins (2013), *supra* note 140 at 7.

396 *See* Balganesh and Parchomovsky (2015), *supra* note 182 at 1268.

397 *See* Nelson (2014), *supra* note 154 at 55.

398 The *acquis communautaire* is the accumulated body of European Union (EU) law and obligations from 1958 to the present day. It comprises all the EU treaties and laws (directives, regulations, decisions), declarations and resolutions, international agreements and the judgments of the Court of Justice. *See* Vaughne Miller, The

Moreover, despite this method of further development of the law by judges, the legislature regularly intervenes by enacting new acts,[399] for instance those passed by the Congress of the United States.[400] Some areas of the law are governed exclusively by statutes.[401] One example is commercial law, which in the US is codified in the Uniform Commercial Code[402] adopted in all 50 US states.[403]

Furthermore, the interpretation and application of the acts is again a matter for the courts. Judicial review was an issue in a well-known case, *Marbury v. Madison*, in which the Chief Justice John Marshall stated that the Supreme Court has the authority to review acts of US Congress and determine whether they are unconstitutional and, therefore, void.[404] In this case, the rule must be repealed.[405]

In contrast, the influence on the development of the law in the common law system exerted by law professors, legal scholarship, and academic writings is less than in the civil law system. While some legal scholars contend that the importance and use of this material by courts will grow in future,[406] *Merryman* states that, even today, the common law is still the law of the judges.[407]

In conclusion, it can be stated that the common law has evolved over time with a systematically organized case system, by overruling precedents and judge-made reinterpretations to give a new understanding of the law, supplemented by legislative statutes in special areas of law, and through the review of those statutes by the judiciary.

b. Development in the Civil Law

In the past, the legal development of the civil law system was subject to two main influences. The first is the function of the legislator to make law. Historically, this authority developed through the codification process and a strict separation of

---

EU's ACQUIS COMMUNAUTAIRE (2011), http://researchbriefings.parliament.uk/ (last visited Sep 24, 2015). *See also* SLAPPER AND KELLY (2017), *supra* note 387 at XII.

399 *See e.g.* UNIFORM COMMERCIAL CODE (UCC), *supra* note 184.

400 US CONST., *supra* note 312 Art. I, § 1. "*All legislative Powers herein granted shall be vested in a Congress of the United States, which shall consist of a Senate and House of Representatives.*"

401 *See* BAST AND HAWKINS (2013), *supra* note 140 at 7.

402 *See* HAY (2011), *supra* note 87 at 9 note 24.

403 *See* BAST AND HAWKINS (2013), *supra* note 140 at 7.

404 *Marbury v. Madison,* 5 US 137, 175 (1803). Chief Justice Marshall explained that *"the essential criterion of appellate jurisdiction"* is *"that it revises and corrects the proceedings in a cause already instituted, and does not create that cause."*

405 *Id.* at 175.; OPINION OF THE COURT | MARBURY V. MADISON, Marshall, C.J., 154–180 180, https://www.law.cornell.edu/supremecourt/text/5/137#writing-USSC_CR_0005_0137_ZO (last visited Dec 12, 2014).

406 *See* A. GILLESPIE, THE ENGLISH LEGAL SYSTEM 53 (5. ed. 2015); MERRYMAN AND PÉREZ-PERDOMO (2007), *supra* note 159 at 57.

407 *See* MERRYMAN AND PÉREZ-PERDOMO (2007), *supra* note 159 at 57.

powers between the legislative, judiciary, and executive.[408] Legislative initiative was introduced by elected representatives of the people or through a referendum in response to altered social circumstances. A mandatory legislative procedure follows.[409] For this reason, the law is created and adopted in the civil law countries by the legislator. Consequently, the judges merely apply and interpret the law. Judicial powers and scope are less than in the common law countries.[410]

A second aspect of legal development is that, contrary to the consistency of the common law system, in the 18th and 19th centuries, the civil law system was modified and reinterpreted due to the increased input from European legal experts and academics.[411] A characteristic feature of the civil law tradition is the method of legal thinking. Legal scholars and academics use abstract terms, scientific legal theory, and methodologies to solve legal problems.[412] Moreover, legal scholars have a highly prestigious standing and their opinions are highly influential.[413] Scholars may influence the judges in two ways: Firstly, the theories and methods of the scholars are used by the courts to help them interpret the law in a specific matter and, secondly, after the decision, academics publish their critical legal opinions of the decision.[414] Furthermore, the legal tradition of writing legal textbooks facilitated the transfer of legal knowledge at the European universities.[415] Hence, in the civil law system, the legal scholars and their legal writings are a dominant factor and have a great impact both on the judges and on the legislator,[416] who use the legal theory put forward by legal scholars when making and applying the law.[417] Thus, legal scholars can also influence the development of the law in the civil law systems.

In conclusion, the role of legal science and academia with its theoretical explanatory, scientific interpretations of the normative material support the legislator or judge in the process of creating or interpreting and applying the law.[418] In addition, legislation responds to changing social circumstances by means of legal theories. Finally, the civil law system evolved exclusively through legislation and legal science through the application of the law by the judiciary.

---

408 *Id.* at 33.

409 *See* in Germany for example: Legislative powers of the Bund and the Länder Grundgesetz (GG) | Basic Law for the Federal Republic of Germany, *supra* note 37 Art. 70.

410 *See* Merryman and Pérez-Perdomo (2007), *supra* note 159 at 38.

411 *See* Dainow (1966), *supra* note 83 at 421.

412 *See* Mousourakis (2015), *supra* note 85 at 302.

413 *See* Merryman and Pérez-Perdomo (2007), *supra* note 159 at 57.

414 *See* O'Connor (2012), *supra* note 240 at 22.

415 *See* Mousourakis (2015), *supra* note 85 at 304.

416 *See* Merryman and Pérez-Perdomo (2007), *supra* note 159 at 60.

417 *Id.* at 60.

418 *See* Lupu (2013), *supra* note 75 at 377.

c. Summary of the Development of both Legal Systems

The three previous sections highlight the specific similarities and differences between the civil law and common law systems similarities. Taking into account the various theories and concepts discussed, the basic distinction between the common and civil law can be succinctly summarized with these words as follows:

> Sec. 570 The most striking difference between the civil and the common law lies in the greater relative importance, which, in the former system, is attributed to the opinions of jurists as compared with prior decisions of the courts.[419]

First and foremost the Anglo-American legal system and the English legal system are built on case law. In other words, the common law is the totality of principles, concepts, and binding decisions set down by the judiciary. Although typically affected by statutory authority, broad areas of the law - most notably relating to property, contracts, and tort, are traditionally part of the common law.[420] These factors confirm that the judiciary's common law authority is established by the decisions made by past generations of judges.[421] Legal scholars also described this approach as "*prior model of judging.*"[422]

Legislation is also subjected to the binding interpretations of the courts. What this means, in practice, is that the legislation is overlaid with the case law.[423] For this reason, the common law system has no statutory basis; because the judges establish common law by applying previous decisions to present cases. However, in some cases, the legislator has regulated the scope of jurisdiction through the creation of new statutes.[424]

In the common law system, there has therefore been no need for legal scholars to devise and develop a comprehensive system of law.[425] In other words, analyzes by legal scholars and legal science do not play any significant role in the development of the law in the common law world. In contrast, the decisive central pillar of the civil law is legislative codification, an approach that has determined the very nature of this legal system.[426] It follows that, in contrast to the year-books and reports in the common law, the codes and legal textbooks possess the highest level of systematics and generalization, based upon a scientific structure and classification of the law. In addition, both the legislative and the judges refer to the

---

419 *See* John C. Gray, The Nature and Sources of the Law 252, New York 1909.

420 *See* http://www.cec.org/lawdatabase/us01.cfm?varlan=english, (last visit Dec 6, 2014)

421 *See* Peter L. Strauss, *Courts or Tribunals? Federal Courts and the Common Law*, 53 Alabama Law Review 891–925, 911 (2002).

422 *Id.* at 925.

423 *See* Hay (2011), *supra* note 87 at 8 note 19.

424 *E.g.* Uniform Commercial Code (UCC), *supra* note 184. *See* Hay (2011), *supra* note 87 at 24 note 9.

425 *See* Apple and Deyling (1995), *supra* note 210 at 34.

426 *See* Dainow (1966), *supra* note 83 at 421.

codes, statutes, and legal commentaries of legal scholars and afford these a great deal of respect and consideration.[427] Thus, it has been recognized that the sources of law in the civil law system comprise a large volume of regulations including the constitution, legislation, statutes, and customs.[428]

While, it might seem that the common law system is slow and unwieldy because the judges rigidly follow established precedents,[429] other authors[430] see the same weakness in the civil law system, where the judges are bound by the codes. However, as has been demonstrated,[431] both the common law and civil law systems have found ways to develop and evolve. Moreover, recent years have shown that altered social and political circumstances can result in modifications and adjustments to government regulations *e.g.* through the transposition of EU directives in the UK and Germany[432] or by the enactment of new acts in both systems.[433]

In conclusion, the common law and civil law system have seen a variety of sources *e.g.* the customary law, judicial precedents, the codes, legislative acts, and legal science.[434] It can be argued that all legal sources of law have revealed their feasibility of development. This ability has evolved through and as a direct response to the multitude and variety of societal issues and historical developments. However, there are also similarities in the two systems in terms of the form taken by such adjustments to social and political influences. Lastly, while formative elements of the law remain tied up in history and tradition, globalization is leading to a steady process of convergence of the two ostensibly opposing systems. Therefore, the next section examines the further development of the law in both the common law and civil law systems.

---

427 *Id.* at 424.

428 *See* Merryman and Pérez-Perdomo (2007), *supra* note 159 at 25.

429 *See* Nelson (2014), *supra* note 154 at 15.

430 *See e.g.* Sarkar (2011), *supra* note 91; Merryman and Pérez-Perdomo (2007), *supra* note 159.

431 *See supra* II., 3., pp. 88 et seq.

432 *See e.g.* Directive 2004/39/EC of the European Parliament and of the Council on markets in financial instruments amending Council Directives 85/611/EEC and 93/6/EEC and Directive 2000/12/EC (MIFID 2004), 32004L0039 L 241/1 (2006). Gesetz zur Umsetzung der Richtlinie über Märkte für Finanzinstrumente und der Durchführungsrichtlinie der Kommission (Finanzmarkt-Richtlinie-Umsetzungsgesetz - FRUG), BGBI. I, p. 1330 (2007).

433 *See e.g.* Sarbanes-Oxley Act of 2002, *supra* note 47. United Kingdom Bribery Act 2010, c. 23 (2010).

434 Dainow (1966), *supra* note 83; Lupu (2013), *supra* note 75 at 375; Merryman and Pérez-Perdomo (2007), *supra* note 159; Mousourakis (2015), *supra* note 85; La Porta, Lopez-de-Silanes, and Shleifer (2008), *supra* note 89; Sarkar (2011), *supra* note 91.

III. Outlook for Further Development

The two systems... are converging from different directions toward roughly equivalent mixed systems.[435]

It has been shown that both legal systems have evolved and adapted over the course of time and that there have also been similarities between the two legal systems.[436] First, the common law world has moved gradually towards greater legislative power. The period since the end of the 19th century has seen a great many more federal statutes due *inter alia* to increased government intervention *e.g.* the US Code,[437] the Foreign Corrupt Practices Act (FCPA)[438], the Sarbanes-Oxley Act 2002,[439] and the UK Bribery Act 2010.[440] Under pressure to respond to a number of high-profile corporate scandals, a number of Western countries, including the US and the UK, established governmental regulatory and standards in fields as diverse as occupational health and safety, the environment, consumer protection, securities, money laundering and foreign corrupt practices in the field of compliance.[441] This has resulted, accordingly, in a more statutory regime that could lead to a "*box-ticking*" approach with the legislature also fostering and enforcing various recommendations. In addition, standards such as the UK Combined Code of Corporate Governance,[442] flexibly offers a "*comply or explain model*" for companies.[443] These examples show an increasing influence of government intervention in the common law.

Secondly, on the other hand, there is an also growing reliance on case law in the civil law system.[444] For instance, in Germany, the judicial decisions of the Federal Labor Court (BAG) are of major significance for the interpretation and practical application of the highly fragmented system of employment law, and, as such, for

---

435 Merryman and Pérez-Perdomo (2007), *supra* note 159 at 126.

436 O'Connor (2012), *supra* note 240 at 34.

437 Uniform Commercial Code (UCC), *supra* note 184.

438 Foreign Corrupt Practices Act 1977 (FCPA), Pub. Law 95-213, 15 USC § 78dd-1 91 Stat. 1494 (1977).

439 Sarbanes-Oxley Act of 2002, *supra* note 47.

440 United Kingdom Bribery Act 2010, *supra* note 433.

441 Christine Parker, *The Ethics of Advising on Regulatory Compliance: Autonomy or Interdependence?*, 28 Journal of Business Ethics 339–351, 339 (2000).

442 Cadbury Committee, The UK Corporate Governance Code (2014) (1992), [hereinafter Cadbury Committee] https://www.frc.org.uk/Our-Work/Codes-Standards/Corporate-governance/UK-Corporate-Governance-Code.aspx (last visited Dec 27, 2014).

443 Sridhar Arcot, Valentina Bruno & Antoine Faure-Grimaud, *Corporate governance in the UK: Is the comply or explain approach working?*, 30 International Review of Law and Economics 193–201, 2 (2010).

444 O'Connor (2012), *supra* note 240 at 34.

the lower labor courts. The reason for this is that, to date, there has been no comprehensive codification of all employment sectors. The great variety of provisions with employment law makes it all more difficult to handle. Hence, in practice, employment law has often been determined largely by judicial decisions. This authority to further develop employment law is set forth in the Labor Court Act (ArbGG).[445] The Federal Labor Court (BAG) has embodied this further development of law in cases concerning the termination of contracts.[446]

Thirdly, the structure of the court systems differs considerably between the two systems. In the civil law countries, there is a distinction between public law and private law.[447] Thus, the civil law system, followed the tradition of the separate codes and built a specialized organization of courts.[448] In contrast, the common law system favored integrated court systems with courts of general jurisdiction. Typically, in the common law countries there is a constitutional review of legislation, which is not customary in civil law countries due to the primacy of legislation there. However, *Merryman* refers to a "*constitutionalization*" in the development of civil law.[449] He argues that the codification process has been completed. Thus, legislative supremacy is bound to decline.[450] Additionally, the civil law countries have also established constitutional courts to review legislation.

Fourthly, particularly in the European countries, another major factor has been the emergence of supranational legal norms, such as the European Union regulations and directives. The development of the European Union and its judicial bodies has had a significant effect in terms of shaping the national law.[451] European law at times overlaps with national laws. In recent years, the adoption of a number of regulatory acts within the EU has resulted in a degree of harmonization of the laws of the Member States. The two families of legal system represented in the EU member states are converging, causing a blurring of the distinction between the civil and common law systems. Legal authors[452] call this phenomenon "*mixed*" or "*hybrid*" legal systems.

Nevertheless, to the present day, a number of fundamental differences and divergent approaches to the law remain between the two legal systems, with the US and the UK common law system on the one side, and the German civil law

---

445 ARBEITSGERICHTSGESETZ (ARBGG) | LABOR COURT ACT, BGBI. I, p. 1267 (1953) § 45 IV. *"Der erkennende Senat kann eine Frage von grundsätzlicher Bedeutung dem Großen Senat zur Entscheidung vorlegen, wenn das nach seiner Auffassung zur Fortbildung des Rechts oder zur Sicherung einer einheitlichen Rechtsprechung erforderlich ist."*(Ger)

446 *See e.g.* BAG v. 20.11.2014 - 2 AZR 664/13, 2015 NZA 931; BAG v. 20.03.2014 - 2 AZR 565/12, 2014 NJW 2219.

447 O'Connor (2012), *supra* note 240 at 15.

448 Apple and Deyling (1995), *supra* note 210 at 37.

449 MERRYMAN AND PÉREZ-PERDOMO (2007), *supra* note 159 at 152.

450 *Id.* at 155.

451 *Id.* at 155.

452 *See e.g.* Apple and Deyling (1995), *supra* note 210; O'Connor (2012), *supra* note 240.

Table 1 *Comparison between the Common Law and Civil Law Systems*

Factors	**Common Law**		**Civil Law**
	US	**UK**	**Germany**
Legal Sources	Judicial Decisions, (Equity)	Judicial Decisions, (Equity)	Legislation
	Precedents	Precedents	Statutes
	Binding cases	Binding cases	Hierarchical Order
	Customary Law	Customary Law	Legal Science
Law Collections	Yearbooks and Reports	Yearbooks and Reports	Comprehensive, Systemized Codes
Doctrine of Good Faith	Corporate and Contract Law, The USC	Not recognized, is owed under a Fiduciary Relationship	Enshrined in law (BGB) as *bona fides*
Court System	Federal and State System, Three-Tiered Unified, Hierarchical System	Four-tier System, Unified, Hierarchical System	Complex, Specialized System
Supreme Court	Original and Appellate Jurisdiction	Original and Appellate Jurisdiction	Appellate Jurisdiction
Formalism	High	High	Very High
Development	By Judges	By Judges	By Legislator
Future Development	Foreign Cases	Foreign Cases, EU Legislation	EU Legislation

system on the other side. Despite the tendencies outlined above (1) increasing legislation in the common law system, (2) the application of case law in specific areas of law within the civil law system, and (3) the convergence of the common law and civil law systems the two distinct legal systems will nevertheless be preserved for the future. *Table 1* summarizes the findings of the comparison of the common law and civil law systems.

B. Discussion of Relevant Literature

The first part of this chapter provided a legal comparison of the common law and civil law systems. In so doing, it included an overview of the main sources of law, the structure of the court systems and a description of the developments in these two systems. To further enhance the understanding of the subject of this book, the role of the compliance officer, this chapter will discuss the relevant literature relating to the German, English and UK compliance function. The aim of this analysis is to identify gaps in the research. Then, the analysis of the American and English literature of the US and UK will continue in the second and third sections with the examination of the present state of research and debate on the compliance officer. Lastly, this part will provide the hypotheses relating to the compliance officer function within companies.

I. The Key Issues Relating to the German Compliance Officer

Prior to 2009, the German literature on compliance was not particularly substantial. The academic debate was centered around the need for compliance within German companies, the implementation of a corporate compliance program as well as the selection of a compliance officer.[453] Following the decision of the Federal Supreme Court (BGH) in 2009,[454] we began to see a broad academic interest and discussion[455] about the legal duties and responsibilities of the compliance officer function. In this judicial decision, the Federal Supreme Court stated that an employee in an executive position has a responsibility under criminal law on account of his or her professional position.[456] Since then, the academic assumption has been that the compliance function justifies a supervisory duty and an obligation to avoid punitive damages.[457] From *Bürkle, Moosmayer, Hauschka* to *Zimmermann*, there is among academic and legal practitioners a far-reaching explanation of the tasks and requirements of this position. An examination of the German literature shows the following key topics relating to the compliance function: (1) What is the scope of responsibility of the compliance function? (2) Should the compliance officer be liable for failing to detect misconduct by employees? (3) Is the compliance officer able to limit his liability? (4) Is there any form of protection against dismissal for compliance officers? (5) How should the employment contract for a compliance officer be drafted?[458]

---

453 *See* Nicola Buffo & Bina Brünjes, *Gesucht wird ein Compliance-Officer – Ein 200.000 Euro-Beispiel aus der Praxis*, CCZ 108–112 (2008); Hauschka (2004), *supra* note 58.

454 BGH, 17.7.2009 - 5 StR 394/08, BGHSt 54, 44; BGH NJW 2009, 3173, *supra* note 25.

455 *See e.g.* Bürkle (2010), *supra* note 28; Dann and Mengel (2010), *supra* note 30; Jörg Fecker & Ulrich-Peter Kinzl, *Ausgestaltung der arbeitsrechtlichen Stellung des Compliance-Officers Schlussfolgerungen aus der BSR-Entscheidung des BGH*, CCZ 13–20 (2010); Gößwein and Hohmann (2011), *supra* note 41; Hauschka (2014), *supra* note 4; Heuking (2014), *supra* note 4; Meier (2011), *supra* note 30; Sünner (2014), *supra* note 44; Wolf (2011), *supra* note 41; Wybitul (2009), *supra* note 28; Zimmermann (2011), *supra* note 28.

456 BGH, 17.7.2009 - 5 StR 394/08, BGHSt 54, 44; BGH NJW 2009, 3173, *supra* note 25 note 22.

457 *See e.g.* José A. Campos Nave, *Strafbarkeit des Compliance Officer aufgrund einer aus dem Aufgabenbereich abgeleiteten Garantenstellung*, BETRIEBS-BERATER 2059, 2059 (2009).

458 *See e.g.* Fecker and Kinzl (2010), *supra* note 455; Gößwein and Hohmann (2011), *supra* note 41; Kirsch (2011), *supra* note 41; Klaus Lackhoff & Martin Schulz, *Das*

However, having surveyed the German literature, it is clear that legal authors are not agreed as to the requirements and liability relating to the compliance function. The current debate centers mainly around the scope of responsibilities and attempts to identify the compliance officer's liability. For this purpose, German legal scholars analyzed the increased criminal and civil liability of the compliance function and its limitation.[459] Other legal authors have explored the scope of responsibilities,[460] the legal employment status of the compliance officer,[461] and models of compliance structures within companies, including the implementation of the compliance function.[462] Since 2012, some authors have discussed the development of the compliance job description.[463] They point out the need for further professionalization of the function. In the financial services sector, for instance, in the view of *Klebeck & Zollinger*[464], the objective behind the AIFM-Directive[465] is to create a European legal framework and to establish an independent and effective compliance function in the post of Alternative Investment Funds Manager (AIFM). According to Art. 37 Sec. 7 (b), (c)[466] the AIFM should appoint a legal representative who is *"sufficiently equipped to perform the compliance function pursuant*

Unternehmen als Gefahrenquelle? Compliance-Risiken für Unternehmensleiter und Mitarbeiter, CCZ 81–88 (2010); Krieger and Günther (2010), *supra* note 30; Volker Rieble, *Zivilrechtliche Haftung der Compliance-Agenten*, CCZ 1–4 (2010); Schulz and Renz (2012), *supra* note 41; Wybitul (2009), *supra* note 28.

459 *See e.g.* Bürkle (2010), *supra* note 28; Tom Giesen, *Die Haftung des Compliance-Officers gegenüber seinem Arbeitgeber – Haftungsprivilegierung bei innerbetrieblichem Schadensausgleich?*, CCZ 102–106 (2009); Wolf (2011), *supra* note 41; Zimmermann (2011), *supra* note 28.

460 *See e.g* Kirsch (2011), *supra* note 41; Nadja Raus & Martin Lützeler, *Berichtspflicht des Compliance Officers – zwischen interner Eskalation und externer Anzeige*, 2012 CCZ 96–101 (2012).

461 *See e.g.* Diana Illing & Karsten Umnuß, *Die arbeitsrechtliche Stellung des Compliance Managers – insbesondere Weisungsunterworfenheit und Reportingpflichten*, CCZ 1–8 (2009); Daniel Meier-Greve, *Zur Unabhängigkeit des sog. Compliance Officers*, 2010 CCZ 216–221 (2010).

462 *See e.g.* Gößwein and Hohmann (2011), *supra* note 41.

463 *See e.g.* Christoph E. Hauschka, Wirnt Galster & Annette Marschlich, *Leitlinien für die Tätigkeit in der Compliance-Funktion im Unternehmen (für Compliance Officer außerhalb regulierter Sektoren)*, 2014 CCZ 242–248 (2014); Hauschka (2014), *supra* note 4; Daniel Sandmann, *Die Compliance-Funktion unter Solvency II – Ein Überblick*, CCZ 70–77 (2015); Sünner (2014), *supra* note 44.

464 *See* Ulf Klebeck & Peter Felix Zollinger, *Compliance-Funktion nach der AIFM-Richtlinie*, Betriebs-Berater 459–464 (2013).

465 Directive 2011/61/EU of the European Parliament and of the Council on Alternative Investment Fund Managers and amending Directives 2003/41/EC and 2009/65/EC and Regulations (EC) No 1060/2009 and (EU) No 1095/201, OJ L 174 p. 1 (2011).

466 *Id.*

to this Directive."[467] The implementation of this Directive could be a further step towards increasing legal requirements relating to this position in the financial services sector.

The discussion[468] specifies the tasks and requirements of the corporate German compliance officer and attempts to establish guidelines for this position. In 2014, the German Federal Association of Compliance Officers (BDCO)[469] published a position paper *"A job description of the compliance officer–minimum requirements of the content, education and development.*"[470] In *Hauschka's* evaluation, these requirements are too far-reaching since they were transferred unaltered from the regulated finance and banking sector into the private sector.[471] Generally, since 2009, the German compliance officer has been the subject of controversial debate.

Furthermore, there is a broad academic debate on the nature and classification of this function. Some authors have argued that this position should be an economic function because the effective compliance officer needs to have an understanding of the business and structure of the company. As such, the appointment of judges and prosecutors as compliance officers, for instance, appears questionable.[472] Other authors identify the significance of legal education and knowledge in being able to properly fulfill this position.[473] They point out that the increasing importance of the legal profession for this function has been recognized in recent years. Mention has also been made of the fact that the compliance officer ought to have both economic and legal expertise.[474] The conclusions of this analysis is the reference to this function as a "*legal manager.*"[475]

---

467 *Id.*

468 *See e.g.* Hauschka (2014), *supra* note 4; Heuking (2014), *supra* note 4; Sandmann (2015), *supra* note 463.

469 German Federal Association of Compliance Officers | Bundesverband deutscher Compliance Officer (BDCO), *supra* note 43.

470 BDCO, BDCO-POSITIONSPAPIER - BERUFSBILD DES COMPLIANCE OFFICERS – MINDESTANFORDERUNGEN ZU INHALT, ENTWICKLUNG UND AUSBILDUNG (2013), hhttp://bdco.de/positionspapier-compliance-officer (last visited Dec 12, 2014).

471 *See* Hauschka (2014), *supra* note 4 at 170.

472 *See e.g.* Jürgen Bürkle, *Compliance-Beauftragte*, in: CORPORATE COMPLIANCE: HANDBUCH DER HAFTUNGSVERMEIDUNG IM UNTERNEHMEN § 8 (Christoph E. Hauschka & Christoph Besch eds., 2. ed. 2010) note 38; Jörg Thierfelder, *Anforderungsprofil für Compliance Officer, in* DER COMPLIANCE OFFICER: EIN HANDBUCH IN EIGENER SACHE § 2, 15–24, 18 (Jürgen Bürkle & Christoph E. Hauschka eds., 1. ed. 2015) note 8; Heuking (2014), *supra* note 4 at 329.

473 *See e.g.* Bürkle (2010), *supra* note 28 at 12; Klaus Moosmayer, *Modethema oder Pflichtprogramm guter Unternehmensführung? – Zehn Thesen zu Compliance*, 2012 NJW 3013–3017, 3014 (2012).

474 *See e.g.* Hauschka (2004), *supra* note 58 at 261.

475 *See e.g.* Moosmayer (2012), *supra* note 473 at 3015.

In 2013, an empirical German study[476] within companies with a random sample of 486 responding compliance mangers revealed the academic education of compliance officers in large firms, active on a global scale. The study found that over 70 percent of compliance officers held an academic degree.[477] Of these, approximately 40 percent have a law degree and approximately 30 percent a degree in economics.[478] In spite of these academic debates, empirical legal research on the function of the compliance officer is largely absent in the German literature and journals. However, it has also been noted that there is a lack of focus on a precise explanation and definition of the compliance function.

Another aspect that the legal authors contributed to the debate is the lack of uniformity and standardization of the compliance function. There is no established official job description for the post of corporate compliance officer.[479] The scope of responsibilities of this function is not enshrined in legislation, neither in accordance with the Vocational Training Act,[480] nor in terms of generally accepted guidelines. In addition, an applicable definition of the compliance function is still lacking.[481] These attitudes are inconsistent with the view taken by *Groß,* who counters that an entirely new and separate job description has in the meantime developed, but she does not actually present this description.[482] However, there is no definition of the compliance function outside the banking sector. This gap in the knowledge is relevant because in recent years and due to international influences, German firms have faced increasingly stringent requirements concerning legally and ethically responsible behavior.[483]

In conclusion, the current German debate among academics and practitioners[484] represents efforts to create a specific job description. In sum, it is acknowledged that there are still many unanswered questions concerning this. There is a need for a generally applicable definition and a modern understanding of the role of the German compliance officer.

---

476 *See* Henning Herzog & Gregor Stephan, Berufsfeldstudie Compliance Manager 2013: Vermessung eines Berufsstandes (Professional Association of Compliance Manager | Berufsverband der Compliance Manager (BCM), 1. ed. 2013).

477 *Id.* at 55. fig. 3.01.

478 *Id.* at 56. fig. 3.02.

479 *See e.g.* Bürkle (2010), *supra* note 472 at 11; Fecker and Kinzl (2010), *supra* note 455 at 15.

480 Berufsbildungsgesetz (BBiG) | Vocational Training Act, BGBI. I, p. 1112 last amended August 2015, p. 1474, 1538 (1969) §§ 4–5.

481 *See e.g.* Hauschka (2014), *supra* note 4; Meier (2011), *supra* note 30; Meier-Greve (2010), *supra* note 461; Raus and Lützeler (2012), *supra* note 460.

482 *See* Gross (2012), *supra* note 42 at 29.

483 *See* Moosmayer (2012), *supra* note 473.

484 Professional Association of Compliance Manager | Berufsverband der Compliance Manager (BCM), *supra* note 43; BDCO | Bundesverband deutscher Compliance Officer, *supra* note 43.

II. The Key Issues Relating to the American Compliance Officer

Having examined the peer-reviewed American Journals and literature dealing with the corporate ethics and compliance officer[485] from 1990 to 2014, it can be noted that a very wide variety of books and articles have been published.[486] American researchers have afforded this position a great deal of interest and attention. For this reason, the subject of compliance[487] is not a new one. There is a rich field of secondary literature on this topic.[488]

One aspect, which illustrates the key issues relating to this position, is the implementation of an ethical and compliance culture and program within American companies. Such programs comprise the designation and the appointment of a high-level officer responsible for ethics and compliance. In addition, ethics researchers have studied the features of compliance professionals, which intended to prevent unethical conduct on the part of the employees. An empirical study by *Weaver, Treviño, and Cochran*[489] summarized the current state of corporate ethics practice in the mid-1990s and found that major American corporations have generally adopted ethical policies and have developed ethics programs within companies in the United States.[490]

Another key issue that has to be considered is that companies have responded to legal requirements by creating an ethics and compliance program and through the appointment of an ethics and compliance officer.[491] More recent research has

485 In the US, the corporate compliance and ethics officer function are often combined as a chief ethics and compliance officer (CECO) in practice. *See* Gnazzo (2011), *supra* note 8 at 534.

486 *See e.g.* Freeman (2007), *supra* note 57; Gnazzo (2011), *supra* note 8; Hoffman, Neill, and Stovall (2008), *supra* note 16; Anthony Pirraglia, *A Tangled Web: Compliance Director Liability Under the Securities Laws*, 8 Fordham J. Corp. & Fin. L. 245–272 (2003); Rosella and Pugliese (2006), *supra* note 13; Heather Traeger, Kris Easter Guidroz & McAllister Jimbo, *Supervisory Liability: The SEC's Scrutiny and Support of Chief Compliance Officers: Part 1 of 2*, 21 The Investment Lawyer 25–33 (2014); Linda Klebe Treviño et al., *Legitimating the legitimate: A grounded theory study of legitimacy work among Ethics and Compliance Officers*, 123 Organizational Behavior and Human Decision Processes 186–205 (2014); Weber and Fortun (2005), *supra* note 4.

487 In the US, the term compliance will examine related to ethics because the two areas penetrate each other. This will be discussed in detail later. *See infra*, pp. 121 et seq.

488 *See e.g.* David Vogel, *The Ethical Roots of Business Ethics*, 1 Business Ethics Quarterly 101, 102 (1991).

489 *See* Gary R. Weaver, Linda Klebe Treviño & Philip L. Cochran, *Corporate Ethics Practices in the Mid-1990's: An Empirical Study of the Fortune 1000*, 18 Journal of Business Ethics 283–294 (1999).

490 *Id.* at 293.

491 *See e.g.* Joshua Joseph, *Integrating Business Ethics and Compliance Programs: A Study of Ethics Officers in Leading Organizations*, 107 Business and Society Review

shown that this development is part of the significant efforts by the federal government to regulate ethical activities.[492] A study by *Weber & Wasieleski* compares the results from previous studies and found that the major pressure to develop and maintain an ethics and compliance program within companies is "*to comply with government laws.*"[493] In addition to these findings, a number of American legal scholars and legal practitioners have acknowledged the increasingly dominant role of federal law in applying the criminal law to ensure corporate compliance with external legal requirements[494] and in regulating directors' duties as "*monitors*" to the compliance issues.[495]

The features of the ethics and compliance function have also been subject to research and have been discussed by a number of different authors. There were two studies[496] relating to the ethics officer's position published before 1990. After that time, a broad debate on the American compliance function, on the role and profile of the ethics and compliance officers also began to take shape.[497] For example, *Izraeli & BarNir*[498] present an *"ideal profile"* of an effective ethics officer. For this purpose, they pointed out five necessary requirements for this position (1) an insider status, (2) independence, (3) professionalism, (4) knowledge of organizational issues, and (5) knowledge of ethical theory.[499] A survey by *Weber and Fortun*[500] supported the

309–347 (2003); Parker (2000), *supra* note 441; Weaver, Treviño, and Cochran (1999), *supra* note 489.

492 *See* James Weber & David M. Wasieleski, *Corporate Ethics and Compliance Programs: A Report, Analysis and Critique*, 112 Journal of Business Ethics 609–626 (2013).

493 *Id.* at 614.

494 *In re Caremark International Inc. Derivative Litigation*, 698 A.2d 959 (Del. Ch. 1996), *supra* note 21 note 969.

495 *See e.g.* H. Lowell Brown, *The Corporate Director's Compliance Oversight Responsibility in the Post Caremark Era*, 26 Delaware Journal of Corporate Law 1–145 (2001); Aaron D. Jones, *Corporate Officer Wrongdoing and the Fiduciary Duties of Corporate Officers under Delaware Law*, 44 American Business Law Journal 475–520 (2007); Paul E. McGreal, *Corporate Compliance Survey*, 67 The Business Lawyer 227–253 (2011); Sale (2007), *supra* note 22.

496 *See* Center for Business Ethics, *Are Corporations Institutionalizing Ethics?*, Journal of Business Ethics 85–91 (1986); Center for Business Ethics, *Instilling Ethical Values in Large Corporations*, 11 Journal of Business Ethics 863–867 (1992).

497 *See also* Gnazzo (2011), *supra* note 8; Dove Izraeli & Anat BarNir, *Promoting Ethics Through Ethics Officers: A Proposed Profile and an Application*, 17 Journal of Business Ethics 1189–1196 (1998); Weber and Fortun (2005), *supra* note 4.

498 *See* Izraeli and BarNir (1998), *supra* note 496.

499 *Id.* at 1192.

500 *See* Weber and Fortun (2005), *supra* note 4. This survey of ethics and compliance officers was carried out under the auspices of to a professional association, the Pittsburgh Ethics Network, located in Pittsburgh, Pennsylvania, and represents a variety of business industries. The survey was conducted in the summer of 2004.

requirement for the ethics and compliance function to have an insider status and provided the following profile:

> ...an ECO is typically a male who is 48 years old. He has been with his company for nearly 14 years and has held the ECO position for about three years.[501]

An earlier survey by *Morf, Schumacher, and Vitell* [502] provided reliable evidence and data: 45 percent of the thirty ethics officers surveyed held this position for one to two years and 77 percent were already employed within in the same company prior to assuming this position.[503] However, the insider status could be a double-edged sword. On the one hand, the majority of insiders have a profound knowledge of the business and structure of the organization; on the other hand, however, they may themselves be entangled in corporate misconduct or professionally blinkered. In addition, there appears to be a lack of influencing factors. In sum, the *"ideal profile"* of an ethics officer presented by *Izraeli & BarNir* appears too simplistic as their profile does not adequately reflect the relevance of links between external and internal factors. In conclusion, there is a lack of social and legal impact factors.

Generally, with a few exceptions, there is very little empirical research available dealing with the positions of the corporate ethics officer and compliance officer.[504] *Smith,* for example, argues that the development of the general characteristics of this position could be generated from the *de facto* or *de jure* working duties and responsibilities.[505] Summon this basis, he uses five key factors to characterize an effective role of the ethics officer with five arguments:

- Reports to the highest levels of the organization,
- Has adequate resources and funding,
- Serves more in a mediation role for employees,
- Communicates employee concerns, and
- Serves as the point person for reaffirming the importance of ethics in the corporation.[506]

---

501 *Id.* at 110.

502 *See* Duffy A. Morf, Michael G. Schumacher & Scott J. Vitell, *A Survey of Ethics Officers in Large Organizations*, 20 JOURNAL OF BUSINESS ETHICS 265–271 (1999). This survey included interviews with thirty ethics officers from Fortune 500 firms in order to develop a database of their duties.

503 *Id.* at 267.

504 *See* Robert W. Smith, *Corporate Ethics Officers And Government Ethics Administrators: Comparing Apples With Oranges or a Lesson to Be Learned?*, 34 ADMINISTRATION & SOCIETY 632–652 (2003).

505 *Id.* at 638.

506 *Id.* at 639.

To further understand the role of the ethics and compliance officer, a study by *Joseph*[507] identified that the major task and responsibility of this position was the implementation of the ethics and compliance programs within companies. He demonstrated that the more recent focus on the role of the ethics officer could be the participation in ethics investigations into misconduct. Apparently, nearly a quarter of the interviewed ethics officers viewed investigative responsibilities as a threat to their programs. In response, *Joseph* suggested that the EO should provide suggestions and insights to make the investigative processes fairer and more transparent to employees.[508] The study by *Joseph* also evaluated the pros and cons of alternative staffing approaches involving employing full-time versus part-time ethics staff members.[509] In conclusion, the study found that a successful ethics and compliance program depends on an awareness of best practices.[510]

Furthermore, an empirical study by *Canary & Jennings*[511] examines the similarities and differences between corporate ethics codes and codes of conduct in the pre- and post-Sarbanes-Oxley era. Their results indicate that the enactment of the SOX[512] would affect the content and structure of codes for public companies.[513] For instance, they found that the terms "*ethics*", "*ethical*", and "*compliance*" converge and the importance of compliance and law is emphasized more in the codes issued in the post-SOX era.[514] Thus, the status of ethics and compliance programs with the adopted component of a compliance officer in the US seems to be warranted. In contrast to this view, other authors[515] have argued that this examination revealed a number of sobering impacts on the effectiveness of ethics and compliance programs. For instance, the content of the codes is considered too generic.[516] The proponents of this line of argument emphasize that all organizations need to be aware that ethics and compliance are at the core of their organizations' values and culture and in the interest of all stakeholders. Furthermore, by analyzing past

507 *See* Joseph (2003), *supra* note 491 at 309. This study includes 26 structured, in-depth interviews with ethics officers at Fortune 500 companies between September 1998 and March 1999.

508 *Id.* at 326.

509 *Id.* at 332–333.

510 *Id.* at 343.

511 *See* Heather E. Canary & Marianne M. Jennings, *Principles and Influence in Codes of Ethics: A Centering Resonance Analysis Comparing Pre- and Post-Sarbanes-Oxley Codes of Ethics*, 80 Journal of Business Ethics 263–278 (2008).

512 Sarbanes-Oxley Act of 2002, *supra* note 47.

513 *See* Canary and Jennings (2008), *supra* note 511 at 275.

514 *Id.* at 275.

515 *See e.g.* Muel Kaptein, *The Effectiveness of Ethics Programs: The Role of Scope, Composition, and Sequence*, 132 Journal of Business Ethics 415–431 (2015); Weber and Wasieleski (2013), *supra* note 492.

516 *See* Weber and Wasieleski (2013), *supra* note 492 at 624.

studies, they found that corporate ethics and compliance programs are significantly influenced by the external environment.[517]

Evidently, the American academic debate identifies the influence of new regulations on the new importance of the role of CECO in the corporate environment.[518] New research by *Adobor, DeStefano, Fanto, Majewski, Miller, Kaptein, Panebianco, Rosella & Pugliese, Sobol, Traeger & Jimbo, Treviño et al.* investigates the performance, effectiveness, independence, and the potential liability of the ethics and compliance function. Their findings show that the role of the CECO is unique because this position deals with multiple (sometimes competing) expectations from different groups or units within the organization.[519]

In addition, the debate also focuses on the prospects and repositioning of the ethics and compliance officer.[520] The current academic debate highlights a new importance, a repositioning and further development of this position. This line of argument follows an ongoing debate concerning the independence of the CECO and on the reporting structure of this function.[521] Another important key issue is the proposal to establish this function as an agent of the board of directors or providing the CECO direct access to the management board.[522] Discussions have held that this proposal could eliminate the conflict of interest and increase the authority and status of the position of the CECO in the company.

In conclusion, in America, the key issues relating to the ethics and compliance function are more far-reaching than those in Germany. It has been mentioned that the American debate centers around four key topics (1) the implementation of an

517 *Id.* at 622–623.

518 *See* Freeman (2007), *supra* note 57.

519 *See e.g.* Adobor (2006), *supra* note 46; DeStefano (2013), *supra* note 14; Fanto (2013), *supra* note 57; Kaptein (2015), *supra* note 515; Majewski (2006), *supra* note 18; Geoffrey P. Miller, *The Compliance Function: An Overview*, No. 14–36 NYU Law and Economics Research Paper (2014); Colette Panebianco, *The after-effect of Rule 203(b)(3)-2: what it means to take on the role of CCO to comply with the controversial measure*, 6 Journal of Investment Compliance 59–62 (2005); Rosella and Pugliese (2006), *supra* note 13; Rob Sobol, *Conversations at the top: the tone of the independent chief compliance officer*, 10 Journal of Investment Compliance 10–15 (2009); Heather Traeger & McAllister Jimbo, *Supervisory Liability: The SEC's Scrutiny and Support of Chief Compliance Officers: Part 1 of 2*, 21 The Investment Lawyer 12–21 (2014); Treviño et al., *supra* note 86.

520 *See* Greenberg (2009), *supra* note 11.

521 *See* Gnazzo (2011), *supra* note 8; Hoffman, Neill, and Stovall (2008), *supra* note 16; Majewski (2006), *supra* note 18.

522 *See e.g.* Michael D. Greenberg, *Culture, compliance, and the C-suite: how executives, boards, and policymakers can better safeguard against misconduct at the top*, (2013); W. Michael Hoffman & Mark Rowe, *The Ethics Officer as Agent of the Board: Leveraging Ethical Governance Capability in the Post-Enron* Corporation, 112 Business and Society Review 553–572 (2007).

ethics and compliance program through the ethics and compliance function within companies, (2) the creation of an ideal job profile, (3) the influence of external factors like business and regulatory environment, and (4) the independence and repositioning of the ethics and compliance officer.

III. The Key Issues Relating to the UK Compliance Officer

Having surveyed the UK literature, it can be stated that there is a distinct lack of material relating to the corporate compliance officer. The analysis of the peer-reviewed journals indicates that the majority of the articles published relating to the UK compliance functions examine the position in the context of the regulated financial sector. For example, *Edwards, Wolfe and Taylor* explore the origins of the function of the compliance officer, how it has evolved over the past 20 years, how the responsibilities are defined for the compliance function, and how the compliance function is expected to change over the coming years.[523] In 1993, *Bosworth-David*[524] analyzed and evaluated the attitudes of the compliance officer in the English financial service industry in the wake of the Financial Services Act 1986.[525] This study, which was conducted with the members of the United Kingdom Association of Compliance Officers, attempted to explore the attitudes of the compliance officer in the financial institutions. The findings indicated that the compliance officers appear to have a weak position within their organizations and that the former system of financial regulation fails to employ compliance officers sufficiently qualified to ensure efficient performance.[526]

In addition to the findings above, *Edwards & Wolfe* concluded that

> The compliance function provides a focal point for compliance in the organisation. Its role is multifunctional. There should be a greater recognition of the complex issues involved in making compliance work in a practical and meaningful way for the benefit of all concerned.[527]

They offered a compliance competence partnership approach within banks. This partnership approach consists of three main elements, which are linked together: (1) good compliance practice, (2) positive regulator relationship, and

---

523 *See* Jonathan Edwards & Simon Wolfe, *The compliance function in banks*, 12 Journal of Financial Regulation and Compliance 216–224 (2004); Jonathan Edwards & Simon Wolfe, *Compliance: A review*, 13 Journal of Financial Regulation and Compliance 48–59 (2005); Jonathan Edwards & Simon Wolfe, *A compliance competence partnership approach model*, 14 Journal of Financial Regulation and Compliance 140–150 (2006); Taylor (2005), *supra* note 13.

524 *See* Bosworth-Davies (1993), *supra* note 4.

525 Financial Services Act 1986, Financial Services Act 1986 c. 60 (1986).(It was repealed 2001 and superseded by the Financial Services and Markets Act 2000)

526 *See* Bosworth-Davies (1993), *supra* note 4 at 356.

527 *See* Edwards and Wolfe (2004), *supra* note 519 at 223.

(3) good ethical practice.[528] The authors believed that this approach facilitates a compliance function capable of enhancing a compliant culture within the organization, as well as boosting the benefits of reputation, the business, and integrity in the financial market.[529]

As previously noted, there is little academic research on the topic of the function of the corporate compliance officer in the UK. Several studies have analyzed the influence of the legal environment on small and-medium sized enterprises (SME) in the UK. For example, an empirical study by *Weir & Laing*[530] examined the effects of Cadbury[531] compliance on UK listed companies.[532] In addition, they found that complete compliance with the model of governance proposed by the Cadbury Committee[533] does not appear be associated with company performance. Furthermore, in recent years several studies by *Arcot et al.* and *Wilson et al.* have examined the influence and effectiveness of environmental legislation on UK SME.[534] Apparently, these studies evaluated only the influence on English legislation of the corporate compliance issue, but not on the compliance function. For example, the analysis by *Arcot et al.*[535] found an increasing trend towards compliance with the Combined

---

528 *Id.* at 221.

529 *See* Edwards and Wolfe (2006), *supra* note 523.

530 *See* Charlie Weir & David Laing, *The Performance-Governance Relationship: The Effects of Cadbury Compliance on UK Quoted Companies*, 4 Journal of Management and Governance 265–281 (2000).

531 *See* Financial Aspects of Corporate Governance - Cadbury Report 1992, (1992).

532 *See* Companies Act 2006, Companies Act 2006 c. 46 (2006)., Part 15, Ch. 1 (2) A *"listed"* or *"quoted company"* means a company whose equity share capital - (a) has been included in the official list in accordance with the provisions of Part 6 of the Financial Services and Markets Act 2000 (c. 8), or (b) is officially listed in an EEA State, or (c) is admitted to dealing on either the New York Stock Exchange or the exchange known as Nasdaq. *See also* http://www.legislation.gov.uk/ukpga/2006/46/part/15/chapter/1/crossheading/quoted-and-unquoted-companies, (last visited Dec. 30, 2014)

533 The Committee recommended that certain internal monitoring mechanisms should be adopted by quoted firms. The Report was published in December 1992 and contained a number of recommendations to raise standards in corporate governance. *See* Financial Aspects of Corporate Governance - Cadbury Report 1992, *supra* note 526.

534 *See e.g.* Arcot, Bruno, and Faure-Grimaud (2010), *supra* note 443; Christopher D. H. Wilson, Ian David Williams & Simon Kemp, *Compliance with Producer Responsibility Legislation: Experiences from UK Small and Medium-sized Enterprises*, 20 Business Strategy and the Environment 310–330 (2011); Christopher D. H. Wilson, Ian David Williams & Simon Kemp, *An Evaluation of the Impact and Effectiveness of Environmental Legislation in Small and Medium-Sized Enterprises: Experiences from the UK: Evaluation of Impact + Effectiveness of Environ Legislation in SMEs*, 21 Business Strategy and the Environment 141–156 (2012).

535 *See* Arcot, Bruno, and Faure-Grimaud (2010), *supra* note 443. They analyzed 245 annual reports of UK non-financial companies.

Code,[536] but frequent use of standard explanations in the event of non-compliance. In contrast to evidence presented by *Arcot et al.*, a study by *Wilson et al.*[537] found that the influence of environmental legislation and surveillance of SME compliance is generally low. They argued that compliance issues were recognized and acknowledged only if identified by a regulator and were regarded as serious only if prosecuted.[538]

There has also been some debate surrounding the modernization and strengthening of corporate criminal laws in the UK. *Djilani* concludes that these developments could create a stronger corporate compliance regime.[539] It can be argued that companies are likely to establish some internal monitoring processes for corporate compliance.[540] This process also includes the establishment of voluntary compliance programs with the assistance of compliance officers.[541] She considers compliance officers reporting duties vis-à-vis external regulators. Similarly, as in the US, UK-based companies could be given credit for reporting wrongdoing if they have created a compliance program.[542] A recent book by *Ward* explores the relationship between regulation and compliance in the UK.[543] She points out the influence of the legal framework and law of the changing face of compliance.[544] In addition, *Stephan* argued that in the event that individual employees are prosecuted, the compliance officer has to weigh up the relationship balance between criminalization and leniency.[545] Furthermore, *Richard* argues that the compliance officers are employees and not directors, even though they are at the front line within their companies.[546] In summary, strong corporate criminal law sanctions

---

536 Cadbury Committee, *supra* note 442. Today the UK Corporate Governance Code, (formerly the Combined Code) sets out standards of good practice in relation to board leadership and effectiveness, remuneration, accountability and relations with shareholders. *See*, https://www.frc.org.uk/Our-Work/Codes-Standards/Corporate-governance/UK- Corporate-Governance-Code.aspx, (last visit Dec 22, 2014)

537 *See* Wilson, Williams, and Kemp (2012), *supra* note 534. They conducted detailed semi-structured interviews with SME management and site staff. In total, 44 businesses were audited in the north-west of England between April and September 2008.

538 *See Id.* at 141.

539 *See* Djilani (2011), *supra* note 62 at 341.

540 *Id.* at 341.

541 *Id.* at 329.

542 *Id.* at 330.

543 *See* Sharon Ward, The changing face of compliance: managing regulatory risk (1. ed. 2015).

544 *Id.*

545 *See* A. Stephan, *Four key challenges to the successful criminalization of cartel laws*, 2 Journal of Antitrust Enforcement 333–362, 360 (2014).

546 Alexander Richards, *Criminal liability of employees of financial intermediaries for money laundering: a British perspective*, 318–339, 318 (1. ed. 2003).

and an increasingly stringent legal environment may also help to achieve corporate reform and foster compliance in UK companies.[547]

To conclude, there has been barely any discussion or examination of the role of the corporate compliance officer in the UK-based academic and practitioner literature. Thus, it appears that the role and profile of the corporate compliance officer in the UK is significantly underresearched. This gap in the research knowledge might be attributable to the absence of cases that directly involve non-financial companies. Another reason could be the non-regulatory environment in the private sector. It is also possible that this is due to the absence or lack of formalization of the corporate compliance role. Nevertheless, it has been noted that the role of the UK compliance officer is often linked with the relationship and reporting duties to external regulators and the handling of regulatory sanctions.

IV. Conclusion and Outlook

First, based on the findings of the literature review above, particularly contributions found in Law Reviews and studies,[548] the general tendency evident in the US and the UK is that an increasingly stringent legal framework and regulatory requirements in the common law system have influenced the evolution of the compliance officer's role in recent years. As a matter of fact, the spread of regulators and rules around the world has been a predominant feature of the last few years in particular.[549] In other words, the legal pressure on firms to act in compliance with the regulations is growing. As a result, the first two assumptions are that the compliance officer will be afforded a more precise profile and a more important role at the high-corporate level within firms.

H1 Due to the legal framework the function of the compliance officer is better defined and standardized in the common law than in the civil law system on account of the specific historical and legal development.

H2 It can be anticipated that the compliance officer emerged with enhanced legal requirements because the legal framework was able to establish a formal position of authority for the compliance officer at a high corporate level within companies.

The examination of the key issues in the US, UK, and Germany has shown that recent years have seen an increasing visibility of the compliance function. One could argue that there is a broad agreement that a strengthened regulatory and legal framework in the corporate environment encourage compliance programs and, thus, the emergence of the compliance officer. In spite of the significance of

547 *See e.g.* COMPANIES ACT 2006, *supra* note 532; UNITED KINGDOM BRIBERY ACT 2010, *supra* note 433.

548 *See e.g.* Brooklyn Law Review, California Law Review, Cornell Law Review, International Review of Law and Economics, Virginia Law Review,...etc.

549 *See* Gareth Adams, *What is Compliance?*, 2 JOURNAL OF FINANCIAL REGULATION AND COMPLIANCE 278–285, 278 (1994).

this function, which is emphasized in the American and German literature, the role of the compliance officer within companies is still undefined. Despite the great importance of the ethics and compliance officer in the US, only 30 percent of surveyed ethics and compliance officers had an employment contract in 2009.[550] Moreover, a European Business Ethics Forum (EBEF) paper shows that most of them are in in voluntary roles if they work outside of the regulated industries, like healthcare or securities.[551]

Second, the findings relating to the key issues in terms of the American, English, and German compliance function reveal that there are a number of differences in the development and importance of this position in the US, UK, and Germany. As mentioned previously, in the course of the last few years, the key issue in Germany as far as the compliance officer is concerned has been the broad academic discussion concerning the criminal duties and responsibilities of the post of compliance officer in the wake of a decision of the Federal Supreme Court on the matter.[552] There is a gap in knowledge between the wide-ranging scope and limitation of the responsibilities of the compliance function. It is precisely the legal position that is the most problematic aspect of the compliance officer's function. Hence, the current role of the compliance officer has been characterized by a number of unclear factors. Evidently, the legal scope of action within companies in which a German compliance officer works is sometimes undefined.[553] Overall, it can be argued that the nature and classification of the German compliance officer are in need of further examination.

In the US, the role of the compliance officer within companies appears more established, more broadly recognized and well integrated. Thus, the academic debate is oriented more towards the repositioning and further development of this function. In contrast, the UK corporate compliance officer has been subject to less attention in the academic debate. However, in general, the consensus is that the compliance officer's role is multifunctional. In recent years, a number of American and English studies have evaluated the influence of legislative and compliance issues within companies.[554] Nevertheless, gaps in the knowledge of this function

---

550 *See* Rebecca Walker, COMPLIANCE AND ETHICS OFFICER POSITIONING: A BENCHMARKING SURVEY 50 (2009), http://www.corporatecompliance.org/Resources/View/ArticleId/262/Compliance-and-ethics-officer-positioning-A-benchmarking-survey.aspx (last visited Dec 22, 2014).

551 *See* Nicole Dando et al. (2013), *supra* note 4 at 13.

552 BGH, 17.7.2009 - 5 StR 394/08- BGHST 54, 44; BGH NJW 2009, 3173, *supra* note 25.

553 *See* Hauschka, Galster, and Marschlich (2014), *supra* note 463 at 243.

554 *See e.g.* Center for Business Ethics (1986, 1992), *supra* note 496; Djilani (2011), *supra* note 62; Panebianco, *supra* note 515; Samuel Richard, *To Bribe a Prince: Clarifying the Foreign Corrupt Practices Act Through Comparisons to the United Kingdom's Bribery Act of 2010*, 37 BOSTON COLLEGE INTERNATIONAL AND COMPARATIVE LAW REVIEW 419–450 (2014); Weir and Laing (2000), *supra* note 530; Wilson, Williams, and Kemp (2012), *supra* note 534.

remain. For instance, *DeStefano* argues that there is little qualitative research on compliance officers in the United States.[555] In addition, *Demott* argues that the role and status of compliance personnel within private-sector firms have been the subject of relatively little examination by scholars although there is a wide-range of academic literature, reviews, and articles referring to the compliance function.[556] Apparently, in Germany there is only one study focusing on the position of the corporate compliance officer.[557] The conclusion from the literature review is that, it is the unclear picture and definition governing the corporate compliance officer's position in the US, the UK, and Germany that triggers the problem statement discussed in this book.

Third, in addition to the literature review, it might be helpful to examine cases in order to explore the concrete responsibility and duties of the compliance officer in practice. For example, in the view of *Jones*, in the US, board decisions are the only legal tool available for regulating officer's conduct and the only means of dismissing the officer in the event of misconduct.[558] Nevertheless, over the last two decades, the corporate governance community and the courts have begun to pay greater attention to the legal obligations incumbent upon corporate officers. One example of this development is the case[559] in which Disney paid $130 million to its president, who was removed for inefficient management a little over a year after he was hired.[560] The court investigated claims that he had wasted money. The Supreme Court of the State of Delaware decided on June 8, 2006 that such a claim could arise only in the rare event of directors irrationally squandering or giving away corporate assets.[561] For this reason, *Jones* concluded that state corporate law, such as Delaware corporate law, remains silent on the relevant legal duties in the context of corporate officers' misconduct.[562] Additionally, in the view of *Murphy*,[563] the case law does not feature any helpful cases concerning the role of compliance officers, since most major companies prefer to agree to a settlement rather than go to trial.[564] However, the Delaware courts have focused on the role of the board members and on the effectiveness of the compliance programs within

555 *See* DeStefano (2013), *supra* note 14 at 77.
556 *See* DeMott (2013), *supra* note 4 at 56.
557 *See* Herzog and Stephan (2013), *supra* note 476.
558 *See* Jones (2007), *supra* note 495 at 477.
559 *In re the Walt Disney Co. Derivative Litig.*, 906 A.2d 27 (Del. 2006).
560 Jones (2007), *supra* note 495 at 475 note 2.
561 *Id.* at 475.
562 *Id.* at 476.
563 *See* Joseph E. Murphy, *The Compliance Officer: Delimiting the Domain, in* Guide to professional development in compliance 19–36, 21 (2001).
564 *See e.g. In re Caremark International Inc. Derivative Litigation*, 698 A.2d 959 (Del. Ch. 1996), *supra* note 21.; *Kennedy, Burlington Industries, Inc. v. Ellerth*, 524 US 742, 97–569 (1998).

companies.[565] It appears that cases involving the personal liability of compliance officers remain relatively rare.

H3 It can be assumed that, due to the limited number of judicial decisions on the compliance officer's role in the common law system, it would be useful to analyze the legal framework pertaining to the corporate compliance officer.

Fourth, another important aspect in the context of the compliance officer that will be examined in this book is the nature of the role within a company. As previously shown, new research has explored the legal environment, reporting duties, independence, the resources available to the compliance departments, the role of supervision, as well as the scope of the responsibilities and tasks incumbent upon the position, but there is still a lack of knowledge about the classification of this position. In the US, legal scholars have attempted to create a profile for the function.[566] In addition, in 1995, *Richard Y. Roberts*, a Commissioner of the US Securities and Exchange Commission, held a speech on "*The Role of Compliance Personnel*".[567] He saw the compliance personnel in "...*the first line of defense against fraud...*."[568] The compliance officer supports the board in monitoring and overseeing the compliance program. Therefore, it is essential for a compliance officer to have authority within the firm to issue sanctions, or even to dismiss rogue employees, it is also vital that the compliance officer obtain appropriate resources to be effective.[569] However, this approach and authority could yield a conflict of interest within the role.

H4 It can be assumed that the compliance officers' post is categorized as a control function in order to implement legal requirements. For this reason, this function is viewed as "corporate cop"[570] or "watchdog" and does not obtain effective and relevant information concerning the business, because employees are wary of them.

Fifth, legal authors have argued that a compliance officer should be able to operate independently of the general counsel or the management. He should be able to perform duties free from any conflicts of interest.[571] The authors concerned pointed out two major potential conflicts: On the one hand, the reporting relationship - to whom does the CO report misconduct? - and on the other hand, the degree of authority that the management has assigned to the compliance officer.[572] They take the view that an independent compliance officer can support the board

---

565 *See* Murphy (2001), *supra* note 563 at 21.

566 *See e.g.* Gnazzo (2011), *supra* note 8; Weber and Fortun (2005), *supra* note 4.

567 *See* Richard Y. Roberts, The Role of Compliance Personnel. (2014), http://www.sec.gov/news/speech/speecharchive/1995/spch030.txt (last visited Dec 16, 2014).

568 *Id.*

569 *Id.*

570 *See* Joseph Weber, *The New Ethics Enforcers - These corporate cops have unprecedented power to throw their weight around*, 4 Business Week 40–41 (2007).

571 *See* Hoffman, Neill, and Stovall (2008), *supra* note 16 at 89.

572 *Id.* at 90.

in its compliance-monitoring role. The authors also make a historical comparison between the CO and the auditor independence of the audited companies.[573] They argue that the Enron case [574] clearly illustrated the weakness of the close relationship between audit firms and clients.[575] However, increasing independence of the compliance officer could give rise to another risk.

H5 It can be assumed that the compliance officer is independent, he may not be sufficiently familiar with the risks of the business, because he is not involved enough in day-to-day business.

If the compliance officer seeks closer ties to the business units and functions, another conflict may arise. If the compensation of the compliance officer is tied to the financial performance of the business, their independence might be undermined. Furthermore, a 2009 study revealed that two- thirds of the surveyed ethics and compliance officers simultaneously held other positions within the company, such as Head of Human Resources, General Counsel, Chief Operating Officer, etc.[576] Therefore, there is a wide-range of job titles for the compliance position[577] and it appears that the compliance function is an add-on responsibility for another function and a multifunctional role.

H6 It can be suggested that, due to this multifunctional role, the function of the corporate compliance officer is unable to develop an independent standalone position, because the responsibilities are not clearly delimited and defined.

It has been recognized that the compliance officer should report to the highest levels within an organization.[578] *Gnazzo* also presents suitable tools such as audits, surveys, and interviews for reporting on the state of compliance.[579] He recommends that the CECO ought to report directly to the board of directors because he protects the stakeholders within companies.[580] This approach protects the CECO from undue influence by senior executives and management and supports them in obtaining senior authority within the company.[581] Moreover, based on this, legal

573 *Id.*

574 The Enron scandal, revealed in October 2001, led to the bankruptcy of the Enron Corporation, an American energy company based in Houston, Texas. *See* The Enron scandal, http://www.ccsenet.org/journal/index.php/ijbm/article/viewFile/7627/5855 (last visited Dec 16, 2014).

575 *See* Hoffman, Neill, and Stovall (2008), *supra* note 16 at 90.

576 *See* Walker, *supra* note 550 at 48.

577 *See* Sally Bernstein & Andrea Falcione, Moving beyond the baseline Leveraging the compliance function to gain a competitive edge 13, www.pwc.com/us/stateofcompliance (last visited Dec 20, 2015).

578 *See* Gnazzo (2011), *supra* note 8 at 533.

579 *Id.* at 539.

580 *Id.* at 551.

581 *See* Michael D. Greenberg, *Directors as guardians of compliance and ethics within the corporate citadel: what the policy community should know*, 3 (Center for Corporate Ethics and Governance ed., 2010).

scholars and legal practitioners argue that the compliance officer should be made an integral part of the corporate management structure.[582] However, a recent study by PWC found that, at present, only around one-third of companies report that the compliance officer is involved in helping to develop or implement corporate strategy.[583] Therefore,

H7 it can be assumed that legislative regulation and a regulatory framework will be necessary to appoint an independent standalone compliance officer at a high- corporate level.

Overall, the review of the academic literature reveals a gap in knowledge concerning the clear definition of the role of the corporate compliance officer. There is a need to evaluate the role and status of the compliance function within companies by examining how this position can help manage risks and contribute to compliance with the applicable laws and regulations.[584] To further define the role of the compliance function, this book will examine in detail the legal and cultural background of the function, the legal framework surrounding the position, as well as the repositioning of the traditional identity of the compliance officer from the role of legal and regulatory supervisor towards effective strategic business partners.[585]

582 *See* Nicole Dando et al. (2013), *supra* note 4 at 13; Hoffman and Rowe (2007), *supra* note 522.

583 State of Compliance Survey 2015 Bernstein and Falcione, *supra* note 570 at 4.

584 *Id.* at 22.

585 *Id.* at 22.

The Origins of Corporate Compliance

Abstract
This chapter provides an overview of the legal and cultural background of compliance and the compliance function in the private sector in America, in the UK, and in Germany. The first step in the legal research is to establish a general understanding of the history of compliance, in order, based thereon, to define the term compliance in the US, UK and in Germany. Then, this chapter will explore the origins of corporate compliance. The third step will be to examine the historical evolution of the compliance function in the US, the UK, and Germany. Thus, the following three parts will provide an overview of the legal history, the development and legal reasons for the emergence of the compliance function. Based on the assumption above that the compliance function did not simply appear and disappear again, the chapter will also examine the changes in the regulatory framework in terms of the compliance function. To understand the role and nature of the compliance function within companies, it is thus essential to examine the entire legal and cultural background. Ultimately, this approach may help to facilitate a better understanding, definition, and classification of the role of the compliance officer.

A. Legal Roots and Cultural Background of Compliance in the US

Focusing on the origins of American compliance, it becomes clear that this issue is the subject of some controversy among legal scholars.[586] In short, they identified several business sectors and areas of law from which compliance seems to have originated. It appears that in the US, the origins of compliance can be traced back to the healthcare sector, securities law, US export regulations, the criminal corporate law of the individual states, and antitrust law.[587]

However, based on a review of the American literature, it can be argued that corporate compliance emerged in the private sector at the beginning of the 19th century as a substantial element of self-regulation within firms. The motivation behind the implementation of self-regulatory company structures has many root causes.[588] For example, a study by

586 *See e.g.* Miriam H. Baer, *Governing Corporate Compliance*, 50 B. C. L. Rev. 949–975 (2009); Alexander Eufinger, *Zu den historischen Ursprüngen der Compliance*, CCZ 21–22 (2012); Fanto (2013), *supra* note 57; Miller (2014), *supra* note 519; Taylor (2013), *supra* note 13.

587 *See* Eufinger (2012) *supra* note 586 at 21.

588 *See* Bettina Palazzo, *U.S.-American and German Business Ethics:An Intercultural Comparison*, 41 Journal of Business Ethics 195–216, 196 (2002). This study compares the US and German cultural background of business ethics.

Palazzo[589] explores the fact that one source seems to have its origins in the basic American religious principle of Protestantism.[590] *Palazzo* states that there is a positive relationship between business and ethics in America attributable to the puritan work ethic, which emphasizes that industriousness and frugality can lead to salvation.[591] Another source that she points out is that Americans appear to have a less extensive personal private sphere than the Europeans.[592] Therefore, it is easier for Americans to accept the declaration of moral norms *e.g.* a code of ethics, or a code of conduct issued by an employer.[593] In fact, as a result of these cultural developments, American business ethics often appear to be rather legalistic. In conclusion, the Americans tend to understand ethics in terms of compliance as a certain set of universal rules. The popularity of checklists, guidelines, and principles in the US is inherent to this understanding.[594] Thus, it can be assumed that the cultural background of corporate compliance could potentially be traced back to the beginning of the 19th century and the American religious values.

Although history has no beginning, *Miller*[595] identifies that the initial legal starting point of corporate compliance might be the Interstate Commerce Act of 1887.[596] In 1890, the drive for industrial expansion, the completion of the railway network, the corporations' need for self-financing, and the need for investment bankers to be financially independent were the first cornerstones of the demands for professionalism in corporate capitalism in the United States. Hence, this historical development was reflected in self-regulatory efforts designed to eliminate corporate corruption and enhance compliance issues within companies.[597]

A further step in the evolution of compliance can be seen in the federal securities laws passed in the wake of the collapse of the financial markets in the US, in 1929. After the Great Depression of 1930, government regulation had a huge

---

589 Palazzo (2002), *supra* note 588.
590 *Id.* at 210. fig. 3.
591 *Id.* at 200.
592 *Id.* at 201.
593 *Id.* at 201.
594 *Id.* at 203.
595 *See* Geoffrey P. Miller, The Law of Governance, Risk Management, and Compliance 138 (1. ed. 2014); Miller (2014), *supra* note 519 at 2.
596 Interstate Commerce Act (ICA), 24 Stat. 379 (1887). This Act was created by a federal administrative agency, the Interstate Commerce Commission (ICC) to regulate the railroad. In 1887, the Congress passed the Interstate Commerce Act, making the railroads the first industry subject to federal regulation. The Act addressed the problem of railroad monopolies by setting guidelines for how the railroads could conduct business. This Act was the first federal law to regulate private industry in the United States. *See* http://www.ourdocuments.gov/doc.php?flash=true&doc=49, (last visit March 28, 2015)
597 *See* Miller (2014), *supra* note 519 at 3.

influence on the development of corporate business and investment banking.[598] Apparently, important legislative origins of compliance were set down in the Banking Act of 1933[599] and the Securities Acts of 1933.[600] In response to the financial crisis, the collapse of the financial markets and the Depression of the 1930s, the US legislative passed statutes exclusively in the area of securities law.[601] It can be argued that these developments indicate the first origins of compliance regulation in the financial services sector. *Fanto*[602] and *Taylor*[603] also emphasized these aspects in their discussion of the evolution of compliance. Ultimately, they concluded that the term compliance refers to the need to adhere to the 1930s securities laws.[604]

In detail, the Exchange Act of 1934[605] empowered the Securities and Exchange Commission (SEC)[606] with broad authority over all aspects of the securities industry.[607] One clear point emphasizing the importance of compliance was that a broker-dealer and its employees must conduct its business in accordance with the legal, regulatory, and professional obligations.[608] Nevertheless, Section 15 (b) (4) (D) allowed the SEC to discipline only the firm, not the violating employee. This problem was resolved with the addition of Sections 15 (b) (4) (E) and 15 (b) (6)[609] in the amendments to the Acts of 1964. Under Section 15 (b) (4) (E), a broker-dealer or an associated person[610] may also be a subject to

598 *See* MAGALI SARFATTI LARSON, THE RISE OF PROFESSIONALISM: A SOCIOLOGICAL ANALYSIS 138–139 (1. ed. 1977).

599 BANKING ACT OF 1933, PUB.L. 73–66, 48 Stat. 162 (1933).

600 SECURITIES ACT OF 1933, PUB. L. 73-22, 15 USC § 77A, 48 Stat. 74 (1933).

601 *See* Miller (2014), *supra* note 519 at 3.

602 *See* Fanto (2013), *supra* note 57 at 11.

603 *See* Taylor (2013), *supra* note 13 at 54.

604 *See* Fanto (2013), *supra* note 57 at 11; Taylor (2013), *supra* note 13 at 54.

605 SECURITIES EXCHANGE ACT OF 1934, PUB. L. 73–291, 15 USC § 78a 48 Stat. 881 (1934).

606 *"The SEC is an administrative agency of the federal government and promulgates detailed administrative rules and regulations, which have the force of law. The SEC has five Commissioners who are appointed by the President of the United States with the advice and consent of the Senate. The mission of the SEC is to protect investors, to maintain fair, orderly, and efficient markets, and facilitate capital formation." See* SEC, SEC | THE INVESTOR'S ADVOCATE: HOW THE SEC PROTECTS INVESTORS, MAINTAINS MARKET INTEGRITY. SEC, http://www.sec.gov/about/whatwedo.shtml (last visited Mar 28, 2015). The term Commission also means the Securities and Exchange Commission as well.

607 *See* SEC, SEC | FEDERAL SECURITIES LAWS SEC, http://www.sec.gov/about/laws.shtml (last visited Mar 28, 2015).

608 *See* Fanto (2013), *supra* note 57 at 11.

609 SECURITIES EXCHANGE ACT OF 1934, *supra* note 605 PUB. L. 88–467,15 USC §§ 78o (b)(4)(E) & (6) (1964).

610 See *Id.*15 U.S.C. § 78o (b) (6) (1964). An *"associated person"* is defined as *"who, among other things, willfully aids and abets a violation of the federal securities laws or who commits a supervisory violation." See also* § 3 (a) (18) *"any partner, officer, director, or*

sanctions.[611] Since the additional provisions came into force, the need for a corporate function for instance compliance, has been reinforced.[612] In addition, the SEC required a financial service firm to have a compliance department and a compliance officer. Over time, this approach has become a model for other companies as well.[613] In conclusion, the main legislative source of compliance was established in the securities laws governing the financial services sector.

The third step in the development of corporate compliance can be traced back to antitrust law. The best-known price-fixing cases in the 1960s were the *"Electrical Equipment Cases,"* which resulted in large fines for the companies concerned.[614] In these cases, the federal grand jury and the government prosecuted a group of heavy electric equipment companies for antitrust violations.[615] It has been suggested that the "*Electrical Cases*"[616] were the landmark cases for the implementation of compliance programs in the private sector in the 1960s.[617] In addition, the Supreme Court stated in previous cases[618] that price-fixing is *per se* illegal under the Sherman Act.[619] However, in a recent case, the court held that Microsoft Corp.[620] had monopoly power in the market for PC operating systems and had violated the Sherman Act.[621] In a broad sense, Microsoft had failed to comply with the required technical standards.[622] Apparently, one reason for the development of compliance is the corporate violation of laws or rules in particular those pertaining to antitrust law. For this reason, US companies have attempted to prevent such violations

branch manager of such broker or dealer (or any person occupying a similar status or performing similar functions).

611 *See* Fanto (2013), *supra* note 57 at 12.

612 *Id.* at 13.

613 *Id.* at 15.

614 *See* Wilbur L. Fugate & Lee H. Simowitz, Foreign commerce and the antitrust laws 342 (5th ed. 1996).

615 *See* DeStefano (2013), *supra* note 14 at 88.

616 *See* Eufinger (2012), *supra* note 586 at 21.

617 *Id.* at 21.

618 *See e.g. United States v. Trenton Potteries Company* 273 US 392 (1927), No. 27 392 (1927).; *United States v. Socony-Vacuum Oil Company* 310 US 150 (1940), No. 346 150 (1940). *"Agreements to fix prices in interstate commerce are unlawful per se under the Sherman Act, and no showing of so-called competitive abuses or evils which the agreements were designed to eliminate or alleviate may be interposed as a defense."*

619 Sherman Antitrust Act, 15 USC §§ 1–7 26 Stat. 209 (1890); Fugate and Simowitz (1996), *supra* note 614 at 342.

620 *United States v. Microsoft Corp.*, 253 F.3d 34, 49 (D.C. Cir. 2001).

621 Sherman Antitrust Act, 15 USC. §§ 1–7, 26 Stat. 209 (1890). *See* William H. Page & Seldon J. Childers, *Measuring Compliance with Compulsory Licensing Remedies in the American Microsoft Case*, 76 Antitrust Law Journal 239–269, 241 (2009).

622 *See* Page and Childers, *supra* note 621 at 250.

before they occur by implementing effective compliance structures.[623] Alongside the enforcement of antitrust law, environmental awareness has increased in the US[624] and the government passed a series of important federal statutes, including the Clean Air Act[625] and the Clear Water Act.[626] In response, a new federal administrative agency was born, the Environmental Protection Agency (EPA), to monitor, standard-setting and enforcement activities to ensure compliance with the environmental regulations.[627]

Thus, the fourth factor in the enhancement of corporate compliance issues were economic reasons linked to corporate scandals and environmental concerns. One reason behind companies' self-regulation lies in the possibility of them being exposed to dramatic and serious losses as a result of fraudulent acts by officers and employees at a lower level of the corporate structure.[628] Hence, the evolution of compliance in the US was further influenced by efforts by the companies themselves to comply with antitrust and environmental law. Thus, self-regulation could be seen as an attempt on the part of the companies to ensure that employees do not violate applicable rules, regulations, or norms.[629] After all, in the US, fraud and misconduct of employees could pose an existential threat for the company due to the separate legal personality[630] of the corporation.[631] In addition, an effective compliance structure could avoid any loss of reputation and may reduce costs of insurance and employee compensation. Furthermore, compliance may help to avoid prosecution or reduce criminal penalties and could provide a significant defense in the event that the board fails to exercise its obligations to supervise compliance risks.[632] In conclusion, it can be noted that self-regulation was the preferred option because it minimized the costs and maximized the independence of companies.

---

623 *See* Theodore L. Banks & Frederick Z. Banks, Corporate legal compliance handbook (2nd ed. 2011) § 4.01.

624 *See* Miller (2014), *supra* note 595 at 139.

625 Clean Air Act (1963), Pub. Law 88-206, 42 USC 77 Stat. 392 (1963).

626 Clean Water Act (1972), Pub. Law 92-500, 33 USC §§ 1251–1387 86 Stat. 816 (1972).

627 EPA, *supra* note 338.

628 *See* Sale (2007), *supra* note 22 at 733.

629 *See* Miller (2014), *supra* note 519 at 1.

630 The right to sue and be sued in its own name. *See* Delaware Code, Del. Code Ann. tit. 12, *supra* note 24, §§ 3801–3862. Provide for strong form legal personality and limited liability.

631 *See* Int'l Business Publications USA, US Company Laws and Regulations Handbook Volume 2 Corporate Laws and Regulation in the Selected States of the US: Delaware Corporation 30 (4. ed. 2009).

632 *See* Banks and Banks (2011), *supra* note 623 § 1.01. *See also* In re *Dow Chemical Company Derivative Litigation*, No. 4349-CC (Del. Ch. 2010), (2010). *"The plaintiffs, stockholders of Dow, brought this action against current directors and officers of the Company, alleging that the defendants had breached their fiduciary duties to the company by point (3) ...to failing to detect and prevent a variety of alleged wrongs,*

The fifth step in the emergence of corporate compliance originated from a larger number of court decisions in corporate law in the 1960s. At that time, there were two different legal perceptions in the US concerning the duties of a company director. In 1963, in *Graham v. Allis-Chalmers Manufacturing Co.*[633] the Delaware Supreme Court rejected the concept that company directors were responsible for implementing a structure that ensured compliance with the law.[634] This court approach also seems consistent with the "*business judgment rule*".[635] While the Delaware courts did not interfere with the internal structure of companies, the legislator enforced the criminal law.[636] From 1996, the Delaware courts re-entered the compliance arena with the landmark case *In re Caremark Derivative Litigation*.[637] In this case, the court concluded that it could not foreclose the director's obligation to be reasonably informed concerning the corporation.[638] Hence, lawyers and legal scholars evaluated the *Caremark* decision as a basis for directors to ensure that monitoring systems were in place to prevent and detect criminal violations.[639]

A further step towards the enforcement of federal law was, that Congress fostered the corporate compliance movement by enacting the Foreign Corrupt Practices Act (FCPA), in 1977.[640] This was a direct response by the legislator to growing concern about corporate bribery in the mid-1970s.[641] In addition, in 1991, the US government enacted the Organizational Sentencing Guidelines for Organizations (FSGO).[642] Under these recommendations, organizations can

---

including bribery, misrepresentation, insider trading, and wasteful compensation." See Chandler, Memorandum Opinion *In re The Dow Chemical Company* in Civil Action No. 4349-CC (2009).

633 *Graham v. Allis-Chalmers Manufacturing Company*, 188 A.2d 125 (Del. 1963), 130 (1963).

634 *See* Baer (2009), *supra* note 586 at 961.

635 "*The business judgment rule is a presumption that a rational business decision of the officers or directors of a corporation is proper unless there exist facts which remove the decision from the protection of the rule, such as self-dealing, conflict of interest, etc." See Schreiber v. Pennzoil Co.*, 419 A.2d 952 (Del. Ch. 1980), 756 (1980). *See supra* footnote 198.

636 *See* Baer (2009), *supra* note 586 at 961.

637 *Id.* at 961.; *In re Caremark International Inc. Derivative Litigation*, 698 A.2d 959 (Del. Ch. 1996), *supra* note 21.

638 *See* Baer (2009), *supra* note 586 at 967; *in re Caremark International Inc. Derivative Litigation*, 698 A.2d 959 (Del. Ch. 1996), *supra* note 21 at 970.

639 *See* Baer (2009), *supra* note 586 at 967.

640 Foreign Corrupt Practices Act 1977 (FCPA), *supra* note 438. *See infra* p. 202

641 *See* Gideon Mark, *Private FCPA Enforcement: Private FCPA Enforcement*, 49 American Business Law Journal 419–506, 422 (2012).

642 US Sentencing Guidelines Manual USSC, Chapter 8, § 8 B2.1. (2004), http://www.ussc.gov/guidelines-manual/2015/2015-chapter-8 (last visited Sep 9, 2015); Freeman (2007), *supra* note 57 at 358.

minimize fines if they have in place an effective compliance program to prevent and detect violations of the law.[643] However, this legislation was not able to prevent the corporate scandals of the early 2000s such as Enron, WorldCom or Adelphia.[644] It was after these scandals that one of the most important governance and compliance statutes came into force, namely the Sarbanes-Oxley Act.[645] The content, relevance, and effects of the FCPA, FSGO, and the SOX with regard to compliance and the compliance function will be discussed in detail later.[646]

These and many other developments point out the legal roots and the cultural background of compliance in America. In short, the cultural background of compliance in the US can be traced back to Protestantism. The industrial revolution and the financial crisis at the beginning of the 20th century led to the enactment of the first legal statutes and administrative regulations governing the corporate and financial services sector. It has been mentioned that, more recently, court decisions have on the one hand enhanced the development of compliance systems within companies while, on the other legislation has encouraged the emergence of compliance issues, for instance in the area of antitrust and anti-corruption laws. *Miller* concluded that this was a fundamental development in American law.[647] He termed this development *"a rise of the administrative state and a judicial model of regulation."*[648] In response, American companies have increased their efforts to protect themselves by implementing compliance structures. To further understand the role of compliance and the compliance officer function the next three sections will examine in more detail the definition of compliance and the emergence of the compliance function in the US.

I. Definitions of Compliance in the US

In order to understand the role of compliance in the US, the term compliance will be outlined. The first explanations of compliance originated in the healthcare sector. In this area, the word compliance was defined as *"the extent to which the patient's behavior matches the prescriber's recommendations."*[649] Thus, the word compliance explains the patients' cooperative behavior in the context of a therapy; in this context, it means adherence to the course of treatment.[650] The healthcare literature has revealed three aspects of compliance: (1) evaluative, (2) rationalization,

643 *See* Freeman (2007), *supra* note 57 at 358.
644 *See* Miller (2014), *supra* note 595 at 139.
645 *Id.* at 139.; Sarbanes-Oxley Act of 2002, supra note 47.
646 *See infra* A., I., pp. 175 et seq.
647 *See* Miller (2014), *supra* note 595 at 140.
648 *Id.* at 140. Under the judicial model of regulation, the government and the regulated organizations were seen as parties on equal footing.
649 *See* Compliance in health care, (R. Brian Haynes, D. Wayne Taylor, & David L Sackett eds., 1979).
650 *Id.*

and (3) acceptance.[651] Today the healthcare sector in the US, is subject to extensive regulation. The relationship of trust between the patient and the physician establishes a special responsibility. Therefore, developments in this area required the development of a professional ethical culture with an ethical structure.[652]

Secondly, as discussed previously, corporate compliance is a creature of federal criminal and antitrust law.[653] When legal scholars explain the matter of compliance, what they actually explore and highlight is the legislation and the implementation of ethics and compliance programs within companies.[654] One study by *Pérezts & Picard* found that researchers have long assumed and described the gap between the adoption of formal regulations and the actual implementation thereof in daily practice.[655] For instance, socio-legal scholars believed that compliance was established within companies and sometimes linked with the external regulators.[656] Meanwhile, other scholars argued that compliance is a complex, political, creative, collective, conflicting, and evolving process between the formal compliance systems and management structure and the perceptions and motivations of individuals in organizations.[657] While, at first glance, these findings might explain the notion of the word compliance, on closer consideration, what they described is the process or procedure of compliance.

Thirdly, in order to describe the US term compliance more precisely it could be helpful to differentiate the meaning of the term ethics. According to *Joyner & Payne* ethics is defined as a core *"set of beliefs and principles."*[658] The term compliance

---

651 *See* Nancy Murphy & Mary Canales, *A critical analysis of compliance*, 8 Nursing Inquiry 173–181, 173 (2001).

652 *See* Mark E. Meaney, *Professional Ethical Development in Health Care Compliance*, *in* Guide to professional development in compliance , 9 (2001).

653 *See supra* A., I., p. 121; *See also* Sherman Antitrust Act, *supra* note 619.

654 *See e.g.* Canary and Jennings (2008), *supra* note 511; Joseph (2003), *supra* note 491; Kaptein (2015), *supra* note 515; Diana E. Murphy, *The Federal Sentencing Guidelines for Organizations: A Decade of Promoting Compliance and Ethics*, 87 Iowa Law Review 698–719 (2002); Weber and Wasieleski (2013), *supra* note 492

655 *See* Mar Pérezts & Sébastien Picard, *Compliance or Comfort Zone? The Work of Embedded Ethics in Performing Regulation*, 131 Journal of Business Ethics 833–852, 833 (2015).

656 *See* Robert A. Kagan, Neil Gunningham & Dorothy Thornton, *Fear, Duty and Regulatory Compliance: Lessons from three research projects*, *in* Explaining Compliance Business Responses to Regulation. 37–58, 37 (1. ed. 2011).

657 *See e.g.* Christine Parker & Sharon Gilad, *Internal Corporate Compliance Management Systems: Structure, Culture and Agency*, *in* Explaining Compliance Business Responses to Regulation. 170–197 (1. ed. 2011); Pérezts and Picard (2015), *supra* note 655.

658 *See* Brenda E. Joyner & Dinah Payne, *Evolution and Implementation: A Study of Values, Business Ethics and Corporate Social Responsibility*, 41 Journal of Business Ethics 297–311, 299 (2002).

can be characterized by observance; conformity; obedience.[659] In this context, it appears that ethics entails more than compliance. The purpose of business ethics is "*to improve the ethical quality of decision making and acting at all levels of business.*"[660] However, ethics and compliance together require that the employees act in accordance with their legal, regulatory and professional obligations.[661] These explanations show that compliance is a concept of what constitutes correct conduct or behavior or, in other words: "*the state or fact of according with or meeting rules or standards*".[662] Thus, compliance is adherence to regulations as an essential part of doing business in today's corporate environment.

Building on these explanations, the business ethics literature often describes compliance as "*adherence with all the laws, regulations, rules, and policies governing an organization.*"[663] In other words, the objective of compliance focuses on obeying and monitoring the existing provisions, rules, and guidelines. Furthermore, *Gnazzo* argued that compliance is an "*oversight*" function.[664] This conclusion has significant importance for the compliance function since it means that the compliance officer ought to be responsible for ensuring that all aspects of compliance are properly managed within organizations.[665]

For this reason, compliance programs within companies address the overall conduct of business activities in accordance with legal and increasingly, ethical and cultural, norms.[666] In recent years, American companies have established compliance departments to monitor and discipline employees who breach law or internal corporate policies.[667] Furthermore, compliance departments assist in the

659 Compliance Facts, information, pictures | West's Encyclopedia of American Law (2005), http://www.encyclopedia.com/topic/Compliance.aspx#4 (last visited Sep 9, 2015).

660 *See* Georges Enderle, *FOCUS: A Comparison of Business Ethics in North America and Continental Europe*, 5 Business Ethics: A European Review 33–46, 37–38 (1996).

661 *See* Fanto (2013), *supra* note 57 at 11.

662 Compliance Facts, information, pictures | The Oxford Pocket Dictionary of Current English (2009), http://www.encyclopedia.com/topic/Compliance.aspx#3 (last visited Sep 9, 2015).

663 *See* Gnazzo (2011), *supra* note 8 at 538. *See also* Ethics Resource Center (ERC), Leading Corporate Integrity: Defining the Role of the Chief Ethics & Compliance Officer (CECO) 48 5 (2007), www.ethics.org/CECO (last visited Dec 12, 2014). "*Compliance…, but also adherence to many other standards designed to regulate the internal operations of the business itself.*"

664 *See* Gnazzo (2011), *supra* note 8 at 538.

665 *Id.* at 538.

666 *See* Baer (2009), *supra* note 586 at 958. *See also* Committee ABA Section of Business Law Corporate Compliance Survey, *Corporate Compliance Survey*, 60 The Business Lawyer 1759–1798, 1759 (2005).

667 *See* Baer (2009), *supra* note 586 at 960.

investigation of wrongdoing. Accordingly, American legal business scholars have provided their definition of the term compliance. They identify compliance as

> ...a system of policies and controls that organizations adopt to deter violations of law and to assure external authorities that they are taking steps to deter violations of law.[668]

All these definitions and explanations mostly highlight the fact that compliance is characterized by its supervisory nature, that it may reduce violation of the law, and that it could help to ensure adherence to internal policies within companies. Finally, it has been mentioned that compliance has existed as long as people have done business.[669]

II. The Historical Evolution of the Compliance Function in the US

To reiterate and to understand the nature of the compliance function within US firms, it is necessary first to explore the ways in which the American compliance function has evolved over the years. The American compliance departments and the independent compliance function were first established in the securities industry in the early 1960s.[670] Before that time, responsibility for compliance was incumbent upon legal departments and the person in charge of compliance often reported to the General Counsel.[671]

In order to assess the role of the corporate compliance function a shift in academic focus to look deeper within private sector firms and the legal environment is necessary. As discussed previously, various federal statutes were enacted in the 1960s and 1970s *e.g.* the Clean Air Act[672] and the Clean Water Act.[673] In addition, a new federal administrative body, the Environmental Protection Agency (EPA),[674] was established. Furthermore, *Chandler* recognized that the roots of the modern-day

---

668 *Id.* at 958.; Corporate Compliance Survey, *supra* note 666 at 1759–1760; Donald C. Langevoort, *Monitoring: The Behavioral Economics of Corporate Compliance with Law*, 71 Colum. Bus. L. Rev, 74 (2002).

669 Corporate Compliance Survey, *supra* note 666 at 1759.

670 *See* Miriam H. Baer, *Confronting the Two Faces of Corporate Fraud*, 66 Florida Law Review 87–156, 142 (2014); Securities Industry Association, Compliance & Legal Division, *The role of compliance*, 6 Journal of Investment Compliance 4–22, 5 (2005).

671 Securities Industry Association, Compliance & Legal Division, *supra* note 670 at 5.

672 Clean Air Act (1963), *supra* note 625.

673 Clean Water Act (1972), *supra* note 626.

674 *"The EPA was born in the wake of elevated concern about environmental pollution, EPA was established on December 2, 1970 to consolidate in one agency a variety of federal research, monitoring, standard-setting and enforcement activities to ensure environmental protection."* *See* EPA, *supra* note 338.

ethics and compliance position can be traced back to the Watergate scandal.[675] The aftermath of the scandal, with the Congressional hearings and investigations into illegal payments, focused public attention on the unethical actions of individual employees. Based on this investigation, more than 400 corporations have admitted to making illegal payments.[676] These developments ultimately encouraged the US federal government to improve the ethical behavior of US corporations by means of legislation.[677] To this end, in 1977, the legislature passed the Foreign Corrupt Practices Act.[678]

A survey of ethics officers at Fortune 500[679] firms by *Morf, Schumacher, and Vitell* found that corporations in the US have established ethics programs for a variety of reasons.[680] For example, they found that General Dynamics was the first corporation to create a new generation of corporate ethics offices in 1985. At the time, General Dynamics was under government investigation for billing irregularities. General Dynamics has in the meantime established an ethics office and an ethics hotline for employees to report ethical problems anonymously.[681]

Furthermore, in 1984, Congress passed the Sentencing Reform Act,[682] which established a set of mandatory federal sentencing guidelines. In 1991, the establishment of the Sentencing Guidelines for Organizations (FSGO)[683] created the first basis for laws relating to corporate compliance programs. This was a significant milestone in advancing corporate compliance. The 2004 amendments of the

675 *See* David Brian Chandler, *Organizations and Ethics: Antecedents and Consequences of the Adoption and Implementation of the Ethics and Compliance Officer Position*, 2011.

676 *Id.* at 14 at note 8.

677 *Id.* at 15. *See also* House of Representatives, Unlawful Corporate Payments Act of 1977 (1977), http://www.justice.gov/sites/default/files/criminal-fraud/legacy/2010/04/11/houseprt-95-640.pdf (last visited Sep 9, 2015).

678 Foreign Corrupt Practices Act 1977 (FCPA), *supra* note 438. *"The FCPA was enacted for the purpose of making it unlawful for certain classes of persons and entities to make payments to foreign government officials to assist in obtaining or retaining business." See* DOJ, Foreign Corrupt Practices Act | Criminal-Fraud | Department of Justice http://www.justice.gov, http://www.justice.gov/criminal-fraud/foreign-corrupt-practices-act (last visited Sep 9, 2015).

679 *"Companies are ranked by total revenues for their respective fiscal years. Included in the survey are companies that are incorporated in the US and operate in the US and file financial statements with a government agency." See* Fortune 500 - Fortune, Fortune 500, http://fortune.com/fortune500/ (last visited Sep 9, 2015).

680 *See* Morf, Schumacher, and Vitell (1999), *supra* note 502 at 265.

681 *Id.* at 265.

682 Sentencing Reform Act (1984), *supra* note 48.

683 United States Sentencing Commission USSC, *supra* note 50. On November 1, 1991, the United States Sentencing Commission (USSC) put into effect the Federal Sentencing Guidelines for Organizations. *See infra* A., I., 3., pp. 236 et seq.

FSGO[684] imposed responsibility for the compliance program on an organization *"governing authority"* or *"high-level personnel."*[685] Thus, the compliance function became a key component of an effective compliance program. The FSGO outlined seven elements of effectiveness.[686] These standards serve as a guide for directors to ensure that compliance is effectively established within firms.[687] Hence, the FSGO developed the first criminal justice framework for an effective corporate compliance program. This was the legal starting point for companies to develop such programs.[688] Finally, under this legislation[689] the companies could impose fines and penalties in cases involving corporate crime.[690] As a result, the guidelines encouraged companies to set up internal structures to help prevent, detect, and report criminal behavior.[691] They also offer incentives for corporations to hire ethics and compliance officers who are in charge of controls to prevent, investigate, and punish wrongdoing and misconduct by employees.[692]

Furthermore, the corporate scandals of the early 2000s led to the enactment of the Sarbanes-Oxley Act (SOX).[693] The SOX was proposed to establish *"significantly higher standards for corporate responsibility and governance"*[694] to protect investors. The SOX requires firms to apply best practice with *e.g.* the enforcement of compliance with professional standards[695] and the establishment of a code of ethics for

---

684 United States Sentencing Commission, USSC, *supra* note 50; USSC, *supra* note 49.

685 *See* Greenberg (2010), *supra* note 581 at 35; USSC, *supra* note 667 § 8 B2.1.b (2) B (2004). *"High-level personnel of the organization shall ensure that the organization has an effective Compliance and Ethics program, as described in this guideline. Specific individual(s) within high-level personnel shall be assigned overall responsibility for the Compliance and Ethics program."*

686 USSC, *supra* note 56.

687 *See* Greenberg (2010), *supra* note 581 at 18.

688 *See* Michael D. Greenberg, *Corporate culture and ethical leadership under the federal sentencing guidelines: what should boards, management and policymakers do now?*, 7 (2012).

689 United States Sentencing Commission, USSC, *supra* note 50.

690 *See* Smith (2003), *supra* note 504 at 634; United States Sentencing Commission, USSC, *supra* note 50 § 994.

691 *See* Smith (2003), *supra* note 504 at 634.

692 *See* Morf, Schumacher, and Vitell (1999), *supra* note 502 at 265.

693 Sarbanes-Oxley Act of 2002, *supra* note 47. *"The Sarbanes-Oxley Act of 2002 is Federal Law and mandatory. All listed organizations must comply. The legislation was enacted in 2002 and introduced major changes to the regulation of financial practice and corporate governance."*; *See* Addison-Hewitt Associates, The Sarbanes-Oxley Act 2002 A Guide To The Sarbanes-Oxley Act, http://www.soxlaw.com/ (last visited Sep 9, 2015).

694 United States Congress, (2002). Senator Sarbanes, 148 Cong. Rec. S7350-04 in: Ethics Resource Center (ERC), *supra* note 663 at 5.

695 Sarbanes-Oxley Act of 2002, *supra* note 47 § 101 (c) (6).

senior financial officers.[696] Hence, this Act tackled issues concerning the role of corporate officers and imposed new legal duties upon those officers.[697] For example, their main tasks are to supervise the day-to-day conduct of business unit activities and to ensure that employees adhere to applicable laws and regulations.[698] It has been mentioned that the focus lies on ensuring legal and ethical norms from the inside out. Hence, the compliance personnel, structure, and processes can be characterized as internal governance mechanisms.[699]

All of these federal statutes were a response to the disclosure of corporate bribery. In addition, following the collapse of insurance and loan institutions and the loss of confidence in the integrity of the American financial system, new banking regulations were enacted. Lastly, the financial crisis of 2007 to 2009 saw the introduction of a number of new statutes, for instance the Dodd-Frank Act of 2010.[700] *Miller* held that the government today possesses greater power of enforcement and authority.[701] He concluded that these developments resulted in a *"tectonic"* change in the American common law system.[702]

Overall, it has been recognized that, nowadays, companies undoubtedly face more compliance issues than they did a century ago.[703] In response, many companies have built strong instituting procedures to internalize law enforcement.[704] The compliance function has evolved over time on the one hand as a component of firms' self-regulatory initiatives in order to avoid corporate scandals and high penalty payments, and on the other hand, on account of the increasingly stringent legal framework.[705] Due to the financial crises, more and more government legislation has been passed over time. In the wake of a number of high-profile corporate scandals, separate compliance departments have also developed within companies outside the financial services sector.[706] Finally, the compliance officer position was established as a result of efforts by organizations to ensure that employees do not violate the applicable laws and the enforcement of legislation.[707] Having examined

---

696 *Id.* § 406.
697 *See* Jones (2007), *supra* note 495 at 476.
698 Securities Industry Association, Compliance & Legal Division, *supra* note 670 at 5.
699 *See* DeMott (2013), *supra* note 4 at 57.
700 Dodd–Frank Wall Street Reform and Consumer Protection Act (2010), Pub. L. 111–203, § 929-Z, 15 USC § 78o 124 Stat. 1376, 1871 (2010); *See* Miller (2014), *supra* note 519 at 3., This was an act *"To promote the financial stability of the United States by improving accountability and transparency in the financial system..."* *See* Dodd-Frank Wall Street Reform and Consumer Protection Act, https://www.gpo.gov/fdsys/pkg/PLAW-111publ203/pdf/PLAW-111publ203.pdf (last visited Sep 9, 2015).
701 *See* Miller (2014), *supra* note 519 at 3.
702 *Id.* at 3.
703 *See infra* A., II., pp. 254 et seq.
704 Miller (2014), *supra* note 519 at 3.
705 *See supra* A., I., p. 124.
706 *See* DeStefano (2013), *supra* note 14 at 74; Smith (2003), *supra* note 504 at 636.
707 *See* Miller (2014), *supra* note 519 at 1.

the historical evolution of this position, the next section will provide a definition of the compliance function in the US.

III. Definition of the Compliance Function in the US

By reviewing the academic literature this section attempts to outline a definition of the US compliance function in the private sector. In the US, the compliance officer function attracts a great deal of public and academic attention.[708] It can be noted, that in the US, the compliance officer is recognized as a member of a profession. As a rule, members of a profession establish their own standards for performing an important function and "*serving a public social goal*".[709] By standardizing of a job description, companies and employers may use determined features for personnel selection and on the other hand, the standards could incentivize the compliance officer for professional self-development.

As the foregoing section demonstrates, compliance officers emerged on the corporate scene in the early 1960s within legal departments. Since then, the US has seen a significant increase in the attention afforded to this position and the number of compliance officers.[710] As discussed previously, over time the compliance function has developed further in response to corporate scandals and to changes in the enforcement of the law, and a new regulatory environment. Hence, the role of the compliance officer has moved to center stage.[711] For instance, the Bureau of Labor Statistics points out that in 2014 a total of 260,300 compliance officers were employed in the US.[712] Additionally, it is expected that this occupation will grow by a further 3.3 percent by 2024. Furthermore, the compliance officer's median annual wage was $ 62,020 and the typical entry-level education of compliance officers is a Bachelor's degree. Surprisingly, a survey by the Health Care Compliance Association (HCCA) found that 72 percent of respondent organizations in the healthcare sector have a female compliance officer.[713] In contrast,

---

708 *See e.g.* Adobor (2006), *supra* note 46; Baer (2009), *supra* note 586; DeMott (2013), *supra* note 4; DeStefano (2013), *supra* note 14; Freeman (2007), *supra* note 57; Gnazzo (2011), *supra* note 8; Majewski (2006), *supra* note 18; Miller (2014), *supra* note 519; Pirraglia (2003), *supra* note 486; Rosella and Pugliese (2006), *supra* note 13; Traeger, Guidroz, and Jimbo (2014), *supra* note 486; Weber and Fortun (2005), *supra* note 4.

709 *See* Meaney (2001), *supra* note 652 at 3–4.

710 *See* Weber and Fortun (2005), *supra* note 4 at 98.

711 Securities Industry and Financial Markets Association SIFMA, The Evolving Role of Compliance | 2013 | White Papers | Correspondence 36 1 (2013), http://www.sifma.org/issues/item.aspx?id=8589942363 (last visited Sep 9, 2015).

712 *See* Bureau of Labor Statistics, United States Department of Labor | Employment Projections (2014), http://data.bls.gov/projections/occupationProj (last visited Sep 9, 2015).

713 Health Care Compliance Officers HCCA, 2008 Annual Survey 22 (2008), http://www.hcca-info.org/Resources/View/ArticleId/781/2008-Annual-Survey.aspx (last visited Sep 10, 2015).

72 percent of the surveyed German compliance officers in the corporate environment are male.[714]

As discussed above,[715] three key reasons for the establishment of the function of ethics and compliance officers in the US have been recognized, (1) as a response to a series of scandals and crises in corporate companies, (2) since then, the FSGO (1991) and the SOX (2002) have provided a criminal justice framework to deter and penalize organizational misconduct, and (3) a growing trend in businesses that promote, enforce, and encourage an ethical climate is needed for effective and profitable companies.[716]

In conclusion, the appointment of a compliance officer position within companies has made a significant contribution of these developments.[717] Since the release of the FSGO[718] in 1991, 54 % of the Fortune 1000[719] has established an ethics or compliance officer function assigned to deal with ethics and conduct measures designed to fulfil the standards.[720] A 2010 survey of more than 1,200 members of the Ethics and Compliance Officers Association (ECOA) by *Weber & Wasieleski* found that 100 percent of the responding organizations[721] have an ethics or compliance officer.[722] They concluded that despite the fact that there is a definite trend towards more ethics and compliance programs within companies, it should be assumed that ethical and compliance efforts still need to be increased.[723]

Having traced the importance of the compliance function, this section will provide the definition of this position proposed by professionals and legal scholars. *Gnazzo*, an early chief compliance officer at United Technologies Corporation describes the compliance function in his own words as follows:

> It should be responsible for ensuring that all aspects of those organizational requirements are being managed properly. Clearly, compliance is an oversight function.[724]
>
> The responsibility of the compliance officer and the compliance function should be one of oversight on behalf of the board of directors.[725]

---

714 *See* HERZOG AND STEPHAN (2013), *supra* note 476 at 265.
715 *See infra* A., II., pp. 254 et seq.
716 *See* Smith (2003), *supra* note 504 at 636.
717 *See* Adobor (2006), *supra* note 46 at 57; Fanto (2013), *supra* note 57 at 1.
718 US SENTENCING GUIDELINES MANUAL USSC, *supra* note 49.
719 *See* Date.com, FORTUNE 1000 FORTUNE 1000 COMPANY LIST (2015), https://connect.data.com/directory/company/fortune/1000 (last visited Sep 10, 2015).
720 *See* Weaver, Treviño, and Cochran (1999), *supra* note 489 at 288.
721 The survey had a 12.8 % response rate.
722 *See* Weber and Wasieleski (2013), *supra* note 492 at 613 Table 2.
723 *Id.* at 624.
724 *See* Gnazzo (2011), *supra* note 8 at 538. *See also* Fanto (2013), *supra* note 57 at 2; Miller (2014), *supra* note 519 at 1.
725 *See* Gnazzo (2011), *supra* note 8 at 539.

Other practitioners explain the daily nature of the function as follows:

> The role has evolved from more of a technical [discipline] to that of a decision science. I think the big shift is in how chief compliance officers interact with and relate to people.[726]

Legal scholars such as *Rostain* and *Freeman* have examined in turn that the compliance function should include

> ...the promulgation of codes of behavior, the institution of training programs, the identification of internal compliance personnel and the creation of procedures and controls to insure company-wide compliance with legal mandates.[727]
>
> The responsibilities of the position [compliance function] often include leading enterprise compliance efforts; ensuring compliance with internal standards and state and federal laws; managing audits and investigations into regulatory compliance issues; and responding to requests for information from regulatory bodies.[728]

In other words, a successful compliance officer will also act as an educator and advisor. *Freeman* concluded that the comprehensive task of the compliance officer is dealing with all levels of management, corporate employees, government regulators and the public with respect, diplomacy, and discretion.[729]

Although *Smith* complained that the precise role of compliance officers often goes undefined in companies, he also argued that it would be helpful to develop a more meaningful definition within corporations.[730] Hence, he believed that it is possible to develop a definition from the *de facto* and sometimes *de jure* job duties and responsibilities.[731] A 2005 survey of ethics and compliance officers conducted by *Weber & Fortun* helpfully provides the following profile of a compliance officer:

> An ECO is typically a male who is 48 years old. He has been with his company for nearly 14 years and has held the ECO position for about three years. His title varies greatly from other ECOs but probably includes the term compliance and is likely a director or officer in the company. His educational background consists of either a JD or MBA or both. His primary job responsibilities most likely include ensuring compliance program oversight, conducting investigations of alleged employee

---

726 Scott Mitchell, CEO of the open compliance and ethics group. *See* Caron Carlson, How the Modern CCO Came to Be | Compliance Week Compliance Week (2008), https://www.complianceweek.com/news/news-article/how-the-modern-cco-came-to-be (last visited Sep 10, 2015).

727 *See* Tanina Rostain, *General Counsel in the Age of Compliance: Preliminary Findings and New Research Questions*, 21 Georgetown Journal of Legal Ethics 465–490, 467 (2008).

728 *See* Freeman (2007), *supra* note 57 at 360.

729 *Id.* at 360.

730 *See* Smith (2003), *supra* note 504 at 635.

731 *Id.* at 638.

misconduct, and carrying out the organization's employee ethics and compliance training program.[732]

These findings suggest that the average US compliance officer has more of an insider status, and is a middle-aged man, despite the findings and figures in the health care sector.[733] In most instances, he has a legal or business background. His main duties comprise the creation of codes of conduct, monitoring of compliance programs, conducting compliance trainings program and ensuring that employees operate the business in adherence with the law. The compliance officer sometimes also participates in internal investigations of alleged breaches by employees. According to these findings, ethics and compliance officers in the corporate world are concerned primarily with overseeing the ethical conduct of all employees.[734] They should ensure that the firm and its employees comply with all applicable laws and regulations.[735] Similarly, *Miller* argued that the compliance function tasks embody the duty and the obligations to prevent illegal activities on the part of the employees.[736] In the view of *DeStefano* and *Parker,* this position should be a combination of compliance detection, prevention, and response policies.[737] In addition, a study[738] by *Rosen, Parker, and Nielsen* found that the compliance function should analyze and influence the company's compliance structures and practices and on the other hand, the costs, benefits and risks of non-compliance.[739] Hence, it has been recognized that a compliance officer is an individual responsible for the detailed revision and monitoring of compliance procedures and policies.

In addition, it has also been noted that the compliance officer occupies a difficult position between business and regulation. On the one hand, he should not engage in the firm's business but nevertheless has to understand the business.[740] On the other hand, he is responsible for revising and monitoring compliance procedures, policies, law, and regulation.[741] These are management tasks.[742] Similarly, *Jones*

---

732 *See* Weber and Fortun (2005), supra note 4 at 110. The results are from a survey of the Pittsburgh Ethics Network members, 37 members of the ethics network were mailed or e-mailed with a two-pages survey. *See Id.* at 100.

733 *See* HCCA, *supra* note 712.

734 *See* Smith (2003), *supra* note 504 at 633.

735 *See* Fanto (2013), *supra* note 57 at 1.

736 *See* Miller (2014), *supra* note 519 at 1.

737 *See e.g.* DeStefano (2013), *supra* note 14 at 93; Parker (2000), *supra* note 441 at 340.

738 This study uses data from a survey of 999 large Australian businesses to examine the professional background of the person in charge of compliance. *See* Robert Rosen, Christine Parker & Vibeke Lehmann Nielsen, *The Framing Effects of Professionalism: Is There a Lawyer Cast of Mind? Lessons from Compliance Programs,* XL Fordham Urban Law Journal 297–367, 297 (2013).

739 *Id.* at 297.

740 *See* Fanto (2013), *supra* note 57 at 2.

741 *Id.* at 2–3.

742 *See* Gnazzo (2011), *supra* note 8 at 540.

considers the dualistic standard applicable to the role of officers due first to their duties of care and second the standard of liability.[743] A theoretical study by *Treviño et al.* pointed out the inherent duality in the compliance officer's approach.[744] They have to balance sensitivity to business needs while having, on occasion to say "no" to potentially profitable new ideas if they would result in the business not complying with the law. In so doing, the role of the compliance officer needs to be effective, and may at times restrict the business creativity and profitability through its rules, procedures and monitoring.[745] On this basis, it has been said that the role of compliance officer is a "*dual-hatted*" position because of their simultaneous business oversight role and supervisory duties.[746]

In conclusion, in the US, there is no single accepted definition of the function of compliance officer' within companies, but the numerous descriptions of the duties and tasks of this position could be helpful to create a definition. The compliance officer's function can be defined as a high-level dual-hatted[747] employee, in charge of managing an effective internal compliance structure in close collaboration with all employees and the management. He diplomatically handles business needs and ensures adherence with the applicable law. Finally, the nature and role of the US compliance function has been defined as a "*dual-hatted*" role and an "*oversight*" function.[748]

B. Legal Roots and Cultural Background of Compliance in the UK

This part traces the legal roots of compliance in the UK and the cultural background of the compliance function within English companies. A review of the English literature shows that there has been little academic and empirical research by legal

743 *See* Jones (2007), *supra* note 495 at 544.
744 *See* Treviño et al. (2014), *supra* note 486 at 196.
745 *See* Fanto (2013), *supra* note 57 at 4.
746 *See e.g.* Baer (2009), *supra* note 586 at 960; Gnazzo (2011), *supra* note 8 at 540; Traeger, Guidroz, and Jimbo (2014), *supra* note 486 at 25–26.
747 *See e.g.* Baer (2009), *supra* note 586; Gnazzo (2011), *supra* note 8; Jones (2007), *supra* note 495; Traeger, Guidroz, and Jimbo (2014), *supra* note 486; Treviño et al. (2014), *supra* note 486.
748 *See e.g.* Adobor (2006), *supra* note 46; Baer (2009), *supra* note 586; DeMott (2013), *supra* note 4; Fanto (2013), *supra* note 57; Freeman (2007), *supra* note 57; Gnazzo (2011), *supra* note 8; Hoffman and Rowe (2007), *supra* note 522; Joseph (2003), *supra* note 491; Miller (2014), *supra* note 519; Securities Industry Association, Compliance & Legal Division, *supra* note 670; Smith (2003), *supra* note 504; Weber and Wasieleski (2013), *supra* note 492.

scholars on the topic of compliance[749] and the function of the corporate compliance officer[750].

The literature on compliance in the UK explains the term compliance as a concept of obedience, observance, deference, governability, amenability, passiveness, non-resistance and submission.[751] Compliance has existed in some form for a long time.[752] The first act governing compliance issues was put on the statute books in the UK in 1697. This Act expired in 1704. Its purpose was to limit the unfair practices of brokers and stock-jobbers.[753] Today, compliance is far more complex and has developed a more professional nature.[754]

However, other authors identified the first step of the development of compliance in the 19th century. During this time, the industrial revolution significantly changed the English economy. There was also a huge growth in the establishment of companies, and in fraudulent actions. Therefore, preventive measures were developed in the form of legal liability.[755] The Joint Stock Companies Act 1844[756] and the Limited Liability Act 1855[757] were enacted at this time. The main purpose behind these Acts was to regulate the registration of companies and the mandatory accounting and auditing requirements. Regulation

749 *See e.g.* Adams (1994), *supra* note 549; Arcot, Bruno, and Faure-Grimaud (2010), *supra* note 443; Pauline Ashall, *The New Settlement under the Financial Services Act 1986*, 1 Journal of Financial Regulation and Compliance 47–55 (1992); Michael Clarke, *What is Compliance? The Moral Dimension*, 3 Journal of Financial Regulation and Compliance 123–125 (1995); Edwards and Wolfe (2004, 2005, 2006), *supra* note 523; Gary Hagland, *Effective Compliance v Regulatory Gestation*, 2 Journal of Financial Regulation and Compliance 11–21 (1993); McMurray (1997), *supra* note 15; Stephan (2014), *supra* note 545; Taylor (2005), *supra* note 13; Weir and Laing (2000), *supra* note 530.

750 *See e.g.* Rowan Bosworth-Davies, *Practical Training for Compliance Officers: An Assessment*, 1 Journal of Financial Regulation and Compliance 34–46 (1992); M. Cruickshanks, *The Role of the Compliance Officer: The Influence of Culture and Company Constitution*, 1 Journal of Financial Regulation and Compliance 376–384 (1993); Samantha Linsley, *SROs: A Compliance Officer's Perspective*, 1 Journal of Financial Regulation and Compliance 364–369 (1993); Gordon McMurray, *The Practical Compliance Officer: Technicality versus Commerciality*, 3 Journal of Financial Regulation and Compliance 141–146 (1995); Stephan (2014), *supra* note 545; Matthew John Weait, *The Role of the Compliance Officer in Firms Carrying on Investment Business*, June, 2005.

751 *Id.*

752 *See* Adams (1994), *supra* note 549 at 278; Edwards and Wolfe (2005), *supra* note 523 at 48.

753 *See* Adams (1994), *supra* note 549 at 278.

754 *Id.* at 278.

755 *See* L. C. B. Gower, *The English Private Company*, 18 Law and Contemporary Problems 535–545, 536 (1953).

756 Joint Stock Companies Act 1844, 7 & 8 Vict., c.110 (1844).

757 Limited Liability Act 1855, 18 & 19 Vict., c. 133 (1855).

was based on the principle of publicity.[758] The legislation manifested a policy both in terms of the companies and the transactions taking place within that company.[759]

In addition, in the UK, it has also been acknowledged that another origin of compliance was the development of a system of self-regulation within companies. The term self-regulation can be characterized, explained, and identified from various different perspectives. At first, the prefix self should be identified. It is possible to argue that self-regulation may consider a system of voluntary self-control. This system was created by companies in order to control risks.[760] In other words, firms implement their own internal rules and procedures to monitor and adjust themselves for non-compliance.[761] *Clarke* identified a risk in self-regulation, namely *"regulatory capture"*.[762] Secondly, at this level of analysis of self-regulation it is important to note that regulation in this context relates to organizational behavior.[763] Seemingly, there is a lack of emphasis on the fact that self-regulation also has a goal. Therefore, self-regulation could be a preventive and evaluative measure to avoid misbehavior of employees. In conclusion, self-regulation explains forward-looking organizational measures of a corporation designed to avoid illegal activities of its employees. It can be said that self-regulation is a model of rules by which a specific organization regulates itself.[764]

The second stage in the modern development of corporate compliance was the division of function at the beginning of the 20th century. The more complex corporations were divided into the owners and the management. Because of this, legislation was introduced in an attempt to ensure that managing directors are accountable.[765] In addition, there is broad public and political interest in the integrity of market participants to carry out financial business in the UK.[766] This led to the introduction and implementation of regulatory techniques and measures in the financial services industry

758 *See* Gower (1953), *supra* note 755 at 537.
759 *See* Weait (2005), *supra* note 750 at 35.
760 *See* Robyn Fairman & Charlotte Yapp, *Enforced Self-Regulation, Prescription, and Conceptions of Compliance within Small Businesses: The Impact of Enforcement*, 27 Law & Policy 491–519, 491 (2005).
761 *See* Ian Ayres & John Braithwaite, Responsive regulation: transcending the deregulation debate 103 (1995).
762 *See* Clarke (1995), *supra* note 749 at 124.
763 *See* Fairman and Yapp (2005), *supra* note 760 at 494.
764 *See* Weait (2005), *supra* note 750 at 65.
765 *Id.* at 37.
766 *See* Steven Prokesch, *Bankruptcy Explanation By Maxwell*, The New York Times, December 18, 1991, http://www.nytimes.com/1991/12/18/business/the-media-business-bankruptcy-explanation-by-maxwell.html (last visited Sep 10, 2015); Weait (2005), *supra* note 750 at 31.

similar to those in the US.[767] Thus, the UK responded by providing legislation governing corporate governance[768] failures in the 1980s.[769] In 1986, this regulation began with the introduction of the Financial Services Bill in 1986.[770] Subsequently, a number of Acts of Parliament were introduced within the financial services industry *e.g.* the Company Directors Disqualification Act 1986[771], the Insolvency Act 1986[772], the Banking Act 1987[773], the Companies Act 1989,[774] and the Criminal Justice Act 1993.[775] *Hagland* noted that such a network of regulations is unprecedented.[776] He argued that this could result in an enforcement of new criminal and civil liabilities.[777]

Before 1986, compliance was considered somewhat of a "*dirty word*".[778] Since the introduction of the Financial Services Bill,[779] however, compliance has undergone a process of continual evolution in the United Kingdom. Since the enactment of this Act, compliance has been recognized as an essential prerequisite in business dealings.[780] With this new legislation, the financial services firms began to realize that the term compliance had gained a new significance and would have an important impact upon their operations.[781] This marked the beginning of the transformation from a self-regulated system to a system of control and the evolution of this concept within the United Kingdom.[782]

In addition, in 2000, the Financial Services Authority (FSA),[783] was established as a central regulatory body for the financial services sector.[784] The FSA was granted

---

767 *See* Weait (2005), *supra* note 750 at 32.

768 "*The term governance means the structure of control within companies and it refers to the processes by which decisions are made.*" *See* MILLER (2014) *supra* note 595 at 2.

769 *See* Arcot, Bruno, and Faure-Grimaud (2010), *supra* note 443 at 94.

770 FINANCIAL SERVICES ACT 1986 (REPEALED), *supra* note 525. It was an Act to regulate the carrying on investment business.

771 COMPANY DIRECTORS' DISQUALIFICATION ACT 1986, c. 46 (1986).

772 INSOLVENCY ACT 1986, c. 45 (1986).

773 BANKING ACT 1987 (REPEALED), c. 22 (1987).

774 COMPANIES ACT 1989, c. 40 (1989).

775 CRIMINAL JUSTICE ACT 1993, c. 36 (1993); Hagland (1993), *supra* note 749 at 11–12.

776 *See* Hagland (1993), *supra* note 749 at 12.

777 *Id.* at 12.

778 *See* Edwards and Wolfe (2005), *supra* note 519 at 52.

779 FINANCIAL SERVICES ACT 1986 (REPEALED), *supra* note 525.

780 *See* Edwards and Wolfe (2005), *supra* note 519 at 52.

781 *See* Taylor (2005), *supra* note 13 at 54.

782 *See* Edwards and Wolfe (2005), *supra* note 519 at 56.

783 Financial Services Authority (FSA) was the UK supervisor of financial market and the authority to regulate the admission of securities to the official listing at the London Stock Exchange (LSE). It has given statutory powers by the Financial Services and Markets Act 2000 in the United Kingdom between 2000 and 2013. One key task of the FSA was making rules.; *See* 25 The North Colonnade The Financial Services Authority, FSA | WHO ARE WE?, http://www.fsa.gov.uk/about/who (last visited Sep 10, 2015).

784 *See* Taylor (2005), *supra* note 13 at 55.

its statutory powers by the Financial Services and Markets Act 2000 (FSMA).[785] This Act sets forth compliance requirements for misleading statements and practices of a person in the financial services sector.[786] For example, in 2011 the FSA has fined a compliance officer at a hedge fund management company with £14,000 because she failed to act with due skill and care.[787] In addition to this Act, the FSA has a number of functions, such as making rules governing admission of securities to the official listing at the London Stock Exchange (LSE), providing guidance, and determining the policies and principles under the FSMA.[788] *Cruickshanks* argued that the compliance officers derive their authority from the FSA.[789] In 2003, the FSA moved to a principles-based regime[790] and regulated the majority of financial services markets, exchanges, and firms. For example, it framed requirements and could take action against firms that failed to meet the required standards. This marked the definitive end of self-regulation, and the advent of statutory regulations within the financial services sector in the UK.[791]

Furthermore, through the impact of international standards as a response to the financial crisis of 2007–09, the Basel Committee on Banking Supervision[792] established ten principles for the compliance functions in banks.[793] Since 2007, the Basel Capital Accord (Basel II) has required banks to manage all of their risks through effective internal risk management procedures.[794] However, another

---

785 Financial Services and Markets Act (2000), c. 8 ff (2000) Chapter 8, part I. "*The Regulator - The body corporate known as the Financial Services Authority, the Authority, is to have the functions conferred on it by or under this Act.*"
786 *Id.* Chapter 8, part XXVII § 397 (1) (2).
787 FSA, FSA fines and bans hedge fund Compliance officer £14,000 (2011), www.fsa.gov.uk/pages/Library/Communication/PR/2011/099.shtml (last visited Jul 15, 2016).
788 *See* Jonathan Fisher, The law of investor protection 18 (2nd ed. 2003). A Practitioner's Guide to the Financial Services Authority Listing Regime, 2012/2013, 4 (25. ed. 2012).
789 *See* Cruickshanks (1993), *supra* note 750 at 379.
790 Cristie L. Ford, *New Governance, Compliance, and Principles-Based Securities Regulation*, 45 American Business Law Journal 1–60, 1 (2008).
791 *See* Taylor (2005), *supra* note 13 at 55.
792 The Basel Committee is the primary global standard-setter for the prudential regulation of banks and provides a forum for cooperation on banking supervisory matters. Its mandate is to strengthen the regulation, supervision, and practices of banks worldwide with the purpose of enhancing financial stability. *See* (BIS) Bank for International Settlements, About the Basel Committee (2011), http://www.bis.org/bcbs/about.htm?m=3%7C14%7C573 (last visited Sep 10, 2015).
793 *See* Edwards and Wolfe (2004), *supra* note 523 at 217; The Basel Committee on Banking Supervision, Compliance and the compliance function in banks (2005).
794 *See* Edwards and Wolfe (2004), *supra* note 523 at 217.

aspect of this approach suggests that there is a lack of analysis of how the compliance function actually works within banks in practice.[795] Ultimately, by means of an international regulatory framework for banks, the increasing importance and significance of compliance has come to the fore in the financial service industry in the UK.

However, it was not only in the UK financial services sector that the significance of compliance was on the rise. In 1992, the Cadbury Report[796], the UK response to the corporate scandals *e.g.* Maxwell Communications,[797] introduced the "*comply or explain*" approach. This approach is characterized by voluntary compliance with the recommended provisions, and mandatory disclosure.[798] This new approach became the cornerstone of UK corporate governance practice.[799] It explained that

> Corporate governance is the system by which companies are directed and controlled. Boards of directors are responsible for the governance of their companies. The shareholders' role in governance is to appoint the directors and the auditors.[.] The board's actions are subject to laws, regulations and the shareholders in general meeting.[800]

The Report made a number of important recommendations relating to internal monitoring mechanisms in UK public limited companies.[801] Some central components of this voluntary code include a clear division of responsibilities at the top, primarily that the position of chairman of the board should be separated from that of chief executive, and the appointment of a company audit committee comprising at least three non-executive directors.[802] The objective was to improve the quality of monitoring by means of a code of practice. The Cadbury Report (1992) was the first

795 *Id.* at 223.

796 Committee on the Financial Aspects of Corporate, The Cadbury Report (1992).

797 Maxwell Communication Corp. plc. was a leading British media business. It was listed on the London Stock Exchange (FTSE 100). It filed for bankruptcy on December 18, 1991. *See* Prokesch, *supra* note 766.

798 *See* Arcot, Bruno, and Faure-Grimaud (2010), *supra* note 443 at 194.

799 The Cadbury Report (1992), *supra* note 796. The UK and the US corporate governance systems are outsider-dominated systems. In these systems, the role of board of directors is important and these systems will tend to inhibit shareholder engagement. *See also* Andrew Tylecote & Paulina Ramirez, *Corporate governance and innovation: The UK compared with the US and 'insider' economies*, 35 Research Policy 160–180, 165 (2006).

800 The Cadbury Report (1992), *supra* note 796 no. 2.5.

801 The Cadbury Report (1992), *supra* note 796 no. 3.1.The Code of Best Practice is directed to the boards of directors of all listed companies registered in the UK.

802 The Cadbury Report (1992) *Id.* no. 4.35 (a) (b).

version of the Code. Since then, the Report has been modified, for example as the Greenbury Report (1995). In 1998, the two Codes were combined in the Combined Code,[803] which was in force from 1998 to 2004.[804] Today the Code is called the UK Corporate Governance Code and aims to:[805]

> set out standards of good practice in relation to board leadership and effectiveness, remuneration, accountability and relations with shareholders.[806]

A study by *Arcot, Bruno, and Faure-Grimaud* analyzed a database of 245 non-financial services companies during the period 1998 to 2004. They found that the Combined Code fostered compliance in the private sector.[807] Seemingly, companies make a fundamental choice between compliance or non-compliance.[808] Furthermore, a study by *Weir & Laing* found that only some of the governance mechanisms recommended by Cadbury had an effect on accounting performance.[809] Finally, they concluded that the public justification *"comply or explain"* could partially account for the increase in compliance.[810] Additionally, a 2009 report carried out by the Financial Reporting Council (FRC)[811] held that the Code promotes high standards of corporate governance and should contribute to better long-term performance by helping a board to discharge its duties.[812]

Overall, in recent years, UK compliance has developed through the enactment of the Financial Service Act,[813] Financial Services and Markets Act 2000[814], and the release of the Cadbury Report[815] as a response to corporate scandals. In contrast to the mandatory system of the Sarbanes-Oxley Act[816] in the US,

---

803 The UK Corporate Governance Code *supra* note 468. See *Id.*
804 *See* Arcot, Bruno, and Faure-Grimaud (2010), *supra* note 443 at 194–195.
805 *See infra* B., I., p. 396.
806 The UK Corporate Governance Code, *supra* note 468.
807 *See* Arcot, Bruno, and Faure-Grimaud (2010), *supra* note 443 at 194.
808 *Id.* at 193.
809 *See* Weir and Laing (2000), *supra* note 530 at 274, Table III.
810 *Id.* at 279.
811 FRC is an important and independent UK regulator responsible for promoting confidence in corporate reporting and governance. *See* FRC, Financial Reporting Council | FRC, https://www.frc.org.uk/About-the-FRC.aspx (last visited Sep 10, 2015).
812 FRC, 2009 Review of the Combined Code Final Report 6 (2009), https://frc.org.uk/Our-Work/Publications/Corporate-Governance/2009-Review-of-the-Combined-Code-Final-Report.aspx (last visited Sep 10, 2015).
813 Financial Services Act 1986 (Repealed), *supra* note 525.
814 Financial Services and Markets Act (2000), *supra* note 785.
815 The Cadbury Report (1992), *supra* note 796.
816 Sarbanes-Oxley Act of 2002, *supra* note 47.

the UK Corporate Governance Code[817] flexibly allows companies to choose whether to comply with its principles or to explain why they do not.[818] Similar to the US agencies, the FSA[819] supported the legislation in the financial services sector. Summing up, the UK has successfully implemented a new and flexible approach known as "*comply or explain*" and tried to enhance corporate compliance.

I. Definition of Compliance in the United Kingdom

This section will outline the definition of compliance in the UK. At first, the academic interest in the word compliance in the UK began in the early nineties by noting that the French use a Greek term for compliance, "*déontologie.*'[820] This term means moral in character[821] or "*deontological ethics.*" The term also could be seen as an expression of a normative ethical position. Examining the term compliance, *Adams* found the following explanations in the British dictionary:

(1) Acquiescence,
(2) A disposition to yield to others,
(3) A measure of the ability of a mechanical system to respond to an applied vibrating force.[822]

Additionally, *Adams* defined compliance as a middle- or front-office function due to its purpose of regulatory risk management.[823] He concluded that compliance is something carried out *by* a firm, not *for* a firm.[824] Moreover, *Adams* pointed out that by characterizing compliance as the management of regulatory risk, there is a better chance of striking a chord and avoiding risks.[825] *Hagland* interpreted the word compliance as a key concept and the observance of the requirements of the general law.[826] That is why he argued that there is a requirement for a company to establish an internal structure and procedures, specifically focused on compliance.[827] However, he did not actually explain the key concept. In 1996,

817 Cadbury Committee, *supra* note 442.
818 *See* Arcot, Bruno, and Faure-Grimaud (2010), *supra* note 443 at 194.
819 The Financial Services Authority (FSA), *supra* note 783.
820 *See* Adams (1994), *supra* note 549 at 279; Clarke (1995), *supra* note 749 at 123.
821 *See* Adams (1994), *supra* note 549 at 279; Clarke (1995), *supra* note 749 at 123.
822 *See* Adams (1994), *supra* note 549 at 279.
823 *Id.* at 284.
824 *Id.* at 284.
825 *Id.* at 284.
826 *See* Hagland (1993), *supra* note 749 at 12.
827 *Id.* at 12.

Lange simply defined compliance as *"fulfilling legal requirements."*[828] She noted that this understanding refers to an abstract level of understanding compliance.[829] Furthermore, *Clarke* categorized the term compliance having either negative or positive connotations - on the one side defensive and hostile, and on the other cooperative and constructive.[830] In addition, *Clarke* suggested that the risk analysis undertaken by many companies and banks are aimed at gaining acceptance of the practical importance of compliance.[831] He concluded that positive compliance is aimed at best practice.[832]

Secondly, a review of the business literature shows that the most important view sees compliance predominantly as a financial corporate decision or relating to concerns of loss of reputation or status.[833] Alternative views see compliance as the consequence of the acceptance or internalization of rules; as the outcome of the learning process or as a result of organizational management.[834] Finally, in 2012, *Miles* suggested from a philosophical point of view that compliance should be characterized "*...as a scale, rather than a binary choice.*"[835]

Thirdly, *Taylor* found that in the UK the term compliance first appeared in the Financial Service Act in 1986.[836] Until this time, the senior management identified executives who should review this legislation. However, it was only later that these executives were referred to as compliance officers.[837] In conclusion, *Taylor* argued that UK compliance refers to financial services legislation and regulation, but there is no official legal definition in the UK.[838] In spite of this legal vacuum, he concluded that in the UK compliance has gradually evolved as a concept over the last years.[839]

---

828 *See* Bettina Lange, *Empirical compliance: A study of waste management regulation in the UK and German*, December, 1996.

829 *Id.* at 1.

830 *See* Clarke (1995), *supra* note 749 at 124.

831 *Id.* at 123.

832 *Id.* at 124.

833 Fairman and Yapp (2005), *supra* note 760 at 494.

834 Ton van Snellenberg & Rob van de Peppel, *Perspectives on compliance: non-compliance with environmental licences in the Netherlands*, 12 European Environment 131–148, 133 (2002).

835 Roger Miles, *From compliance to coping: Experiences of Chief Risk Officers in UK banks 2007–2009*, July 4, 2012.

836 Taylor (2005), *supra* note 13 at 54. Financial Services Act 1986 (Repealed), *supra* note 525 Ch. 3, 12 compliance orders.

837 Taylor (2005), *supra* note 13 at 54.

838 *Id.* at 57.

839 *Id.* at 58.

Furthermore, the English legal scholars have adopted the American terminology of compliance. According to the American definition, the English literature also describes the term compliance as *"...the adherence by the regulated to rules and regulations laid down by those in authority..."*[840] However, in a broader sense, the English scholars supplemented the argument that compliance also links to other aspects of duties. Compliance links both to business and the consumer and was first established in the financial services sector. For example, investment businesses (*e.g.* banks, insurance companies, building societies and others) are required to comply with the conduct and business requirements set out by the FSA.[841] Hence, the term also includes concepts of *e.g.* obedience, observance, deference, governability... etc.[842]

As has been noted, the financial services sector has been significantly influenced by the enforcement of regulation and, as a result, the emergence of compliance in the UK. Simultaneously, recent studies[843] shed new light on an increasing trend in compliance relating to the Combined Code of Corporate Governance, also referred to simply as the Code.[844] As discussed previously,[845] these studies found that the Code fostered compliance by implementing internal monitoring mechanisms in listed firms.[846] For example, in 2004, more than half of the FTSE 350[847] companies were fully compliant with all provisions of the Code.[848] In addition, *Weir & Laing* examined the relationship between governance structures and performance in 1992 and in 1995.[849] Their conclusion was that the number of firms adopting

840 *See e.g.* Edwards and Wolfe (2005), *supra* note 523 at 48; Edwards and Wolfe (2006), *supra* note 523 at 141.

841 *See* Edwards and Wolfe (2006), *supra* note 523 at 141. *See* FSA The Financial Services Authority, *supra* note 783. The FSA is renamed the Financial Conduct Authority (FCA). *See* FCA, HANDBOOK | FINANCIAL CONDUCT AUTHORITY (FCA), http://www.fca.org.uk/handbook (last visited Sep 10, 2015).

842 *See* Edwards and Wolfe (2006), *supra* note 523 at 141.

843 *See e.g.* Arcot, Bruno, and Faure-Grimaud (2010), *supra* note 443; Weir and Laing (2000), *supra* note 530.

844 THE CADBURY REPORT (1992), *supra* note 796; The UK Corporate Governance, *supra* note 465.

845 *See supra* p. 152.

846 *See* Weir and Laing (2000), *supra* note 530 at 265.

847 FTSE is a London Stock Exchange Index of the largest 350 companies by capitalization. *See* London Stock Exchange, FTSE 350 CONSTITUENTS SHARES PRICES - LONDON STOCK EXCHANGE, http://www.londonstockexchange.com/exchange/prices-and-markets/stocks/indices/summary/summary-indices-constituents.html?index=NMX (last visited Sep 10, 2015).

848 *See* Arcot, Bruno, and Faure-Grimaud (2010), *supra* note 443 at 193.

849 They used a sample of 200 firms. Company names were taken from the Times 1000 for 1992 and 1995. The Times 1000 lists are the firms with the largest sales in the UK. For each year, 200 nonfinancial, fully quoted UK companies were randomly selected. *See* Weir and Laing (2000), *supra* note 530 at 269.

the governance structures recommended by Cadbury has increased.[850] The authors saw the reason in the public justification of explaining companies' governance policies.[851]

Furthermore, the evidence highlights that the composition of the board with non-executive directors is seemingly associated with better performance.[852] However, an American meta-analytic review of board composition[853] found that there is no consistent link between the board structures and the company's financial performance because outside directors lacked the requisite information and did not appear to fully understand the business.[854] In sum, it can be noted that the adopted governance structure could lead to improved compliance with the law, but there does not appear to be any reliable evidence of higher financial performance of a company as a result. The reason for this might be the high costs of implementation and maintenance of this structure.

Fourthly, compliance in the English private sector developed in response to corporate scandals without prescriptive and legislative regulation – a different approach to that implemented in the Sarbanes-Oxley Act in the US.[855] The United Kingdom's Bribery Act was passed in 2010.[856] *Richard* compared the US Foreign Corrupt Practices Act (FCPA)[857] structure and key provisions with the United Kingdom Bribery Act.[858] In his view, the UKBA anti-bribery provisions are more extensive than the FCPA provisions in the US. For instance, this Act holds corporations strictly liable for preventing persons from committing bribery.[859] The Act establishes potential criminal liability for corporations, their officers, employees, and shareholders. Thus, since 2010, strict bribery legislation has also been enacted in the private sector in the UK. Therefore, English and foreign companies that are active in the UK must ensure conformity with the law by means of internal control systems or compliance structures to prevent potential violations of the law. In addition, the UKBA 2010 Guidance provides recommendations for companies on forms of external verification of the effectiveness of anti-bribery

---

850 *Id.* at 265.

851 *Id.* at 279.

852 So-called outside directors, *See Id.* at 279.

853 *See* Dan R. Dalton et al., *Meta-analytic reviews of board composition, leadership structure, and financial performance*, 19 Strategic Management Journal 269–290, 269 (1998). This meta-analysis provided 54 relevant empirical studies of board composition and financial performance.

854 *See* Weir and Laing (2000), *supra* note 530 at 267.

855 *See* Arcot, Bruno, and Faure-Grimaud (2010), *supra* note 443 at 194.

856 United Kingdom Bribery Act 2010, *supra* note 433. *See* Richard (2014), *supra* note 554 at 437.

857 Foreign Corrupt Practices Act 1977 (FCPA), *supra* note 438.

858 *See* Richard (2014), *supra* note 554.

859 *Id.* at 439.

procedures in instances where an offence could be prosecuted.[860] For this reason, *Ernst & Young* recommend that companies should undertake a proper risk assessment and build an effective anti-corruption compliance program.[861]

In conclusion, it has been highlighted that the first steps in corporate compliance were the development of a model of corporate self-regulation and the introduction of the *"comply or explain"* approach with the Code. To summarize, the legal development of compliance began with the enactment of the Financial Service Act in 1986 and a number of other financial regulations, with the establishment of regulators, then with the creation of the UK Corporate Governance Code and reached its highpoint with the UKBA in 2010. Therefore, the UK legislator enhanced corporate compliance by introducing a formal statute to combat foreign bribery. Between 1985 and today, a number of items of far-reaching legislation have been passed in the UK, creating a legal framework for the development of compliance. One reason for this strong legislation might be the English importation of American corporate compliance by strengthening corporate criminal laws in recent years.[862]

Based on the above, answering the question of how English corporate compliance is defined continues to pose a challenge. Other than the two studies[863] evaluating the impact of the Code on corporate compliance, there is very little research on the topic of compliance. As mentioned previously, there is no legal definition of the term compliance in the UK and the general definition of UK compliance is more abstract than the American description. Similar to US compliance, UK compliance has evolved through self-regulation within companies. Nevertheless, today, the majority of English legal scholars view compliance as a compulsory exercise or scale necessary to fulfil legal requirements.

II. The Historical Evolution of the Compliance Function in the UK

As explained previously, over the last thirty years UK compliance has evolved through legislation within the financial services sector and subsequently also in the private sector. As we have seen, in the UK the compliance function originated from the Financial Services Act.[864] However, some concerns concerning compliance have remained. Despite the introduction of the Financial Service Act 1986, there

---

860 Ministry of Justice, THE BRIBERY ACT 2010 - GUIDANCE 31, https://www.justice.gov.uk/downloads/legislation/bribery-act-2010-guidance.pdf (last visited Sep 11, 2015) [hereinafter THE BRIBERY GUIDANCE].

861 ERNST & YOUNG, THE UK BRIBERY ACT: DEVELOPING AN ANTI-CORRUPTION COMPLIANCE FRAMEWORK 16 3 (2011).

862 *See* Djilani (2011), *supra* note 62 at 303.

863 *See* Arcot, Bruno, and Faure-Grimaud (2010), *supra* note 443; Weir and Laing (2000), *supra* note 530.

864 FINANCIAL SERVICES ACT 1986 (REPEALED), *supra* note 525; Taylor (2005), *supra* note 13 at 54. *See supra* p. 106.

are still many different perceptions of the compliance officer's role.[865] For instance, initially, the description of the job profile was not clear - neither to the public nor to the compliance officers themselves.[866] However, *Cruickshanks* identified that the role and authority of compliance officer derives from the legislation.[867] For example, the self-regulatory organizations (SROs) such as the LAUTRO[868] required that its members *"shall appoint one of its officers"*[869] to be a compliance officer with general responsibility for overseeing the member's compliance procedures. Initially, these executives were not called compliance officers.[870] Generally, members of the board who were close to retirement age were selected to perform this new compliance function.[871] There was little knowledge or staff expertise. In the UK, the first wave of compliance officers had to understand the new legislation, the new regulations of the self-regulatory organizations (SROs) and to obtain authorization for their firms.[872] However, *Taylor* pointed out that in recent years the compliance function has changed radically, with widening responsibilities set forth in new legislation. For example, in 2007, the EU Markets in Financial Instruments Directive (MiFID) required that the compliance function be independent from internal audit and risk management functions.[873] Based on this, *Taylor* concluded that the compliance function should be more adaptable in the future.[874]

Another milestone in the development of the compliance function in the financial services sector in the UK was further supported by a consultative document by the Basel Committee on Banking Supervision.[875] In April 2005, it published ten principles for the compliance function in banks.[876] The paper defined this function as:

865 *See* Cruickshanks (1993), *supra* note 750 at 376.
866 *Id.* at 376.
867 *Id.* at 377.
868 *See e.g.* Life Assurance and Unit Trust Regulatory Organization (LAUTRO) *See* John Black, Life Assurance and Unit Trust Regulatory Organization | LAUTRO A Dictionary of Economics (3. ed. 2009), http://www.oxfordreference.com/view/10.1093/acref/9780199237043.001.0001/acref-9780199237043-e-1804 (last visited Sep 10, 2015). "*A UK self-regulating organization responsible for regulating organizations offering life assurance and unit trusts as principals.*" *See infra* note 920, p. 148.
869 *Id.* Rule Book, Rule 2.12(3). In: Cruickshanks (1993), *supra* note 750 at 377.
870 *See* Taylor (2005), *supra* note 13 at 55.
871 *Id.* at 55.
872 *Id.* at 55.
873 Commission Directive 2006/73/EC, ABI. 2006 L 241/26 (2006) Article 6 2., which implemented Directive 2004/39/EC of the European Parliament and of the Council on markets in financial instruments amending Council Directives 85/611/EEC and 93/6/EEC and Directive 2000/12/EC (MIFID 2004), *supra* note 432.
874 *See* Taylor (2005), *supra* note 13 at 58.
875 Bank for International Settlements, *supra* note 792.
876 The Basel Committee on Banking Supervision, *supra* note 793.

> An independent function that identifies, assesses, advises on, monitors, and reports on the bank's compliance risk, [...] to comply with all applicable laws, regulations, and codes of conduct and standards of good practice.[877]

The paper highlighted two principles of the compliance function: First, the role and responsibilities should be clearly identified, and secondly, the function should be independent from the business activities of the bank.[878] Therefore, *Edwards & Wolfe* concluded that this consultation paper provides a high-level approach to business in banks and can enhance a compliant competent culture within an organization.[879] At the same time, they criticized the fact that the complex compliance issues need to taken into consideration in day-to-day business.[880]

By contrast with the apparently mandatory nature of the compliance officer's function within the financial services sector, the emergence of the compliance function in the English private sector has no legal origins. One aspect of the evolution of this function identified by *Cruickshanks* is commercial and competitive pressure on a company.[881] The next aspect that can be identified is the increasing influence of the investors. The author demonstrated this aspect, citing the increase in investor's complaints,[882] for instance, the bankruptcy of Maxwell fueled skepticism regarding the self-regulatory system.[883] Hence, at the same time investors have made greater use of complaints.[884] In sum, he argued that the standards of service are likely to have a significant influence on the commercial success of companies in the future. The complaints should initially be addressed directly to the compliance officer. As a result, contributions by compliance officers are likely to be afforded greater importance.[885] However, there are still many challenges facing this function. For example, *Cruickshanks* noted that there are various different perceptions of the compliance officer's role.[886] He concluded that due to the lack of concrete specification of this role, it is difficult to clearly define and describe precisely what it entails.[887]

In addition to these considerations, *Miles* pointed out that if self-regulation were purely voluntary, internal compliance officers could be *"more capable [but] not*

---

877 *Id.* at 3. para. 10.
878 *Id.* at 9–10.; Edwards and Wolfe (2004), *supra* note 523.
879 *See* Edwards and Wolfe (2004), *supra* note 523 at 223.
880 *Id.* at 223.
881 *See* Cruickshanks (1993), *supra* note 750 at 377.
882 *Id.* at 378.
883 *See* Prokesch, *supra* note 766. *"Robert Maxwell diverted millions of pounds of the firm employees' pension funds for his own purpose." See also* In: Annie Mills & Peter Haines, Essential strategies for financial services compliance (2nd ed. 2015).
884 *See* Cruickshanks (1993), *supra* note 750 at 378.
885 *Id.* at 379.
886 *Id.* at 376.
887 *Id.* at 376–377.

necessarily more willing to regulate effectively" than the regulator's own agents.[888] For example, in the absence of any formal authority like in the financial services sector, companies have to establish some form of internal control. The role has evolved through the legitimate self-interest of the private sector and the market seems to have chosen compliance as a standard.[889]

Furthermore, the emergence of corporate compliance and the compliance function in the UK was also influenced by the UK takeover regime.[890] The Takeover Code regulates takeovers and mergers[891] and while it does not have statutory force, the Companies Act of 2006 affords it considerable clout.[892] The purpose of the company law reform was to codify the principles underpinning directors' duties under common law.[893] In addition, under Section 9A of the Company Directors Disqualification Act 1986,[894] the Office of Fair Trading (OFT)[895] and the regulators have the power to apply to the court for an order disqualifying a director from being involved in the management of a company, if there has been a breach of UK or EU competition law by the company.[896] In addition, the OFT Guidance 1341[897] encouraged all companies to comply with competition law using a risk-based, four- step process for achieving a compliance culture.[898] This process includes step one: risk identification, step two: risk assessment, step three: risk mitigation; and step four: review.[899] Moreover, the guidance recommended that the company should reinforce a compliance culture by appointing *"compliance champions"* within business units.[900]

---

888 *See* Miles (2012), *supra* note 835 at 63.

889 *See* Arcot, Bruno, and Faure-Grimaud (2010), *supra* note 443 at 200.

890 The Panel on Takeovers and Mergers (the "Panel") is an independent body, established in 1968, whose main functions are to issue and administer the City Code on Takeovers and Mergers (the "Code") and to supervise and regulate takeovers and other matters to which the Code applies. Its central objective is to ensure fair treatment for all shareholders in takeover bids. *See* The Takeover Panel, The Panel on Takeovers and Mergers (the "Panel"), http://www.thetakeoverpanel.org.uk/ (last visited Sep 12, 2015).

891 *See* Mills and Haines (2015), *supra* note 883 at 13.

892 Companies Act 2006, *supra* note 532. This Act is the primary source of UK company law and codifies certain existing common law principles, such as those relating to general duties of directors (Ch. 2) and to the disqualification of directors'.

893 *Id.* Ch. 2.

894 Company Directors' Disqualification Act 1986, *supra* note 771 § 9A.

895 OFT, Company directors and competition law - Directors' guidance (2011), https://www.gov.uk/government/uploads/system/uploads/attachment_data/file/284410/oft1340.pdf (last visited Sep 12, 2015) [hereinafter Directors' guidance].

896 *See* Banks and Banks (2011), *supra* note 623 at 24.

897 Directors' guidance, *supra* note 895.

898 *Id.* at 4.

899 *Id.* at 9.

900 *Id.* at 13.

However, as mentioned previously,[901] before the enactment of the UK Bribery Act 2010,[902] the English law system consisted of a collection of legislation and voluntary codes.[903] Fortunately, the UKBA includes a defense from criminal liability for corporations.[904] A commercial organization is not liable for failing to prevent bribery if it *"had in place adequate procedures designed to prevent persons associated with [the corporation] from undertaking such conduct."*[905] Furthermore, the UKBA pointed out that

> The Secretary of State must publish guidance about procedures that relevant commercial organizations can put in place to prevent persons associated with them from bribing.[906]

Nevertheless, this guidance gives no recommendations concerning the implementation of the compliance function.[907]

In conclusion, the new UK legislation and the growing responsibilities of the corporate management have combined the practice of business with legal requirements and have strongly supported the transformation of the compliance manager into a self-regulatory function within UK companies.[908] The purpose behind the UK compliance function is to be involved in the interests of developing the most conducive compliance culture within companies.[909] Similar to the US, the UK compliance function originated from the financial services legislation. In contrast to the US, however, it has been recognized that the UK compliance officer is a relatively new phenomenon.

III. Definition of the Compliance Function in the United Kingdom

Linked to the findings above, an examination of the historical evolution of the compliance officer in the UK shows that the UK compliance function is still a young position and there is no generally accepted or legal definition of the corporate compliance officer.[910] This section will now explore the characteristics and features of the position within companies in the UK. *Edwards & Wolfe* already identified the

---

901 *See supra* B., II., p. 143.
902 United Kingdom Bribery Act 2010, *supra* note 433.
903 *See* Richard (2014), *supra* note 554 at 438.
904 *Id.* at 439.
905 United Kingdom Bribery Act 2010, *supra* note 433 § 7(2).
906 *Id.*§ 9 (1). *See* The Bribery Guidance, *supra* note 860.
907 The Bribery Guidance, *supra* note 860.
908 *See* Christine Parker, The open corporation: effective self-regulation and democracy 168 (1. ed. 2002).
909 *See e.g.* Bosworth-Davies (1992), *supra* note 750; Cruickshanks (1993), *supra* note 750; Edwards and Wolfe (2004), *supra* note 523; McMurray (1995), *supra* note 750.
910 *See* Mills and Haines (2015), *supra* note 883 at 15.

objectives, targets and techniques of the compliance function within banks.[911] The objectives and techniques of the corporate compliance function can be examined analogous to those findings. *Edwards & Wolfe* found that there are some difficulties in terms of defining this function. At first, internally, within a company the objectives of the compliance function might be determined by its compliance policy.[912] In the UK, regulators[913] additionally have defined responsibility for businesses.[914] Often, the senior management delegates daily responsibility for compliance to the compliance department.[915] Secondly, the size of companies, their scope of business and their corporate objectives differ and the scope of responsibilies of the compliance officer varies accordingly.[916] However, they agree with the key principle put forward by the Committee,[917] which was that the compliance function should be independent from business activities of the company units.[918] In other words, compliance staff should not be directly involved in the activities they are required to monitor.

In addition, *Hagland* argued that the compliance officer should have the power, status, authority, and personality to challenge anyone about any action within the company to effectively control and monitor the firm.[919] In the UK, one important aspect of the compliance function is the contact to the self-regulatory organizations (SROs)[920] in order to obtain pertinent informal guidance.[921] The compliance officer should be familiar with the rulebooks and guidance of the SROs.[922] *Ward* suggests a balancing role of compliance between the objectives,

---

911 Edwards and Wolfe (2004), *supra* note 519 at 218 Table 1.

912 *Id.* at 218.

913 *See supra* note 783, p. 135 *e.g.* the FSA later the FCA.

914 FCA, The principles - Financial Conduct Authority, The FCA principles of good regulations. http://www.fca.org.uk/about/operate/principles (last visited Sep 12, 2015).

915 *See* Mills and Haines (2015), *supra* note 883. *See e.g.* FCA, *supra* note 907. "*A firm's senior management is responsible for the firm's activities and for ensuring that its business complies with regulatory requirements.*"

916 *See* Edwards and Wolfe (2004), *supra* note 523 at 218.

917 The Basel Committee on Banking Supervision, *supra* note 793.

918 *See* Edwards and Wolfe (2004), *supra* note 523 at 218. *See also* Hagland (1993), *supra* note 749 at 13.

919 *See* Hagland (1993), *supra* note 749 at 12–13.

920 "*A non-governmental organization that has the power to create and enforce industry regulations and standards. The priority is to protect investors through the establishment of rules that promote ethics and equality.*" *See* Self-Regulatory Organization (SRO) Definition, Investopedia (2004), http://www.investopedia.com/terms/s/sro.asp (last visited Sep 22, 2015).

921 *See* Hagland (1993), *supra* note 749 at 13.

922 *See e.g.* The Bribery Guidance, *supra* note 860; Directors' guidance, *supra* note 895.

purposes, and needs of the regulators on the one side, and of the board of directors on the other.[923] Lastly, the compliance officer has to establish a regulatory infrastructure within the firm.[924]

Another key aspect is the handling of his actions following the establishment of wrongdoing by employees within the company.[925] The compliance officer's conduct will have a major impact upon the nature, quality, and credibility of his evidence if called upon to testify at a tribunal.[926] Hence, *Hagland* concluded that taking compliance issues seriously requires that the compliance officers have the necessary skills and adopts the power and authority to apply the complex tasks and duties inherent to their function.[927] To further strengthen this function, the compliance officer should deal with the establishment of a compliance culture within the firm.[928] Generally, the compliance culture could arise through announcement imposed top-down and training of employees and compliance staff.[929] *Mills & Haines* drew up a list summarizing the key responsibilities of the compliance officer.[930] They pointed out that regardless of which firm the compliance officer works for, his activities encompass an understanding of that company.[931] The compliance officer should identify and determine best practice standards applicable with respect to compliance with law, regulations, and the corporate goals in order to document and keep records of the compliance steps; he must monitor and measure compliance risks and should advise the employees and the management accordingly.[932] Based on these multiple tasks, *Taylor* identified the compliance function as a "*multifunctional*" role.[933]

Finally, the UK definition of the corporate compliance officer can be summarized with a flexible description by *Mills & Haines*, which could apply for each company in the UK:

> Compliance officers are there to help stop things going wrong from a regulatory perspective, and to help to deal with them if they do.[934]

---

923 *See* Ward (2015), *supra* note 543 at 60.
924 *See* Mills and Haines (2015), *supra* note 883 at 21.
925 *See* Hagland (1993), *supra* note 749 at 18.
926 *Id.* at 18.
927 *Id.* at 18.
928 *See* McMurray (1995), *supra* note 750 at 142.
929 *Id.* at 143.
930 *See* Mills and Haines (2015), *supra* note 883 at 23.
931 *Id.* at 23.
932 *Id.* at 23.
933 *See* Taylor (2005), *supra* note 13 at 223.
934 *See* Mills and Haines (2015), *supra* note 883 at 19.

C. Legal Roots and Cultural Background of Compliance in Germany

The two previous parts explored the emergence and definition of compliance and the compliance function in the US and UK respectively. This part will introduce the German legal roots of compliance and examine whether there is a definition of compliance and the compliance function in Germany.

A review of the German literature shows that there is little explanation on the cultural background and legal origins of compliance in Germany. Apparently, the emergence of compliance is attributable predominantly to external factors. One reason for this could be that the term compliance is relatively new outside the financial services sector and has been subject of extended debate and discussion for only around ten years.[935] The German academic debate has recognized that the term compliance is derived from the Anglo-American terminology.[936] For more than a century, the management boards of American companies have been dealing with the issues of to prevent and detect corporate crime and misconduct.[937] Hence, even before legislation was introduced to regulate compliance issues, American companies had implemented voluntary codes of conduct, policies, and a corporate compliance culture. This self-regulated system developed mainly in the US and in the UK.[938] Compared to companies in continental Europe, the American firms have by preference tended towards formal rules controlling employees in line with Taylor's principles.[939] In contrast, Taylor's theory of management[940] was never as popular in German companies as in America.[941] Therefore, ethical

---

935 *See* Eberhard Vetter, *Compliance im Unternehmen*, *in* Compliance in der Unternehmerpraxis: Grundlagen, Organisation und Umsetzung 1–18, 1 (G. Wecker & B. Ohl eds., 3. ed. 2013).

936 *See e.g.* Eufinger (2012), *supra* note 586 at 1; Hauschka (2004), *supra* note 58 at 257; Thomas Rotsch, *Compliance*, *in* Handbuch Wirtschaftsstrafrecht 45–78, 50 (Hans Achenbach, Andreas Ransiek, & Katharina Beckemper eds., 3. ed. 2012); Vetter (2013), *supra* note 935 at 1.

937 *See supra* A., I., p. 121.

938 *See supra* A., I., p. 121, II., p. 143.

939 *See* Palazzo (2002), *supra* note 588 at 204.

940 *See* Taylorism is a system of scientific management advocated by Fred W. Taylor. In Taylor's view, the task of factory management was to determine the best way for the worker to do the job, to provide the proper tools and training, and to provide incentives for good performance. He broke each job down into its individual motions, analyzed these to determine which were essential, and timed the workers with a stopwatch. With unnecessary motion eliminated, the worker, following a machinelike routine, became far more productive. *See* Taylorism | scientific management system, Encyclopedia Britannica (2015), http://www.britannica.com/topic/Taylorism (last visited Sep 24, 2015).

941 *See* Palazzo (2002), *supra* note 588 at 205.

behavior and rules are usually introduced informally in German companies.[942] As a result, *Palazzo* argued that Americans think and work towards achieving unity between ethics and profit. Ethics and compliance issues are connected to formal codes, and are equated to good business practice.[943] By contrast, European companies are more community-oriented. *Palazzo* argued that European companies prefer more moral orientations in the field of relationships than US firms. Moral principles and behavior depend more on the concrete situation, and less on absolute and universalistic norms.[944] Thus, *Palazzo* concluded that German companies rely more on informal mechanisms of social control.[945]

As previously discussed, the legal origins of American corporate compliance can be traced back to American antitrust compliance at the beginning of the 1960s.[946] In contrast to the development of compliance in the US, the initial starting point for the German compliance debate centered around the keyword "*corporate governance*"[947] in the 1990s.[948] In Germany, the first legal objective of compliance related to the financial services sector within securities services companies.[949] At first, there were voluntary guidelines to support self-regulation within securities services companies.[950] In 1994, the transposition of the European Investment Services Directive enshrined the term compliance in German law.[951] However, *Eufinger* concluded that the transfer of compliance within various areas is fluent.[952] He argued

942 *Id.* at 205.

943 *Id.* at 210.

944 *Id.* at 204.

945 *Id.* at 204.

946 *See e.g.* Eufinger (2012), *supra* note 586 at 22; Rotsch (2012), *supra* note 936 at 50 margin note 10.

947 In Germany, corporate governance means corporate constitution and explains the regulatory framework for the management and supervision of German listed companies. *See* The German Corporate Governance Code (DCGK), (2015) Foreword. The German corporate governance system is seen as an *"insider-dominated"* system in which the stakeholders are included and more engaged in governing the company. [hereinafter THE GERMAN CODE 2015]; *See* Tylecote and Ramirez (2006), *supra* note 799 at 163.

948 *See e.g.* Jürgen Bürkle, *§ 1 Einleitung*, in Der Compliance Officer: ein Handbuch in eigener Sache 1–13, 3 (Jürgen Bürkle & Christoph E. Hauschka eds., 1. ed. 2015) margin note 6; Christoph E. Hauschka, *Corporate Governance und Compliance, in* Corporate Compliance: Handbuch der Haftungsvermeidung im Unternehmen § 1, (Christoph E. Hauschka & Christoph Besch eds., 2. ed. 2010) margin note 1; Rotsch (2012), *supra* note 936 at 50 margin note 10.

949 *See* Rotsch (2012), *supra* note 936 at 53 margin note 17.

950 *Id.* at 53 margin note 17.

951 *Id.* at 53 margin note 17; Directive on Investment Services 93/22/EEC, OJ 141 of 11.6.1993 (1993); Wertpapierhandelsgesetz (WpHG) | Securities Trading Act, WpHG BGBI. I, p. 1749 (1994) § 33.

952 *See* Eufinger (2012), *supra* note 586 at 23.

that the compliance organizational structures of the securities services organizations are also applicable to various other areas.[953] Based on the above, it has been suggested that compliance will pervade other sectors as well.[954] Meanwhile, the evidence suggests that compliance influences not only the banks and investment services companies within the financial services sector, but also companies in the private sector.[955] Nevertheless, not all of the research shows that this transfer runs smoothly and without adjustments.[956]

In Germany, corporate scandals also focused attention on corporate compliance. In 2008, a German company listed in the US, Siemens AG and several of its subsidiaries were accused of bribery. Siemens AG and its subsidiaries were involved in offering bribes totaling more than $1.4 billion to foreign officials in various countries all over the world.[957] Siemens ultimately agreed to pay $800 million in fines and penalties.[958] Since then, Siemens has undergone a fundamental compliance transformation and the term compliance entered the public arena in Germany.[959] The enforcement of compliance through the globalization of economic transactions, growing economic pressure, and increasingly complex international legal norms and regulations also led to the need for the implementation of appropriate values and patterns of behavior within German companies.[960] In contrast, *Parker* argued that German companies are still reluctant to address normative questions publicly.[961]

Following the decision of the Federal Supreme Court (BGH) in criminal matters of July 17, 2009 a comprehensive and far-reaching academic and practical debate has begun to develop around the issues of corporate compliance and the compliance officer function.[962] The head of the internal audit and legal department at a

953 *Id.* at 23.

954 *See* Rotsch (2012), *supra* note 936 at 54 margin note 17.

955 *See* Bürkle (2015), *supra* note 948 at 4 margin note 8.

956 *See* Hauschka (2014), *supra* note 4; Sünner (2014), *supra* note 44.

957 PRESS RELEASE DOJ, SIEMENS AG AND THREE SUBSIDIARIES PLEAD GUILTY TO FOREIGN CORRUPT PRACTICES ACT VIOLATIONS AND AGREE TO PAY $450 MILLION IN COMBINED CRIMINAL FINES (2008), http://www.justice.gov/archive/opa/pr/2008/December/08-crm-1105.html (last visited Sep 12, 2015).

958 *See* Mike Koehler, *Revisiting a Foreign Corrupt Practices Act Compliance Defense*, WISCONSIN LAW REVIEW 609–659, 612 (2012); B. SIEBLER, CRIMINAL-COMPLIANCE IM INTERDISZIPLINÄREN KONTEXT: DIE LEGITIMIERUNG VON COMPLIANCE-TÄTIGKEITEN UND MASSNAHMEN SOWIE DEREN VERWERTBARKEIT IM DEUTSCHEN STRAFVERFAHREN 3 (1. ed. 2014); *See also* BGH, 29. 8.2008 - 2 StR 587/07 - Siemens Case, Bildung verdeckter Kassen als Untreue (Ger), 2009 NStZ 95–100 (2008).

959 *See* Koehler (2012), *supra* note 958 at 613.

960 *See* PARKER (2002), *supra* note 908 at 195.

961 *Id.* at 195.

962 BGH, 17.7.2009 - 5 StR 394/08, BGHST 54, 44; BGH NJW 2009, 3173, *supra* note 25 - Responsibility under criminal law on account of professional position.

public cleaning service company was found guilty of failure to take appropriate measures on evidence of customer overcharging.[963] However, he was not a compliance officer. Nevertheless, this decision by the German Federal Court could establish compliance officers' criminal liability for violation of their duties, and creating a challenge for compliance measures within companies.[964] The Court classified the compliance officer as a guarantor pursuant to criminal law.[965] The court decided that the head of the internal audit and legal department was responsible under law to ensure that a specific outcome does not occur.[966] He thus bears a special responsibility.[967] As a result, the Court leans in favor of the transfer of criminal prevention within the companies.[968] Over the past five years, legal scholars have criticized this attempted shift.[969] However, in the German academic legal literature, this decision had a broad impact[970] on the advisory and supervisory tasks of the compliance function within companies.[971] An EBEF paper surmised that although such legal cases are rare, they suggest a trend relating to compliance and the compliance function, and demonstrate a need for clarity in terms of the scope and limitation of the responsibilities and liabilities of this function.[972]

Moreover, in 2013, the Munich I Regional Court decided another compliance case.[973] In that case, the court initially decided in a civil judgment on the compliance

---

963 *See* Dando et al. (2013), *supra* note 4 at 6.

964 Ralf-Friedrich Fahrenbach et al., The Compliance Officer's Function within a Company Mayer Brown (2009), http://www.mondaq.com/x/91716/ (last visited Sep 22, 2015).

965 Strafgesetzbuch (StGB) | German Criminal Code, BGBI. I, 3322 (1998) § 13 (1). *See also infra* p. 449.

966 BGH, 17.7.2009 - 5 StR 394/08, BGHSt 54, 44; BGH NJW 2009, 3173, *supra* note 25 note 31.

967 *Id.* note 23.

968 *See e.g.* Bürkle (2015), *supra* note 948 at 5 margin note 11; Bürkle (2010), *supra* note 28 at 4; Meier (2011), *supra* note 30 at 779.

969 *See e.g.* contra Campos Nave (2009), *supra* note 457 at 2548; Wolf (2011), *supra* note 41 at 1358; pro Dann and Mengel (2010), *supra* note 30 at 3267.

970 *See e.g.* Bürkle (2010), *supra* note 28; Campos Nave (2009), *supra* note 457; Dann and Mengel (2010), *supra* note 30; Fecker and Kinzl (2010), *supra* note 455; Giesen (2009), *supra* note 459; Hauschka, Galster, and Marschlich (2014), *supra* note 463; Hauschka (2004), *supra* note 58; Heuking (2014), *supra* note 4; Illing and Umnuß (2009), *supra* note 461; Kirsch (2011), *supra* note 41; Klebeck and Zollinger (2013), *supra* note 464; Krieger and Günther (2010), *supra* note 30; Lackhoff and Schulz (2010), *supra* note 458; Meier-Greve (2010), *supra* note 461; Raus and Lützeler (2012), *supra* note 460; Rieble (2010), *supra* note 458; Wolf (2011), *supra* note 41; Wybitul (2009), *supra* note 28; Zimmermann (2011), *supra* note 28.

971 *See* Bürkle (2010), *supra* note 28 at 8.

972 *See* Dando et al. (2013), *supra* note 4 at 7.

973 LG München I, 10.12.2013 - 5 HK O 1387/10 - Pflichten des Vorstands einer AG, 2014 NZG 345–349 (2013); Handelsblatt, *Heinz-Joachim Neubürger: Ex-Siemens-Finanzchef*

duties of the management board.[974] *Bürkle* argued that this decision will have a considerable impact on day-to-day compliance. It can be recognized as a landmark decision in terms of internal liability of the management board in instances of non-compliance.[975] The court argued that the management board is responsible for monitoring and supervising in order that no legal violations can arise from the employees.[976] In its decision, the court explained that compliance issues were not new.[977] In addition, *Bürkle* pointed out that the court had to failed to take account of the organizational approach of compliance.[978] He concluded that the responsibility includes the application of this approach in daily practice.[979] The risk of such judgment[980] is that hysterical compliance activities will begin.[981]

Evidently, like many other trends, compliance issues were introduced from the US to Europe and Germany.[982] It has been recognized that the concept of compliance was historically transferred from the US to Germany as a result of the legal handling of the outcomes of corporate scandals.[983] As previously discussed, in accordance with the strict legislation in force there, American companies have developed a very specific way of dealing with the norms and have introduced so-called compliance programs as a self-regulatory system.[984] In spite of the different cultural backgrounds in the US and Germany, the US transportation of compliance has led to the implementation of formal business compliance programs in German listed companies. On the assumption that German firms need to remain competitive, they will increasingly be required to comply with more and more requirements in terms of adherence to legal provisions. For example, over time and as a result of pressure from the Sarbanes-Oxley Act 2002[985] on German companies

---

soll Millionen zahlen, HANDELSBLATT, December 10, 2013, http://www.handelsblatt.com/unternehmen/management/heinz-joachim-neubuerger-ex-siemens-finanzchef-soll-millionen-zahlen/9200546.html (last visited Sep 22, 2015).

974 *See* Jürgen Bürkle, *Compliance als Aufgabe des Vorstands der AG – Die Sicht des LG München I*, CCZ 52–55, 52 (2015); Bürkle (2015), *supra* note 948 at 5 note 13.

975 *See* Bürkle (2015), *supra* note 974 at 52.

976 LG München I, 10.12.2013 - 5 HK O 1387/10, NZG 2014, *supra* note 973 at 346; AKTIENGESETZ (AKTG) | GERMAN STOCK CORPORATION ACT, BGBI. I, 1089 (1965) § 91 (II).

977 LG München I, 10.12.2013 - 5 HK O 1387/10, NZG 2014, *supra* note 973 at 346.

978 *See* Bürkle (2015), *supra* note 948 at 6 note 15.

979 *Id.* at 6. note 15.

980 LG München I, 10.12.2013 - 5 HK O 1387/10, NZG 2014, *supra* note 973.

981 *See* Bürkle (2015), *supra* note 948 at 5 note 13.

982 *See* Palazzo (2002), *supra* note 588 at 196.

983 *See e.g.* SIEBLER (2014), *supra* note 958 at 4.

984 *See* Rotsch (2012), *supra* note 936 at 60 margin note 10.

985 SARBANES-OXLEY ACT OF 2002, *supra* note 47.

listed in the US and the detailed rules and regulations of the SEC,[986] compliance also infiltrated German companies.[987] In conclusion, it can be stated that corporate compliance has no German cultural and legal origin, and that compliance was an *"Importation of American corporate compliance."*[988]

I. Definition of Compliance in Germany

As discussed above, according to many German authors[989] the term compliance originated from the Anglo-American legal terminology. That is why in Germany compliance also means *"...the adherence, observance, accordance, and fulfilment of determined bids."*[990] However, the word compliance has simply been adopted into the German legal terminology without translation. As such, it constitutes a so-called *"legal transplant."*[991] The word represents a generic term, originating from the English verb *"to comply with."*[992] Hence, in a strict sense, compliance means *"to be in compliance with the law."*[993] In practice, compliance requires that corporations and companies should act in accordance with the applicable laws.[994] In *Hauschka's* view, this is an obvious principle under the rule of law in all states.[995] As such, it describes an implicit understanding: The corporation and every employee should always act in compliance with the applicable laws.[996]

However, standing by this narrow definition would render compliance a mere platitude.[997] For this reason, the term compliance will be considered in a broader sense. *Rotsch* argued that compliance is a tool for monitoring and supervising a system.[998] The term is therefore clarified as comprising a set of measures in order to ensure the legal conduct of the employees.[999] *Bürkle* defines compliance as a package of organizational activities, which guarantee that the employees adhere

986 United States Sentencing Commission, USSC, *supra* note 50.
987 *See* Meier (2011), *supra* note 30 at 779.
988 *See* Djilani (2011), *supra* note 62.
989 *See e.g.* Eufinger (2012), *supra* note 586; Gößwein and Hohmann (2011), *supra* note 41; Gross (2012), *supra* note 42; Hauschka, Galster, and Marschlich (2014), *supra* note 463; Siebler (2014), *supra* note 958.
990 *See* Hauschka (2010), *supra* note 948 § 1 note 2.
991 *See* Gross (2012), *supra* note 42 at 34.
992 *See* Siebler (2014), *supra* note 958 at 3.
993 *See* Rotsch (2012), *supra* note 936 at 47 margin note 1.
994 *See* Hauschka (2010), *supra* note 948 § 1 note 2.
995 *Id.* § 1 note 2.
996 *See* Rotsch (2012), *supra* note 936 at 47 margin note 1.
997 *See* Hauschka (2004), *supra* note 58 at 257; Rotsch (2012), *supra* note 936 at 47 margin note 2; Uwe H. Schneider, *Compliance als Aufgabe der Unternehmensleitung*, ZIP 645–650, 646 (2003).
998 *See* Rotsch (2012), *supra* note 936 at 47 margin note 3.
999 *See e.g.* Frank Maschmann, *Haftungsvermeidung durch Gesetzetreue - Compliance und Arbeitsrecht*, 15 *in* Corporate Compliance und Arbeitsrecht | Mannheimer

to internal and external requirements.[1000] In short, he defines compliance as *"organized legal conformity."*[1001] In addition, *Gößwein & Hohmann* point out that compliance requires an organizational model with procedures and structures, which facilitate adherence to corporate policies.[1002] Moreover, *Benz & Klindt* conclude that, today, the general term compliance includes all aspects of risk management, auditing, and various areas of law *e.g.* antitrust law, criminal law and product liability law.[1003] In short, compliance pervades a number of areas of law.

Furthermore, it should be noted that compliance measures must always themselves be compliant.[1004] For example, the recent corporate emissions scandal involving VW illustrates a spectacular failure on the part of the compliance department and measures.[1005] Following the first scandal in 2005, the CCO reported directly to the chairman of the executive board under the renewed VW-compliance structure.[1006] However, the current structure revealed a common weakness in the compliance system within corporations. Seemingly, the sets of measures are biased toward corruption and compliance staff are too far removed from the day-to-day business.[1007] These assumptions ought to be taken into consideration in any review of the existing compliance structures in German companies. This most recent scandal shows that the structure of the compliance organization must be established effectively.[1008]

ARBEITSRECHTSTAG 2009 7–10, 7 (Frank Maschmann ed., 1. ed. 2009); Rotsch (2012), *supra* note 936 at 48 margin note 4; Schneider (2003), *supra* note 997 at 646.

1000 *See* Bürkle (2015), *supra* note 948 at 2 note 3.

1001 *Id.* at 3. note 3. *See also infra* in detail p. 415.

1002 *See* Gößwein and Hohmann (2011), *supra* note 41 at 963.

1003 *See* Jochen Benz & Thomas Klindt, Compliance 2020 – ein Blick in die Zukunft, 49 BB 2977–2980, 2977 (2010).

1004 *See* Maschmann (2009), *supra* note 999 at 9.

1005 Christopher Grundler, director of the EPA said "*that VW manufactured and installed software in the electronic control module of these vehicles that sensed when the vehicle was being tested for compliance with EPA emissions standards.*" *See*, Jana Kasperkevic, *Head of VW in US will tell Congress he knew of emissions rigging in early 2014*, THE GUARDIAN, October 8, 2015, http://www.theguardian.com/business/2015/oct/07/vw-president-ceo-congress-knew-emissions-rigging-early-2014-michael-horn (last visited Sep 22, 2015).

1006 *See* Geertje Oldermann, COMPLIANCE: VOLKSWAGEN ÜBERARBEITET STRUKTUR UND BERUFT LEITER ARBEITSRECHT ALS CCO JUVE (2011), http://juve.de/nachrichten/namenundnachrichten/2011/02/compliance-volkswagen-uberarbeitet-struktur-und-beruft-leiter-arbeitsrecht-als-cco (last visited Sep 22, 2015).

1007 *See* Newsdesk, *Zwei Gründe, warum die interne Kontrolle bei VW erneut versagt hat*, MANAGER MAGAZIN, September 28, 2015, http://www.manager-magazin.de/unternehmen/autoindustrie/zwei-gruende-warum-die-interne-kontrolle-bei-vw-erneut-versagt-hat-a-1054967.html (last visited Sep 22, 2015).

1008 *See e.g.* Gößwein and Hohmann (2011), *supra* note 41 at 966; Hauschka, Galster, and Marschlich (2014), *supra* note 463 at 245; Lackhoff and Schulz (2010), *supra* note 458 at 88; Moosmayer (2012), *supra* note 473 at 3016.

Despite the definition of compliance in the academic literature and the landmark case[1009] establishing responsibility under criminal law on account of a professional position, it is difficult to find legal norms relating to corporate compliance in Germany. However, the academic debate often refers to the Administrative Offences Act,[1010] the Stock Corporation Act,[1011] the Federal Immission Control Act,[1012] the German Banking Act[1013], the Securities Trading Act,[1014] and the implementing provision.[1015] In line with the American and English origins of the legal definition of compliance and the appointment of a compliance function in the securities laws, it is not surprising that the German codification was enacted in the Banking Act[1016] and Securities Trading Act.[1017] Thus, financial services and investment services organizations must appoint a compliance function are required to have in place a properly established internal business organization, which guarantees adherence to the legal provisions.

However, it is uncertain whether this legislation[1018] includes organizational requirements of the implementation of corporate compliance structures and the compliance function within companies in the private sector.[1019] Nevertheless,

---

1009 BGH, 17.7.2009 - 5 StR 394/08, BGHSt 54, 44; BGH NJW 2009, 3173, *supra* note 25.

1010 Gesetz über Ordnungswidrigkeiten (OWiG) | Act on Regulatory Offences, *supra* note 42 §§ 9, 30, 130.

1011 Aktiengesetz (AktG) | German Stock Corporation Act, *supra* note 976 § 91 (II).

1012 Bundes-Immissionsschutzgesetz (BImSchG) | Federal Immission Control Act, BGBI. I, p. 721 (1974) § 52 (II).

1013 Gesetz über das Kreditwesen (KWG) | German Banking Act, RGBl. I, 1203 (1935) § 25a.

1014 Wertpapierhandelsgesetz (WpHG) | Securities Trading Act, *supra* note 951 § 33 I 2 No. 5.

1015 Wertpapierdienstleistungs-Verhaltens- und Organisationsverordnung (WpDVerOV) | Securities Trading Implementing Provision, BGBI. I, 1432 (2007) § 12.

1016 Gesetz über das Kreditwesen (KWG) | German Banking Act, *supra* note 1013 § 25a.

1017 Wertpapierhandelsgesetz (WpHG) | Securities Trading Act, *supra* note 951 § 33 (I) No. 5; Wertpapierdienstleistungs-Verhaltens- und Organisationsverordnung (WpDVerOV) | Securities Trading Implementing Provision, *supra* note 1015 § 12.

1018 Aktiengesetz (AktG) | German Stock Corporation Act, *supra* note 976 § 91 (II); Gesetz über Ordnungswidrigkeiten (OWiG) | Act on Regulatory Offences, *supra* note 42 §§ 9, 30, 130.

1019 *See e.g.* Gößwein and Hohmann (2011), *supra* note 41 at 963; Hauschka (2010), *supra* note 948 § 1 note 21; Hauschka (2014), *supra* note 4 at 168; Moosmayer (2012), *supra* note 473 at 3013; Rotsch (2012), *supra* note 936 at 53 margin note 17; Schneider (2003), *supra* note 997 at 645; Konstantin von Busekist & Oliver Hein, *Ein praktischer Compliance Standard in den USA? Eine Analyse von Prosecution Agreements mit dem Department of Justice*, CCZ 185–191, 191 (2013).

there is also an academic debate[1020] on the legal obligation to implement a compliance structure within companies according to Sections 9, 30, 130 of the Act on Regulatory Offences (OWiG).[1021] *Hauschka* pointed out that there appears to be a legal obligation. For example, the compliance officer is responsible for avoiding offences by employees. This could be described as the supervisory duty of the compliance officer.[1022]

Furthermore, in Germany the term compliance is explained in the German Code 2015.[1023] Hence, the DCGK term compliance describes a requirement of or a task performed by the management board.[1024] The DCGK primarily refers to listed corporations.[1025] The legislative commission claimed that through the declaration of conformity pursuant to Section 161 German Stock Corporation Act (AktG),[1026] the code has a legal basis.[1027] In contrast, legal scholars have argued that the legal nature of the DCGK is not entirely clear.[1028] At the beginning of the 1990s, due to the international corporate governance development and the resultant emergence of codes, guidelines, principles, reports, statements, and standards of good practice, as well as due to a number of German corporate scandals,[1029] the German legislator recommended the draft of a Corporate Governance Code.[1030] On February

1020 *See pro* Moosmayer (2012), *supra* note 473; Schneider (2003), *supra* note 997; von Busekist and Hein (2013), *supra* note 1019; *See contra* Hauschka (2010), *supra* note 948; Rotsch (2012), *supra* note 936.

1021 GESETZ ÜBER ORDNUNGSWIDRIGKEITEN (OWIG) | ACT ON REGULATORY OFFENCES, *supra* note 42.

1022 *See* Hauschka (2014), *supra* note 4 at 168.

1023 THE GERMAN CODE 2015, *supra* note 947 at 6 Number 4.1.3. "*The Management Board ensures that all provisions of law and the enterprise's internal policies are abided by and works to achieve their compliance by group companies (Compliance).*"

1024 *See* Hauschka, Galster, and Marschlich (2014), *supra* note 463 at 243; Peter Hemeling, *Compliance im Erst- und Rückversicherungsunternehmen*, CCZ 21–25, 21 (2010).

1025 AKTIENGESETZ (AKTG) | GERMAN STOCK CORPORATION ACT, *supra* note 976 § 161.

1026 *Id.*§ 161 inserted on July 25, 2002, BT 2682.

1027 The German Government Commission, DEUTSCHER CORPORATE GOVERNANCE KODEX (DCGK) | THE GERMAN CORPORATE GOVERNANCE CODE DCGK, http://www.dcgk.de/en/code.html (last visited Sep 21, 2015). *See also supra* in detail pp. 482 et seq.

1028 Henrik-Michael Ringleb, *Vorbemerkung*, in: KOMMENTAR ZUM DEUTSCHEN CORPORATE GOVERNANCE KODEX: KODEX-KOMMENTAR (Thomas Kremer, Marcus Lutter, & Axel von Werder eds., 5. ed. 2014) [hereinafter: Commentary on the DCGK] note 54; Rotsch (2012), *supra* note 936 at 55 margin note 20.

1029 *E.g.* PHILIPP HOLZMANN AG was a German construction group and a global player. It was located in Frankfurt am Main. In 2002, it declared its bankruptcy.

1030 Introduction of the DCGK | Commentary on the DCGK, *in* KOMMENTAR ZUM DEUTSCHEN CORPORATE GOVERNANCE KODEX: KODEX-KOMMENTAR (Thomas Kremer et al. eds., 6. ed. 2016) [hereinafter: Commentary on the DCGK] note 1–8.

26, 2002, the DCGK was published on the website of the Commission.[1031] Similar to the UK Corporate Governance Code, the DCGK[1032] and Section 161 German Stock Corporation Act include a *"comply or explain"* approach. Although the Code is voluntary, German listed companies must explain their governance policies and give reasons for not complying with the recommendations of the DCGK. However, this international framework of corporate governance is not a primary source of law, but so-called *"soft law"*.[1033] Simarly, the German Code is not a primary source of law.[1034]

In so doing, Germany has no formal legal definition of the term compliance. The Code only provides an explanation of the term compliance, but even the case-law does not provide any definitive answer as to what compliance entails or requires the implementation of compliance tools such as risk analysis, or a code of conduct.[1035] Due to this legal gap, the academic literature has attempted to define the term. To summarize all the definitions mentioned in this section, compliance is more than simply adherence to the law; the term also encompasses rules of conduct, the avoidance of violations, and an organizational concept with appropriate measures. Ultimately, all of these organizational measures serve to ensure lawful conduct by the company and its employees.

II. The Historical Evolution of the German Compliance Function

Considering the evolution of compliance in the US and the UK, the compliance function did not simply appear. Similarly, in Germany, this development was a result of legal enforcement and changes in the European regulatory environment in the financial services and securities sectors. In recent years, specific requirements of compliance and the compliance function have been put into place. For example, the EU Directives[1036] have to be implemented into national law. In contrast, the EU regulations have direct effect and are binding on all EU member states.[1037] Based on the MiFID-Directive[1038] for instance, the German legislator inserted the European requirements of compliance and the compliance function

---

1031 *See* The German Code 2015, *supra* note 947.

1032 *Id.* at 2. Foreword.

1033 Commentary on the DCGK (2016), *supra* note 1030 note 5.

1034 *See* Ringleb in: Commentary on the DCGK (2014), *supra* note 1028 note 54.

1035 *See* Bürkle (2010), *supra* note 472 at 6 note 15.

1036 Consolidated versions of the Treaty on European Union and the Treaty on the Functioning of the European Union, OJ EC No. C 115 (2009) Article 288.

1037 *See* Jürgen Bürkle, *Der Compliance Officer in regulierten Finanzsektoren*, in: Der Compliance Officer: ein Handbuch in eigener Sache 315–342, 325 (Jürgen Bürkle & Christoph E. Hauschka eds., 1. ed. 2015) note 28.

1038 Commission Directive 2006/73/EC, *supra* note 873.

into the German Securities Trading Act (WpHG)[1039] and the Securities Trading Implementing Provision,[1040] which established binding compliance requirements in the securities sector.[1041] These provisions require the appointment of a compliance officer as a permanent, effective, and independent compliance function[1042] within financial services companies.[1043] In addition, in 1999 the Federal Banking Supervisory Authority (Bafin)[1044] provided a Directive specifying the organizational duties.[1045] For example, no. 4.1 determined that the executive board must establish a compliance position to monitor organizational duties.[1046] This function should operate independently from the other business units and report directly to the executive management.[1047]

Just like in the UK, since 2005, the impact of international regulation has grown significantly. The Basel Capital Accord (Basel II)[1048] has provided non-binding recommendations on the establishment of a compliance function in the financial services sector.[1049] In accordance with these recommendations, the German banks must manage all of their risks through an effective internal risk management procedure. As a result, the Federal Financial Supervisory Authority (Bafin) published its minimum requirements for the compliance function in a newsletter (MAComp)

1039 Wertpapierhandelsgesetz (WpHG) | German Securities Trading Act, *supra* note 951 § 33 (I) 2 No. 1.

1040 Wertpapierdienstleistungs-Verhaltens- und Organisationsverordnung (WpDVerOV) | Securities Trading Implementing Provision, *supra* note 1015 § 12 (4).

1041 *See* Bürkle (2015), *supra* note 1037 at 325 note 30.

1042 Wertpapierhandelsgesetz (WpHG) | German Securities Trading Act, *supra* note 951 § 33 (I) 2 No. 1.

1043 The definition of the financial services companies is enshrined in the *Id.* § 2 (4); Gesetz über das Kreditwesen (KWG) | German Banking Act, *supra* note 1013 § 53 (1) 1.

1044 This is an autonomous public-law institution and is subject to the legal and technical supervision of the Federal Ministry of Finance. *See* BaFin | Federal Banking Supervisory Authority, http://www.bafin.de/EN/BaFin/bafin_node.html (last visited Sep 22, 2015).

1045 Directives of the Federal Banking Supervisory Authority in order to specify the organizational obligations of investment services companies according to the German Securities Trading Act (WpHG), § 33 Abs. 1 of October 25, 1999. *See* BaFin, Richtlinie des Bundesaufsichtsamtes für den Wertpapierhandel zur Konkretisierung der Organisationspflichten von Wertpapierdienstleist ungsunternehmen gemäss § 33 Abs. 1 WpHG (1999), https://www.uni-leipzig.de/bankinstitut/files/dokumente/1999-10-25-01_0.pdf (last visited May 22, 2015).

1046 *Id.* at 4. no. 4.1.

1047 *Id.* at 4. no. 4.2.

1048 Bank for International Settlements, *supra* note 785.

1049 The Basel Committee on Banking Supervision, *supra* note 793.

in June 2010.[1050] However, these recommendations merely include guidelines and administrative rules for the compliance position, but are not legally binding on courts.[1051] For example, the proposals suggest that the compliance officer should be independent and discrimination should be prevented by the appointment being for a 24-month period and with a 12-month notice period for termination of the employment contract.[1052]

In January 2014, a huge European regulatory package implementing Basel III entered into effect, the Capital Requirements Directive IV (CRD IV)[1053] and the Capital Requirements Regulation (CRR).[1054] The provisions set out in the CRR and the technical standards are thus binding throughout the EU.[1055] Although there are no explicit requirements of compliance and the compliance function, the German legislator enshrined these provisions in law.[1056] Thus, the German Banking Act[1057] includes a mandatory compliance function within credit institutions.[1058] Lastly, today it is evident that due to the European legal framework there are now legal provisions in the German financial services and investment service sectors, which require all securities firms to appoint a compliance officer within credit institutions and financial services companies.

In contrast, outside the financial services sector there are no legal provisions on the implementation and establishing of a compliance function within companies.[1059] However, the legal obligation of the establishment of the compliance function has been the subject of much discussion in the academic debate in recent

---

1050 Minimal Requirements for Compliance (MaComp), *See* BaFin, BaFin | 4/2010 (WA) | Minimum Requirements for the Compliance Function and Additional Requirements Governing Rules of Conduct, Organisation and Transparency pursuant to Sections 31 et seq. of the Securities Trading Act (2010), https://www.bafin.de/SharedDocs/Veroeffentlichungen/EN/Rundschreiben/rs_1004_macomp_en_wa.html (last visited Sep 23, 2015).

1051 *See* Schulz and Renz (2012), *supra* note 41 at 2511.

1052 BaFin, *supra* note 1045 MaComp B.T. 1.3.3.4 Measures of Ensurance the independence of the Compliance function.

1053 Directive 2013/36/EU of the European Parliament and of the Council (CRD IV Directive), ABl. 2013 L 176/338 (2013).

1054 Regulation (EU) No 575/2013 of the European Parliament and of the Council, OJ L 176, 2013, 1, L 321/6 (2013).

1055 Birgit Höpfner, *CRD IV: New regulatory package for banks in force*, January 15, 2014, https://www.bafin.de/SharedDocs/Veroeffentlichungen/EN/Fachartikel/2014/ (last visited Sep 22, 2015).

1056 *See* Bürkle (2015), *supra* note 1037 at 329 note 47–48.

1057 Gesetz über das Kreditwesen (KWG) | German Banking Act, *supra* note 1013 § 25a (I) s. 3 No. 3 (c).

1058 The definition of the credit institutions provides Section 1 of the German Banking Act. *See Id.* § 1.

1059 *See* Schulz and Renz (2012), *supra* note 41 at 2512.

years.[1060] For example, for large companies *Hauschka* recommended the implementation of the compliance function,[1061] while *Moosmayer*[1062] argued that compliance is a primary task of the management board to conduct a risk analysis and to implement appropriate compliance measures according to the Stock Corporation Act (AktG)[1063] or the Act on Regulatory Offences (OWiG).[1064] In addition, he pointed out that the case-law has provided minimum standards for appropriate compliance measures such as (1) the organizational duty, (2) the supervisory duty, and (3) the examination duty.[1065] A number of authors suggest that every company should have an appropriate compliance structure with a compliance function to protect against the risk of loss of reputation and assets.[1066]

Lastly, nowadays German companies are confronted with international competition and an increasing legal framework in the European environment, resulting in greater pressure to implement compliance measures to meet legislative regulations and internal guidelines. The compliance officer should be responsible for fulfilling these requirements.[1067] Since 2000, the emergence of the German compliance officer has been attributable to the binding regulatory requirements in the financial services sector. In the private sector, the compliance officer function has been implemented voluntarily for several reasons.[1068] Seemingly, the increasing influence of international regulations and the court decisions concerning organizational duties have influenced German companies. Similarly, to the US, the emergence of this function also appears to have been a response to public pressure due to corporate scandals.

III. Definition of the Compliance Function in Germany

As previously discussed, the development of compliance and the compliance function occurred in stages. The academic literature has focused on the current

1060 *See e.g. Pro* Lackhoff and Schulz (2010), *supra* note 458; Moosmayer (2012), *supra* note 473 at 3013; *Contra* Fecker and Kinzl (2010), *supra* note 455 at 15; Gößwein and Hohmann (2011), *supra* note 41 at 964; Illing and Umnuß (2009), *supra* note 461 at 2.

1061 *See* Hauschka (2010), *supra* note 948 § 8 note 7.

1062 *See* Klaus Moosmayer, Compliance: Praxisleitfaden für Unternehmen (3. ed. 2015) note 10.

1063 Aktiengesetz (AktG) | German Stock Corporation Act, *supra* note 976 §§ 93 (I) (1) and 91 (II) – Duty of Care.

1064 Gesetz über Ordnungswidrigkeiten (OWiG) | Act on Regulatory Offences, *supra* note 42 §§ 9, 30, 130 – Organizational Duties.

1065 *See* Moosmayer (2015), *supra* note 1062 note 11–13; *See e.g.* OLG Stuttgart, 7.9.1976 - 3 Ss 526/76 - Überwachungspflicht des Betriebsinhabers, 1977 NJW 1410 (1976).

1066 *See e.g.* Schulz and Renz (2012), *supra* note 41 at 2512.

1067 *See* Meier (2011), *supra* note 30 at 779.

1068 *See* Bürkle (2015), *supra* note 948 at 7 note 20.

trend in compliance. Since the well-known court decision[1069] on the criminal liability of the compliance officer, the attention afforded to and the significance of this position has increased.[1070] The classification of the compliance officer as a guarantor for the purposes of criminal law[1071] will have far-reaching consequences for their daily practice.[1072] For this reason, it is necessary to identify and define the specific role and nature of this position within firms. For example, *Deister* argued that the current position of the compliance function is a separate role as an executive more "*general controller*" of the management board.[1073] In some cases, this classification might be too simple. First, it could be useful to analyze the importance and the content of compliance work. For example, the academic literature describes six essential issues relating to the significance of the German compliance officer:[1074]

(1) The scope of the tasks and duties,
(2) The criminal and civil liability of this function,
(3) Duties in the case of a lack of or non-specific job description,
(4) Limitation of responsibilities of this function,
(5) The standards of the profession of the compliance officer, and
(6) The further development of the compliance function.

Although the responsibilities of the compliance officer depend on the size and structure of the company in which he works, he is generally responsible for organizing the internal compliance program.[1075] In other words, the compliance officer plays a key role in the compliance system.[1076] Nevertheless, there are many recurring tasks in his daily work. To provide a general overview, it is useful to divide the different nature of compliance work into separate categories. In the view of *Renz & Wybitul*, the compliance officer's work comprises three main tasks: (1) the advisory function, (2) review and control function, and (3) the reporting function.[1077] In addition, *Hauschka* points out that the scope and diversity

---

1069 BGH, 17.7.2009 - 5 StR 394/08, BGHSt 54, 44; BGH NJW 2009, 3173, *supra* note 25.

1070 *See* Thomas Rotsch, *Grundfragen der Criminal Compliance, in* Criminal Compliance: Handbuch (Katharina Beckemper & Thomas Rotsch eds., 1. ed. 2015) § 2 note 13.

1071 BGH, 17.7.2009 - 5 StR 394/08, BGHSt 54, 44; BGH NJW 2009, 3173, *supra* note 25 note 19(b).

1072 *See* Bürkle (2015), *supra* note 948 at 5 note 11.

1073 *See* Jochen Deister & Anton Geier, *Der UK Bribery Act 2010 und seine Auswirkungen auf deutsche Unternehmen*, CCZ 12–18, 17 (2011).

1074 *See e.g.* Campos Nave (2009), *supra* note 457 at 2059; Wolf (2011), *supra* note 41 at 1353–1360; Hartmut Renz & Tim Wybitul, *Im Blickpunkt: Das Berufsbild des Compliance-Beauftragten Ein modernes Verständnis von Compliance*, BB, VI (2012).

1075 *See* Hauschka (2010), *supra* note 948 § 8 note 8.

1076 *Id.* § 8 note 23.

1077 *See* Renz and Wybitul (2012), *supra* note 1074 at VI.

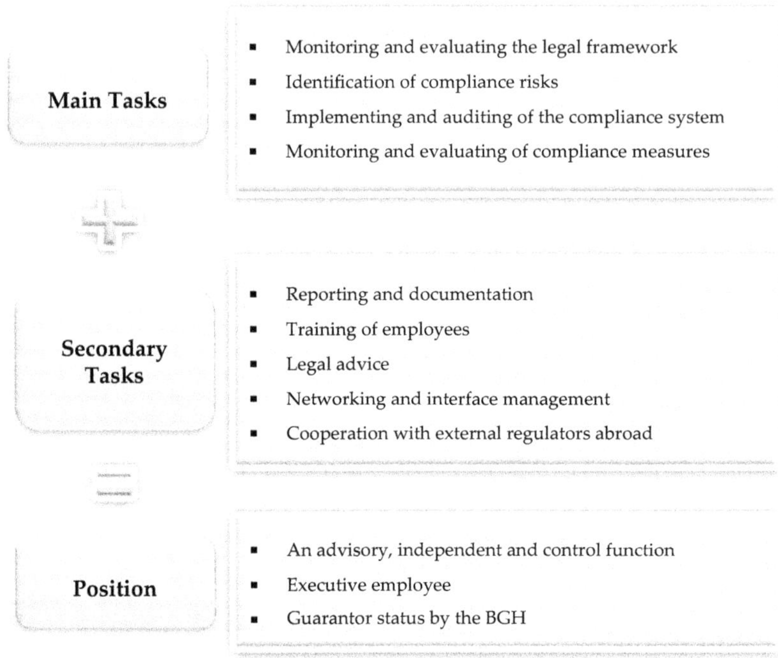

Figure 7 *Field of Activities of the German Compliance Officer following*[1078]

of compliance work includes training and information of employees, and support of the whistleblower-hotline.[1079] Furthermore, *Schulz & Renz* emphasized the documentation of employee activities and the activities of compliance officers themselves.[1080] Moreover, *Kirsch* presented the responsibilities in terms of law *e.g.* antitrust law, prevention of corruption, competition law, data protection law and other regulations.[1081] *Hastenrath* provides a broad overview of the various fields of activity. She divides the field of activity into five pillars, (1) the law and standard, (2) the knowledge of processes, (3) the risk audits, (4) the interface management,

---

1078 *See e.g.* Bürkle (2010), *supra* note 28; Dann and Mengel (2010), *supra* note 30; Gößwein and Hohmann (2011), *supra* note 41; Hastenrath (2015), *supra* note 1081; Illing and Umnuß (2009), *supra* note 461; Klebeck and Zollinger (2013), *supra* note 464; Krieger and Günther (2010), *supra* note 30; Meier (2011), *supra* note 30; Meier-Greve (2010), *supra* note 461; Renz and Wybitul (2012), *supra* note 1074; Schulz and Renz (2012), *supra* note 41; Sünner (2014), *supra* note 44; Wolf (2011), *supra* note 41.

1079 *See* Hauschka (2010), *supra* note 948 § 8 note 26.

1080 *See* Schulz and Renz (2012), *supra* note 41 at 2515.

1081 *See* Kirsch (2011), *supra* note 41.

and (5) the communication.[1082] It has been noted that there is a lack of knowledge of the compliance officer's work. They should also be able to network internally and diplomatically cooperate with external regulators abroad. The general tasks of the compliance officer are summarized in *Figure 7* above. This overview does not claim to be exhaustive and does not present any ranking of the compliance officer's tasks.

Finally, it has been mentioned that there is no legal or academic definition of the corporate compliance position in Germany.[1083] The reason for this may be that the role as such is difficult to define because it is a product of circumstances and situations. A review of the German literature shows a broad field of activities of this function. On that note, the German compliance officer is an executive employee responsible for the implementation, monitoring, and evaluation of the compliance system and for advising and monitoring other employees to prevent legal violation by the firm.

D. Conclusion

Based on the results of the literature analysis, it can be concluded that in the US, UK and in Germany, the legal origins of compliance lie in the securities legislation. Additionally, in the US and the UK compliance can be traced back to a form of corporate self-regulation. By surveying the literature and applicable provisions, it is notable that the compliance function was first established by statute in laws governing the financial services sector. Accordingly, in the US the compliance function originated from the securities laws,[1084] in the UK from the Financial Services Act,[1085] and in Germany from the German Securities Trading Act and German Banking Act.[1086]

Hence, this development was supported by legislation. The legislation and the creation of regulators arose on account of the importance of the financial services sector in the US and the UK, the global financial crisis, and numerous corporate scandals. Furthermore, the American system provides a legal definition of compliance and the compliance officer. Since the birth of the FSGO in 1991, the US has begun to continue to fill the legal gap. Thus, the legal framework of compliance set forth in the American legislation has had a significant influence on the global trade and, thus, also on European companies. For example, in recent years the British legislator has reevaluated the laws and procedures on corporate crime. In an effort to modernize and strengthen corporate provisions, criminal laws and procedure from the US have been examined and, in some cases, "*imported*" to the UK.[1087] *Djilani* referred to this phenomenon as the *"Importation of American*

1082 *See* Katharina Hastenrath, *Bestellung und Pflichtendelegation, in* Der Compliance Officer: ein Handbuch in eigener Sache , 28 (Jürgen Bürkle & Christoph E. Hauschka eds., 1. ed. 2015) note 5.

1083 *See* Meier (2011), *supra* note 30 at 779.

1084 *See supra* A., II., p. 124.

1085 *See supra* B., II., p. 143.

1086 *See supra* C., II., p. 159.

1087 *See* Djilani (2011), *supra* note 62 at 303.

Corporate Compliance."[1088] Nevertheless, in the UK and in Germany there are no legal provisions specifically governing the position of corporate compliance officer.

The comparative development in US, UK and German compliance legislation at the beginning of the 19th century with the situation today shows that over the last twenty years, there has been an extraordinary increase in the scope and complexity of regulations.[1089] Since 1960, the administrative enforcement of compliance has occurred in three waves: First, with the foreign corrupt practice and environmental awareness in the US, second with the regulation in the financial services industry in the UK, and third with the legislative response to recurring corporate scandals in the US, UK, and Germany. The next diagram summarizes the number of landmarks, the number of acts, regulations, codes, and landmark court decisions, which were created and took place regarding compliance and the compliance function in the US, in the UK, and in Germany.

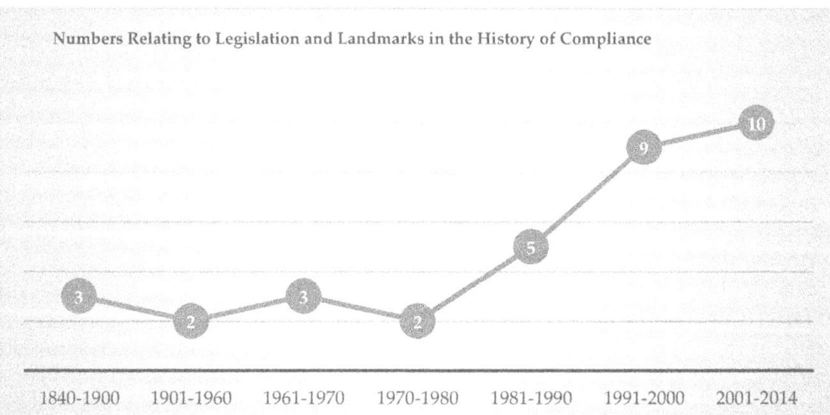

Figure 8 *Numbers Relating to Legislation and Landmarks in the History of Compliance*

As we have seen, there is a great increase in legislation and court decisions pertaining to compliance in recent years. In the US, the term compliance, compliance efforts of companies, and the debate on organizational ethical culture are rooted in a longstanding tradition. There, the first origins of corporate compliance can be traced back to the 18th century. By contrast, in Germany, the nascence of corporate compliance began in the wake of corporate scandals since 2008. Compliance issues were highlighted in the landmark case decided in 2009.[1090] Consequently, in

1088 *Id.* at 303. *See supra* B., I., p. 139.
1089 *See* Miller (2014), *supra* note 595 at 141.
1090 BGH, 17.7.2009 - 5 StR 394/08, BGHSt 54, 44; BGH NJW 2009, 3173, *supra* note 25; *See also supra* C., III., p. 162.

Germany companies began to deal with compliance issues through transportation from the US, through European and national legislation in the financial services sector, and under pressure from court decisions and corporate scandals over the last ten years. On account of this late development, Germany still does not have a definitive official definition of the compliance officer. The findings of the legal origins of the term compliance and the compliance function are presented in a brief overview in Table 2 below:

Table 2 – *Overview of Legal Roots of Compliance and the Compliance Function*

	US		*UK*		*Germany*	
	Compliance	**CO**	**Compliance**	**CO**	**Compliance**	**CO**
Origins	Railroads 1887	Watergate Scandal	Since new legislation 1986		Since the Federal Supreme Court (BGH) *obiter dictum* in 2009	
Legal and Cultural Background	Taylors Principles 1909, Self-regulated companies, Ethics issues based in Protestantism		Self-regulated system, European regulatory environment, Importation of American Corporate Compliance		Importation of American and British Corporate Compliance, European regulatory environment, Corporate scandals	
Legal Roots in the Financial Services Ind.	Federal Sec. Law 1933, 1934	Amendments of the Federal Sec. Law 1964	Fin. Service Bill 1986, FSMA 2000, MiFID 2004	Basel II	German Banking Act, Securities Trading Act (1994)	Basel II, III, KWG § 25a, WpDVerVO, § 12 IV. s. 1
Regulator	ICC, SEC, EPA		FSA, FCA, LAUTRO		Bafin	
Legal Roots in the Private Sector	Antitrust Law, FCPA 1977, FSGO 1991, SOX 2002	Since 2004 by FSGO	UKBA 2010 § 7 (2)	No origin	No origin	No origin
Legal Definition or Guidelines in the Private Sector	USSC § 8 B2.1 2004	USSC § 8 B2.1.b (2)B 2004, 2010	Companies Act 2006, Takeover Code Comb. Code	No origin	DCGK (2002)	No origin
Department	Legal or Compliance Department		Usu. Compliance Department		Usu. Compliance Department	
Role	Self-regulation, Risk-management	Dual-hatted, Oversight Function	Self-regulation, Risk-management	Multi-functional	Risk-management	Guarantor status, Control Function

In conclusion, the review of the literature shows a number of theoretical findings that provide a narrow definition of the term compliance. However, many authors view the term in a broader sense and include concepts of obedience, observance, deference, governability, the organizational aspects,...etc. It has been mentioned that defining corporate compliance is a difficult task. In brief, compliance could be defined as obedience to the law. However, this definition could be too restrictive. Compliance acknowledges not only adherence to rules and law, but also engagement with business risks. In addition, compliance should also deal with its legal and ethical responsibilities.

Finally, this section summarizes both the narrow and the broader understanding of the term compliance in order to highlight the particular challenges facing companies. As has been noted, when business and legal scholars explore the question of compliance, they are actually interested in understanding the implementation and adoption of compliance programs within organizations. However, compliance is more than integration into the day-to-day business and confirmation that employees have to comply with the law. Ultimately, this section provides a fairly broad definition of corporate compliance, which will apply throughout the rest of this book:

> **Compliance** is a package of formal and informal structures to ensure that all employees in the organization adhere to all applicable laws, regulations, internal and external policies to avoid loss of reputation and avoid penalties, with the goal of increasing the benefits for stake- and shareholders.

Figure 9 illustrates the broad definition of the term corporate compliance. As the figure shows, the academic debate has considered the compliance function in a broad sense. As mentioned in the preceding discussions, although the empirical research regarding this function is limited, there is a degree of diversity in the German literature in the interpretation of the applicable day-to-day activities and responsibilities.[1091] To summarize all the findings in the literature on the corporate compliance officer, as outlined above, this function will be defined as follows:

> A corporate **compliance officer** is an oversight function and a high-level employee, who is responsible for implementation and organization of the compliance structure such as an compliance management system (CMS), for advising and reviewing of employees to prevent legal violations by the firm, and for diplomatic dealing with external regulators.

Although it could be argued that this definition is general and comprehensive, the daily business of the compliance officer is complex and has a far-reaching significance for the company. In order to fill the gap between the nature and role of the German corporate compliance officers it is important to obtain a broader understanding of their integration and identification within companies. In short,

---

1091 *See supra* Figure 7, p. 164.

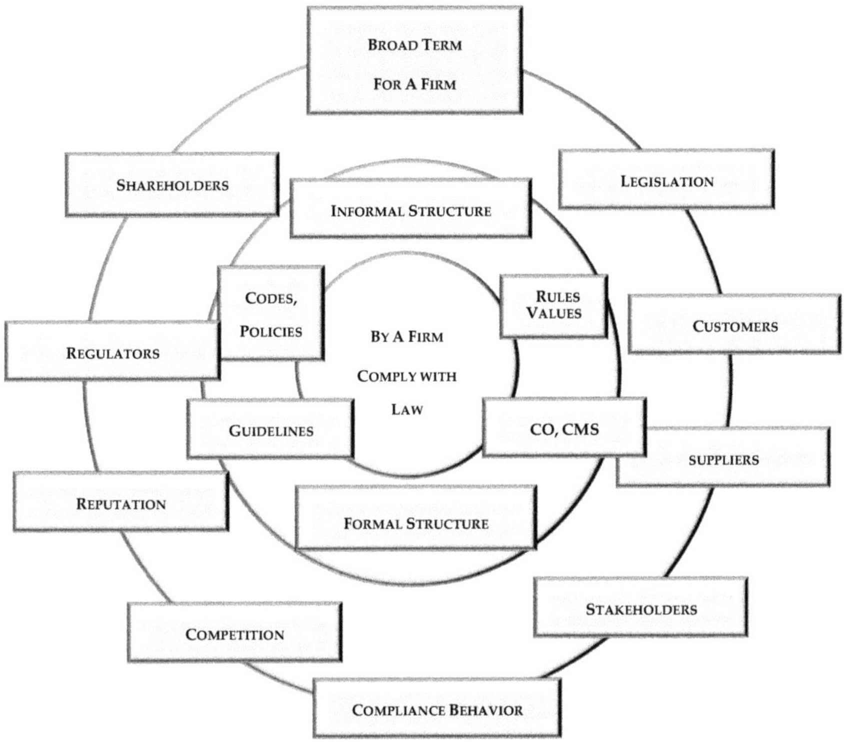

Figure 9 *The Term Corporate Compliance in a Broader Sense*

a modern and dynamic role of the German compliance officer can be established only by means of a precise definition.

To conclude, this chapter has focused on the legal roots and the cultural background of the compliance officer in the US, UK, and Germany. It has established the definition of corporate compliance and the corporate compliance officer that will apply throughout this book. Having introduced these definitions, the next chapters first will introduce the legal framework with regard to the American, British, and German compliance function and secondly present the models of the corporate compliance officers.

The American Legal Framework of Corporate Compliance

Abstract
The challenge for the next sections will be to examine the American legal framework and landmark cases relating to compliance and, more specifically, to the corporate compliance function. In addition, this chapter will explore the role of the corporate compliance officer and his relationships, duties and responsibilities within the US corporate structure. The following sections will address the key provisions, definitions under US federal law, state law and court decisions on corporations and and the effects thereof on the corporate compliance function. Considering the power of administrative and executive branch agencies, regulators, and guidelines, which are closely tied to compliance and the American compliance officer this chapter outlines the particularities of the US compliance function. To this end, it also explores the state corporation law and employment laws under which corporate officers could incur civil and criminal liability if they fail to implement appropriate corporate structures or to supervise employees. The findings will form the basis for the development of the changing and evolving model of the US corporate compliance officer at the end of chapter three.

A. The Importance of the Legal Framework for American Compliance

At the end of chapter two, the term compliance was defined as follows:

> ....a package of formal and informal structures [...] the organization adherence with all the laws... [ ]."[1092]

Thus, compliance refers to a concept of internal control and to a process that has gradually evolved under pressure of the tightening of the legal framework as well as the relationships with suppliers, customers, capital markets, insurers, and stakeholders.[1093] However, in the US, the legal framework of compliance comprises not only the body of rules for instance regulations such as *"hard-law"*, but also recommendations from the administrative and executive branch agencies *e.g.* the SEC.[1094] This legal framework has a profound influence on the law of US

1092 *See supra* D, p. 168.
1093 *See supra* Figure 9, p. 169; *See also* Miller (2014), *supra* note 519 at 3.
1094 *See supra* note 352, 44 USC, § 3502 (1); *See also* Jerry Ellig & Hester Peirce, *SEC Regulatory Analysis: "A Long Way to Go and a Short Time to Get There,"* 8 BROOK. J. CORP. FIN. *&* COM. L. 361–437, 364 (2014).

compliance.[1095] Hence, companies have a strong incentive to internalize the law and to establish a supervisory compliance function.[1096] While one could argue that this view is too biased, a number of scholars have acknowledged that the consequences of failure to comply with the applicable laws could be serious and far-reaching.[1097] This is why many corporations have chosen to enhance the control of their business in a legal way and thereby enforce their compliance approach.[1098] An earlier study[1099] examined the importance of law to business in general.[1100] The findings of this study showed that an understanding of the legal framework could be useful for the executive officers responsible for corporate actions in a legal context.[1101] Based on these findings, a further study by *Siedel* presented six forces that determine the competitive advantage of a company including the importance of compliance. These forces are *inter alia*: (1) government regulation, (2) litigation as traditional forces, (3) compliance, (4) entrepreneurship, (5) globalization, and (6) technology as accelerating forces.[1102] The study describes the accelerated development of compliance as follows: Although many companies historically have had compliance programs, the enactment of the Federal Sentencing Guidelines in 1991[1103] enforced the further development of these programs.[1104] Lastly, the study concludes that the correct handling of the legal framework is beginning to play an increasingly important role in the success of the firm.[1105]

In addition, in 1988, *Schipani & Siedel* found that, with increasing liability for directors and officers, it is imperative that directors and officers know and understand

---

1095 *See* Miller (2014), *supra* note 519 at 3.

1096 *Id.* at 3.

1097 *See e.g.* Constance E Bagley, *What's Law Got to Do With It?: Integrating Law and Strategy*, 47 American Business Law Journal 587–639 (2010); Sara Sun Beale, The Development and Evolution of the US Law of Corporate Criminal Liability 32 (2014), http://papers.ssrn.com/abstract=2375318 (last visited Oct 2, 2015); Fairman and Yapp (2005), *supra* note 760; Sharon Oded, *Inducing corporate compliance: A compound corporate liability regime*, 31 International Review of Law and Economics 272–283 (2011); L. S. Paine, *Managing for Organizational Integrity*, 72 Harvard Business Review 106–117 (1994).

1098 *See* Fairman and Yapp (2005), *supra* note 760 at 491.

1099 *See* Frank C. Pierson, *The Education of American Businessmen: A Study of University-College Programs*, Business Administration 266–267 (1959).

1100 *See* George J. Siedel, *Six Forces and the Legal Environment of Business: The Relative Value of Business Law among Business School Core Courses*, 37 American Business Law Journal, 729 (2000).

1101 *Id.* at 729.

1102 *Id.* at 734. fig. 2.

1103 US Sentencing Guidelines USSC, *supra* note 58.

1104 *See* Siedel (2000), *supra* note 1100 at 737.

1105 *Id.* at 738.

their legal responsibilities.[1106] Given the significant influence on observance of the legal framework, the executive officer[1107] should also consider this when developing the strategy of the company. For example, *Paine* describes a strategic concept of compliance as *"a shared set of values and guidance principles"* driven by organizational leadership.[1108] She presented five elements of a compliance strategy from the Martin Marietta Corp., a US aerospace and defense contractor, in 1985.[1109] At that time, the defense industry was under pressure due to mismanagement. For this reason, the management switched to an integrity-based program from self-governance with five elements:

(1) Ethos – in conformity with externally imposed standards,
(2) Objective – to prevent criminal misconduct,
(3) Leadership – lawyer-driven,
(4) Methods such as education, auditing, controls, and penalties,
(5) Behavioral assumptions for leading and guiding employees.[1110]

In her view, the general purpose of compliance is "*to avoid legal sanctions.*"[1111] She points out that for an organizational life, it is better to obey the law with appropriate internal programs and structures than for external authorities to impose constraints.[1112] Overall, she concluded that the task of the management is to define and create a legal environment that supports ethical behavior.[1113] The weakness of this concept is the focus solely on the development of internal corporate structures relating to compliance, while the relationship between internal and external parties is absent.

Additionally, *Bagley* argues that the academic discussion has already recognized the growing significance of the legal framework for companies. However, she finds that companies´ active management of the legal environment of business is less well-developed.[1114] In her view, law affects every-single activity in the value chain. This comprises IT-Infrastructure, the Human Resource Management, Technology

---

1106 *See* Cindy A. Schipani & George J. Siedel, Legal Liability: The Board of Directors, 1 Family Business Review 279–285, 279 (1988).

1107 In this part, the term officer means a corporation's president, chief financial officer, chief accounting officers, vice presidents of principal business units and any person with significant policy-making functions. This word is used in accordance with the definition of officer in Rule 16a-1 under the Securities Exchange Act of 1934. *See* Securities Exchange Act of 1934, *supra* note 605, 15 USC § 78a, 17 CFR 240.16a-1.

1108 *See* Paine (1994), *supra* note 1097.

1109 *Id.* at 112.

1110 *Id.* at 113.

1111 *Id.* at 111.

1112 *Id.* at 111.

1113 *Id.* at 111.

1114 *See* Bagley (2014), *supra* note 1097 at 587.

Development, Procurement, Logistics, Marketing, Sales, and Service activities of each firm.[1115] She asserts that a complete model of the resource-based view of the company must also include the legal environment.[1116] Thus, she attempts to combine earlier theories[1117] into a comprehensive theory of the law and strategy and proposes a conceptual framework for understanding the law and strategy.[1118] This approach centers around the senior management team. She finds that this unit is the most critical resource for deciding a successful compliance strategy. This strategy is influenced by four elements: (1) public law, (2) company resources, (3) activities in the value chain, and (4) competitive environment.[1119] However, she states that this model has taken a "*dynamic*" approach.[1120] For example, public law will change in response to the altered ethical conduct of firms, or the competitive environment will change in response to the altered legal environment, etc.[1121] In conclusion, this model sheds new light on the mutual influence of various and legal internal and external factors of the company. *Bagley´s* findings indicate that the most decisive importance of the law for companies lies in their understanding and correct application of the law. This could be a source of sustained competitive advantage for companies.[1122] Nevertheless, the model fails to consider the definition of the term "*top management team*." It is not clear whether the term applies to the board of directors, or to the executive officers. This model reflects the fact that the law is more than merely a force that constrains the management team. Finally, this concept provides a fit between the companies' legal, competitive, and social responsibility for the understanding of the law.[1123]

To summarize the above, the recent corporate legal environment can be described as complex. Companies often operate in international legal transactions and have to deal with various internal and external factors and parties. The participants involved are the executive officers, employees, agents, investors, and regulators. Misconduct, non-compliance, law breaking, or violation of law by the employees and executives could give a rise to serious negative consequences for firms, resulting in criminal liability for their organizations.[1124] In fact, the mere adherence to the letter of the law is no longer sufficient. Compliance entails more than obeying the law. Overall, the strategy of the board management needs to ensure that adherence to the law pervades the entire business conduct within the company.

1115 *Id.* at 605, fig. 1.
1116 *Id.* at 606.
1117 *See e.g.* Kalman J. Cohen & Richard M. Cyert, *Strategy: Formulation, Implementation, and Monitoring*, 46 The Journal of Business 349–367 (1973).
1118 *See* Bagley (2014), *supra* note 1097 at 624 fig. 2.
1119 *Id.* at 624–625.
1120 *Id.* at 623.
1121 *Id.* at 625.
1122 *Id.* at 599, 601, Table 1.
1123 *Id.* at 639.
1124 *See* Greenberg (2012), *supra* note 688 at 1.

For this reason, the challenge for the next sections will be to examine the American legal framework and landmark cases relating to compliance and specifically to the corporate compliance function. In addition, the next sections also explore the circumstances under which corporate officers could incur civil and criminal liability if they fail to implement corporate structures or to supervise employees.[1125] This examination will also include the *"doctrine of respondeat superior"*[1126] and the *"employment at-will doctrine"*[1127] since the courts have used this theory and this doctrine in various cases.[1128] However, to present the background of US Federal Law, it will first be traced in chronological order from 1970 to 2010 in more detail.[1129] Specifically, the following sections will examine the FCPA, the SOX and the FSGO. The Dodd-Frank Wall Street Reform and Consumer Protection Act is a comprehensive and complex bill, which includes huge changes in the regulation of financial institutions and financial products and contains hundreds of pages.[1130] The Act also provides a new regulatory framework for consumer protection and remittance transfers.[1131] It will not be discussed here since it is still a

---

1125 *See* Martin Petrin, *The Curious Case of Directors' and Officers' Liability for Supervision and Management: Exploring the Intersection of Corporate and Tort Law*, 59 American University Law Review 1161–1715, 1162 (2010).

1126 *"Under the doctrine of respondeat superior an employer is liable for the negligent acts or omissions of his employee which are committed within the scope of his employment. Liability based on respondeat superior requires some evidence that a master-servant relationship existed between the parties. The test to determine if respondeat superior applies is whether the person sought to be charged as a master had the right or power to control and direct the physical conduct of the other in the performance of the act. If there is no right to control, there is no liability." See Wilson v. United States, 989 F.2d 953, 958 (8th Cir. 1993). See infra* in detail I., 1., a., p. 183.

1127 *"This refers to the presumption that employment is for an indefinite period of time and may be terminated either by employer or employee. This is the historical approach that courts have taken in interpreting employment relationships. By the end of the twentieth century, state courts found other exceptions to the doctrine of "at- will" employment." The late twentieth century saw many states abandoning the "at-will" doctrine and an increase in protection of employee rights at work." See* John C. Busby, Employment-at-will Doctrine LII / Legal Information Institute (2009), https://www.law.cornell.edu/wex/employment-at-will_doctrine (last visited Apr 14, 2016). *See infra* in detail II., p. 254.

1128 *See* Petrin (2010), *supra* note 1125 at 1674.

1129 *See also supra* A., pp. 115 et seq.

1130 Dodd–Frank Wall Street Reform and Consumer Protection Act (2010), *supra* note 700. The Act was enacted as the response to the financial crisis that began in 2008 and became Public Law No: 111–203 on July 21(st), 2010. In 2017 and 2018, under the presidency of Donal Trump, the Republican made several efforts to withdraw some of the consumer-protection provisions laid down in the Dodd-Frank Act.

1131 *Id.* 15 USC § 1693o-1.

source of political debates and issues that fall beyond the scope and the purpose of this book.

I. The Development of US Federal Legislation

> Corporate bribery is bad business. In our free market system, it is basic that the sale of products should take place on the basis of price, quality, and service.[1132]

The enforcement of the federal law relating to compliance in the US can be seen as a response to a number high-profile corporate bribery scandals and corruption in the 1960s and 1970s.[1133] As a result, the US government's objective was to enable US corporations to compete in the global economy under fair conditions. The Department of Justice (DOJ)[1134] cited an example put forward by the World Bank Institute, which estimated the annual costs of corruption and bribery at approximately one trillion US$ globally - three percent of the world economy.[1135] Moreover, US Congress emphasized that corruption undermines efficiency and good business practices.[1136] It also argued that bribery harms American business and creates foreign policy problems.[1137] In addition, the US Senate stated that corporate bribery is bad business.[1138] Conversely, *Richard* argued that enhancing US bribery law could provide foreign corporations with an unfair advantage over US corporations.[1139]

1132 Foreign Corrupt Practices and Domestic and Foreign Investment Improved Disclosure Acts of 1977, 4 (1977).

1133 *See supra.*, p. 125, The Watergate scandal and the following investigation. *See also* Court E. Golumbic & Jonathan P. Adams, *Dominant Influence Test: The FCPA's Instrumentality and Foreign Official Requirements and the Investment Activity of Sovereign Wealth Funds, The*, 39 Am. J. Crim. L. 1–51 (2011); Richard (2014), *supra* note 554.

1134 "*The Department of Justice (DOJ). The Department of Justice belongs to the executive branch. It works to enforce federal law and to defend the interests of the United States according to the law. The Office of the Attorney General was created by the Judiciary Act of (1789). In its strategic plan for 2014 – 2018 the DOJ decribes itself as an agency with unique authorities, opportunities, and capabilities,with the goal e.g. to prevent crime, protect the rights of the American people, and enforce federal law.*" *See* Office of the Attorney General DOJ, Strategic Plan Fiscal Years 2014–2018 | DOJ | Department of Justice, http://www.justice.gov/about/strategic-plan-fiscal-years-2014-2018 (last visited Oct 20, 2015). *See* Committee on the Judiciary House of Representatives, Hearing before the Subcommittee on Crime, Terrorism, and Homeland Security 6 (201AD), http://judiciary.house.gov/_files/hearings/printers/112th/112-47_66886.PDF (last visited Oct 20, 2015).

1135 *See* Mark (2012), *supra* note 641 at 424.

1136 Committee on the Judiciary House of Representatives, *supra* note 1134 at 6.

1137 *Id.* at 3.

1138 Foreign Corrupt Practices and Domestic and Foreign Investment Improved Disclosure Acts of 1977, *supra* note 1132.

1139 *See* Richard (2014), *supra* note 554 at 420.

Despite these concerns, in 1977 Congress enacted the Foreign Corrupt Practices Act (FCPA) to combat foreign bribery.[1140]

The Defense Industry Initiative (DII) on Ethics and Conduct introduced the second stage of legal enforcement in 1986. During the 1980s, as a result of government mismanagement, President Reagan established his Blue Ribbon[1141] Commission on Defense Management.[1142] The purpose of this Commission was to explore the issues of defense management and organization, and to report its findings and recommendations to the President.[1143] In its final report,[1144] which intended to facilitate the legislative and executive branch, the Chairman recommended that excellence in management must displace systems and structures that measure quality by regulatory compliance.[1145] These results were generally considered to be the starting point of formal organizational ethics and compliance programs.[1146] Furthermore, these recommendations led to additional efforts to promote an ethical culture with formal codes and structures within government-owned industry.[1147]

Additionally, in 1984, US Congress created the United States Sentencing Commission (USSC).[1148] The Commission formulated national sentencing guidelines, the Federal Sentencing Guidelines (FSG),[1149] to provide certainty and fairness in sentencing and to avoid unwarranted sentencing disparities.[1150] Moreover, in 1991 the USSC extended the Federal Sentencing Guidelines[1151] to

1140 Foreign Corrupt Practices Act 1977 (FCPA), *supra* note 438.

1141 Ronald Reagan, Executive Order 12526 - President's Blue Ribbon Commission on Defense Management (1985).

1142 *See* The National Association of College and University Attorneys | NACUA, *The Case for Compliance Programs: The Legal and Policy Mandates*14, 3 (2011).

1143 Reagan, *supra* note 1141 Sec. 2. (a).

1144 David Packard, Final Report of the President's Blue Ribbon Commission on Defense Management 147 (1986), http://www.ndia.org/Advocacy/AcquisitionReformInitiative/Documents/Packard-Commission-Report.pdf (last visited Oct 20, 2015).

1145 *Id.* Foreword.

1146 NACUA (2011), *supra* note 1142 at 4.

1147 Examples include new structures in the Department of Defense (DoD).

1148 The US Sentencing Commission ("the Commission") was created by the Sentencing Reform Act (1984), *supra* note 47., Provisions of the Comprehensive Crime Control Act of 1984. The US Supreme Court decided in *Mistretta v. United States, 488 US 361 (1989)* the constitutionality of the Commission. Hence, it is an independent agency in the judicial branch of government. Its major purpose is to establish sentencing policies and practices for the federal courts. *See* USSC, USSC | United States Sentencing Commission, http://www.ussc.gov/about (last visited Feb 2, 2016).

1149 The sentencing guidelines went into effect November 1, 1987. *See* USSC, *supra* note 1148.

1150 NACUA (2011), *supra* note 1142 at 4.

1151 *See* United States Sentencing Commission, USSC, *supra* note 50.

include a new chapter on organizational crime and intended to encourage the scope of traditional compliance - *"encourage ethical conduct and a commitment to compliance with the law."*[1152] This extended Chapter 8 codified the components for an effective compliance program.[1153] Since then, additional standards have been added to define the elements of an effective compliance program and to highlight the role of US ethics and compliance officers in daily business practice.[1154] Hence, they have gained more visibility and attention within companies and among legal scholars. *Murphy* argued that the Guidelines have created an entirely new job description for the ethics and compliance officer.[1155] Many authors have found that, in response to the FSG, a number of companies have begun to enhance their corporate compliance programs.[1156] Other critical voices assert that the Guidelines' extrinsic, incentive-based approach has led to the persistence of ineffective compliance.[1157] However, there is no evidence documenting features and reliable data on effective compliance programs within companies.

The third stage began with a huge change in the American federal law shortly before the beginning of the new millennium. Despite government efforts in the 1990s to encourage compliance, a number of high- profile corporate corruption scandals, such as the Enron[1158] and WorldCom accounting scandals [1159] and their auditor Arthur Andersen, terrified the public and highlighted persistent accounting and governance problems.[1160] In the spring of 2002, additional revelations were discovered concerning other firms. One example was Adelphia, Inc., the sixth-largest US cable company. This scandal[1161] involved one of the most extensive cases of

---

1152 *See* US Sentencing Guidelines USSC, *supra* note 58 Ch. 8, § 8B2.1.

1153 *See* Greenberg (2009), *supra* note 11 at 1.

1154 *See* Greenberg (2012), *supra* note 688 at 1.

1155 *See* Murphy (2002), *supra* note 654 at 710.

1156 *See e.g.* DeStefano (2013), *supra* note 14 at 92–93; Greenberg (2012), *supra* note 688 at 1; Paine (1994), *supra* note 1097 at 106.

1157 *See e.g. Maurice E. Stucke, In Search of Effective Ethics & Compliance Programs* 77 (2014), http://www.ssrn.com/abstract=2366209 (last visited Feb 2, 2016).

1158 The Enron Board of Directors failed to safeguard Enron shareholders [...] by allowing Enron to engage in high risk accounting. *See* in: Mark S. Schwartz, Thomas W. Dunfee & Michael J. Kline, *Tone at the Top: An Ethics Code for Directors?*, 58 Journal of Business Ethics 79–100, 80 (2005).

1159 *"WorldCom, an US large long distance phone company, submitted the largest bankruptcy filing in United States history."; See* Romero and Atlas (2002), *supra* note 6; Tran, *supra* note 6.

1160 *See e.g.* Jonathan Shirley, *International Law and the Ramifications of the Sarbanes-Oxley Act of 2002*, 27 B.C. Int'l & Comp. L. Rev 501–528, 502 (2004).NACUA (2011), *supra* note 1142 at 10.

1161 *"Adelphia disclosed Thursday that the debt incurred by the Rigas family is $ 3.1 billion – instead of the $ 2.3 billion Adelphia previously reported. The level of self-dealing is extremely serious." See* Robert Frank & Deborah Solomon, *Adelphia and Rigas*

insider dealing ever.[1162] In the aftermath of these scandals, Congress came under increasing pressure to pass the Sarbanes-Oxley Act of 2002.[1163] This legislative response developed rapidly. On July 24, 2002, the Conference Committee of the House and Senate drafted the final bill. It passed in Congress the following day. The President signed the Act into law five days later.[1164] President Bush asserted that this Act was the *"most far-reaching reform of American business practices since the time of Franklin Delano Roosevelt."*[1165] He also stated that "*The era of low standards and false profit is over*" and "*No boardroom in America is above or beyond the law*."[1166]

Since then, the consequences of the SOX for corporations have been far-reaching and pronounced. First, this Act made best practices in corporate governance among public companies mandatory.[1167] The term best practices is explained in in Section 406 (c) of the SOX with such standards including *e.g.* (1) *"honest and ethical conduct,"* (2) *"full, fair, accurate, timely, and understandable disclosure in the periodic reports"*, and (3) "*compliance with applicable governmental rules and regulations.*"[1168] Secondly, the Act imposed significant changes in accounting and auditing companies' rules, as well as with respect to the monitoring of public accounting.[1169] Thirdly, the SOX required a Management Assessment of Internal Controls,[1170] which includes the requirement that public companies must adopt and publish a code of ethics. Furthermore, the Act addresses the criminal penalties for altering

---

Family Had A Vast Network of Business Ties, Wall Street Journal, May 24, 2002, http://www.wsj.com/articles/SB1022168448423792680 (last visited Nov 3, 2015).

1162 *See* Shirley (2004), *supra* note 1160 at 504.

1163 Sarbanes-Oxley Act of 2002, *supra* note 47. The Sarbanes-Oxley Act (SOX) was passed in the House and Senate on July 25, 2002 and enacted in 2002.

1164 *See* Shirley (2004), *supra* note 1160 at 505.

1165 *See* Elisabeth Bumiller, *CORPORATE CONDUCT: THE PRESIDENT; Bush Signs Bill Aimed at Fraud In Corporations*, The New York Times, July 31, 2002, http://www.nytimes.com/2002/07/31/business/corporate-conduct-the-president-bush-signs-bill-aimed-at-fraud-in-corporations.html (last visited Nov 3, 2015).)

1166 *Id.*

1167 *See* David C. Fischer, *Responsibilities of principal executive officers under the Sarbanes-Oxley Act of 2002: A compliance checklist*, 5 Journal of Investment Compliance 97–105, 97 (2004). Public companies in terms of the SOX means an issuer as defined in Section 3 of the Securities Exchange Act of 1934, 15 USC. 78c. *See* Sarbanes-Oxley Act of 2002, *supra* note 47 § 2 (7).

1168 Sarbanes-Oxley Act of 2002, *supra* note 47 § 406 (c), 15 USC § 7264.

1169 *See* Fischer (2004), *supra* note 1167 at 97.

1170 Sarbanes-Oxley Act of 2002, *supra* note 47 § 404 (a) (1). *"The Commission shall prescribe rules requiring each annual report required by Section 13(a) or 15(d) of the Securities Exchange Act of 1934 (15 USC §§ 78m or 78o(d)) to contain an internal control report, which shall-(1) state the responsibility of management for establishing and maintaining an adequate internal control structure and procedures for financial reporting."*

and destroying corporate audit records[1171] and extends the timeline[1172] under which any accountant is required to maintain, audit or review reports.[1173] Overall, the two legal goals of this Act were to improve the quality of financial reporting and to bolster investor confidence.[1174]

Although the US legislator was responding to domestic corporate scandals, its impact is global.[1175] The new Act caused a ripple effect overseas, prompting critics to claim that the costs would drive foreign companies away from the United States.[1176] Nevertheless, legal scholars argued that this effect was only justified in the short term and that it was of a temporary nature only, since the SEC had not yet finalized its rules for SOX.[1177] Moreover, they stated that for companies, the rewards for listing on the NSYE are higher because foreign companies obtain access to a huge pool of capital.[1178] In 2006 the number of listed German companies on the NSYE was still seventeen.[1179] In contrast, by 2010 only four German companies were listed on the NSYE; Deutsche Bank, Fresenius Medical Care, SAP and Siemens due to the withdrawal from the NSYE by Infineon, Bayer, BASF and E.ON in 2009.[1180] In 2010, Daimler Benz also ended its stock-exchange listing in New York.[1181] According to its statement, the reason was to save administrative expenses and fees. Even the New York Times stated that:

1171 *Id.* § 802, 18 USC §§ 1519, 1520.

1172 *Id.* § 802 (a) (2), 18 USC § 1520.

1173 *See* Shirley (2004), *supra* note 1160 at 511.

1174 *See* Peter Iliev, *The Effect of SOX Section 404: Costs, Earnings Quality, and Stock Prices*, 65 THE JOURNAL OF FINANCE 1163–1196, 1163 (2010).

1175 *See* Shirley (2004), *supra* note 1160 at 511.

1176 *Id.* at 527.

1177 *Id.* at 527.

1178 *See* Hudson Hollister, *Shock Therapy' for Aktiengesellschaften: Can the Sarbanes-Oxley Certification Requirements Transform German Corporate Culture, Practice and Prospects?*, 25 NW. J. INT'L L. & BUS 453, 481 (2005); Shirley (2004), *supra* note 1160 at 528.

1179 *See* WHISTLE BLOWING UND CONCERN-MANAGEMENT: NEUE HERAUSFORDERUNGEN FÜR UNTERNEHMER UND IHRE PRÜFER, 4 (Matthias Wolz ed., 1. ed. 2007).

1180 *See* Mark Pitzke, *Wall Street und Co.: Amerikaner fürchten um ihre Börsenmacht*, SPIEGEL ONLINE, November 22, 2010, http://www.spiegel.de/wirtschaft/unternehmen/wall-street-und-co-amerikaner-fuerchten-um-ihre-boersenmacht-a-729965.html (last visited Feb 3, 2015).

1181 n-tv Nachrichtenfernsehen, *Nicht mehr unter SEC-Fuchtel: Daimler verlässt NYSE*, N-TV.DE, 2010, http://www.n-tv.de/wirtschaft/Daimler-verlaesst-NYSE-article873265.html (last visited Feb 3, 2015).)

> There is no question that the costs of complying with Section 404 of the law – requiring audits of corporate internal controls – has scared executives in the United States and abroad.[1182]

In addition, a study by *Doidge et al.* found that 59 companies dropped their American registration at the NSYE in 2007.[1183] The reason behind this was a change brought about by a new rule, referred to as the Exchange Act Rule 12h-6.[1184] The authors argued that this rule makes it easier for foreign firms to deregister from the NSYE.[1185] The other reasons they put forward were both the new SOX requirements for listed companies, as well as other regulatory developments in the US. Overall, these factors have made it more costly for foreign firms to maintain an US listing.[1186] The authors referred to this phenomenon as the "*loss of competitiveness theory*."[1187] They concluded that the value of a listing became negative for the leaving firms.[1188] However, *Doidge et al.* held that the sample of 59 deregistering firms was small and that there was no reliable evidence that foreign listed firms had suffered from the introduction of SOX.[1189]

In spite of these misgivings, the SOX entered into force and today provides the framework for the SEC's oversight of the securities markets.[1190] To ensure that the intent of the legislation is carried out in specific situations, the SEC is also involved in rule-making.[1191] For example, in 2003, the SEC implemented amendments to Section 404 of the SOX,[1192] which requires that companies periodically carry out test procedures that monitor the internal systems.[1193] The aim of this monitoring is to ensure accurate financial reports. Furthermore, Section 404 mandates that outside auditors have to attest to the findings of management.[1194] Thus, this provision determines the responsibility of management for establishing and maintaining an adequate internal control structure and financial reporting procedures.[1195] Hence,

---

1182 Floyd Norris, *Reasons Some Firms Left the US*, The New York Times, August 7, 2008, http://www.nytimes.com/2008/08/08/business/08norris.html (last visited Feb 3, 2015).

1183 Craig Doidge, George Andrew Karolyi & Rene M. Stulz, Why Do Foreign Firms Leave US Equity Markets? An Analysis of Deregistrations Under SEC Exchange Act Rule 12h-6 1 (2008).

1184 *See* Doidge, Karolyi, and Stulz (2008), *supra* note 1183. *See also* Securities Exchange Act of 1934, *supra* note 605, 17 CFR 240.12h-6.

1185 *Id.* at 1.

1186 *Id.* at 1.

1187 *Id.* at 28.

1188 *Id.* at 28.

1189 *Id.* at 28.

1190 SEC, *supra* note 603.

1191 *Id.*

1192 Securities Act of 1933, *supra* note 600 § 404, 15 USC § 7262.

1193 *See* Iliev (2010), *supra* note 1174 at 1163.

1194 *Id.* at 1163 note 1.

1195 Sarbanes-Oxley Act of 2002, *supra* note 47 § 404 (a) (1), 15 USC § 7262.

the amendments imposed through the SOX created new legal duties for corporate executive officers such as the CEO and CFO and aimed to increase accountability. In 2007, the Senate passed a further amendment to Section 404.[1196] This amendment aimed to reduce uncertainty about the requirements and to limit the burdens placed on small and mid-sized public companies.[1197]

The last stage in the enhancement of the US federal legislation was the amendments to the Federal Sentencing Guidelines for Organizations (FSGO) in 2004 and 2010.[1198] In accordance with Section 805 of the SOX, the United States Sentencing Commission shall review and amend so that the Guidelines that apply to organizations in United States Sentencing Guidelines are sufficient to deter and punish organizational criminal misconduct.[1199] Hence, the first amendment enforced effective compliance programs in organizations by adding an eighth element. It requires that the organization periodically assess the risk of criminal conduct.[1200] The second amendment fostered compliance programs through reporting requirements for the high-level personnel with direct access to the board[1201] and the organizations' appropriate response following criminal conduct.[1202] Therefore, with the 2010 releases, the Commission enhanced the independence of the function of US compliance and ethics officer.[1203] In conclusion, one of the major aims of the FSGO has been to encourage compliance structural change within organizations.[1204]

Notwithstanding the enhancement of the federal law, the next step suggested should be the true engagement and consistent support from the board for the compliance and ethics officers' activities.[1205] The structural compliance goal envisioned by the FSGO might be achieved through governmental support for the compliance and ethics officer function by incentivizing compliance.

In conclusion, over the last thirty years, the American federal law relating to compliance has developed to protect investors in response to corporate bribery and misleading corporate disclosures. In recent years, the landscape of corporate

---

1196 Amendments to rules regarding management's report on internal control over financial reporting. SARBANES-OXLEY ACT OF 2002, *supra* note 47 SEC Release no. 8809.

1197 *See e.g.* Cindy R. Alexander et al., *Economic effects of SOX Section 404 compliance: A corporate insider perspective*, 56 JOURNAL OF ACCOUNTING AND ECONOMICS 267–290 (2013) at 283; Iliev (2010), *supra* note 1174 at 1164.

1198 US SENTENCING GUIDELINES MANUAL USSC, *supra* note 49 § 8 B2.1 (2004), (2010).

1199 SARBANES-OXLEY ACT OF 2002, *supra* note 47 § 805 (a) (5), 28 USC § 994.

1200 US SENTENCING GUIDELINES MANUAL USSC, *supra* note 49 (2004), § 8 B2.1 (c). § 8 B2.1 is called as a model template for a compliance and ethics program.

1201 US SENTENCING GUIDELINES MANUAL *Id.* (2010), § 8 B2.1 (b) (2)(C).

1202 *Id.* (2010), § 8 B2.1 (b) (7).

1203 *See* Greenberg (2012), *supra* note 688 at 8.

1204 *Id.* at 1.

1205 *Id.* at 12.

compliance has begun to change significantly. The increasing influence of government legal resolutions have affected corporate compliance structures and, thus, corporate compliance has become a professionalized discipline in the US. This development has had a huge global impact. Therefore, both listed domestic and foreign firms have had to develop efficient compliance structures too. While the establishment of corporate compliance structures is expensive, it gives firms the opportunity to invest in their reputation to gain credibility among the public, investors, and shareholders. Lastly, the companies that establish a compliance structure are able to obtain benefits and remain competitive.

The next sections will examine the statutes, administrative regulations, and landmark cases relating to the position of compliance officer in the US. The following three sections are structured as follows: The first step analyzes American hard law: the Federal State Law, specifically the Foreign Corrupt Practices Act, the Sarbanes-Oxley Act, and the FSGO. The second step comprises an examination of the impact of the administrative agencies; *e.g.* the DOJ or SEC, and their case law concerning compliance and the compliance officer. The results provide an overview of the American legal framework and the most important provisions in relation to the corporate compliance officers' function, which companies should take into consideration.

1. The Key Provisions of the FCPA

The most relevant statute referring to bribery and corruption is the Foreign Corrupt Practices Act of 1977 (FCPA), which addresses bribery and improper record keeping.[1206] Generally, the Act comprises three main provisions: (1) anti-bribery provisions,[1207] (2) accounting provisions,[1208] and (3) provisions on other related legal issues *e.g.* money laundering, reporting, and tax violations.[1209] Under this Act, it is unlawful for any issuer and their officers, directors, employees, or agents to offer, payment, or promise to pay of payments to a foreign official, political party, or candidate for office in order to influence any act or an official decision.[1210] Hence, the main purpose of the FCPA is to prohibit companies and individuals from corruptly providing, offering, or promising anything of value to foreign government officials to obtain or retain a business advantage.[1211]

Firstly, the purview and definitions of the anti-bribery provisions need to be considered. After a rigorous analysis of the FCPA, the Court of Appeals for the

---

1206 Foreign Corrupt Practices Act 1977 (FCPA), *supra* note 438, 15 USC §§ 78dd-1, et seq.

1207 *Id.*§ 102, 15 USC §§ 78dd-1, 78dd-2, 78dd-3 (2006).

1208 *Id.*§ 102, 15 USC §§ 78m(b)(4)–(5) (2006).

1209 *See* Mark (2012), *supra* note 641 at 427.

1210 Foreign Corrupt Practices Act 1977 (FCPA), *supra* note 438, 15 USC § 78dd–1, (a) (1) -(3).

1211 *See* Mark (2012), *supra* note 641 at 427.

Fifth Circuit stated that the scope for obtaining or retaining business pursuant to the FCPA could be broad.[1212] In its opinion, the Court was required to construe the scope of statute in order to bring a sufficient indictment.[1213] Finally, it held that "*illicit payments to foreign officials*" in order to avoid a significant part of customs duties, sales taxes and retain business *"could (but not necessarily)"* be a bribe and be covered by the scope of the FCPA.[1214] Furthermore, the anti-bribery provisions of the FCPA could apply to all US individuals and foreign issuers of securities.[1215] For example, Section 78dd–3 (a) stipulates:

> It shall be unlawful for any person other than an issuer that is subject to section 78dd-1 of this title or a domestic concern (as defined in section 78dd-2 of this title), or for any officer, director, employee,[ ], while in the territory of the United States, corruptly to make use of the mails or any means or instrumentality of interstate commerce or to do any other act in furtherance of an offer, payment, promise to pay, or authorization of the payment of any money, or offer, gift, promise to give, or authorization of the giving of anything of value to...
>
> (1) any foreign official for purposes of—
>
> (A)(i) influencing any act or decision of such foreign official in his official capacity, (ii) inducing such foreign official to do or omit to do any act in violation of the lawful duty of such official, or (iii) securing any improper advantage; or....

The provisions of the FCPA define the term foreign official as:

> ....any officer or employee of a foreign government or any department, agency, or instrumentality thereof, or of a public international organization, or any person acting in an official capacity for or on behalf of any such government or department, agency, or instrumentality, or for or on behalf of any such public international organization.[1216]

Despite this definition of the term foreign official, a heated debate on this term has emerged among legal scholars.[1217] Further to the legal definition set forth in

---

1212 *See e.g. United States v. Kay*, 513 F.3d 432 (5th Cir. 2007), 440 (2007). In this case the Court of Appeals concluded "*in diametric opposition to the district court, ..."[,] that bribes paid to foreign officials in consideration for unlawful evasion of customs duties and sales taxes could fall within the purview of the FCPA's proscription, ...*"

1213 *See United States v. Kay*, Opinion 56, 2 (2004).

1214 *Id.*

1215 DOJ, *supra* note 673; Richard (2014), *supra* note 554 at 423.

1216 Foreign Corrupt Practices Act 1977 (FCPA), *supra* note 438 § 102, 15 USC § 78dd–3 (f), (2006).

1217 *See e.g.* Golumbic and Adams (2011), *supra* note 1133; Alexander G. Hughes, *Drawing Sensible Borders for the Definition of "Foreign Official" Under the FCPA*, 40

the FCPA, legal scholars discuss various definitions of a foreign official under the FCPA.[1218] *Hughes*, for example, argues that the DOJ considers every employee - regardless of rank or position – to be a foreign official.[1219] Therefore, the scope of these provisions includes not only domestic companies, but also any stockholders, officers, directors, agents of companies, and employees.[1220] Scholars have attempted to clarify the question of precisely who is a foreign official, since in their view there is a lack of *de minimis* exception and consistent judicial definition.[1221] Simultaneously, although there is no consensus among judicial definitions of foreign official, the DOJ appears to apply this term very broadly.[1222]

The nature and scope of the FCPA is that it is both a civil statute and a criminal statute. Furthermore, it is part of the federal securities laws.[1223] Therefore, administrative agencies both the DOJ and the SEC, have enforced authority.[1224] Although the scope of their enforcement powers differ, they often simultaneously pursue FCPA proceedings against the same issuer.[1225] The term issuer is legally defined as *"any person who issues or proposes to issue any security."*[1226] Hence, an issuer is an entity[1227] that is required under the Securities Exchange Act of 1934[1228], to register

---

American Journal of Criminal Law 254–278 (2013); Koehler (2012), *supra* note 958; Richard (2014), *supra* note 554.

1218 *See e.g.* Golumbic and Adams (2011), *supra* note 1133; Hughes (2013), *supra* note 1217.

1219 *See* Hughes (2013), *supra* note 1217 at 15.

1220 *See* Golumbic and Adams (2011), *supra* note 1133 at 15.

1221 *See e.g.* Hughes (2013), *supra* note 1217 at 255; Mark (2012), *supra* note 641 at 28.

1222 *See e.g.* Richard (2014), *supra* note 554 at 424.; Lanny A Breuer & Att'y Gen. DOJ Crim. Div., Prepared Keynote Address to The Tenth Annual Pharmaceutical Regulatory and Compliance Congress and Best Practices Forum (2009), http://www.justice.gov/criminal/pr/speeches-testimony/documents/ll-1209breuer-pharmaspeech.pdf (last visited Oct 3, 2015). *"[ ] under certain circumstances and in certain countries, that nearly every aspect of the approval, manufacture, import, export, pricing, sale and marketing of a drug product in a foreign country will involve a "foreign official" within the meaning of the FCPA."*

1223 Foreign Corrupt Practices Act 1977 (FCPA), *supra* note 438, 15 USC §§ 78m-1, 78dd-1, 78dd-2, 78dd-3, 78 ff (2010).

1224 Department of Justice DOJ, US Department of Justice (2016), http://www.justice.gov/ (last visited Feb 8, 2016); Securities Exchange Commission SEC, *supra* note 604.

1225 *See* Mark (2012), *supra* note 641 at 426–428.

1226 Foreign Corrupt Practices Act 1977 (FCPA), *supra* note 438, 15 USC § 78 (a) (8). In addition, the term person means a natural person, company, government, or political subdivision, agency, or instrumentality of a government. § 78 (a)(9).

1227 *"An entity is often referred to as 'juridical person' in the context of statutes, regulations, and legal texts. Generally, the term includes not only, a corporation, a limited liability company, or no-profit organization." See* in: S.H. Deming, The Foreign Corrupt Practices Act and the New International Norms 74 (2. ed. 2010) n. 49.

1228 Securities Exchange Act of 1934, *supra* note 605, 15 USC §§ 78aff (2010).

under Section 78, or to file reports pursuant to section 78.[1229] In general, publicly traded companies on a national exchange in the United States are issuers.[1230] Therefore, the scope of the FCPA also includes foreign companies listed on the NSYE or NASDAQ. Traditionally, the DOJ handles all criminal actions against entities or individuals while the SEC handles civil actions limited against issuers and individuals such as officers, directors, employees, agents, and shareholders of issuers.[1231] Other civil enforcements, for example violations of the anti-bribery provision of the FCPA are left to the DOJ.[1232] Additionally, other authors point out that the government's broad interpretation of jurisdiction under this Act:

> … includes US companies and their employees, US investors in a non-US entity, foreign subsidiaries of US-based companies, and non-US companies and nationals (non-US persons) who commit an act in furtherance of bribery of a foreign official while in the territory of the United States.[1233]

Hence, the FCPA also applies to non-US citizens and companies who act in the US. Overall, under the FCPA a company who acts in the US, an US citizen, or their agents will be liable to prosecution if they obtain their business by bribery of a governmental official of another country or a publicly traded US company.[1234] Nonetheless, it is striking that it is not a crime for an US company to pay bribes in foreign countries where bribes are not illegal.[1235] Regardless, it has been acknowledged that the local law must provide that bribes are legal.[1236] However, such law has never been found.[1237] In the same way, it has been recognized that *"facilitating*

1229 *See* Deming (2010), *supra* note 1227 at 8; Mark (2012), *supra* note 641 at 427. *See also* Foreign Corrupt Practices Act 1977 (FCPA), *supra* note 438, 15 USC §§ 78m (a) (2) (2010).

1230 *See* Deming (2010), *supra* note 1227 at 8.

1231 *See* Deming (2010), *supra* note 12278 at 75; Mark (2012), *supra* note 641 at 427; Foreign Corrupt Practices Act 1977 (FCPA), *supra* note 438, §§ 78m-1(c)(2)(E), 78dd-1(e)(1), 78dd-2(f)(1) (2010).

1232 *See* Deming (2010), *supra* note 1227 at 75.

1233 *See* Zack Harmon, Confronting the New Challenges of FCPA Compliance: Recent Trends in FCPA Enforcement and Practical Guidance for Meeting These Challenges, in Foreign Corrupt Practices Act compliance issues: leading lawyers on responding to recent FCPA enforcement actions, maintaining an effective compliance program and navigating risk in emerging markets. 62–63 (1. ed. 2010).

1234 *See* M.T. Biegelman *&* D.R. Biegelman, Foreign Corrupt Practices Act Compliance Guidebook: Protecting Your Organization from Bribery and Corruption (1. ed. 2010).

1235 Foreign Corrupt Practices Act 1977 (FCPA), *supra* note 438, 15 USC § 78dd–3 (b)(c), (2010).

1236 *See* Lawrence J. Trautman & Kara Altenbaumer-Price, *The Foreign Corrupt Practices Act: Minefield for Directors*, 6 Virginia Law *&* Business Review, 157 (2011).

1237 *Id.* at 157.

or expediting payments"[1238] like simple expenditure *e.g.* gifts, travel and entertainment expenses, do not fall under the purview of the law.[1239] Additionally, there are options for companies to protect themselves. For example, firms could defend themselves with a compliance program and by including specific clauses in their contracts. In these contract terms, local agents and partners would be required to confirm that they will not violate the law, particularly under the FCPA.[1240] These recommendations with respect to compliance and enforcement of the FCPA are provided to companies of all shapes and sizes in a Resource Guide to the FCPA issued by the DOJ; it does not, however have force of law.[1241]

Secondly, accounting provisions also need to be considered. In fact, the issuers are required to:

> (A)...make and keep books, records, and accounts, which, in reasonable detail, accurately and fairly reflect the transactions and dispositions of the assets of the issuer;
> (B)... devise and maintain a system of internal accounting controls...[1242]

The aim of these provisions is to make accounting more transparent for investors and to expose illegal payments more easily.[1243] It has been stated that these provisions apply only to issuers of securities[1244] registered on US stock exchanges.[1245] Since 1977, the accounting provisions of the FCPA have, however, also applied to certain foreign issuers.[1246] The FCPA Resource Guide also describes issuer as a company with a class of securities registered pursuant to Section 78 of the Exchange Act.[1247] On December 31, 2011, 965 foreign companies were registered under Section 78 of the Exchange Act.[1248] Specifically, the FCPA Guide points out that officers, directors, employees, agents, or stockholders acting on behalf of an issuer or a

1238 Foreign Corrupt Practices Act 1977 (FCPA), *supra* note 438, 15 USC § 78dd–3 (c) (2010).

1239 *See* Richard (2014), *supra* note 554 at 424.

1240 *See* Biegelman and Biegelman (2010), *supra* note 1234.

1241 DOJ *&* SEC, A Resource Guide to the US Foreign Corrupt Practices Act (2012), http://www.sec.gov/spotlight/fcpa.shtml (last visited Feb 5, 2016), [hereinafter FCPA Resource Guide].

1242 Foreign Corrupt Practices Act 1977 (FCPA), *supra* note 438, 15 USC 78m (b) (2)(A)(B) (2012).

1243 *See* Richard (2014), *supra* note 554 at 423.

1244 Foreign Corrupt Practices Act 1977 (FCPA), *supra* note 438, 15 USC § 78m (a) (2012). As defined previously, the term issuers means publicly traded companies.

1245 *See* Richard (2014), *supra* note 554 at 423.

1246 Foreign issuers include both US public companies, as well as foreign companies whose shares trade on US exchanges. *See* in Trautman and Altenbaumer-Price (2011), *supra* note 1236 at 149 note 10.

1247 FCPA Resource Guide DOJ and SEC, *supra* note 1241 at 11; Foreign Corrupt Practices Act 1977 (FCPA), *supra* note 438, 15 USC § 78dd-l.

1248 FCPA Resource Guide DOJ and SEC, *supra* note 1241 at 11.

domestic concern[1249] could also be prosecuted under the FCPA.[1250] Finally, considering the essential conditions of violation the anti-bribery provisions of the FCPA are as follows:[1251]

(a) An individual such an officer, director, employee, agent, or stockholder of an issuer thereof acting on behalf of an issuer or a domestic concern, to make use of the mails or any means or instrumentality of interstate commerce corruptly in furtherance of an offer,[1252]
(b) Willfully,[1253]
(c) Making an offer, payment, promise to pay, or authorization of the payment of any money, or offer, gift,[1254]
(d) To any foreign official, to any foreign political party, or to any person,[1255]
(e) Corruptly,[1256]
(f) For the purpose of influencing any act or decision of such foreign official, political party, or person,[1257]
(g) In order to obtain or retain business.[1258]

Overall, the DOJ must show that the company has knowingly and willfully through its employees and agents violated any provision of the FCPA. Since 1977 the DOJ has determined these conditions in a large number of criminal corporate enforcement actions. The prosecutors investigate and prosecute cases under the FCPA, which are listed in a chronical order available on the DOJ's website. One example is the well-known and largest FCPA settlement by the DOJ with Siemens AG. Siemens is a German corporation organized under German law with its headquarters in Berlin and Munich.[1259] In 2008, Siemens AG pleaded guilty to violations

1249 *Id.* "*The term domestic concern means any individual who is a citizen, national, or resident of the United States; and any corporation, [.], which has its principal place of business in the United States, or which is organized under the laws of a State of the US.*" *See* Foreign Corrupt Practices Act 1977 (FCPA), *supra* note 438, 15 USC § 78dd-2 (h)(1)(A)(B) (2010).
1250 Foreign Corrupt Practices Act 1977 (FCPA), *supra* note 438, 15 USC § 78dd-2 (a),(g) (2010); FCPA Resource Guide DOJ and SEC, *supra* note 1241 at 11.
1251 *See* Deming (2010), *supra* note 1227 at 13.
1252 Foreign Corrupt Practices Act 1977 (FCPA), *supra* note 438, 15 USC § 78dd-2 (a) (2010).
1253 *Id.*15 USC § 78 dd-2 (g)(2)(A) (2010).
1254 *Id.*15 USC § 78 dd-2 (a) (2010).
1255 *Id.*15 USC § 78 dd-2 (a)(1)(2)(3) (2010).
1256 *Id.*15 USC § 78 dd-2 (a) (2010).
1257 *Id.*15 USC § 78 dd-2 (a)(1)(A)(i) (2010).
1258 *Id.*15 USC § 78 dd-2 (a)(1)(B) (2010).
1259 DOJ, *United States v. Siemens Aktiengesellschaft,* (2008), http://www.justice.gov/sites/default/files/criminal-fraud/legacy/2013/05/02/12-15-08siemensakt-plea.pdf (last visited Feb 5, 2016).

of FCPA bookkeeping, records keeping, and internal control requirements and agreed to pay US$ 800 million.[1260] As explained previously, issuers are corporations whose securities are listed on US exchanges. As such, both domestic and foreign issuers are subject to the FCPA.[1261] The accounting provisions exclude only foreign subsidiaries that are not issuers of securities on the US stock exchange.[1262]

Thus, the findings have shown that the legal scope of the FCPA is far-reaching. Hence, US companies and listed foreign companies in the US ought to closely comply with the provisions of the FCPA. The best way of handling the FCPA's statute for the company is to reduce bribery and thus, increase public confidence.[1263] For this purpose, it is necessary for both corporate officers and directors to become experts in the FCPA.[1264] In conclusion, another factor in preventing corporate bribery could be for companies to have an effective anti-corruption compliance program. This compliance program should also consider the anti-corruption law and policies in other countries and generally, reduce improper conduct. In other words, nowadays FCPA expertise and compliance are inextricably linked.[1265] For this reason, the next section will examine affirmative corporate defenses provided by the FCPA and its Guidance.

a. The Hallmarks of an Effective Corporate Compliance Program

This section will outline the legal consequences that follow for companies guilty of violating provisions of the FCPA. Then, it will examine which requirements specified by the DOJ and SEC are likely to be relevant for a company's compliance procedures and structure as a preventive measure to tackle bribery and misconduct. These measures are referred to as the hallmarks of an effective corporate compliance program.

The FCPA itself provides two corporate affirmative defenses: first, the payment is legal in the foreign official's home country and second, it is a facilitating or expediting payments expense.[1266] However, the FCPA provides different criminal, civil penalties and collateral consequences for companies and individuals for violations of its rules. For example, corporations could be subject to a fine of up to US$ 2 million for each violation of the anti-bribery provisions of the FCPA.[1267] Moreover,

---

1260 *See* Trautman and Altenbaumer-Price (2011), *supra* note 1236 at 164.
1261 *Id.* at 150.
1262 *Id.* at 152.
1263 *See* Koehler (2012), *supra* note 958 at 609.
1264 *See* Trautman and Altenbaumer-Price (2011), *supra* note 1236 at 180.
1265 *Id.* at 180.
1266 Foreign Corrupt Practices Act 1977 (FCPA), *supra* note 438, 15 USC § 78dd–3 (c) (1) (2).
1267 Foreign Corrupt Practices Act 1977 (FCPA), *supra* note 438, 15 USC §§ 78dd-2(g) (1)(A), 78dd-3(e)(1)(A), 78 ff(c)(1)(A); FCPA Resource Guide DOJ and SEC, *supra* note 1241 at 68.

pursuant to Sections 78dd-2(g)(2)(A), 78dd-3(e)(2)(A), 78 ff(c)(2)(A) individuals, including officers, directors, stockholders, and agents of companies could be subject to a fine of up to US$ 250,000 and imprisonment of up to five years.[1268] As discussed above, the DOJ has the authority to pursue criminal actions and civil action against foreign nationals and companies for violations of the FCPA,[1269] while the SEC may pursue civil actions against issuers and their officers, directors, employees, agents, or stockholders for violations of the anti-bribery and accounting provisions.[1270] In addition to criminal, civil penalties or imprisonment pursuant to the FCPA, individuals and companies may also face collateral consequences, including suspension from contracting with the federal government, or exclusion from certain export privileges.[1271] Thus, the legal consequences for individuals and companies could be considerable. Overall, the penalties and consequences outlined above demonstrate that companies are under tremendous pressure to deter illegal behavior such as bribery or falsification of records.

Secondly, as a result, the FCPA Guide provides helpful information for companies of all sizes.[1272] However, the recommendations set forth in the Guide are non-binding. The FCPA Guide outlines the hallmarks of an effective corporate compliance program in detail.[1273] Simultaneously, the DOJ and SEC admit that there is no *"one-size-fits-all program."*[1274] The DOJ itself acknowledges that

> ...no compliance program can ever prevent all criminal activity by a corporation's employees..."[1275]

In other words, a *"check-the-box"* approach may be inefficient because each compliance program should be targeted specifically to a company's size, specific needs, risks, and challenges.[1276] The Guide recommends ten principles for a robust and enforced compliance program.[1277] Nevertheless, the compliance function is considered

---

1268 Foreign Corrupt Practices Act 1977 (FCPA), *supra* note 438, 15 USC §§ 78dd-2(g)(2)(A), 78dd-3(e)(2)(A), 78 ff(c)(2)(A); FCPA Resource Guide DOJ and SEC, *supra* note 1241 at 68.

1269 *See e.g.* DOJ, *United States & SEC v. KPMG Siddharta & Harsono, et al.,* No. 01-cv-3105 (2001). The company paid bribes to Indonesian government official and violated Sections 15 USC §§ 78 dd-1 (a); 15 USC §§ 78m (b) (2) (A); 15 USC §§ 78m (b) (2) (B).

1270 FCPA Resource Guide DOJ and SEC, *supra* note 1241 at 69.

1271 FCPA Resource Guide *Id.* at 69–70.

1272 FCPA Resource Guide *Id.* Foreword.

1273 FCPA Resource Guide *Id.* at 52 et seq.

1274 FCPA Resource Guide *Id.* at 56 et seq.

1275 DOJ, Principles of Federal Prosecution of Business Organizations | [hereinafter US Attorneys' Manual], http://www.justice.gov/sites/default/files/opa/legacy/2008/08/28/corp-charging-guidelines.pdf (last visited Feb 5, 2016).

1276 FCPA Resource Guide DOJ and SEC, *supra* note 1241 at 56.

1277 FCPA Resource Guide *Id.* at 56–62.

in Chapter 7 of the Guide, which features a list of anonymized cases of companies prosecuted by the DOJ and SEC.[1278] For example, in case two, the DOJ and SEC declined to take enforcement actions against a public US company because

> The company reorganized its compliance department, appointed a new compliance officer dedicated to anti-corruption, improved the training and compliance program, and undertook a review of all of the company's international third-party relationships.[1279]

The example cases cited in the Guide focus on two main tasks of a compliance officer relating to the FCPA provisions (1) to abide by anti-corruption law and (2) to carry out due diligence on vetting distributors, suppliers and local partners.[1280] It is difficult to see how a FCPA compliance program should work with regard to the prevention of bribery. For this reason, corporations should also consider the DOJ's Principles of Prosecution of Business Organizations, which are found in the US Attorneys' Manual.[1281] For example, companies should think about the general principle that the prosecutors apply the same factors when charging a company as when prosecuting individuals.[1282] In the course of an investigation, the DOJ and SEC will consider the following factors (1) the nature and seriousness of the offense, (2) the degree of pervasiveness of the misconduct, (3) the history of the company, (4) the prompt processing and voluntary disclosure of wrongdoing, and (5) the existence and effectiveness of the corporation's pre-existing compliance program.[1283] The SEC and DOJ confirm that the general principles of corporate liability apply also in the event of FCPA violation by an individual, acting within the scope of their employment.[1284] In the event of misconduct by an employee, it will assume a lack of managerial oversight. One aspect of failure of oversight could be that the directors and executive officers' due diligence was incomplete.[1285] Thus, the idea of a rogue employee is often rejected.[1286] For this reason, it is vital that companies ensure that they have appropriate compliance procedures in place.

1278 FCPA Resource Guide *Id.* at 77–78.
1279 FCPA Resource Guide *Id.* at 78.
1280 FCPA Resource Guide *Id.* at 63–64.
1281 US Attorneys' Manual DOJ, *supra* note 1275 Title 9, 9-28.000.
1282 US Attorneys' Manual *Id.* Title 9, 9-28.300 - Factors to Be Considered.
1283 US Attorneys' Manual *Id.* 9-28.300.
1284 FCPA Resource Guide DOJ and SEC, *supra* note 1241 at 27.
1285 FCPA Resource Guide *Id.* at 65.
1286 The law enforcement agencies do not recognize this theory; but sometimes they do not reject this theory in some cases. *See* American Bar Association Section of Antitrust Law, Antitrust Compliance: Perspectives and Resources for Corporate Counselors 33 (2005).

However, the Manual points out that the prosecutors will evaluate the effectiveness of a compliance program in terms of whether it is designed for maximum effectiveness in order to prevent and detect misconduct and whether the management of the company enforces this program.[1287] Nevertheless, the US courts have held that a corporate compliance program does not absolve the corporation from criminal liability. For example in *United States v. Potter* the Court stated that "*the case law has rejected arguments that the corporation can avoid liability by adopting abstract rules.*"[1288] Under the doctrine of respondeat superior a company can be held liable for the illegal acts of its directors, officers, employees, and agents.[1289] As discussed previously,[1290] the US government and US courts[1291] do not agree with arguments based on a rogue executives theory.[1292] In general, the conduct

---

1287 US Attorneys' Manual DOJ, *supra* note 1275, 9-28.800.

1288 *United States v. Potter* 463 F.3d 9, 25 (1st Cir. 2006); US Attorneys' Manual *Id* 9-28.800.

1289 *Respondeat superior* (Latin: "let the master answer) *"is a legal doctrine, which states that, in many circumstances, an employer is responsible for the actions of employees performed within the course of their employment. The common-law doctrine of 'respondeat superior was established in 17th century in England to define the legal liability of an employer for the actions of an employee. The doctrine was adopted in the United States and has been a fixture of agency law. The legal relationship between an employer and an employee is called agency. A principle of agency law which holds that a principal (or employer) is vicariously liable (also known as derivative liability) for the torts of his agent (or employee) which occur during the course of the agent's (or employee's) actions on behalf of the principal (or employer). The employer is called the principal when engaging someone to act for him. The person who does the work for the employer is called the agent. The theory behind respondeat superior is that the principal controls the agent's behavior and must then assume some responsibility for the agent's actions."* *See* Respondeat Superior Definition, Duhaime's Law Dictionary, http://www.duhaime.org/LegalDictionary/R/Respondeatsuperior.aspx (last visited Feb 6, 2016); Wolfram Müller-Freienfels, Agency Theory Encyclopedia Britannica, http://www.britannica.com/topic/agency-law (last visited Feb 6, 2016). *See also United States v. Potter* 463 F.3d 9 (1st Cir. 2006), *supra* note 1288 at 26. "*The principal is held liable for acts done on his account by a general agent, which are incidental to or customarily a part of a transaction, which the agent has been authorized to perform. And this is the case, even though it is established fact that the act was forbidden by the principal.*"

1290 *See supra* A., p. 175.

1291 *See e.g. United States v. Ionia Management, S.A.* 537 F. Supp.2d 321 (D. Conn. 2008), (2008)., The Second Circuit Court of Appeals shooting down attempts to change the way corporations are held liable for the criminal acts of their employees. The respondeat superior doctrine has a great impact on enforcement of the Foreign Corrupt Practices Act against corporations. *See also* Richard L. Cassin, Naked Corporate Defendants | The FCPA Blog The FCPA Blog (2009), http://www.fcpablog.com/blog/2009/1/22/naked-corporate-defendants.html#sthash.ZPktNvPJ.dpuf (last visited Feb 6, 2016).

1292 *See* Murphy (2001), *supra* note 563 at 25.

of employees that appears in conjunction with his work will usually be considered to be within the scope of employment.[1293] Contrary to the civil law system, corporations are legal persons, capable of suing and being sued, and capable of committing crimes.[1294] Hence, the established approach is that the company is liable if officers are involved in wrongdoing, regardless of how well the compliance program and the compliance officer work.[1295]

In contrast, more recently the DOJ has implemented a number of new policies,[1296] for example those introduced by Deputy Attorney General Sally Yates,[1297] to focus on efforts to secure evidence against individuals responsible for corporate wrongdoing. The new approach suggests six key steps to strengthen the DOJ's pursuit of individual corporate wrongdoing.[1298] *Yates* explains this approach in a speech following the announcement of the new policies that cooperation credit now comprises *"all or nothing,"* and there is *"[n]o more partial credit for cooperation that doesn't include information about individuals."*[1299] Legal scholars have taken these words to represent a new direction in governmental policy.[1300] In practice, it remains to be seen how the DOJ will identify and prosecute criminal behavior by employees.

One limitation of the evaluation of an effective corporate compliance program is that the DOJ has no specifically formulated requirements with regard to such programs.[1301] One recommendation is that the directors of the corporation should carry out an independent review and supervision by means of internal audit functions.[1302] The most important question is whether the compliance program is

1293 Respondeat superior Definition, *supra* footnote 1289, p. 192.

1294 US Attorneys Manual DOJ, *supra* note 1275, 9-28.200.

1295 *See* Murphy (2001), *supra* note 563 at 25.

1296 John F. Savarese, DOJ Adopts New Requirements for Corporations Seeking Credit for Cooperation Harvard Law School Forum on Corporate Governance and Financial Regulation (2015), https://corpgov.law.harvard.edu/2015/09/14/doj-adopts-new-requirements-for-corporations-seeking-credit-for-cooperation/ (last visited Feb 6, 2016).

1297 Deputy Attorney General Yates & DOJ, Memorandum for Assistant Attorney General | Individual Accountability for Corporate Wrongdoing (2015), http://www.wlrk.com/docs/IndividualAccountabilityforCorporateWrongdoing.pdf (last visited Feb 6, 2016).

1298 *Id.* at 2. For example, the first step (1) *"In order to qualify for any cooperation credit, corporations must provide to the Department all relevant facts relating to the individuals responsible for the misconduct,[...]"*

1299 *See e.g.* Memorandum Yates and DOJ, *supra* note 1297; Savarese, *supra* note 1296.

1300 *See e.g.* Savarese, supra note 1296.

1301 US Attorneys' Manual DOJ, *supra* note 1275, 9-28.800.

1302 US Attorneys' Manual *Id.*9-28.800; *in re Caremark International Inc. Derivative Litigation*, 698 A.2d 959 (Del. Ch. 1996), supra note 21 at 968–70.

merely a "*paper program*" or whether it is designed, implemented, and reviewed in an effective manner.[1303] With respect to this question, the Principles of Federal Prosecution of Business Organizations refer to Chapter 8 for factors determining an effective corporate compliance program.[1304] Nevertheless, the FCPA has no legal obligation to consider these factors when deciding whether a prosecuted company will benefit from its commitment to compliance and any pre-existing compliance program.[1305]

A further aspect could be that the DOJ or SEC take into consideration the compliance program as a preventing or mitigating factor. Actually, there is no consensus in the DOJ on these considerations. A number of authors[1306] agree that the DOJ may consider a compliance program as a potential mitigating factor when prosecuting, but the Department is under no obligation to do this. In addition, the FCPA Guide itself points out that

> In appropriate circumstances, DOJ and SEC may decline to pursue charges against a company based on the company's effective compliance program, or may otherwise seek to reward a company for its program, even when that program did not prevent the particular underlying FCPA violation that gave rise to the investigation.[1307]

The SEC and DOJ argue that their Guidance includes the basic elements of a compliance program, which the government will evaluate and seek to reward in the case of a FCPA violation.[1308] These elements comprise the following hallmarks of an effective compliance program (1) commitment from senior management, (2) code of conduct, (3) oversight, autonomy, and resources, (4) risk assessment, (5) training and advice, (6) incentives and disciplinary measures, and (7) third-party due diligence and payments.[1309] In fact, the FCPA Guide contains general characteristics and features of an effective compliance program but does not define the term effectiveness. In the event of an investigation, both the SEC and DOJ will consider these elements of a corporate compliance program when deciding what action to take against the prosecuted company.[1310]

1303 US Attorneys' Manual DOJ *Id.* 9-28.800.

1304 US Sentencing Guidelines USSC, *supra* note 667 § 8 B2.1; US Attorneys' Manual *Id.* at 7, 9-28.800.

1305 *See e.g.* Miriam H. Baer, *Organizational Liability and the Tension between Corporate and Criminal Law*, 19 Journal of Law and Policy 1–14, 8 (2011); Koehler (2012), *supra* note 958 at 616.

1306 *See e.g.* Beale (2014), *supra* note 1097; Stucke (2014), *supra* note 1157.

1307 FCPA Resource Guide DOJ and SEC, *supra* note 1241 at 56.

1308 FCPA Resource Guide *Id.* at 56–60.

1309 FCPA Resource Guide *Id.* at 56–60.

1310 FCPA Resource Guide *Id.* at 56.

In addition, in 2003, in the THOMSON MEMO, the Deputy Attorney General of the DOJ outlined nine *"factors to be considered"* when the DOJ is determining whether to charge a corporation.[1311] The fifth factor that was pointed out is *"the existence and adequacy of the corporation's compliance program."*[1312] That means a corporate compliance program should be

> established by corporate management to prevent and to detect misconduct and to ensure that corporate activities are conducted in accordance with all applicable criminal and civil laws, regulations, and rules.[1313]

Finally, the program has to be implemented and enforced carefully and seriously to ensure that the company could be enabled to prevent violations, discover those that do occur, and combat them appropriately.[1314] The question is thus if the compliance program works appropriately.[1315]

b. Compliance Reforms through N/DPA Agreements?

In addition to financial penalties and custodial sentences pursuant to the FCPA, the Criminal Division of the Justice Department's deals with and resolves cases through deferred prosecution (DPA) or non-prosecution agreements (NPA).[1316] A DPA is filed with the court, while an NPA is filed by the parties without formal charges.[1317] If the company agrees to obey the governmental demands, such as

---

1311 Deputy Attorney General Thompson & DOJ, THOMPSON MEMO | PRINCIPLES OF FEDERAL PROSECUTION OF BUSINESS ORGANIZATION (2003), http://federalevidence.com/pdf/Corp_Prosec/Thompson_Memo_1-20-03.pdf (last visited Feb 8, 2016).

1312 THOMPSON MEMO *Id.* at 3. II.

1313 THOMPSON MEMO *Id.* at 7. VII. General Principle.

1314 FCPA RESOURCE GUIDE DOJ AND SEC, *supra* note 1241 at 57.

1315 *"The answer is that the prosecutor should consider the comprehensiveness of the compliance program; the extent and pervasiveness of the criminal conduct; the number and level of the corporate employees involved; the seriousness, duration, and frequency of the misconduct; and any remedial actions taken by the corporation, including restitution, disciplinary action, and revisions to corporate compliance programs." See* THOMPSEN MEMO, *supra* note 1311 at 8. VII.

1316 *"N/DPAs are contractual arrangements between the government and corporations that allow the government to impose sanctions against the respective company and set up institutional changes in exchange for the government's agreement to forego further investigation and corporate criminal indictment." See* June Rhee, THE EFFECT OF DEFERRED AND NON-PROSECUTION AGREEMENTS ON CORPORATE GOVERNANCE HARVARD LAW SCHOOL FORUM ON CORPORATE GOVERNANCE AND FINANCIAL REGULATION (2014), https://corpgov.law.harvard.edu/2014/09/23/the-effect-of-deferred-and-non-prosecution-agreements-on-corporate-governance/ (last visited Feb 8, 2016).

1317 *See* DEMING (2010), *supra* note 1227 at 79.

restitution and structural changes, it could avoid criminal indictment and an costly trial.[1318] The most commonly cited reason for N/DPAs in the US is the negative effects brought about by the disintegration of the auditing and consulting firm Arthur Andersen.[1319]

However, in the US, these agreements by the federal prosecutors are the subject of heated debate since they are decided not by judges or the legislature.[1320] Despite the objections, however, the authors point out that the N/DPAs provide for the creation of compliance reforms through the enhancement of corporate internal investigation, while avoiding costly litigation.[1321] Irrespective of the political debate on the legitimacy of the N/DPAs, there is little consensus among scholars that these agreements have led to changes in governance of leading public corporations and entire industries.[1322] A study by *Kaal & Lacine* underlined this development from 1993 to 2013.[1323] They found that the DOJ and SEC have broadly expanded their traditional role by the D/NPAs.[1324] Thus, the DOJ and SEC shifted in their prosecutorial approach to an ex-ante consideration of compliance.[1325] The authors gathered their results by coding all publicly available N/DPAs [N=271] and by evaluating the impact of N/DPAs on corporate governance structures.[1326] Their results showed that 97.41 percent [N=264] of these public N/DPAs contained mandated changes of corporate governance structures within these companies in the following areas: (1) business changes, (2) board changes, (3) senior management changes, (4) monitoring, (5) cooperation, (6) compliance program.[1327]

Another empirical study by *Garrett* examined the terms in N/DPAs from 2003 to 2007, which showed an increasing trend toward compliance features and revealed the imposition of deep structural corporate reforms.[1328] *Garrett* coded terms from thirty-five deferred and non-prosecution agreements, derived from

---

1318 *See* Wulf A. Kaal & Timothy Lacine, *The Effect of Deferred and Non-Prosecution Agreements on Corporate Governance: Evidence from 1993–2013*, 70 The Business Lawyer 1–60, 3 (2014).

1319 *See Arthur Andersen LLP v. United States*, 544 US 696 (2005). *"In 2002, the firm surrendered its licenses to practice as Certified Public Accountants in the United States after being found guilty of criminal charges with a loss substantial loss of firm value and 28,000 jobs." See* Kaal and Lacine (2014), *supra* note 1318 at 10.

1320 *See* Kaal and Lacine (2014), *supra* note 1318 at 1.

1321 *Id.* at 4.

1322 *See e.g.* Golumbic and Adams (2011), *supra* note 1133; Koehler (2012), *supra* note 958; Trautman and Altenbaumer-Price (2011), *supra* note 1236.

1323 *See* Kaal and Lacine (2014), *supra* note 1318.

1324 *Id.* at 2.

1325 *Id.* at 2.

1326 *Id.* at 8.

1327 *Id.* at 9.

1328 *See* Brandon L. Garrett, *Structural Reform Prosecution*, 93 Virginia Law Review 853–957 (2007).

federal organizational prosecutions und identified twenty-four ordered compliance programs (69 percent).[1329] He found that in ten of the non-examined eleven agreements, the corporation had already implemented a compliance program.[1330] For example, in 2005, the DOJ provided a deferred prosecution agreement for radical structural change at KPMG. Ultimately, KPMG agreed to

> ...implement and maintain an effective compliance and ethics program, to install an independent, government-appointed monitor who will oversee KPMG's compliance with the deferred prosecution agreement for a three-year period...[1331]

Apparently, the DOJ follows the guidelines of the THOMPSON MEMO in emphasizing compliance.[1332] However, only in one of the coded N/DPAs by *Garrett*, did the DOJ require the creation of a position of chief compliance officer.[1333] Overall, legal scholars consider the prosecutors' approach as the most important development in changes of corporate structures and the federal and corporate law in recent years.[1334] *Garrett* criticizes that structural reform by prosecutors creates both benefits and problems that are unique to the role of prosecutors in the US federal system.[1335] His main criticism is that, on the one hand, there could be a lack of legal remedy and a lack of discretion on the part of prosecutorial exercises.[1336] On the other hand, the enforcement by the prosecutors could constrain the courts.[1337] Notwithstanding academic criticism and skepticism leveled at this approach, the prosecutorial focus on compliance looks set to continue to increase.

In conclusion, although there is a political debate on the legal power of the prosecutors' D/NPAs, corporate compliance programs have emerged and been adopted through requirements enforced by both the DOJ and the SEC in the US. This approach led to structural corporate changes within the prosecuted companies. Additionally, the DOJ Principles of Federal Prosecution of Business Organizations, set forth in Chapter 9 of the US ATTORNEYS' MANUAL,[1338] and the THOMPSON MEMO provide recommendations for *"the existence and effectiveness of*

1329 *Id.* at 894–895. Table 1.

1330 *Id.* at 895.

1331 *See* DOJ, KPMG TO PAY $456 MILLION FOR CRIMINAL VIOLATIONS IN RELATION TO LARGEST-EVER TAX SHELTER FRAUD CASE (2005), http://www.justice.gov/archive/opa/pr/2005/August/05_ag_433.html (last visited Feb 8, 2016).

1332 *See* Garrett (2007), *supra* note 1328 at 896.

1333 *Id.* at 952. University of Medicine and Dentistry of New Jersey, (December 2005).

1334 *Id.* at 937.

1335 *Id.* at 913.

1336 *Id.* at 913.

1337 *Id.* at 913.

1338 U.S. ATTORNEYS' MANUAL Mark Filip & Deputy Attorney General DOJ, PRINCIPLES OF FEDERAL PROSECUTION OF BUSINESS ORGANIZATIONS (2008), http://www.justice.gov/sites/default/files/dag/legacy/2008/11/03/dag-memo-08282008.pdf (last visited Feb 10, 2016); THOMPSON MEMO Thompson and DOJ, *supra* note 1311.

the corporation's pre-existing compliance program." However, domestic and foreign corporations, defined as issuers listed on the US stock exchanges should take account of the findings above in order to help prevent bribery and misconduct. These companies should be aware that in the event of an investigation, the prosecutors have the authority to define and require the framework of a compliance program in the D/NPAs. However, it has been noted that the corporate compliance function is not explicitly required. Hence, the FCPA Resource Guide and the DOJ Principles do not take account of the nature and role of the compliance function.

c. FCPA Settlements Review Related to the Compliance Function

In according with the findings in the section above, this section will examine a number of examples of FCPA Settlements to establish whether there are any requirements as to the effectiveness of the compliance program relating to the compliance function within companies. Under the legal mandate of the FCPA, the DOJ and SEC have struggled to enforce the federal law.[1339] A study on international trends in the fight against bribery and corruption by *Cleveland et al.* found that the DOJ initiated only 16 prosecutions between 1977 and 1995.[1340] Within this period, the US was the only country to have such provisions in force against bribery.[1341] However, recent trends and patterns in FPCA enforcement have shown that there has been an extraordinary increase in both DOJ and SEC actions since 1998.[1342] The authors found that the number of SEC and DOJ enforcement actions rose to 37 in 2007.[1343] The largest fine imposed on a company was US$ 1.6 billion, which Siemens AG[1344] was required to pay in 2008.[1345] Hence, the study confirmed the growing trend toward prosecution enforcement.

In recent years, the DOJ and SEC prosecutions led to high-profile settlements including AIG, America Online, Boeing, Bristol-Myers Squibb Co., Computer Associates, HealthSouth, KPMG, MCI, and Merrill Lynch & Co.[1346] However, these

1339 Foreign Corrupt Practices and Domestic and Foreign Investment Improved Disclosure Acts of 1977, *supra* note 1132, 15 USC §§ 78d, 78dd-2 (e).

1340 *See* Margot Cleveland et al., *Trends in the International Fight Against Bribery and Corruption*, 90 Journal of Business Ethics 199–244, 205 (2009).

1341 *Id.* at 205.

1342 *Id.* at 210.

1343 *Id.* at 211. Table IV.

1344 SEC, SEC Files Settled Foreign Corrupt Practices Act Charges Against Siemens AG for Engaging in Worldwide Bribery With Total Disgorgement and Criminal Fines of Over $1.6 Billion (2008), https://www.sec.gov/litigation/litreleases/2008/lr20829.htm (last visited Feb 8, 2016).

1345 *See* Cleveland et al (2009), *supra* note 1340 at 211 Table IV.

1346 *See* Garrett (2007), *supra* note 1328 at 853.

FCPA Settlements have already been examined by *Garrett*.[1347] To further examine the requirements and structural changes in terms of the compliance function, this examination gathered publicly available N/DPAs for the period from 2010 until 2015. Initially, the keyword *"compliance officer"* was searched in order to code the N/DPAs across the DOJ website.[1348] After coding, a number of agreements were identified, particularly those involving banking organizations like JP Morgan, HSBC, BNP or private companies like Genzyme Corp., Transocean Inc. and Monsanto in which organizations agreed to enhanced compliance obligations including the compliance function. This section explores four of these in detail below.

The first DOJ agreement which will be examine is the DPA of HSBC Holdings Plc., a UK corporation headquartered in London and in the US.[1349] From 2001 through 2006, the HSBC Bank USA repeatedly told the senior compliance officers at HSBC Group that the use of cover payments constituted illegal payment transactions made through the US financial system.[1350] Hence, the HSBC Group violated the IEEPA[1351] by failing to maintain an effective anti-money laundering program. The bank was prosecuted by the Criminal Division of the DOJ. HSBC, agreed to enhance its compliance structures in 2012.[1352] The DPA requires that the HSBC replace almost all of its senior management and compliance officers within a five-year period and has to implement structural changes across its entire global operations.[1353]

In January 2005, the Monsanto company, a Delaware corporation, accepted and acknowledged violations of the FCPA provisions, having falsified books and records.[1354] The company entered into a DPA with the Criminal Division of the DOJ, which provides the framework for an effective FCPA compliance program.[1355]

1347 *See* Garrett (2007), *supra* note 1328.

1348 *See* DOJ, US Department of Justice (2016), http://www.justice.gov/ (last visited Feb 8, 2016).

1349 Office of Public Affairs DOJ, HSBC Holdings Plc. and HSBC Bank USA N.A. Admit to Anti-Money Laundering and Sanctions Violations, Forfeit $1.256 Billion in Deferred Prosecution Agreement | OPA | Department of Justice (2012), http://www.justice.gov/opa/pr/hsbc-holdings-plc-and-hsbc-bank-usa-na-admit-anti-money-laundering-and-sanctions-violations (last visited Feb 9, 2016).

1350 *Id.*

1351 International Emergency Economic Powers Act | IEEPA, 50 US Code §§ 1701–1708 (1977). *"If the President declares a national emergency, he may be exercised to deal with any unusual and extraordinary threat and can regulate commerce."*

1352 HSBC DPA, DOJ, *supra* note 1349.

1353 *Id.*

1354 Foreign Corrupt Practices Act 1977 (FCPA), *See supra* note 438, 15 USC § 78dd-I; § 78m(b)(2) & (5).

1355 DOJ, United States v. Monsanto Company Deferred Prosecution Agreement (2005), http://www.justice.gov/sites/default/files/criminal-fraud/legacy/2011/02/16/01-06-05monsanto-agree.pdf (last visited Feb 9, 2016).

In Appendix B, Monsanto agreed to improve its existing compliance program. This compliance program is required to comprise, at a minimum *e.g.* the following components:

1. A clearly articulated corporate policy against violations of the Foreign Corrupt Practices Act and other applicable anti-bribery law.
2. The assignment to one or more senior Monsanto corporate officials of responsibility for oversight of compliance with policies, standards, and procedures. Such officials shall have the authority and responsibility to implement and utilize monitoring and auditing systems.[1356]

Monsanto already had a compliance program in place, but was required to extend it further, as well as to perform a risk assessment throughout its internal compliance structures.[1357] According to this agreement, Monsanto is required to carry out detailed audits of the books and records of each operating unit, audits of selected agents, consultants, contractors, sub-contractors, and joint ventures, and interviews with relevant employees, consultant, agents, contractors, subcontractors, and joint venture partners.[1358] In addition, the company was ordered to periodically conduct rigorous FCPA audits of its operations.[1359] Furthermore, an independent compliance expert is required to certify the policies and procedures, monitor the implementation of compliance and report his findings to Monsanto's corporate compliance officer.[1360]

The third DPA examined was settled by the US Department of Justice with the Genzyme Corporation, an American biotechnology company, which was acquired by the Sanofi Group in 2011. Both agreed to the terms set forth in Attachment B in order to enhance compliance measures and continue to maintain compliance policies and procedures.[1361] This Attachment specifically states the enhancement and maintaining of a compliance program, including the tasks and scope of authority of the compliance function and policies and procedures on the following subjects: *e.g.* sales compensation and incentives, off-label promotion, etc.[1362]

> Besides the requirements of maintaining an Sanofi compliance program, the firm has established a compliance committee which is met al least quarterly, and a Sanofi **compliance officer**. The compliance committee has to ensure the effectiveness of all components of the Sanofi compliance program. The Sanofi **compliance officer** has to report to the Global compliance officer of the parent company. He is responsible

1356 United States v. Monsanto DPA *Id.* Appendix B.
1357 United States v. Monsanto DPA *Id.* at 6.
1358 United States v. Monsanto DPA *Id.* Appendix B.
1359 United States v. Monsanto DPA *Id.* Appendix B.
1360 United States v. Monsanto DPA *Id.* at 7.
1361 DOJ, Genzyme Corporation | DPA Attachment B (2015), http://www.justice.gov/opa/file/767296/download (last visited Feb 9, 2016).
1362 Genzyme Corporation DPA, *Id.* at 2.

> for overseeing the administration and implementation of the Compliance program and has direct access to the senior executives with the authority to direct and implement necessarily compliance changes in the organization. Moreover, he has also the authority to assess compliance-related matters and to seek advice from independent legal counsel and outside experts. In addition, the compliance officer is authorized to report any issues of any kind directly to officers and directors of Sanofi.[1363]

Furthermore, the board of directors[1364] is required to review the effectiveness of the compliance program related to sales, marketing and promotion. This review must include reports and updates by the compliance officer and other personnel with regard to compliance matters.[1365] Lastly, the board of directors has to submit to the US government a *"board resolution"* including a written explanation that Sanofi has implemented an effective compliance program pursuant to the United States Sentencing Guidelines Manual,[1366] and as set forth in this Attachment B.[1367]

The fourth DPA that was examined is an agreement between the DOJ and the Transocean Inc.,[1368] a large offshore drilling contractor headquartered in Switzerland that rents floating mobile drill rigs together with the equipment and personnel required for operations. The firm acknowledged having violated the provisions of the FCPA[1369] and accepted a DPA that comprises relevant considerations with regard to a compliance program over a period of three years.[1370]

> The subsidiary of Transocean Ltd. has to consider about hiring a new chief compliance officer with a substantial expertise in corporate ethics and anti-corruption compliance policies and the compliance officer of Transocean Ltd. is responsible for the oversight of compliance for Transocean Ltd. and all of its subsidiaries.[1371]

1363 Genzyme Corporation DPA, *Id.* at 2.

1364 *"The board of directors is responsible for governing a corporation." See* Miller (2014), *supra* note 595 at 27; tit. 8 Delaware Code, *supra* note 24, § 141 (a) (b). *"The business and affairs of every corporation shall be managed by or under the board of directors." "The board of directors of a corporation shall consist of one or more members, each of whom shall be a natural person. The number of directors shall be fixed by, or in the manner provided in, the bylaws." See also* Miller (2014), *supra* note 595 at 31. *"The board members are appointed for a term of office, which is also defined in the bylaws of the company. Usually, all members of the board are elected annually."*

1365 Genzyme Corporation DPA, DOJ, supra note 1361 at 10.

1366 US Sentencing Guidelines Manual USSC, *supra* note 49 Chapter 8.

1367 Genzyme Corporation DPA, DOJ, supra note 1361 at 10.

1368 DOJ, United States v. Transocean Inc. | DPA (2010), http://www.justice.gov/sites/default/files/criminal-fraud/legacy/2011/02/16/11-04-10transocean-dpa.pdf (last visited Feb 9, 2016).

1369 Foreign Corrupt Practices Act 1977 (FCPA) *see supra* note 438,15 USC § 78dd-l and § 78m.

1370 United States v. Transocean Inc., DOJ, supra note 1368

1371 United States v. Transocean Inc., *Id.* at 7.

In Attachment C to this DPA, the Transocean Inc. agreed to conduct a corporate compliance program in order to address any deficiencies in compliance with the FCPA.[1372] The company is required to adopt a rigorous, clearly formulated, and visible anti-corruption compliance code, and to develop, review, and promulgate compliance standards at all levels of the company.[1373] In addition, the company has to assign responsibility to one or more senior executives for the implementation, communication, training, and oversight of these standards.[1374] Furthermore, the company is required to establish an effective training system for guidance and advising agents, business partners and officers and directors on complying with compliance standards and policies and ensure disciplinary procedures to address violations of the anti-corruption law.[1375] Moreover, the company was ordered to include standard provisions to prevent violations of anti-corruption law in agreements, contracts, and renewals with all agents and business partners. Lastly, in Attachment D the Transocean Inc. agreed to a periodic review and to report to the DOJ in terms of the Attachment C.[1376]

The review of the small sample of settlements between the DOJ and the four companies reveals a huge shift in the internal corporate structure and in the business operations on the one hand, as well as rigorous and far-reaching staffing changes on the other. For example, the prosecutor even demanded that the company had to replace the compliance function or the board of directors or to appoint a new compliance officer.[1377] Hence, these contractual agreements, which are sometimes referred to as a pretrial diversion method, influence the internal corporate structure, human resources, the relationship to business partners, the contracts and the core business of the corporation.[1378] In sum, the prosecuted domestic and foreign corporations listed in the US not only have to abide by the anti-corruption law (FCPA) but also with the requirements set forth in the governmental contractual agreements such as DPAs. Therefore, all companies listed on the US exchanges

---

1372 United States v. Transocean Inc., *Id.* Attachment C (C1–C7).
1373 United States v. Transocean Inc., *Id.* Attachment C (C1–C7).
1374 United States v. Transocean Inc., *Id.* Attachment C (C1–C7).
1375 United States v. Transocean Inc., *Id.* Attachment C (C1–C7).
1376 United States v. Transocean Inc., *Id.* Attachment D (D1–D2).
1377 *See e.g.* HSBC DPA DOJ, *supra* note 1349; United States v. Monsanto DPA DOJ, *supra* note 1355; United States v. Transocean Inc. DOJ, *supra* note 1368.
1378 *"It is a method to avoid an expensive trial. Diversion, any of a variety of programs that implement strategies seeking to avoid the formal processing of an offender by the criminal justice system. Although those strategies, referred to collectively as diversion, take many forms, a typical diversion program results in a person who has been accused of a crime being directed into a treatment or care program as an alternative to criminal prosecution and imprisonment." See* Carrie A. Weise-Pengelly, diversion | criminal justice system Encyclopedia Britannica (2015), http://www.britannica.com/topic/diversion (last visited Feb 9, 2016).

should seriously design and implement an effective working compliance program in accordance with Chapter 8 and appoint a compliance officer who is in charge of continuously supervising and controlling this program, employees and contract partners.[1379] As discussed previously, an effective existing compliance program and a present compliance function with a defined purview of tasks and periodic reporting lines to the board of directors is unlikely to completely avoid all misconduct of directors, officers, employees, business partner, and agents. However, these structures required by the prosecutor would contribute to limiting criminal conduct, to prompt disclosures and responses to misconduct, which is reflected as credit for sentencing and hence, can help to avoid financial risks for companies. The changes to corporate structures made by US prosecutors will be explored in terms of the 2008 FCPA Siemens AG case in the next section.[1380]

d. The FCPA Siemens AG Case and the Huge Changes of Corporate Structures

Among the FCPA cases against companies, the Siemens case played a significant role in the history of the FCPA.[1381] Siemens, a German engineering company with over 400,000 employees operates in 191 countries.[1382] In 2001, Siemens was listed on the New York Stock Exchange and was an issuer pursuant to the FCPA provisions.[1383] As a publicly traded corporation, it was registered pursuant to Section 78 of the Securities Exchanges Act 1934.[1384] In 2008, it was alleged that Siemens had been engaged in a pattern of bribery *"unprecedented in scale and geographic reach."*[1385] Siemens was guilty as an issuer of making illegal payments to foreign government officials in exchange for business and for inaccurate internal

1379 US Sentencing Guidelines Manual, USSC, *supra* note 49.

1380 *United States v Siemens AG* (2008), 08-CR-367-RJL.

1381 *See e.g.* JGC Corporation (Japan) $218.8 million in 2011, BAE (UK): $400 million in 2010, KBR / Halliburton (USA): $579 million in 2009, Alstom (France): $772 million in 2014. *See* Richard L. Cassin, Our Top Ten List didn't change in 2015 (but here's when it did change) The FCPA Blog (2016), http://www.fcpablog.com/blog/2016/1/5/our-top-ten-list-didnt-change-in-2015-but-heres-when-it-did.html (last visited Feb 15, 2016).

1382 DOJ, Sentencing Memorandum | Siemens Sentencing Memo 1 (2008), http://www.justice.gov/sites/default/files/opa/legacy/2008/12/19/siemens-sentencing-memo.pdf (last visited Feb 15, 2016).

1383 Foreign Corrupt Practices Act 1977 (FCPA), *supra* note 438, 15 USC § 78-c (a) (8).

1384 Securities Exchange Act of 1934, *supra* note 605, 15 USC § 78l.

1385 DOJ, Siemens AG and Three Subsidiaries Plead Guilty to Foreign Corrupt Practices Act Violations and Agree to Pay $450 Million in Combined Criminal Fines (2008), http://www.justice.gov/archive/opa/pr/2008/December/08-crm-1105.html (last visited Feb 15, 2016); Koehler (2012), *supra* note 958 at 612.

controls, books, and records.[1386] As early as 2006, investigations began into possible bribery of foreign public officials and falsification of corporate books and records. Since then, Siemens' entire corporate structure-compliance, legal, internal audit, corporate finance, and business units have come under the scrutiny of US prosecutors. Furthermore, the role of the management board[1387] and supervisory board[1388], known as a "*two-tier system*" of the board structure, were also the subject of comprehensive investigations.[1389] Siemens' new compliance function was established in 2001. The corporate compliance officer worked part-time and was staffed with two lawyers.[1390] In 2004, a corporate compliance office based in Erlangen and Munich was set up.[1391] Until 2006, several lawyers were responsible for compliance issues while regional compliance officers, as employees with other full-time responsibilities, were responsible for compliance within the regional groups.[1392] These individuals received minimal training or direction in terms of compliance issues.[1393] Despite Siemens having both an audit committee, responsible for the supervision of accounting and risk management, and a compliance program, the company failed to comply with the anti-corruption legislation.[1394] The investigation revealed, for instance, that several Siemens AG subsidiaries made significant "*kickback payments*" to the Iraqi government.[1395] Overall, the evidence showed that Siemens was engaged in a systematic effort to bribe and to falsify its books and records from 1995 to 2007.[1396] Ultimately, the DOJ was able to prosecute Siemens for the misconduct of its managers under respondeat superior theory.[1397]

In this case, it was clear that the reasons for the failure to comply with the law were attributable to significant control weaknesses. It transpired in the course of the DOJ investigations that the Siemens compliance program existed on paper

1386 Foreign Corrupt Practices Act 1977 (FCPA), *supra* note 438, 15 USC §§ 78m(b)(2), 78(b)(5), and 78 ff(a).

1387 Known in Germany as the "Vorstand". According to the German Stock Corporation Act (AktG) German stock corporations boards are consist of a so named "*two-tier system*", the management board and the supervisory board.

1388 "*The highest-level board within Siemens AG, the supervisory board, was composed of twenty members, ten of whom were elected by the shareholders and ten of whom were elected by the employees. It has the authority to appoint and remove members of the management board." See United States v Siemens AG* (2008), *supra* note 1380 at 3.

1389 Siemens Sentencing Memo DOJ, *supra* note 1382 at 2.

1390 *United States v Siemens AG* (2008), *supra* note 1380 at 12.

1391 *United States v Siemens AG* (2008) *Id.* at 4.

1392 *United States v Siemens AG* (2008) *Id.* at 5.

1393 *United States v Siemens AG* (2008) *Id.* at 5.

1394 *United States v Siemens AG* (2008) *Id.*

1395 Siemens Sentencing Memo DOJ, *supra* note 1382 at 3. *See also* the German case BGH, 29.8.2008 - 2 StR 587/07, NStZ 2009, 95, *supra* note 958.

1396 Siemens Sentencing Memo DOJ, *supra* note 1382 at 4.

1397 US Attorneys' Manual Filip and DOJ, *supra* note 1322; Koehler (2012), *supra* note 958 at 615; Respondeat Superior Definition, *supra* note 1289.

only.[1398] There was also a lack of effectiveness on the part of the regional compliance officers. For example, they reported to Siemens that there were no business consulting agreements with other regions and that no potential violations were visible.[1399] As a rule, the regional compliance officers are required to sign off on consulting agreements and attach a due diligence questionnaire as part of the process.[1400] Although a lack of effectiveness of this process by regional compliance officers was reported, there was no search for missing documents.[1401]

Prior to the investigations, in 2005, Siemens additionally compared its compliance resources and structure with that of General Electric Company (GE). The benchmarking analysis found that the Siemens compliance office team was extremely understaffed in proportion to the numbers of employees.[1402] The analysis furthermore showed that the GE program was more efficient than Siemens in diffusing compliance principles.[1403] Despite these findings, Siemens took no action to enhance its compliance structure and to improve the quality of the regional compliance officer until the opening of the US investigation. Siemens finally agreed to plead guilty to (1) having knowingly failed to implement sufficient anti-bribery compliance policies and procedures, (2) having knowingly failed to discipline employees involved in making illegal payments, and (3) having failed to establish a competent corporate compliance office.[1404]

Moreover, in its statement of offense, Siemens agreed to maintain an ethics and compliance program that comprises the minimum elements set forth in Attachment 1.[1405] These minimum elements include *e.g.* a clearly articulated corporate policy against violations of the FCPA, promulgation of compliance standards and procedures, one or more senior corporate officials of Siemens AG to be responsible for the implementation and oversight of compliance with direct access to the Audit Committee or the Supervisory Board of Siemens AG, periodic training for all directors, officers, employees, and business partners, an effective system to report criminal conduct, due diligence to oversee business partners and standard provisions in contracts with all agents and business partners.[1406] Moreover,

---

1398 *United States v Siemens AG* (2008), *supra* note 1380 at 19.

1399 *United States v Siemens AG* (2008) *Id.* at 20.

1400 *United States v Siemens AG* (2008) *Id.* at 20.

1401 *United States v Siemens AG* (2008) *Id.* at 20.

1402 *United States v Siemens AG* (2008) *Id.* at 19.

1403 *United States v Siemens AG* (2008) *Id.* at 20.

1404 Criminal Division DOJ & United States Attorney's Office, United States v. Siemens Aktiengesellschaft | Plea Agreement 15th December 2008 36 (2008), http://www.justice.gov/sites/default/files/criminal-fraud/legacy/2013/05/02/12-15-08siemensakt-plea.pdf (last visited Feb 15, 2016).

1405 United States v. Siemens Aktiengesellschaft | Statement of Offense, 40 (2008) Attachment 1.

1406 United States v. Siemens Aktiengesellschaft | Statement of Offense *Id.* at 40–42. Attachment 1.

Siemens agreed to a four-year independent program monitoring by the DOJ in order to review the effectiveness of its internal controls and ongoing compliance with the anti-corruption laws.[1407]

Since then, Siemens' compliance structures have been radically reorganized and a revamped compliance system put into place over a period of two years.[1408] In the course of 2007, the members of the management board were replaced.[1409] At that time, there were more than 500 compliance employees working full time worldwide at Siemens.[1410] Until 2010, a chief compliance officer was responsible for all compliance matters and reported directly to the general counsel and the chief executive officer.[1411] Siemens also implemented new compliance policies, for example, a new business partner policy including web-based tools for compliance matters, a compliance helpdesk, and a confidential communications channel for employees to report misconduct.[1412] A new compliance audit function was also established to review implementation of the compliance system while an anti-corruption toolkit improved financial controls.[1413] In addition, since 2007, over 300,000 employees worldwide received compliance training.[1414] Finally, today the Siemens compliance system is designed to systematically evaluate and improve continuously its process.[1415]

In conclusion, the Siemens FCPA case by the DOJ provides strong evidence that the prosecution agreements lead not only to a settlement with huge fines, but also to radical changes in the corporate structure. Siemens has enforced its internal controls with a strengthened role for the compliance personnel, the implementation of new compliance structures, tools, trainings, and review processes for business partners. The described examples of dealing with a corporate investigation by administrative agencies and prosecutors above have shown that N/DPA agreements will continue to change the internal corporate structure, to enhance compliance issues and strengthen the corporate compliance function.

1407 United States v. Siemens Aktiengesellschaft | Statement of Offense, *Id.* Attachment 2.

1408 *See e.g.* Koehler (2012), *supra* note 958 at 613; Klaus Moosmayer & Josef Winter, The Siemens Compliance System: "Prevent – Detect – Respond and Continuous Improvement" 3 (2011).

1409 *See* Moosmayer and Winter (2011), *supra* note 1408 at 4.

1410 *See* Koehler (2012), *supra* note 958 at 613; Klaus Moosmayer, *„Die Neuausrichtung heißt Compliance Ownership Culture"*, compliance-manager.net, December 12, 2014, http://www.compliance-manager.net/fachartikel/die-neuausrichtung-heisst-compliance-ownership-culture-1534 (Ger) (last visited Feb 15, 2016).

1411 *See* Moosmayer and Winter (2011), *supra* note 1408 at 5.

1412 *See* Koehler (2012), *supra* note 958 at 613.

1413 *Id.* at 614.

1414 *See* Moosmayer and Winter (2011), *supra* note 1408 at 9.

1415 *Id.* at 14.

e. The Changing FCPA Enforcement Policy of the DOJ

As discussed previously, the DOJ is charting a new direction as far as its policy on individual liability in matters of corporate wrongdoing is concerned.[1416] This includes new principles and a new approach seeking accountability from the individuals who perpetrated the wrongdoing. This new tendency was outlined for DOJ prosecutors.[1417] *Yates* cites the deterrent effect for future illegal activities, the enhancement of corporate behavior, the identification of the responsible individual and the promotion of public confidence in the US justice system as the reasons behind this approach.[1418] In her MEMO, she states six specific steps to holding individual corporate wrongdoers accountable. Additionally, the DOJ will revise several of the guidance documents, including the US Attorneys' Manual and the principles of federal prosecution of business organizations.[1419] In her remarks at New York University School of Law, Yates claims: *"The rules have just changed."*[1420] In practice that means *"...if a company wants any credit for cooperation, any credit at all, it must identify all individuals involved in the wrongdoing ..."* and *"It's all or nothing."*[1421] Moreover, she announces that this new threshold requirement does not mean that the DOJ will wait for the company to deliver information on individual wrongdoers.[1422] In contrast, ... *"the department attorneys will be actively investigating individuals at every step of the process."*[1423] Her final note on this point was a call for all defense lawyers to be actively involved in discussions with the DOJ concerning the scope of what is required.[1424] The shift from corporate liability to individual liability in the DOJ approach may be the result of a recent study, which gathered data from records of the DOJ and federal courts.[1425] The study found that more than 1.6 million defendants were criminally prosecuted between 2004 and

1416 Deputy Attorneys' Gen. Yates & DOJ, DEPUTY ATTORNEY GENERAL SALLY QUILLIAN YATES DELIVERS REMARKS AT NEW YORK UNIVERSITY SCHOOL OF LAW ANNOUNCING NEW POLICY ON INDIVIDUAL LIABILITY IN MATTERS OF CORPORATE WRONGDOING | OPA | DEPARTMENT OF JUSTICE (2015), http://www.justice.gov/opa/speech/deputy-attorney-general-sally-quillian-yates-delivers-remarks-new-york-university-school (last visited Feb 9, 2016). *See supra* I., 1.a., p. 193.

1417 MEMORANDUM Yates and DOJ, *supra* note 1297 at 1.

1418 MEMORANDUM Yates *Id.* at 1.

1419 REMARKS Yates and DOJ, *supra* note 1416.

1420 REMARKS Yates *Id.*

1421 REMARKS Yates *Id.*

1422 REMARKS Yates *Id.*

1423 REMARKS Yates *Id.*

1424 REMARKS Yates *Id.*

1425 DOJ, JUSTICE DEPARTMENT DATA REVEAL 29 PERCENT DROP IN CRIMINAL PROSECUTIONS OF CORPORATIONS (2015), http://trac.syr.edu/tracreports/crim/406/ (last visited Feb 9, 2016).

2014.[1426] By means of illustration, 99.8 percent of these prosecutions were aimed at individuals; only two tenths, or one in 500, involved companies.[1427]

The American academic debate views the new policy direction of the DOJ as a short-term political move.[1428] The focus on individual corporate agents is discussed critically. Some authors compare this direction with the peculiar analogy of the *"street crime enforcement model."*[1429] They argue that those informants are *"notoriously unreliable"* and the DOJ might have underestimated the complexity of misconduct and decision-making in daily corporate practice.[1430] They explain that the informants can identify only people whom they know and that there is the risk of focusing on people whom they dislike.[1431] In addition, they concluded that the new DOJ policy would not actually provide the prosecutor the desired information on high-level officials.[1432] Finally, other authors argue that the federal prosecutors' investigations have the potential to become either more resource intensive, or much longer, involving the building of multiple cases against both corporations and individuals.[1433]

In September 2015, simultaneous with *Yates'* announcement, Volkswagen AG, a German car manufacturer, was forced to admit responsibility for using software designed to manipulate the light-duty test results in vehicles in real-world-conditions.[1434] This marked the beginning of a criminal investigation by the DOJ against VW, since the Clean Air Act (CAA)[1435] gives the federal regulator Environmental Protection Agency (EPA)[1436] the power to fine VW for a possible

1426 *Id.*

1427 *Id.* fig. 3.

1428 *See* Elizabeth E. Joh & Thomas Wuil Joo, *The Corporation as Snitch: The New DOJ Guidelines on Prosecuting White Collar Crime*, 101 Virginia Law Review 51–59, 52 (2015).

1429 *Id.* at 54.

1430 *Id.* at 55.

1431 *Id.* at 58.

1432 *Id.* at 59.

1433 Daniel P. Chung, Individual Accountability for Corporate Wrongdoing Harvard Law School Forum on Corporate Governance and Financial Regulation (2015), https://corpgov.law.harvard.edu/2015/09/21/individual-accountability-for-corporate-wrongdoing/#more-71670 (last visited Feb 9, 2016).

1434 Bill Vlasic & Aaron M. Kessler, *It Took E.P.A. Pressure to Get VW to Admit Fault*, The New York Times, September 21, 2015, http://www.nytimes.com/2015/09/22/business/it-took-epa-pressure-to-get-vw-to-admit-fault.html (last visited Feb 9, 2016).

1435 This Act (CAA) is the comprehensive federal law that regulates air emissions from stationary and mobile sources. This law authorizes the EPA to establish National Ambient Air Quality Standards. The EPA works with its federal, state regulatory partners to monitor and ensure compliance with clean air laws and regulations in order to protect human health and the environment. *See* Clean Air Act (1963), *supra* note 625.

1436 EPA, *supra* note 338.

total fine of US$ 18 billion[1437] pursuant to Sections 204 and 205 of the Clean Air Act (CAA).[1438] In the wake of the announcement of the manipulated software, VW CEO resigned from his position on the board.[1439] American legal scholars[1440] noted that this scandal could be the first major test of the DOJ's recently announced guidelines[1441] focusing on individual accountability in white-collar criminal investigations. In 2017, Volkswagen AG pleaded guilty to violating the Clean Air Act (CAA) and has been ordered to pay US$4.3 billion, the statutory maximum fine, in criminal and civil penalties.[1442] In addition, six German executives and employees have been indicted in connection with conspiracy to cheat US emissions tests. They are named in a public press release published on the DOJ website.[1443]

Another aspect of the complexity of misconduct could arise from corporate practice. The majority of the agreements between the DOJ and corporations were signed by CEOs, other board members or the general counsel of the company. Thus, these persons are highly likely to simply accuse lower-level employees of offences. In addition, in practice, corporations have already identified individual corporate misconduct through internal investigations. As a result, these employees are likely to have had their contracts terminated or to have been disciplined in internal investigations. However, the complex legal issue of whether a corporation can be held liable for the acts of its agents remains.[1444]

The impact this new approach will have on compliance programs and how it will involve the compliance function is uncertain. The pressure on the compliance function to promptly report individual misconduct to the prosecutor and the board of director may increase. This would require the compliance officer to weigh the relevance of information. Furthermore, it is important for compliance officers to identify the responsibilities of each individual in the company and the relevant business to identify where risks are most likely to appear. In addition, corporations will have to select appropriate personnel more carefully and review their daily business in more detail. In conclusion, the new DOJ policy will enforce corporate

1437 Vlasic and Kessler, *supra* note 1434; *United States v. Volkswagen AG, Audi AG*, Civil Action No. 16-CR-20394, https://www.justice.gov/usao-edmi/page/file/930026/download (last visited Feb 2, 2017).

1438 Clean Air Act (1963), *supra* note 625, 42 USC §§ 7523 and 7524, §§ 204, 205.

1439 Winterkorn legt Amt als Audi-Aufsichtsratschef nieder, Welt Online, November 12, 2015, http://www.welt.de/wirtschaft/article148751371/Winterkorn-legt-Amt-als-Audi-Aufsichtsratschef-nieder.html (last visited Feb 9, 2016) (Ger).

1440 *See e.g.* Joh and Joo, *supra* note 1428.

1441 Memorandum Yates and DOJ, *supra* note 1297.

1442 *See United States v. Volkswagen AG, Audi AG, supra* note 1437.

1443 *See* DOJ, DOJ Release | Press Release Number: 17-037 Department of Justice (201AD), https://www.justice.gov/opa/pr/volkswagen-ag-agrees-plead-guilty-and-pay-43-billion-criminal-and-civil-penalties-six (last visited Jul 2, 2017).

1444 *See e.g.* Joh and Joo, *supra* note 1428 at 55; *See also United States v. Potter* 463 F.3d 9 (1st Cir. 2006), *supra* note 1288; Respondeat superior Definition, *supra* note 1289.

compliance programs and strengthen the compliance function by means of periodic reporting, review, evaluation, and monitoring.

In October 2017, the DOJ reviewed and revised a number of its corporate enforcement policies, including the Yates Memo. Thereafter, a new FCPA Corporate Enforcement Policy was announced, which reflected the DOJ's practice in criminal and civil cases.[1445] These policy changes encompass *e.g.* releasing individuals from civil liability when resolving civil corporate cases and giving companies "*credit for voluntary self-disclosure, full cooperation, and timely and appropriate remediation in FCPA matters.*"[1446] According to that approach, the DOJ will provide additional credits to companies based on their corporate behavior. A recent non-prosecution agreement between the DOJ and Fresenius Medical Care AG & Co. KGaA states that the department will not criminally prosecute the company for any crimes under the FCPA (except for criminal tax violations) based *inter alia* on its voluntary disclosure credit and the company received partial credit for its cooperation with the DOJ investigation.[1447] This case demonstrates the DOJ's application of its new policy. It is also interesting to note that in Attachment B and C Fresenius is also required to agree with the adoption of a new or modification of existing internal controls, compliance code, policies, and procedure and to an independent compliance monitorship.[1448] It remains to be seen how the DOJ will continue its FCPA enforcement policy.

f. Conclusion - The Compliance Officer's Work under FCPA

The following section summarizes the findings of the FCPA law and its enforcement through the DOJ with regard to the compliance function and the shaping of this role within companies. This section therefore highlights the compliance officer's work under the FCPA.

The Foreign Corrupt Practices Act (1977) is now well-established US law, which must be observed by both US corporations and foreign issuers listed on the US Stock exchanges.[1449] The consequences of non-compliance with the FCPA

1445 Justice Manual (JM), § 9–47.120 – FCPA Corporate Enforcement Policy – "*The JM was previously known as the United States Attorneys' Manual (USAM). It was comprehensively revised and renamed in 2018.*" *See* DOJ, Justice Manual (2018), https://www.justice.gov/jm/justice-manual (last visited Apr 8, 2019).

1446 Justice Manual *Id.* at 1

1447 Criminal Division DOJ, Fresenius Medical Care AG & Co. KGAA | NPA (2019), https://www.justice.gov/criminal-fraud/fcpa/cases/fresenius-medical-care-ag-co (last visited Apr 8, 2019).

1448 Fresenius Medical Care AG & Co. KGAA | NPA, *Id.* Attachments B (B-1) and C (C-1) at 36 et seq.

1449 Foreign Corrupt Practices Act 1977 (FCPA), *supra* note 438, 15 USC § 78dd-1, §§ 78m(b)(2)(A) and (B).

law are far-reaching and can prove costly. For example, the FCPA Blog[1450] shows and provides a ranking of the top ten FCPA cases involving financial penalties.[1451] Only two of the companies penalized are US corporations.[1452] *Cassin* identified six reasons why foreign issuers, non-US firms, dominate this list:[1453] First, the DOJ stated that these companies did not have an effective anti-bribery compliance program. Second, they use bribery to operate in global business. Third, these companies are not aware of FCPA compliance requirements. Fourth, they do not cooperate with the DOJ in full. Fifth, the countries of origin of these companies have a weak enforcement record. However, when senior executives are responsible for the misconduct, their country is more likely to appear on the list. This applies to both US and non-US firms.[1454] Overall, these reasons show that misconduct occurs around the globe and that many companies still underestimate the risk of non-compliance with the applicable legal rules.

Apparently, the DOJ might consider the existence of an effective compliance program as a mitigating factor.[1455] However, the DOJ opposes a *formal* or *de facto* compliance defense.[1456] The compliance program has to be effective in stopping bribery. However, it is difficult to see how a FCPA compliance program should work effectively in order not to be evaluated as a purely paper compliance program.[1457] Nevertheless, it has been mentioned that the DOJ *de facto* recognizes a compliance defense through its N/DPA settlement agreements. The company has to demonstrate its efforts to tailor its own FCPA compliance policies and procedures.[1458] For example, in the DPA during the Monsanto investigation, the DOJ required an effective element of the compliance program by *"using objective measures"* to identify high-risk countries or regions in which Monsanto periodically does business.[1459] In the Agreement with the Genzyme/Sanofi Corporation, the DOJ stated that the board should confirm that Sanofi US has implemented an effective compliance

---

1450 The FCPA Blog founded by Richard L. Cassin, a publisher and editor founder. He was a senior partner in a major international law firm and the head of its Asia practice. *See* Richard L. Cassin - The FCPA Blog The FCPA Blog, http://www.fcpablog.com/richard-l-cassin/ (last visited Feb 16, 2016).

1451 *See* Cassin, *supra* note 1381.

1452 *Id.* KBR / Halliburton (US) $579 million in 2009, Alcoa (US) $384 million in 2014.

1453 *See* Richard L. Cassin, From Alstom: Six reasons why non-US companies dominate the FCPA top ten list - The FCPA Blog - The FCPA Blog The FCPA Blog (2015), http://www.fcpablog.com/blog/2015/1/5/from-alstom-six-reasons-why-non-us-companies-dominate-the-fc.html (last visited Feb 15, 2016).

1454 *Id.*

1455 U.S. Attorneys' Manual Mark Filip & Deputy Attorney General DOJ, Principles of Federal Prosecution of Business Organizations (2008), *supra* note 1338.

1456 *See* Koehler (2012), *supra* note 958 at 645.

1457 *Id.* at 646.

1458 *Id.* at 649; *See supra* p. 228

1459 Monsanto Company DPA, *supra* note 1331 at 6 no. 12.

program, as defined in the United States Sentencing Commission Guidelines Manual, Chapter 8.[1460] Having surveyed the five DPAs, the following seven minimum elements of a compliance program were identified, which in general should include:[1461]

(1) a rigorous anti-corruption compliance code and clearly articulated and visible corporate internal policies to deter bribery,
(2) develop and promulgate compliance standards and procedures for all directors, officers, employees, agents and business partners which include an effective system for reporting suspected criminal conduct,
(3) periodic internal control and monitoring of these compliance standards,
(4) the assignment of one or more senior corporate executives of the company who is responsible for the implementation and oversight of the compliance standards with direct reporting access to the board,
(5) periodic trainings and provide guidance for all directors, officers, employees, agents and business partners,
(6) appropriate documented risk-based due diligence and compliance requirements and oversight of all agents and business partners,
(7) include standard provisions in agreements, contracts, and renewals with all agents and business partners to prevent violations of the anti-corruption laws.[1462]

As has been noted, the fourth element relates to the compliance function. Additionally, in the DPA Attachment B of the Genzyme/Sanofi Corporation, the DOJ pointed out that the compliance officer should have direct access to the board with the authority to implement compliance changes within the company as necessary.[1463] He also has the authority to obtain independent advice in compliance issues from external experts.[1464] The compliance officer must report his activities and the effectiveness of the compliance program to the board.[1465] The findings of these agreements show that the requirements of the compliance program and compliance officer function are similar and make reference to the elements of an effective

1460 Genzyme Corporation | DPA DOJ, *supra* note 1345 at 10 Attachment B; U.S. Sentencing Guideline Manual USSC, *supra* note 625.

1461 Genzyme Corporation | DPA DOJ, *supra* note 1345; HSBC Holdings Plc. and HSBC Bank USA N.A. DOJ, *supra* note 1333; Monsanto Company | DPA DOJ, *supra* note 1339; Transocean Inc. | DPA DOJ, *supra* note 1352; United States v. Siemens Aktiengesellschaft | Statement of Offense, *supra* note 1405.

1462 Genzyme Corporation | DPA DOJ, *supra* note 1345; HSBC NA DOJ, *supra* note 1333; United States v. Monsanto DPA DOJ, *supra* note 1355; United States v Transocean DPA DOJ, *supra* note 1352; United States v. Siemens Aktiengesellschaft | Statement of Offense, *supra* note 1405.

1463 Genzyme Corporation | DPA DOJ, *supra* note 1382 at 2. Attachment B.

1464 Genzyme Corporation | DPA *Id.* at 2. Attachment B.

1465 Genzyme Corporation | DPA *Id.* at 10. Attachment B.

compliance program set forth in Chapter 8 of the US Sentencing Guidelines Manual.[1466]

Overall, there are three key incentives and aspects for US corporations and foreign issuers listed on the US Stock exchanges to establish FCPA compliance policies and procedures. First, the DOJ will consider "*the existence and effectiveness of the corporation's pre-existing compliance program*" as a mitigating factor in the course of investigations.[1467] Second, the corporations ought to follow the recommended hallmarks of a corporate compliance program, which the FCPA Guide states in Chapter 5.[1468] Lastly, the effectiveness of a compliance and ethics program should be adapted in line with the requirements in Chapter 8, § B2.1.[1469] *Table 3* on the next page summarizes the most important FCPA recommendations relating to corporate compliance and the compliance function.

In addition, the compliance officer and the general counsel must ensure that every international contract includes clear FCPA terms. These terms are non-negotiable.[1470] Furthermore, the compliance staff needs to be aware of requirements and restrictions of the FCPA provisions. The compliance officer must communicate and train the management and every employee on FCPA standards, policies, and processes.[1471] In other words, the company should appoint a compliance officer who should conduct a risk assessment and guide the management, employees, and business partners on FCPA standards.[1472] *Klehm & Roseman* emphasize the fact that a compliance officers benefits from having a written job description that describes his scope of authority in terms of compliance issues.[1473] Finally, the compliance officer needs to get to ensure that the compliance program works in practice.

1466 US Sentencing Guidelines Manual USSC, *supra* note 49 Chapter 8, § B2.1.
1467 US Attorneys' Manual DOJ, *supra* note 1275, Title 9, 28.300.
1468 FCPA Resource Guide DOJ and SEC, *supra* note 1241 at 56–60.
1469 US Sentencing Guidelines Manual *Id.* Chapter 8, § B2.1.
1470 *See* Stephen Clayton, Top Ten Basics of Foreign Corrupt Practices Act Compliance for the Small Legal Department ACC | Association of Corporate Counsel (2011), http://www.acc.com/legalresources/publications/topten/SLD-FCPA-Compliance.cfm (last visited Feb 16, 2016).
1471 *See* Jones Day | Ten Questions Henry Klehm & Joshua S. Roseman, Jones Day | Ten Questions Every Director Should Ask About FCPA Compliance Jones Day Publications (2010), http://www.jonesday.com/ten_questions/ (last visited Feb 16, 2016).
1472 *See* Anti-Corruption Ethics and Compliance Handbook Oecd, Unodc *&* World Bank, Anti-Corruption Ethics and Compliance Handbook for Business 74, https://www.unodc.org/documents/corruption/Publications/2013/Anti-CorruptionEthicsComplianceHandbook.pdf (last visited Feb 16, 2016).
1473 *See* Jones Day | Ten Questions Klehm and Roseman, *supra* note 1472.

Table 3 *FCPA Recommendations for Issuers with Respect to Compliance and the Compliance Function*[1474]

Sources	Compliance Program	Compliance Function
FCPA Resource Guide, DOJ and SEC, Ch. 5	Hallmarks of an effective compliance program,	Example cases:
	Existence and effectiveness of a pre-existing compliance program as a mitigating factor, ex-ante considerations.	Identify and assess bribery risk of business within the company,
		Due diligence to oversee business partners.
		Design and review contracts that incorporate FCPA and anticorruption terms.
Principles of Prosecution of Business Organizations	Existence and adequacy of an effective compliance program,	New approach
• **US Attorneys' Manual (2003)**	Refers to Ch. 8, § 8 B2.1	Individual Accountability for Corporate Wrongdoing,
• **Thompson Memo (2008)**		Identify the compliance responsibilities within the company,
• **Yates Memo (2015), Six key steps**		Weigh the relevance of information,
• **FCPA Enforcement Policy**		Promptly report misconduct to the board and to the prosecutors.
• **JM since (2018)**		
N/DPAs impact on corporate structures	Changes in the corporate governance structure:	Changes in the personnel structure:
	Clearly articulated anti-bribery policy or code,	Replacement of senior management, or CCO,
	Establish a Compliance Committee	Appointment of senior executives for oversight of compliance, or CCO,
	Implement and maintain a compliance program pursuant to Ch. 8, § 8 B2.1,	Establish reporting structure, CCO should have direct access to the CEO, or to the board,

1474 Table 3 summarizes the findings accordingly to *supra* I., 1.a.-d., pp. 173 et seq.

Table 3 *Continued*

Sources	Compliance Program	Compliance Function
	Periodic reviews and audits.	CCO responsible for implementing, communication, training on FCPA standards and compliance program,
		To ensure disciplinary procedures,
		Independent compliance expert to certify the policy and compliance procedure.

In conclusion, the findings above have shown that the FCPA legislation with its emphasis on anti-bribery, trends in enforcement and penalties, has wakened many companies to the need to implement and maintain effective compliance programs.[1475] It has been established that the main tasks and duties of compliance officers under the FCPA provisions comprise (1) identifying and assessing bribery risk of business within the company, (2) identifying and evaluating bribery risk of business of third-party relationships, (3) improving the training on standards, and (4) implementing, maintaining, and improving the compliance system, (5) overseeing the periodic review process on the compliance program. Under the FCPA agreements, the compliance officers have the authority and are under an obligation to report compliance activities and matters directly to the board and to implement compliance changes within the company as necessary. Legislation such the FCPA and its application by administrative agencies have made the compliance function necessary to manage and maintain the compliance programs within companies.[1476] Therefore, it can be stated that the FCPA has strengthened the role and nature of the compliance officer.

2. The Sarbanes-Oxley Act

This part introduces the second wave of US federal legislation at the beginning of the 21st century. Furthermore, it examines whether the second wave by means of the Sarbanes-Oxley Act (SOX), has strengthened the importance of the compliance function in the US. Therefore, it also aims to clarify the relevant definitions and provisions of this Act[1477] with regard to compliance and the compliance officer, and its impacts on domestic and foreign companies, public companies,[1478] which

1475 *See* Cleveland et al. (2009), *supra* note 1340 at 223.

1476 *See* Freeman (2007), *supra* note 57 at 357.

1477 Sarbanes-Oxley Act of 2002, *supra* note 47.

1478 *"A public company is a company that has issued securities through an initial public offering (IPO) and is traded at one stock exchange. Public companies are highly*

list securities on the US Stock exchanges.[1479] Among other traditional securities regulations,[1480] the SOX seeks to increase and to recover the confidence of investors in the US capital market.[1481] The Sarbanes-Oxley Act is Federal Public Law and, thus, mandatory.[1482] All listed companies must comply. The legislation introduced major changes to the regulation of financial accounting practice and corporate governance.[1483] As has been mentioned, this Act was the legislative response to several further corporate accounting and governance scandals like WorldCom, Adelphia, and Enron.[1484] Therefore, the SOX aims to establish higher standards for corporate accounting and governance.[1485] The new approach of the SOX has made corporate responsibilities and disclosure obligations mandatory through written standards.[1486] The SOX also targets corporate corruption and seeks to protect

---

regulated. Public companies must meet stringent reporting requirements set out by the Securities and Exchange Commission (SEC), including the public disclosure of financial statements and annual 10-k reports discussing the state of the company. The shareholders elect a board of directors who oversees the operations of the company." *See* Public Company Definition, INVESTOPEDIA (2003), http://www.investopedia.com/terms/p/publiccompany.asp (last visited Mar 1, 2016).

1479 *See e.g.* New York Stock Exchange (NYSE), *See* The Editors of Encyclopædia Britannica, NEW YORK STOCK EXCHANGE (NYSE) | STOCK EXCHANGE, NEW YORK CITY, NEW YORK, UNITED STATES ENCYCLOPEDIA BRITANNICA, http://www.britannica.com/topic/New-York-Stock-Exchange (last visited Feb 17, 2016); The New York Stock Exchange | NYSE, , https://www.nyse.com/index (last visited Feb 17, 2016).and the National Association of Securities Dealers Automated Quotations (Nasdaq), See NASDAQ's Homepage for Retail Investors, NASDAQ.COM, http://www.nasdaq.com/ (last visited Feb 17, 2016).

1480 SECURITIES ACT OF 1933, *supra* note 600; SECURITIES EXCHANGE ACT OF 1934, *supra* note 605.

1481 *See* Shirley (2004), *supra* note 1160 at 528.

1482 *See supra* A., p. 171; The history and significance of the SOX has already been explained.

1483 *See supra* footnote 768, p. 135, *See also* Ravij Prabhakar, CORPORATE GOVERNANCE | BUSINESS ENCYCLOPEDIA BRITANNICA, http://www.britannica.com/topic/corporate-governance (last visited Mar 1, 2016). US corporate governance refers to the important legal relationship that exists between shareholders, management, auditors, and the board of directors. *See* Shirley (2004), *supra* note 1160 at 508.

1484 *See supra* p. 121; Yael V. Hochberg, Paola Sapienza & Annette Vissing-Jørgensen, *A Lobbying Approach to Evaluating the Sarbanes-Oxley Act of 2002*, 47 JOURNAL OF ACCOUNTING RESEARCH 519–583, 526 (2009).

1485 *See e.g.* Principles-Based Accounting Standards – Generally Accepted Accounting Principles US GAAP, SECURITIES EXCHANGE ACT OF 1934, *supra* note 605, 17 CFR 228, 229, 240, 249 and 274; *See also* ETHICS RESOURCE CENTER (ERC), *supra* note 663 at 5.

1486 *See* Fischer (2004), *supra* note 1167 at 97; SARBANES-OXLEY ACT OF 2002, *supra* note 47 §§ 301–308, 401–409.

investors.[1487] Overall, it focuses on corporate disclosure, risk management, auditing and financial reporting.[1488]

a. The Composition of the SOX

The SOX is organized into eleven titles. There are a number of provisions dealing specifically with compliance and professional standards.[1489] The following sections examine *inter alia* the three most significant provisions of the SOX in terms of compliance. The next section contains the key definitions used in this Act. The examination will go on focus on Section 302 of the SOX concerning the certification of accuracy of periodic financial disclosures as well as Section 404 on the responsibility of management for establishing and maintaining an adequate internal control structure.[1490] The last section stipulates the rules of professional responsibilities for attorneys pursuant to Section 307 and the shifting in corporate responsibilities between the attorneys and compliance officers.[1491]

Specifically, the SOX first makes it

> unlawful knowingly to alter, destroy, mutilate, conceal, cover up, falsify, or makes a false entry in any record, and document or to obstruct and influence the investigation of the federal agency.[1492]

Second, any accountant who conducts an audit of an issuer shall maintain all documents relating to the audit or review for a period of five years from the end of the fiscal period.[1493] The knowing and willful destruction of records carries a maximum penalty of ten years' imprisonment.[1494] Furthermore, any person who knowingly defrauds other persons in connection with any security of an issuer could be imprisoned for up to twenty-five years.[1495] For these reasons, violations of this Act could constitute a criminal offence under SOX and individuals may face imprisonment for a period of up to twenty-five years.[1496] Therefore, similarly to the FCPA, the SOX includes a number of provisions pertaining to financial reporting and the quality and control of such audits. In addition, the SOX also includes a number of independent standards.[1497].

1487 *See* Freeman (2007), *supra* note 57 at 359.

1488 *Id.* at 359.; Sarbanes-Oxley Act of 2002, *supra* note 47, §§ 101–109.

1489 Sarbanes-Oxley Act of 2002, *supra* note 47, §§ 301, 401, 404, 406, 806.

1490 *Id.* § 302 - Corporate Responsibility for financial reports, *Id.* § 404 - Management assessments of internal controls.

1491 Sarbanes-Oxley Act of 2002, *supra* note 47, § 307 (1)(2), 15 USC 7245.

1492 *Id.* § 802, 18 USC § 1519.

1493 *Id.* § 802, 18 USC § 1520 (a) (1).

1494 *Id.* § 802, 18 USC § 1520 (b).

1495 *Id.* § 807, 28 USC 994, § 1348.

1496 *Id.* § 802, 18 USC § 1519.

1497 *Id.* § 108, 15 USC 7218 - Accounting standards, *Id.* § 103, 15 USC 7213 - Auditing, quality control, and independence standards and rules.

b. Important Definitions of the SOX

The SOX as well as the FCPA contains a number of important definitions. The first term explicitly defined in the SOX is the Commission. This means the Securities and Exchange Commission (SEC).[1498] The SEC was established by the Securities Exchange Act of 1934, when the bill passed into law on June 1, 1934.[1499] As discussed previously, the main purpose of securities laws was also to revive investor confidence in the US capital markets following the stock market crash in October 1929.[1500] This Act empowers the SEC with considerable authority over the securities industry. For example, the SEC can require periodic reporting by companies with publicly traded securities.[1501] Since then, the SEC has overseen the activities of over 20,000 financial firms and other US exchange listed companies.[1502] The SEC consists of five commissioners who are appointed by the President.[1503] The SEC is divided into five divisions and twenty-three offices and employs approximately 3,500 staff.[1504] Staff in the enforcement division conduct investigations into possible violations of the federal securities laws, and can recommend that the Commission file civil actions or complaints in the federal courts.[1505] Investigations may concern conduct by misrepresentation or omission of important information about securities.[1506] Nevertheless, just like the DOJ – the SEC settles many cases out of court. The Commission could take a second procedural step, an administrative action in which the court can exclude companies from stock exchanges or, following due process and hearing, exclude a corporate officer or director from employment with a registered firm.[1507] The third possibility is that the Commission seeks a criminal prosecution, if fraud or other willful, criminal misconduct has been established.[1508]

1498 Sarbanes-Oxley Act of 2002, *supra* note 47, § 2 (a)(6). "*The SEC [hereinafter also referred to as the Commission] is the primary overseer and regulator of the US securities markets with the goal to protect investors, maintain fair, orderly, and efficient markets, and facilitate capital formation. It regulates the US securities markets as an independent regulatory agency.*" *See also* SEC, *supra* note 606.

1499 Securities Exchange Act of 1934, *supra* note 605, § 4; Rowan Bosworth-Davies, *The SEC: An Examination of its Structures, Powers and Procedures*, 2 Journal of Financial Regulation and Compliance 31–41, 33 (1993).

1500 *See also supra* footnote 607, p. 117.

1501 Federal Securities Law SEC, *supra* note 632; Securities Exchange Act of 1934, *supra* note 605, § 13 (1934), § 78m (2012).

1502 *See* Ellig and Peirce (2014), *supra* note 1094 at 361.

1503 *See also supra* footnote 607, p. 117.

1504 SEC, Securities and Exchange Commission Organization Chart, http://www.sec.gov/images/secorg.pdf (last visited Feb 17, 2016).

1505 SEC, Sec | Division of Enforcement, https://www.sec.gov/enforce (last visited Feb 17, 2016).

1506 *See also supra* footnote 607, p. 117.

1507 *See* Bosworth-Davies (1993), *supra* note 1499 at 38.

1508 *Id.* at 38.

The SEC also has the power to impose penalties, or to demand the return of illegal profits.[1509]

The SEC also has an office of compliance inspections and examinations (OCIE). This office conducts examinations to facilitate compliance with the securities laws and to detect violations of the law.[1510] The OCIE is responsible for (1) improving compliance, (2) preventing fraud, (3) monitoring risk, and (4) informing policy.[1511] The Commission applies the results of these examinations to initiate rule-making intentions.[1512]

The SOX specifically authorizes the SEC to begin with rule-making activities.[1513] For instance, the SEC's rule-making activity established a new whistleblowing regime.[1514] This is why the SEC describes itself as a law enforcement agency.[1515] Lastly, the American financial regulator SEC has developed a degree of American regulatory control and a pragmatic approach that applies a set of minimum standards.[1516]

The next term, which this section will explain is the Public Company Accounting Oversight Board, also known as the PCAOB or the Board.[1517] The Board was established pursuant to Section 101.[1518] The Board is responsible for overseeing the preparation of informative, accurate, and independent audit reports of public companies that are subject to the securities laws.[1519] It is subject to action by the Commission under Section 107.[1520] As a result, the Commission has oversight and enforcement authority over the Board. Therefore, the Commission also has oversight responsibility for all of the activities of the PCAOB, including the approval of its annual budget.[1521]

1509 *See also supra* footnote 607, p. 117.

1510 *Id.*

1511 SEC, Sec | About Office of Compliance Inspections and Examinations, https://www.sec.gov/ocie/Article/about.html (last visited Feb 17,2016).

1512 *Id. "Rule-making is the process by which federal agencies implement legislation passed by Congress and signed into law by the President." See e.g.* concept releases, proposed rules, final rules, interpretive releases, and policy statements. *See* SEC, Sec | Regulatory Actions, http://www.sec.gov/rules.shtml (last visited Feb 18, 2016).

1513 *See* Hochberg, Sapienza, and Vissing-Jørgensen (2009), *supra* note 1484 at 526.

1514 *See* Ellig and Peirce (2014), *supra* note 1094 at 363; Sarbanes-Oxley Act of 2002, *supra* note 47, § 806 (a), 18 USC § 1514 A - Whistleblower Protection for Employees of Publicly Traded Companies.

1515 *See also supra* footnote 607, p. 117.

1516 *See* Bosworth-Davies (1993), *supra* note 1499 at 39.

1517 Sarbanes-Oxley Act of 2002, *supra* note 47, § 101, 15 USC 7211; SEC, *supra* note 632.

1518 Sarbanes-Oxley Act of 2002, *supra* note 47, § 101 (a), 15 USC 7211.

1519 *Id.*§ 101 (c), 15 USC 7211.

1520 *Id.*§ 107, 15 USC 7217 - Commission oversight of the Board.

1521 *See also supra* footnote 607, p. 117.

The SOX also considers the term issuer,[1522] which is defined in the Securities Exchange Act of 1934.[1523] Thus, the SOX applies when an issuer becomes subject to US registration requirements and must register its securities in the United States.[1524] Additionally, SEC Rule 3b-4 explains the term foreign private issuer. This means a company organized outside the US, with more than 50 percent of its voting shares owned by US citizens, where the majority of the executive officers are US citizens and the business is generally administered in the US.[1525] However, there is an permanent academic and political debate on the extraterritorial application of US laws in securities fraud actions. Legal scholars refer in this context to the financial service regulation of 1934.[1526] It provides that

> Sec. 10 It shall be unlawful for any person, directly or indirectly, by the use of any means or instrumentality of interstate commerce or of the mails, or of any facility of any national securities exchange-
>
> (b) To use or employ, in connection with the purchase or sale of any security registered on a national securities exchange or any security not so registered, or any securities based swap agreement any manipulative or deceptive device or contrivance in contravention of such rules and regulations as the Commission may prescribe as necessary or appropriate in the public interest or for the protection of investors.[1527]

In order to classify the extraterritorial range of the US Securities Law, the US Code defines Interstate Commerce as follows:

> ...trade, commerce, transportation, or communication among the several States, or between any foreign country and any State, or between any State and any place or ship outside thereof.[1528]

However, *Heminway* argued that this is a blurred definition and it is not explicitly clear that Section 10(b) has an extensive extraterritorial range.[1529] This legal issue

---

1522 *See supra* I., 1, p. 185.

1523 Sarbanes-Oxley Act of 2002, *supra* note 47, § 2 (a) (7). *"The term issuer means any person who issues or proposes to issue any security..." See* Securities Exchange Act of 1934, *supra* note 605, 15 USC 78c (8). *"The term person means a natural person, company, government, or political subdivision, agency, or instrumentality of a government." See Id.* 15 USC 78c (9).

1524 Sarbanes-Oxley Act of 2002, *supra* note 47, § 2 (a) (7); Shirley (2004), *supra* note 1160 at 523.

1525 Securities Exchange Act of 1934, *supra* note 605, 17 CFR 240.3b-4.

1526 *See e.g.* Joan MacLeod Heminway, The Extraterritorial Application of US Securities Fraud Prohibitions in an Increasingly Global Transactional World (2012).

1527 Securities Exchange Act of 1934, *supra* note 605, § 10 (b), 17 C.F.R. § 240.10b-5 (2011).

1528 *Id.* 15 USC § 78c (a) (17).

1529 Heminway (2012), *supra* note 1526 at 3.

was also dealt with in a recent US Supreme Court decision.[1530] In its opinion, the Supreme Court defined the extraterritorial reach of Section 10(b) as follows:

> The canon or presumption that federal law is not meant to have extraterritorial effect is applicable in all cases, whenever party seeks to give any federal legislation extraterritorial effect, including cases arising under the Securities Exchange Act.[1531]

In the view put forward by *Heminway*, this court opinion affects international business law and practice.[1532] Before *Morrison v. Nat'l Austl. Bank Ltd*, the US federal courts consistently followed a line of cases law with a test that assessed the involvement of the defendant to justify the exercise of jurisdiction.[1533] The courts evaluated the conduct and effects of the defendant's activities in the US and the impact on US markets and investors.[1534] However, a number of commentators have criticized this judicial test because it has no textual basis.[1535] *Heminway* argued that the decision in *Morrison v. Nat'l Austl. Bank Ltd.* defines a clearer and narrower rule of the extraterritorial range of Section 10(b) and Rule 10b-5.[1536] Therefore, the US Supreme Court has created more stringent limits for the extraterritorial application of Section 10(b) and Rule 10b-5 in securities fraud actions.[1537]

Although given the blurred interpretations relating to the extraterritorial range, consequently, the SOX will apply to issuers who have securities registered on the US Stock exchanges and are required to file reports.[1538] In 2003, there were more than 1,300 foreign companies with securities listed on the US Stock exchanges.[1539] As a result, the SOX has led to the creation of a complex legal environment for the foreign companies concerned. In 2004, thirty-one German companies were registered.[1540] At that time, Germany held the top spot on the list of European countries listed on both NSYE and NASDAQ.[1541] Today, as mentioned previously,

---

1530 *Morrison v. Nat'l Austl. Bank Ltd.*, 130 S. Ct. 2869 (2010). In this case foreign investors brought action against Australian banking corporation, alleging securities fraud as to foreign transaction. *See also* in: Heminway (2012), *supra* note 1526 at 2.

1531 *Morrison v. Nat'l Austl. Bank Ltd.*, 130 S. Ct. 2869 (2010), *supra* note 1530. The US Supreme Court held that *"Section 10(b) reaches the use of a manipulative or deceptive device or contrivance only in connection with the purchase or sale of a security listed on an American stock exchange, and the purchase or sale of any other security in the United States." Id.* note 2888. *See also* in: Heminway (2012), *supra* note 1526 at 7.

1532 *See* Heminway (2012), *supra* note 1526 at 7.

1533 *Id.* at 8.

1534 *Id.* at 8.

1535 *Id.* at 9.

1536 *Id.* at 9.

1537 *Id.* at 19.

1538 Sarbanes-Oxley Act of 2002, *supra* note 47, § 2 (a) (7).

1539 *See* Shirley (2004), *supra* note 1160 at 511.

1540 *Id.* at 512.

1541 *Id.* at 512.

only five German companies are still listed on the US Stock Exchanges.[1542] Hence, the SOX and its extraterritorial range does not have such a significant effect on German companies. Despite this fact, the next sections examine the effects of the SOX provisions as regards compliance issues and the compliance function within foreign corporations in order to identify standards for corporate structures.

c. Section 302 of the Sarbanes-Oxley Act

One of the major goals of Section 302 of the Sarbanes-Oxley Act of 2002 was to improve the quality of corporate reporting in the United States and, thus, recover investors' confidence.[1543] The requirements of this Section relate not directly, but indirectly to compliance issues. The chief executive officer (CEO) and the chief financial officer (CFO), or persons, performing similar functions, have to sign each annual or quarterly accounting report.[1544] Before doing so, they must fulfill six requirements stipulated in Section 302: (1) must have reviewed the report, (2) ensure that the report does not contain any untrue statement, (3) financial information included in the report is fairly current, (4) responsibility for establishing and maintaining internal controls, (5) disclosure to the issuer's auditors and the audit committee[1545] of the board of directors, and (6) indicate in the report any significant changes in internal controls or in other factors.[1546] These certifications refer to Rule 13a-14 of the SEC.[1547] Every issuer has to report and file to the SEC separate Forms 10-Q, 10-K or 10-KSB[1548] for each foreign private issuer under Section 13(a) of the 1934 Act.[1549] The certification required by

1542 Aixtron, Deutsche Bank, Fresenius Medical Care, SAP, Voxeljet. *See* The Complete List of German ADRs Trading on the US Markets | TopForeignStocks.com, TopForeignStocks.com (2015), http://topforeignstocks.com/foreign-adrs-list/the-german-adrs-trading-on-the-us-markets/ (last visited Feb 20, 2016).

1543 Sarbanes-Oxley Act of 2002, *supra* note 47, § 302, 15 USC 7241 - Corporate responsibility for financial reports.

1544 *Id.* § 302 (a).

1545 *Id.* § 202 (3). The audit committee is present in every public company. The SOX requires that the audit committee is staffed by independent directors. *"Each audit committee must have the authority to engage independent counsel and other advisers, as it determines necessary to carry out its duties. It has to establish procedures regarding accounting, internal accounting controls, or auditing matters." See also* Securities Exchange Act of 1934, *supra* note 605, 17 CFR 240.10A-3 - Listing standards relating to audit committees.

1546 Sarbanes-Oxley Act of 2002, *supra* note 47 § 302 (a) (1)-(6).

1547 Securities Exchange Act of 1934, *supra* note 605 § 240.13a-14 Certification of disclosure in annual and quarterly reports.

1548 SEC, Sec | Form 10-K, http://www.sec.gov/answers/form10k.htm (last visited Feb 19, 2016).

1549 Securities Exchange Act of 1934, *supra* note 605 § 78m (a) (2012).

paragraph (d) of this Section must be signed by each chief executive officer and each chief financial officer of the issuer.[1550] Therefore, this SOX provision refers directly to the conduct of corporate directors and officers.[1551] For example, in Form 20-F, the company is required to disclose annually that it has adopted a code of ethics that applies to the registrant's chief executive officer, chief financial officer, chief accounting officer, or chief controller.[1552] The term code of ethics means written standards that are reasonably designed to deter wrongdoing and to promote *e.g.* (1) honest and ethical conduct, (2) compliance with applicable governmental laws, rules and regulations, and (3) prompt internal reporting of violations of the code to an appropriate person.[1553] The issuer should design disclosure controls or procedures to ensure that the necessary information is communicated to the management.[1554]

Overall, it is important to note that Section 302,[1555] the requirement for CEO and CFO certification of financial statements, provides no exemptions for foreign issuers and the rule specifically emphasizes that the Act requires a no exemption policy.[1556] Another aspect to be taken into account under Section 302 is that the CEOs and CFOs could be held personally liable for any misstatements in their firms' financial periodic reports.[1557] Thus, this provision could distract top management focus from business issues towards compliance with rules.[1558] The next section will analyze the Section 404 of the SOX relating to compliance.

d. **Section 404 of the Sarbanes-Oxley Act**

In 2003, the SEC implemented Section 404 of SOX.[1559] Similar to Section 302 of the SOX, Section 404 requires companies to put in place a periodic monitoring and

1550 *Id.*17 CFR 240.13a-14(a).

1551 *See* Fischer (2004), *supra* note 1167 at 101.

1552 SEC, SEC | FORM 20-F, http://www.sec.gov/about/forms/form20-f.pdf (last visited Feb 19, 2016) Item 16B Code of Ethics.

1553 *Id.* Item 16B Code of Ethics.

1554 SECURITIES EXCHANGE ACT OF 1934, *supra* note 605, 17 CFR 240.13a-14(a).

1555 SARBANES-OXLEY ACT OF 2002, *supra* note 47 § 302.

1556 *See* Joseph D. Piotroski & Suraj Srinivasan, *Regulation and Bonding: The Sarbanes-Oxley Act and the Flow of International Listings*, 46 JOURNAL OF ACCOUNTING RESEARCH 383–425, 392 (2008).

1557 *See e.g.* Alexander et al. (2013), *supra* note 1197 at 275; T. Jean Engebretson & Heidi Hylton Meier, *The Perceived Effectiveness of the Officer Certification Requirement under Sarbanes-Oxley*, 15 INTERNATIONAL JOURNAL OF AUDITING 176–190, 178 (2011).

1558 *See* Piotroski and Srinivasan (2008), *supra* note 1556 at 393.

1559 SARBANES-OXLEY ACT OF 2002, *supra* note 47 § 404 - Management assessment of internal controls; FINAL RULE: MANAGEMENT'S REPORT ON INTERNAL CONTROL

assessment of their internal systems to ensure accurate financial reports.[1560] This provision states, *inter alia*, that the management is responsible for establishing and maintaining an adequate internal control structure and procedures for financial reporting.[1561] In addition, Section 404 requires that an independent outside auditor attests to the management's assessment of the company controls.[1562] According to the final SEC Rule, the internal control report should include:

> a statement to identify the framework used by management to evaluate the effectiveness of the company's internal control over financial reporting.[1563]

The SEC explains the term internal controls and procedures for financial reporting as follows:[1564]

> It means controls that pertain to the preparation of financial statements for external purposes that are fairly presented in conformity with generally accepted accounting principles as addressed by the codification of statements on auditing standards.[1565]
>
> Under the supervision of, the issuer's principal executive and principal financial officers, or persons performing similar functions, [...] to provide reasonable assurance regarding the reliability of financial reporting and the preparation of financial statements for external purposes in accordance with generally accepted accounting principles.[1566]

Therefore, Section 404 of the SOX lays down a number of internal monitoring requirements, accounting and auditing standards, and disclosure requirements on issuers.[1567] Hence, companies need to invest time and resources in both Section 404

Over Financial Reporting and Certification of Disclosure in Exchange Act Periodic Reports; Rel. No. 33-8238, 17 CFR 210, 228, 229, 240, 249, 270 and 274 (2003).

1560 *See* Iliev (2010), *supra* note 1174 at 1163.

1561 Sarbanes-Oxley Act of 2002, *supra* note 47, § 404 (a) (1).

1562 *See* Iliev (2010), *supra* note 1174 at 1163.

1563 Final Rule: Management's Report on Internal Control Over Financial Reporting and Certification of Disclosure in Exchange Act Periodic Reports; Rel. No. 33-8238, *supra* note 1559; Securities Exchange Act of 1934, *supra* note 605, 15 USC 78, 17 CFR 240.13a-15 - Controls and procedures.

1564 Final Rule: Management's Report on Internal Control Over Financial Reporting and Certification of Disclosure in Exchange Act Periodic Reports; Rel. No. 33-8238, *supra* note 1559.

1565 *Id.* The AICPA Statements and Standards - this codification supersedes all existing non-SEC accounting standards. *See* ICAEW, Aicpa Statements and Standards | Accounting standards | Library | Icaew, http://www.icaew.com/en/library/subject-gateways/accounting-standards/us-accounting-standards/aicpa-statements-and-standards (last visited Feb 19, 2016).

1566 Securities Exchange Act of 1934, *supra* note 605, 15 USC 78, 17 CFR 240.13a-15 (f).

1567 *See* Sale (2007), *supra* note 22 at 724.

compliance and in their compliance programs to prevent wrongdoing. The compliance officer of the issuers should read carefully the legislation and the rules to enable him to provide support and assistance for senior management and boards of directors faced with having to interpret SEC disclosure rules.[1568]

Since the implementation of Section 404 of the SOX, a large part of the debate has centered on the costs incurred by publicly traded companies in order to comply with its requirements.[1569] This was the beginning of a new counter debate among business and legal scholars on the advantages and disadvantages of the Act. The data from a recent survey by *Alexander et al.* examined the cost and benefits of compliance with Section 404 of the SOX within companies.[1570] They found that the effects of compliance depend on firm complexity, but are for the most part unrelated to the firm's structure.[1571] Furthermore, they established out that more than two-thirds of the respondents acknowledge positive effects from compliance, but the costs of compliance far outweigh the benefits.[1572] Nevertheless, other authors *e.g. Hollister,* argued that investors are likely to reward corporations that comply with the standards, including the certification requirements.[1573]

An analysis of a web survey data study by the SEC in 2009 found that there appears to be a general downward trend in Section 404 compliance costs, irrespective of the company size.[1574] Nevertheless, other empirical results by *Iliev* evidenced that the implementation of Section 404 led to a significant increase in costs for both domestic and foreign firms, particularly with regard to small firms.[1575] In addition, a study by *Hochberg et al.* evaluated the impact of the SOX on shareholders.[1576] They found that investors expected that the legislation would increase the shareholder value.[1577] Furthermore, they noted that significant increases in compliance costs as a result of SOX were causing concern among many firms.[1578]

1568 *See* Preeti Choudhary, Jason D. Schloetzer & Jason D. Sturgess, *Boards, Auditors, Attorneys and Compliance with Mandatory SEC Disclosure Rules*, 34 MANAGERIAL AND DECISION ECONOMICS 471–487, 9 (2013).

1569 SEC, STUDY OF THE SARBANES-OXLEY ACT OF 2002 SECTION 404 INTERNAL CONTROL OVER FINANCIAL REPORTING REQUIREMENTS 137 37 (2009), https://www.sec.gov/news/studies/2009/sox-404_study.pdf (last visited Feb 4, 2016).

1570 *See* Alexander et al. (2013), *supra* note 1197. This survey included a sample of managers from 2,901unique US public companies and was conducted from 2008 until 2009.

1571 *Id.* at 267.

1572 *Id.* at 288.

1573 *See* Hochberg, Sapienza, and Vissing-Jørgensen (2009), *supra* note 1484 at 481.

1574 SEC, *supra* note 1187 at 43–44 Table 8.

1575 *See* Iliev (2010), *supra* note 1174 at 1193.

1576 *See* Hochberg, Sapienza, and Vissing-Jørgensen (2009), *supra* note 1484.

1577 *Id.* at 565.

1578 *Id.* at 574.

Due to the political and academic debate[1579] on the costly effects of Section 404, small US companies and foreign companies were granted a *"stay of execution"* for a reasonable period from 2002 until 2004.[1580] Small companies with a public float[1581] under US$ 75 million were required to file their first management report for the fiscal year 2007.[1582] Foreign companies with a public float of less than US$ 700 were not required to file an auditor's attestation to the report in the first year, namely 2006.[1583]

In addition to the increased cost incurred as a result of Section 404, there are also other consequences for companies. A study by *Nagy & Cenker* revealed that the internal audit within companies *"shifted toward a compliance focus."*[1584] Their findings present expected benefits for internal auditors, like job security and increased pay, but it is possible that the compliance workload could increase and reduce professionalism as a result.[1585]

Today, however, Section 404 and its regulations set forth elements of internal monitoring requirements and standards that the compliance officer also needs to give careful consideration.[1586] The result within companies could be the more conscious handling of compliance issues. Therefore, the next section introduces the enforcement of compliance followed by a summary of the enhanced responsibilities of the compliance officer's work under the SOX.

e. The Shifting in Responsibility for Compliance Tasks

Despite the fact that the SOX rules do not provide any section referring directly to the compliance officer, Section 307 points out the professional role and responsibilities of corporate attorneys in the disclosure process.[1587] For example, attorneys should assist the senior management[1588] with the preparation of SEC disclosure

---

1579 *See also supra* A., I., pp. 176 et seq.

1580 *See* Iliev (2010), *supra* note 1174 at 1165.

1581 *"Also known as public equity float. The portion of a company's outstanding shares that is in the hands of public investors, as opposed to company officers, directors, or stockholders that hold controlling interests. These are the shares that are available for trading."* See PLC - Public Float, http://us.practicallaw.com/6-382-3723 (last visited May 24, 2016); *See also* Category of Filer SEC, *supra* note 1569.

1582 *See* Iliev (2010), *supra* note 1174 at 1165.

1583 *Id.* at 1165.

1584 *See* Albert L. Nagy & William J. Cenker, *Internal Audit Professionalism and Section 404 Compliance: The View of Chief Audit Executives from Northeast Ohio*, 11 International Journal of Auditing 41–49, 41 (2007). *"This study is based upon the responses from interviews conducted with 17 Chief Audit Executives (CAEs) of large US public companies."*

1585 *Id.* at 41–42.

1586 *See* Sale (2007), *supra* note 22 at 724.

1587 Sarbanes-Oxley Act of 2002, *supra* note 47, § 307, 15 USC 7245.

1588 Examples including the executive officers, CEO and CFO.

documents.[1589] The Sarbanes-Oxley requires the SEC to set minimum standards of professional conduct, as for lawyers.[1590] In accordance with the SEC Rule pursuant to Section 307, the attorney has a duty to report evidence of a material violation to the issuer's chief legal officer or chief executive officer.[1591] Therefore, the SEC requires attorneys with evidence of material violations of federal securities laws to report misconduct to the chief legal counsel or the chief executive officer of the company.[1592] In the event of no response from the chief legal officer or chief executive officer within a reasonable time, the attorney shall report the evidence of a material violation to the audit committee or another committee or the board of directors.[1593] An attorney who violated these requirements shall be subject to civil penalties and remedies in an action by the SEC.[1594] Exemptions apply to attorneys practicing outside the US.[1595]

In addition, the SEC requires that mandatory disclosure be made on time.[1596] For example, the annual reports on Form 10-K must be filed within 60, 75, or 90 days of the fiscal year end.[1597] In 2005, the SEC filed approximately 80 enforcement actions against corporate attorneys' pursuant to Section 307.[1598] The total number of SEC enforcement actions increased from 676 in 2013 to 807 in 2015.[1599] These actions include prosecution on grounds of accounting violations, misstating financial results, disclosure failures, suspending accountants for bad auditing or the liability of attorneys, accountants and other executive officers for failures to comply with professional standards.[1600]

Although many companies in the US today have a senior officer responsible for compliance, originally, the general counsel was the corporate compliance officer.[1601] However, in recent years their responsibilities have passed into

---

1589 Form 10-K, SEC, *supra* note 1548; Form 20-F, SEC, *supra* note 1552.

1590 *See* Stephen M. Cutler, SEC Speech: The Themes of Sarbanes-Oxley as Reflected in the Commission's Enforcement Program (2004), https://www.sec.gov/news/speech/spch092004smc.htm (last visited Feb 24, 2016).

1591 Sarbanes-Oxley Act of 2002, *supra* note 47, § 307 (1), 15 USC 7245; Securities Exchange Act of 1934, *supra* note 605, 17 CFR 205.3.

1592 *See* Cutler, *supra* note 1590., *See also* Sarbanes-Oxley Act of 2002, *supra* note 47, § 307 (1).

1593 Sarbanes-Oxley Act of 2002, *supra* note 47, § 307 (2), 15 USC 7245; Securities Exchange Act of 1934, *supra* note 605, 17 CFR 205.3 (3).

1594 Securities Exchange Act of 1934, *supra* note 605, 17 CFR 205.6 (a).

1595 *Id.* 17 CFR 205.6 (d).

1596 *See* Choudhary, Schloetzer, and Sturgess (2013), *supra* note 1568 at 18.

1597 Securities Exchange Act of 1934, *supra* note 605, 17 CFR 240.12b-2.

1598 *See* Choudhary, Schloetzer, and Sturgess (2013), *supra* note 1568 at 10.

1599 SEC, Sec Announces Enforcement Results For fy 2015, http://www.sec.gov/news/pressrelease/2015-245.html (last visited Feb 24, 2016).

1600 *Id.*

1601 *See supra* A., I., p. 117; Miller (2014), *supra* note 519 at 8; Miller (2014), *supra* note 595 at 129.

the hands of the compliance personnel.[1602] Generally, the corporate attorneys are classic gatekeepers within the corporate environment because their services are often needed to achieve corporate objectives.[1603] A gatekeeper is:

> An independent professional who plays one or two distinct roles, which tend to overlap in practice. First, the gatekeeper may be a professional who is positioned so as to be able to prevent wrongdoing […]. Second an agent who acts as a reputational intermediary to assure investors as to the quality of the 'signal' sent by the corporate issuer.[1604]

Coffee identifies four basic factors that comprise the gatekeeper function; liability, regulation, reputational resources and supervision by a principal.[1605] One theory by *Kraakman* describes the gatekeeper as an actor with the capacity to monitor, to control, and thus to deter wrongdoing.[1606] Generally, gatekeepers are considered to be actors who are able to deter corporate wrongdoing.[1607]

However, there is some debate in America surrounding the question of whether the corporate lawyer ought to actually have compliance gatekeeping responsibilities.[1608] *DeStefano* argues that it is difficult to describe *"where legal ends and compliance begins"*[1609] and, therefore, it could be argued that law and compliance go hand in hand.[1610] Similarly, *Langevoort* does not acknowledge any clear distinction between legal advice and compliance oversight.[1611] Nevertheless, nowadays, large American corporations have ethics and compliance officers with separate departments from the legal department.[1612] Hence, the enforcement of corporate responsibilities distinguishes the compliance function from the legal department.[1613] In spite of this development, both legal and compliance functions rely on legal expertise to perform their duties.[1614] Additionally, the compliance personnel are responsible for risk

---

1602 *See* MILLER (2014), *supra* note 595 at 129.

1603 *"The gatekeeper has control over the gate. The gate is a metaphor, which separates the company from corporate objective." See Id.* at 296.

1604 *See* J.C. COFFEE, GATEKEEPERS: THE PROFESSIONS AND CORPORATE GOVERNANCE 2 (1. ed. 2006).

1605 *See* COFFEE, *supra* note 1604.

1606 *See* Reinier H. Kraakman, *Corporate Liability Strategies and the Costs of Legal Controls*, 93 THE YALE LAW JOURNAL 857, 890 (1984).

1607 *See* Andrew F. Tuch, *Multiple Gatekeepers*, 96 VIRGINIA LAW REVIEW 1583–1672, 1590 (2010).

1608 Pro SEC, *supra* note 625, the American Bar Association (ABA)

1609 *See* DeStefano (2013), *supra* note 14 at 91.

1610 *See* Donald C. Langevoort, *Getting (Too) Comfortable: In-House Lawyers, Enterprise Risk and the Financial Crisis*, WISCONSIN LAW REVIEW 495–519, 500 (2011).

1611 *Id.* at 500.

1612 *Id.* at 500.

1613 *See* DeStefano (2013), *supra* note 14 at 71.

1614 *Id.* at 91.

assessment and for communicating and providing training on the legal regulations to employees.[1615] However, having a law degree is not a prerequisite for becoming a compliance officer.[1616] Finally, *Tuch* emphasized the multiple gatekeeper phenomenon within companies.[1617] Nowadays, the boundaries between legal, accounting, and financial skills are blurring within the corporate environment.[1618] Overall, the question that arises from the developments outlined above is whether the compliance officer is considered to be a gatekeeper. While there is currently no academic debate on this consideration, the compliance officer should be aware that he has the capacity to monitor, to control, and thus to deter wrongdoing.

Furthermore, governmental agencies such as such as the Office of Inspector General (OIG) of the SEC and the Department of Health and Human Services (DHHS) promote the separation between legal and compliance departments with governmental agreements. When corporations are involved in governmental investigations, the SEC emphasizes the formal structure and compliance programs within companies.[1619] For example, in the corporate integrity agreement[1620] between Grace Healthcare and the OIG, the company was required to establish and maintain a compliance program and appoint an individual as compliance officer.[1621] In addition, the OIG requires:

> The compliance officer shall be a member of senior management of Grace, shall report directly to the chief executive officer of Grace, shall make periodic (at least quarterly) reports regarding compliance matters directly to the board of directors of Grace, and shall be authorized to report on such matters to the board of directors at any time. The compliance officer shall not be or be subordinate to the general counsel or chief financial officer.[1622]

In addition, a 2013 survey by PWC of 800 chief compliance officers in UK and US-based companies found an emerging trend in US companies for the CCO to first report to the chief executive officer.[1623] These results showed that the CEO

1615 *Id.* at 96.
1616 *Id.* at 101.
1617 *See* Tuch (2010), *supra* note 1577 at 1607.
1618 *Id.* at 1601.
1619 *See* DeStefano (2013), *supra* note 14 at 110.
1620 DHHS, OIG, Corporate Integrity Agreement (CIA) between the Office of Inspector General (OIG) of the United States Department of Health and Human Services (HHS) (2013), http://oig.hhs.gov/fraud/cia/agreements/Grace_Healthcare_03042013.pdf.
1621 *Id.* at 2.
1622 *Id.* at 3.
1623 Sally Bernstein, Barbara Kipp & Tracey Groves, PwC-2013-Survey | Deeper Insight for greater Strategic Value | State of Compliance 2 (2013) [hereinafter PWC Study 2013], http://www.pwc.com/us/en/risk-management/assets/

is beginning to play a greater role in compliance oversight.[1624] The study confirmed that the role of compliance has evolved via the formality of compliance structures.[1625] The study also found a growing demand from both regulators and the board for effectiveness of the compliance program.[1626] A study by the Society of Corporate Compliance and Ethics and Health Care Compliance (SCCE) examined the relationship between the board of directors and the compliance officer.[1627] The results showed that among publicly traded companies the percentage reporting to the board has increased from 41 % to 53 % since 2010.[1628]

Hence, it can be stated that the enforced legislation and rule-making activities by regulators enhanced the independent, separate compliance function and changed the reporting structure within both US and foreign listed companies. In contrast to the general counsel, the compliance officer must remember to report wrongdoing not only to the board, but also to the government in order to obtain credit.[1629] Thus, the legal framework and requirements of the SOX and the SEC rule-making activities have supported the separate development of a standalone corporate compliance function since compliance tasks and responsibilities have increased significantly since 2002.

f. The SEC cases against Compliance Officers

The results of a survey of SEC enforcement actions against chief compliance officers and compliance officers showed that from 2003 to 2015, the SEC brought five actions against CCOs at investment advisers within the financial services sector who were involved in violations of compliance-related rules.[1630] The research did not yield any SEC actions or cases against corporate compliance officers. As well as providing an understanding of the SEC's enforcement approach towards compliance officers, this section examines in detail one of these cases against CCOs involving investment advisers. This could be helpful in showing specific types of misconduct in order to clarify the compliance officers' duties and define the role of this function outside the

---

pwc-soc-survey-2013-final.pdf (last visited Feb 25, 2016). Twenty percent of the CCO reported to the CEO in 2012 versus 28 percent in 2013.

1624 PWC Survey 2013 *Id.* at 9.

1625 *Id.* at 7.

1626 *Id.* at 7.

1627 SCCE, The Relationship between the Board of Directors and the Compliance and Ethics Officer (2014), http://www.corporatecompliance.org/ (last visited Feb 25, 2016).

1628 SCCE Survey 2014 *Id.* at 2.

1629 *See* DeStefano (2013), *supra* note 14 at 124.

1630 Over the term of this period, the total amount of the SEC actions was 8,000 and 807 in 2015. SEC, Select SEC and Market Data Fiscal 2015 3, https://www.sec.gov/reportspubs/select-sec-and-market-data/secstats2015.pdf (last visited May 25, 2016).

financial services sector. The corporate compliance officer needs to consider how the administrative agencies lead their enforcement activities.

In the SEC cases against compliance officers within the financial services sector, the SEC held the CCO responsible for the compliance failures of his firm.[1631] The director of the Division of Enforcement made it clear that

> Being a CCO does not provide immunity from liability.[1632]

The results of these cases reveal that the SEC targets compliance officers for securities law violations in particular. However, the number of actions against chief compliance officers under compliance-related rules is small. For example, in 2015, the SEC brought two actions against registered investment advisers. Some commentators argue that the last two SEC actions[1633] against CCOs seem to indicate to a policy change on the part of the SEC and conclude that enforcers in other industries are liable to follow.[1634] In the SEC action against *SFX*, the CCO was charged because the required policy was not effectively implemented.[1635] In the second SEC action, the firm failed to conduct timely annual compliance program reviews and to implement and enforce certain provisions of its procedures and the code of ethics.[1636] The chief compliance officer joined the investment adviser in November 2006 to fill a variety of roles, including backup trader, backup trade reconciliation, research analyst, and portfolio manager.[1637] However, the CCO had no compliance background and no compliance staff.[1638] He learned at a compliance conference in 2008 and wanted to improve the efficiency of the compliance program.[1639] Additionally, the CEO knew that the CCO had limited experience and

---

1631 Andrew Ceresney & Division of Enforcement, SEC | 2015 National Society of Compliance Professionals, National Conference: Keynote Address (2015), http://www.sec.gov/news/speech/keynote-address-2015-national-society-compliance-prof-cereseney.html (last visited Feb 25, 2016). In 2015, the SEC brought two actions against CCOs of Adviser firms, BlackRock (BLK) Advisers and LLC SFX Financial Advisory Management Enterprises Inc.

1632 *Id.*

1633 SEC, *United States before the SEC v. Pekin Singer Strauss Asset Management Inc.*, et al., Release No. 31688 (2015); SEC, *United States before the SEC v. SFX Financial Advisory Management Enterprises, Inc. and Eugene S. Mason,* No. 3-16591 (2015).

1634 Ben DiPietro, SEC Actions Stir Concerns Over Compliance Officer Liability (2015), http://blogs.wsj.com/riskandcompliance/2015/06/24/sec-actions-stir-concerns-over-compliance-officer-liability/ (last visited Feb 25, 2016).

1635 SEC, *United States before the SEC v. SFX Financial Advisory Management Enterprises, Inc. and Eugene S. Mason,*) *supra* note 1633.

1636 *United States v Pekin Singer,* SEC, *supra* note 1633 at 2.

1637 *Id.* at 3.

1638 *Id.* at 4.

1639 *Id.* at 4.

training in compliance issues.[1640] Nevertheless, the compliance program was not a priority for the firm or the board.[1641] As a result, the investment firm violated the Advisers Act[1642] and the SEC charged the adviser's president based on these violations.[1643] The CCO was not charged since he received no support from the board in his attempts to improve compliance issues.[1644]

The Director of the Division of Enforcement of the SEC made it clear that the SEC will bring actions against CCOs as soon as they become involved in misconduct, in fraudulent activity or other conduct that harms investors and is unrelated to their compliance function.[1645] Secondly, the SEC charges CCOs who obstruct or mislead the Commission staff.[1646] Thirdly, the SEC charges CCOs who fail to carry out their responsibilities, such as under rule 206(4)-7 and other compliance-related rules.[1647]

To conclude, the SEC cases against CCOs at investment advisers and the declared approach of the SEC show that the corporate compliance officer is under an obligation to familiarize himself with and establish effective compliance policies and procedures. In in the majority of cases, the chief compliance officer was also in charge of other roles in the company.[1648] In the event of the compliance officers' failure to establish an effective compliance program, he could be held liable. However, in the event of any lack of support or resources from the board, the compliance officer should document his proposals on the improvement of compliance policies and procedures. Considering this SEC approach examined above, the corporate compliance officer ought to pay attention to the course of action of the SEC within the financial services sector, to the SEC rules and to the responsibilities under the SOX.

1640 *Id.* at 4.

1641 *Id.* at 4.

1642 Investment Advisers Act of 1940, Pub. L. 112-90, 15 USC. § 80b-1-80b-21 (1940).

1643 *See* Richard L. Cassin, SEC: We protect compliance officers, except when we prosecute them, The FCPA Blog (2015), http://www.fcpablog.com/blog/2015/11/9/sec-we-protect-compliance-officers-except-when-we-prosecute.html (last visited Feb 25, 2016).

1644 *Id.*

1645 *See* Ceresney and Division of Enforcement, *supra* note 1631.

1646 *"The SEC brought an action against a former Wells Fargo Advisors compliance officer who allegedly altered a document before it was provided to the SEC during an investigation." See Id.*; SEC, SEC Announces Enforcement Action Against Former Wells Fargo Advisors Compliance Officer for Altering Document (2014), http://www.sec.gov/News/PressRelease/Detail/PressRelease/1370543175814 (last visited Feb 25, 2016).

1647 *See* Ceresney and Division of Enforcement, *supra* note 1631; Investment Advisers Act of 1940, *supra* note 1642 17 CFR 275.206(4)-7(a) *"Adopt and implement written policies and procedures reasonably designed to prevent violation, by you and your supervised persons, of the Act and the rules that the Commission has adopted under the Act."*

1648 *Id.*

g. Conclusion - The Compliance Officers Work under SOX

Legislation such as the Sarbanes-Oxley Act has improved the accounting and reporting responsibility for the chief executive officers within companies. Although this Act is part of federal law, it also affects corporate structures within publicly traded companies and issuers, that are listed on the US Stock exchanges. The main SOX provisions address certified periodic financial reporting by CEOs and CFOs,[1649] internal control structure of the financial reporting,[1650] corporate and lawyer accountability,[1651] disclosure requirements,[1652] the role of the independent auditor of the issuer,[1653] and criminal penalties.[1654] The SOX also created the Public Company Accounting Oversight Board (PCAOB)[1655] to regulate and oversee the auditing practices of listed companies. Overall, this legislation as well as the FCPA affects corporate structures, increases reporting and disclosures obligations, and compliance responsibilities. The responsibilities for the executives' officers under the Sarbanes-Oxley Act are stated in a checklist, *Table 4*, below:

Table 4 *Checklist - The SOX Responsibilities for Executives Officers*

Requirements under SOX	Compliance with SEC Rules	Responsibilities for Executive Officer
Section 302 Certification Corporate Responsibility for Financial Reports	17 CFR 240.13a-14 Certification of disclosure in annual and quarterly reports - filed on Form 10-Q, Form 10-K, Form 20-F.	Signed by an issuer's principal executive and principal financial officers, CEO or CFO.
Section 404 Management Assessment of Internal Controls	17 CFR 240.13a-15 (e)(f) Every issuer must maintain disclosure controls and procedures, and internal control over financial reporting, required to file an annual report.	Under the supervision of the issuer's principal executive and principal financial officer. The reports have to be communicated to the issuer's management by a body or group.

1649 Sarbanes-Oxley Act of 2002, *supra* note 47, § 302, 15 USC 7241.
1650 *Id.* § 404, 15 USC 7262.
1651 *Id.* § 302, 15 USC 7241; § 307, 15 USC 7245.
1652 *Id.* §§ 401–403, 15 USC 7261.
1653 Securities Exchange Act of 1934, *supra* note 605, § 3, 15 USC 78(c); Sarbanes-Oxley Act of 2002, *supra* note 47, § 2 (a) (7), 15 USC 7201.
1654 Sarbanes-Oxley Act of 2002, *supra* note 47, § 807, 18 USC 1348.
1655 Sarbanes-Oxley Act of 2002, *supra* note 47, § 101, 15 USC 7211.

Table 4 *Continued*

Requirements under SOX	Compliance with SEC Rules	Responsibilities for Executive Officer
Section 307 Rules of Professional Responsibility for Attorneys	17 CFR 205.3, 205.4, 205.5, 205.6 Duty to report evidence of a material violation, responsibilities of supervisory attorneys, sanctions and discipline, civil law penalties and remedies.	The attorney is required to report any material violation of securities law or breach of fiduciary duty to the chief legal counsel or the chief executive officer. In the case of no response, the attorney is required to report to the audit committee of the board of directors.

A number of US companies and foreign listed companies responded with a shift in compliance responsibilities and the separation of the legal and compliance department, with the appointment of a compliance officer[1656] and with changes to the internal reporting structures also in less regulated[1657] industries. Both the requirements of the SOX and the rule-making activities of the SEC have a considerable influence on the work of the executive officers, particularly of the CEO and CFO, attorney and indirectly of the compliance officer. Since the enactment of the SOX, the responsibilities and duties of these functions have increased markedly.[1658]

To conclude, the challenges that arose in the SEC actions against compliance officers in the financial services sector are wide-ranging and include challenges for the corporate compliance officer. The compliance officer's abilities require a diverse set of skills *e.g.* legal, accounting, financial, and communication skills.[1659] The compliance officer has to continuously improve compliance policies and procedures, to oversee reporting deadlines, to provide information on compliance issues to the board or CEO, to manage audits and investigations into regulatory compliance issues, to establish and maintain excellent relationships with regulators, and to respond to requests for information from administrative agencies.[1660]

1656 *E.g.* 82 percent of tech companies, 80 percent of manufacturing companies have appointed a CCO in 2013. *See* PWC Survey 2013 Bernstein, Kipp, and Groves, *supra* note 1624 at 8.

1657 In the US, the regulated industries are for example, the financials service industry and the health care industry.

1658 *See supra* A., I., 2.d., p. 223.

1659 *See supra* A., I., 2.f., p. 230.

1660 *See supra* A., I., 2.f., p. 230; *See also* Freeman (2007), *supra* note 57 at 360.

The compliance officer should be aware that he could be held liable, charged, and fined by the SEC, for violating the federal law. The SEC held that if a compliance officer has a sufficient position of influence and resources within a firm, he might be responsible for actively deterring misconduct. Overall, the compliance officer needs to ensure and document that the compliance policies and procedures work effectively within the company. Hence, the function of the compliance officer is beginning to develop separately, to become more independent and more visible.

For these reasons, the compliance officer is required to establish and document clear lines of supervision within the firm.[1661] He should know who is responsible for supervising the employee or agent in the event of wrongdoing.[1662] Furthermore, the compliance officer should periodically review the firm's policies. If there are any policies that are not followed, he should repeal these.[1663] Even in the event of investigation, the compliance officer is required continue the periodic compliance review.[1664] The evidence highlights that holding multiple functions besides the compliance function can lead to inefficiency.[1665] A compliance officer with a *"two or more hats"* role could result in difficulties and conflicts of interests. As a result, in their enforced actions against firms and individuals such as the CCO, the SEC requires prosecuted firms to establish a separate and standalone compliance department, to appoint a CCO with his own reporting structure and lines directly to the board of director or the CEO.[1666] In brief, the requirements of the compliance function have increased and extended since the SOX and the actions of the SEC have increased the responsibilities for chief executive officers as follows:

(1) Shift in corporate responsibilities for compliance,
(2) Increased pressure to separate corporate legal and compliance function,
(3) Improved legal, accounting, financial and communication skills of the compliance function,
(4) Periodically review and document compliance policies and procedures,
(5) Establish and document clear lines of supervision within the firm,
(6) Oversee reporting deadlines,
(7) Manage audits and investigations into regulatory compliance issues,
(8) Establish and maintain excellent relationships with regulators,
(9) Demand a standalone compliance function.[1667]

1661 *See supra* A,. I., 2.f., p. 230; *See also* Richard D. Marshall, BNA INSIGHTS: COMPLIANCE OFFICER LIABILITY-- SEC JUDGE SIDES WITH THE COMPLIANCE PROFESSION BLOOMBERG LAW (2015), http://www.bna.com/bna-insights-compliance-n17179935485/ (last visited Feb 26, 2016).

1662 *Id.*

1663 *Id.*

1664 *Id.*

1665 *Id.*

1666 *See supra* A,. I., 2.f., p. 230.

1667 *See supra* A,. I., 2.a.-f., pp. 217 et seq.

Although, to the present date, the SEC has prosecuted only CCOs who work within financial services companies, such as investment advisors, and broker-dealers, under the Investment Adviser Act and Investment Companies Act, all issuers need to adhere to the provisions of the SOX Act. The SEC could also use its compliance-rules[1668] as a model for unregulated industries.[1669] In conclusion, the overall role of the compliance officer that emerges from the above is a separate function with growing responsibilities and duties within firms. Therefore, the SOX, the compliance rules and actions of the SEC look likely to further strengthen the corporate compliance function within companies.

3. The Federal Sentencing Guidelines for Organizations (FSGO)

Considering the fact that both the FCPA Guide and the N/DPA Agreements of the DOJ refer to the USSC in order to point out an effective corporate compliance program and the design of the compliance function,[1670] there follows an overview of the guidelines, standards, and recommendations regarding all aspects of the compliance officer. Specifically, this section provides a brief history of the organizational guidelines[1671] and reviews their impact on the sentencing of organizations in court cases involving compliance issues.[1672]

At the beginning of the 1980s, Senate passed the Sentencing Reform Act (SRA)[1673] as a *"legislative effort to deal with sentencing disparity."*[1674] The actual purpose of this Act was to reject the belief that *"prisons could reform all criminals merely by isolating them from society."*[1675] Hence, this Act pursues three major goals

1668 *See* Investment Advisers Act of 1940, 17 CFR 275.206(4)-7, *supra* note 1642.

1669 *See* Fanto (2013), *supra* note 57 at 37.

1670 *See supra* A,. I., 1.a.,c.,.f., pp. 217 et seq.

1671 *"Federal Sentencing Guidelines for organizations (FSGO), which apply to corporations, partnerships, labor unions, pension funds, trusts, non-profit entities, and governmental units." See* Paula Desio & Deputy General Counsel USSC, An Overview of the Organization Guidelines, http://www.ussc.gov/sites/default/files/pdf/training/organizational-guidelines/ORGOVERVIEW.pdf (last visited Mar 8, 2016).

1672 *See* United State Code 18 USC, *supra* note 352, § 18; US Sentencing Guidelines Manual USSC, *supra* note 49, § 8 A1.1., Commentary 1. The term organizations includes corporations, partnerships, associations, joint-stock companies, unions, trusts, pension funds, unincorporated organizations, governments and political subdivisions thereof, and non-profit organizations.

1673 Sentencing Reform Act (1984), *supra* note 47.

1674 *See* Senator Kennedy, 1984, Simplification Draft Paper | United States Sentencing Commission, http://www.ussc.gov/research-and-publications/working-group-reports/simplification/simplification-draft-paper-2 (last visited Mar 2, 2016).

1675 ABA, April 2011 Cases | Public Education Preview of US Supreme Court Cases (2011), http://www.americanbar.org/publications/preview_home/april_2011.html#tapia (last visited Mar 2, 2016). *See e.g. Tapia v. United States* 131 S. Ct. 2382,

(1) fulfilling the purposes of sentencing listed in the statute for instance punishment, deterrence, incapacitation, and rehabilitation; (2) providing certainty and fairness among similar cases, and (3) reflecting "*advancement in knowledge of human behavior as it relates to the criminal justice process.*"[1676] It also establishes an independent commission in the judicial branch of the United States - the United States Sentencing Commission (USSC),[1677] which creates sentencing policies and practices for the Federal criminal justice system.[1678] The Commission has the power to develop guidelines and policy statements to help secure the purposes of sentencing pursuant to Section 3553 (a)(2).[1679] Furthermore, the Sentencing Reform Act of 1984 empowers the Commission to monitor the guidelines and submit to Congress appropriate modifications of the guidelines.[1680] Although the guidelines of the Commission are not set forth in law, the Commission states that the importance of these guidelines is acknowledged by the US Supreme Court in *United States v. Booker.*[1681] The Court held in this case that the enhanced application of the federal sentencing guidelines can be justified by the judge's determination of the "*real conduct underlying the crime of conviction.*"[1682] The court concluded that the guidelines were not unconstitutional, but they were considered to be an "*advisory guideline system*".[1683]

Originally, the Guidelines were used by courts when sentencing individuals. The Guidelines for individuals focus on punishment.[1684] In contrast, the organizational guidelines focus on providing restitution.[1685] However, the statistics have shown that a small number of organizations have been sentenced each year.[1686] During the period from 1984 to 1990, the Commission conducted an empirical analysis of organizational sentencing practices and drafted and implemented supplementary organizational guidelines.[1687] The Commission found a lack of consideration among

---

180 L. Ed. 2d 357, (2011). The question that was presented to the United States Supreme Court: Does 18 USC § 3582(a) allow a district court, when setting the length and term of imprisonment, to consider an individual defendant's need for an in-prison drug treatment program?

1676 *See supra* note 350, United States Code 18 USC, *supra* note 318 § 3553 - Imposition of a sentence. *See also* April 2011 Cases, ABA, *supra* note 1675.

1677 United States Sentencing Commission, USSC, *supra* note 50, 28 USC §§ 991–998.

1678 *Id.*28 USC § 991 (a)(b)(1).

1679 *Id.*28 USC § 991 (b)(1)(A); 18 USC, *supra* note 352, § 3553 (a)(2).

1680 United States Sentencing Commission, USSC, *supra* note 50, 28 USC § 995.

1681 *United States v. Booker*, 543 US 220 (2005).

1682 *Id.* at 250.

1683 *Id.* at 265–266.

1684 *See* Murphy (2002), *supra* note 654 at 702.

1685 *Id.* at 703.

1686 *Id.* at 698–699.

1687 USSC, Supplementary Report on Sentencing Guidelines for Organizations 2 (1991), [hereinafter supplementary report] http://www.ussc.gov/sites/default/

scholars with regard to how organizations ought to be sentenced and a great disparity in sentencing practices for organizations.[1688] In 1988, a working group of private defense attorneys was established to develop a set of practical principles for sentencing organizations.[1689] This working group submitted its *"recommendations regarding criminal penalties for organizations"* to the Commission.[1690] At the end of this, the Commission used three approaches to organize guidelines for narrow ranges within organizations. First, the statutory maxima based on pecuniary loss or gain[1691], second the statutory maxima based on class of offense[1692] and third the statutory maxima based on type of offense.[1693]

The US Code includes provisions on the sentencing of organizations.[1694] Since there are literally hundreds of criminal statutes in the United States Code, the Commission attempted to examine the application of these provisions, framed ranges of categories, and placed them in a rational order.[1695] Finally, on May 1, 1991, following many years of research and debate, the Commission promulgated an entirely new Chapter 8 to the guidelines for organizations pursuant to Section 994 (a).[1696]

a. Chapter 8 - Sentencing of Organizations

One of the objectives of the new organizational sentencing guidelines is to prevent and deter organizational criminal conduct by providing organizations credit for an effective compliance program.[1697] The importance of these amended guidelines (1991) is that it gives corporations the opportunity to reduce criminal penalties if they are able to prove that they had established compliance procedures and programs within the firm.[1698] The Federal Sentencing Guidelines of Organizations

---

files/pdf/training/organizational-guidelines/selected-articles/OrgGL83091.pdf (last visited Mar 2, 2016).

1688 *See* Murphy (2002), *supra* note 654 at 700.

1689 Supplementary Report , *supra* note 1687 at 3.

1690 Supplementary Report *Id.* at 3.

1691 Supplementary Report *Id.* at 10.; 18 USC., *supra* note 352, § 3571 (d) *"the defendant may be fined not more than the greater of twice the gross gain or twice the gross loss."*

1692 Supplementary Report *Id.* at 12; 18 USC, *supra* note 352 *e.g.* § 3571 (c) (5) *"for a Class A misdemeanor that does not result in death, not more than $200,000."*

1693 Supplementary Report *Id.* at 12; 18 USC, *supra* note 352 *e.g.* § 3571 (c) (5) "for a felony, not more than $500,000."

1694 18 USC, *supra* note 352, § 3571 (c) Fines for Organizations.

1695 United States Sentencing Commission, USSC, *supra* note 50.

1696 US Sentencing Guidelines Manual USSC, *supra* note 49 Chapter 8; United States Sentencing Commission, USSC, *supra* note 50, 18 USC. § 994 (a).

1697 US Sentencing Guidelines Manual Chapter 8 *Id.*§ 8 B2.1, Commentary 1. NACUA (2011), *supra* note 1142 at 4.

1698 *See* Smith (2003), *supra* note 504 at 637.

(FSGO) set forth seven minimum criteria for an effective compliance program as follows:

(1) The organization shall exercise due diligence to prevent and detect criminal conduct,
(2) The board of directors should be competent for exercising reasonable oversight of the content and operation of the compliance and ethics program,
(3) High-level personnel of the organization must be involved in oversight tasks,
(4) Specific individual(s) shall be delegated day-to-day responsibility and appropriate authority for the compliance and ethics program,
(5) Effective communication to ensure that the organization's compliance program is followed to all level of employees,
(6) Standards must be consistently enforced,
(7) Reasonable steps to respond appropriately to the criminal conduct and to prevent further similar criminal conduct.[1699]

Corporations need to meet these requirements. Furthermore, the commentary has added three more factors that ought to be considered when sentencing organizations; first, applicable governmental regulation and industry practice; second, the size of the organization; and third, repetition of similar misconduct in prior history of the company.[1700] Thus, Chapter 8 outlines a culpability score that determines the factors that could mitigate sentencing. This system begins with five points then proceeds through subsections (b) through (g) and at the end, adds or subtracts points to determine the applicable fines.[1701] The offense level fine table ranges between six or less points with US$ 8,500 and 38 or more points with US$ 150,000,000.[1702] Finally, the courts also have to ensure that organizations remedy any harm caused by the offense.[1703]

b. The FSGO Amendments in 2004 and 2010

Despite the introduction of the FCPA and the FSGO in 1991, as outlined above, further high-profile corporate scandals involving Enron and WorldCom revealed a crucial gap in the effectiveness of corporate compliance efforts.[1704] In response,

1699 *See* Megan Barry, *Why Ethics & Compliance Programs can fail*, 23 Journal of Business Strategy 37–40, 38 (2002); *See also* Murphy (2002), *supra* note 654 at 703–704. US Sentencing Guidelines Manual USSC, *supra* note 49 Chapter 8 § 8 B2.1.;

1700 US Sentencing Guidelines Manual USSC, *supra* note 49, Chapter 8 § 8 B2.1, Commentary 2.

1701 US Sentencing Guidelines Manual *Id.*§ 8 C2.5. (a)-(g).

1702 US Sentencing Guidelines Manual *Id.*§ 8 C2.4.

1703 US Sentencing Guidelines Manual *Id.* Introductory Commentary.

1704 NACUA (2011), *supra* note 1142 at 5.

the 2004 Amendments to the FSGO added an eighth new element for an effective compliance program. This states:[1705]

> (c) ...the organization shall periodically assess the risk of criminal conduct and shall take appropriate steps to design, implement, or modify each requirement set forth in subsection (b) to reduce the risk of criminal conduct identified through this process.[1706]

Therefore, the FSGO defined the term effective for a compliance program, which is absent from the FCPA Resource Guide.[1707] Based on this, an organization needs to periodically assess the risk of criminal conduct, including assessing the following aspects: first, the nature and seriousness of such criminal conduct, second, the nature of the organization's business - for example, in sales business, the organization should establish standards and procedures designed to prevent and detect price-fixing; and lastly, the prior history of the types of criminal conduct which occurred within the organization.[1708] In the view of the Commission, Section 8 B2.1 sets forth the requirements for an effective compliance and ethics program and responds to Section 805(a)(5) of the Sarbanes-Oxley Act, which determines that the Commission shall review and amend the guidelines that apply to organizations in Chapter 8.[1709] The guidelines have to ensure that they are *"sufficient to deter and punish organizational criminal misconduct."*[1710]

Furthermore, the 2004 Amendments clarified the leadership responsibilities relating to compliance.[1711] First, the board of directors should be familiar with the content and operation of the compliance program and exercise reasonable oversight in terms of compliance issues.[1712] Second, the director, the executive officer, and the individual in charge of a business or functional unit of the organization must ensure that the company has an effective compliance program as described in the guidelines and a specific individual should be responsible for the compliance program.[1713] Third, this individual should be responsible for the day-to-day operations of the compliance program and should have adequate resources, appropriate authority, and direct access to the board of directors.[1714] Therefore, the board of directors must take extra efforts to ensure compliance. Compliance issues must

---

1705 *Id.* at 5.
1706 US Sentencing Guidelines Manual USSC, *supra* note 49, § 8 B2.1. (c) (2004).
1707 FCPA Resource Guide DOJ and SEC, *supra* note 1241 Ch. 5 - Hallmarks of an effective compliance program. *See supra* A., I., 1.a., p. 189.
1708 US Sentencing Guidelines Manual *Id.*§ 8 B2.1. Commentary 7.
1709 US Sentencing Guidelines Manual *Id.*§ 8 B2.1. Commentary 7.
1710 Sarbanes-Oxley Act of 2002, *supra* note 47, § 805 (a)(5); United States Sentencing Commission, USSC, *supra* note 50, 28 USC § 994.
1711 ERC, ECOA & SCCE, Leading Corporate Integrity: Defining the Role of the Chief Ethics & Compliance Officer (CECO) 32 (2007).
1712 US Sentencing Guidelines Manual USSC, *supra* note 49, § 8 B2.1 (b) (2) (A).
1713 US Sentencing Guidelines Manual *Id.* § 8 B 2.1 (b) (2) (B) (2004).
1714 US Sentencing Guidelines Manual *Id.* § 8 B 2.1 (b) (2) (C) (2004).

be placed on the board's agenda, with time reserved for compliance records, and the compliance officer needs to have at his disposal adequate resources and appropriate authority.[1715] Thus, these Amendments made it clear that a direct relationship between the board and the compliance officer is a key element in ensuring the board's oversight duty of compliance.[1716] In return, the compliance officers themselves have to seek a direct reporting line to the board.[1717] In addition, they have to ensure that the code of conduct and compliance standards will continue to be promoted and apply to agents,[1718] business partners, and others serving the organization.[1719] According to the federal sentencing guidelines, both the board of directors and the compliance officer should work closely together. Moreover, the 2004 Amendments also provide additional guidance with respect to the implementation of compliance and ethics programs by small organizations with fewer than 200 employees.[1720]

In 2010, the guidelines were amended again with several changes regarding the sentencing of organizations. For example, Section 8 C2.5 (f) was amended by inserting:

> (1) If the offense occurred even though the organization had in place at the time of the offense an effective compliance and ethics program, as provided in § 8B2.1 (Effective Compliance and Ethics Program), subtract 3 points.[1721]

In addition, this section also comprises a mitigating factor if the individual with operational responsibility for the compliance program has direct reporting obligations to the governing authority or an appropriate subgroup thereof *e.g.* an audit committee or the board of directors.[1722] This obligation includes reporting promptly on any matter involving criminal conduct or potential criminal conduct.[1723] Furthermore, the organization could be given credit for promptly reporting

---

1715 Leading Corporate Integrity ERC, ECOA, and SCCE, *supra* note 1711 at 33.

1716 *See* Greenberg (2010), *supra* note 581 at 22.

1717 Leading Corporate Integrity ERC, ECOA, and SCCE, *supra* note 1711 at 34.

1718 The term agent relating to the guidelines means *"any individual, including a director, an officer, an employee, or an independent contractor, authorized to act on behalf of the organization." See* US Sentencing Guidelines Manual USSC, *supra* note 49 § 8 A1.2. Commentary.

1719 Leading Corporate Integrity ERC, ECOA, and SCCE, *supra* note 1711 at 34.

1720 USSC, 2011 Federal Sentencing Guidelines Manual - Appendix C - Volume III - Amendments to the Guidelines Manual 120 (2011), http://www.ussc.gov/sites/default/files/pdf/guidelines-manual/2011/manual-pdf/Appendix_C_Vol_III.pdf (last visited Mar 7, 2016), Amendment 674 (2004).

1721 US Sentencing Guidelines Manual USSC, *supra* note 49 § 8 C2.5 (f) (2010).

1722 US Sentencing Guidelines Manual, *Id.* § 8 C2.5 (f) (3) (C) (2010); USSC, *supra* note 1675 at 358, Amendment 744 (2010).

1723 US Sentencing Guidelines Manual USSC, *Id.* § 8 C2.5 (f) (3) (C) (2010), Application Notes.

the offense to appropriate governmental authorities; and if the compliance program revealed the offense before it went public and none of the compliance personnel involved willfully ignored the committal of the offense.[1724]

In sum, these four criteria could allow an organization to be granted a decrease in sentencing. Overall, the FSGO Amendments 2010 respond to the question as to how effective the compliance officer is within a company. Such effectiveness could be achieved through direct reporting duties and adequate resources. These will strengthen the compliance officers' role and authority within the firm and integrate this function into strategic decision-making.[1725] To whom the compliance officer reports will continue to determine his position in the company.

c. The Impact of the Organizational Guidelines (FSGO)

The academic view is that the main aim of the Guidelines is to promote good corporate governance and best practice by encouraging the implementation of effective compliance programs within companies.[1726] For instance, a study by *Murphy* found that the organizational guidelines influence four areas: sentencing practice, corporate culture, government enforcement and regulation, and corporate law.[1727] Firstly, the study compares the level of fines imposed in the pre-and post-era of the organizational guidelines from 1990 to 2000.[1728] Although the number of organizations sentenced does not vary greatly, the results show an upwards trend in terms of fines imposed. The median of the fine imposed rose from US$ 15,000 to US$ 100,000 between 1990 and 2000.[1729] Apparently, these results represent a move by the courts away from pre-guidelines sentencing practice for organizations.[1730]

An evaluation of the sourcebooks of the Commission for the number of organizations sentenced pursuant to Section 8 B2.1 shows the number of cases in which the guidelines on the imposition of fines were applied to organizations over the period from 2004 to 2014. *Table 5* presents a comparison of the number and percentage of cases in which the guidelines were applied and the number and percentage of cases in which the guidelines were not applied.[1731] The chart in *Figure 10* shows the figure for each percentage.[1732]

1724 US Sentencing Guidelines Manual *Id.* § 8 C2.5 (f) (3) (C) (i)-(iv); Amendment 744 (2010).

1725 *See* Greenberg (2010), *supra* note 581 at 23.

1726 *See e.g.* Baer (2009), *supra* note 586; DeStefano (2013), *supra* note 14; Murphy (2002), *supra* note 654 at 706.

1727 *See* Murphy (2002), *supra* note 654 at 707.

1728 *Id.* at 708.

1729 *Id.* at 708.; USSC & Office of Public Affairs, Sourcebook 2000 | United States Sentencing Commission (2000), Table 52.

1730 *See* Murphy (2002), *supra* note 654 at 708 n. 47.

1731 *See infra* Table 5, p. 243.

1732 *See infra* Figure 10, p. 244.

Table 5 *Number of Organizations Sentenced Pursuant to § 8 B 2.1*[1733]

Year	Cases	Applied	Not Applied	Percent Applied	Percent Not Applied
2004	86	54	32	62.79 %	37.21 %
2005	45	22	23	48.89 %	51.11 %
2006	217	122	95	56.22 %	43.78 %
2007	197	90	107	45.69 %	54.31 %
2008	199	98	101	49.25 %	50.75 %
2009	177	96	81	54.24 %	45.76 %
2010	149	60	89	40.27 %	59.73 %
2011	160	74	86	46.25 %	53.75 %
2012	187	69	118	36.90 %	63.10 %
2013	172	70	102	40.70 %	59.30 %
2014	162	57	105	35.19 %	64.81 %
Average	**159.18**	**73.82**	**91.73**	**46.94 %**	**53.06 %**
Median	**172**	**70**	**95**	**46.25 %**	**53.75 %**

Table 5 above provides a comparison of the percentage of cases (organizations) in which the FSGO were applied and those in which the guidelines were not applied.[1734] The results reveal that, in 2004, the percentage of cases in which the FSGO were applied was twice that of the cases in which they were not applied. This situation has reversed since 2010 and in 2014, the number of cases in which the FSGO were not applied was two times higher than the number of the cases in which the guidelines were applied.[1735]

These results could be attributable to the Amendments of the Guidelines in 2010. These Amendments introduced a new element to the compliance and ethics program and tightened the sentencing conditions.[1736] Conversely, this means that the courts imposed restrictive probation conditions of the fulfillment of the requirement to implement and maintain an effective compliance program. Companies, thus, have to consider compliance issues more seriously. Lastly, as these findings

---

1733 *Sources*: USSC & Office of Public Affairs, Annual Reports & Sourcebooks Archives | United States Sentencing Commission, http://www.ussc.gov/research-and-publications/annual-reports-sourcebooks/annual-reports-sourcebooks-archives (last visited Mar 22, 2016).

1734 *See supra* Table 5, p. 243.

1735 *See supra* Table 5, p. 243.

1736 US Sentencing Guidelines Manual USSC, *supra* note 49, § 8 B2.1 (b) (5) (c) (2010).

Proportion of the Cases in which the FSGO were applied and to those they were not applied from 2004 to 2014 (Source: US Sentencing Commission, Sourcebooks)

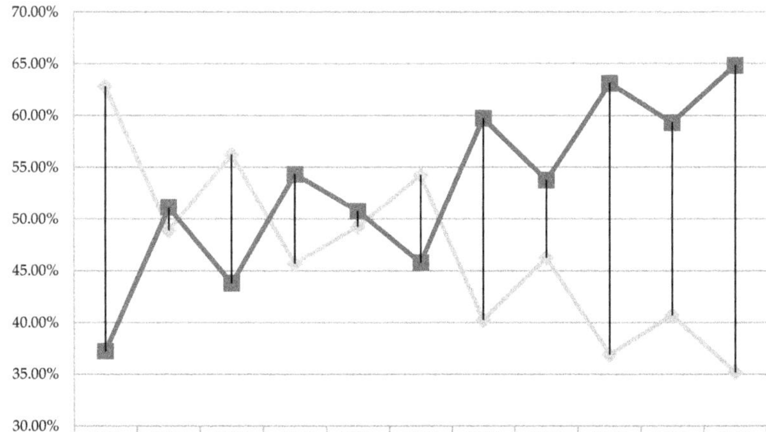

	2004	2005	2006	2007	2008	2009	2010	2011	2012	2013	2014
Percent App.	62.79%	48.89%	56.22%	45.69%	49.25%	54.24%	40.27%	46.25%	36.90%	40.70%	35.19%
Percent Not	37.21%	51.11%	43.78%	54.31%	50.75%	45.76%	59.73%	53.75%	63.10%	59.30%	64.81%

Figure 10 *Proportion of the Cases in which FSGO were applied and to those they were not applied*[1737]

illustrate, the impact of the organizational guidelines on sentencing has been both significant and costly.

Secondly, at the beginning of the 1990s, the organizational guidelines supported the creation of an entirely new job description: that of the corporate compliance officer.[1738] The compliance officer is responsible for developing, implementing, maintaining, and reviewing an effective compliance program.[1739] As discussed previously, the corporate compliance function includes creating and managing policies and procedures around compliance issues in order to uncover and prevent misconduct.[1740] Hence, over time, a new corporate compliance structure has developed.[1741] Furthermore, if the company is able to demonstrate that an effective compliance program is in place, the organizational sentencing guidelines mitigate corporate criminal penalties.[1742]

1737 Sources: *See supra* note 1733.
1738 *See* Murphy (2002), *supra* note 654 at 710.
1739 *Id.* at 710.
1740 *See* DeStefano (2013), *supra* note 14 at 87.
1741 *Id.* at 84.
1742 US Sentencing Guidelines Manual USSC, *supra* note 49, § 8 C2.5 (f).

However, a number of academics state a critical distinction between compliance programs that have the designated features on paper only and merely served as *"window dressing,"* like those at Enron or Anderson.[1743] In addition, in several cases, the court has actually found that the corporate compliance program was no more than a *"paper program."*[1744] In 2012, a report by the Ethics Resource Center (ERC) conducted an independent assessment of the experience of the organizational guidelines over the past twenty years, as well as the effectiveness of those guidelines.[1745] In this report, the authors acknowledged that the guidelines have achieved significant success in reducing workplace misconduct by enhancing compliance issues.[1746] Additionally, a study by *Weber & Fortun* stated that the business landscape has changed dramatically since the promulgation of the organizational guidelines. Corporations have responded by creating compliance programs and establishing the function of the compliance officer.[1747] In 2013, a study by *Weber & Wasieleski* found similar results to the effect that the Federal Organization Sentencing Guidelines (FSGO) support the creation of an internal reporting mechanism and shape the current state of compliance programs within companies.[1748] Overall, the 2012 ERC report summarized a list of criteria for a compliance program to be considered by companies, for instance:[1749]

- The FCPA compliance program requirements imposed by DOJ in recent N/DPAs and the hallmarks of an effective compliance program in the FCPA Resource Guide,[1750]
- The Sarbanes-Oxley Act compliance provisions,[1751]

1743 *See e.g.* Beale (2014), *supra* note 1097 at 20; Virginia Bodolica & Martin Spraggon, *An Examination into the Disclosure, Structure, and Contents of Ethical Codes in Publicly Listed Acquiring Firms*, 126 Journal of Business Ethics 459–472, 460 (2015); Greenberg (2009), *supra* note 11 at 27 Appendix C; Oded (2011), *supra* note 1097 at 276; Stucke (2014), *supra* note 1157 at 80.

1744 *See* Oded (2011), *supra* note 1097 at 276 n. 21; *See e.g. United States v. LBS Bank-New York, Inc.*, (E.D.PA. 1990), 757 F. Supp. 496 (E.D. Pa. 1990), Crim. A. No. 88-00516-05 (1990).

1745 Ethics Resource Center (ERC), The Federal Sentencing Guidelines for Organizations at twenty years a call to action for more effective promotion and recognition of effective compliance and ethics programs. (2012).

1746 *Id.* Foreword.

1747 *See* Weber and Fortun (2005), *supra* note 4 at 97.

1748 *See* Weber and Wasieleski (2013), *supra* note 492 at 617.

1749 Ethics Resource Center (ERC), *supra* note 1745 at 58.

1750 FCPA Resource Guide DOJ and SEC, *supra* note 1241; *See supra* A., I., 1a.-e., pp. 189 et seq.

1751 Sarbanes-Oxley Act of 2002, *supra* note 47; *See supra* A., I., 2.a.-f., pp. 217 et seq.

- The elements of the Federal Sentencing Guidelines for Organizations,[1752]
- The NYSE and/or NASDAQ listing standard requirements for issuers.[1753]

Thirdly, the Federal Sentencing Guidelines influence the prosecutorial policy of the DOJ.[1754] In their memos, the Deputy Attorney Generals listed a number of factors for consideration when charging corporations.[1755] Both memos include *"the existence and adequacy of the corporation's compliance program."*[1756] Thus, an effective compliance program can help defer federal prosecution and mitigate criminal penalty.[1757] In addition, in practice, the DOJ provides the framework of an effective compliance program in their N/DPAs with prosecuted firms.[1758] In these agreements, the DOJ refers to Section 8 B2.1. in order to shape the framework and conditions of the effectiveness of this program. Thus, it can be seen that the Federal Sentencing Guidelines have a major impact on government enforcement and regulation in terms of corporate compliance structures.

Fourthly, the last significant influence of the guidelines can be seen in their application by the courts. For instance, in the 1996 landmark case, *Caremark*,[1759] the organizational guidelines expanded corporate directors' potential liability vis-à-vis their shareholders.[1760] In this decision, the court applied the guidelines, citing:

> The Guidelines offer powerful incentives for corporations today to have in place compliance programs to detect violations of law, promptly to report violations to appropriate public officials when discovered, and to take prompt, voluntary remedial efforts.[1761]

To conclude, it has been highlighted that the Federal Sentencing Guidelines have shaped more clearly corporate compliance structures, have supported the creation

1752 US Sentencing Guidelines Manual USSC, *supra* note 49, § 8 B2.1.; *See supra* A., I., 3.a.-b., pp. 236 et seq.

1753 *See e.g.* Nasdaq, Initial Guide Listening | Nasdaq (2016), https://listingcenter.nasdaq.com/assets/initialguide.pdf (last visited Mar 4, 2016).

1754 *See* Murphy (2002), *supra* note 654 at 712.

1755 Eric Holder & DOJ, Deputy Attorney General, Memorandum | Bringing Criminal Charges Against Corporations (1999), https://www.justice.gov/sites/default/files/criminal-fraud/legacy/2010/04/11/charging-corps.PDF (last visited Mar 4, 2016); Thomson Memo Thompson and DOJ, *supra* note 1296.

1756 Holder and DOJ, Deputy Attorney General, *supra* note 1755; Thompson and DOJ, *supra* note 1296.

1757 *See* Murphy (2002), *supra* note 654 at 712.

1758 *See supra* A., I., 1.c., p. 198.

1759 *In re Caremark International Inc. Derivative Litigation,* 698 A.2d 959 (Del. Ch. 1996), *supra* note 21.

1760 *See* Murphy (2002), *supra* note 654 at 713.

1761 *In re Caremark International Inc. Derivative Litigation*, 698 A.2d 959 (Del. Ch. 1996), *supra* note 21 at 969; Murphy (2002), *supra* note 654 at 714.

of direct reporting mechanisms within companies and, therefore, have strengthened the compliance officer's position.

d. Conclusion – The Compliance Officer's Work under the FSGO

The FSGO and the amendments thereto were designed with two key sentencing purposes in mind: (1) *"punishment"* and (2) *"deterrence."*[1762] A number of authors view the guidelines as an important step in the development of corporate compliance because they provide firms incentives to adopt compliance programs.[1763] These guidelines lead the organizations to measures of preventing and detecting crime through the eight elements of an effective compliance program. By means of appropriate features of compliance, such as the appointment of a compliance officer responsible for the daily compliance operations with direct access to the board of directors, the company can be given credit in sentencing practice. In brief, the guidelines led to a new focus on compliance structure, board oversight, and independent compliance reporting.[1764] However, this approach does not offer precise details for implementation; instead, it flexibly enables organizations to act in designing their own appropriate compliance program, giving due consideration to the defined framework.[1765] It has been recognized that the Federal Sentencing Guidelines for Organizations have set standards for corporate compliance programs, compliance structure, and compliance reporting.[1766] Under the FSGO, the compliance officer is required to immediately bring compliance problems to the attention of the board of directors and establish a direct reporting relationship with the board. In supporting the board with compliance issues, the compliance officer should propose to the board the establishment of a compliance committee.

However, recent studies by PWC illustrate that only approximately 40 percent of US companies from the consumer or retail sectors actually have and use a compliance committee.[1767] In contrast, in the regulated sectors (financial services or healthcare) approximately 60 percent of organizations have a compliance committee.[1768] While the 2014 study by PWC found that investors' expectations concerning compliance issues rank higher in terms of priority than its priority at board

1762 An Overview of the Guidelines Desio and USSC, *supra* note 1671.

1763 *See e.g.* Koehler (2012), *supra* note 958 at 618; Miller (2014), *supra* note 595 at 269; Murphy (2002), *supra* note 654 at 706; Weber and Fortun (2005), *supra* note 4 at 97.

1764 *See* Greenberg (2011), *supra* note 11 at 1.

1765 An Overview of the Guidelines Desio and USSC, *supra* note 1671.

1766 *See e.g.* Greenberg , *supra* note 669 at 1; Greenberg (2013), *supra* note 522 at 3; ERC, ECOA, and SCCE, *supra* note 1683 at 5; Weber and Wasieleski (2013), *supra* note 492.

1767 PWC Study 2013, *supra* note 1623 at 10; PWC Study 2014, *supra* note 8 at 5. This specialized committee operates separately from the audit committee and it is usually composed of a majority of independent directors. *See* Miller (2014), *supra* note 595 at 83.

1768 PWC Study 2013, *supra* note 1623 at 10.

level,[1769] regulatory compliance is not particularly high on the list of priorities for either boards or investors.[1770] A subsequent study by PWC with 1,102 responses from compliance executives of companies from 23 US industry sectors, states that, today, only 35 percent of chief compliance officers are actively involved in strategic planning.[1771] For this reason, the compliance officer needs to use the regulatory framework to embed compliance messages into board and management reports in order to bring compliance into the consciousness of the board member.[1772] The board of directors has to understand that strengthening the authority of the compliance officer could help to support the board in fulfilling its responsibility for compliance oversight.[1773] The board should see the compliance officer as a primary supporter in overseeing compliance.[1774] An empowered role of the compliance officer could also provide a defense against directors' liability.[1775]

In addition, in order to achieve these goals, compliance officers should provide compliance issues and ensure that the board of directors implements compliance into the business strategy of the company.[1776] Thus, the compliance officer could initiate measures to combine compliance with corporate goals.[1777] In so doing, he would be able to familiarize himself with the business and could evaluate and discover compliance risks in corporate business more effectively.[1778] Furthermore, in order to address compliance risk and to handle compliance tasks, the compliance officer needs to be provided with appropriate staff resources and budgets.

Evidently, laws, regulations, and guidelines may help to facilitate and to enhance the role of the compliance officer, but compliance officers themselves noted that strong government mandates for corporate compliance have resulted in some instances in a "*check-the-box*" mentality within corporations.[1779] A number of compliance officers mentioned that the establishment by the Commission of a "*specific individual*" responsible for dealing with corporate

---

1769 PWC Study 2014, *supra* note 1767 at 13.

1770 PWC Study 2014 *Id.* at 13.

1771 Sally Bernstein & Andrea Falcione, PwC-2015 Compliance Survey | Moving beyond the baseline Leveraging the compliance function to gain a competitive edge 4 (2015), [hereinafter PWC Study 2015] www.pwc.com/us/stateofcompliance. This survey includes 1,102 responses to the 2015 survey from compliance executives (compliance officers, chief compliance and ethics officers) from companies of the industry sector.

1772 PWC study 2014, *supra* note 1767 at 13.

1773 *See* Greenberg (2009), *supra* note 11 at 6. The duty of oversight of the board will be discussed later in this chapter. *See infra* II., a., p. 254.

1774 *Id.* at 7.

1775 *Id.* at 8.

1776 PWC study 2014, *supra* note 1767 at 12.

1777 PWC Study 2014 *Id.* at 12.

1778 PWC Study 2014 *Id.* at 12.

1779 *See* Greenberg (2009), *supra* note 11 at 14.

compliance issues as a point of contact for compliance officers could help facilitate better communication and reporting lines within companies and between industry and government.[1780]

In conclusion, over the past twenty years, the sentencing guidelines for organizations have further refined the role of the compliance function in the US. With respect to organizations, the original targets of the FSGO - to provide certainty and fairness among similar cases - were expanded to include directing companies to establish effective compliance procedures and structures. The guidelines aim to integrate compliance responsibilities into strategic business objectives, both in the corporate structure and in the consciousness of the board.[1781]

4. The Line of Federal Law and the Challenges Posed by the Role of Compliance Officers

Having examined the line of relevant federal law over the course of more than 100 years, particularly with regard to the private sector, it can be seen that a strong and complex legislation has evolved also in the financial service sector with respect to compliance issues and the compliance officers' function in the US. In the wake of various corporate scandals, cases of bankruptcy and stock market crashes, both the government and the regulators have enforced legislation and compliance requirements for corporations. This line of legislation began with the introduction of the Interstate Commerce Act of 1887[1782] and the Sherman Antitrust Act of 1890,[1783] which were designed to regulate the private sector. Following the Great Depression on the stock market, the government introduced additional far-reaching legislation for publicly traded companies in order to regulate the offer and sale of securities and to restore investors' confidence.[1784] The Foreign Corrupt Practices Act of 1977[1785] was enacted with the objective of making it unlawful for US persons and foreign issuers of securities to make payments to foreign government officials in return for business.[1786] After a number of high profile corporate scandals at the beginning of the new century, Congress passed the Sarbanes-Oxley Act in 2002. In recent years, the enforcement of legislation culminated in signing of the Dodd–Frank Wall Street Reform and Consumer Protection Act as a response

---

1780 *Id.* at 14.

1781 Leading Corporate Integrity ERC, ECOA, and SCCE, *supra* note 1711 at 17.

1782 Interstate Commerce Act (ICA), *supra* note 579.

1783 Sherman Antitrust Act, *supra* note 619.

1784 Securities Act of 1933, *supra* note 600; Securities Exchange Act of 1934, *supra* note 605; Investment Advisers Act of 1940, *supra* note 1642; Investment Company Act of 1940, *supra* note 1599.

1785 Foreign Corrupt Practices Act 1977 (FCPA), *supra* note 438.

1786 FCPA | Criminal Fraud DOJ, *supra* note 659.

to the global economic downturn in 2010.[1787] This extensive legislation empowered the regulators with broad authority over all aspects of the securities industry.

To summarize the line of enforcement of Federal Law, *Table 6* shows the scope of the federal statutes.

Table 6 *Overview of the Extent of Federal Legislation*

Legislation	United State Code	Number of Sec., Pages
Interstate Commerce Act	Terminated in 1995	n.a.
Sherman Antitrust Act	15 USC §§ 1–7	Three Sections
Securities Act (1933)	15 USC §§ 77a-77aa	22 pages
Securities Exchanges Act	15 USC §§ 78a-78pp	28 pages
Investment Advisers Act	15 USC §§ 80b 1–21	10 pages
Investment Comp. Act	15 USC §§ 80a 1–64	58 pages
FCPA	15 USC §§ 78dd-1	3 pages
SOX	15 USC, 18 USC	65 pages
Dodd Frank	12 USC, 15 USC	848 pages

Accordingly, the legal environment of companies has been expanded. Companies and their directors, officers, employees, agents, and business partners have to deal with the altered legal framework every day. The ongoing enhancement of federal law has changed and increased the responsibilities for corporate compliance. In today's complex regulatory environment, corporate reputations or indeed an entire company can stand and fall with the issue of compliance. Additionally, more recently, regulators such as the DOJ and the SEC have required effective corporate compliance policies, procedures, and even the designation of a chief compliance officer position. As a result, the compliance officer now faces new challenges in order to avoid governmental investigations, fines, and expensive settlements for the company. For this reason, legal scholars have named the compliance officer "*gatekeepers*" or the "*second defense line*"[1788] after the business units within a company. The following tabular comparison between the FCPA, SOX and FSGO, all of which were examined above, sets up the recommendations on required compliance responsibilities with respect to the compliance function within companies.

1787 DODD–FRANK WALL STREET REFORM AND CONSUMER PROTECTION ACT (2010), *supra* note 700.

1788 *See e.g.* Miller (2014), *supra* note 519 at 4; Traeger, Guidroz, and Jimbo (2014), *supra* note 486 at 25.

Table 7 - *Comparison between the FCPA, SOX and FSGO Recommendations with Respect to the Compliance Function*[1789]

FCPA, Resource Guide, DOJ, N/DPA	SOX and the SEC cases	FSGO, Manual Chapter 8, § 8 B2.1
Clearly articulated policy against corruption by the management	Periodic improvement of compliance policies and procedures	High-level personnel of the organization shall ensure that the organization has an effective compliance program
Code of conduct and compliance policies and procedures	Maintain disclosure controls and procedures, and internal control over financial reporting, file an annual report	Promotion of an organizational culture that encourages ethical conduct and a commitment to compliance with the law
Oversight, autonomy, and resources of a company's compliance program	Increase of, *e.g.* legal, accounting, financial, and communication skills of the compliance officer	Compliance program shall be reasonably designed, implemented, and enforced
Risk assessment to develop an effective compliance program	Shift in corporate compliance responsibilities, separation between the legal and compliance department	The organization shall periodically assess the risk of criminal conduct to reduce the risk of criminal conduct.
Training and continuing advice on anti-bribery regulations	Manage audits and investigations into regulatory compliance issues,	Reasonable steps to communicate and conduct effective training programs
Incentives and disciplinary measures	Establish and maintain excellent relationships with regulators, and respond to requests for information	Specific individual(s) within the organization shall be delegated day-to-day operational responsibility for the compliance program
Third-party due diligence and payments, designing anti-bribery contract terms, ongoing monitoring and reviewing	Establish and document clear lines of supervision within the firm	Exercise due diligence to prevent and detect criminal conduct
Confidential reporting and internal investigation	Oversee reporting deadlines, Provide information on compliance issues to the board or CEO	Individual(s) with operational responsibility shall report periodically to high-level personnel and, as appropriate, to the governing authority.

1789 *See generally* A., I., 1. to 3., pp. 183 et seq.

As we have seen, in response to an increased line of federal law and the rule making activities by regulators, corporate compliance departments were assigned more responsibilities for compliance issues and an effective compliance program to reduce violations of law and fines in the event of an offense. While the recommendations of the FCPA do not specifically mention or require the compliance function, since 1991 the FSGO have required an effective program with specific *"high-level personnel"* of the organization to be responsible for the compliance and ethics program.[1790] Individuals who have *"day-to-day operational responsibility"* have to report regularly to high-level personnel *"on the effectiveness of the compliance and ethics program,"* and shall obtain *"adequate resources, appropriate authority, and direct access to the governing authority."*[1791] The FCPA required the risk assessment to develop an effective compliance program without defining the effectiveness of such a program. In addition to the FCPA and the SOX, the FSGO required and created the position of the corporate compliance officer with a specific reporting structure to the CEO or board. Furthermore, the SOX, the FSGO, and the Rules of the SEC have actually defined the effectiveness with periodic risk assessment and periodic reporting and disclosure obligations to reduce criminal conduct. Hence, federal law places new legal duties on corporate officers aimed at increasing reporting and disclosure accountability. Over time, though each new legislative act, the requirements applicable to the compliance officers' and executive officers' responsibilities have increased and extended. Most recently, the regulators have additionally been encouraging the separation between the legal and compliance function and have changed corporate structures by means of N/DPAs.

As a result of this line of federal law, there are three key aspects of the compliance officer's role that need to be carefully considered by the board of directors and executive officers to ensure that this function provides an effective and successful response to the legal environment.

(1) Separation between the Legal and the Compliance Function
A growing body of legislation has meant an increase in corporate compliance tasks and duties. As such, it is becoming increasingly difficult to fulfill these tasks and duties on the side. What this means in practice is that, given the clearly defined duties and tasks for the compliance officer, this position can be a full-time employment with focus on compliance issues. At the same time, there continues to be an academic debate on the separation between the general counsel and the compliance officer; the examined corporate settlement agreements by prosecutors place the compliance officer function in a direct reporting line to the board and provide new guidance and standards for this function.[1792] Thus, the regulator sets standards for the corporate compliance officer within the private sector. Overall, the prevalence of the corporate

1790 US Sentencing Guidelines Manual USSC, *supra* note 49, § 8 B2.1 (b)(2)(B).
1791 *Id.* § 8 B2.1 (b)(2)(C).
1792 *See generally* A., I., 1.b., p. 195.

compliance officer as a separate and standalone function looks set to continue to rise in view of these developments and standards.[1793] Therefore, the "*multi-functional*" or "*dual hatted*" role of the compliance officer should be gradually transforming into a standalone corporate function.

(2) Changes in Corporate Reporting Structures
Due to the separation of the compliance officer from the legal function and based on the requirements of the 2010 amendments to the FSGO, *"direct reporting obligations to the governing authority,"* the compliance officer should have direct access to the board.[1794] It is important that the quality of relevant information does not change reporting through and to third parties such as the general counsel. In order to establish an effective compliance program, the day-to-day compliance issue should reach the board unfiltered. The reporting lines should be clearly determined, periodically timed and communicated within the company.[1795] Furthermore, the compliance officer should have formal and informal connections with the business units and functions of the company. He should be invited to important business meetings such as risk meetings, review meetings, and planning meetings.

(3) Corporate Authority for the Effective Compliance Officer
In order to be effective and to carry out his extended responsibilities under US Federal Law, the compliance officer should have authority to establish, maintain, and review periodically corporate compliance policies and procedures. He can gain authority through unfiltered board access, adequate budgets and resources, as well as sufficient compliance staff. Through the increase in authority, the effectiveness of the compliance officer will continue to improve. Thus, the compliance officer will become increasingly visible within the company.[1796]

These three essential aspects of the compliance officers' role could be applied by all companies irrespective of the size, corporate purpose, risk profile, and industry to help deal with the challenges of this function. However, PWC Studies from 2012 to 2015 have shown, in practice, that there are still many hurdles for companies to overcome if they wish to successfully and effectively integrate the compliance officer function.[1797]

After analyzing the US federal legal framework and its Guidelines in terms of the compliance officers' role and work, the next section introduces the US State Corporations Law, landmark cases, and US Employment Law with respect to the compliance officers' role, duties and liability.

1793 PWC Study 2013, *supra* note 1623 at 16; PWC Study 2014, *supra* note 1767 at 11.

1794 *See supra* Table 7, p. 291, US Sentencing Guidelines Manual USSC, *supra* note 49, § 8 B2.1 (f)(3)(C).

1795 *See supra* A.,I.,3.a.-d., pp. 236 et seq.

1796 *See supra* A.,I.,3.a.-d., pp. 236 et seq.

1797 PWC Study 2012, *supra* note 10; PWC Study 2013, *supra* note 1623; PWC Study 2014, *supra* note 1767; PWC Study 2015, *supra* note 1771.

II. State Corporation Law and the Development of Directors and Officers Duties

As examined previously, case law is also a major source of common law in the US. The corporate law is further embodied in judicially decided cases. The holdings in court decisions may differ from the applicable state corporation law. The applicable law is determined by the internal affairs doctrine.[1798] Internal affairs include, for example, the procedural matters and transactions of the company.[1799] Under this rule, the company is governed by the law of the state, in which the company was incorporated.

Generally, corporation law governs the creation, organization, and regulation of corporations. The term corporation is defined as follows:

> A corporation is a legal entity created through the laws of its articles of incorporation. The corporation is treated as a legal person. [1800]

In the US, the majority of corporation law takes the form of state corporation law and, thus, varies from state to state. The corporation law of each state in the US comprises the articles of incorporation and bylaws for forming a corporation.[1801] US State Corporation Law is a primary source relating to corporate directors' and officers' liability.[1802] Pursuant to corporate law, directors, and officers have a

---

1798 *See e.g. CTS Corp. v. Dynamics Corp. of America,* (US Supreme Court), 481 69, 78 (1987). Finally, the US Supreme Court addressed the internal affairs doctrine, a "*principle of conflict of laws*" ... designed to make sure that the law of only one state shall govern the internal affairs of a corporation or other association.

1799 *See* Pat K. Chew, Directors' and officers' liability 9 (4. ed. 1993).

1800 *See in:* US Legal Inc., *supra* note 1.

1801 *See* Chew, *supra* note 1799 at 9. "*The articles of incorporation must include the corporation's name, whether the corporation will exist for a limited period of time or perpetually, the lawful business purpose of the corporation, the number of shares that the corporation will issue to shareholders as well as the types and preferences of the shares, the corporation's registered agent and address for the purpose of accepting service of process in the event that the corporation is sued, and the names and addresses of the corporation's directors and incorporators."'Bylaws' are rules that dictate how the corporation is going to be run. Bylaws are fairly easy to amend. They may include rules regarding the conduct of corporate officers, directors, and shareholders, and typically they designate times, locations, and voting requirements for corporate meetings.*" *See also* US Legal Inc, Forming a Corporation – Corporations US Legal, https://corporations.uslegal.com/basics-of-corporations/forming-a-corporation/ (last visited Jul 7, 2015).

1802 *See* Chew, *supra* note 1799 at 8. Under corporation law the term directors includes the "*governing body of a corporation who are usually elected by the shareholders. The roles of corporate officers comprise the corporation's president, vice presidents, treasurer, and secretary, are defined by the corporate bylaws, and*

number of duties that may give rise to liability.[1803] These duties establish standards and if these standards are neglected, directors and officers could be held liable.[1804] In addition, approximately one half of the US States base their corporation laws on the Model Business Corporations Act (MBCA), which was approved by the American Bar Association (ABA).[1805] The MBCA of the ABA is often used as an exemplary source of corporate law principles.[1806]

The majority of publicly traded companies are incorporated in Delaware.[1807] For this reason, the following part introduces the most important definitions and provisions of Delaware Corporation Law and the Model Business Corporations Act, as far as corporate directors, officers, and their duties and liabilities, their possible indemnification, are concerned, the landmark decisions with respect to the fiduciary duties of directors and officers since this obligation has become important in the era of corporate scandals in the assessment of responsibility to shareholders for their actions in the Delaware courts, and the applicable standards.[1808] This part also outlines the findings of an examination of the American board structure and an analysis of the corporate (compliance) officers' agreements.

1. Relevant Definitions and Provisions Relating to US Corporation Law

Corporate law implies that directors and officers are the fiduciary[1809] of the company.[1810] The general and federal statute, the United State Code, provides a broad definition of fiduciary and includes the following:

---

articles of incorporation. They act as agents of the corporation." See US Legal Inc, Officers – Corporations US Legal, https://corporations.uslegal.com/basics-of-corporations/shareholders-directors-and-officers/officers/, https://corporations.uslegal.com/basics-of-corporations/shareholders-directors-and-officers/officers/ (last visited Jul 7, 2015).

1803 *See* Chew, *supra* note 1799 at 8; *See infra* B., IV., pp. 303 et seq.

1804 *Id.* at 8; *See infra* B., IV., p. 307.

1805 Model Business Corporation Act, 4th Edition Business Corporation Act (2010), (1950). It contains model corporate law provisions and it was first published and approved in 1950 by the American Bar Association (ABA). A number of model provisions are adopted by twenty-four states in the US. *See* US Legal Inc, Laws Governing Corporations – Corporations US Legal, https://corporations.uslegal.com/basics-of-corporations/laws-governing-corporations/, https://corporations.uslegal.com/basics-of-corporations/laws-governing-corporations/ (last visited Jul 7, 2015).

1806 *See* Chew, *supra* note 1799 at 8.

1807 *Id.* at 10.

1808 *See* McMillan (2013), *supra* note 198 at 521.

1809 29 USC, *supra* note 351 § 1002.

1810 *See* Chew, *supra* note 1799 at 24.

A fiduciary is a person, who

(i) exercises any discretionary authority or discretionary control respecting management of such plan or exercises any authority or control respecting management or disposition of its assets,
(ii) renders investment advice for a fee or other compensation, direct or indirect, with respect to any moneys or other property of such plan, or has any authority or responsibility to do so, or
(iii) has any discretionary authority or discretionary responsibility in the administration of such plan.[1811]

This definition is set forth in title 29, labor law, Chapter 18 Employee Retirement Income Security Act (ERISA)[1812] - a complex statutory regime that will be discussed later.[1813] One element that must be maintained under a plan is that of a named fiduciary.[1814] Therefore, named directors and officers are liable as fiduciaries.[1815] In addition, a number of cases have held that *"officers and directors owe fiduciary duties to the corporation and its shareholders."*[1816]

Furthermore, the core idea of liability is the theory of the good faith obligation of directors and officers.[1817] As previously discussed, the duty of good faith has long been incorporated into the statutes.[1818] In addition, Sections 8.30 and 8.42 of the Model Business Corporation Act (MBCA) comprise general standards for directors and officers.[1819] When a director or officer is discharged of his duty, he shall act in good faith.[1820] Hence, a number of corporate statutes impose a duty of good faith on directors and officers.[1821] While these statutes do not precisely define this duty, the ABA Guidebook includes *inter alia* the task of *"establishing and monitoring effective*

1811 *Id.* at 162.; 29 USC, *supra* note 351 § 1002 (21)(A).

1812 Employee Retirement Income Security Act (ERISA), Pub. L. 114-38, 29 USC §§ 1001-1461 USC 88 Stat. 829 (1974).

1813 *See supra* III., 1., p. 274.

1814 *See* Chew, *supra* note 1799 at 162; 29 USC, *supra* note 352, § 1105 (c)(1).

1815 *See* Chew, *supra* note 1799 at 162; 29 USC., *supra* note 352, § 1105 (c)(2).

1816 *See e.g. Guth v. Loft, Inc.*, (Del 1939), A.2d 5 503, 510 (1939); *In re Walt Disney Co. Derivative Litig.*, (Del. Ch. 2004), 38 (2004)... *"the fiduciary relationship that an officer or director owes to the corporation and its shareholders has long been recognized in Delaware jurisprudence."*

1817 *See* Sale (2007), *supra* note 22 at 723.

1818 *See supra* footnote196, p. 73; *See e.g.* Commercial law Uniform Commercial Code (UCC), *supra* note 184, § 1–203; Contract law *Id.* § 205.

1819 Model Business Corporation Act, 4th Edition, *supra* note 1805 § 8.30 (a) (1), § 8.42 (a) (1).

1820 *Id.* § 8.30 (a) (1), § 8.42 (a) (1).

1821 *See e.g.* Delaware Code, *supra* note 24 § 145 (a) (b); New York Business Corporation Law, N.Y. Bus. Corp. Law (1890) § 717 (a); Eisenberg (2006), *supra* note 199 at 4.

compliance systems and policies for ethical conduct."[1822] Hence, corporate monitoring systems form part of the directors' oversight duty.[1823] Directors derive their information they need to make important decisions from those established systems.[1824]

The duty of good faith has also long been recognized in case law in the form of the business judgment rule.[1825] The business judgment rule was established in a number of Delaware judicial decisions[1826] and based on the good faith obligation.[1827] Seemingly, courts tend to recognize the business judgment rule as a standard of liability.[1828] It has been recognized that in conscious decisions by directors, the business judgment rule is implied.[1829] A decision is present, for example, when directors participate in board meetings, discuss, consult, or reject a proposal.[1830] The purpose of the business judgment rule is that directors need flexibility, discretion, and autonomy to make business decision.[1831] Hence, the directors need all relevant and material information. Sometimes, a number of decisions have to be made under pressure.[1832] Thus, it is difficult and inappropriate for courts to assess director's judgment.[1833] However, the case law has shown that the business judgment rule does not protect any decisions by directors that are made involving unlawful conduct, fraudulent conduct or which present a conflict of interest for the directors.[1834] A conflict of interest could generally arise when directors have a personal financial interest, as it was the case in *Gantler v. Stephens.*[1835]

Similarly, under Delaware Corporation Law,[1836] directors are not held liable for corporate losses if they act and make decisions on behalf of a company with good intentions.[1837] The Supreme Court of Delaware confirmed that under Delaware law

---

1822 American Bar Association Committee on Corporate Laws & American Bar Association Section of Business Law, 5. Corporate Director's Guidebook 12 (2007).

1823 *See* Sale (2007), *supra* note 22 at 724.

1824 *Id.* at 724.

1825 *See supra* footnote 635; p. 120; Eisenberg (2006), *supra* note 199 at 4.

1826 *See* McMillan (2013), *supra* note 198 at 521.

1827 Good faith, West's Encyclopedia of American Law (The Gale Group, Inc., 2. ed. 2008), http://legal-dictionary.thefreedictionary.com/good+faith (last visited Mar 24, 2016).

1828 *See* McMillan (2013), *supra* note 198 at 529.

1829 *See* Chew, *supra* note 1799 at 30.

1830 *Id.* at 30.

1831 *Id.* at 30.

1832 *Id.* at 30.

1833 *Id.* at 30.

1834 *Id.* at 29–30.

1835 *Gantler v. Stephens*, 965 A.2d 695 (Del. 2009), *supra* note 23.

1836 *See e.g.* 8 Delaware Code, *supra* note 24, § 141 (a).

1837 *Id.*

the business judgment rule is a fundamental principle, codified in Section 141(a).[1838] Furthermore, in *Aronson v. Lewis,* the court explained the rule as follows:

> The rule itself "is a presumption that in making a business decision, the directors of a corporation acted on an informed basis, in good faith and in the honest belief that the action taken was in the best interests of the company."[1839]

Nevertheless, *McMillan* argues that the rule constitutes a type of immunity.[1840] In practice, the courts have used it as a test to determine whether the directors or officers' conduct leads to personal liability.[1841] The courts also examined the duty of loyalty and the duty of care in the context of the standard of liability while assessing the fiduciary duties of directors. In 1985, for example, in the context of a proposed merger, the Delaware Supreme Court defined the duty of care in *Smith v. Van Gorkom* as follows:

> In the specific context of a proposed merger of domestic corporations, a director has a duty under Del. Code Ann. tit. 8, § 251(b), along with his fellow directors, to act in an informed and deliberate manner in determining whether to approve an agreement of merger before submitting the proposal to the stockholders.[1842]

The court concluded that the directors were uninformed and thus, the decision of the Trans Union Corp board's to sell the company was grossly negligent.[1843] Hence, under the business judgment rule the directors' liability is predicated upon concepts of gross negligence.[1844] Therefore, the majority of director's decisions are protected by the business judgment rule.[1845]

The powers of directors are codified in Section 141 (a) of the Delaware Code:

> (a) The business and affairs of every corporation organized under this chapter shall be managed by or under the direction of a board of directors, except as may be otherwise provided in this chapter or in its certificate of incorporation.[1846]

The powers and duties of directors as determined in the statutes, are specified in the bylaws of the company. For example, the general power provision includes the following:

> The business and affairs of the corporation shall be managed, and all corporate powers shall be exercised by or under the direction of, the board of directors.[1847]

1838 *Smith v. Van Gorkom,* 488 A.2d 858, 872 (Del. 1985).
1839 *Aronson v. Lewis,* 473 A.2d 805, 812 (1984).
1840 *See* McMillan (2013), *supra* note 198 at 521.
1841 *Id.* at 529.
1842 *Smith v. Van Gorkom,* (Del. 1985), *supra* note 1838 at 873.
1843 *Id.* at 884.
1844 *Id.* at 873.; *Aronson v. Lewis, supra* note 1839 at 812.
1845 *See* Chew, *supra* note 1799 at 41.
1846 tit. 8 *Id.*§ 141 (a).
1847 Bylaws of a Holding, Inc., State of California, (2009) Sec. 3.1.

In addition, the bylaws determine the specific duties of the directors:

> (a) Select and remove all officers, agents, and employees of the Corporation; prescribe any powers and duties for them that are consistent with law, with the Articles of Incorporation, and with these bylaws; fix their compensation; and require from them security for faithful service.
> (b) Adopt, make, and use a corporate seal; prescribe and alter the forms of certificates of stock.
> (c) Borrow money and incur indebtedness on behalf of the Corporation, and cause to be executed and delivered for the Corporation's purposes, in the corporate name, promissory notes, bonds, debentures, deeds of trust, mortgages, pledges, hypothecations, and other evidences of debt and securities.[1848]

Conversely, US State Courts have not unequivocally ruled on whether the business judgment rule should apply to officer's decisions.[1849] It appears that State Corporation Law does not cover officers' limited liability.[1850] In the US, there is sometimes a degree of uncertainty regarding who is classified as an officer.[1851] As has been mentioned, State Corporation Law does not make any clear distinction between the fiduciary duties of corporate directors and those of corporate officers.[1852] Generally, the provisions of these statutes describe the powers of directors and officers as follows:

> (a) In addition to the powers enumerated in § 122 of this title, every corporation, its officers, directors and stockholders shall possess and may exercise all the powers and privileges granted by this chapter or by any other law or by its certificate of incorporation.[1853]

Therefore, the duties of officers are not clearly defined in State Corporation Law such as in the Delaware Code:

> (a) Every corporation organized under this chapter shall have such officers with such titles and duties as shall be stated in the bylaws or in a resolution of the board of directors.[1854]

or such as in the Florida Business Coordination Act:

> Each officer has the authority and shall perform the duties set forth in the bylaws or, to the extent consistent with the bylaws, the duties prescribed by the board of

---

1848 Bylaws of a Holding, Inc. *Id.*
1849 *See e.g. Gantler v. Stephens*, 965 A.2d 695 (Del. 2009), *supra* note 23.
1850 *See e.g.* tit. 8 DELAWARE CODE, *supra* note 24, § 102 (b) (7).
1851 *See* CHEW, *supra* note 1799 at 19.
1852 CALIFORNIA CORPORATION CODE (CORP), CAL. CORP. CODE (1947) §§ 204 (a) (10) (C), 309; tit. 8 DELAWARE CODE, *supra* note 24, §§ 141 (a), 142 (a).
1853 tit. 8 DELAWARE CODE, *supra* note 24, § 121 (a).
1854 tit. 8 DELAWARE CODE, *supra* note 24, § 142 (a).

directors or by direction of any officer authorized by the bylaws or the board of directors to prescribe the duties of other officers.[1855]

2. *Directors and Officers Indemnification*

In order to provide an initial overview of whether there is any legal protection for directors and officers against the risks inherent to decision-making, this part will further examine State Corporation Law concerning possible indemnification. Indemnification implies reimbursement for the costs of litigation. If directors and officers are personally liable, they could be required to pay a large amount of money. These costs could include:

(1) Fines, judgments, or settlement payments,
(2) Case initiation, expenses of trial, expenses against claims,[1856]
(3) Attorneys' fees.[1857]

A review of State Corporation Law highlights that a number of states have adopted provisions governing when the company has power or may indemnify its officers and directors *"against expenses including attorneys' fees, judgments, fines, and amounts paid in settlement"*, if they *"acted in good faith."*[1858] The Supreme Court of Delaware refers to Section 145 of the Delaware Code and states that *"any person a director, officer, employee or agent of a corporation"* can be indemnified *"against expenses including attorneys' fees, judgments, fines and amounts paid in settlement"* when "*they acted in good faith and in the best interest of the corporation."*[1859]

Generally, these provisions distinguish between (1) mandatory indemnification, (2) permissive indemnification, and (3) court indemnification.[1860] The Delaware indemnification provisions are expressly applicable to *"officers, directors, employees, and agents"*[1861] while the New York indemnifications provisions apply to directors and officers.[1862] Nevertheless, there are many requirements for indemnification of

---

1855 Florida Business Coordination Act, Fla. Stat. Ann. (2015) Ch. 606 § 607.0841.

1856 In 2013, the median cost of litigation by liability are approximately $54,000 and by malpractice $122,000 including initiate, settlement and trial costs but without attorney fee. *See e.g.* Paula Hannaford-Agor & Nicole L. Waters, Estimating the Cost of Civil Litigation 7 (2013) Figure 2.

1857 *See* Chew, *supra* note 1799 at 230.

1858 *Id.* at 231.; *See also* tit. 8 Delaware Code, *supra* note 24 § 145 (a)-(e); Model Business Corporation Act, *supra* note 1805, § 8.56; New York Business Corporation Law, *supra* note 1821 § 722.

1859 tit. 8 Delaware Code, *supra* note 24 § 145 (a)(b*); See* in: *In re Walt Disney Co. Derivative Litigation,* (Del. 2006), *supra* note 552 at 65.

1860 *See* Chew, *supra* note 1799 at 231. The wording within the provisions are: *"shall"* is mandatory and *"may"* is permissive.

1861 tit. 8 Delaware Code, *supra* note 24, § 145.

1862 New York Business Corporation Law, *supra* note 1821 § 722.

directors. For mandatory indemnification, the MBCA states *"a corporation shall indemnify a director who was wholly successful."*[1863] Under the MBCA, this means the result of the litigation must be that the director was not found liable. If the director appeals, the decision is not final.[1864] By contrast, the Delaware Corporation Law requires that the director or officer *"has been successful on the merits or otherwise in defense of any action, suit, or proceeding."*[1865] However, in *Merritt-Chapman & Scott Corporation v. Wolfson* the court states that *"the statute does not require complete success."*[1866] Therefore, it allows partial indemnification for partial success.[1867] Furthermore, in the same case, when directors achieve a settlement without any admission of liability, the courts tend to interpret statutes similarly to the Delaware approach.[1868] Nevertheless, in *Galdi v. Berg*, the court stated in the event of dismissal of an action without prejudice that, *"an indemnification award would be premature and contrary to the spirit of the statute."*[1869] In accordance with the provision *"has been successful on the merits or otherwise,"*[1870] the court held that *"the director is entitled to indemnity if he is vindicated on the merits or otherwise."*[1871] In addition, under the MBCA, a director may also apply for a court-ordered indemnification or an advance for expenses.[1872] Delaware Corporation Law determines that *"the Court of Chancery may summarily determine a corporation's obligation to advance expenses including attorneys' fees."*[1873] Often, the indemnification provisions set forth in the State Corporation Law are non-exclusive statutes.[1874] For example, Delaware companies may be entitled to other indemnification rights under the bylaws, agreements, or by vote of stockholders.[1875] According to State Corporation Law, directors and officers may be entitled to corporate and court indemnification if they are held liable. Whether and how much indemnification they could be awarded depends on the applicable statutes, bylaws, or agreements.[1876]

1863 Model Business Corporation Act, *supra* note 1805 § 8.52.
1864 *See* Chew, *supra* note 1799 at 234.
1865 tit. 8 Delaware Code, *supra* note 24 § 145 (c).
1866 *Merritt-Chapman & Scott Corporation v. Wolfson*, 321 A.2d 138, 141 (Del. Super. Ct. 1974).
1867 *See* Chew, *supra* note 1799 at 234; *Merritt-Chapman & Scott Corporation v. Wolfson*, (Del. Super. Ct. 1974), *supra* note 1866 at 141.
1868 *Safeway Stores, Inc. v. National Union Fire Insurance Company of Pittsburgh*, 64 F.3d 1282 (9th Cir. 1995).
1869 *Galdi v. Berg*, 359 F. Supp. 698, 702, (D. Del. 1973).
1870 tit. 8 Delaware Code, *supra* note 24 § 145 (c).
1871 *Galdi v. Berg*, (D. Del. 1973), *supra* note 1869 at 701.
1872 *See* Chew, *supra* note 1799 at 235–236; tit. 8 Delaware Code, *supra* note 24 § 145 (e); Model Business Corporation Act, *supra* note 1805 § 8.51 (a).
1873 tit. 8 Delaware Code, *supra* note 24 § 145 (k).
1874 tit. 8 *Id.* § 145 (f); New York Business Corporation Law, *supra* note 1821 § 721.
1875 tit. 8 *Id.* § 145 (f).
1876 *See* Chew, *supra* note 1799 at 241–242.

3. The Line of Cases Relating to Corporate Directors and Officers

Having defined relevant terms and having examined State Corporation Law provisions as they relate to directors' and officers' duties and their possible indemnification, there follows a brief overview of key cases with respect to directors' and officers' compliance duties. To begin, the most important, most cited,[1877] and most analyzed decision in the academic literature was the Delaware Court decision *in re Caremark International, Inc. Derivative Litigation,*[1878] which marks the initial starting point at which the court shifts from the duty of care to monitoring and oversight obligations of directors.[1879] This landmark case was the beginning of a line of cases concerning the duty of oversight of the board of directors.[1880] In these Delaware cases, the court established standards of conduct for directors requiring them to act in the best interests of the corporation, with a view towards maximizing corporate profit and shareholder gain.[1881] The duty of care and the duty of oversight are part of the director's legal responsibility.[1882] As previously discussed, directors are fiduciaries[1883] and, as such, owe their company and shareholders a fiduciary duty.[1884] In *Caremark,* the Delaware Chancery Court examined whether the board of directors was guilty of breaching their fiduciary duty as a result of their failure to monitor and oversee the corporation's legal compliance efforts and risks.[1885] The holding of the Delaware Court of Chancery in this case was that directors can be held liable for losses resulting from the corporation's failure to comply with applicable legal standards.[1886] This responsibility for adherence to the

1877 *See e.g.* Baer (2009), *supra* note 586; Brown (2001), *supra* note 495; Mark (2012), *supra* note 641; Sale (2007), *supra* note 22.

1878 *See supra* note 22. *In re Caremark International Inc. Derivative Litigation* (698 A.2d 959), note 961–962. Caremark realized significant revenues from third party payments, including payments from insurers and Medicare reimbursements.

1879 *See* Sale (2007), *supra* note 22 at 719.

1880 This duty was established in the *Caremark* case and is based on the concept of good faith. *See infra* pp. 263 et seq.

1881 *See* Eisenberg (2006), *supra* note 199 at 5.

1882 *See* Miller (2014), *supra* note 595 at 49.

1883 Additionally, Miller defines the term fiduciary as *"a person who is in charge under the law with making decisions fundamental to the welfare of someone else." See Id.* at 49. This term was often discussed in court decision beginning with *Meinhard v. Salmon* 249 N.Y. 458, 164 N.E. 54, (1928). In this case, the court held that partners in a business have a fiduciary duty to each other. See *Id.* at 546.; *See* in: Miller (2014), *supra* note 595 at 49.

1884 *In re Caremark International Inc. Derivative Litigation*, 698 A.2d 959 (Del. Ch. 1996), *supra* note 21.

1885 *See e.g.* Mark (2012), *supra* note 641 at 479; McGreal (2011), *supra* note 495 at 134; Miller (2014), *supra* note 519 at 55. This means the directors duty of oversight that the company complies with applicable law and regulation.

1886 *See* Brown (2001), *supra* note 495 at 1.

law could form a substantial part of management duties; in other words, the board of directors is responsible for compliance.[1887] This has triggered an academic debate on the board's role in ensuring compliance.[1888]

a. The Caremark Litigation and the Duty of Oversight

Caremark, today CSV Health Corporation, a Delaware corporation, is a large US pharmacy services provider and is listed on the NYSE. The company is headquartered in Woonsocket, Rhode Island and at present employs nearly 215,000 employees in 47 US states.[1889] The history of the *Caremark* case began in 1991. At that time, Caremark came under an extensive four year investigation by the Department of Health and Human Services.[1890] One year later, the DOJ joined the investigation to include Caremark's billing practices and inadequate record keeping.[1891] In the course of the government investigation, Caremark designed an internal audit plan, intended to ensure adherence with business policies.[1892] In addition, Caremark employed an outside auditor, PWC.[1893] In 1993, PWC attested that there was no significant weakness in Caremark's control structure.[1894] Furthermore, the audit and ethics committee of Caremark implemented a new audit charter that requires a review of compliance policies and the chief financial officer was appointed as Caremark's compliance officer.[1895] Despite these efforts, on August 4, 1994, a federal grand jury in Minnesota charged two Caremark officers with having made illegal payments.[1896] They were accused of possible unlawful "*kickback*" payments to physicians in exchange for referrals for treatment to Caremark facilities.[1897] The Anti-Referral Payments Law (ARPL)[1898] prohibits health care providers from paying any form of remuneration.[1899]

In June 1995, Caremark approved a plea agreement with the DOJ. In this agreement Caremark pleaded guilty and paid approximately US$ 161 million in

---

1887 *See* Miller (2014), *supra* note 595 at 55.
1888 *See* Brown (2001), *supra* note 495 at 1.
1889 CSV Health, Corporate Social Responsibility Report 7 (2014).
1890 *See* Brown (2001), *supra* note 495 at 17.
1891 *See* Miller (2014), *supra* note 595 at 55.
1892 *In re Caremark International Inc. Derivative Litigation,* 698 A.2d 959 (Del. Ch. 1996), *supra* note 21 at 963; Miller (2014), *supra* note 595 at 56.
1893 *Id.* at 963.
1894 *Id.* at 963.; Miller (2014), *supra* note 595 at 56.
1895 *In re Caremark International Inc. Derivative Litigation,* 698 A.2d 959 (Del. Ch. 1996), *supra* note 21 at 963.
1896 *Id.* at 963–964.
1897 *Id.* at 961–962.; Sale (2007), *supra* note 22 at 725.
1898 Physician Self-Referral (Stark II), Anti-Kickback Laws and Safe Harbor Regulations
1899 *In re Caremark International Inc. Derivative Litigation,* 698 A.2d 959 (Del. Ch. 1996), *supra* note 21 at 961–962.

criminal fines, civil restitution and damages for kickbacks and fraud.[1900] Together, with other agreements, Caremark paid a total of US$ 250 million.[1901] After the conclusion of the agreement with the DOJ, the federal and state proceedings were concluded and no senior officers or directors were individually charged with wrongdoing in the Government Settlement Agreement.[1902]

However, this did not mark the end of the case; in the meantime, five shareholder derivative actions had been filed.[1903] These actions alleged that Caremark's directors had breached their duty by failing to monitor their employees.[1904] The shareholders claimed that the breach of duty involved violations by Caremark employees of federal and state laws and regulations applicable to health care providers.[1905] They argued that directors should be aware of what is going on in the company and need to be more active in monitoring the employees.

i. The Legal Principles of *Caremark* and the Impact Thereof

At that time, the US courts and legal scholars followed the traditional corporate model,[1906] meaning that the board of directors has the power to manage the company.[1907] Based on this position of power, the directors are viewed as fiduciaries with obligations towards all shareholders and are required to act in good faith.[1908] During the court proceedings, the Chancellor first stated that the Court would attempt to protect the best interests of the corporation.[1909] The Delaware Court then went on to specifically examine the potential liability for directorial decisions. In so doing, the Chancellor made it clear that there are only two *"distinct contexts"* in which a breach of the directors' oversight duty may arise.[1910] The first is in instances in which a board decision is *"ill advised"* or *"negligent"* and results in

1900 DOJ, #342 CAREMARK BRIEFING RELEASE (1995), https://www.justice.gov/archive/opa/pr/Pre_96/June95/342.txt.html (last visited Mar 23, 2016).
1901 *In re Caremark International Inc. Derivative Litigation*, 698 A.2d 959 (Del. Ch. 1996), *supra* note 21 at 961.
1902 *Id.* at 964.; Brown (2001), *supra* note 495 at 18.
1903 *Id.* at 964.
1904 *Id.* at 964.
1905 *Id.* at 960.
1906 *See* Brown (2001), *supra* note 495 at 7.
1907 *Id.* at 7.
1908 *Alpert v. 28 Williams St. Corp.*, 63 N.Y.2d 557 (N.Y. 1984), 557 (1984) 568–569. The New York Court of Appeal viewed the fiduciary role as "*guardians of the corporate welfare.*"
1909 *Id.* at 966.
1910 *In re Caremark International Inc. Derivative Litigation,* 698 A.2d 959 (Del. Ch. 1996), *supra* note 21 at 967.

a loss.[1911] The second context is when the loss arises from an "*unconsidered failure*" of the board of directors.[1912]

Furthermore, the Court pointed out that *"the business judgment rule is process oriented"* and with *"a deep respect for all good faith board decisions."*[1913] It refers to the statement in *Barnes v. Andrews* and identifies this statement as *"the core element of any corporate law duty of care."*[1914]

> True, he was not very suited by experience for the job he had undertaken, but I cannot hold him on that account. After all, it is the same corporation that chose him that now seeks to charge him... Directors are not specialists like lawyers or doctors... They are the general advisors of the business and if they faithfully give such ability as they have to their charge, it would not be lawful to hold them liable. Must a director guarantee that his judgment is good?[1915]

Secondly, the Chancellor examines the liability for failure to monitor when the loss is caused by *"unconsidered inaction."*[1916] He considers the question of what the board's responsibility is with respect to monitoring the company and its employees.[1917] In his answer, he weighs the fact that this question has become more increasingly important in recent years under federal law. The broader interpretation of *Graham v. Allis Chalmers,*[1918] namely that of the board of directors is under no responsibility to ensure that the management establishes an information and reporting system, was not accepted by the Delaware Supreme Court in 1996.[1919] In order to cope with this responsibility, the directors should be informed of the facts and law relating to a corporate decision.[1920] Hence, directors have a duty of oversight. However, the Delaware Court has established a high threshold for directors' liability.[1921] In fact, the Chancellor cites the phrases *"utter failure"* and *"sustained or systematic failure."*[1922] In his view, only such a test of liability will establish a

---

1911 *Id.* at 967.
1912 *Id.* at 967.
1913 *Id.* at 968.
1914 *Id.* at 968.
1915 *Barnes v. Andrews,* 208 App. Div. 856 (S.D.N.Y. 1924) in: *In re Caremark International Inc. Derivative Litigation*, 698 A.2d 959 (Del. Ch. 1996), *supra* note 21 at 968.
1916 *Id.* at 968.
1917 *Id.* at 969.
1918 *Graham v. Allis-Chalmers Manufacturing Company,* 188 A.2d 125 (Del. 1963), *supra* note 633.
1919 I*n re Caremark International Inc. Derivative Litigation,* 698 A.2d 959 (Del. Ch. 1996), *supra* note 21 at 970.
1920 *See* Brown (2001), *supra* note 495 at 9.
1921 *See* McGreal (2011), *supra* note 495 at 136.
1922 *See* Brown (2001), *supra* note 495 at 31; McGreal (2011), *supra* note 495 at 135; *In re Caremark International Inc. Derivative Litigation,* 698 A.2d 959 (Del. Ch. 1996), *supra* note 21 at 971.

lack of good faith and a lack of standard for the board's compliance oversight responsibility.[1923]

In addition, scholars have pointed out that there should be "*specific indicia suggesting misconduct,*" for instance "*red flags*" concerning the directors' and officers' conduct.[1924] The discussion of *Caremark* included a consideration of when directors' liability can arise. Ultimately, the liability may be established where a "*loss eventuates not from a decision but, from unconsidered inaction.*"[1925]

The commentators concluded that the Delaware Court established the standard for determining liability based on a director or officer's failure to fulfill oversight responsibility.[1926] Since federal law began to pay attention to internal corporate procedures, the Delaware courts have had to establish their own directors' and officers' theory of liability.[1927] American legal scholars refer to these legal principles as the *Caremark theory*.[1928] *Jones* concluded that the Delaware Court took a stance that courts would pay greater attention to the law of director and officer misconduct in the coming years.[1929] In general, since the *Caremark* decision, the federal and state courts have recognized a cause of action against directors for the failure to exercise oversight and failure to take minimal steps to achieve legal compliance.[1930]

Furthermore, the established standards of liability for a breach of directors' oversight duty had great influence in subsequent cases such as *Stone v. Ritter*[1931] and *Gantler v. Stephens*[1932]. In these cases, the court formally confirmed the *Caremark* standard for oversight liability.[1933]

> We hold that Caremark articulates the necessary conditions predicate for director oversight liability: (a) the directors utterly failed to implement any reporting or information system or controls; or (b) having implemented such a system or controls, consciously failed to monitor or oversee its operations thus disabling themselves from being informed of risks or problems requiring their attention.[1934]

1923 *In re Caremark International Inc. Derivative Litigation,* 698 A.2d 959 (Del. Ch. 1996), *supra* note 21 at 971.
1924 *See e.g.* Brown (2001), *supra* note 495 at 15.
1925 *Id.* at 24.
1926 *See* Mark (2012), *supra* note 641 at 479.
1927 *See* Jones (2007), *supra* note 495 at 477.
1928 *Id.* at 477.
1929 *Id.* at 477.
1930 *See* McGreal (2011), *supra* note 495 at 134.
1931 *Stone v. Ritter,* 911 A.2d 362 (Del. 2006), *supra* note 197.
1932 *Gantler v. Stephens,* 965 A.2d 695 (Del. 2009), *supra* note 23 at 708–709.
1933 *Stone v. Ritter,* 911 A.2d 362 (Del. 2006), *supra* note 197 at 370.
1934 *Id.* at 370.

Here, the court directly addressed compliance issues. First, a director of a company violated the *Caremark* duty by failing to take any action directed toward establishing a compliance program.[1935] Second, the court stated that there is an ongoing duty to address compliance.[1936] That means, for instance that the board of directors has to request reports on the design, implementation, and operation of the program itself.[1937]

ii. The Holding in *Caremark* and the Settlement

Although the Delaware Chancery Court shifts away from the *"no responsibility"* of directors to establish and to monitor reporting systems and despite its analysis of a director's responsibility to fulfill a monitoring role, it concluded, *"there is a very low probability that the directors of Caremark breached any duty to appropriately monitor and supervise the company."*[1938] It refers to the active consideration and handling of the Caremark board in terms of the establishment of corporate policies and structure, prior to 1996.[1939] In its view, there was no knowing violation of the ARPL law and no systematic or sustained failure of the board to exercise oversight.[1940]

However, the Court proposed a settlement that resulted in the terms, including (1) that Caremark and its employees and agents complies with the ARPL law, (2) that the board shall discuss all relevant material changes in government healthcare regulations, (3) that the board will establish a compliance and ethics committee of four directors, with two non-management directors, which will meet four times a year and directly report compliance issues by each business segment to the board, and (4) that corporate officers responsible for business segments shall serve as compliance officers who must report semi-annually to the compliance and ethics committee with the review of existing and new contracts.[1941] Finally, the court approved this settlement because it facilitated the assurance of shareholders that Caremark will continue to implement an active supervisory system in the future.[1942]

iii. Significance of *Caremark* and the Consequences thereof

In his opinion, the Chancellor derives a compliance duty from the business judgment rule.[1943] He states that the traditional rule does not protect directors in case of an *"utter"* or *"systematic"* failure to exercise proper supervision and oversight

1935 *See* McGreal (2011), *supra* note 495 at 135.
1936 *Id.* at 135.
1937 *Id.* at 135.
1938 *In re Caremark International Inc. Derivative Litigation*, 698 A.2d 959 (Del. Ch. 1996), *supra* note 21 at 961.
1939 *Id.* at 961.
1940 *Id.* at 971.
1941 *Id.* at 966.
1942 *Id.* at 972.
1943 *See* Miller (2014), *supra* note 595 at 60.

or from *"unconsidered inaction."* Hence, the Delaware Chancery Court establishes a fiduciary duty, in particular the duty of oversight or compliance duty, over and above this, as well as standards of directors' liability.[1944] As a result, the good faith obligation is increasingly becoming a subject of federal law.[1945] Under the SOX, the CEO and CFO are required to disclose all significant information and reports in the design or operation of internal controls to the audit committee of the board of directors before filing.[1946] Therefore, the board of directors is under an obligation to fulfil its compliance duty.[1947]

Caremark was a decision by the Delaware Chancery Court; the opinion by the Chancellor was influential, but its scope and precedential effect did not become clear until some time later.[1948] Critics have also argued that it was an unpublished opinion that then evolved into a key opinion.[1949] A later decision[1950] by the Delaware Supreme Court confirmed the standards of *Caremark's* liability under Delaware law.[1951] This *Caremark* liability is known as the *Caremark theory* and legal scholars cite it as a landmark decision.[1952] Since this case was decided, US federal and state courts have recognized a cause of action against directors for their failure to exercise oversight to ensure legal compliance.[1953]

A 2010 study by *Erickson* found that more than ninety percent of 141 derivative suits filed in federal district courts against public companies over a twelve-month period in 2005 and 2006 involved *Caremark* claims or other good faith claims.[1954] Thus, compliance issues have entered into the courtroom. Nevertheless, the study showed that only two of forty-one derivative suits of private companies provided favorable judgments; eleven provided a settlement; twenty-four were dismissed, and four were still pending at that time.[1955] None of the 141 public company suits actually reached the stage of a judgment being passed.[1956] Overall, forty-two suits

1944 *Id.* at 60.
1945 *See* Sale (2007), *supra* note 22 at 720.
1946 SARBANES-OXLEY ACT OF 2002, *supra* note 47 § 302 (a) (5), 15 USC § 7241.
1947 *See* MILLER (2014), *supra* note 595 at 60.
1948 *Id.* at 63.
1949 *See* Sale (2007), *supra* note 22 at 720.
1950 *Stone v. Ritter*, 911 A.2d 362 (Del. 2006), *supra* note 197.
1951 *See* MILLER (2014), *supra* note 595 at 63.
1952 *See e.g.* ERC PAPER, *supra* note 3 at 10; Mark (2012), *supra* note 641 at 479; Murphy (2002), *supra* note 654 at 714.
1953 *See* McGreal (2011), *supra* note 495 at 134.
1954 *See* Jessica Erickson, *Corporate Governance in the Courtroom: An Empirical Analysis*, 51 WILLIAM & MARY LAW REVIEW 1749, 1756, 1770, 1777 (2010).
1955 *Id.* at 1797. Table 1.
1956 *Id.* at 1798. Table 2.

(29.8 percent) were settled.[1957] Ninety-one of the public company suits (64.5 percent) were dismissed.[1958] Eight suits (5.7 percent) were still pending at that time.[1959]

These results show that, in court, an oversight claim *"is possibly the most difficult theory in corporation law upon which a plaintiff might hope to win a judgment."*[1960] It has been noted that *Caremark* duties are hard to violate.[1961] Nevertheless, under the settlements in the courts, private and public companies are required to establish an effective compliance structure. Thus, corporate directors could be subject to liability when they (1) *"utterly"* fail to implement reporting or information system, or (2) having implemented such a system, they consciously fail to oversee business operations. In addition to the federal law regulations and the application thereof, the decisions of the courts in the US continue to contribute to corporate structural reform.

b. The Confirmation of Oversight Liability

In October 2006, two AmSouth shareholders brought a derivative action on behalf of the AmSouth Bancorporation, a Delaware corporation, against the bank's directors for breach of their fiduciary duties through failure to monitor internal controls to guard against violations of the Bank Secrecy Act[1962] and anti-money laundering regulations.[1963] On January 26, 2006, the Delaware Court of Chancery dismissed the derivative litigation under Court of Chancery Rule 23.1.,[1964] since the plaintiffs failed to plead facts demonstrating any lack of adequate board and management oversight.[1965] The subsequent appeal was also dismissed. The Delaware Supreme Court also stated a shortcoming in the plaintiffs' argument that the directors did not exercise their oversight responsibility in good faith.[1966] Only a sustained or systematic failure of management oversight will result in liability.[1967] The Court clearly pointed out *"that good faith in the context of oversight must be measured by the directors' actions"* to obtain reasonable information about the reporting system and not by evaluating results *"after the occurrence of*

1957 *Id.* at 1798. Table 2.

1958 *Id.* at 1798. Table 2.

1959 *Id.* at 1798. Table 2.

1960 *In re Caremark International Inc. Derivative Litigation*, 698 A.2D 959 (DEL. CH. 1996), *supra* note 21 at 967.

1961 *See* Mark (2012), *supra* note 641 at 480.

1962 BANK SECRECY ACT OF 1970, PUB. LAW 91-508, 31 USC. § 1051 84 Stat. 1114-2 (1970).

1963 *Stone v. Ritter*, 911 A.2d 362 (Del. 2006), *supra* note 197 at 365.

1964 Rules of the Delaware State Courts - Delaware Courts - State of Delaware, http://courts.delaware.gov/Rules/ (last visited Apr 7, 2016).

1965 WILLIAM B. CHANDLER, OPINION | *Stone, et al. v. Ritter, et al.* (2006).

1966 *Stone v. Ritter*, 911 A.2d 362 (Del. 2006), *supra* note 197 at 373.

1967 *Id.* at 369.

employee conduct."[1968] The Delaware Supreme Court argued that *Caremark* states the *"necessary conditions"* for director oversight liability:

> ... (a) the directors utterly failed to implement any reporting or information system or controls; or (b) having implemented such a system or controls, consciously failed to monitor or oversee its operations thus disabling themselves from being informed of risks or problems requiring their attention.[1969]

In this case, the Supreme Court of Delaware applied the *Caremark theory* and ultimately dismissed the plaintiffs' derivative complaint.[1970] Hence, the Supreme Court of Delaware affirmed the judgment of the Court of Chancery and, thus, confirmed the *Caremark* standard of oversight liability.[1971]

c. What is an Officer's Duty?

A review of the Delaware Courts' decisions shows that only a minority of cases specifically involve compliance officers' duties.[1972] The research at the Delaware Courts found only one case between 1990 and today in which a compliance officer was involved as a party and his duties were discussed.[1973] In two other cases, *Hampshire Group, Limited v. Kuttner*[1974] and *Ironworkers District Council of Philadelphia & Vicinity Retirement & Pension Plan v. Andreotti,*[1975] the Court of Chancery of Delaware examined the duties of corporate officers in general.

In this context, it is necessary first to establish precisely who is an officer and secondly, what an officer's duties are. According to Delaware Corporation Law, an officer is anyone who:

> (1) Is or was the president, chief executive officer, chief operating officer, chief financial officer, chief legal officer, controller, treasurer or chief accounting officer of the corporation at any time during the course of conduct alleged in the action or proceeding to be wrongful;

1968 *Id.* at 373.
1969 *Id.* at 370.
1970 *Id.* at 373.
1971 *Id.* at 373.
1972 Court of Chancery of Delaware and Supreme Court of Delaware.
1973 *Gantler v. Stephens*, 965 A.2d 695 (Del. 2009), *supra* note 23.
1974 *Hampshire Group, Limited v. Kuttner*, C.A. No. 3607-VCS (Del. Ch. 2010). *"Generally, like directors, both directors were expected to pursue the best interests of the company in good faith (for instance to fulfill their duty of loyalty) and to use the amount of care that a reasonably prudent person would use in similar circumstances (for instance to fulfill their duty of care)."*
1975 *Ironworkers District Council of Philadelphia & Vicinity Retirement & Pension Plan v. Andreotti* (Del. Ch. 2015), C.A. No. 9714-VCG (2015).

(2) Is or was identified in the corporation's public filings[1976] with the United States Securities and Exchange Commission because such person is or was one of the most highly compensated executive officers of the corporation at any time during the course of conduct alleged in the action or proceeding to be wrongful; or
(3) Has, by written agreement with the corporation, consented to be identified as an officer for purposes of this section.[1977]

Furthermore, Section 142 (a) states that

> Every corporation organized under this chapter shall have such officers with such titles and duties as shall be stated in the bylaws or in a resolution of the board of directors.[1978]

Although the compliance officer is not explicitly enumerated in Section 3114 (b)(1), he could be an officer under Section 3114 (b)(2) or (3). However, in the event that the chief legal compliance officer is responsible for compliance issues, he could be included indirectly. Even in the case that the chief compliance officer is identified as a corporate officer in a written agreement, he will be considered as an officer under Delaware Corporation Law.

Furthermore, pursuant to Section 8.40 of the MBCA, a person is an officer, if:

> (a) A corporation has the officers described in its bylaws or appointed by the board of directors in accordance with the bylaws.[1979]

To summarize, an officer is a person with various titles, appointed by the board, described in the bylaws, identified in the public filings of the SEC[1980] or by a written agreement with the company. The officers or senior executives are referred to as the management of the company.[1981] They are given their power by the board of directors, which has the power to delegate much of its management authority.[1982] In general, officers are responsible for day-to-day operation and have the authority to legally bind the company in contracts on behalf of the corporation.

However, the duties of the officers are not clearly explained under Delaware Corporation Law. For this reason, the research must focus on other legal sources. For example, both the MBCA and the CEO Guide recommend that an officer's duty shall include informing the board of director of the affairs of the corporation

---

1976 *See e.g.*Form 10-K SEC, *supra* note 1579.
1977 tit. 10 DELAWARE CODE, *supra* note 24, § 3114(b).
1978 tit. 8 *Id.* § 142 (a).
1979 MODEL BUSINESS CORPORATION ACT, *supra* note 1805 § 8.40 (a).
1980 *See e.g.* FORM 10-K SEC, *supra* note 1568, "*All officers are appointed annually by the board of directors and, subject to existing employment agreements (of which there is currently one), serve at the discretion of the board.*"(This statement is included and published in 10-K SEC form in a company within the healthcare industry).
1981 *See* MILLER (2014), *supra* note 595 at 103.
1982 tit. 8 DELAWARE CODE, *supra* note 24, §§ 141(a), 142.

and about probable material breaches of duty by other officers.[1983] In addition, as previously discussed,[1984] in the case of publicly traded companies, the most important compliance responsibility of the management consists in establishing and maintaining an adequate internal control structure and procedures for financial reporting and an assessment of this structure under Federal Law.[1985] For particular executives, like the CEO or CFO, Section 302 of the SOX requires that they certify in the annual and quarterly reports and that they have disclosed all significant deficiencies in the design or operation of internal controls.[1986] However, one question remains: Where does Federal or State Law regulate the corporate compliance officer's duties? Although corporate officers' misconduct has been linked to corporate scandals, their duties are underdeveloped and legally unenforced.[1987]The previous research reveals this corporate officer is afforded limited specific attention under State and Federal Corporate Law.[1988] Therefore, a useful approach might be to analyze the case *Gantler v. Stephens* in order to specify the officers' duties. This decision is worth discussing because the Court clarified *"that the fiduciary duties of officers of Delaware corporations are the same as those of directors."*[1989]

In 2009, a fiduciary duty action of shareholders by a corporation was appealed to the Delaware Supreme Court in which the plaintiffs alleged that the defendants, the officers and directors of the corporation, violated their fiduciary duties by rejecting a valuable opportunity to sell the company for the purpose of retaining the benefits of continued incumbency.[1990] The corporation, a Delaware company, headquartered in Ohio, is a holding that owns the Savings and Loan Association.[1991] One of the defendants was the compliance officer during the sale process period from 2003 until 2006; he had worked as a full-time employee in both institutions since 1996.[1992] Nevertheless, the Court of Chancery *inter alia* dismissed the claim against the compliance officer [defendant] under Court of Chancery Rule 12

1983 Chief Executive Group, CEO Legal Guide 6–6 (2012); Model Business Corporation Act, *supra* note 1805 § 8.42 (b) (1)(2).

1984 *See supra* I., 2.d., p. 223.

1985 *See* Miller (2014), *supra* note 595 at 104; Sarbanes-Oxley Act of 2002, *supra* note 47 § 404 (a) (1) (2), 15 USC 7262.

1986 *See* Miller (2014), *supra* note 595 at 108; Sarbanes-Oxley Act of 2002, *supra* note 47 § 302 (a) (2) (3), 15 USC 7241.

1987 Megan W. Shaner, *The (Un)Enforcement of Corporate Officers' Duties*, 48 UC Davis Law Review 271–336, 276 (2014).

1988 *Id.* at 276.

1989 *Gantler v. Stephens,* 965 A.2d 695 (Del. 2009), *supra* note 23 at 709.; Petrin (2010), *supra* note 1125 at 1691.

1990 *Gantler v. Stephens,* 965 A.2d 695 (Del. 2009), *supra* note 23 at 704.

1991 *Id.* at 699.

1992 Memorandum Opinion | Gantler v. Stephens, 2008 WL 401124, (Del. Ch. 2008); *Gantler v. Stephens,* 965 A.2d 695 (Del. 2009), *supra* note 23 at 699.

(b) (2)[1993] because he was not a director, did not hold an officer position pursuant to Delaware Corporate Law and was not identified as an executive officer by the company.[1994] Nevertheless, according to the company's website, there was a notice at that time that:

> The [defendant] has served Home Federal as compliance officer since 1996, as Vice President since 2007, and as a director since 2006.[1995]

In contrast, the Delaware Supreme Court stated that, "*fiduciary duties of officers are the same as those of directors.*"[1996] In the Court's view, both have identical fiduciary duties; this has long been an articulated principle of Delaware Law.[1997] Despite this principle, the consequences of a fiduciary breach by directors or officers would not necessarily be the same.[1998] Under Delaware Corporate Law, it is possible to adopt a provision in the certificate of incorporation that eliminates or limits "*the personal liability of a director to the corporation or its stockholders for monetary damages for breach of fiduciary duty as a director.*"[1999] However, there is no statutory provision of comparable exculpation of corporate officers.[2000] In *Gantler v. Stephens,* there were no indications of a provision of exculpation of these directors. Hence, the Supreme Court of Delaware considered the legal sufficiency of this action against these directors. Although the Court examined the decision of the board to reject the "*First Place*" bid under the business judgment rule, it concluded that the directors and officers of this corporation breached either their duty of loyalty or their duty of care.[2001] The decision was reached for the following reasons: first, the reclassification proxy admits a conflict of interest on the part of the company's directors and officers.[2002] They could structure the reclassification in order to benefit from their interest, contrary to the interest of the unaffiliated stockholders.[2003] Second, an analysis of the corporation's board of directors showed that a majority of the board was conflicted.[2004] The members of the board were attempting to maintain their financial interests. For example, the CEO never responded to a due diligence request and failed

---

1993 Rules of the Delaware State Courts - Delaware Courts - State of Delaware, *supra* note 1964.

1994 *Gantler v. Stephens,* 965 A.2d 695 (Del. 2009), *supra* note 23 at 704; 10 Delaware Code, *supra* note 24, § 3114(b).

1995 Home Federal Savings and Loan Association of Niles | Board of Directors, , http://www.homefedniles.com/asp/services/service_4_5.asp (last visited Apr 12, 2016).

1996 *Gantler v. Stephens,* 965 A.2d 695 (Del. 2009), *supra* note 23 at 699.

1997 *See e.g. Cede & Co. v. Technicolor, Inc.*, 634 A.2d 345 (Del. 1993), 361 (1993).

1998 *Gantler v. Stephens,* 965 A.2d 695 (Del. 2009), *supra* note 23 at 37.

1999 *Id.* at 37.; tit. 8 Delaware Code, *supra* note 613§ 102 (b) (7).

2000 *Gantler v. Stephens,* 965 A.2d 695 (Del. 2009), *supra* note 23 at 37.

2001 *Id.* at 706.

2002 *Id.* at 707.

2003 *Id.* at 707.

2004 *Id.* at 707.

to deliver the necessary due diligence materials and information.[2005] Hence, the Court concluded that these directors and officers had a personal interest to *"sabotage"* the Sales Process and were in breach of their duty of loyalty.[2006] Therefore, the Supreme Court allowed the appeal and overruled the judgment of the lower court.

To conclude, the most notable aspects of this decision were that it imposed the same duties on corporate officers as those imposed on members of the board and examined the conflicts of interest in terms of the business judgment rule. Thus, a corporate officer could have the same duties, such as a duty of care, a duty of loyalty and a duty of oversight. However, there is little case law on the officers' fiduciary duties and the Delaware Courts have not clarified whether the business judgment rule should apply to officers.[2007] Therefore, the potential scope of officer' duties, including the compliance officer's duties, remains uncertain under Delaware Corporation Law.[2008] For this reason, the next sections will examine the duties of the corporate compliance officer and his legal status under US Employment Law.

III. Is the Compliance Officer Covered by the Employment-At-Will Doctrine?

A more detailed understanding of the legal status and the duties of the compliance officer could be achieved by turning to employment law, in particular individual employment law. For this purpose, this part explores the role and status of corporate directors, officers and compliance officers under employment law and their protection against unfair dismissal in the US. The applicable legal rules can be found in employment law and case law.[2009] In addition, it is necessary to take a closer look at the corporate employment relationship.

The employment relationship by law involves the "*employment at-will doctrine*."[2010] Therefore, this section provides an explanation of the "*employment at-will doctrine*," followed by a brief overview of Federal and State Employment Law, the case law concerning the question of whether compliance officers are "*at-will*" employees, a summary of similarities and differences between directors and officers, and lastly an examination of termination provisions applicable to compliance officer contracts.

A number of American commentators consider the "*at- will*" rule and its approach to constitute the *"exceptionalism of American employment law"* and call for

---

2005 *Id.* at 707.

2006 *Id.* at 709.

2007 Chief Executive Group, *supra* note 1983 at 6–5.

2008 Chief Executive Group, *supra* note 1983 at 6–6.

2009 *See* Jones (2007), *supra* note 495 at 487.

2010 *"At- will"* means the legal default, if the matter is not specified contractually. *See Id.* at 487 at 60.

the rule to be reconsidered.[2011] A 2013 comparative study found that the absence of a constitutional, statutory, or secondary legislation or ruling restricting the grounds for termination in the US is unique in comparison to twelve countries including France, Germany, Italy or the even the UK.[2012] American authors argue that such a rule would prevent greater labor-market flexibility and, thus, a productive economy.[2013] Hoewever, there is one exception in the case of collective dismissal, but this issue falls outside the scope of this examination and, as such, will not be discussed any further.[2014]

In fact, in 2016 the Bureau of Labor Statistics presented the actual employment figures for February.[2015] The number of hires increased to 5.4 million, the highest level since November 2006, and the number of layoffs and discharges was 1.7 million.[2016] Hence, the number of layoffs was smaller than the number of hires.

1. US Employment Law

Traditionally, there is no uniform regulation under employment law in the US. American employment law consists of a variety of federal, state and local regulations, which are not harmonized and frequently overlap. The employment law includes a collection of federal statutes.[2017] The States can fill the areas of employment law, which are not govern by federal law, but on the other hand federal employment law can allow the States to enact provisions which are more favorable for workers.[2018] Hence, the States for example can issue their own minimum wages and maximum hours rules, which are not lower than the federal requirements.[2019]

Originally, employment law comprised principles and rules of common law. As discussed above, the original and most important principle of American labor law is the "*employment at- will doctrine.*"[2020] This doctrine is the historical approach

2011 *See* Samuel Estreicher & Jeffrey M. Hirsch, *Comparative Wrongful Dismissal Law: Reassessing American Exceptionalism*, 92 North Carolina Law Review 343–480, 348 (2013).

2012 *Id.* at 480. Appendix, Table 13.

2013 *See generally* Richard A. Epstein, *In Defense of the Contract at Will*, 51 University of Chicago Law Review 947–982 (1984) - He tends to the maintenance of the at-will rule; In: Estreicher and Hirsch (2013), *supra* note 2011 at 8.

2014 Employers with over 100 employees have to provide at least sixty days' notice to employees, before closings and mass layoffs. *See* 29 USC, *supra* note 352 § 2102 (a).

2015 US Dep't of Labor, News Release |Bureau of Labor Statistics (2016).

2016 *Id.*

2017 Wilma B. Liebman, *Labor Law and the Trump Effect*, 35. NZA 227–233, 228 (2019).

2018 *Id.* at 228.

2019 *Id.* at 228.

2020 *See* Hay (2011), *supra* note 87 at 245 note 666; *See* Busby, Definition, Employment-at-will Doctrine, *supra* note 1127.

that courts have taken when interpreting employer/employee relations.[2021] That is why, an employer can at any time, and for any reason, or no reason terminate an "*at- will*" employee and the courts will as a rule not protect the employee. Only one state, Montana, has an unfair dismissal statute, the Montana Wrongful Discharge from Employment Act.[2022] Every other state uses the "*at- will*" doctrine.[2023]

In addition, since 1935, federal and state antidiscrimination laws have developed. This federal regulation focuses on matters such as minimum wage and maximum hour requirements, as well as exemptions from the employment *"at- will"* doctrine.[2024] US labor law has seen two major developments since its beginning. The first step was the enactment of the National Labor Relations Act (NLRA) in 1935,[2025] which is a statute of United States employment law.[2026] The purpose of this Act is to protect the national interests of the United States as regards labor within the country. It defines the interests and protects the rights of employers, employees, and labor unions.[2027] However, this Act has not been essentially amended since 1947.[2028] The second step was the enactment of the Civil Rights Act of 1964 (CRA), which stated, for example, that it is unlawful

> to discriminate against, any individual because of his race, color, religion, sex, or national origin, or to classify or refer for employment any individual on the basis of his race, color, religion, sex, or national origin.[2029]

These two statutes had a huge impact on the at-will doctrine and pervade the employment case law.[2030] The US employment relationship is governed by contractual agreements. Similar to situation in the UK and Germany this relationship is based on a contract of employment.[2031] This contract can be agreed in written, oral or implied. Contrary to the UK and Germany an employment contract between

---

2021 *See* in: *Payne v. Western & Atlantic Railroad Company,* 81 Tenn. 507, 519–520 (1884)*"All may dismiss their employes at- will, be they many or few, for good cause, for no cause or even for cause morally wrong, without being thereby guilty of legal wrong."*; Busby EMPLOYMENT-AT-WILL DOCTRINE, *supra* note 1127.

2022 MONTANA CODE AN., MONTANA WRONGFUL DISCHARGE FROM EMPLOYMENT ACT (1987) §§ 901–914.

2023 *See* Estreicher and Hirsch (2013), *supra* note 2011 at 443.

2024 FAIR LABOR STANDARDS ACT OF 1938 (FSLA), PUB. L. 114-38, 29 USC, §§ 201-219 Chapter 8 (1938).

2025 NATIONAL LABOR RELATIONS ACT (NLRA), PUB. L. 49 STAT. 449, 29 USC §§ 151–169 ch. 372 (1935).

2026 *See* Epstein (1984), *supra* note 2013 at 947.

2027 John C. Busby, NATIONAL LABOR RELATIONS ACT (NLRA) LII / LEGAL INFORMATION INSTITUTE (2009), https://www.law.cornell.edu/wex/national_labor_relations_act_nlra (last visited Apr 14, 2016).

2028 *See* Liebman (2019), *supra* note 2017 at 228.

2029 CIVIL RIGHTS ACT, PUB. L. 114-38, 42 USC §§ 2000E–17 78 Stat. 253 (1964).

2030 *See* Epstein (1984), *supra* note 2013 at 947.

2031 *Compare* A., IV., p. 373; A. IV., p. 467.

an employer and an executive officer is an exception.[2032] Whether there is an employment contract between the two parties, the term employ must be defined. It *"includes to suffer or permit to work."*[2033] Section 203 of the FSLA also explain the terms employer and employee, but these terms are not clearly legally defined.[2034] Therefore, similar to Germany, the US Courts apply an overall picture of factors to decide if a person falls in the scope of the FSLA. Two of those factors are:

> (1) the degree of the alleged employer's right to control the manner in which the work is to be performed, and (2) the alleged employee's opportunity for profit or loss depending upon his managerial skill.[2035]

From that the courts conclude that, without being an employee, the person is qualified as an independent contractor.[2036]

As we have seen, under the American employment at- will doctrine, it is permissible for both the employer and the employee to end an employment contract without cause or notice.[2037] For this reason, courts have taken this approach in interpreting employment relationships.[2038] Furthermore, over the years, the courts have developed a growing number of statutory and common law exceptions.[2039] Nowadays, state courts tend to abandon the at- will doctrine and lean towards greater protection of employee rights under a variety of theories.[2040] This may also be important for compliance officers, in the event that they refuse to violate the law at the employer's request or report violations of the law to administrative agencies or regulators. Therefore, the next section examines the kind of agreements into which corporate officers enter in practice in order to identify their specific duties, their termination terms, and to show whether they may benefit from protection against dismissal.

2. The Employment Agreements of Corporate Officers

In practice, it seems that, unlike normal employment relationships, corporate officers negotiate *"cause"* and *"good reason* "contracts.[2041] An empirical analysis of CEO employment contracts found that three-quarters of the sample were employment agreements and that the most common defined causes were *"willful misconduct"*,

---

2032 Executive officers are only subordinate to the members of the board.
2033 Fair Labor Standards Act of 1938 (FSLA), *supra* note 2024 § 203(g).
2034 *Id.* § 203 (d) (e).
2035 *Real v. Driscoll Strawberry Associates Inc. D J*, F.2d 748, 603 (1979).
2036 *Real v. Driscoll Strawberry Associates Inc. D J*, F.2d 748, 603 (1979).
2037 *See* Estreicher and Hirsch (2013), *supra* note 2011 at 343.
2038 *See* Busby Employment at- will doctrine, *supra* note 1127.
2039 *Id.* at 349.
2040 *See* Busby Employment at- will doctrine, *supra* note 1127; *See e.g.* in: *Wieder v. Skala*, 80 N.Y.2d 628 (1992) The Courts consider the unique characteristic of the legal profession and the special releationshipt to a law firm. *See also supra* footnote 2063, p. 283.
2041 *See* Jones (2007), *supra* note 495 at 489.

"moral turpitude", "failure to perform duties" and *"fiduciary breach."*[2042] By surveying the public corporate information as filed and published by the SEC in the EDGAR database, it appears that, although the companies had appointed directors or officers, like CEO, CFO, COO or CCO, approximately sixty-seven percent (two-thirds) of companies did not enter into a written employment agreement with their directors or officers.[2043] A search in the EDGAR database for employment agreements proved difficult on account of the researcher having to know the filing date, filing number and form in which the contract is incorporated. Thus, thirty-three companies with employment agreements with directors and officers is likely to be higher than the number found. Ultimately, seventy-one contracts of corporate officers were found and analyzed.[2044] Additionally, in the course of the search, a number of consulting agreements, brief confidential agreements, non-competition agreements, and stock option agreements were found; however, but not examined here.

For the purpose of obtaining an informative and complete picture of the common reason for terminating provisions in employments agreements of corporate officers, the provisions of the agreements were structured and codified. In the sample, the majority of employment agreements referred to the CEO, CFO, COO and CTO. Only in two companies was a chief compliance officer appointed and entered into a written employment contract. It has been mentioned that the CEO and CFO may simultaneously hold various positions, such as President, Vice-President, treasurer, or secretary. The majority of the companies appointed two officers: CEO and CFO. This is necessary for signing and certifying the certification of the CEO pursuant to Section 302 and the certification of the CEO and CFO pursuant to Section 906 of the Sarbanes Oxley Act.[2045] Only three of the sixty-eight appointed officers were female. Two of them were the CCO and General Counsel and one the CFO. In this sample, the average basic salary of the officers was US$ 245,828 and the average age was 53 years.[2046]

Overall, by analyzing the termination terms of officer's employment agreements, four kinds of termination were identified. They can be categorized as follows:

(1) With cause or just-cause agreements (28; 41 percent)[2047]
(2) Without cause agreements (19; 28 percent)
(3) Good reasons agreements. (17; 25 percent)
(4) At- will Employment (4; 6 percent)

2042 *See* Stewart J. Schwab & Randall S. Thomas, *What Do CEOs Bargain For? An Empirical Study of Key Legal Components of CEO Employment Contracts*, 63 Washington and Lee Law Review 231–270, 242, 249 (2006) Table 3.

2043 For the purpose of this book, the search examined the filings of SEC Form 10-K and a sample of one hundred US registered (publicly traded) companies from all sectors, which were filed within two days in April 2016.

2044 *See supra* Table 8, p. 281.

2045 Sarbanes-Oxley Act of 2002, *supra* note 47, §§ 302, 906; 15 USC 7241, § 1350.

2046 *See supra* Table 8, p. 281.

2047 *See supra* Table 8, p. 281.

Thus, approximately one third of the employment agreements are without cause agreements, while only six percent are at- will employments. Most of the contracts were concluded for a definite term. The range varies from two, three, and five years.[2048] Moreover, the vast majority of termination provisions are just-cause agreements in the event that officers are involved in fraud, dishonesty, or moral turpitude or when they are indicted or charged with a felony or crime. Willful misconduct, refusal to perform employee's duties and breach of a fiduciary duty follow. Thus, the officers can assess the circumstances under which they may be laid off. *Figure 11* presents a chart on the distribution of causes within the officers' employment agreements.

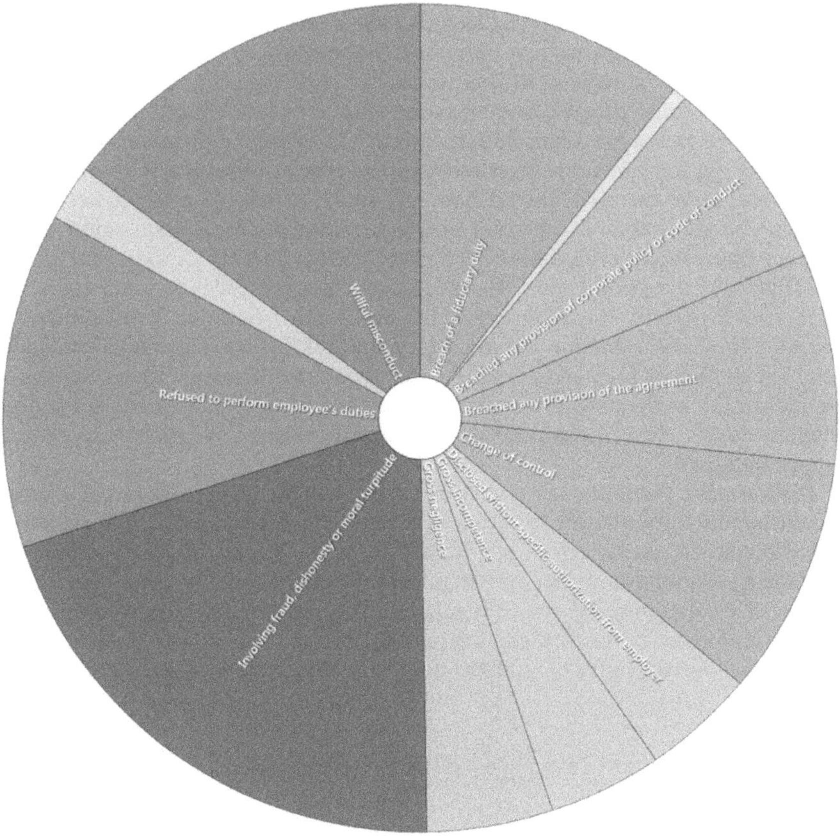

Figure 11 *Distribution of Causes within Officers' Employment Agreements*[2049]

2048 *See supra* Table 8, p. 281.

2049 *See supra* Table 8, p. 281 - The two missing causes within were: uses illegal drugs and alcohol and breach of information of the board.

Interestingly, in seventeen agreements there is a cause provision *"change in or of control."* For example, in the event of a sale of all, or substantially all of the assets of the company or any of its affiliates or any division, the company can terminate the agreement without financial disadvantage. In addition, eight contracts feature a provision on disclosure of information by officers. This means disclosure of proprietary or confidential information without specific authorization from the employer. Poor performance and incompetence on the job rarely constitutes cause in the officers' contracts. Only eight agreements include this cause. Finally, only one contract includes the cause *"breach of duty to inform the board,"* which means the officer failed to resolve any act or omission that purportedly formed the basis for the board's determination. Although the recognition by courts since *Caremark* that a cause of action could be given against directors on account of their failure to exercise oversight, it seems that this cause is rarely afforded any attention in practice. Furthermore, it is interesting to note that a breach of fiduciary duties is subject to termination only for cause and not for damages. In general, in the event of termination with cause, the officers leave the company without any severance compensation. Seventeen agreements allow the officer to terminate the contract for a good cause, but it appears that officers would be in breach of their contracts in the event of termination without good cause. The most important instances of good cause are a material breach by the company of the agreement, material diminishment of position, material reduction in base salary, and relocation of geographical location. The review of the agreements showed that the officers are given severance compensation in the case of termination for good cause and when they are fired without cause. Nevertheless, no agreement comprises any protection against unfair dismissal.

Furthermore, the terms of these agreements state the officers' duties. The range of contractual duties varies from not becoming involved in fraud, dishonesty or moral turpitude, no breach of a fiduciary duty, no breach of policies until the board has been informed. The duty to inform the board could be adopted from the increased legislation and enforced regulation. This term could be significant for the compliance officer in the forthcoming period.

Table 8 shows the range of reasons for termination stated in officers' agreements.

Table 8 Range of Causes of Termination

Causes Agreements	**28**
Breach of a fiduciary duty	19
Breach of information of the Board	1
Breached any provision of corporate policy or code of conduct	14
Breached any provision of the agreement	15
Change of control	17
Disclosed without specific authorization from employer	8
Gross incompetence	8
Gross negligence	9
Involving fraud, dishonesty or moral turpitude	37*)
Refused to perform employee's duties	24
Uses illegal drugs or alcohol	4
Willful misconduct	27
Good Cause Agreements	**17**
Material breach by the Company of the agreement	15
Material diminishment of position	17
Material reduction in base salary	14
Relocation of the geographical location	11

*) This cause comprises more provisions such as fraud, dishonesty etc.

Two of the seventy-one agreements provide for the fullest extent of indemnification permitted by State Corporation Law for directors and officers. Three agreements comprise an indemnification and limitation on liability of directors and officers. Overall, it appears that corporate officers could minimize their risk of damage by means of employments agreements. On the other hand, however, there are advantages for the companies as well. In cases where officers have an employment agreement, this is justified with the profit and benefit for the company. For example, a company within the food industry explained as follows:

> The loss of the services of our CEO, other senior officers or other key employees could have a material adverse effect on our business and plans for future development. We have no reason to believe that we will lose the services of any of these individuals in the foreseeable future; however, we currently have no effective replacement for any of these individuals due to their experience, reputation in the industry and special role in our operations.[2050]

2050 *See e.g.* Form 10-K (2016) SEC, *supra* note 1571 Statement from a food company.

In conclusion, evidently officers have power to negotiate employment agreements and their terms and, it appears that compliance officers are not employed exclusively under the employment at-will doctrine.[2051] Hence, they could negotiate terms in their agreements, for example an indemnification against fines, judgments or settlements but negotiate a term of dismissal protection could be difficult. Additionally, in order to clarify whether the US compliance officer enjoys specific protection under the common law employment at-will doctrine, the next section provides two examples of employment law cases involving compliance officers.

a. The New York At- Will Employment Doctrine

In 2012, the Court of Appeals of New York marked a move contrary to federal regulation. The Court of Appeal affirmed the lower court's decision that New York common law does not recognize any cause of action for the wrongful discharge of an at-will employee.[2052] The plaintiff was a 15 percent partner, the executive vice president, treasurer, secretary, chief operating officer, and chief compliance officer of a hedge fund.[2053] The defendant was the majority owner, chief executive officer, and president.[2054] The plaintiff claimed for wrongful termination after he provided information to a lawyer concerning a proposed agreement that would have eliminated his ownership interest.[2055] He confronted the defendant about improper trading and emphasized the importance of federal regulation for registered investment advisers.[2056] The plaintiff pointed out his duty to avoid improper trading as chief compliance officer under federal securities laws and the company's Code of Ethics.[2057] The SEC requires every investment company and investment adviser registered to adopt and implement written policies, and designates a chief compliance officer to be responsible for administering the policies and procedures, but it provides no protection for wrongful termination of the compliance officer.[2058] However, the Court did not acknowledge any reason for wrongful termination, on the grounds that the plaintiff was not a full-time compliance officer. He had four other titles and even held a 15 percent share in the hedge fund.[2059] Thus, he had many other responsibilities and employment duties.[2060] the plaintiff acted in

---

2051 *See e.g.* Jones (2007), *supra* note 495 at 489; Schwab and Thomas (2006), *supra* note 2042 at 266.
2052 *Sullivan v. Harnisch,* 19 N.Y.3d 259, 261 (2012).
2053 *Id.* at 261.
2054 *Id.* at 261.
2055 *Id.* at 262.
2056 *Id.* at 264.
2057 *Id.* at 262.
2058 Investment Advisers Act of 1940, *supra* note 1642; Investment Company Act of 1940, *supra* note 1636, 17 CFR § 270.38a-1.
2059 *Sullivan v. Harnisch,* 19 N.Y.3d 259, *supra* note 2052 at 264.
2060 *Id.* at 264.

his own interest, and failed to report to the SEC, which was why the Court did not apply the federal law[2061] to his's conduct and confirmed the application of the employer-employee relationship.[2062] For these reasons, the Court of Appeal did not recognize the application of an exception as in *Wieder v. Skala.*[2063] In this case, the plaintiff, a lawyer, sued his former employer, a law firm, for wrongfully discharging him as an associate.[2064] He was fired after reporting on unethical conduct of another associate. The Court of Appeals of the State of New York recognized the unique characteristics of the legal profession and the special relationship of an associate to a law firm.[2065] The Court concluded that the plaintiff's employment differs in several aspects from other corporate employments.[2066] For example, each lawyer and judge has the duty to report to the Disciplinary Committee of the Appellate Division any potential violations of the Disciplinary Rules (DR 1-103 (A)).[2067] Hence, the Court held that the plaintiff had a valid claim for breach of his contract. This was the only time that the New York State Court of Appeals has recognized an exception from the employment-at-will doctrine.[2068]

Finally, the Court pointed out that the *Wieder* exception is a *"narrow one"*[2069] and declined an exception to that rule for the compliance officer of a hedge fund.[2070] Therefore, under the employment at- will doctrine[2071] the defendant was authorized to fire the plaintiff at any time for any reason or for no reason because the Court did not recognize that regulatory compliance, "*was at the very core and, indeed, the only purpose*" of the plaintiff's employment,[2072] since he had four other titles.[2073]

2061 Dodd–Frank Wall Street Reform and Consumer Protection Act (2010), *supra* note 700, § 922 (a), 15 USC § 78u-6.

2062 *Sullivan v. Harnisch*, 19 N.Y.3d 259, *supra* note 2052 at 265.

2063 *Wieder v. Skala*, *supra* note 2040.

2064 *Id.* at 628.

2065 *Id.* at 637.

2066 *Id.* at 635.

2067 *Id.* at 636. The rule provides: *"A lawyer possessing knowledge, not protected as a confidence or secret, of a violation of DR 1-103 that raises a substantial question as to another lawyer's honesty, trustworthiness or fitness in other respects as a lawyer shall report such knowledge to a tribunal or other authority empowered to investigate or act upon such violation."*

2068 *Sullivan v. Harnisch*, 19 N.Y.3d 259, *supra* note 2052 at 263.

2069 *Id.* at 263.

2070 *Id.* at 261.

2071 The judicially created New York at- will employment doctrine was initially recognized in 1895 in the case of *Martin v. New York Life Ins. Co., 148 N.Y. 117 (1895).*

2072 *Sullivan v. Harnisch,* 19 N.Y.3d 259, *supra* note 2052 at 261, 264; *Murphy v. Am. Home Prod.*, 58 N.Y.2d 293, 297 (1983).

2073 *Sullivan v. Harnisch,* 19 N.Y.3d 259, *supra* note 2052 at 264.

However, critics argue that the non-recognition of the exception for compliance officers provided a misleading sign to companies intending to improve their compliance and risk management functions.[2074] In conclusion, this decision confirmed that compliance officers fall within the scope of the at- will employment doctrine and that better protection could be established through the conclusion of full- employment agreements.

b. *Mayers v. Stone* and the Employment Agreement

In this case, the plaintiff was the company's general counsel, chief compliance officer and a member of the board of Stone Castle Partners, LLC, an equity fund.[2075] He had an employment agreement. In addition to his employment with Stone Castle Partners, LLC, the plaintiff established his own company called TP Investments, LLC, which also dealt with collateralized debt obligations. When Stone Castle Partners became aware of his company and trading, the board confronted the plaintiff about his dealings and provided him two choices: (1) to sell his TP Investment or (2) if he refused, termination for cause.[2076] The plaintiff sold his TP Investment. Nevertheless, he was fired for cause. Hence, he claimed *inter alia* for breach of the employment agreement for termination without cause and for breach of the duty of good faith.[2077]

The Supreme Court of New York County examined the terms of the plaintiff's LLC Agreement. Under Section 6.01 of this agreement, the plaintiff was required to "*devote substantially all of his full professional time to the performance of his duties as an employee of the company*" and under Section 5.01 "*to disclose any conflict of interest*" as a board member.[2078] Furthermore, the termination clause stipulated in the agreement stated that the board could terminate his agreement for cause at any time.[2079] For this reason, he was not able to claim good faith, since the terms of a contract govern the parties, not an implied covenant of good faith.[2080] The court concluded that the plaintiff had the right to challenge whether his conduct was the reason for his termination, but that he was unable to replace the terms with a claim of good faith.[2081] In the end, the court dismissed the plaintiff's claims.

In conclusion, cases concerning compliance officers' agreements are rare. Both cases show that there is no specific protection against dismissal for the compliance officer. Under the employment at- will doctrine, the New York Court of Appeal granted protection for lawyers only in an exceptional case. Thus, the compliance

---

2074 *See* Clearly Gottlieb, New York's Employment At-Will Doctrine Puts Private Company Compliance Personnel At Risk 5 (2012).
2075 *Mayers v. Stone Castle Partners, LLC*, No. 650410/2013 (US N.Y. 2014).
2076 *Id.*
2077 *Id.*
2078 *Mayers v. Stone Castle Partners, LLC, supra* note 2075.
2079 *Id.*
2080 *Id.*
2081 *Id.*

officer position has the same legal nature as other corporate officers under the State Corporation Law and under Employment Law.

3. Conclusion – The Compliance Officers Work under US State Corporation Law and Employment Law

Additionally to the US federal law, in the last thirty years State Corporation Law and the Courts have responded to focus greater attention on the role of corporate officers and on the legal duties of officers. Delaware Corporation Law clearly states that corporate officers such as directors are fiduciaries. In a number of Delaware cases, the courts concluded, *"officers and directors owe fiduciary duties to the corporation and its shareholders.'"*[2082] Although both officers and directors are fiduciaries, for a long time it was unclear what the corporate officers' fiduciary duties actually entail. Specifically, a definition of the officers' duties and the duties of the compliance officer are absent from the State Corporation Law.

Since 1996, the Delaware Courts have developed a line of cases which have clarified the compliance duties of directors and officers, as summarized below.[2083]

Table 9 *The Line of Delaware Cases Relating to Corporate Compliance*

Line of Delaware Cases	Compliance Issue
1996 *Caremark*[2084]	Recognition of shareholders litigation against corporate directors for fail to exercise oversight,
	Established standards for liability, breach of directors oversight with necessary conditions "systematic failure", "utter failure" or " unconsidered inaction",
	Development of a new duty of oversight or compliance duty for directors,
	Development of the *Caremark* standard or *Caremark* theory
	Ongoing duty to address compliance
2006 *Stone v Ritter*[2085]	Confirmation of duty of oversight for directors and the *Caremark* standard of oversight liability.
2009 *Gantler v Stephen*[2086]	Officers owe the same fiduciary duties as directors such as the duty of oversight.

2082 *See e.g. Guth v. Loft, Inc.*, 5 A.2d 503 (Del 1939), *supra* note 1816 at 510; *In re Walt Disney Co. Derivative Litig.*, (Del. Ch. 2004), *supra* note 1816 at 16.

2083 *See supra* A., II., 3.a.-c., pp. 262 et seq.

2084 In re Caremark International Inc. Derivative Litigation, 698 A.2d 959 (Del. Ch. 1996), supra note 21.

2085 *Stone v. Ritter*, 911 A.2d 362 (Del. 2006), *supra* note 196.

2086 *Gantler v. Stephens*, 965 A.2d 695 (Del. 2009), *supra* note 23.

While the compliance duties of directors and officers are now clearly defined under corporation case law, the protection from liability or from wrongful termination for officers, specifically for compliance officers, remains uncertain. Corporate law provides statutory provisions of exculpation for directors, but not for officers. In addition, the business judgment rule generally applies to decisions within a director's authority. However, it seems that officers do not have protection under the rule. For this reason, two recent cases with respect to the compliance officer under employment case law were examined.[2087]

Table 10 *The Employment Law with Respect to Wrongful Termination of Compliance Officer*

Employment Law Cases	Wrongful Termination of Compliance Officers
2012 *Sullivan v. Harnisch*[2088]	No exception from the employment at- will doctrine due to the employment relationship,
	The plaintiff was not a full-time compliance officer,
	Under at-will doctrine he could be terminated without cause or notice.
2014 *Mayers v Stone*[2089]	The plaintiff was a general counsel and a compliance officer,
	Due to his employment agreement he breached his duty of loyalty, he had a conflict of interest,
	The court confirmed the cause of termination without specific protection for the compliance officer.

The case law does not support the application of the business judgment rule to officers on the same basis as directors. In their employment agreements, directors negotiate precise termination and indemnification terms. Since the vast of majority of corporate officers are at- will employees, they fall under the employment at- will doctrine meaning that the employer can terminate their contracts for any reason at any time.[2090] Generally, under the common law at-will doctrine, courts did not recognize any cause for actions for wrongful discharge in the US. Thus, no specific dismissal protection for compliance officers was found under the US Employment Law.

2087 *See supra* A., III., 2.a.-b., pp. 282 et seq.
2088 *Sullivan v. Harnisch,* 19 N.Y.3d 259, *supra* note 2052.
2089 Mayers v. Stone Castle Partners, LLC, supra note 2075.
2090 This is not applicable to the executive officers such as CEO, CFO, etc. *See infra* Table 11, p. 287.

B. The Model of the Corporate Compliance Officer in the US

Having examined US State Corporation Law, US Employment Law and landmark cases with respect to compliance and compliance officers, this section will now identify the role and the model of the corporate compliance officer by examining the corporate bylaws and other sources together with his responsibilities, duties, and liability in practice in order to present a model of the US compliance officer at the end of this chapter.

First and foremost, by reviewing the bylaws of companies, they prescribe that *"The officers of the corporation shall be elected by, and serve at the pleasure of, the board"* or *"The board may appoint such other officers and agents as it shall deem necessary."*[2091] The findings of the review of ten bylaws of companies in recent SEC filings showed a variety of officer titles. These bylaws also outline the responsibilities and duties in terms of the corporate purpose. The following list identifies the core duties of the selected and examined bylaws:

Table 11 – Officers' Duties in the Bylaws[2092]

Officers Appointed in the Bylaws	No.	Officers Duties (Examples)
Chief Executive Officer	8	General power to execute bonds, deeds, and contracts in the name of the Corporation, to appoint or designate all employees and agents of the Corporation, shall be a member of the Board and shall have general charge and supervision of the business of the Corporation, shall have general management and control over the policy, business and affairs of the corporation.
Chief Financial Officer	4	He shall render to the Board of Directors, whenever the Board may require, an account of the financial condition of the corporation, shall be responsible for the system of financial control of the corporation, including internal audits, the maintenance of its accounting records, and the preparation of the corporation's financial statements.

2091 Form 10-K SEC, *supra* note 1528 The bylaws of companies were found in the SEC Filings in the EDGAR database. The sample includes six small companies and four corporations at the Fortune 500 list. *See* Fortune 500, footnote at 679; The corporate names and the names of their officers will not disclosed to ensure privacy.

2092 See also *Id.*

Table 11 *Continued*

Officers Appointed in the Bylaws	No.	Officers Duties (Examples)
Chief Operating Officer	2	He shall be the officer of the Corporation charged with supervision and management of the daily operations of the Corporation in support of the Chief Executive Officer.
General Counsel	2	The GC shall supervise and direct the legal affairs of the Corporation, Whenever an applicable statute, decree, rule, or regulation requires a document to be subscribed by a particular officer of the Corporation, such document may be signed on behalf of such officer, shall advise the board of directors and officers on legal matters, except those relating to taxes.
Other Officer	5	Any other elected officer shall have such powers and perform such duties as may from time to time be granted, or assigned by the Board or, subject to the control of the Board, by a committee thereof or by the Executive Committee.
Secretary	8	The Secretary shall attend to the giving of notice of all meetings of stockholders and of the Board of Directors and shall keep and attest true records of all such proceedings, The Secretary shall have charge of the corporate seal and have authority to attest any and all instruments or writings to which the same may be affixed and shall keep and account for all books, documents, papers, and records of the Corporation relating to its corporate organization.
Treasurer	5	The Treasurer shall have the care and custody of all moneys, funds, and securities of the Corporation, and shall deposit or cause to be deposited all funds of the Corporation. The Treasurer shall have power to sign stock certificates, to indorse for deposit or collection, or otherwise, all checks, drafts, notes, bills of exchange, or other commercial paper payable to the Corporation, and to give proper receipts therefore.

The reviewed bylaws of the companies do not show any appointed standalone compliance officer. However, in this sample of large publicly traded corporations (Fortune 500), the issues of compliance are within the purview of the legal department. The general counsel has multiple responsibilities for law, governance, and compliance, as specified in the 10-K file. One aspect of his duties is to advise the board of directors and officers on legal matters, except those relating to taxes.

Secondly, as we have seen, US courts tend to deal with the duties of both directors and officers together.[2093] However, there are a number of pronounced distinctions. Pursuant to State Corporation Law, directors are elected and can be removed by stockholders.[2094] Officers are usually elected or appointed by the board of directors and can be removed from office by the directors.[2095] *Sale* identifies corporate officers as counterparts to the directors.[2096] She compares the number of decisions taken in day-to-day activity.[2097] Directors have to make strategic decisions and to oversee the corporation's affairs and business.[2098] Hence, this position includes a variety of responsibilities, which are described in the Corporate Director's Guidebook.[2099] Therefore, pursuant to the view put forward by *Sale*, monitoring systems are within the directors' purview since they are responsible for approving and overseeing them.[2100] In contrast, officers manage daily business operations.[2101] They are responsible for maintaining and improving corporate procedures and business.

Thirdly, however, State Corporation Law allows the board of directors to delegate its own managerial responsibility to the senior officers. Nevertheless, Section 141(a) of Delaware Corporation Law permits a board of directors to delegate

2093 *See supra* A., II.,.1. to 3., pp. 255 et seq.; *See also* CHEW, *supra* note 1799; Eisenberg (2006), *supra* note 199 at 3; *Guth v. Loft, Inc.*, 5 A.2d 503 (Del 1939), *supra* note 1816 at 510. *"Corporate officers and directors are not permitted to use their position of trust and confidence to further their private interests. While technically not trustees, they stand in a fiduciary relation to the corporation and its stockholders."*

2094 tit. 8 DELAWARE CODE, *supra* note 24, § 211 (b); MODEL BUSINESS CORPORATION ACT, *supra* note 1805 § 7.28 (a).

2095 *See* Lyman Johnson & David Millon, *Recalling Why Corporate Officers Are Fiduciaries*, 46 WILLIAM & MARY LAW REVIEW 1597, 1605 (2005).

2096 *See* Sale (2007), *supra* note 22 at 724.

2097 *Id.* at 723.

2098 *See* Brown (2001), *supra* note 495 at 14.

2099 CORPORATE DIRECTOR'S GUIDEBOOK, *supra* note 1822 at 12. *"The overall responsibilities of directors are, e.g. monitoring the corporation performance with regard to operating, financial, and other significant plans, strategies and objectives; selecting the CEO and other senior executives; understanding the corporations risk profile, reviewing and overseeing the risk management programs; monitoring the internal financial program; establishing and monitoring effective compliance programs; etc."*

2100 *See* Sale (2007), *supra* note 22 at 724.

2101 *See* Johnson and Millon (2005), *supra* note 2095 at 1601.

managerial duties to officers of the corporation, except to the extent that the corporation's certificate of incorporation or bylaws may limit or prohibit such delegation.[2102] For example, bylaws of a Delaware company states the following:

> the Board of Directors may delegate to the Chief Executive Officer the right to appoint such Executive Vice Presidents, Senior Vice Presidents, Vice Presidents, Assistant Vice Presidents, Assistant Secretaries, Assistant Treasurers and agents, as the Chief Executive Officer shall deem appropriate and necessary from to time.[2103]

According to these bylaws, the Chief Executive Officer can also delegate his responsibilities to other corporate officers:

> The Chief Executive Officer shall have the power to execute any and all instruments and documents on behalf of the corporation and to delegate to any other officer of the corporation the power to execute any and all such instruments and documents.[2104]

In addition, the courts have confirmed that directors are not required to supervise every detail of business operation.[2105] Instead, the directors can delegate to officers limited responsibilities relating to day-to-day business.[2106] Specifically, the Delaware Court examined the scope of delegation by a CEO. The employment agreement provides that the CEO "*shall be responsible for the general management of the affairs of the company.*"[2107] Therefore, the board of directors delegated the general management to the CEO. The Court concluded that this term of the agreement is contrary to law and the bylaws.[2108] This term was "*void as a matter of law.*"[2109] Furthermore, such delegation does not relieve directors of their general duty of care.[2110]

Fourthly, a small number of scholars disagree with the theory that officers are fiduciaries. They argue that officers are agents since they are appointed by

---

2102 tit. 8 Delaware Code, *supra* note 24 § 141 (a) "*If any such provision is made in the certificate of incorporation, the powers and duties conferred or imposed upon the board of directors by this chapter shall be exercised or performed to such extent and by such person or persons as shall be provided in the certificate of incorporation.*"

2103 Bylaws of a Delaware Corporation, Art. IV, Sec. 1.

2104 Bylaws of a Delaware Corporation *Id.* Art. IV, Sec. 7.

2105 *See. e.g. Myers & Chapman, Incorporated v. Thomas G. Evans,* 374 S.E.2d 385, 392 (N.C. 1988) "*Directors are not ... insurers of the honesty and integrity of the officers and agents. Neither are they required to personally supervise all the details of business transactions.*"

2106 *See* Petrin (2010), *supra* note 1125 at 1677 at 90.

2107 *Grimes v. Donald,* 673 A.2d 1207, 1210 (Del. 1996).

2108 *Id.* at 1211, 1214. Directors may not delegate duties which lie "*at the heart of the management of the corporation.*"

2109 *Id.* at 1212.

2110 *Lowell Hoit & Co. v. Detig*, 50 N.E.2d, 602, 603 (111. App. Ct. 1943).

the board.[2111] The principal source of agency law is the Third Restatement by the American Law Institute (ALI), which defines the term agency as the

> fiduciary relationship that arises when one person (a "principal") manifests assent to another person (an "agent") that the agent shall act on the principal's behalf and subject to the principal's control, and the agent manifests assent or otherwise consents so to act.[2112]

Hence, whenever one person acts on behalf of another, the principles of agency define the relationships and the responsibilities of both parties. Furthermore, this person is subject to the principal's control.[2113] Therefore, according to this theory, officers are subject to the control of directors acting on behalf of the corporate principal, the director.[2114] Notwithstanding this, as agents, corporate officers owe also a number of fiduciary duties.[2115] For example, the agent must act loyally for the principal's benefit.[2116] Moreover, the agent owes a duty of performance, a duty of care, a duty to provide information, and a duty of good conduct.[2117] Thus, the officer as an agent has a duty to inform the principal using *"reasonable effort to provide the principal with facts that the agent knows, has reason to know, or should know."*[2118] The MBCA adopted the duty to provide information in section 8.42 (b) (1).[2119] In fact, in *Smith v. Van Gorkom* the court concluded that Van Gorkom, a Chairman and Chief Executive Officer, had violated his disclosure obligation by withholding material information from the board and stockholders.[2120]

Another example seen in corporate scandals like Enron shows that the court-appointed examiner held that the corporate officers owed a fiduciary duty of good faith, duty of care and duty of loyalty to Enron.[2121] In that case, "*knowing dissemination of false information about the financial condition of the company*" constituted

---

2111 *See e.g.* Eisenberg (2006), *supra* note 199 at 47 *"Officers are a special class of agents, and the rule has long been established in agency law that agents have a duty to duly inform their principals."*; *See Generally* Johnson and Millon (2005), *supra* note 2095.

2112 ALI American Law Institute, Third Restatement of the Law | Agency (2006) § 1.01 [hereinafter Third Restatement].

2113 *Id.*§ 1.01.

2114 *See* Johnson and Millon (2005), *supra* note 2095 at 1607.

2115 Third Restatement, *supra* note 2112 § 8.01.

2116 Third Restatement, *Id.* § 8.01.

2117 *Id.* §§ 8.07-8.12.

2118 *Id.* § 8.11.

2119 Model Business Corporation Act, *supra* note 1805 § 8.42 (b)(1) "*The duty of an officer includes the obligation: (1) to inform the superior officer to whom, or the board of directors or the committee thereof to which, the officer reports of information about the affairs of the corporation known to the officer.*"

2120 *Smith v. Van Gorkom*, (Del. 1985), *supra* note 1838 at 893.

2121 Neal Batson, *In re Enron Corporation, et al.*, Case No. 01-16034 (AJG) (S.D.N.Y.), Third Interim Report of Neal Batson, Court-appointed Examiner, 24 (2003).

a breach of the officer's fiduciary duties.[2122] *Eisenberg's* view confirmed that an officer who fails to provide material information is in violation of his duty of good faith.[2123] In so doing, officers may also be guilty of breaching their duty of loyalty. In *Hampshire Group, Limited v. Kuttner,* the Delaware Court held that two former officers and employees of Hampshire breached their fiduciary duties by having knowingly falsified financial records of the company.[2124] Moreover, *Johnson & Millon* argue that officers have a duty to establish adequate internal monitoring procedures and have primary responsibility for the corporation's business activities and financial reporting.[2125] While State Corporation Law does not clearly describe the role of officers, Federal Law governs a number of duties incumbent upon officers under the SOX.[2126] With respect to current developments in Federal Law, the agent theory should be given due consideration.

The conclusion from the foregoing is that corporate officers' duties and liabilities are discussed in conflicting contexts and they are not always clear. The officers' fiduciary duties are original and derive from Agency Law, not only from the board's delegation of powers to oversee the company's daily business.[2127] Hence, some legal scholars and some courts argue that the business judgment rule applies also at that time to officers and their decisions.[2128] If the courts do not apply the business judgment rule to officers, they could probably be held personally liable more often for breaching their duties.[2129] In addition, it has been mentioned that there is no need for any transplant into Corporation Law, because Agency Law also comprises the officers' relationship with the corporation.[2130]

I. The Compliance Officer within the Corporate Structure

This section presents the position of the corporate compliance officer within the structure of a typical US corporation. This model is a simplified representation of the averaged structure within a large corporation. Generally, the corporate structure consists of two main groups at the high-level personnel, which were examined above: directors and officers. The first group, the board of directors,

2122 *Id.* at 24.
2123 *See* Eisenberg (2006), supra note 199 at 50.
2124 *Hampshire Group, Limited v. Kuttner, C.A.* No. 3607-VCS (Del. Ch. 2010), *supra* note 1974.
2125 *See* Johnson and Millon (2005), *supra* note 2095 at 1636.
2126 *Id.* at 1636.; SARBANES-OXLEY ACT OF 2002, *supra* note 47 §§ 302, 906.
2127 *See* Johnson and Millon (2005), *supra* note 2095 at 1638.
2128 *Id.* at 1642.; Lyman Johnson, *Corporate Officers and the Business Judgment Rule,* 60 BUSINESS LAWYER, 440 (2005); *Cede & Co. v. Technicolor, Inc.*, 634 A.2d 345 (Del. 1993), *supra* note 1997 at 367–368.
2129 *See* CHEW, *supra* note 1799 at 20.
2130 *See* Johnson and Millon (2005), *supra* note 2095 at 1638.

is generally responsible for supervision and oversight of corporate affairs.[2131] As determined previously, the board of directors can delegate certain responsibilities to board committees.[2132] Furthermore, the board of directors has the option of delegating partial tasks to executive officers.[2133] The US unified board of directors is referred to as *"one-tier"* board and comprises the CEO, executives directors, a chairman, and independent directors.[2134] Large corporations have established additionally a number of committees, such as audit, compensation, risk or compliance committees. If the corporation does not have a specific compliance committee, the audit committee is the most important committee in the context of compliance.[2135] In general, directors are selected to committees based on their qualifications, such as skills, expertise, and background.[2136]

Studies have shown that board size tends to correlate with the company's revenues.[2137] The average board size in small firms with revenue of less than US$ 10 million revenue is seven directors, while in larger firms with more US$ 10 million revenue, the average is twelve directors.[2138] This number is often stated in the certificate of incorporation or bylaws.[2139] The directors are elected for terms defined in the certificate of incorporation or bylaws of the company. Usually, the directors elect a chairman who leads the board and exerts a great deal of authority.[2140] The

---

2131 *See supra* A, II.,1., p. 255; tit. 8 DELAWARE CODE, *supra* note 24, § 141 (a).

2132 *See supra* A., II., pp. 254 et seq.; "All State Corporation Laws allow for the establishment of board committees." *See* MILLER (2014), *supra* note 595 at 27.

2133 *See supra* A., II., pp. 254 et seq.; tit. 8 DELAWARE CODE, *supra* note 24, §§ 141 (a), 142; and based on corporation's certificate of incorporation or bylaws.

2134 *See* David Block & Anne-Marie Gerstner, *One-Tier vs. Two-Tier Board Structure: A Comparison Between the United States and Germany*, Paper 1 COMPARATIVE CORPORATE GOVERNANCE AND FINANCIAL REGULATION, 6 (2016).

2135 *See* MILLER (2014), *supra* note 595 at 73.

2136 David F. Larcker & Brian Tayan, BOARD OF DIRECTORS: STRUCTURE AND CONSEQUENCES (2015), https://www.gsb.stanford.edu/sites/gsb/files/publication-pdf/cgri-quick-guide-05-board-directors-structure-consequences.pdf (last visited Jun 4, 2016).

2137 *See* Jeffrey Coles, Naveen D. Daniel & Lalitha Naveen, *Boards: Does one size fit all*, 87 JOURNAL OF FINANCIAL ECONOMICS 329–356 (2008); David Yermack, *Higher market valuation of companies with a small board of directors*, 40 JOURNAL OF FINANCIAL ECONOMICS 185–211 (1996).

2138 Board of Directors Larcker and Tayan, *supra* note 2136.

2139 BYLAWS OF THE MERCK & CO., INC., (2015) Art. II, Sec. 1; RESTATED CERTIFICATE OF INCORPORATION OF SCHERING-PLOUGH CORPORATION (MERCK & CO, INC.), (2009) Art. VI, Art. XII *"The number of directors of the Corporation shall be such number, not less than three nor more than eighteen, as may, from time to time, be determined in accordance with the bylaws."*

2140 *See* MILLER (2014), *supra* note 595 at 66–67.

chairman has the power, for example, to call special meetings of the shareholders and also sets the agenda for board meetings.[2141]

The second corporate group at the high-level personnel comprises the corporation's officers, who oversee the day-to-day business operations. At the annual meeting, the board of directors elects the officers for the transaction of business.[2142] These officers are referred to as the *"executive officers"* or *"management"* of the company.[2143] These titles are stated in the bylaws. The most important are the president, vice-president, secretary, treasurer, CEO, CFO, COO, and sometimes the GC, who has also compliance responsibilities.[2144] For publicly traded companies, the compliance requirements for the management are set forth in Section 404 (a) of the SOX.[2145] Special corporate responsibility for financial reports is required for the CEO and CFO, who are required to certify each annual or quarterly report filed under the SOX.[2146] The chief compliance officer is not specifically named in the sample bylaws examined.[2147] Hence, the responsibilities delegated from the board are not clearly defined. Generally, the CCO act as staff to the CEO and compliance committee.[2148] As discussed previously, their key responsibility is to oversee and monitor the compliance program.[2149] The CCO should report all efforts, results, or irregularities relating to compliance issues to the compliance committee or directly to the board.

To conclude, as the study above shows, the corporate compliance officer is not specifically integrated in the structure set out in the bylaws or certificate of incorporation and their role is not always clear. The compliance officers themselves have to clarify their responsibilities and tasks by means of job descriptions or employment agreements. Although the US legislation and the regulators have repeatedly attempted to enforce the position of the corporate compliance officer, there is no federal or state statutory provision that clearly requires a designation of or which stipulates in detail what the duties of the corporate compliance officer are. The FSGO only provides that *"high-level personnel of the organization"* are responsible for an effective compliance program.[2150]

2141 Bylaws of the Pico Holding, Inc., Exhibit 3.1, *supra* note 1827 Art. II, Sec. 2.3.
2142 Bylaws of the Boeing Company, Exhibit 3.2, *supra* note 2256 Art. II, Sec. 4.
2143 *See* Miller (2014), *supra* note 595 at 103.
2144 *See supra* Table 11, pp. 287–288.
2145 *See supra* A., II., 2.d., p. 223; Sarbanes-Oxley Act of 2002, *supra* note 47 § 404 (a), 15 USC 7262.
2146 *Id.* § 302 (a), 15 USC 7241.
2147 *See supra* Table 11, pp. 287–288.
2148 *See* Miller (2014), *supra* note 595 at 128.
2149 *See supra* A., I., 3. p. 236; *Id.* at 128.
2150 *See supra* A., I., 3. p. 236; US Sentencing Guidelines Manual USSC, *supra* note 49, § 8 B2.1 (b)(2)(B).

II. The Role of the Corporate Compliance Officer

The resulting question is: Where is the role of the corporate compliance officer defined? Some Corporation Law statutes identify a variety of officers' titles. Generally, these include a president, vice-president, a secretary and a treasurer, as well as other officers determined in or provide for in the bylaws.[2151] Meanwhile other statutes state only that

> A corporation shall have the officers described in its bylaws or appointed by the board of directors in accordance with the bylaws.[2152]

Thus, State Corporation Law and the sample of corporation bylaws[2153] make no mention of compliance officers. The reason for the absence in law of specifically defined officers could be the stronger focus on the duties of the highest corporate management, such as the directors and executive officers, rather than on titles.[2154] However, when dealing with cases concerning fiduciary duties, the courts tend to refer to *"key employees."* Key employees have positions that are comparable to enumerated officers in the law and bylaws.[2155] The courts examine whether these individuals have access to confidential business information and increased authority.[2156] Based on this, they could be subject to a fiduciary duty. Therefore, the next section first looks at instances in which the compliance function is incorporated into the corporate structure and, second, which are the main duties of corporate compliance officers.

In US corporations, traditionally, the general counsel took the compliance officer position.[2157] As examined previously, the responsibility for compliance often lies with the vice-president or the general counsel.[2158] The general counsel continues to perform this position to this day in a number of companies.[2159] In other companies, the role of the corporate compliance officer illustrates that general counsels with a *"dual-role"*[2160] are appointed as corporate executives with responsibility for compliance issues at large publicly-traded corporations.[2161] A 2005 survey by the

2151 *See e.g* NEW YORK BUSINESS CORPORATION LAW, *supra* note 1821 § 715.

2152 *See e.g.* FLA. STAT. ANN. (2015), *supra* note 1971 § 607.08401; ILLINOIS BUSINESS CORPORATION ACT (ILCS), 805 ILCS 5/ (1983) 805 ILCS 5/8.50.

2153 *See supra* Table 11, pp. 287–288.

2154 *See* CHEW, *supra* note 1799 at 20.

2155 *Id.* at 20.

2156 *Id.* at 20.

2157 *See* MILLER (2014), *supra* note 595 at 129.

2158 *See supra* A., III., 2., pp. 277 et seq.

2159 *Id.* at 129.

2160 *ASSOCIATION OF CORPORATE COUNSEL ACC, COMPLIANCE PROGRAM AND RISK ASSESSMENT BENCHMARKING SURVEY 2005 8 (2005). "The general counsel of companies has daily operational responsibility for the compliance and ethics function 40 % of the time."; See supra* Table 11, pp. 287–288.

2161 *See supra* Table 11, pp. 287–288.

ACC confirmed that the person who deals with daily operational responsibility for compliance activities is the general counsel (forty percent) and the chief compliance officer (twenty percent).[2162] In addition, the survey found that the *"primary driver"* of compliance programs is the general counsel's office or the legal department and the CEO or the board of directors.[2163] Following on from this, a study by PWC shows that the legal department is in charge of oversight for compliance.[2164] The majority of responsibilities for compliance are assumed by the senior vice president (forty-seven percent) and by other executives (twenty-four percent).[2165] There thus appears to be a lack of breadth in the compliance officers' function.[2166]

However, in recent years, the role of the general counsel - just like the role of the compliance officer, has evolved within companies.[2167] Compliance issues are no longer exclusively a legal task.[2168] For example, the requirements of an effective compliance program, the establishment, the processing, the monitoring, and the auditing of internal compliance structures, codes, and policies cannot be met by a department staffed solely by lawyers.[2169] Furthermore, as previously discussed, the administrative agencies such as the SEC and DOJ enforce the separation between legal and compliance structures.[2170]

Instead, of simply listing the tasks of the corporate compliance officer, this section discusses the role of this function, which is often described as wearing *"two or multiple hats."* The compliance officers with *"two or more hats"* themselves note that it is sometimes challenging to have enough time to properly coordinate and handle compliance issues.[2171] In addition, a number of studies show that the range of titles and responsibilities varies widely.[2172]

There is an academic and political debate on the separation of the compliance function from that of the general counsel. Critics argue that compliance is not a biased subject and that it comprises a number of areas: "*competition law, employment law, environmental law, labor and employment law, international law, accounting rules, and disclosure law,*" etc.[2173] For this reason, all experts in areas of formal rules

---

2162 Benchmarking Survey 2005 ACC, *supra* note 2159 "*The representation was broken down with 15 percent coming from foreign-based corporations and 85 percent from U.S-based corporations in all major industries. Nearly 60 percent of the* companies represented by *survey participants are publicly-traded on a major US stock exchange.*"

2163 *Id.* at 27.

2164 PWC Study 2013, *supra* note 1623 at 17, In forty percent of the US Companies, the oversight for compliance resides with the legal department.

2165 PWC Study 2013 *Id.* at 18.

2166 *See* DeStefano (2013), *supra* note 14 at 126.

2167 *See* Miller (2014), *supra* note 595 at 129.

2168 *Id.* at 129.

2169 *Id.* at 129.

2170 *See supra* A., I.,1.d., p. 203.

2171 PWC Study 2014, *supra* note 1767 at 10.

2172 PWC Study 2014, *supra* note 1767; PWC Study 2015, *supra* note 1771.

2173 Ben W. Heineman, Don't Divorce the GC and Compliance Officer Harvard Law School Forum on Corporate Governance (2010), https://corpgov.law.

and legal should report to the general counsel.[2174] However, they acknowledge that lawyers have legal and ethical expertise but less procedural skills.[2175] Other authors argue that the compliance and the legal function have different objectives and specific tasks.[2176] The compliance officer on the one hand has to monitor business activity and employee conduct in order to detect and prevent misconduct and to cooperate with the government and should have open relationship with regulators. On the other hand, the general counsel has to provide legal analysis, advise and defend the company.[2177] In contrast, the compliance position is a control function. Despite this, the compliance officer and the general counsel should collaborate closely. Combining the two functions could, however, cause conflict.[2178]

The evidence shows that larger companies are more likely than smaller companies to have a standalone chief compliance officer on account of their larger resources and budgets.[2179] Smaller companies also have simpler business structures. Nevertheless, in a number of large companies, the compliance function remains in the legal department because the general counsel is the *de facto* compliance officer at 48 percent of the surveyed companies that do not have a named chief compliance officer.[2180] However, maintaining and reviewing compliance policies and procedures will continue to be a primary responsibility of compliance officers. Finally, the enhancement of the regulatory environment, enforcement by the regulator and the shift in focus toward greater accountability will lead to a more standalone, *"one-hatted"* and equal role of the compliance officer.

Another aspect derived from the corporate structure is that the compliance officer rarely reports to the CEO or to the board of directors, because *"...that is what the CEO wants."*[2181] A compliance study by PWC and Compliance Week found that only three percent of chief compliance officers report to the board of directors while thirty-five percent report to the general counsel.[2182] This number had not significantly changed

harvard.edu/2010/12/26/dont-divorce-the-gc-and-compliance-officer/ (last visited Jun 3, 2016).

2174 *Id.*

2175 *Id.*

2176 PWC Study 2014, *supra* note 1767 at 11; Traeger, Guidroz, and Jimbo (2014), *supra* note 486 at 25.

2177 PWC Study 2014, *supra* note 1767 at 11.

2178 PWC Study 2014 *Id.* at 11.; José A. Tabuena & Jennifer L. Smith, *The Chief Compliance Officer versus the General Counsel: Friends or Foes? Part II*, Journal of Health Care Compliance 13–18, 16 (2006).

2179 PWC Study 2013, *supra* note 1623 at 5; PWC Study 2014, *supra* note 1767 at 7.

2180 PWC Study 2015, *supra* note 1771 at 12.

2181 *See* DeStefano (2013), *supra* note 14 at 126. This study carried out telephone interviews with general counsels. This is a response from a general counsel and compliance officer.

2182 PWC Study 2012, *supra* note 10 at 17 Chart 4. "*Survey data supporting the Compliance Week-PwC State of Compliance 2012 Study was collected from February*

by 2015. Thirty-one percent of compliance officers report to the general counsel, and twenty-one percent report to the board of directors.[2183] The general counsel has a great deal of power, influence, and credibility.[2184] Hence, the CEO tends to trust the legal advice provided by the general counsel. In contrast, the compliance officers themselves explain that they are often viewed as *"cops," "watchdogs,"* or *"outsiders."*[2185] However, due to its duty of oversight, the board of directors would be well-advised to assure itself that the compliance officer provides objective information, analyzes, and recommendations on compliance procedures.[2186]

However, the key problem is that the compliance officer may not recognize *ex ante* the effectiveness of a compliance program, and the prosecutors instead decide *ex post* if the compliance program was effective.[2187] In 2005, a study by *Weber & Fortun* found that approximately half of the compliance officers surveyed had no direct reporting responsibilities. Furthermore, the average ethics and compliance departments has 3.58 employees.[2188] In contrast, in 2012, the compliance study[2189] by PWC and Compliance Week showed an increased number of full-time staff including a CCO, working in the compliance department. Sixty-one percent of the compliance executives surveyed had more than six employees in their compliance department.[2190] In short, the majority of compliance officers describe the compliance structure in their companies as a *"centralized leadership with dedicated central resources supported by remote resources embedded in the business reporting."*[2191]

However, critics view the structural corporate compliance changes as nothing more than *"cosmetic compliance"* or *"window-dressing."*[2192] The reason for this is that they see the weaknesses in enforcement through an *"informal quasi-adjudicative process"* by the government.[2193] A number of scholars refer to the governmental compliance regulation as *"adjudicative compliance."* They argue that it is a procedural shortcoming process leading to significant costs.[2194] They conclude that, despite strengthened governmental focus on compliance, companies nowadays are

---

28 through April 6, 2012. The survey instrument was directed to senior-level compliance officers at US corporations with annual revenue of $1 billion or more." See Id. at 18.

2183 PWC STUDY 2015, *supra* note 1771 at 12.

2184 *See* DeStefano (2013), *supra* note 14 at 127.

2185 *Id.* at 129.; Freeman (2007), *supra* note 57 at 360.

2186 *See* Tabuena and Smith (2006), *supra* note 2178 at 17.

2187 *See* Baer (2009), *supra* note 586 at 997.

2188 *See* Weber and Fortun (2005), *supra* note 4 at 109.

2189 PWC STUDY 2012, *supra* note 10.

2190 PWC STUDY 2012 *Id.* at 17. Chart 2.

2191 PWC STUDY 2013, *supra* note 1623 at 29.

2192 *See e.g.* Baer (2009), *supra* note 586 at 952; Beale (2014), *supra* note 1097 at 20; Oded (2011), *supra* note 1097 at 276; Rosen, Parker, and Nielsen (2013), *supra* note 738 at 361.

2193 *See* Baer (2009), *supra* note 586 at 952.

2194 *Id.* at 975.

no more transparent than in the past.[2195] Instead, the administrative agencies use companies to obtain information about individual employees for investigations and prosecutions.[2196] Finally, as discussed previously, the governmental response is to attempt to restore investors' confidence by means of periodic statutory disclosure obligations and recommended corporate structures, which then taken into consideration when sentencing companies.[2197]

The compliance officer also has to deal with governmental agencies and regulators like the DOJ and SEC.[2198] For this reason, the compliance officers find themselves stuck in the middle between the demands of the board management and the employees. Sometimes, they have to make decisions to the detriment of their own colleagues in charge of operations, procurement, business acquisition, and contracting in order to comply with the law.[2199] As a result, this post is highly complex and complicated to handle. However, the SEC supports the corporate compliance function in the private sector.[2200] *Ceresney*, the director of the SEC Division of Enforcement, considers the following questions with respect to the compliance function within companies:

(1) Are compliance personnel included in critical meetings?
(2) Do compliance officers report to the CEO and have significant visibility with the board?
(3) Is the compliance department viewed as an important partner in the business and not simply as a support function or a cost center?
(4) Is compliance given the personnel and resources necessary to fully cover the entity's needs?[2201]

The SEC has recognized the absence of real compliance involvement in company considerations, for example that there is sometimes a lack of resources and information for the compliance function.[2202] On these grounds, the SEC enforces and encourages companies to afford compliance the prominence and resources it needs in order to be effective.[2203]

In conclusion, in practice, it appears that the corporate compliance officer often occupies a dual-hatted or multifunctional role rather than a standalone function. In most instances, legal departments carry out the responsibilities of oversight

2195 *Id.* at 952.
2196 *Id.* at 956.
2197 *Id.* at 956.; FCPA GUIDANCE DOJ AND SEC, *supra* note 1275; US SENTENCING MANUAL USSC, *supra* note 667, § 8 B2.1; SARBANES-OXLEY ACT OF 2002, *supra* note 47.
2198 *See* Fanto (2013), *supra* note 57 at 2; *See supra* A., I., II., pp. 171 et seq.
2199 *See* Greenberg (2009), *supra* note 11 at 34.
2200 SEC 2015 National Society of Compliance Professionals Ceresney and Division of Enforcement, *supra* note 1631.
2201 SEC 2015 NATIONAL SOCIETY OF COMPLIANCE PROFESSIONALS *Id.*
2202 SEC 2015 NATIONAL SOCIETY OF COMPLIANCE PROFESSIONALS *Id.*
2203 SEC 2015 NATIONAL SOCIETY OF COMPLIANCE PROFESSIONALS *Id.*

for compliance issues. The compliance officer title is not enumerated in State Corporation Law and precedents involving corporate compliance officers are few and far between. Nevertheless, the administrative agencies like the DOJ and SEC will enforce the integration and creation of a standalone position of the compliance officer. The role of the compliance officer looks set to continue to remain separate from the general counsel's role in future.

III. Development of Responsibilities and Duties of the Compliance Officer

The conclusion from the above is that the challenges for the corporate compliance officer work have increased significantly in the US. Due to the enhanced legal framework of federal law, the development of compliance standards by the courts and the rule-making activities by regulators, the responsibilities for compliance officers have increased, more duties pertaining to compliance officers have emerged and, therefore, more personally liability can arise. After the enactment of the FCPA, the SOX and the promulgation of the FSGO, corporate compliance officers' key responsibilities have established as followed:[2204]

Table 12 - *Key Responsibilities for Corporate Compliance Officers*

FCPA	SOX	FSGO
Identify and assess bribery risk of business within the company,	Implement and maintain disclosure controls and procedures, and internal control over financial reporting,	Promotion of an organizational culture that encourages ethical conduct and a commitment to compliance with the law,
Conduct periodic training for all directors, officers, employees, agents and business partners,	Improve legal, accounting, financial and communication skills,	Reasonably design and implement a compliance program,
Document appropriate risk-based due diligence and compliance requirements and oversee all agents and business partners,	Periodically review and document compliance policies and procedures,	Periodically assess the risk of criminal conduct to reduce the risk thereof,
Include standard provisions in agreements, contracts, and renewals with all agents and business partners to prevent violations of the anti-corruption laws.	Oversee reporting deadlines.	Periodically report to high-level personnel on the effectiveness of the compliance program.

2204 *See generally* A., I., 1. to 3., pp. 183 et seq.

As the overview shows, the SOX and the FSGO added a new time element for the risk-assessment, the periodic review, audit and monitoring of the compliance program. The setting of time standards aims to require companies to evaluate periodically the effectiveness of their internal controls and their compliance programs.[2205] Hence, the compliance officers should improve their legal and financial skills, and develop a resubmission system in order to oversee reporting deadlines to regulators. Additionally, the FSGO added a new periodic reporting line for individuals with operational responsibility for the compliance program such as the compliance officer, to high-level personnel such as the CEO or the board, on the effectiveness of the compliance program.[2206] Additionally, the SEC and DOJ have extended the reporting obligations of companies and the need to document compliance responsibilities within companies. Therefore, the legislation, the guidelines and regulations increased the number of responsibilities for the corporate compliance function at the same time. This development also influenced the case law, particularly in the area of corporation law. The Delaware Courts developed a new duty of oversight or compliance duty for directors and corporate officers.[2207] In addition, if the courts consider the compliance officer to be an agent of the company, he has a duty to provide material information to the principal under the agency law. Agency law also supports the required reporting responsibilities for compliance officers to report the material information of compliance issues to the CEO or the board. The most important responsibility of the compliance officer should be one of oversight on behalf of the board of directors, but the overall responsibility remains with the board.[2208]

On account of these responsibilities and duties the corporate compliance officer can face supervisory liability or liability for breach of the duty of oversight. The SEC has applied the statutory supervisory liability against compliance officers in the financial services sector. However, to this day, the US courts have not held a corporate compliance officer liable for failing to oversee an effective compliance program or supervise subordinates for misconduct.[2209]

Due to the absence of statutory codification or definitions of the duties of the corporate compliance officer, which are conversely discussed, the relevant duties and responsibilities can derive from requirements, guidelines, agreements by prosecutors or from the definition of compliance. In a narrow sense, compliance can be understood as a form of internal control.[2210] Hence, the compliance function

---

2205 *Compare* Sarbanes-Oxley Act of 2002, *supra* note 47, § 302 (a)(4)(C), 15 USC 7241; US Sentencing Guidelines Manual USSC, *supra* note 49, § 8 B2.1 (b)(5)(B).

2206 US Sentencing Guidelines Manual USSC, *supra* note 49, § 8 B2.1 (b)(2)(C).

2207 *See supra* Table 9, p. 285.

2208 *See generally* A., pp. 171 et seq.

2209 *See generally* A., pp. 171 et seq.

2210 *See* Miller (2014), *supra* note 519 at 3.

is *"a form of internalized norm enforcement within companies."*[2211] Sometimes, this function is compared with that of a policymaker who has to devise the compliance system in the company.[2212] In this narrow, internal context, the key duties of the compliance officer include establishing, implementing, maintaining, overseeing, and monitoring the corporate compliance program, if the board has approved the program.[2213] Furthermore, this function includes a periodical reporting duty of compliance issues to the CEO or the board. In other words, this position includes the operational responsibilities for the compliance program. In addition, this function also comprises an external component. The compliance officer has to ensure that the board of directors, executive officers, employees, and agents of the company adhere to the law and rules of regulators.[2214] He has to uncover any illegal business practices or misconduct. For this reason, this function is dependent on connections with and insights into other business units.

Subject to the condition that the court considers that the compliance officer operates as a fiduciary as a key employee, he has to act in the best interests of the company. In this case, the compliance officer has a duty of care, a duty of loyalty and, since *Caremark,* a duty of oversight. The duty of oversight of the compliance officer comprises the management and assessment of all compliance risks. The compliance officer should directly provide all compliance responsibilities and issues to the CEO and the board within the company.[2215] If the court considers that the compliance officer is covered by agent theory, compliance officers also owe fiduciary duties. The agent owes a duty of care and has a duty to provide material information to the principal. Before reaching a decision, the court will examine the scope of the delegation by the board and the terms of agreements with the compliance officer.

A recent study by PWC[2216] measures the order of priority and the primary accountability of the compliance officers' function. First and foremost, the corporate compliance officer is responsible for the code of conduct (86 percent), then for the ethics and compliance program (84 percent), and thirdly for anti-bribery and anti-corruption issues under the FCPA (76 percent).[2217] These are followed by responsibilities for investigations, hotlines, compliance audits, policy process management, and lastly, responsibility for customs and trade compliance.[2218] To conclude, compliance officers' responsibilities and duties are as varied as their titles.[2219]

2211 *See* Miller (2014), *supra* note 595 at 137.
2212 *Id.* at 138.
2213 *Id.* at 128.
2214 *Id.* at 128.
2215 PWC Study 2015, *supra* note 1771 at 17.
2216 PWC Study 2015, *supra* note 1771.
2217 PWC Study 2015 *Id.* at 6.
2218 PWC Study 2015 *Id.* at 6.
2219 *See supra* Table 11, pp. 287–288.

The scope of duties and responsibilities of the compliance officer can vary significantly based on such factors as company size, sector, and specific risks. Another study by *Weber & Fortun* shows a wide range from ensuring compliance with internal standards and state and federal laws, conducting investigations, to carrying out trainings, managing, and performing audits.[2220] The compliance officer is often viewed as an educator with respect to policies and standards.[2221] Moreover, compliance officers and their teams write, revise, promote codes of business conduct, and monitor and discipline employees.[2222] Together with the general counsel, compliance departments support the investigation of wrongdoing by employees.[2223]

However, there are forerunners for establishing legal duties and responsibilities of compliance officers, for example in the financial services under Federal Law, its regulators like the SEC, and in the SEC cases against compliance officers.[2224] Additionally, the SOX established duties and responsibilities for CEOs and CFOs within publicly-traded companies. Furthermore, the FSGO set up standards for compliance officers' reporting duties. Nevertheless, the corporate compliance officer should be aware that the regulatory requirements relating to compliance officers in the financial services sector could provide a model for the private sector in future. In the same way, it is possible that the compliance officer could be required to annually report and certify the effectiveness of the compliance program to the regulators. In brief, it seems that one important legal duty of the compliance officer is to provide regular information about compliance issues within the given reporting line in the company.

In conclusion, the compliance officer should have a comprehensive overview of compliance obligations throughout the company. In addition, the compliance officer needs to know who carries following compliance responsibility within the company. An appropriate solution might be an agreement on the scope and details of responsibilities. Ultimately, it appears that the most important legal duties of this function are (1) to manage and to oversee all compliance issues within the company, and (2) to provide timely material information about compliance issues to the CEO or board of directors.

IV. The Liability of the Corporate Compliance Officer

As discussed previously, US Federal Law and State Corporation Law impose broad new duties on directors and officers.[2225] Today, directors and officers *inter alia* have

2220 *See also* Freeman (2007), *supra* note 57 at 360; Weber and Fortun (2005), *supra* note 4 at 107 Figure 3.
2221 *See* Fanto (2013), *supra* note 57 at 1.
2222 *See* Baer (2009), *supra* note 586 at 960.
2223 *Id.* at 961.
2224 *US SEC v. Pekin Singer* SEC, *supra* note 1644; *US SEC v. SFX* SEC, *supra* note 1644.
2225 *See supra* II., 1.-3., pp. 255 et seq.

a duty of oversight in relation to the company.[2226] Consequently, a personal liability based on inadequate management or failure to supervise and manage corporate affairs and subordinates could follow.[2227] In addition, the general agency principle states that an agent is subject to liability to a third party for all torts he commits, notwithstanding that the person acts as an agent or as an employee.[2228]

1. Statutory Supervisory Liability

The title of compliance officer alone does not establish liability on the part of this position.[2229] Under common law, *"officers are not personally liable for torts of a company or of any other agent due to their position."*[2230] The courts require additional facts and circumstances to make a judgment.[2231] Hence, the court examines and focuses on whether any duty of the officers has been breached.[2232] This means that corporate officers could be subject to statutory liability, but the plaintiffs would have to prove a breach of duty, citing material facts. For example, in 2010, *In re Dow Chemical Co. Derivative Litigation,*[2233] the plaintiffs alleged that directors and officers of Dow Chemical had failed to detect and prevent FCPA bribery.[2234] The court dismissed this claim because

> ....the plaintiffs have failed to allege facts suggesting that the Dow board "*utterly failed*" to supervise insiders, or that any director acted with anything other than good faith.[2235]

2226 *See supra* II., 1., p. 255.

2227 *See* Petrin (2010), *supra* note 1125 at 1662.

2228 *See e.g. Bowles v. Ruppel,* (3d Cir. 1946), 157 F.2d 944, 946 (1946) *"Nor is it an excuse from legal liability generally that one has acted, in what he did, as agent for another."*; Petrin (2010), *supra* note 1125 at 1666 note 17; Third Restatement, *supra* note 2112 § 7.01.

2229 *See e.g.* SEC Compliance FAQ SEC Division of Trading and Markets:, Frequently Asked Questions about Liability of Compliance and Legal Personnel at Broker-Dealers under Sections 15(b)(4) and 15(b)(6) of the Exchange Act (2013), http://www.sec.gov/divisions/marketreg/faq-cco-supervision-093013.htm (last visited May 6, 2016) Question 3.

2230 *See e.g. Bernstein v. Starrett City, Inc.,* (2d Dept. N.Y.2003), 303 A.D.2d 530, 532 (2003). "It is well settled that a corporate officer may not be held liable for the negligence of the corporation merely because of his or her official relationship to it." *See also Felder v R&K Realty,* 295 A.D.2d 560 (2002); *Clark v Pine Hill Homes,* 112 A.D.2d 755 (1985)."; Petrin (2010), *supra* note 1125 at 1667 note 22.

2231 *See* Petrin (2010), *supra* note 1125 at 1667.

2232 *Id.* at 1667.

2233 *In re Dow Chemical Company Derivative Litigation,* No. 4349-CC (Del. Ch. 2010), *supra* note 615.

2234 *Id.*

2235 *Id.*

The pleading standard is rigorous when a plaintiff alleges breaches of the ongoing duty to oversee compliance.[2236] In the view of the legal scholars, the Delaware standards for the directors' duty are very low.[2237] However, it has not yet been conclusively decided whether a director is individually liable for losses resulting from a failure to oversee and monitor the corporation's activities.[2238]

Furthermore, officers can be liable under US Federal Law, and statutes like the FCPA, and the SOX.[2239] Additionally, nowadays, the regulators are beginning to focus on individual accountability.[2240] As discussed above, this assumption is encouraged by several SEC cases against compliance officers. The SEC has enforced actions against compliance officers in the financial services sector.[2241] Two recent SEC cases have shown that a compliance officer could be potentially liable.[2242] In one case, the SEC held a compliance officer of an investment adviser liable for failure to implement compliance policies, failure to conduct an annual review, and responsible for a material misstatement in an SEC Form filing.[2243] This leaves compliance officers in a potentially vulnerable position. Although there is no specific case law relating to personal liability of a corporate compliance officer, there is an expectation that potential personal liability of this function is likely to increase.[2244]

However, *Traeger et al.* identified three potential indications of personal liability under Federal Securities Law:

> (1) a person violates the federal securities laws or rules, (2) this person is a subject to the supervision of another individual, and (3) the supervising individual does not reasonably fulfill his or her supervisory responsibilities.[2245]

Hence, supervisory obligations of a compliance officer could arise under federal securities laws. The Investment Advisers Act defines a *"supervised person"* as

> Any partner, officer, director (or other person occupying a similar status or performing similar functions), or employee of an investment adviser, or other person

---

2236 *See* McGreal (2011), *supra* note 495 at 136.

2237 *Id.* at 135.

2238 *See* Brown (2001), *supra* note 495 at 15.

2239 *See supra* A., I., pp. 171 et seq.

2240 *See supra* A., I., 1.d., p. 203; *See also* Keynote Ceresney and Division of Enforcement, *supra* note 1631; Remarks Yates and DOJ, *supra* note 1416.

2241 *See supra* A., I., 2.f., p. 230.

2242 *US SEC v Pekin Singer* SEC, *supra* note 1630; *US SEC v SFX* SEC, *supra* note 1632.

2243 *See e.g. US SEC v. SFX* SEC, *supra* note 1632; Investment Advisers Act of 1940, *supra* note 1642, § 203 (e)(f)(k); Securities Exchange Act of 1934, *supra* note 605, 17 CFR 275.206(4)-7 (2003).

2244 BNA Insights Marshall, *supra* note 1661; By surveying the US Supreme Court Cases and the Delaware Court Ceases between 1990 and 2016 there was no specific case, in which a corporate compliance officer was held personal liable.

2245 *See* Traeger, Guidroz, and Jimbo (2014), *supra* note 486 at 26.

> who provides investment advice on behalf of the investment adviser and is subject to the supervision and control of the investment adviser.[2246]

Specifically, In *re John H. Gutfreund, et al.*, the SEC examines, at which point a compliance professional becomes a *"supervisor."*[2247] The criteria of this analysis are acknowledged as the *"Gutfreund Standard."*[2248] Under Federal Securities Law, the SEC does not presume, for example, *"broker-dealer's compliance or legal personnel are supervisors solely of their compliance or legal functions."*[2249] The SEC determined that, under certain circumstances, persons who occupy positions in the compliance departments of broker-dealers are supervisors for the purposes of Sections 78o (b)(4)(E) and 78o (b)(6).[2250]In fact, the SEC argued that compliance personnel of broker-dealers who have *"a requisite degree of responsibility, ability, or authority to affect the conduct of the employee"* could become supervisors.[2251] Additionally, the SEC identified a number of criteria of supervisory authority, such as the power to hire, reward, or to punish others, and the power to prevent illegal behavior.[2252]

For instance, in the case In *re John H. Gutfreund, et al.*, the legal and compliance officer discovered that an employee had violated the securities laws and informed three senior executives.[2253] All of them failed to supervise *e.g.* to conduct an investigation, failed to discipline and failed to limit the activities of this employee.[2254] The SEC concluded, based on the circumstances of this case, the role and influence of the legal and compliance officer position, that such a person becomes a supervisor for the purposes of securities law.[2255] Hence, this person *"is obligated to take affirmative steps to ensure that appropriate action is taken to address the misconduct."*[2256] However, the findings of this case are applicable only to this proceeding and are not binding on any other persons.[2257]

2246 Investment Advisers Act of 1940, *supra* note 1642, 15 USC § 80b-2 (a)(25) (2010).

2247 In *re John H. Gutfreund, et al.* | Exchange Act Release No. 34-31554, 51 SEC 93 (1992); *See* in: Traeger, Guidroz, and Jimbo (2014), *supra* note 486 at 27.

2248 *See* Traeger, Guidroz, and Jimbo (2014), *supra* note 486 at 27.

2249 Division of Trading and Markets:, *supra* note 2190.

2250 *In re John H. Gutfreund, et al.* | Exchange Act Release No. 34-31554, supra note 2247 at [Fn25].

2251 In *re John H. Gutfreund, et al.* | Exchange Act Release No. 34-31554, *supra* note 2247 at [Fn24];

2252 Frequently Asked Questions FAQ Division of Trading and Markets:, *supra* note 2229 Question 2.

2253 In *re John H. Gutfreund, et al.* | Exchange Act Release No. 34-31554, *supra* note 2247 at [Fn2].

2254 *Id.* at [Fn19].

2255 *Id.* at [Fn25].

2256 *Id.* at [Fn25].

2257 *Id.* at [Fn2].

In conclusion, Federal Securities Law requires that firms registered as broker-dealers, investment advisers, or investment companies designate a chief compliance officer charged with overseeing compliance tasks. If the chief compliance officer has to supervise subordinates who committed illegal acts, he could be liable (1) due to failure to perform supervisory obligation, and (2) for failure to maintain an effective compliance program under Federal Securities Law. Hence, in the financial services sector, the compliance officer could have enforced duties as supervisor.

In a broader sense, the National Labor Relations Act (NLRA) defines a statutory definition of the term supervisor as follows:[2258]

> The term supervisor means any individual having authority, in the interest of the employer, to hire, transfer, suspend, lay off, recall, promote, discharge, assign, reward, or discipline other employees, or responsibly to direct them, or to adjust their grievances, or effectively to recommend such action, if in connection with the foregoing the exercise of such authority is not of a merely routine or clerical nature, but requires the use of independent judgment.[2259]

Despite this legal definition in the area of employment law, the Court of Appeals for the Sixth Circuit concluded in the case *Am. Fed. of Tele. & Radio v. Storer Broadcasting*:

> There are no bright lines controlling the determination of whether a particular position comes within the definition of supervisor under the NLRA.[2260]

Hence, the ambiguity of the application of the compliance officers' position will remain. In the context of holding a compliance officer in other industry liable for the actions of others, it is uncertain which definition - the financial service or employment law definition - of the term supervisor the courts will prefer and apply. In the event that a corporate compliance officer is recognized as a supervisor and subjected to liability, it could lead to undesirable inaction.

2. Liability for Breach of Duty of Oversight

A fundamental legal principle under common law is *"without duty, there is no liability."*[2261] The requirement of duty is *"fundamental to the whole concept of tort liability."*[2262] Courts could impose liability on corporate officers who negligently fail to oversee daily business transactions.[2263] Generally, the negligent supervision is

2258 National Labor Relations Act (NLRA), *supra* note 2025.
2259 *Id.* 29 USC § 152 (11).
2260 *Am. Fed. of Tele. & Radio v. Storer Broadcasting* 745 F.2d 392, 399 (6th Cir. 1984).
2261 *Troy Robillard v. Asahi Chem. Indus. Co.,* (Conn. Super. Ct. 1995), 44, 510, 524.
2262 *Id.* at 524.
2263 *See* Petrin (2010), *supra* note 1125 at 1676.

likely to consist in an omission rather than an action.[2264] Although there is no recent case concerning the liability of the corporate compliance officer, in *re World Health Alternatives Inc.*, the United States Bankruptcy Court held a corporate general attorney personally liable for corporate misconduct through failure of oversight.[2265] In 2008, the plaintiffs alleged that a corporate officer, specifically the general attorney, was responsible for failing to implement an internal monitoring system.[2266] According to Section 307 of the SOX, the general attorney must observe minimum standards of professional conduct.[2267] This standard requires "*an attorney to report evidence of a material violation of securities law or a breach of fiduciary duty.*"[2268] The plaintiffs asserted that the general attorney has a duty to be aware of corporate wrongdoings and to report such misconduct.[2269] The attorney was not actively engaged in the alleged wrongful activities, but he knew, or should have known, about the mismanagement.[2270] The Court confirmed that other courts have also recognized *"both officers and directors owe fiduciary duties to the corporation."*[2271] The court also expands the *Caremark* duty to include the general attorney and he was held personally liable in that case for corporate fraud and misconduct because he failed to implement an adequate monitoring system. This is also confirmed by a study by *Erickson*, which found that, in derivative litigation between 2005 and 2006, corporate officers like the CEO, CFO and COO are also named.[2272] Plaintiffs even named lower-ranking officers like general counsels.[2273]

Following these approaches, the courts have held corporate officers personally liable for *e.g.* corporate misconduct and wrongful activities by directors, other officers, and employees. The courts tend also to apply liability for failure of the duty of oversight to corporate officers. This could imply that the courts also intend to apply this duty to corporate compliance officer in the future. Nevertheless, the focus on the personal liability of compliance officers is increasing.

3. Increasing Personal Liability of the Corporate Compliance Officer

The US regulatory environment covering areas as varied as investors' protection, reporting and disclosures obligation, and foreign corrupt practices, establish increasing liability of corporate officers, sentencing, and settlement incentives

2264 *Id.* at 1676.
2265 *In re World Health Alternatives, Inc.*, 385 B.R. 576, 590 (B.R. Del. 2008).
2266 *Id.* at 590.
2267 *Id.* at 590.; SARBANES-OXLEY ACT OF 2002, *supra* note 47 § 307, 15 USC 7245.
2268 SARBANES-OXLEY ACT OF 2002, *supra* note 47 § 307 (1), 15 USC 7245.
2269 *In re World Health Alternatives Inc.*, (B.R. Del. 2008), *supra* note 2265 at 590.
2270 *Id.* at 593.
2271 *Id.* at 593.
2272 *See supra* A., II., 3.c., p. 270; Erickson (2010), *supra* note 1954 at 1772.
2273 *Id.* at 1772.

for the voluntary implementation of effective corporate compliance policies and procedures.[2274] A study by *Engebretson & Meier* shows that the executive officers expect that the certification requirements of the SOX will establish personal liability for the information that is reported.[2275] As previously discussed,[2276] under the FSGO, companies are required to have specific *"high-level personnel"* in the organization responsible for the compliance and ethics program.[2277] The *"day-to-day operational responsibility"* for the compliance program shall be delegated to specific individuals who shall report to periodically to *"high-level personnel."*[2278] Hence, the corporate compliance officer is charged with overseeing compliance tasks. The company's governing authority shall *"exercise reasonable oversight"* of *"the implementation and effectiveness of the compliance program."*[2279] Additionally, regulators are putting more pressure and liability on corporate officers. Furthermore, the courts have established personal liability for corporate directors and officers when they have failed to avoid corporate misconduct and non-compliance with the law through effective compliance policies and procedures.[2280]

Although the courts have confirmed that officers' duties are the same as directors', the consequences are not the same. A company can use a provision in its certificate of incorporation to exculpate its directors from personal liability for breach of fiduciary duty as a director under Delaware Law Section 102.[2281] In fact, there is no statutory provision governing comparable exculpation of corporate officers.[2282] What remains is the possibility of indemnification. The company can provide indemnification for directors and officers *e.g. "against all expense, liability, and loss including attorneys' fees, judgments, fines, taxes or penalties, and amounts paid in settlement"* in its bylaws.[2283]

However, how can a corporate compliance officer establish any form of self-protection? In practice, the compliance officer could potentially face personal liability if he *"directly participated in the misconduct, mislead or obstructed regulators, ignored*

2274 *See* Parker (2000), *supra* note 441 at 339.
2275 *See* Engebretson and Meier (2011), *supra* note 1557 at 187–188.
2276 *See supra* A., I., 3., pp. 236 et seq.
2277 *See supra* A., I., 3., pp. 236 et seq.; US SENTENCING GUIDELINES MANUAL *supra* note 49 § 8 B 2.1(b)(2)(B).
2278 *See supra* A., I., 3., pp. 236 et seq.; US SENTENCING GUIDELINES MANUAL *Id.*§ 8 B 2.1(b)(2)(C).
2279 *See supra* A., I., 3., pp. 236 et seq.; US SENTENCING GUIDELINES MANUAL *Id.*§ 8 B 2.1(b)(2)(A).
2280 *See supra* B., IV., 2., p. 307.
2281 tit. 8 DELAWARE CODE, *supra* note 24, § 102 (b)(7).
2282 *Gantler v. Stephens*, 965 A.2d 695 (Del. 2009), *supra* note 23 at 37.
2283 *See e.g.* BYLAWS OF THE BOEING COMPANY, (2015) SEC. 3.1; BYLAWS OF THE OFFICE DEPOT, INC., Art. VII, Sec. 1.

their compliance responsibilities, or wore multiple hats."[2284] The SEC will focus on the compliance officers' responsibilities and how the compliance officer handles misconduct when it occurs within the company.[2285] Thus, the scope of liability that compliance officers face is broad. As such, the compliance officer should take the following measures recommended by the SEC:

(1) Document every decision, which was made after an occurrence of misconduct,
(2) Document every decision during an investigation by prosecutors,
(3) Document every disciplinary measure *e.g.* terminate agents for criminal misconduct, and illegal activities,
(4) Be active not inactive in the event of misconduct.[2286]

Overall, the SEC in its cases[2287] against and statements[2288] does not establish any clear standard of liability for corporate compliance officers.[2289] In light of this uncertainty, *Marshall* proposed that the corporate compliance officers should take reasonable measures to protect themselves:

(1) Identify compliance risks in all business units and develop and document clear compliance responsibilities,
(2) Identify and document the line of supervisory within the company,
(3) Identify and review periodically the compliance policy and procedure,
(4) Identify problematic activities, take measures and escalate compliance issues immediately to the senior management,
(5) Identify possibilities to avoid a multifunctional role and try to get a standalone compliance function,
(6) Identify standards by prosecutors and follow them,
(7) Identify possibilities to obtain adequate indemnification.[2290]

In response to the increasingly complex legal environment and regulatory requirements, companies now pay greater attention to and provide larger budgets for executive oversight of compliance issues.[2291] This ought to allow compliance departments and compliance personnel to maintain and review compliance

2284 Keynote Ceresney and Division of Enforcement, *supra* note 1631; Jaclyn Jaeger, *The Real State of CCO Legal Liability*, 2015 Compliance Week 28–30, 29 (2015).
2285 *See* Jaeger (2015), *supra* note 2284 at 29.
2286 *Id.* at 29.
2287 *US SEC v Pekin Singer* SEC, *supra* note 1634; *US SEC v SFX* SEC, *supra* note 1632.
2288 Keynote Ceresney and Division of Enforcement, *supra* note 1631.
2289 BNA Insights Marshall, *supra* note 1661.
2290 BNA Insights *Id.*
2291 PWC Study 2012 Kelly, *supra* note 7 at 9 "In the 2011 State of Compliance survey, nearly one-third of respondents had budgets of less than $1 million last year. In 2012, that group dropped to 20 percent."

policies and procedures more effectively and enable compliance officers to address compliance risks more efficiently and thereby prevent potential liability.

V. The Evolving Model of the US Corporate Compliance Officer

As a middle line, on the one hand, between the business units and the oversight and control compliance department, and on the other hand, between the company and the regulators, the corporate compliance officers face a difficult and complex job. An additional aggravating factor is that the appointment of a corporate compliance officer is not required by statute, but the estimated appointment through recommendations and the FSGO. Hence, in practice, the corporate compliance officer often holds various titles and has to fulfil a multifunctional or dual-hatted role within smaller companies in particular. It is a frequent business practice in smaller companies for an officer to serve as the CEO, CFO, vice-president, and secretary while simultaneously having compliance responsibilities.[2292] An officer holding multiple positions can have supervisory duties with respect to his supervisory responsibility for subordinate employees.[2293] The same duties can arise from the dual-hatted role of the general counsel who wears a legal and a compliance hat when he has to carry out supervisory tasks in a reasonable manner, preventing violations of corruption and of other areas of law and rules. However, the SEC does not view compliance and legal personnel as supervisors of business line personnel solely for purposes of securities law because they occupy compliance or legal positions.[2294] Combining the two functions of general counsel and compliance officer is unlikely to be expedient. The general counsels owe their professional and legal duties to the best interest of the company. They have to act loyally to their clients.[2295] In contrast, the compliance officer could be subject to a broader public interest such as the regulators.[2296] Therefore, it is difficult for the dual-hatted role of the compliance officer to be aware of all potential conflicts and to be effective in managing them.

Over the years, the role of the compliance officer has changed from a mere administrating, policing role to an active advising, training, overseeing, and communicating role. Each of the business units must be responsible for compliance with both external and internal rules, policies, and laws affecting their

2292 *See supra* Table 11, pp. 287–288.

2293 *See supra* B., II., p. 295; Traeger, Guidroz, and Jimbo (2014), *supra* note 486 at 26–27; *In re John H. Gutfreund, et al.* | Exchange Act Release No. 34-31554, *supra* note 2247 at [24].

2294 *See supra* B., II., p. 295; Frequently Asked Questions FAQ Division of Trading and Markets:, *supra* note 2229 Question 3; *In re John H. Gutfreund, et al.* | Exchange Act Release No. 34-31554, *supra* note 2247.

2295 *See* Miller (2014), *supra* note 519 at 8.

2296 *Id.* at 8.

function. Therefore, the compliance department should play a larger role as a business support function. Additionally, the compliance officer should provide guidance, direction, and reports to the board or the CEO on related matters. It is important for the compliance officer to have an excellent and thorough understanding of all processes, products, and supervisory lines within the company. As we have seen, in particular, the SOX and the FSGO as well as the regulators rule making activities and N/DPAs require and incentivize companies to assign a standalone function, the compliance officer, with clearly defined reporting lines and direct access to the board.[2297] Over the course of the last twenty years, the enhanced regulatory framework and landmark cases pertaining to compliance have developed a new duty of oversight for directors and officers. For this reason, US corporations face widening compliance responsibilities. That is why the board has to ensure compliance and thus, corporate officers are assigned with compliance tasks.

The perspective of compliance officers shows an ambivalent picture. The majority of authors and regulators assume that the compliance officers' role will evolve into an independent standalone function.[2298] Today, compliance is a control function rendered through various monitoring and reviewing procedures and activities.[2299] As the role of compliance evolves to reflect the enforced legal environment, many companies have assumed the compliance functions to provide greater responsibility and accountability.[2300] Hence, new regulations have assigned more accountability and involved the compliance function in new areas of responsibility for risk assessments, oversight, monitoring, internal investigations, regulatory examinations and investigations, education and training.[2301] However, practice shows that the majority of companies in the small sample did not name a standalone chief compliance officer in their bylaws.[2302]

Figure 12 shows a model of the compliance officer and the classification of the CCO and CO within a typical US corporate structure. The connections between the first and second corporate group are depicted by reporting lines (green) and possible lines of delegation lines (blue).

2297 *See supra* A., I., 3. p. 236; Transocean DPA DOJ, *supra* note 1352; US Sentencing Guidelines Manual USSC, *supra* note 49.

2298 *See e.g.* Dando et al. (2013), *supra* note 4 at 10; DeStefano (2013), *supra* note 14 at 74; Greenberg, *supra* note 710 at 21; Greenberg (2009), *supra* note 11 at 1; Majewski (2006), *supra* note 18 at 23; Tabuena and Smith (2006), *supra* note 2178 at 14.

2299 The Evolving Role of Compliance SIFMA, *supra* note 692 at 4.

2300 The Evolving Role of Compliance *Id.* at 18.

2301 The evolving Role of Compliance *Id.* at 4.

2302 *See supra* Table 11, pp. 287–288.

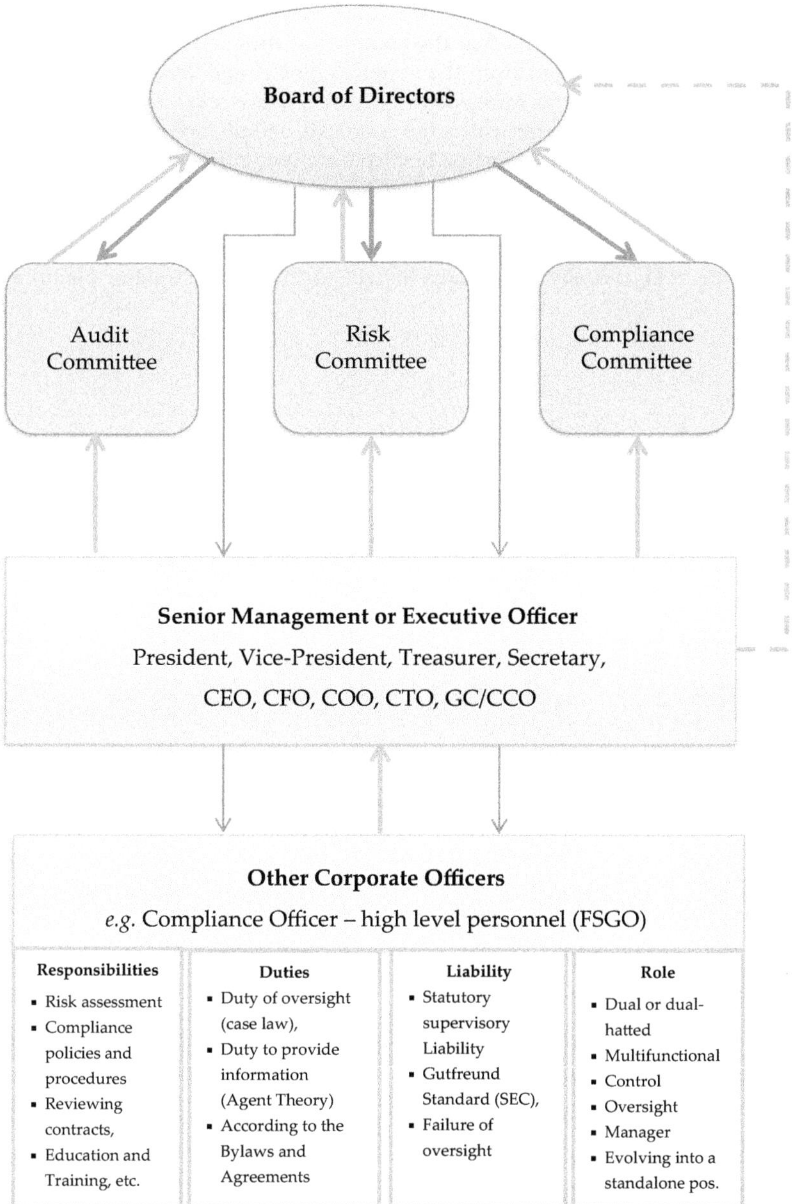

Figure 12 *The Model of the US Corporate Compliance Officer*

The findings of the examined studies and surveys of compliance officers in US corporations show a trend that the compliance function will become a stand-alone position, independent from the general counsel and legal department with appropriate resources and authority.[2303] However, it seems that without legal requirements for the appointment of the corporate compliance function, such as in securities laws in the federal law or in corporate law, compliance responsibilities will remain in a number of various executives' hands. Nevertheless, the development of this function will continue to change into a business partner in every business unit. The corporate compliance officer will understand the business risks and operate as an risk advisor. Finally, he will participate in strategic planning.

2303 *See supra* B., I., pp. 292 et seq.

The UK Legal Framework of Compliance

Abstract

This chapter now provides a general overview of the nature of the UK legislative framework for the function of the compliance officer, of the various self-regulatory organizations (SROs) and the common law governing UK companies. The common law applicable to companies comprises the rules of the courts and judgments related to companies, compliance, and the compliance officer. This chapter will examine the duties, responsibilities, and liability of corporate directors and company secretaries relating to compliance tasks. For this purpose, an examination, analysis, and comparison of the legal framework of compliance in the areas of company, bribery, criminal law, and employment law follows, as well as a research for landmark cases with respect to compliance and compliance officers, additional guidelines and principles to outline the role and position of the compliance officer under common law in the UK. The findings of this examination will be used to establish an UK role model of the corporate compliance officer under common law.

A. The Importance of the Legal Framework for UK Compliance

As discussed previously, the UK Legal Framework has evolved over several centuries. While the main source of law in the UK is case law, there is also a legislative framework in place with respect to compliance.[2304] Therefore, the legal framework comprises two main sources of law: the common law, created by judges and statutes, created by Parliament.[2305] Unlike the US and Germany, the United Kingdom does not have a written constitution, but an unwritten unitary constitution.[2306] The cornerstones of the constitution are the rule of law and the principle of parliamentary sovereignty.[2307] Parliament in the UK has three functions: (1) to legislate, (2) to deal with public finance, and (3) to provide a forum.[2308] A further principle

---

2304 The examination in this book of the legal framework with respect to compliance and the compliance officer focuses on the law as it applies in England, Wales and Northern Ireland. The terms English law and UK law are used synonymously.

2305 *See* Gary Slapper *&* David Kelly, *supra* note 387; *See also supra* Ch. 1, p. 57.

2306 Commission of the European Communities, Communication from the Commission to the Council, the European Parliament, the Economic and Social Committee and the Committee of the Regions on certain Community measures to combat discrimination 3 (1999).

2307 *See* Slapper and Kelly (2017), *supra* note 387 at 49, 190. *"The rule of law requires that all people and organisations are subject to law."*

2308 *See* Wilson et al.(2014), *supra* note 303 at 35.

of the constitutional doctrines is the separation of powers between the executive, legislative and judicial.[2309] This separation supports the guarantee of continued independence of the judiciary.[2310] In England, the law is divided into private and public law. One form of private law is the civil law, while criminal law is a form of public law.[2311] The structure of the English Courts reflects this distinction.[2312] Today, the UK has an organized system of appeals in criminal cases in law reports.[2313] Nevertheless, as in the US, the legislation plays an important role in maintaining social order.

Besides the legal system, both the UK and the US have highly developed stock markets and, thus, strictly regulated securities markets. Since the enactment of the Financial Services Act 1986, all investment businesses have been subject to authorization.[2314] Likewise, similar to the US, there is a huge regulatory environment in the UK financial service sector for organizations. Traditionally, regulators are also involved in the financial service sector in the UK.[2315] Under the Financial Services Act 1986 and later the Financial Services and Markets Act (FSMA) 2000, a number of self-regulating organizations (SROs)[2316] such as the Investment Management Regulatory Organization Ltd (IMRO) or the Life Assurance and Unit Trust Regulatory Organization (LAUTRO) were established as regulators for specific sectors in the financial services industry.[2317] They provide governance standards and rules to promote the interests of shareholders and other stakeholders.[2318] Financial regulators, such as the Financial Conduct Authority (FCA)[2319] and its predecessor, the Financial Services Authority (FSA), have established a principles-based regulation.[2320] The FCA is empowered to issue delegated legislation.[2321] Its

---

2309 *See* Slapper and Kelly (2017), *supra* note 387 at 42, 76.

2310 *Id.* at 76; Constitutional Reform Act 2005, *supra* note 284 § 3(1).

2311 *Id.* at 7–8.

2312 *Id.* at 10.

2313 *Id.* at 137 et seq.

2314 *See* Ashall (1992), *supra* note 749 at 47.

2315 *See* Alexander Kern, *UK Corporate Governance and Banking Regulation: The Regulator's Role as Stakeholder*, 33 Stetson L. Rev. 991, 993 (2003).

2316 SRO's such as the Serious Fraud Office SFO and Financial Conduct Authority FCA. *See infra* III., 2., p. 360; IV., 3., a, b, p. 377.

2317 *See e.g.* Ashall (1992), *supra* note 749 at 48; Linsley (1993), *supra* note 750 at 364.

2318 *See* Kern (2003), *supra* note 2315 at 993.

2319 "*The FCA is the regulator for 56,000 financial services firms and 125,000 approved persons and financial markets in the UK. It was established on April 1, 2013, taking over responsibility for conduct and relevant prudential regulation from the Financial Services Authority.*" *See* FCA, FCA UK | Our role (2016), https://business-plan-2016-17.the-fca.org.uk/1-our-role (last visited Jun 10, 2016).

2320 *See* I.H.Y. Chiu, Regulating (From) the Inside: The Legal Framework for Internal Control in Banks and Financial Institutions (2015).

2321 *See* D. French, S.W. Mayson & C. Ryan, Mayson, French & Ryan on Company Law 12 (32 ed. 2015).

general functions are rule making, preparing and issuing codes, and the provision of general guidance.[2322] The FCA will also take enhanced actions against firms and individuals that fail to act in compliance with the rules.[2323] However, unlike the SEC, the FCA does not often pursue actions.[2324]

Although the UK has a similar financial system to the US federal securities law, its company law differs significantly.[2325] The centralized UK legal system has one set of laws relating to corporate governance; the US has a decentralized State Corporation Law for each US State.[2326] Similar to the situation in the US, the UK legal framework for companies has increased in volume over the past 30 years. The legislation includes the Companies Directors' Disqualification Act 1986,[2327] the Insolvency Act 1986,[2328] the Financial Services and Markets Act 2000[2329], the Enterprise and Regulatory Reform Act 2013[2330], and the amended Companies Act.[2331] For example, the amended UK Companies Act 2006 has expanded the fiduciary duties of directors.[2332] The Companies Act was accompanied by a comprehensive review of the Company Law Review Steering Group.[2333] Chapter 4 of the Companies Act 2014 sets out the statutory role and advisory responsibilities of the Review Group.[2334] The Group aims to modernize the law to bring it *"into line with today's business needs."*[2335] Furthermore, on March 26, 2015, Parliament enacted the Small Business, Enterprise, and Employment Act 2015 with the aim of improving access to finance for businesses and individuals.[2336] In addition, in the UK there is a set of non-binding self-regulatory

---

2322 Financial Services and Markets Act (2000), *supra* note 785 § 1 (4)(a)(b)(c).

2323 (FCA) The Financial Conduct Authority, Annual Report and Accounts 2014/15 - Financial Conduct Authority 15 (2015), https://www.fca.org.uk/your-fca/documents/corporate/annual-report-14-15 (last visited Jun 20, 2016).

2324 FCA Annual Report 2014/15 *Id.* at 64. Figure 26.

2325 *See* Tylecote and Ramirez (2006), *supra* note 799 at 167.

2326 *Id.* at 167.

2327 Company Directors' Disqualification Act 1986, *supra* note 771.

2328 Insolvency Act 1986, *supra* note 772.

2329 Financial Services and Markets Act (2000), *supra* note 785.

2330 Enterprise and Regulatory Reform Act 2013, c.24 (2013).

2331 Companies Act 2006, *supra* note 532.

2332 Great Britain et al., Any of our business? Human rights and the UK private sector: First report of session 2009–10. Vol. 2, Vol. 2, 155 (2009).

2333 The Company Law Review was established by the Department of Trade and Industry (DTI) in March 1998 in order to modernize the company law and to make recommendations for an effective framework for carrying out business. *See* French, Mayson, and Ryan (2015), *supra* note 2321 at 12. *See also* Statutory Role - Company Law Review Group, http://www.clrg.org/About-Us/Statutory-Role/ (last visited Jun 9, 2016).

2334 Statutory Role - Company Law Review Group (CLRG), *supra* note 2363.

2335 Corporate Law and Governance Directorate & Department of Trade and Industry, Company Law Reform 3 (2005).

2336 Small Business, Enterprise and Employment Act 2015, c. 26 (2015).

standards such as the UK Listing Rules,[2337] the Turnbull Guidance,[2338] or the City Code on Takeovers and Mergers.[2339] Moreover, the UK Corporate Governance Code sets out principles, standards of good practice and reporting duties for governing corporations.[2340] All listed companies in the UK are required under the Listing Rules to report in their annual report and accounts on how they have applied the Code.[2341]

Furthermore, since it joined the European Union (EU) January 1, 1973, the UK has also been subject to EU law.[2342] On June 23, 2016, however, a referendum was held in the UK on whether to remain part of the European Union, which resulted in a vote to leave.[2343] Withdrawal negotiations pursuant to Article 50 of the Treaty on the Functioning of the European Union are underway.[2344] The UK must conclude an agreement setting out the arrangements for its withdrawal and the framework for its future relationship with the EU in accordance with Article 218.[2345] The legal consequences of withdrawal from the EU, are as follows: EU law will continue to have an effect on UK law, since many aspects of EU law bind UK companies doing business in the EU, including competition rules regarding mergers.[2346] The EU laws that were transposed into UK law will remain in force until they are repealed by an act of Parliament.[2347] Thus, the final settlement could result in continued application of EU law in the UK or lead to primary and secondary EU law ceasing to apply.[2348]

During its period of membership of the EU, European law was a source of English law and affected many aspects of business activity in the private and financial service

---

2337 The Listing Rules of the UKLA (the UK Listing Authority) can be found in the FCA Handbook. *See in:* LSE, Rules and regulations | London Stock Exchange | Admission and Disclosure Standards 5 (2016).

2338 Financial Reporting Council FRC, Revised Turnbull Guidance 2005 | Revised Guidance for Directors on the Combined Code (2005).

2339 *See* Saleem Sheikh, A guide to the Companies Act 2006 371 (3. ed. 2008).

2340 UK Corporate Governance Code (2014) Cadbury Committee, *supra* note 442.

2341 Financial Conduct Authority FCA, LR 9.8 Annual financial report | FCA Handbook (2014), https://www.handbook.fca.org.uk/handbook/LR/9/8.html (last visited Jun 10, 2016).

2342 *See* Slapper and Kelly (2017), *supra* note 387 at 190.

2343 Jessica Elgot, *Brexit, the fallout and the UK's future: what we know so far*, The Guardian, June 24, 2016, http://www.theguardian.com/politics/2016/jun/24/brexit-fallout-what-we-know-so-far (last visited Jun 25, 2016).

2344 Consolidated versions of the Treaty on European Union and the Treaty on the Functioning of the European Union, C326/01-C326/407 (2012) Art. 50 (2).

2345 *Id.* Art. 218.

2346 The Law Society, The EU and the Legal Sector 5 (2015), www.lawsociety.org.uk.

2347 *Id.* at 26.

2348 Peter Bußjäger & Österreichische Gesellschaft für Europapolitik, Brexit, was wäre wenn... Szenarien rund um das EU-Austrittsreferendum im Vereinigten Königreich 4 (2015), http://www.oegfe.at/cms/uploads/media/OEGfE_Policy_Brief-2015.26.pdf (last visited Jun 25, 2016).

sector. However, the response in Europe to the high-profile corporate scandals was much more lax than that in the US.[2349] In order to establish a common market for goods and services, the EU aims to ensure the harmonization of company law across the EU Member States.[2350] This harmonization is facilitated by Directives on company law, which are usually implemented by an act of Parliament in the UK.[2351]

Moreover, since 2000, the EU has instigated a series of reforms of corporate governance.[2352] In 2003, the EU developed an Action Plan to meet the following two objectives: (1) strengthening shareholders' rights and third party protection, and (2) fostering efficiency and competitiveness of business.[2353] This Plan comprises the requirement that listed EU companies *e.g.* enhance corporate governance disclosure in their annual report and accounts.[2354] However, a 2002 comparative study of corporate governance codes carried out on behalf of the European Commission found that only two EU member states - Belgium and the United Kingdom - had merged or consolidated codes for disclosure purposes at that time.[2355] This led to the adoption in 2006 of a new Article 46a of Directive 78/660/EEC, which requires companies on the stock exchanges to include a corporate governance statement in their annual report.[2356] Further, if a company decides not to apply any provisions of a corporate governance code, it must state its reasons for not doing so.[2357] This approach is the opposite of the mandatory approach of the US SOX.[2358]

2349 *See* MASSIMO BELCREDI & GUIDO FERRARINI, THE EUROPEAN CORPORATE GOVERNANCE FRAMEWORK: ISSUES AND PERSPECTIVES 5 (2013).

2350 TREATY ON THE FUNCTIONING OF THE EUROPEAN UNION (TFEU), Art. 50 (2) (g); *See* FRENCH, MAYSON, AND RYAN (2015), *supra* note 2321 at 21.

2351 *See* FRENCH, MAYSON, AND RYAN (2015), *supra* note 2321 at 21.

2352 *See* BELCREDI AND FERRARINI (2013), *supra* note 2349 at 5; Corporate Governance, *supra* note 1463.

2353 Commission of the European Communities, MODERNISING COMPANY LAW AND ENHANCING CORPORATE GOVERNANCE IN THE EUROPEAN UNION - A PLAN TO MOVE FORWARD C5-0378-03 COM (2003) 284 FINAL 8–9 (2003).

2354 *Id.* at 12.

2355 The Combined Code CADBURY COMMITTEE, *supra* note 442; (WG&M) WEIL, GOTSHAL & MANGES LLP, COMPARATIVE STUDY OF CORPORATE GOVERNANCE CODES RELEVANT TO THE EUROPEAN UNION AND ITS MEMBER STATES 26 (2002).

2356 DIRECTIVE 2006/46/EC OF THE EUROPEAN PARLIAMENT AND OF THE COUNCIL OF 14 JUNE 2006 AMENDING COUNCIL DIRECTIVES 78/660/EEC ON THE ANNUAL ACCOUNTS OF CERTAIN TYPES OF COMPANIES, 83/349/EEC ON CONSOLIDATED ACCOUNTS, 86/635/EEC ON THE ANNUAL ACCOUNTS AND CONSOLIDATED ACCOUNTS OF BANKS AND OTHER FINANCIAL INSTITUTIONS AND 91/674/EEC ON THE ANNUAL ACCOUNTS AND CONSOLIDATED ACCOUNTS OF INSURANCE UNDERTAKINGS, OJ L 224 (2006) Art. 1 § 7 (1).

2357 *Id.* Art. 1 § 7 (1)(b).

2358 *See infra* B., III., pp. 407 et seq., Comparison between the US SOX and the UK Code.

In the UK, the financial services sector is one of the most important sectors for the economy.[2359] The City of London, specifically the Square Mile or City of London Corporation, is the greatest financial center in the world and the ninth largest economy in the EU.[2360] It generates a trade surplus greater than all other exporting industries combined.[2361] Just like the private sector, the financial services sector has been affected by European Law. A research paper by the House of Commons Library found that from 1980 to 2009, 186 UK Acts, - 14.3 percent - included the incorporation of one or more EU obligations.[2362] For instance, through the implementation of EU Directives, the requirement for banks that carry out investment business to establish a compliance function was introduced.[2363] The FSA extended these requirements to all regulated organizations such as banks and credit institutions. Under EU reforms, the concept of *"financial stability"* comprises internal control by the financial services sector.[2364] Internal control is defined as including *e.g.* a compliance function.[2365] In order to fulfill this requirement, the senior management must appoint executives to review the expanding legislation in order to understand the implications thereof for the company's business.[2366] Finally, the impact of European social and employment law in the UK is also extremely important and highly complex.[2367]

In conclusion, the UK legal framework with respect to compliance plays an equally important role as its US counterpart, specifically for organizations in the financial services sector. However, in contrast to the US, company law in the UK developed in a centralized way with a highly-developed corporate governance

2359 The Law Society, *supra* note 2346 at 14.

2360 *Id.* at 14.

2361 *Id.* at 14.

2362 House of Commons Library, How much legislation comes from Europe? 19 (2010). The research based on data from the UK Statute Law database.

2363 Directive 2004/39/EC of the European Parliament and of the Council on markets in financial instruments amending Council Directives 85/611/EEC and 93/6/EEC and Directive 2000/12/EC (MIFID 2004), *supra* note 432 Art. 6 (3) (b).

2364 *See* Chiu (2015), *supra* note 2320.

2365 *Id.* at 59.

2366 *See* Taylor (2005), *supra* note 13 at 54.

2367 The Law Society, *supra* note 2346 at 49; *See e.g.* Council Directive 89/654/EEC of 30 November 1989 concerning the minimum safety and health requirements for the workplace (first individual directive within the meaning of Article 16 (1) of Directive 89/391/EEC), L393/1-393/12 (1989); Directive 2002/14/EC of the European Parliament and of the Council of 11 March 2002 establishing a general framework for informing and consulting employees in the European Community - Joint declaration of the European Parliament, the Council and the Commission on employee representation, L080/29-080/34 (2002).

regime encompassing various standards and rules for listed companies. In addition, for the last forty years European Law has influenced all areas of UK laws.

I. The Development of Company Law in the UK

This section provides an overview of the development of company law in the UK in order to understand and define firstly the liability of company members, secondly, the enhancement of the protection of shareholders, creditors, and investors; and thirdly, the requirements on companies or their directors and then the duties and responsibilities of companies directors and officers relating to compliance. It goes on to analyze the main provisions of the recently amended UK Companies Act 2006 with regard to the duties of directors and officers applicable to compliance. To help explain and understand the importance of English Company Law, it should be borne in mind that English Company Law was the first codification of the law on corporations in the world.[2368] Originally, this Act was created for large companies with a great number of investors.[2369] Nowadays, the majority of companies have five or fewer shareholders.[2370]

1. The Roots of Legislation in UK Company Law

Initially, UK Company Law was fragmented and included case law, principles of contract law, self-regulation rules, best practices, and a number of legislative acts.[2371] The Bubble Act of 1720[2372] allowed the issue of transferable shares and the limitation of liability only with a royal or parliamentary charter.[2373] Since then, a variety of companies in a number of business sectors such as banking, insurance, textiles, paper and metal manufacturing have been established as joint-stock companies.[2374] While a number of legal historians view the Bubble Act as the promotion of joint- stock companies as a legitimate form of business corporation, only a few consider the Act itself.[2375] The first provisions stipulated the incorporation of two marine insurance companies.[2376] The eighteenth provision of the Act regulated the transferring of shares without legal authority by Parliament or by any charter

2368 *See* Sheikh (2008), *supra* note 2339 at 2.
2369 *Id.* at 2.
2370 *Id.* at 2.
2371 *Id.* at 1.
2372 The Bubble Act of 1720, 6 Geo, I. c. 18 (1720).
2373 *See* Mark Freeman, Robin Pearson *&* James Taylor, The Politics of Business: Joint Stock Company Constitutions in Britain, 1720-1844 1; Gower (1953), *supra* note 755 at 535.
2374 *See* Freeman, Pearson, and Taylor, *supra* note 2373 at 1.
2375 *See* Ron Harris, Industrializing English law: entrepreneurship and business organization, 1720–1844 60 (2000).
2376 *Id.* at 67.

from the Crown.[2377] These actions were illegal and void. The next three provisions set forth penalties and remedies.[2378] Scholars consider this to be the first attempt to legislate for companies although there were also a number of other statutes, though these were less widely-known statutes.[2379] The formal process of incorporation was slow and cumbersome and as a result many partnerships and unincorporated associations with a large number of members[2380] used the unincorporated deed of settlement companies to do business.[2381] One of the greatest risks of this approach was that the members were personally liable for the obligations of the association without any limitation of liability.[2382]

2. The Joint Companies Act of 1844 and 1856

On account of the bureaucratic incorporation procedure and the increase in the number of companies, there was a rise in fraudulent activities at the beginning of the nineteenth century.[2383] In response, the legislature attempted to develop new methods to improve members' legal liability.[2384] These attempts affected the Joint Stock Companies Act of 1844.[2385] This Act was founded on the principle of publicity.[2386] Under the Act, unincorporated associations could be incorporated by registering their constitution by means of a deed of settlement at Companies House.[2387] Thus, the first legislation governing the incorporation of companies came into effect in 1844. As a result, legislation is the primary source of UK company law.[2388] According to the Act, the members of the incorporated company could held be personally liable for debts of the company.[2389]

2377 *Id.* at 67.
2378 *Id.* at 67.
2379 *See* R. H. Watzlaff, *The Bubble Act of 1720*, 7 ABACUS 8–28, 8 (1971).
2380 *"A registered company is been seen as an association of persons (natural or legal) who are called the members' of a company. The membership of a company is based on holding company's shares. That's why the terms member and shareholders are synonymous." See* in FRENCH, MAYSON, AND RYAN (2015), *supra* note 2321 at 6; *See* also COMPANIES ACT 2006, *supra* note 532, §§ 8(1)(b), 16(2).
2381 *See* Gower (1953), *supra* note 755 at 535; SHEIKH (2008), *supra* note 2339 at 11.
2382 *See* Gower (1953), *supra* note 755 at 536.
2383 *Id.* at 536.
2384 *Id.* at 536. "*The members of an English company are the shareholder and directors*".
2385 JOINT STOCK COMPANIES ACT 1844, *supra* note 735; SHEIKH (2008), *supra* note 2339 at 3.
2386 *See* Gower (1953), *supra* note 755 at 537.
2387 Companies House - GOV.UK, https://www.gov.uk/government/organisations/companies-house (last visited Jun 27, 2016); *See also* Gower (1953), *supra* note 755 at 536; SHEIKH (2008), *supra* note 2339 at 11.
2388 *See* FRENCH, MAYSON, AND RYAN (2015), *supra* note 2321 at 11.
2389 *Id.* at 54.; Gower (1953), *supra* note 755 at 536.

Since then, there has been an ongoing debate on how company law ought best to regulate and establish limited liability.[2390] Company members' liability was first limited with the introduction by Parliament of the Limited Liability Act of 1855.[2391] The limitation of liability must always be indicated with the abbreviation Ltd. as the last word of the company's name.[2392] This means that liability is assumed by the registered company, not its members.[2393] However, after a few months, the 1844 Act and the 1855 Act were repealed and consolidated into the Joint Stock Companies Act of 1856.[2394] Thereafter, two main kinds of companies have been established in England: the incorporated, registered company with a minimum of seven members with limited liability and the unincorporated partnership with unlimited members' liability.[2395] The Act of 1856 thus excluded the one-man business or the small family partnership.[2396] Under the common law, limited partnerships had no root in England until the end of the 20th century.[2397] In contrast, in civil law countries such as Italy, the introduction of limited partnerships derived from the French *commandite* or *commenda* began in the early 19th century.[2398]

The issue of limited liability of members of small registered companies was the subject of a court decision in 1897 when the House of Lords[2399] overruled a decision by the Court of Appeal ([1895] 2 Ch. 323) in a landmark case in UK company law *Salomon v. Salomon*.[2400] The House of Lords held that it was not contrary to the

2390 *See* SHEIKH (2008), *supra* note 2339 at 12.

2391 LIMITED LIABILITY ACT 1855, *supra* note 736; *See also* FRENCH, MAYSON, AND RYAN (2015), *supra* note 2321 at 54; Gower (1953), *supra* note 755 at 536.

2392 *"Ltd. is short for limited, or a limited company. This structure is used mostly in European countries and Canada."* Gower (1953), *supra* note 755 at 537; The Difference Between Inc. & Ltd. & Co., http://smallbusiness.chron.com/difference-between-inc-ltd-co-38627.html (last visited Jul 2, 2016).

2393 *See* FRENCH, MAYSON, AND RYAN (2015), *supra* note 2321 at 55.

2394 JOINT STOCK COMPANIES ACT 1856, 19 & 20 Vict. c. 47 (1856); Gower (1953), *supra* note 755 at 536.

2395 *See* Gower (1953), *supra* note 755 at 537.

2396 *Id.* at 537.

2397 *Id.* at 537; Charles R. Hickson & John D. Turner, PARTNERSHIPS 6 (2005).

2398 *See* Hickson and Turner (2005), *supra* note 2397 at 6.

2399 *"The House of Lords is the upper chamber of Great Britain's bicameral legislature. Originated in the 11th century, when the Anglo-Saxon kings consulted counsels composed of religious leaders and the monarch's ministers, it emerged as a distinct element of Parliament in the 13th and 14th centuries. One element the Law Lords, consisting of the judges of the Supreme Court of Judicature (the Court of Appeal and the High Court of Justice), acted as Britain's final court of appeal (except for Scottish criminal cases) until 2009, when the Law Lords were abolished and the Supreme Court of the United Kingdom came into being." See* House of Lords | British government, https://www.britannica.com/topic/House-of-Lords (last visited Jul 4, 2016).

2400 *Salomon v. Salomon* [1896] UKHL 1, [1897] AC 22, [1897] A.C. 22-58 22 (1896); *See* in Gower (1953), *supra* note 755 at 538.

Companies Act of 1862[2401] for a trader [the respondent] to sell his solvent business in order to limit his liability to a limited company.[2402] This registered company comprised only himself and six members of his own family.[2403] Over time, the company was wound up and there was not enough money to pay the creditors, but the respondent had been appointed as managing director.[2404] Hence, the business belonged to the company and he was its agent.[2405] The House of Lords concluded that the sale process met all the requirements of the Companies Act 1862.[2406] Thus, the transfer was not fraudulent in respect of the creditors and the respondent was not liable to indemnify the company against the creditors' claims.[2407] This decision confirmed the legality of small registered companies as well as of large publicly registered companies and strengthened the separate corporate entity principle.[2408]

3. Current Legislation and Company Law Reform

Since the 19th century, the Act has been reformed from time to time with several enhancements that have greatly increased its volume. Section 121 of the 1908 Act comprised a first statutory definition of the meaning private company.[2409] This is a company, which by its articles:

(a) restricts the right to transfer its shares; and
(b) limits the number of its members to 50; and
(c) prohibits any invitation to the public to subscribe for any shares or debentures of the company.[2410]

The Act of 1908 states that a private company needs to have only two members instead of a minimum of seven.[2411] The purpose of these provisions was to take account of the concerns of small family-run businesses.[2412] In addition, the Act required the publication of a balance sheet.[2413] Thus, the legislation attempted to

---

2401 Companies Act 1862, 25 & 26 Vict. c. 89 (1862) §§ 6, 8, 30, 43.
2402 *Salomon v. Salomon* [1897] AC 22, *supra* note 2400 at 22.
2403 *Id.* at 22.
2404 *Id.* at 22.
2405 *See* Gower (1953), *supra* note 755 at 539.
2406 *Salomon v. Salomon* [1897] AC 22, *supra* note 2400 at 23.
2407 *Id.* at 23.
2408 *"The separate entity principle was firstly established in R v Arnaud [1846] 9 QB 806 case. It means that a company is a separate entity with distinct legal personality." See* The separate entity principle | Law Teacher, http://www.lawteacher.net/free-law-essays/company-law/the-separate-entity-principle.php (last visited Jul 4, 2016).
2409 *See* Gower (1953), *supra* note 755 at 540.
2410 Companies (Consolidation) Act 1908, c. 69 (1908) § 121 (1) (a)-(c).
2411 *Id.* § 115.
2412 *See* Gower (1953), *supra* note 755 at 540.
2413 Companies (Consolidation) Act 1908, *supra* note 2410 § 90.

improve the protection of shareholders, creditors, and potential investors. In accordance with the efforts of the legislator to impose further statutory restrictions and requirements on companies or their directors, the Companies Act was extended in its complexity and volume by formal measures of corporate control of directors and company management. The Act of 1948 comprised a total of 462 sections.[2414] Government committees were set up with the purpose of facilitating reforms to Company Law.[2415] For example, the Cohen Committee[2416] and the Jenkins Committee[2417] developed proposals for reforms. In June 1962, the Jenkins Committee reported to the Parliament through the President of the Board of Trade upon the provisions and workings of the Act of 1948.[2418] Specifically, this Committee considered the duties of directors and the rights of shareholders.[2419] Nevertheless, the Jenkins Committee was not able to reduce the number of provisions of the Act because of the growing and changing challenges facing companies.[2420] For example, the Jenkins Committee recommended the *"inclusion of a general statement of the director's fiduciary duties to his company in the Act"* despite the rule in *Percival v. Wright.*[2421] Furthermore, it encouraged an increased disclosure of company information.[2422]

While UK corporate governance rules aim to increase shareholder value, traditionally, UK Company Law comprised the principle that directors owe a duty of loyalty to the company, not to individual shareholders.[2423] In *Percival v. Wright*[2424] the High Court established this principle concerning directors' duties.[2425] The court held that directors of a company owe a duty of loyalty to the company, and that

2414 COMPANIES ACT 1948, c. 38 (1948); REPORT OF THE COMPANY LAW COMMITTEE 1962, http://www.takeovers.gov.au/content/Resources/other_resources/downloads/jenkins_committee_v2.pdf [hereinafter JENKINS COMMITTEE 1962] (last visited Jun 27, 2016).

2415 *See* SHEIKH (2008), *supra* note 2339 at 14.

2416 REPORT OF THE COMMITTEE ON COMPANY LAW AMENDMENT (COHEN REPORT 1945), (1945), http://www.takeovers.gov.au/content/Resources/other_resources/Cohen_Committee.aspx (last visited Jul 5, 2016).

2417 In 1959, the President of the Board of Trade appointed persons to form a Committee to review and report upon the provisions and working of the Companies Act. *See* JENKINS COMMITTEE 1962, *supra* note 2414.

2418 *Id.*

2419 *Id.*; SHEIKH (2008), *supra* note 2339 at 18.

2420 JENKINS COMMITTEE 1962, *supra* note 2414.

2421 *Id.* at 89.; *Percival v. Wright* [1902] 2 Ch. 401, (1902). In this case, the court held that a company's directors do not owe a fiduciary duty to individual shareholders *"and may purchase their shares without disclosing pending negotiations for the sale of the company." See* in Kern (2003), *supra* note 2315 at 1002.

2422 JENKINS COMMITTEE 1962, *supra* note 2414; SHEIKH (2008), *supra* note 2339 at 18.

2423 *See* Kern (2003), *supra* note 2315 at 1001–1002.

2424 *Percival v. Wright* [1902] 2 Ch. 401, (1902), *supra* note 2421.

2425 *Id.* at 425–426.

they were not in breach of duty in respect of the individual shareholders.[2426] The House of Lords followed this principle in *Johnson v. Gore Wood & Co.*[2427] However, nowadays this principle is beginning to change. For example, in *Re Chez Nico (Restaurants) Ltd,*[2428] the court doubted that there was no legal requirement to disclose the circumstances of the acquisition to the shareholders.

In addition, the Jenkins Commission concluded that the law should protect each person who suffers loss because a director breached a duty.[2429] Regarding fiduciary duties, the Committee recommended that the duties of directors should be strengthened in the Act. Furthermore, there should be enforcement of the duties imposed upon companies and their directors and officers.[2430] However, the legislator did not adopt all of the proposals put forward by the Jenkins Committee into law and overall, the Jenkins Committee did not result in any extensive reforms.[2431] Today, as a result of the Committee and the Company Law Review Group (CLRG), the Companies Act 2006 has largely superseded the Companies Act 1985.[2432] The CA 2006 has been fully in force since 2009.[2433] Nevertheless, some provisions in part 14, 15 and 18 of the CA 1985 continue to apply.[2434] Hence, the CA 2006 also comprises:

> (b) Part 2 of the Companies (Audit, Investigations and Community Enterprise) Act 2004, and[2435]
>
> (c) the provisions of the Companies Act 1985 and the Companies Consolidation (Consequential Provisions) Act 1985 that remain in force.[2436]

The Companies Acts as defined by this Act (see Section 2) also extends to Northern Ireland.[2437] The companies covered by this act are called registered companies. These companies are incorporated and have legal personality.[2438] The public markets in

2426 *See* Kern (2003), *supra* note 2315 at 1002.
2427 *Johnson v. Gore Wood & Co.* [2000] UKHL 65; [2001] 1 All ER 481; [2001] 2 WLR 72 (14th December, 2000), (2000).
2428 *Re Chez Nico Ltd.*, [1992] BCLC 192 (1991).
2429 Jenkins Committee 1962, *supra* note 2414 at 89.
2430 *Id.* at 504.
2431 Jenkins Committee 1962, *supra* note 2414; Sheikh (2008), *supra* note 2339 at 18.
2432 *See e.g.* Company Law Reform Corporate Law and Governance Directorate and Department of Trade and Industry, *supra* note 2335; Modern Company Law Company Law Review Steering Group, Modern Company Law for a Competitive Economy: Developing the Framework (2000) [hereinafter Company Law Review Steering Group]; Jenkins Committee Jenkins Committee 1962, *supra* note 2414. *See also* footnote 2333, p. 371.
2433 *See* French, Mayson, and Ryan (2015), *supra* note 2321 at 11.
2434 *Id.* at 11. *"These parts are concerned with investigations of a company."*
2435 Companies Act 2006, *supra* note 532, § 2 (1)(b).
2436 *Id.*§ 2 (1)(c).
2437 *Id.*§ 1284.
2438 Companies Act 2006, *supra* note 532, § 15 (1).

company shares are under legislative control of the Financial Services and Markets Act (FMSA) 2000.[2439]

In conclusion, the development of English Company Law comprises the limitation of liability of company members of registered corporations. On the other hand, the most recent amendments to English Company Law again attempted to improve shareholders' rights by strengthening the duties of company directors. Hence, the legislation on company law has grown into a complex and detailed code of rules.[2440] The CA 2006 has 1,300 Sections and 16 schedules.[2441] Such comprehensive legislation runs the risk of people acting in ignorance of some important provisions.[2442] Even before the CA 2006 entered into force, solicitors with extensive experience wrongly advised their clients on the Companies Acts *e.g.* with respect to substantial property transactions.[2443] Such erroneous advice could result in individuals being liable to pay more than £1 million.[2444]

Since this extensive legislation was enacted, the Companies Act has played a key role in governing the responsibilities of corporate directors. For this reason, the following section will examine in detail the enforcement of directors' and officers' duties and explore their liability with respect to compliance over the course of the development of company law.

II. The Enforcement of Duties under Company Law

Contrary to US State Corporation Law, English Company Law[2445] is codified in detail. Unlike the separate State Corporation Law in the US, the UK has a centralized, uniform company law. English Company Law is based on legislation, common law and equitable principles. It is also affected by European Law and soft law, such as codes, rules, and recommendations.[2446] However, since the structure

---

2439 Financial Services and Markets Act (2000), *supra* note 785; *See* in French, Mayson, and Ryan (2015), *supra* note 2321 at 12.

2440 *See* French, Mayson, and Ryan (2015), *supra* note 2321 at 15.

2441 Companies Act 2006, *supra* note 532; French, Mayson, and Ryan (2015), *supra* note 2321 at 15.

2442 *See* French, Mayson, and Ryan (2015), *supra* note 2321 at 15.

2443 *British Racing Drivers Club Ltd v Hextall Erskine & Co,* [1996] 3 All E.R. 667, [1996] B.C.C. 727, [1997] 1 B.C.L.C. 182, [1996] P.N.L.R. 523, (1996); *See* in: French, Mayson, and Ryan (2015), *supra* note 2321 at 15.

2444 *See* French, Mayson, and Ryan (2015), *supra* note 2321 at 15.

2445 The Companies Acts extend to the whole of Great Britain. The Act provides for a single company law regime applying to the whole of the UK, so that companies will be UK companies. *See* Companies Act 2006, *supra* note 532 Explanatory Notes, Territorial Extent and Devolution.

2446 *See* P. Mäntysaari, Comparative Corporate Governance: Shareholders as a Rule-maker 82 (1. ed. 2006).

of the limited company was created by an act of parliament, the primary source of company law in the UK is legislation.[2447]

Sometimes, UK Company Law is complex and difficult to navigate.[2448] Therefore, over the years, various groups of legal experts, practitioners, and business people have tried to make the law more reliable, effective and unequivocal.[2449] In the course of this extensive revision and reform process, one of the main points of focus has been directors' duties.

As in the US, directors' duties originate from equitable principles.[2450] They were based on the equitable principles of fiduciary duty and the common law of negligence.[2451] In order to make the law in this area more accessible and transparent, the codification of directors' duties under the common law was a major concern for the legislator.[2452] In the CA 1985, the number of mandatory provisions applicable to duties of directors and officers increased markedly compared to its predecessor.[2453] The Act comprised *e.g.* reporting duties,[2454] disclosure duties,[2455] duties on serious loss of capital[2456] and provisions on criminal liability for untrue statements.[2457] The Law Commissions of England, Wales, and Scotland supported this important reform and reviewed the CA 1985 particularly with regard to the duties owed by directors in respect of their company.[2458] Today, directors' duties, which apply to all company directors, are set forth in seven provisions in the CA 2006.[2459] The following sections provide a brief overview of these principles and introduce the codified provisions stating the seven general duties of directors in the Companies Act 2006.[2460]

2447 *"These companies are the creature of statute" See* Lord Macnaghten in *Welton v Saffery* (HL 1897) [1897}, 299 AC 66, 326 (1897); *See* in: French, Mayson, and Ryan (2015), *supra* note 2321 at 11.

2448 Company Law Reform Corporate Law and Governance Directorate and Department of Trade and Industry, *supra* note 2335 at 5; Mäntysaari (2006), *supra* note 2446 at 82.

2449 *See e.g.* Law Commission & Scottish Law Commission, Company Directors: Regulating Conflicts of Interests and Formulating a Statement of Duties (1998); Corporate Law and Governance Directorate and Department of Trade and Industry, *supra* note 2335.

2450 *See* French, Mayson, and Ryan (2015), *supra* note 2321 at 478.

2451 *Id.* at 477.

2452 *See* Allister Hudson, Understanding Company Law 7 (2nd ed. 2013) para 6.1.

2453 *See* Mäntysaari (2006), *supra* note 2446 at 87.

2454 Companies Act 1985, c. 6 (1985), § 234.

2455 *Id.* §§ 314, 324.

2456 *Id.* § 142.

2457 *Id.* § 70.

2458 Law Commission & Scottish Law Commission, *supra* note 2449.

2459 Companies Act 2006, *supra* note 532, §§ 171–177.

2460 Companies Act 2006, *supra* note 532, §§ 171–177.

1. Equitable Principles of Directors' Fiduciary Duties

Section 154 of the CA 2006 requires that a private company must have one director, while a public company must have at least two directors.[2461] Generally, a director is a person who is officially appointed according to the company's articles.[2462] Pursuant to this, a company's director holds an office, not an employment.[2463] The UK company is governed by the board of directors and the shareholders' meeting.[2464] Section 250 states that a director includes any person occupying the position of director, by whatever name.[2465] However, a distinction is made between *de facto* directors and *shadow* directors.[2466] A *de facto* director is firstly a person who is validly appointed as a director; secondly, a person who acts as director, although not validly appointed as such, may nevertheless be treated as a director *de facto*.[2467] In the CA 2006 a *shadow* director is defined as *"a person in accordance with whose directions or instructions the directors of the company are accustomed to act."*[2468]

However, the English Courts have always regarded directors to be fiduciaries.[2469]

> A fiduciary is someone who has undertaken to act for, or on behalf of, another person in a relationship of trust and confidence, which equity protects by imposing on the fiduciary a duty of loyalty. A fiduciary must act in good faith.[2470]

The equitable principles of directors' duties are classified in various ways.[2471] The most conventional approach is the classification of fiduciary duties of directors under the following topics: loyalty, good faith, proper purpose, the duty to act in accordance with the company's constitution, or the duty to deal fairly as between different classes of shareholders, etc.[2472] All of these principles govern the relationship between directors and the company.

2461 *Id.*§ 154 (1) (2).

2462 *See* French, Mayson, and Ryan (2015), *supra* note 2321 at 439.

2463 *Id.* at 479.

2464 *"The company itself can only act through directors." See* in *Ferguson v Wilson* (LJJ 1866) LR 2 Ch App 77, 36 LJ Ch 67, 89–90 (1866).

2465 Companies Act 2006, *supra* note 532, § 250.

2466 *See* Mäntysaari (2006), *supra* note 2446 at 221.

2467 *See e.g. Holland v Revenue and Customs & Anor* [2011] Bus LR 111, [2010] UKSC 51, [2011] 1 All ER 430, [2010] WLR 2793, [2010] 1 WLR 2793, [2011] BCC 1, [2010] STI 3074, 29 (2010).

2468 Companies Act 2006, *supra* note 532, § 251 (1).

2469 *See e.g. Mothew (Stapley & Co) v Bristol & West Building Society* [1996] 4 All ER 698, [1998] Ch 1, [1996] EWCA Civ 533, [1997] PNLR 11, [1997] 2 WLR 436, (1996).

2470 *Id.* at 158.

2471 Law Commission & Scottish Law Commission, *supra* note 2449 at 214 para 11.4.

2472 *Id.* at 214. para 11.4.

Similar to the situation in the US, the UK director of a company owes a duty of good faith to the company, which means he is required to act in good faith and in the best interests of the company.[2473] The general rule of equity means that the fiduciary duty precludes the individual from entering into engagements in which a personal conflict of interest could arise.[2474] This rule was first applied in *Aberdeen Railway Company v. Blakie* to a director of a railway company.[2475] The House of Lords stated that a director of a railway company is a trustee, *"and, as such, is precluded from dealing, on behalf of the company, with himself, or with a firm of which he is a partner."*[2476] Furthermore, Lord Cranworth pointed out that the duty to manage the general affairs of the company is delegated to directors.[2477] A corporate body can act only through its agents and those agents have to act in the best interest of the company.[2478] For this purpose, this rule applies to agents, as for example directors, when they act in a fiduciary capacity.[2479]

Later, the House of Lords, characterized the relationship between the company and the director as follows:

> Directors, no doubt, are not trustees, but they occupy a fiduciary position towards the company whose board they form.[2480]

The directors as trustees were specified in the case *Bairstow & Ors v. Queens Moat Houses Plc* in 2001, in which the court concluded,:

> ..although company directors are not strictly speaking trustees, they are in a closely analogous position because of the fiduciary duties which they owe to the company.[2481]

This principle was now confirmed.[2482] The background to this appeal was a claim for payment to the company on account of unlawful dividends to directors.[2483] The Court of Appeal considered the *Flitcroft's case* in which the court concluded that if the directors, who are *quasi*-trustees for the company, improperly pay

2473 *See* Kern (2003), *supra* note 2315 at 1006.
2474 *Regal (Hastings) Ltd v. Gulliver* [1942] 1 All ER 378, [1967] 2 AC 134, [1942] UKHL 1, 3 [3] (1942).
2475 *Aberdeen Railway Company v. Blakie, Brothers* [1854] UKHL 1_Macqueen_461, 461, 461.
2476 *Id.* at 461.
2477 *Id.* at 471.
2478 *Id.* at 471.
2479 *Id.* at 3 [3].
2480 *Regal (Hastings) Ltd v. Gulliver* [1942], *supra* note 2474 at [22].
2481 *Bairstow & Ors v. Queens Moat Houses Plc.* [2001] 2 BCLC 531, [2001] EWCA Civ 712, [2002] BCC 91, 50, (2001).
2482 *Id.* at 50.
2483 *Id.* at 3.

away the assets, and then they could be liable to replace them.[2484] The Court ultimately dismissed the appellants' appeal for relief in that case.[2485] The remedy of the fiduciary duty of directors is to confiscate the profit made by the breach and to transfer it to the company.[2486] The breach of a fiduciary duty is described as fraud.[2487]

Furthermore, a directors' duty of skill and care has evolved under common law. This duty addresses the implications of the director's position within the company.[2488] Traditionally, the standard of this duty in the UK was not high and was not classified as a fiduciary duty.[2489] Members of a company have no right to expect any reasonable standard from the company's managing directors.[2490] The duty does not depend on any contract, but a contract could determine the extent and the nature of it.[2491] In particular, the duty of care arises from the responsibility for the property or affairs of the company.[2492] Today, it aims to ensure that directors devote sufficient time to manage the company, to act only on an informed basis, possess the necessary skills and experience to make and consider business decisions carefully.

The English Courts have recognized that directors must rely on employees to inform them accurately of material information with respect to the company's affairs.[2493] The Earl of Halsbury states in *Dovey v. Cory*

> I cannot think that it can be expected of a director that he should be watching either the inferior officers of the company or verifying the calculations of the auditors himself.[2494]

2484 *Id.* at 28; *In re Exchange Banking Company* (1882) LR 21 Ch D 519, 534.

2485 *Id.*

2486 *See* French, Mayson, and Ryan (2015), *supra* note 2321 at 479.

2487 *Armitage v. Nurse & Ors* [1997] 2 All ER 705, [1998] Ch 241, [1997] EWCA Civ 1279, [1997] Pens LR 51, [1997] 3 WLR 1046, (1997); *See* in French, Mayson, and Ryan (2015), *supra* note 2321 at 479.

2488 *See* John Davies, A guide to directors' responsibilities under the Companies Act 2006 31 (2007) para 6.17.

2489 *Id.* at 31. para 6.17; *Mothew (t/a Stapley & Co) v. Bristol & West Building Society* [1996] 4 All ER 698, [1998] Ch 1, [1996] EWCA Civ 533, [1997] PNLR 11, [1997] 2 WLR 436.

2490 *Re Elgindata Ltd* [1991] BCLC 959, 994; *See* in French, Mayson, and Ryan (2015), *supra* note 2321 at 499.

2491 *See* French, Mayson, and Ryan (2015), *supra* note 2321 at 499.

2492 *Id.* at 499.

2493 *Id.* at 500.

2494 *Dovey v. Cory* [1901] AC 477, 70 LJ Ch 753, 486 (1901); *See* in French, Mayson, and Ryan (2015), *supra* note 2321 at 500.

In addition, similar to the US, company directors have a supervisory duty in the event of any delegation of their responsibilities. This is confirmed by the Court of Appeal in the case *Re Barings plc* with the statement

> ... the exercise of power of delegation does not absolve a director from the duty to supervise the discharge of this function.[2495]

To conclude, under common law , the most important directors' duties thus consist of two parts: the directors' duty of care and skill, and fiduciary duties. Company directors in the UK are subject to similar duties as under the common law principle in the US. Under Delaware Corporation Law, directors and officers additionally owe a duty of oversight for implementing and maintaining an internal control system. Thus, the personal responsibilities of directors and officers for adequate monitoring were established under the *Caremark* standard.[2496] Although English company directors have to carry out supervisory duties, a duty of oversight is not found anywhere in the English common law.

2. Statutory Directors' Duties under Company Law

The nature of the director's role is central to the English Company Law.[2497] In a private company, the director can be both a substantial shareholder as well as the company's manager.[2498] This can potentially lead to conflicts of interest. In a public company, the directors usually hold fewer shares proportionate to the total shareholding.[2499] The two main types of company, private and public companies, are defined in Section 4 of the Companies Act 2006.[2500] Public companies are registered and *"limited by shares"* or *"limited by guarantee and having a share capital."*[2501] In contrast to a public company,

> A private company is any company that is not a public company.[2502]

The Companies Act of 1985 provides a legal framework stipulating that companies are also managed in the interests of the shareholders.[2503] Section 309 states that directors must give due regard to the interests of employees, as well as the interests of its members. Nevertheless, the most important amendments to the CA 1985 were

---

2495 *Re Barings plc* (No. 5) [1999] 1 BCLC, [2000] 1 BCLC 523, 433; *See* in French, Mayson, and Ryan (2015), *supra* note 2321 at 500.
2496 *See* Chiu (2015), *supra* note 2320 at 235.
2497 *See* Hudson (2013), *supra* note 2452 at 7.
2498 *Id.* at 7.
2499 *Id.* at 7.
2500 Companies Act 2006, *supra* note 532, § 4.
2501 *Id.* § 4 (2).
2502 *Id.* § 4 (1).
2503 Companies Act 1985, c. 6 (1985), §§ 89, 90, 309.

effected in 1989, 2004, and 2006.[2504] These developments of the law represented the attempt to reconsider the legal position of companies within the business and social environment.[2505]

Simultaneously, in the last thirty years, the number of incorporated companies has grown from 785,688 in 1980 to 3,678,860 in May 2016.[2506] Moreover, the UK has introduced reforms to allow the Secretary of State to lodge disqualification proceedings against directors for breaches of duty and breaches of legislation.[2507] The reason for this is that the disqualification of directors is rooted in public interest.[2508] Pursuant to Section 5 of the Company Directors Disqualification Act 1986, the legislation has inserted Part 9 into the Small Business, Enterprise and Employment Act 2015 in order to protect businesses and society as a whole from unfit directors and to enhance confidence in the UK's business environment.[2509]

Furthermore, to bolster the competiveness of companies, the Company Law Review Steering Group proposed that the directors' duty of loyalty should appear in a statutory provision.[2510] The proposed formulation was:

(1) Compliance and loyalty

a) A director must exercise his powers honestly and for their proper purpose, and in accordance with the company's constitution and decisions taken lawfully under it [or under the general law].[2511]

Therefore, the Steering Group intended to extend the law to include a new compliance duty.[2512] In its view, both compliance and proper purpose duties override the duty of loyalty.[2513] Nevertheless, the legislator restricted the proposed formulation in Section 171 and codified the duty of loyalty as follows:

2504 Companies Act 1989, *supra* note 774; Companies (Audit, Investigations and Community Enterprise) Act 2004, c. 27 (2004); Companies Act 2006, *supra* note 532.

2505 *See* Davies (2007), *supra* note 2488 at 28 para 6.4.

2506 Companies House, Incorporated companies in the UK | May 2016 9 (2016) Chart 3.

2507 *See* Chiu (2015), *supra* note 2320 at 235; Department for Business and Innovation & Skills, Transparency *&* Trust: Enhancing the Transparency of UK Company Ownership and Increasing Trust in UK Business 55 (2014) para 223.

2508 *See* Chiu (2015), *supra* note 2320 at 235.

2509 *Re Sevenoaks Stationers (Retail) Ltd* [1991] BCLC 325., Transparency & Trust Department for Business and Innovation & Skills, *supra* note 2507 at 52 para 203.

2510 *See* Sarah Worthington, *Reforming Directors' Duties*, 64 Modern Law Review 439–458, 6 (2001).

2511 Company Law Review Steering Group, *supra* note 2432 at 29 para 3.40.

2512 Company Law Review Steering Group *Id.* at 32. para 3.46.

2513 Company Law Review Steering Group *Id.* at 33. para 3.48.

A director of a company must–
(a) act in accordance with the company's constitution, and
(b) only exercise powers for the purposes for which they are conferred.[2514]

This provision is based on the equitable principle that a director has the duty to exercise the company's powers for its purpose.[2515] For example, in *Howard Smith Ltd v Ampol Petroleum Ltd* the Supreme Court of South Wales states that the directors' power under an article of the constitution is a fiduciary power and must be exercised for the purpose for which it was conferred.[2516]

The vast majority of statutory directors' duties are based on the equitable principles of fiduciary duty.[2517] Section 170 stipulates to whom the duties should apply:

(1) The general duties specified in sections 171 to 177 are owed by a director of a company to the company.

Additionally, for an understanding of the application of the general statutory duties, Section 170 states that they have taken effect in place of those common law rules and equitable principles.[2518] It could thus be assumed that they have replaced the pre-existing case law. However, Section 170 furthermore states that *"the general duties shall be interpreted and applied in the same way as common law rules or equitable principles."*[2519] Furthermore, the English Courts can develop and adjust equitable principles and common law of negligence through the rules of precedents.[2520] Legal scholars view this approach as a new way of interpreting a statute and it will be interesting to see how the courts will apply Section 170 (4).[2521]

Today, the Companies Act 2006 states seven general directors' duties that need to be taken into account.[2522] The CA 2006 codifies directors' statutory duties as follows:

§ 171.Duty to act within powers
§ 172.Duty to promote the success of the company
§ 173.Duty to exercise independent judgment
§ 174.Duty to exercise reasonable care, skill and diligence

2514 Companies Act 2006, *supra* note 532 § 171.
2515 *See* French, Mayson, and Ryan (2015), *supra* note 2321 at 481.
2516 *Howard Smith Limited v. Ampol Petroleum Limited and Others* [1974] 2 WLR 689, 118 SJLB 330, [1974] AC 821, [1974] UKPC 3, [1974] 1 All ER 1126; *See* in: French, Mayson, and Ryan (2015), supra note 2321 at 482.
2517 Companies Act 2006, *supra* note 532 §§ 171–173, §§ 175–177, Section 174 codifies the common law of negligence. *See* in: French, Mayson, and Ryan (2015), *supra* note 2321 at 478.
2518 Companies Act 2006, *supra* note 532, § 170 (3).
2519 *Id.*§ 170 (4).
2520 *See* French, Mayson, and Ryan (2015), *supra* note 2321 at 477.
2521 *Id.* at 477.
2522 *Id.* at 477.

§ 175.Duty to avoid conflicts of interest
§ 176.Duty not to accept benefits from third parties
§ 177.Duty to declare interest in proposed transaction or arrangement.[2523]

Therefore, the company is the proper plaintiff in relation to claims for any breach of such a duty to act within powers, to promote the success of the company, to exercise reasonable care, skill, and diligence, etc. by a director.[2524]

In conclusion, today, the UK has a strong substantive company law.[2525] Following years of ongoing reforms, the Companies Act of 2006 for the first time clearly stipulated directors' duties.[2526] The scope and nature of general duties owed by a director of a company to the company are specifically stated in Sections 171 to 177 of the Companies Act 2006.[2527] UK company directors *inter alia* have a duty of reasonable care and fiduciary duties.[2528] The duties *"are based on certain common law rules and equitable principles."*[2529] However, the situation has changed. Today, Section 174 of the CA 2006 expects a higher standard of directors' duties of skill and care.[2530] For example, a director is now required to act within the scope of the company's constitution. Any decision made outside the constitution, will be void.[2531] The director is also bound by contractual agreements. However, the English Courts have not ruled on any explicit oversight duty or compliance duty of directors similar to that in the US. Contrary to US corporation law, the CA 2006 explicitly states that any provisions to exempt a director of a company from any liability are void.[2532]

3. The Legal Definition and General Role of Company Officers

This section will explore whether company officers are also subject to the common law and equitable rules and, hence, to rules regarding fiduciary duties.

2523 Companies Act 2006, *supra* note 532 §§ 171–177.
2524 *See* Hudson (2013), *supra* note 2452 at 7.
2525 John Armour et al., *Private Enforcement of Corporate Law: An Empirical Comparison of the United Kingdom and the United States: Private Enforcement of Corporate Law: United Kingdom vs. United States*, 6 Journal of Empirical Legal Studies 687–722, 721 (2009).
2526 *See* B. Horrigan, Corporate Social Responsibility in the 21st Century: Debates, Models and Practices Across Government, Law and Business 229 (1. ed. 2010).
2527 Companies Act 2006, *supra* note 532, § 170 (1).
2528 *Id.* § 170 (4).
2529 *Id.* § 170 (3).
2530 *Id.* § 174 (1) (2) *"A director of a company must exercise reasonable care, skill and diligence."*
2531 *See* Mäntysaari (2006), *supra* note 2446 at 110.
2532 *Id.* § 232 (1).

The position of company officers is no different from that of directors.[2533] Thus, the question of who is a company officer in the UK is not easy to answer, since there is no clear distinction between directors and officers. In accordance with the CA, company directors and secretaries are referred to as officers.[2534] Officers may be an employee while directors are appointed by members *e.g.* shareholders or the board. The articles of association of a company may allow directors to appoint one or more managing directors or executive officers and to delegate to them the day-to day management.[2535] The CLRG made, *"proper"* act of delegation will not remove potential liability from those delegating.[2536] The CLRG concluded that decisions on this legal matter *"can only be decided on a case by case basis."*[2537]

However, the control of the management should remain with the board.[2538] As mentioned previously, this principle is set forth in the case *Re Barings plc (No. 5)* concerning directors' duties of care and skill.[2539] So, while directors are entitled, in accordance with the articles of association of the company, to delegate particular functions to those below them in the management chain, and to trust in their competence and integrity to a reasonable extent, the exercise of the power of delegation does not absolve a director from the duty to supervise the discharge of the delegated functions.[2540] Therefore, the directors have to monitor the functioning of the managing directors or executive officers.[2541] However, the scope of function of the managing directors is not clear, since it is not stipulated anywhere in the law.[2542] The House of Lords held that a person with a title managing director has no particular power, since these depend on the terms of his appointment.[2543]

The main legislative provisions that govern company officers are Sections 270–280, 485–539, 589–604, 1121, 1132 and 1173 of the CA 2006. Section 1121 includes any director, manager or secretary, and any person who is to be treated as an officer of the company to take all reasonable steps to prevent the contravention.[2544] The

2533 *See* Worthington (2001), *supra* note 2510 at 16.

2534 Companies Act 2006, *supra* note 532 § 1121 - Commentary on Section 1121 – "*An officer of a company is defined as including a director, manager or (company) secretary.*"

2535 *See* Mäntysaari (2006), *supra* note 2446 at 99.

2536 Company Law Reform *Id.* at 38. para 4.6.

2537 Company Law Reform *Id.* at 38. para 4.6.

2538 *See* Mäntysaari (2006), *supra* note 2446 at 99.

2539 *See supra* A, II., 1., p. 332, *supra* note 2495.

2540 *Re Barings plc* (No. 5) [1999] 1 BCLC, [2000] 1 BCLC 523, *supra* note 2495 at 489.

2541 *See* Mäntysaari (2006), *supra* note 2446 at 100.

2542 *Id.* at 100.

2543 *Harold Holdsworth & Co (Wakefield) Ltd v Caddies* [1955] 1 WLR 352.

2544 Companies Act 2006, *supra* note 532, § 1121 (2)(a)(b).

auditor is absent from this list, but the Companies Act provides that the auditor is a person who "*holds office in accordance with the terms of their appointment*".[2545] The compliance officer and other officers' titles are also absent, but the English Courts have decided on the liability of officers in each case of an individual who is considered to be an officer in default.[2546]

Nevertheless, the list in Section 1121 does not mean that every person whose title includes the word manager is covered. Section 1121 (2) of the CA 2006 should be interpreted narrowly in the context of officers' liability under Section 1121. This was determined in the case *R v. Baol* in which the court states that the provisions apply only to a person who has a position of real authority, the management of the company's affairs and the power and responsibility to decide corporate policy and strategy.[2547] However, in contrast to *R v. Boal,* in the case *Re a Company,* the court interpreted the application of the office relating to the officers of a body corporate in Section 1173 (1) in a wider sense.[2548] The court held that, in this context, the term means that every person in charge of supervisory control is a manager. Shaw L.J. points out for the purposes of Section 1132:

> The expression manager should not too narrowly construed. It is not to be equated with a managing or other director or a general manager. As I see it, any person who in the affairs of the company exercises a supervisory control which reflects the general policy of the company for the time being or which is related to the general administration of the company is in the sphere of management. He need not be a member of the board of directors.[2549]

This case has shown that there is reasonable cause to assume that the departmental manager, who committed an offence, was covered by Section 1132 as an officer of the company.[2550] In conclusion, these two example cases demonstrate that each case needs to be considered on its own individual merits and circumstances.[2551] The courts must look at what the person's role is within the company, as opposed to their job title, how this fits into the corporate structure and how it affects the

2545 Companies Act 2006, *supra* note 532, § 487 (1).

2546 *Id.*§ 1121 (2)(a)(b); *See supra* p. 378.

2547 *R v. Boal* (CA 1992), [1992] QB 591, [1992] 2 WLR 890, (1992); *See* in French, Mayson, and Ryan (2015), *supra* note 2321 at 529.

2548 *Re a Company* [1980] Ch 138, [1980] 2 WLR 241; *See* in French, Mayson, and Ryan (2015), *supra* note 2321 at 529.

2549 *Re a Company* [1980] Ch 138, [1980] 2 WLR 241, *supra* note 2548 at 144; *See* in French, Mayson, and Ryan (2015), *supra* note 2321 at 529.

2550 *See* French, Mayson, and Ryan (2015), *supra* note 2321 at 529.

2551 *See* Tania Clench, Being Concerned in the Management of a Company–What Does it Mean? 29–31 31 (2012).

enterprise.[2552] Finally, there is no clear legal definition of the post of the company officer in UK Company Law such as in the Delaware Corporation Law. Although the UK has a detailed system of regulation and comprehensive company law provisions, there is no clear distinction between a director and an officer, and their roles depend on the specific facts of their authority, power and responsibilities within a company.

a. Officers in Default

The statutory provisions in the CA 2006 provide a legal framework to clarify when a company officer under specific circumstances could be liable for a breach of any provision of the Companies Act.[2553] As discussed previously, it is interesting to note that:

> For this purpose, 'officer' includes–
> (a) any director, manager or secretary, and
> (b) any person who is to be treated as an officer of the company for the purposes of the provision in question.[2554]

Therefore, all directors, managers, and the company secretary are considered to be officers of their company.[2555] However, there is a distinction between directors and officers particularly with regard to their liability. Generally, directors are liable when they authorize, participate in, or fail to take active preventative steps including monitoring failures.[2556] Secretaries should be liable for the same default if directors have properly charged them with the relevant function.[2557]

The Companies Act 2006 lists a great number of offences referring to directors and officers, which are derived from the CA 1985.[2558] Annex A states every provision classified by certain types of offence *e.g.* (1) information relating to company constitution, (2) company names, (3) trading disclosures, etc., in which parties are liable.[2559] In the majority of the offences, the liable parties are the company and every officer who is in default.[2560] Thus, the company and every company officer

---

2552 *Id.* at 31.

2553 Companies Act 2006, *supra* note 532, §§ 1121–1123; Company Law Reform Corporate Law and Governance Directorate and Department of Trade and Industry, *supra* note 2335 at 37.

2554 Companies Act 2006, *supra* note 532, § 1121 (2).

2555 *See* Davies (2007), *supra* note 2488 at 11 para 2.5.

2556 Company Law Reform Corporate Law and Governance Directorate and Department of Trade and Industry, *supra* note 2335 at 37.

2557 Company Law Reform *Id.* at 37.

2558 Annex A Companies Act 2006 | Schedule of Company Offences.

2559 *Id.*

2560 *Id.*

can be prosecuted for the majority of these offences.[2561] In the event of a breach of a statutory duty, the officers in default will face a fine and, in some cases, imprisonment.[2562]

In Section 1121 (3) the CA 2006 states that

> an officer is in default for the purposes of the provision if he authorizes or permits, participates in, or fails to take all reasonable steps to prevent, the contravention.[2563]

This is a broad definition and takes the opposite approach to that under the Companies Act 1985, which covered any officer of the company who "*knowingly and willfully*" authorized or permitted the contravention.[2564] The expression *"fails to take all reasonable steps to prevent the contravention"* in particular appears difficult to handle in daily practice. The following examination will show which impact this new legal definition will have in the English Courts.

A search of the British and Irish Legal Information Institute case database from English and Welsh Courts with coding of the exact phrase *"officers in default"* found eighteen cases from 2006 to 2016. These cases were selected relating to a criminal breach of the Companies Act 2006. In eight cases, an officer was in default for the purposes of a provision of the Companies Acts.[2565] The other ten cases refer to financial services companies, such as broker-dealers, banks, and traders. These cases will not be taken into consideration here. However, only in one of these eight cases was a company charged with four offences under Section 501(1) of the Companies Act 2006.[2566] This provision refers to the auditor's rights to information:

> (1) A person commits an offence who knowingly or recklessly makes to an auditor of a company a statement (oral or written) that—
> (a) conveys or purports to convey any information or explanations which the auditor requires, or is entitled to require, under section 499, and
> (b) is misleading, false or deceptive in a material particular.

2561 *See* Davies (2007), *supra* note 2488 at 88 para 10.32.

2562 Companies Act 2006, *supra* note 532, § 26 (4).

2563 Companies Act 2006, *supra* note 532, § 1121 (3).

2564 Companies Act 1985, *supra* note 2488, § 730 (5).

2565 *See AMG Global Nominees (Private) Ltd v. SMM Holdings Ltd & Anor.* [2008] EWHC 221 (Ch), (2008); *Id.*; *Anglo Petroleum Ltd & Anor v. TFB (Mortgages) Ltd* [2007] EWCA Civ 456, (2007); *Cox v. Cox & Anor* [2006] EWHC 1077 (Ch), (2006); *Estafnous v. London & Leeds Business Centres Ltd.* [2009] EWHC 1308 (Ch), (2009); *Gyrus Group Ltd & Anor, R v.* [2014] EW Misc B57 (CC), (2014); *Hamid (t/a Hamid Properties) v. Francis Bradshaw Partnership* [2013] EWCA Civ 470, (2013); *Paros Plc v. Worldlink Group Plc* [2012] EWHC 394 (Comm), (2012), https://www.bailii.org/ (last visited Aug. 15, 2016).

2566 *Gyrus Group Ltd & Anor, R v.* [2014] EW Misc B57 (CC), *supra* note 2565; Companies Act 2006, *supra* note 532 § 501 (1).

Section 499 (2)(a) of the CA 2006 states that

> (2) Those persons are—
> (a) any officer or employee of the company;...

In this case the judge states

> Likewise, it is the company which is responsible for sending copies of its annual report and accounts to its members (see s423). Consequently, the company itself (as well as every officer in default) is explicitly criminally liable if this does not occur (see s425). On the other hand, it is the duty of the company's directors – and not the duty of the company – to file the company's annual accounts with the register (see s441). Consequently, criminal liability for failing to comply with this duty explicitly lies with the directors only and not with the company (see s451(1)).[2567]

The company, through its officers, made misleading statements to the auditors during the 2009 and 2010 audit process.[2568] However, this case has not yet been decided since the Crown Court in its judgment concluded that this proceeding *"is inevitably doomed as a matter of law."*[2569]

However, the other seven cases which were found deal with offences under Sections 151, 351 and 359 of the Companies Act 1985, as the full CA 2006 only entered into in force in 2009. In the vast majority of these cases, the officers were in default of provisions of Section 151[2570] and Sections 348, 349 and 351 of the CA 1985.[2571] Nevertheless, this sample did not include any court cases in which a compliance officer was involved. The majority of directors and officers involved were the vice-president or executive officers.

In conclusion, it remains to be seen how the English Courts will decide in practice on the issue of officers in default. This legislative approach to sanctioning is seen as an overarching in default framework, but it is in line with the recommendation of

---

2567 *Gyrus Group Ltd & Anor, R v.* [2014] EW Misc B57 (CC), *supra* note 2565 at 23 iv).

2568 *Id.* at 10.

2569 *Id.* at 44.

2570 *See e.g. AMG Global Nominees (Private) Ltd v Africa Resources Ltd* [2008] EWCA Civ 1262, (2008); *AMG Global Nominees (Private) Ltd v. SMM Holdings Ltd & Anor.* [2008] EWHC 221 (Ch), *supra* note 2565; *Cox v. Cox & Anor* [2006] EWHC 1077 (Ch), *supra* note 2565; *Estafnous v. London & Leeds Business Centres Ltd.* [2009] EWHC 1308 (Ch), *supra* note 2565; *Paros Plc v. Worldlink Group Plc* [2012] EWHC 394 (Comm), *supra* note 2565. Section 151 of the CA 1985 provided as follows: *"It is not lawful for the company or any of its subsidiaries to give financial assistance directly or indirectly for the purpose of that acquisition before or at the same time as the acquisition takes place."*

2571 *Hamid (t/a Hamid Properties) v. Francis Bradshaw Partnership* [2013] EWCA Civ 470, *supra* note 2565.

the CLRG.[2572] Ultimately, the compliance officer is likely to be viewed just like an officer in default according to Section 1121 of the CA 2006.

b. Company Managers

The CA 2006 also lists the manager of a company.[2573] A manager means a senior employee who is also in a fiduciary relationship with the company.[2574] This could be a chief accountant,[2575] president, vice-president, or executive officer.[2576] In the majority of cases, it was held that these managers owe the same fiduciary duties as directors.[2577] Therefore, senior managers are subject to the same fiduciary duties as those upon which the statutory duties of directors are based.[2578]

c. Company Secretaries

The CA 2006 also refers to the company secretary in the event of the contravention of an enactment in relation to a company as well as the director and officer.[2579] Furthermore, Section 271 states that there is a need for public companies to have a secretary.[2580] In contrast, *"private companies are not obliged to have a company secretary."*[2581] In addition, the proposed officer for registration of a private and public company should be the director or the first secretary.[2582]

The company's directors must ensure that the secretary of a public company has the requisite knowledge and experience to discharge the function. That means he should have the following qualifications *e.g.* a barrister, advocate or solicitor or a member of any of the bodies specified in Section 273 (3).[2583] In the view of the Secretary of State for Trade and Industry, this requirement to

---

2572 Company Law Reform Corporate Law and Governance Directorate and Department of Trade and Industry, *supra* note 2335 at 37 para 4.6.

2573 Companies Act 2006, *supra* note 532, § 1121 (2)(a).

2574 *See* French, Mayson, and Ryan (2015), *supra* note 2321 at 547.

2575 *Agip (Africa) Ltd. v. Kingsley & Ors* [1990] EWCA Civ 2 (1990), [1991] Ch 547, 24 (1990). The judge said: *"There is no difficulty about that in the present case since the accountant must have been in a fiduciary relationship with the company. He was the Chief Accountant of the company and was entrusted with the signed drafts or orders upon BdS."*

2576 *See* French, Mayson, and Ryan (2015), *supra* note 2321 at 547.

2577 *See e.g. Green v. Bestobell Industries Ltd* [1982] WAR 1, *See* in French, Mayson, and Ryan (2015), *supra* note 2321 at 547. *"In this case the manager had the complete control of human, financial and contractual resources according to his letter of appointment."*

2578 *See supra* II., 2., p. 332.

2579 Companies Act 2006, *supra* note 532, § 1121 (2)(a).

2580 Companies Act 2006, *supra* note 532, § 271.

2581 *See* Davies (2007), *supra* note 2488 at 21 para 4.14.

2582 Companies Act 2006, *supra* note 532, §§ 12 (1)(a-c).

2583 *Id.* § 273 (1)(2)(3).

employ a qualified company secretary ensures that public companies have a *"company officer who focuses on legal requirements, thus improving compliance and reducing risk of penalty."*[2584] In addition, another provision provides that the appointment and the removal of the company secretary should be a matter for the board.[2585]

Pursuant to the CA 2006 and the Combined Code, a company secretary is a:

> [ ] mere servant; his position is that he is to do what he is told, and no person can assume that he has any authority to represent anything at all; [ ][2586]

For listed companies, the UK Corporate Code states the responsibilities as follows:

> The company secretary should be responsible for advising the board through the chairman on all governance matters. All directors should have access to the advice and services of the company secretary, who is responsible to the board for ensuring that board procedures are complied with.[2587]

There are also common law rules on the duties of company secretaries. In addition, in recent years, the responsibilities and duties of company secretaries have increased in the legislation. A number of reporting duties of company secretaries are enshrined in the CA 2006 *e.g.* they have to sign the directors' accounting report[2588] and the directors' remuneration report.[2589] The company secretary is also responsible for a number of matters concerned with administration *e.g.* sending the registrar a copy of the articles as amended,[2590] providing constitutional documents to company members,[2591] changing the company's name if so required,[2592] trading disclosures,[2593] keeping a register of secretaries,[2594] etc. These responsibilities apply to the company and every officer in default.[2595] In conclusion, in accordance with common law principles, the extent of authority and responsibilities of secretary were strengthened.

A company secretary can also represent the company in its dealings with third parties.[2596] The power of the company's secretary varies, depending on the size of

---

2584 Company Law Reform Corporate Law and Governance Directorate and Department of Trade and Industry, *supra* note 2335 at 279.
2585 UK Corporate Governance Code, Cadbury Committee, *supra* note 442 B.5.2.
2586 *Barnett, Hoares & Co v. South London Tramways Co* [1887] 18 QBD, 815, 817 (1887).
2587 Cadbury Committee, *supra* note 442 B.5.2.
2588 Companies Act 2006, *supra* note 532, § 419 (1).
2589 *Id.*§ 422 (1).
2590 *Id.*§ 26.
2591 *Id.*§ 32.
2592 *Id.*§§ 63, 64, 68, 75, 76.
2593 *Id.*§§ 82, 113.
2594 *Id.*§ 275.
2595 *See supra* II, 1., p. 329.
2596 *See* Mäntysaari (2006), *supra* note 2446 at 102.

the company, but is generally extensive.[2597] In the case *Panorama Developments (Guildford) Ltd v. Fidelis Furnishing Fabrics Ltd*, the Lord Justice stated, *"the company secretary had ostensible, or apparent, authority to enter in agreements"* regarding administrative matters.[2598] The company secretary hired a number of cars for the business in the absence of his managing director. The court held that the company was bound by the contract.[2599]

In order to describe the role of a company secretary, the professional Institute for Chartered Secretaries (ICSA) views ensuring compliance with corporate law, regulations, and the company's constitution as a key element of his duties.[2600] The Cadbury Committee also evaluates the company secretary as a key role player *"in ensuring that board procedures are both followed and regularly reviewed."*[2601] He is also referred to as "*the chief administrative officer of the company.*"[2602] Furthermore, the duties of a company secretary are usually enshrined in an employment agreement.[2603] The Company Law Review in its final report recommended "*that the test for liability of secretaries should be the same as that for directors, where directors have properly charged the secretary with e.g. administrative function.*"[2604]

Finally, it appears that company secretaries are officers with extensive responsibilities and duties.[2605] They have certain legal duties and responsibilities with respect to the administration of the company and compliance with company law and the company's constitution. In public companies, they also have to ensure compliance with all rules concerning the listing of the shares. In addition, their task is to advise the board on governance matters.

4. Theories of Company Liability in the UK

To understand and distinguish the concepts of a company's liability and individual liability under company law, this section analyzes the relevant theories of liability in the UK. English Company Law addresses two groups of cases company liability which are inherent parts of the structure of companies: firstly, the principle of limited corporate liability for the company's shareholders, and secondly, the

2597 *Id.* at 102.
2598 *Panorama Developments (Guildford) Ltd v. Fidelis Furnishing Fabrics Ltd* [1971] 2 QB 711, [1971] 3 All ER 16; *See* in French, Mayson, and Ryan (2015), *supra* note 2321 at 635.
2599 *Id.*
2600 Roger Dickinson (ICSA), The company secretary in the UK, http://www.ebrd.com/downloads/legal/corporate/icsa.pdf (last visited Jul 24, 2016).
2601 The Cadbury Report (1992) Cadbury Committee, *supra* note 796 para 4.25.
2602 *Panorama Developments (Guildford) Ltd v. Fidelis Furnishing Fabrics Ltd* [1971] 2 QB 711, [1971] 3 All ER 16, *supra* note 2598.
2603 *See* Mäntysaari (2006), *supra* note 2446 at 111.
2604 Company Law Review Steering Group, *supra* note 2432 at 318 para 15.41.
2605 *See* Mäntysaari (2006), *supra* note 2446 at 103.

individual default rule.[2606] The first principle is the liability that could arise between the company's management and the shareholders as a class.

Under common law, it has been recognized that a company has a dual nature. On the one hand, it is an association of its members and on the other, a person separate from its members.[2607] In practice, this means the company is viewed as a separate person, who enters into contracts, conducts business and owns the company's property.[2608] This fundamental principle was established in the leading case *Salomon v. Salomon.*[2609] In this case, Lord Halsbury said:

> .[...]once the company is legally incorporated it must be treated like any other independent person with its rights and liabilities appropriate to itself,.[...][2610]

In addition, the Serious Fraud Office (SFO)[2611] defines a company *"as a legal person, which could be prosecuted and should not be treated differently from individuals."*[2612] In the event of a corporate criminal prosecution, the SFO will first and foremost consider the provisions of the statute.[2613] The difficult question in criminal law is then how a legal entity such as a company can actually be held responsible.[2614]

Under common law, there are three theories concerning the criminal responsibility of companies. The first theory is the agency theory, as described previously.[2615] In the US, this theory is referred to as the respondeat superior doctrine.[2616] Equally, under UK agency law, when an agent makes his principal party to a

---

2606 *See* Paul L. Davies, The Board of Directors: Composition, Structure, Duties and Powers 4 (2000).

2607 *See* French, Mayson, and Ryan (2015), *supra* note 2321 at 126.

2608 *Id.* at 126.

2609 *Salomon v. Salomon* [1897] AC 22, *supra* note 2400; *See* in: French, Mayson, and Ryan (2015), *supra* note 2321 at 126.

2610 *Salomon v. Salomon* [1897] AC 22, *supra* note 2400 at 30–31; *See* in: French, Mayson, and Ryan (2015), *supra* note 2321 at 127.

2611 *See infra* III., p. 413, The SFO *"is part of the UK criminal justice system covering England, Wales and Northern Ireland, but not Scotland, the Isle of Man or the Channel Islands."* The SFO can be seen as the English counterpart to the United States Department of Justice (DOJ). *See* SFO, Serious Fraud Office | About us Serious Fraud Office, https://www.sfo.gov.uk/about-us/ (last visited Jul 26, 2016).

2612 SFO Guidance Serious Fraud Office SFO, Guidance on Corporate Prosecutions 1 (2009), https://www.skadden.com/eimages/Guidance_on_Corporate_Prosecutions.pdf [hereinafter SFO Guidance](last visited Jul 25, 2016) para 4.

2613 SFO Guidance *Id.* at 3. para 15.

2614 *See* Wells, *Criminal Responsibility of Legal Persons in Common Law Jurisdictions, in* Paper prepared for OECD Anti-Corruption Unit 10, 2 (2000).

2615 *See supra* A., I.a, p. 192, *See also* Agency Theory Müller-Freienfels, *supra* footnote 1289.

2616 Michael Litvin, Doctrine of Respondeat Superior LII / Legal Information Institute (2009), https://www.law.cornell.edu/wex/

contract, the agent does not himself become party to that contract and, hence, is not liable for any breach of the contract by the principal.[2617] Therefore, as an agent of the company, the director or officer is not held liable for the breach of the contract.[2618] This principle encompasses the rule that the company is liable for the wrongful acts of all its employees.[2619] This basic principle was established in the case *Said v. Butt* where the court held that the managing director was not personally liable, because he was acting within his authority as a director.[2620] Contrary to this principle, for certain torts, such as fraudulent misrepresentation, for instance a director, who fraudulently states that the company is creditworthy can be held personally liable.[2621] In the case *Standard Chartered Bank v. Pakistan National Shipping Corp* the Lord Justice stated that:

> He is liable not because he was a director but because he committed a fraud.[2622]

In addition, the other Lord Justice said

> [.] directors or employees acting as such will only be liable for tortious acts committed during the course of their employment. In the event that a director or an employee himself commits the tort he will be liable.[2623]

It could be argued that a hallmark of common law is that the courts examine the facts and circumstances of each case individually. Traditionally, the English common law limits the application of vicarious liability to certain kinds of torts.[2624] That means, "*when an employee commits a tort, the employer, whether an individual or a company, may be held vicariously liable.*"[2625] For example, companies may also

---

quotation/%5Bfield_short_title-raw%5D_123 (last visited Jun 19, 2016); Respondeat Superior Definition, *supra* note 1289; *Wilson v. United States* (8th Cir. 1993), *supra* note 1126.

2617 *Compare also* in the UK: *See* French, Mayson, and Ryan (2015), *supra* note 2321 at 639 Immunity when acting for a company.

2618 *Id.* at 639.

2619 *"Under the doctrine of respondeat superior an employer is liable for the negligent acts or omissions of his employee which are committed within the scope of his employment."A principle of agency law, which holds that a principal, or employer is vicariously liable for the torts of his agent, or employee, which occur during the course of the agent's, or employee's actions on behalf of the principal, or employer." See e.g.* Litvin, *supra* note 2616; Respondeat Superior Definition, *supra* footnote 1289.

2620 *Said v. Butt* [1920] 3 KB 497; *See* in: French, Mayson, and Ryan (2015), *supra* note 2321 at 639.

2621 *Standard Chartered Bank v. Pakistan National Shipping Corp* [2002] UKHL 43, [2003] 1 AC 959, (2002); *See* in: French, Mayson, and Ryan (2015), *supra* note 2321 at 641.

2622 *Standard Chartered Bank v. Pakistan National Shipping Corp* [2002] UKHL 43, [2003] 1 AC 959, *supra* note 2621 at 22.

2623 *Id.* at 34.

2624 *See* Wells (2000), *supra* note 2614 at 3.

2625 *See* French, Mayson, and Ryan (2015), *supra* note 2321 at 641.

be liable *"for offences requiring mens rea*[2626] *by application of the identification principle."*[2627] However, in the event that a company is vicariously liable for the tort of an employee, notwithstanding this, the agent or employee can also be sued.[2628]

The second theory of liability that has gained prevalence in recent years comprises the identification of a limited layer of senior officers within the company as its brains.[2629] This theory is called the identification theory. The thoughts behind this theory are that *"liability attaches only to persons who have requisite knowledge."*[2630] The leading case for that theory is *Tesco Supermarkets Ltd v. Nattrass,*[2631] in which, the Lord Justice stated

> Normally the board of directors, the managing director, and perhaps other superior officers of a company carry out the functions of management and speak and act as the company.[2632]

The House of Lords compared the vicarious liability with the identification principle as follows:

> The vicarious responsibility is very different from identification. There are some officers of a company who may for some purposes be identified with it, as being or having its directing mind and will, its centre and *ego,* and its brains.[2633]

However, in this case, the House of Lords held

> But here the board never delegated any part of their functions. The acts or omissions of shop managers were not acts of the company itself.[2634]

Therefore, this case restricts the application of the identification principle to the board of directors, the managing director, and other executive officers.[2635] In essence, the identification theory qualifies *"the acts and state of mind of those*

2626 Mens rea is *"an element of criminal responsibility, a guilty mind; a guilty or wrongful purpose; a criminal intent. Guilty knowledge and willfulness." See e.g., Mens Rea The Gale Group, Inc.,* MENS REA WEST'S ENCYCLOPEDIA OF AMERICAN LAW (2. ed. 2008).

2627 SFO GUIDANCE SFO, *supra* note 2612 at 4 para 17.

2628 *Standard Chartered Bank v. Pakistan National Shipping Corp* [2002] UKHL 43, [2003] 1 AC 959, *supra* note 2621.

2629 *See* Wells (2000), *supra* note 2614 at 3.

2630 *See* FRENCH, MAYSON, AND RYAN (2015), *supra* note 2321 at 642.

2631 *Tesco Supermarkets Ltd v Nattrass* [1971] 2 All ER 127, [1971] 2 WLR 1166, [1971] UKHL 1, 69 LGR 403, [1972] AC 153, 1 (1971).

2632 *Id.* at 4.

2633 *Id.* at 19.

2634 *Id.* at 7.

2635 *Tesco Supermarkets Ltd v. Nattrass* [1971] 2 ALL ER 127, [1971] 2 WLR 1166, [1971] UKHL 1, 69 LGR 403, [1972] AC 153, *supra* note 2631; *See* in: SFO GUIDANCE SFO, *supra* note 2612 at 4 para 18.

individuals who are part of the "directing mind and will" of the company."[2636] Hence, this theory includes two steps. At first, it *"identifies the perpetrator of the crime, and then asks whether he or she is a person who can be said to embody the company's mind and will."*[2637]

The third theory identifies the fault in the procedures, operating systems, or culture of a company by prosecuting corporate homicide offence.[2638] The application of this third theory depends on the nature of offence. In addition, there are other conditions limiting corporate liability *e.g.* the type of the offence and the sanction must be a fine.[2639] Rape, for example, is excluded.[2640]

However, legal scholars have held the distinction between these three theories to have less substance than it first appears.[2641] For example, in both vicarious and identification liability, the individual employee can be prosecuted, and in each case, the company can be liable only if the fault is found in one individual.[2642] However, the phrase "*directing mind and will*" has been interpreted in various ways.[2643] Hence, identification theory appears weak. Some argue that this theory is a restricted version of the vicarious liability theory.[2644] Even today, a wide-ranging academic debate on principles of company liability continues.[2645]

In practice, the SFO Guidance sets out the general principles for prosecuting companies, for corporate liability, and the identification principle.[2646] In the understanding of the SFO, the prosecution of a company is not a substitute for the prosecution of criminally liable individuals, such as directors, officers, or employees.[2647] If individuals are prosecuted, a possible liability of the company should also be considered.[2648] In the view of the SFO, the best practice is to prosecute all offenders

---

2636 ARCHBOLD 2010: FULL TEXT AND SUPPLEMENTS: CRIMINAL PLEADING, EVIDENCE AND PRACTICE, (James Richardson ed., Revised ed. 2009) para 30.

2637 *See* James Gobert, *Corporate criminality: four models of fault*, 14 LEGAL STUDIES 393–410, 395 (1994).

2638 *See* Wells (2000), *supra* note 2614 at 4.

2639 SFO GUIDANCE SFO, *supra* note 2612 at 3 para 11, 12.

2640 SFO GUIDANCE *Id.* at 3. para 12.

2641 *See* Wells (2000), *supra* note 2614 at 6.

2642 *Id.* at 6.

2643 THE LAW COMMISSION, CRIMINAL LIABILITY IN REGULATORY CONTEXT 104 (2010) para 5.81, [hereinafter THE LAW COMMISSION].

2644 *See* G. R. Sullivan, *The Attribution of Culpability to Limited Companies*, 55 THE CAMBRIDGE LAW JOURNAL 515 (1996).

2645 THE LAW COMMISSION, *supra* note 2643 at Ch. 5 Appendices A, B, and C by Black, Cartwright, and Wells.

2646 SERIOUS FRAUD OFFICE (SFO), GUIDANCE ON CORPORATE PROSECUTIONS (2009), [hereinafter SFO Guidance] https://www.skadden.com/eimages/Guidance_on_Corporate_Prosecutions.pdf (last visited Jul 25, 2016).

2647 SFO GUIDANCE *Id.* at 2. para 8.

2648 SFO GUIDANCE *Id.* at 2. para 8.

at the same time.[2649] The prosecution practice can be important for companies and their employees because the Law Commission provides that there were increasing numbers of criminal offences between 1989 and 2008.[2650]

In conclusion, the UK uses various theories for company liability for criminal offences. Ultimately, however, the general principle that a company can be prosecuted for a criminal offence has long been accepted and the courts have rarely applied the vicarious or identification doctrine.[2651] Similar to the situation in the US, it is well established that a company may be held vicariously liable for the crimes committed by its employees within the scope of their employment. The US courts read criminal statutes to impose liability on corporations under a theory on the doctrine of respondeat superior. However, nowadays, the DOJ pursues a new policy with a new approach of individual liability in matters of corporate wrongdoing.

5. Factors to be Considered when Charging Companies

In the UK, in accordance with the approach of the Director of Public Prosecution (DPP), the guidance provides a defense of adequate corporate procedures and factors, which are viewed with benevolence by the prosecutors and the English Courts.[2652] The DPP is a special agency that prosecutes corporate offenders.[2653] In 2009, the guidance of the DPP announced an enforcement of prosecution against corporate offenders in order to protect the public business practice and to increase the public confidence in the criminal justice system.[2654]

The guidance defines the term company as follows:

> A legal person, capable of being prosecuted, and should not be treated differently from individual because of its artificial personality.[2655]

2649 SFO GUIDANCE *Id.* at 2. para 9.

2650 THE LAW COMMISSION, *supra* note 2643 at 5 para 1.17. The Law Commission states that *"more than two and a half times as many pages were needed in Halsbury's Statutes to cover offences created in the 19 years between 1989 and 2008 than were needed to cover the offences created in the 637 years prior to that."*

2651 *See* Wells (2000), *supra* note 2614 at 10.

2652 *"The office (DPP) was created by the Prosecution of Offences Act 1985 and is appointed by the Attorney General."* SFO GUIDANCE SFO, *supra* note 2612; PROSECUTION OF OFFENCES ACT 1985, c. 23 (1985) § 2 (1); The Director of Public Prosecutions, INBRIEF.CO.UK, http://www.inbrief.co.uk/legal-system/director-of-public-prosecutions/ (last visited Sep 6, 2016), [hereinafter GUIDANCE ON CORPORATE PROSECUTION].

2653 GUIDANCE ON CORPORATE PROSECUTION, *supra* note 2652 at 1 para 3.

2654 GUIDANCE ON CORPORATE PROSECUTION *Id.* at 2. para 7.

2655 GUIDANCE ON CORPORATE PROSECUTION *Id.* at 1. para 4.

Legally, it means a company formed and registered under the Companies Act 2006, or its predecessors.[2656] In the UK, there are some public interest factors in charging companies that the prosecutor needs to consider. Given the prospect of a company's conviction, the prosecutor should balance the following factors: the loss of the company, the risk of harm to the public, the employees, the creditors, the shareholders, and detrimental effects on the confidence and stability of the financial market and international trade.[2657] Furthermore, *"the offending in other countries should be taken into account."*[2658] In conclusion, there are also public interest factors in the impact on the prosecutor's decision on whether to prosecute a company.[2659] Here too, the decision depends on the specific facts of each case.[2660]

Factors listed by the DPP as being taken into consideration against prosecution are enumerated as follows:[2661]

a) A seriously proactive approach by the corporate management team, which involves self-reporting and remedial actions,
b) A lack of previous offences in the company's history,
c) The existence of a seriously proactive and effective corporate compliance program,
d) The availability of other civil or regulatory appropriate alternative remedies,
e) It is an isolated offence by individuals like a director,
f) The prosecutor should consider the commercial consequences under European Law also.[2662]

These are the summarized factors against prosecution. However, the Guidance also lists factors in favor of prosecution, such as a history of similar conduct or an ineffective corporate compliance program at the relevant time.[2663] Therefore, the English Courts may take into account an effective corporate compliance program as a mitigating factor.[2664] However, the Guidance on corporate prosecution does not define the meaning of a *"proactive and effective"* compliance program. It seems that the wording has been adopted from the US Sentencing Guidelines Manual.[2665]

A search of criminal cases regarding the matter of compliance in the British and Irish Legal Information Institute case law database where individuals were convicted of fraudulent trading pursuant to Section 458 of the Companies Act

2656 Companies Act 2006, *supra* note 532 § 1(1).
2657 Guidance on Corporate Prosecution, *supra* note 2652 at 6 para 30.
2658 Guidance on Corporate Prosecution *Id.* at 7. para 30.
2659 Guidance on Corporate Prosecution *Id.* at 7. para 31.
2660 Guidance on Corporate Prosecution *Id.* at 7. para 32.
2661 Guidance on Corporate Prosecution *Id.* at 8 to 9. para 32 a. to h.
2662 Guidance on Corporate Prosecution *Id.* at 8 to 9. para 32 a. to h.
2663 Guidance on Corporate Prosecution *Id.* at 7 to 8. para 32 a. to f.
2664 *See infra* III., 3., p. 424.
2665 US Sentencing Guidelines Manual, *supra* note 49 Chapter 8, § 8B2.1.

1985 Section or Section 993 of the Companies Act 2006 found seventeen cases between 2006 and 2016. In one case, *Ravjani & Ors, R. v.*, the Court of Appeal considered the compliance procedure within a company.[2666] The financial director and qualified accountant of the group of companies, who had influence and importance in the companies, was convicted of conspiracy to cheat the public revenue and was sentenced to 11 years' imprisonment.[2667] The director concerned changed the compliance procedures, which deviated markedly from the lawful procedures in place before his arrival.[2668] The court concluded that his role in authorizing many fictitious changes was pure *"window dressing."*[2669] However, this term also appears to have been adopted from the American literature.[2670] In conclusion, the corporate compliance program needs to be more than a symbolic gesture or formal compliance structure; it should comprise a set of well-drafted supervisory procedures to ensure that the company and all its employees comply with the applicable law, rules, and codes within UK companies.

6. Compliance in English Company Law

Following an examination of English Company Law, it is clear that one of the major results of the company law reform process was the codification of the principles underpinning directors' duties under the common law.[2671] Companies, their directors, and officers are subject to the diverse range of compliance obligations under Company Law and personal liability.[2672] Hence, the reform considered responsible corporate behavior in the 21st century and recognized *"the trend of the courts in recent years by expecting higher standards of skills and care from company directors."*[2673] Nevertheless, the new Companies Act 2006 and the codified directors' duties have not yet been the subject of any legal guidance from the English Courts.[2674]

2666 *Ravjani & Ors, R. v.* [2012] EWCA Crim 2519, (2012), https://www.bailii.org/ (last visited Sep. 12, 2016).

2667 *Id.* at 3.

2668 *Id.* at 33.

2669 *Id.* at 33.

2670 *See e.g.* Baer (2009), *supra* note 586 at 952; Beale (2014), *supra* note 1097 at 20; Erickson (2010), *supra* note 1954 at 1824; Weber and Wasieleski (2013), *supra* note 492 at 610.

2671 *See* Davies (2007), *supra* note 2488 at 28 para 6.1.

2672 *Id.* at 104. para 12.11.

2673 *Id.* at 8. para 1.3.

2674 David Chivers, The Companies Act 2006: Directors' Duties Guidance 4 (2007), http://corporate-responsibility.org/wp-content/uploads/2013/11/directors_guidance_final.pdf (last visited Sep 14, 2016). [hereinafter Directors' Duties Guidance].

Pursuant to English Company Law, compliance means ensuring adherence with the provisions on the administration of company affairs.[2675] These provisions also include disclosure requirements *e.g.* duty to prepare a directors report.[2676] In essence, directors, company officers, managers, secretaries, and any person who is to be treated as an officer of the company, are liable when they authorize, participate in, permit, or fail to take active steps to prevent a default pursuant to the Companies Acts.[2677] Section 1121 of the CA 2006 comprises a broad category of persons acting on behalf of the company, who are charged with compliance to the Act. They must ensure that all of their decisions are taken in accordance with the Act.[2678] Therefore, they should have in place a proper procedure.[2679] A directors' guidance recommends submitting those procedures for review to the board on an annual basis and reporting immediately any departure from or failure in the agreed procedures.[2680] On the other hand, the board should ensure that directors have a proper flow of information in order to comply with their statutory duties.[2681]

Additionally, the CLRG argues

> that the requirement to employ a company secretary ensures that there is at least one company officer who focuses on legal requirements, thus improving compliance and reducing risk of penalty.[2682]

However, there is no requirement to employ a compliance officer under English Company Law. It appears that the company secretary should carry out compliance tasks. The Guidance recommends that the company secretary, or other designated person, should report directly to the chief executive.[2683] Finally, the Guidance argues that an appropriate reporting procedure should pass vertically through corporate structures.[2684]

7. Comparison between UK and US Compliance under Corporation Law

English Company Law is centralized and regulated in detail. The English Parliament implemented changes to substantive company law in England to strengthen the government's ability to combat corporate crime and to institute

---

2675 *See* Davies (2007), *supra* note 2488 at 8 para 1.6.
2676 Companies Act 2006, *supra* note 532, § 418 - Disclosure to auditors.
2677 *Id.*§ 1121 (2)(a)(b).
2678 Directors' Duties Guidance Chivers, *supra* note 2674 at 4.
2679 Directors' Duties Guidance *Id.* at 16.
2680 Directors' Duties Guidance *Id.* at 16.
2681 Directors' Duties Guidance *Id.* at 18.
2682 Company Law Reform Corporate Law and Governance Directorate and Department of Trade and Industry, *supra* note 2335 at 279.
2683 Directors' Duties Guidance Chivers, *supra* note 2674 at 16.
2684 Directors' Duties Guidance *Id.* at 19.

corporate reforms.[2685] In the US, the legislator passed various federal statutes, such as the FCPA and the SOX, to prosecute corporate offences.[2686] Therefore, the evidence highlights that there is a need for a centralized legal framework to deal with corporate compliance.

In the last ten years, the UK has introduced reforms to allow the Secretary of State to direct the company to comply with the provisions of the CA 2006. Failure to do so constitutes an offence, and failure on the part of the officers in default who have been implicated in breaches of duty and breaches of legislation. The English legislator codified directors' duties and also applied the same duties to the company officers. Similar to the US, UK company directors are considered to be fiduciaries. Their fiduciary duties were developed by the courts through common law and equitable principles. The US State Courts, especially the Delaware Court, developed a compliance or oversight duty of directors. Under Delaware law, directors are duty bound to monitor delegated activities.[2687] It must be considered that personal liability for a breach of such duty could arise if an internal corporate control system has not been put in place.[2688] Hence, the responsibilities of directors and officers in terms of delegated oversight and monitoring could be seen to have been discharged if an internal control system is implemented under the *Caremark* standard.[2689] In contrast to the UK, the common law and equitable principles with regard to directors' duties have not hitherto been codified in US State Corporation Law. In the US, it appears that, nowadays, compliance is influenced more by common law rules, federal law and by the efforts of prosecutors. In the UK, compliance is effected to a greater degree through legislation, with the support of prosecutors. Nevertheless, neither US State Corporation Law and English Company Law explicitly require companies to employ a compliance officer or to establish a compliance program.

Overall, it seems that there are no fundamental differences between the general legal framework of corporate liability culpability in both the US and the UK.[2690] The US courts apply an expansive theory of corporate criminal liability according to current federal law; simultaneously, the English Courts are hesitant to impose liability on companies for the acts of employees.[2691] Although the two legal systems retain differences in the scope of liability *e.g.* various theories of company liability,

---

2685 *See supra* II, pp. 327 et seq.

2686 *See supra* A., I., pp. 171 et seq.

2687 *See* Chiu (2015), *supra* note 2320 at 234.

2688 *Id.* at 234.

2689 *In re Caremark International Inc. Derivative Litigation,* 698 A.2d 959 (Del. Ch. 1996), *supra* note 21; *See* in: Chiu (2015), *supra* note 2320 at 234.

2690 *Compare* A., II., pp. 254 et seq.; II, 4. pp. 343 et seq.; *See also* Jessica de Grazia, Review of the Serious Fraud Office 2 (2008), http://library.college.police.uk/docs/JdeGrazia-Final-Review-of-SFO.pdf (last visited Jul 29, 2016); Djilani (2011), *supra* note 62 at 306.

2691 *See* Djilani (2011), *supra* note 62 at 308.

over the last ten years, UK Parliament has passed new legislation broadening and codifying the scope of liability for companies and for directors' duties.[2692] In conclusion, it appears that English Law attempts to restrict company criminal liability unless the highest level of management is involved in and responsible for the wrongdoing.

III. The Enforcement of Compliance in the UK - The Bribery Act 2010

New legislation in the form of the introduction of the United Kingdom Bribery Act (UKBA) 2010, an item of anti-corruption legislation with significant jurisdictional reach, met with considerable international interest.[2693] The Act applies to the entire United Kingdom of Great Britain: England, Scotland, Wales and Northern Ireland.[2694] In addition, this Act has an *"expansive jurisdictional reach"* and is more far-reaching than the US Foreign Corrupt Practices Act of 1977.[2695] The UK Bribery Act 2010 entered into force on July 1, 2011.[2696]

Also Courts based on English law confirmed that

> Bribery is an evil practice which threatens the foundations of any civilised society.[2697]

The bribery legislation reform was not introduced to echo the US bribery legislation, but in response to criticism for failing to adequately implement the OECD Convention on Combating Bribery of Foreign Officials in International Business Transactions.[2698] In 2005, the lead examiners of the Working Group on Bribery recommended that the UK should enact legislation on bribery that clearly included bribery of a foreign public official, because "*the absence of specific case law on the*

2692 *Id.* at 306.

2693 Marcus Sohlberg, The United Kingdom Bribery Act 2010 | Law Library of Congress, https://www.loc.gov/law/help/uk-bribery-act.php#introduction (last visited Sep 24, 2016); United Kingdom Bribery Act 2010, *supra* note 433. The Act received Royal Assent on 8 April 2010.

2694 United Kingdom Bribery Act 2010, *supra* note 433 Explanatory Notes, Territorial Extent.

2695 *Id.*§ 12 (5) "*An offence is committed under section 7 irrespective of whether the acts or omissions which form part of the offence take place in the United Kingdom or elsewhere.*" *See also* Sohlberg, *supra* note 2693; Ernst & Young (2011), *supra* note 861 at 1.

2696 *See* Djilani (2011), *supra* note 62; Koehler (2012), *supra* note 958 at 636; Sohlberg, *supra* note 2693.

2697 *See e.g. AG for Hong Kong v. Reid* [1993] UKPC 2, Privy Council Appeal No. 44 of 1992 (1993).

2698 OECD, Convention on Combating Bribery of Foreign Public Officials in International Business Transactions (2011), http://www.oecd.org/daf/anti-bribery/ConvCombatBribery_ENG.pdf (last visited Sep 25, 2016); *See* in: Sohlberg, *supra* note 2693.

bribery of foreign public officials makes it difficult to evaluate how effectively the current system works."[2699] Nevertheless, bribery before the UKBA was also subject to the pre-existing law, specifically the Prevention of Corruption Act 1906, which was repealed in 2010. As a result of the new Act, the Working Group recognized that major English companies have taken important steps to adopt compliance programs to prevent bribery amongst their employees and agents abroad, but recommended that increased efforts to prevent bribery should be undertaken among SME's.[2700]

Currently, the new Bribery Act has two main objectives: Firstly, effectively to prevent the increasing use of bribery and secondly, to make it easier to prosecute bribery by individuals and companies.[2701] Under the Criminal Justice Act 1987, the Serious Fraud Office (SFO) was constituted for England and Wales and Northern Ireland.[2702] The Attorney General appoints the Director of the SFO.[2703] The Director has the power to investigate serious or complex fraud.[2704] The amendments of Schedule 1 of the Bribery Act state the "*pre-investigation powers in relation to bribery and corruption: foreign officers*" of the Director of the SFO in terms of an offence under Sections 1 or 2 of the Act.[2705] Hence, the SFO also enforces the Act internationally.[2706] The SFO could be seen as the UK "*counterpart*" to the DOJ in the US.[2707] In 2011, the SFO and the UK Crown Prosecution Service published final guidance on prosecuting under the Bribery Act, which English and foreign companies should consider seriously.[2708] This Guidance provides procedures which companies can put into place to prevent bribery.[2709] The following sections will examine these procedures alongside the six Guidance principles and the key provisions of the Bribery Act.

2699 Directorate for Financial and Enterprise Affairs OECD, Report on the Application of the Convention on Combating Bribery of Foreign Public Officials in International Business Transactions and the 1997 Recommendation on Combating Bribery in International Business Transactions 14 (2005) para 15 and 43; *See* in: Sohlberg, *supra* note 2693.
2700 OECD, *supra* note 2698 at 15 para 43.
2701 *See* Sohlberg, *supra* note 2693.
2702 Criminal Justice Act 1987, c. 38 (1987) § 1 (1).
2703 *Id.*§ 1 (2).
2704 *Id.*§ 1 (3).
2705 United Kingdom Bribery Act 2010, *supra* note 433 Schedule 1, Consequential Amendments.
2706 Ernst & Young (2011), *supra* note 861 at 1.
2707 *See* Djilani (2011), *supra* note 62 at 303.
2708 The Bribery Guidance, *supra* note 860; Sohlberg, *supra* note 2693.
2709 The Bribery Guidance, *supra* note 860.

1. The Key Provisions of the UKBA 2010

The Act includes four main provisions in terms of criminal offences such as bribing another person (active bribery) or receiving a bribe (passive bribery); bribing foreign officials; and company liability for failing to prevent bribery.[2710] Section 1 clearly defines the criminal offence of bribery of another person as: *"it applies to the person who offers, promises or gives a financial or other advantage to another."*[2711]

The Commentary states that the meaning of financial or other advantage is left to be determined by the courts.[2712] The Section distinguishes two cases: Case one concerns the situation when a person intends the advantage to induce or to reward a person to perform and for the performance of an improper relevant function or activity.[2713] Case two applies where the person offering the bribe knows or believes that the acceptance of the advantage would itself constitute the improper performance.[2714] The term improper performance is defined in Sections 3, 4 and 5 of the Act.[2715] In brief, it means performance which amounts to a breach of an expectation that a person will act in good faith.[2716] The Guidance provides one example under Section 1 where hospitality is not intended as a bribe:

> An invitation to foreign clients to attend a Six Nations match at Twickenham as part of a public relations exercise designed to cement good relations or enhance knowledge in the organisation's field is extremely unlikely to engage Section 1 as there is unlikely to be evidence of an intention to induce improper performance of a relevant function.[2717]

However, it is irrelevant whether the advantage is offered, promised or given by the person directly or through a third party.[2718]

In addition, Section 2 lists further instances, namely Case three to Case six, in which a person could be guilty of an offence, when receiving a bribe.[2719] Cases three, four and five require that the person *"requests, agrees to receive or accepts"* an advantage, whether or not the person actually receives it.[2720] Cases three, four, and five consider three forms of improper performance. The English Courts will have jurisdiction over offences set forth in Section 1 and 2 committed in any part of the UK, but they will also have jurisdiction over offences when the person

2710 *See* United Kingdom Bribery Act 2010, *supra* note 433, §§ 1, 2, 6, 7.
2711 *Id.* § 1 (2) (a), Commentary on Sections.
2712 *Id.* Commentary on Section 1.
2713 *Id.* § 1 (2) (a) (b) (i)(ii), Commentary on Section 1.
2714 *Id.* § 1 (3) (a) (b), Commentary on Section 1.
2715 *Id.* §§ 3, 4, 5.
2716 *See especially Id.* § 4 (1) (a) (b).
2717 The Bribery Guidance, *supra* note 860 at 10 para 20.
2718 United Kingdom Bribery Act 2010, *supra* note 433 § 1 (5).
2719 *Id.* § 2 (1) - (5).
2720 *Id.* § 2 (2) - (5), Commentary on Section 2.

commmitted the offence outside the United Kingdom and has a close connection with the United Kingdom.[2721]

Section 6 defines a specific, standalone, or separate criminal offence of bribery of a foreign public official, where the person intended to obtain or retain business, or an advantage in the conduct of business, and the person offers, promises or gives any financial or other advantage to another person.[2722] The term foreign public official is defined in Subsection 5 as an individual who holds a legislative, administrative or judicial position of any kind of a country or territory outside the UK and *"exercises a public function, or is an official or agent of a public international organization"* such as the UN or the World Bank.[2723] Legal scholars have criticized the far-reaching scope of this definition. They contend that the broad definition of the term results in uncertainty regarding interpretations.[2724] In this broader definition, the senior management of private companies whose shares are owned primarily by foreign governments could also be included.[2725] Finally, the recommendation is that UK companies should be alert when dealing with companies in foreign countries.[2726]

Section 6 contains two elements of the offence, a conduct element and a fault element.[2727] The conduct is set forth in Subsection 3.[2728] This Subsection states that this kind of bribery is committed when the person

> offers, promises or gives any advantage to a foreign public official, and the written law applicable to the foreign public official neither permits nor requires the foreign public official to be influenced in his or her capacity as a foreign public official.[2729]

The term written law is defined as the law of the relevant part of the UK, or the law of the country or territory in terms of which the foreign public official is hold his office.[2730] Subsections 1, 2 and 4 determine the fault element of the offence.[2731] They describe what a person must intend in order to commit the offence.[2732] In essence, the fault element includes influence on the performance of the foreign

2721 *Id.*§ 12 (1) (2) (a)-(c); The Bribery Guidance, *supra* note 860 at 9 para 15.
2722 United Kingdom Bribery Act 2010, *supra* note 433, § 6 (1) (2)(3).
2723 *Id.*§ 6 (5) (a)(b)(c), (6); The Bribery Guidance, *supra* note 860 at 11 para 22.
2724 Gordon Belch, An Analysis of the Efficacy of the Bribery Act 2010 6 (2014), https://www.abdn.ac.uk/law/documents/An_Analysis_of_the_Efficacy_of_the_Bribery_Act_2010.pdf (last visited Oct 4, 2016).
2725 *Id.* at 6.
2726 *Id.* at 6.
2727 United Kingdom Bribery Act 2010, *supra* note 433 § 6.
2728 United Kingdom Bribery Act 2010, *supra* note 433 § 6, Commentary on Section 6.
2729 *Id.*§ 6 (3), Commentary on Section 6.
2730 *Id.* § 6 (7) (a) (c), Commentary on Section 6.
2731 *Id.* § 6 (1) (2)(4).
2732 *Id.* § 6 (1) (2) (4), Commentary on Section 6.

public official in order to obtain or retain business or an advantage in the conduct of business.[2733] The term business includes what is done in the course of a trade or profession.[2734] In addition, the Guidance outlines that *e.g.* bona fide corporate hospitality and promotional activities intended to improve the image of the company or to present products and services of the company are recognized as a part of doing business.[2735] However, there is another critical discussion on which hospitality may be considered as a bribe by the SFO.[2736] The difficult question that arises in this context is where the SFO and the courts will draw the line between criminal and legitimate hospitality.[2737]

However, companies are invited and able to prevent bribery. Section 7 introduces a corporate defense, which entails proving that the company *"had in place adequate procedures"* designed to prevent bribery.[2738] While the Act does not itself define these adequate procedures the Bribery Guidance of the Secretary of State outlines which procedures will be recognized as adequate.[2739] Section 7 seems to be the most problematic section of the UKBA 2010 with regard to the definition of the terms relevant commercial organization and associated person.[2740] Section 7 sets forth that

> A relevant commercial organization ("C") is guilty of an offence under this section if a person ("A") associated with C bribes another person.[2741]

A relevant commercial organization is defined in Section 7(5)

> (a) a body which is incorporated under the law of any part of the United Kingdom and which carries on a business (whether there or elsewhere), or
> (b) any other body corporate (wherever incorporated) which carries on a business, or part of a business, in any part of the United Kingdom.[2742]

Therefore, a relevant commercial organization also includes all international corporations within the private and financial services sector, which are involved in business in the UK or when they have some business presence in the UK.[2743] Hence, this definition and the UKBA 2010 have a more far-reaching territorial application

---

2733 *Id.* § 6 (1) (2) (4), Commentary on Section 6.
2734 *Id.* § 6 (8), Commentary on Section 6.
2735 The Bribery Guidance, *supra* note 860 at 12 para 26.
2736 *See* Belch, *supra* note 2724 at 7.
2737 *Id.* at 7.
2738 United Kingdom Bribery Act 2010, *supra* note 433, § 7 (2).
2739 The Bribery Guidance, *supra* note 860 at 20, The Six Principles which will explain below.
2740 United Kingdom Bribery Act 2010, *supra* note 433, § 7 (1); Belch, *supra* note 2724 at 8.
2741 United Kingdom Bribery Act 2010, *supra* note 433, § 7 (1).
2742 United Kingdom Bribery Act 2010, *supra* note 433, § 7 (5) (a) (b).
2743 *See* Belch, *supra* note 2724 at 8; Sohlberg, *supra* note 2693.

than the US Foreign Corrupt Practices Act of 1977.[2744] Belch sets out an example, *"a Dutch business with retail outlets in the UK, which pays bribes in France could in theory face prosecution in the UK."*[2745] In addition, the Guidance refers to the courts as the final arbiter.[2746] They have to consider, based on the particular facts in each individual case, whether an organization does indeed *"carry on a business"* in the UK.[2747]

Furthermore, a commercial organization could be liable under Section 7 if a person associated with it bribes another person.[2748] The meaning of an associated person is defined in Section 8.[2749] It provides that a person is associated with the organization where the person performs services for, or on behalf of the organization. Accordingly, the person could be, for example, the organization's employee, agent, or subsidiary.[2750] The concept of an associated person is also broad in scope because it includes the whole range of persons, even other contractual partners like contractors, consultants, or suppliers, who are connected to an organization.[2751] However, there is no guidance about the degree of this connection to the organization.[2752] Hence, the term associated person appears somewhat of imponderability for companies. In conclusion, it is essential for companies to initiate correct due diligence and keep records on any associated persons who are engaged with the company.[2753]

For this purpose, the Guidance sets out six principles on the required *"adequate procedures"*, which are flexible and outcome-focused, to reflect the huge variety of circumstances and all kinds of sizes of companies.[2754] First, the procedures should be "*proportionate*" to the bribery risks that the organization faces.[2755] The Guidance provides the meaning of the term proportionate. The company should first and foremost consider a risk assessment.[2756] The identified risks will be linked to the size of the company, and the nature and complexity of its business.[2757] The second principle requires a top-level commitment to the determination of bribery prevention procedures.[2758] This commitment should include an internal and external

---

2744 *See* Sohlberg, *supra* note 2693.
2745 *See* Belch, *supra* note 2724 at 8.
2746 The Bribery Guidance, *supra* note 860 at 15 para 34.
2747 The Bribery Guidance *Id.* at 15. para 34; United Kingdom Bribery Act 2010, *supra* note 433, § 7 (5) (a) (b).
2748 The Bribery Guidance, *supra* note 860 at 16 para 37.
2749 United Kingdom Bribery Act 2010, *supra* note 433, § 8 (1).
2750 *Id.* § 8 (1) (3).
2751 The Bribery Guidance, *supra* note 860 at 16 para 38, 39.
2752 *See* Belch, *supra* note 2724 at 8.
2753 *Id.* at 8.
2754 The Bribery Guidance, *supra* note 860 at 20.
2755 *Id.* at 21. Principle 1.
2756 *Id.* at 21. Principle 1.
2757 *Id.* at 21. Principle 1.
2758 *Id.* at 23. Principle 2.

communication of the company's anti-bribery stance, and an appropriate degree of involvement of the top-level management in this matter.[2759] Principle three sets out the nature of the company's risk assessment in detail.[2760] The assessment should be periodic, informed and documented.[2761] It also includes the oversight of the risk assessment by top-level management.[2762] Furthermore, the risk assessment should include a due diligence by internal or external experts in order to prevent bribery.[2763] Principle five provides that the bribery prevention communication should pervade completely throughout the whole company including, training in the company's bribery prevention policies and procedures for all employees, and associated persons.[2764] Finally, the last Principle sets out that the company has to review and monitor periodically its bribery prevention procedures and adapt them where necessary under changed circumstances.[2765]

The courts have serious concerns regarding the Bribery Act, although in a recently decided case, *R v. Innospec Ltd*, the Lord Justice stated:

> There can be no doubt that corruption of foreign government officials or foreign government ministers is at the top end of serious corporate offending both in terms of culpability and harm. It is deliberate and intentional wrongdoing. It causes serious harm.[2766]

A UK company and a wholly-owned subsidiary of a Delaware company, pleaded guilty to making corrupt payments to public officials of the Government of Indonesia in order to secure contracts.[2767] The Crown Court at Southwark had to consider two issues: (1) the level of criminality in the offence of corruption of a foreign government, and (2) the way in which a prosecutor, the SFO, and a court should approach sentencing.[2768] There is a draft agreement between the company and the SFO with respect to compliance, monitoring, and the appointment of a compliance monitor.[2769] In the US, the company also made a plea agreement on compliance and monitoring.[2770] The management of the company has changed and the company has put in place an enhanced compliance program.[2771] Ultimately, the

---

2759 *Id.* at 23. Principle 2.
2760 *Id.* at 25. Principle 3.
2761 *Id.* at 25. Principle 3.
2762 *Id.* at 25. Principle 3.
2763 *Id.* at 27. Principle 4.
2764 *Id.* at 29. Principle 5.
2765 *Id.* at 31. Principle 6.
2766 *R v. Innospec Ltd* [2010] EW Misc 7 (EWCC), 30 (2010); *See* in: Sohlberg, *supra* note 2693.
2767 *R v. Innospec Ltd* [2010] EW Misc 7 (EWCC), *supra* note 2766 at 1.
2768 *Id.* at 2.
2769 *Id.* at 17.
2770 *Id.* at 20.
2771 *Id.* at 40.

Court approved this agreement, but simultaneously emphasized clearly that there will be no precedent for the future.[2772] The company was fined $12.7m.[2773]

Overall, Section 7 of the new Act is especially important for compliance managers for two reasons. First, the legal scope is substantially different from the FCPA, meaning that companies subject to both the FCPA and the Bribery Act must adjust their anti-bribery and compliance programs accordingly.[2774] Secondly, unlike the FCPA, the Bribery Act provides an affirmative defense for companies with adequate procedures designed to prevent bribery and a compliance program.[2775] In conclusion, the UKBA 2010 established a far-reaching anti-bribery legislation not only in the UK, but also for the rest of the world. Despite the Guidance issued by the Ministry of Justice uncertainty regarding interpretation of some terms still remains. In response to these uncertainties, companies are required to establish stringent procedures such as a compliance policy and program to minimize their risk of incurring criminal liability for corrupt behaviors under the UKBA.

2. Prosecution under the UKBA 2010

Similar to the US, in the UK there are also specific agencies to investigate and prosecute *e.g.* serious or complex fraud, bribery, money laundering and corruption by corporate offenders under the statutory framework.[2776] One such body is the Serious Fraud Office (SFO), which was constituted under the Criminal Justice Act (CJA) 1987 and established in 1988.[2777] The SFO is a law enforcement agency, not a regulator, and deals with large economic crime cases.[2778] As a result, since 2008 the SFO has undergone extensive structural changes and amendments to its procedures for dealing with corporate wrongdoers.[2779] Further, introduced in 2008, Section 2A of the CJA 1987 enables the director of the SFO to exercise his powers *"before a formal investigation has begun relating to overseas bribery and corruption*

2772 *Id.* at 48.

2773 *Id.* at 47.

2774 *See* McGreal (2011), *supra* note 495 at 147; Richard (2014), *supra* note 554 at 421.

2775 *Id.* at 147; The Bribery Guidance, *supra* note 860 at 20–31; United Kingdom Bribery Act 2010, *supra* note 433, § 7 (2).

2776 SFO GUIDANCE SFO, *supra* note 2612.

2777 Criminal Justice Act 1987, *supra* note 2702 § 1 (1). The SFO describes itself as a *"small independent non-ministerial Government department under the superintendence of the Attorney General." See in* SFO, Annual Report and Accounts 2015–2016 (2016), https://www.sfo.gov.uk/publications/ (last visited Jul 27, 2016) [hereinafter SFO Report].

2778 Alun Milford, Speech to compliance professionals | SFO General Counsel (2016), https://www.sfo.gov.uk/2016/03/29/speech-compliance-professionals/ (last visited Jul 28, 2016) [hereinafter SFO Speech].

2779 *See* Djilani (2011), *supra* note 62 at 314.

cases."[2780] Therefore, the SFO is the lead agency in England, Wales and Northern Ireland concerning the investigation and prosecution of corruption.[2781] Prosecution under the Act in England, Wales and Northern Ireland can only be brought with the consent of the Director of the SFO.[2782]

However, relief from the offence of bribery is on the balance of probabilities.[2783] It is a matter for the courts, on a case by case basis, to decide whether a procedure is adequate within a relevant commercial organization.[2784] For example, a single offence does not necessarily mean that the anti-bribery procedure is inadequate.[2785] The court and the prosecutor will consider when an employee acts willfully and knowingly contrary to a well-implemented procedure or instructions within the company.[2786]

The penalties under Sections 1, 2 or 6 of the Bribery Act for an individual could be a fine or imprisonment for up to ten years, or both.[2787] An offence under Sections 1, 2 or 6 committed by a person other than an individual is punishable by a fine up to the statutory maximum, currently £5,000 in England, Wales or Northern Ireland.[2788] On indictment, the maximum penalty could be an unlimited fine with collateral consequences, such as director disqualification and asset confiscation for companies.[2789]

To summarize, there are two uncertainties in terms of the UKBA 2010, namely the interpretation of certain terms and, secondly, the penalties that companies face when they have committed an offence under the Act. To clarify these points, the next section will examine the cases, including the SFO cases, which the courts have decided in relation to the UKBA 2010 to date.

3. Bribery Cases and Actions under the UKBA 2010

The Guidance of the SFO provides whether the defense of adequate procedures will be a matter for the courts to decide on a case by case basis.[2790] The prosecutors

2780 Criminal Justice Act 1987, *supra* note 2702 § 2 (1A); SFO, SFO historical background and powers Serious Fraud Office, https://www.sfo.gov.uk/publications/corporate-information/sfo-historical-background-powers/ (last visited Jul 29, 2016).

2781 *See* Belch, *supra* note 2724 at 5.

2782 United Kingdom Bribery Act 2010, *supra* note 433 § 10 (1) (b), (2) (b), Commentary on Section 10.

2783 Bribery Act Guidance, *supra* note 2818 at 10.

2784 Bribery Act Guidance *Id.* at 10.

2785 Bribery Act Guidance *Id.* at 10.

2786 Bribery Act Guidance *Id.* at 10.

2787 United Kingdom Bribery Act 2010, *supra* note 433 § 11 (1) (a) (b).

2788 *Id.* § 11 (2) (a) (b), Commentary on Section 11.

2789 *See* Sohlberg, *supra* note 2693; United Kingdom Bribery Act 2010, *supra* note 433 § 11 Commentary on Section 11.

2790 SFO Guidance SFO, *supra* note 2612 at 10.

also have to evaluate carefully all the circumstances, including the adequacy of any anti-bribery procedures.[2791]

Since the enactment of the UKBA in 2011, there have been some cases in which an individual was found guilty of taking bribes[2792] or was guilty of bribing another person.[2793] The first prosecution and conviction of an individual under the Bribery Act 2010 was a court clerk, who works at a Magistrates' Court.[2794] He was found guilty of taking bribes to systematically alter driving offence records.[2795] This activity provided a lucrative second income.[2796] Two further cases involving British individuals attempting to bribe another person resulted in prison sentences.[2797] In the course of the last five years, there were also some cases relating to corporate offences under the Bribery Act 2010 and its predecessor, the Corruption Act 1906.[2798] Although the new Bribery Act entered into force in 2011, there are still cases under the Corruption Act 1906 that have not yet been decided. One such case is the prosecution of suspected offences of bribery of foreign public officials and misconduct in the execution of administrative duties, corruption, false accounting, and money laundering within a large Company Group.[2799] The investigation of bribery at the Company's Group was considered in the case *Burgin & Anor v Commission of Police* in which the Holding Ltd and the Director of the Serious Fraud Office took part as interested parties.[2800] The Company Group has approximately 80,000 employees worldwide and about 30 trading locations in the UK employing more than 4,000 people.[2801] A great number of the Company Group are registered in the UK, in London.[2802] It is expected that the payment of bribery involving this company has an excess of €90 million in the UK and approximately €1.7 million in Switzerland.[2803] The investigation focused on the activities of seven

2791 SFO GUIDANCE *Id.* at 10.
2792 UNITED KINGDOM BRIBERY ACT 2010, *supra* note 433 § 2.
2793 *Id.*§ 1.
2794 *R v. Patel* [2012] EWCA Crim 1243.
2795 *See* BELCH, *supra* note 2724 at 9.
2796 *Id.* at 9.
2797 *Id.* at 9–10.; UNITED KINGDOM BRIBERY ACT 2010, *supra* note 433 § 1.
2798 *See e.g. McKenzie, R v. Director of the SFO* [2016] EWHC 102, CO/4888/2015 (2016); *Soma Oil And Gas Ltd, R v. Director of the SFO* [2016] EWHC 2471, (2016); *Tchenguiz & Anor v. Director of the Serious Fraud Office* [2014] EWHC 1315, (2014); *UBS AG (London Branch) & Anor v. Kommunale Wasserwerke Leipzig GMBH* [2014] EWHC 3615, 2010 Folio 505 (2014); *West & Anor, R v.* [2016] EWCA Crim 742, 201500057 B5 (2016), https://www.bailii.org/ (last visited Aug. 23, 2016).
2799 *See in Burgin & Anor v Commission of Police for the Metropolis & Ors* [2011] EWHC 1835, CO/5723/2010, CO/6227/2010, 4 (2011).
2800 *Burgin & Anor v Commission of Police for the Metropolis & Ors* [2011] EWHC 1835, *supra* note 2793.
2801 *Id.* at 6–7.
2802 *Id.* at 7.
2803 *Id.* at 100.

individuals, who are company executives, and two companies of this company Group.[2804] The offences relate to transport projects in India, Poland, and Tunisia.[2805] While the offences were already committed between August 2000 and August 2006, the trial is only set to commence only at Southwark Crown Court in 2017.[2806] There is another company that has been under criminal investigation by the SFO since 2014.[2807] It is clear that investigations into bribery take considerable time due to the complex nature of the documentary evidence.[2808]

Nevertheless, the first corporate prosecution under the UKBA 2010 was the conviction of fraudulent trading and bribery of three former directors of the Company Group following an investigation by the Serious Fraud Office in December 2014.[2809] It was determined in the course of the investigation of the Sustainable Growth Group that the directors also committed criminal acts contrary to Section 2 (1) and (2) of the Bribery Act 2010.[2810] Finally, in December 2014, they were convicted of offences of bribery at the Crown Court at Southwark.[2811] The defendants were sentenced to several years imprisonment, disqualified from being a company director, and were ordered to pay a confiscation order.[2812] Their appeal against both conviction and sentence was dismissed in March 2016 at the Royal Courts of Justice.[2813]

The practice of the SFO in the course of criminal prosecution was reviewed in the case *McKenzie, R v. Director of the Serious Fraud Office.*[2814] In June 2015, the director of a company was arrested on suspicion of committing an offence contrary to Section 1 of the UKBA 2010.[2815] A number of electronic devices, an USB stick, a

---

2804 SFO, Alstom Network UK Ltd *&* Alstom Power Ltd Serious Fraud Office (2015), https://www.sfo.gov.uk/cases/alstom-network-uk-ltd-alstom-power-ltd/ (last visited Oct 23, 2016).

2805 *Id.*

2806 *Id.*

2807 SFO, SFO opens investigation into Solar Energy Savings Limited Serious Fraud Office (2014), https://www.sfo.gov.uk/2014/12/05/sfo-opens-investigation-solar-energy-savings-limited/ (last visited Oct 26, 2016).

2808 *See* Belch, *supra* note 2724 at 10.

2809 *See* Companies Act 2006, *supra* note 532 § 993 Offence of fraudulent trading; United Kingdom Bribery Act 2010, *supra* note 433 § 2; Belch, *supra* note 2724 at 10; SFO, Sustainable Agroenergy Plc and Sustainable Wealth Investments UK Ltd Serious Fraud Office, https://www.sfo.gov.uk/cases/sustainable-agroenergy-plc-sustainable-wealth-investments-uk-ltd/ (last visited Oct 23, 2016).

2810 SFO, *supra* note 2803; United Kingdom Bribery Act 2010, *supra* note 433 § 2 (1) (2).

2811 *West & Anor, R v.* [2016] EWCA Crim 742, *supra* note 2798 at 1–3.

2812 SFO, *supra* note 2803; *West & Anor, R v.* [2016] EWCA Crim 742, *supra* note 2798 at 1–3.

2813 *West & Anor, R v.* [2016] EWCA Crim 742, *supra* note 2798 at 69.

2814 *McKenzie, R v. Director of the SFO* [2016] EWHC 102, *supra* note 2798.

2815 *Id.* at 5.

mobile telephone, and a laptop were seized from him.[2816] In this case, the director as the claimant submits the proposition that the approach of the SFO was unlawful in the course of the investigation because the SFO dealt with material potentially subject to legal professional privilege which was embedded in the seized electronic devices.[2817] Hence, it could be that the defendant, the SFO, could use this material to the claimants' disadvantage.[2818] However, the Court decided to dismiss this proposition and thus, the claim that the preliminary review of electronic material must be conducted by third parties.[2819]

One feature of the SFO is that it does not announce all of its criminal investigations, unless a company, for instance, is required to inform the market.[2820] For example, in 2015, the SFO opened criminal investigations into bribery and corruption offences by an Oil and Gas Limited, which operates in Somalia.[2821] It is an interesting and extraordinary fact that in August 2016 there was a claim submitted to require the SFO to bring the investigation of the company to an end.[2822] The SFO stated that the company's involvement in making "*capacity building*" payments to Somali public officials could constitute criminal offences under Section 6 and 7 of the UKBA 2010.[2823] However, the company denied any criminal offence of its business because there was an agreement between the company and the Somali Ministry of Petroleum and Natural Resources and the "*capacity building*" payments were a contractual obligation.[2824] Additionally, an internal investigation within Somalia concluded that there was no evidence of wrongdoing and that the company acted in good faith.[2825] The Court also considered the difficult market with competing commercial and political interests and the geographical context in Somalia.[2826] In August 2016, the SFO concluded that there is *"currently insufficient evidence of criminality on the part in relation to the capacity building payments"* of the company.[2827] Accordingly, the Court concluded that the SFO's decision to terminate this investigation was fair and responsible.[2828]

2816 *Id.* at 5.
2817 *Id.* at 1.
2818 *Id.* at 3.
2819 *Id.* at 40.
2820 SFO, SFO OPENS INVESTIGATION INTO SOMA OIL & GAS SERIOUS FRAUD OFFICE (2015), https://www.sfo.gov.uk/2015/07/31/sfo-opens-investigation-into-soma-oil-gas/ (last visited Oct 30, 2016).
2821 *Id.*
2822 *Soma Oil And Gas Ltd, R v. Director of the SFO* [2016] EWHC 2471, *supra* note 2798 at 1.
2823 *Id.* at 6.
2824 *Id.* at 7–8.
2825 *Id.* at 9.
2826 *Id.* at 9.
2827 *Id.* at 18.
2828 *Id.* at 37.

Similar to the US, in 2015, a case was closed in a first landmark UK Deferred Prosecution Agreement (DPA)[2829] between the SFO and a bank institut resulting in a total penalty of £16.8m.[2830] Under Section 45 and Schedule 17 of the Crime and Courts Act 2013, a designated prosecutor and a person such as a "*body corporate, a partnership or an unincorporated association*" are enabled to enter into a DPA in England and Wales.[2831] Hence, in the UK, the DPA is regulated by law. For example, paragraph 5 sets out that each agreement must include an expiry date.[2832] This date is a mandatory requirement.[2833] Nevertheless, the Schedule also provides an illustrative list of potential terms and conditions that may be included in a DPA, which are not prescriptive.[2834] The list includes a range of issues that a DPA may impose *e.g.* from the payment of financial penalties to the implementation of a compliance program or the alteration of an existing compliance program.[2835] It follows that the implementation of a corporate compliance program could be a mitigating factor in sentencing a company when the program is proportionate to the bribery risks.[2836] Both the SFO and the Crown Court will consider the program in the course of an investigation, prosecution, and criminal proceeding conducted by the Court, particularly in an agreement between the SFO and the prosecuted company.[2837]

Furthermore, the DPA has to be approved by the Crown Court to clarify that

(a) the DPA is in the interests of justice, and
(b) the terms of the DPA are fair, reasonable and proportionate.[2838]

Thus, the DPA takes effect only when the court has made its final declaration.[2839] In the event that the company has failed to comply with the terms of the DPA, the

2829 The SFO defines the term UK DPA as follows: "*A UK Deferred Prosecution Agreement (DPA) is an agreement reached between a prosecutor and an organisation which could be prosecuted, under the supervision of a judge. The agreement allows a prosecution to be suspended for a defined period provided the organisation meets certain specified conditions. DPAs can be used for fraud, bribery and other economic crime. They apply to organisations, never individuals.*" *See* SFO, Deferred Prosecution Agreements Serious Fraud Office, https://www.sfo.gov.uk/publications/guidance-policy-and-protocols/deferred-prosecution-agreements/ (last visited Oct 27, 2016).

2830 SFO Report *Id.* at 4.; DPA | Standard Bank Plc DPA | SFO v Standard Bank PLC (now known as ICBC Standard Bank Plc), (2015).

2831 Crime and Courts Act 2013, c. 22 (2013) § 45, Schedule 17 para 1 and 4.

2832 *Id.*§ 45, Schedule 17 para 5 (2).

2833 *Id.*§ 45, Commentary on Schedule 17 para 5 (2).

2834 *Id.*§ 45, Commentary on Schedule 17 para 5 (3).

2835 *Id.*§ 45, Schedule 17 para 5 (3).

2836 *Id.*§ 45, para 5 (3) (e); United Kingdom Bribery Act 2010, *supra* note 33 § 7; The Bribery Guidance, *supra* note 860 at 21 Principle 1.

2837 Crime and Courts Act 2013, *supra* note 2831 § 45, Schedule para 5 (3) (e).

2838 *Id.* § 45, Schedule 17 para 8 (1) (a) (b).

2839 *Id.* § 45, Commentary on Schedule 17 para 8 (3).

Agreement could be terminated, at which point the prosecutor can proceed with the criminal prosecution.[2840]

For example, the bank institut agreed that it failed to prevent bribery, contrary to Section 7 of the UKBA 2010, and also agreed to the payment of a financial penalty, and, additionally, agreed to an independent review of its existing internal anti-bribery and corruption controls within the next three years.[2841] Furthermore, the Bank is required to conduct a review including the implementation of its existing internal controls, policies, and procedures regarding compliance with the Bribery Act 2010.[2842] The requirements of the DPA include the implementation of a corporate compliance program within six months and an independent report by PWC on the scope of its current anti-bribery and corruption policies and the effectiveness of the anti-bribery and corruption training, which should be provided to the SFO.[2843] However, the DPA requires that the ultimate responsibility for identifying, assessing, and addressing risks remains with the board of directors of the Bank.[2844] In the event of any failure by the Bank to meet a term of this DPA, the SFO will consider making an application to the court.[2845] This agreement requires judicial approval to become effective both as to the principle of the DPA and its precise terms.[2846]

Overall, the number of criminal corporate prosecutions opened and investigated by the SFO appears to be lower than by the DOJ and SEC in the US.[2847] In addition, the SFO stated that the number of cases concerning prosecutions under Section 993 of the Companies Act 2006 has increased from one case in 2011 to four cases in 2014.[2848] Between 2015 and 2016, the SFO opened 12 criminal investigations into individuals and companies and three civil investigations.[2849] *Table 13* presents enforced proceedings against seven companies and 51 individuals in eleven current criminal cases and one civil case, which were found on the SFO website.[2850] The number of individuals shows that the SFO prosecuted subsequently identified individuals for bribery, fraud, and corruption within companies. The titles

---

2840 *Id.* § 45, Commentary on Schedule 17 para 9 (3) (b), 2 (3).

2841 DPA | Standard Bank Plc DPA | SFO v Standard Bank PLC (now known as ICBC Standard Bank Plc), *supra* note 2830 para 1, 6; United Kingdom Bribery Act 2010, *supra* note 433, § 7 (1).

2842 DPA | Standard Bank Plc DPA | SFO v Standard Bank PLC (now known as ICBC Standard Bank Plc), *supra* note 2830 para 27.

2843 DPA | Standard Bank Plc *Id.* para 28 a.

2844 DPA | Standard Bank Plc *Id.* para 31.

2845 DPA | Standard Bank Plc *Id.* para 34.

2846 SFO Speech Milford, *supra* note 2771.

2847 SFO Report SFO, *supra* note 2770 at 4.

2848 SFO, Section 993 of the Companies Act 2006 (2015), https://www.sfo.gov.uk/publications/ (last visited Jul 27, 2016).

2849 SFO Report SFO, *supra* note 2770 at 4.

2850 *See* Table 13, p. 367.

Table 13 *Current SFO Cases from 2015 until 2016*[2851]

Case	Companies	Individuals
Company one	2	7
Company two		2
Company three		1
Company four		11
Company five		7
Company six		6
Company seven		3
Company eight	3	
Company nine		6
Company ten	1	6
Company eleven	1	
Company twelve		3
Total	**7**	**51**
Median	**1,5**	**6**
Average	**1,75**	**5,1**

of the prosecuted individuals vary from partner, director, CEO, and employee. Nevertheless, there is no case where a compliance officer was involved with respect to a criminal offence like bribery or fraud.

Criticism of the productivity of the SFO came from a comparison between its US counterpart, the DOJ, based on the number of defendants prosecuted and its conviction rate. A review report by *de Grazia* in 2008, an Assistant District Attorney in Manhattan in the US, revealed that the SFO does not work effectively measured both in terms of its productivity (the number of defendants prosecuted) and its conviction rate.[2852] According to this review report by *de Grazia*, the DOJ concluded 88 prosecutions with a conviction rate of 91 percent in 2006, the SFO concluded 166 prosecutions with a conviction rate of 61 percent from 2003 until 2007.[2853] There are major differences between the length of time for investigation and conviction. The review compared one case in terms of time between the

2851 SFO, Our cases Serious Fraud Office, https://www.sfo.gov.uk/our-cases/ (last visited Oct 30, 2016).

2852 *See* de Grazia, *supra* note 2690; Djilani (2011), *supra* note 62 at 316.

2853 *See* de Grazia, *supra* note 2690 at 5, Chart - Summary of comparative conviction rates.

opening of the investigation and the indictment with the size of the prosecution team.[2854] Although the UK team comprised 31 in contrast to eight in the US, the time period between the opening and indictment was 41 months in the UK and 11 months in the US.[2855] As a result of the findings of this report, the SFO has undergone internal structural changes from improving the effectiveness of the SFO leadership to improvements in hiring, promoting, training, policy and standards of the SFO prosecutors.[2856] Hence, it appears that the SFO had a *"damaged reputation."*[2857] After the enactment of the UKBA 2010, there was great public pressure on the SFO to secure a first corporate conviction under the Act.[2858] Lastly, it can be argued that there are still difficulties of proving criminal corporate liability under the current legislation. As discussed previously, the problems can be found in bribery and corruption investigation, where complex documentary evidence has to review, for instance thousands of pages, which necessitates significant time resources to secure a conviction. Another time resource is the hearing of witnesses and their testimony.

In conclusion, the new bribery legislation in the UK was a response to international criticism and the role model effect of the FCPA. Despite the enactment and wide extraterritorial reach of the UKBA 2010, there is still a lack of legal certainty surrounding the interpretation of several terms of the Act and the number of corporate convictions.[2859] In essence, the UKBA 2010 without defining what an associated person is holds companies, guilty of an offence when a person associated with the company bribes another person.[2860] This establishes potential criminal liability for companies for the actions of officers and employees. Nevertheless, as has been examined, the Bribery Act sets out a corporate offence of failure to prevent bribery. The company has to prove that it has implemented adequate procedures to prevent bribery. Although the Bribery Act does not provide the requirement of implementing a compliance function, or other indications of any elements of what such adequate procedures would entail, a compliance program could be a bribery-prevention tool or adequate procedure for companies.

Finally, the possibility of defense encourages greater in corporate compliance with the UKBA 2010. As a result, it is important that domestic and foreign companies which carry on a business in the United Kingdom review their anti-corruption procedures to ensure compliance with all relevant provisions of this

2854 *Id.* at 37, para 2, Both US Allied Deals Inc. and UK Allied Deals were based in London and New York. In the US and in the UK, the investigation began at the same time related to fraudulent trading involving a metals trading group of companies.
2855 *Id.* at 39, Chart I.
2856 *See* DE GRAZIA, *supra* note 2690.
2857 *See* BELCH, *supra* note 2724 at 11.
2858 *Id.* at 12.
2859 *Id.* at 13.
2860 UNITED KINGDOM BRIBERY ACT 2010, *supra* note 433 § 7 (1) (a)(b).

Act. In addition, as regards the first UK DPA, the number of cases investigated by the SFO is expected to increase and a DPA should be a more *"resource-efficient prosecution tool"* as compared with a case at trial.[2861]

4. Comparison between the FCPA and UKBA 2010 Compliance Requirements

As examined above, the UKBA 2010 makes the bribery of foreign public officials an offence and extends beyond company employees to include those acting on behalf of a company. Furthermore, the Act comprises all bribery, not only bribery of foreign officials, but also giving or receiving a bribe from another person.[2862] Unlike the FCPA, the Bribery Act covers both domestic and foreign companies that do business in the UK.[2863] The anti-bribery provisions of the FCPA focus on improper payments to foreign officials; the Bribery Act additionally prohibits improper payments to both domestic officials and foreign public officials as well as bribes in the conduct of business.[2864] Under the UKBA 2010, there is no exception relating to facilitating or expediting payments such as under the FCPA.[2865] With such a wide-ranging scope, the statutory provisions of the UKBA 2010 are much broader than the provisions of the FCPA although the UKBA does not include any false accounting provision.[2866] The provisions of false accounting and false statements are separately enshrined in the Theft Act.[2867] Furthermore, unlike the FCPA, the UKBA 2010 provides a defense for companies able to prove that they have in place an adequate procedure such as a compliance program.[2868]

However, both statutes apply to offers and payments and allow payments that are legal under the written law of a foreign country.[2869] In addition to both

2861 *See* DPA | SFO v Standard Bank PLC (now known as ICBC Standard Bank Plc), *supra* note 2830; Belch, *supra* note 2724 at 13.

2862 United Kingdom Bribery Act 2010, *supra* note 433 §§ 1, 2.

2863 *Compare* Foreign Corrupt Practices Act 1977 (FCPA), *supra* note 438, 15 USC § 78dd-1, 78dd-2, 78dd-3; United Kingdom Bribery Act 2010, *supra* note 433 § 6.

2864 *Compare* Foreign Corrupt Practices Act 1977 (FCPA), *supra* note 438, 15 USC § 78dd-1; United Kingdom Bribery Act 2010, *supra* note 433 §§ 1, 3, 6.

2865 *Compare* Foreign Corrupt Practices Act 1977 (FCPA), *supra* note 438, 15 USC 78dd-1 (b) Exception for routine governmental action; United Kingdom Bribery Act 2010, *supra* note 433 § 6.

2866 *See e.g.* McGreal (2011), *supra* note 495 at 147; Richard (2014), *supra* note 554 at 438; Foreign Corrupt Practices Act 1977 (FCPA), *supra* note 438 § 102, 15 USC §§ 78m(b)(4)–(5) (2006).

2867 Theft Act 1968, c. 60 §§ 17, 19.

2868 United Kingdom Bribery Act 2010, *supra* note 433 § 7 (2).

2869 *Compare* Foreign Corrupt Practices Act 1977 (FCPA), *supra* note 438 § 104, 15 USC § 78dd-2 (2006); United Kingdom Bribery Act 2010, *supra* note 433 § 6; *See also* McGreal (2011), *supra* note 495 at 147.

statutes, the FCPA and the UKBA 2010, there is published Guidance in order to provide helpful information and recommendations to companies of all sizes, for example the hallmarks of an effective compliance program or the six Principles, which are not prescriptive.[2870] While the Principles of the Bribery Act consider adequate bribery-prevention procedures, which is not explicitly called a compliance program, the FCPA Guide sets out hallmarks of an effective compliance program.[2871] Consequently, every company that does business in the UK and every issuer listed on the exchange in the US has to adjust its anti-bribery procedure or compliance program to take account of the particular provisions of the Bribery Act and the FCPA.

To understand the differences between the recommendations of the bribery-prevention of the FCPA and the UKBA *Table 14* below compares the FCPA Resource Guide's hallmarks of an effective compliance program with the six Principles of the UK Bribery Act Guidance.

Table 14 *Comparison between FCPA and UKBA Guidance of Compliance*

UK Bribery Act Guidance Six Principles	**FCPA's Hallmarks of Effective Compliance Programs**
Proportionate procedures	Commitment from Senior Management
Top-Level commitment	Code of Conduct and Compliance Policies and Procedures
Risk Assessment	Oversight, Autonomy, and Resources
Due diligence	Risk Assessment
Communication (including training)	Training and Continuing Advice
Monitoring and Review	Incentives and Disciplinary Measures
	Third-Party Due Diligence

As this comparison shows, the hallmarks of the FCPA Guide comprise more requirements for companies to prevent bribery *e.g.* to implement a code of conduct, oversight, autonomy, resources, incentives, and disciplinary measures than the principles of the UKBA.[2872] Nevertheless, the core elements of the requirements,

2870 *Compare* FCPA Resource Guidance DOJ and SEC, *supra* note 1269 Ch. 5; The Bribery Guidance, *supra* note 860 at 20–31.

2871 *Compare* FCPA Resource Guide DOJ and SEC, *supra* note 1241 at 56–60 Ch. 5; The Bribery Guidance, *supra* note 860 at 20–31.

2872 *Compare* FCPA Resource Guide DOJ and SEC, *supra* note 1241 at 56–60 Ch. 5; The Bribery Guidance, *supra* note 860 at 20–31.

like a commitment from the senior management, the risk assessment, a due diligence and communication and training in order to prevent bribery, are included in both Guides.[2873] Therefore, a company, wherever incorporated, which is listed on a US exchange and carries on a business, or part of a business, in any part of the United Kingdom should implement both compliance requirements to prevent and detect agent misconduct.

Similar to the DOJ in the US, the SFO is currently adopting DPAs in prosecuting criminal corporate conduct, for example any illegal payments.[2874] However, contrary to the US DPA model, the UK DPA is set forth in law.[2875] Despite importing such American procedure, the SFO has also been successful in court in achieving corporate reform through the use of agreements between a prosecuted company and the government, like the DOJ.[2876] These agreements can contribute as an incentive to companies to set up a self-reporting policy of wrongdoing to the government.[2877] One characteristic of an agreement in the UK was that the Crown Court at Southwark held that the SFO lacks the authority to set the penalty amount of such agreements.[2878] In the case *R v. Innospec Ltd,* where the prosecutor struck a plea agreement between a defendant and the government, the Lord Justice said:

> The Practice Direction reflects the constitutional principle that, save in minor matters such as motoring offences, the imposition of a sentence is a matter for the judiciary.[2879]

Today, under the Crime and Courts Act 2013, the content of a DPA may provide *"to pay to the prosecutor a financial penalty."*[2880] However, the penalty must be *"comparable to the fine that a court would have imposed on conviction for the alleged offence following a guilty plea."*[2881]

2873 *Compare* FCPA Resource Guide DOJ and SEC, *supra* note 1241 at 56–60 Ch. 5; The Bribery Guidance, *supra* note 860 at 20–31.
2874 *See e.g.* DPA | SFO v Standard Bank PLC (now known as ICBC Standard Bank Plc), *supra* note 2830.
2875 Crime and Courts Act 2013, *supra* note 2831 § 45, Schedule 17.
2876 *See* Djilani (2011), *supra* note 62 at 305.
2877 *Id.* at 317.
2878 *R v. Innospec Ltd* [2010] EW Misc 7 (EWCC), *supra* note 2766 at 26.
2879 *Id.* at 27.
2880 Crime and Courts Act 2013, *supra* note 2831 § 45, Schedule 17 para 5 (3) (a).
2881 *Id.*§ 45, Schedule 17 para 5 (4).

Table 15 *Comparison between US and UK DPAs*

Terms of the US N/DPA[2882]	Terms of the UK DPA[2883]
The company admits to wrongdoing.	A DPA must contain a statement of facts relating to the alleged offence.
The company waives the statute of limitations.	A DPA must specify an expiry date.
The company agrees that the agreement is admissible in court.	A DPA may impose a cooperation requirement in any investigation related to the alleged offence.
The company agrees that it will no longer violate the law.	A DPA may impose the disgorgement of any profits made from the alleged offence.
The company assists the government in prosecuting individuals associated with the crimes.	A DPA may impose the requirement to donate money to a charity or other third party.
The company pledges that employees will not violate the terms of the agreement.	A DPA may impose the payment of compensation to victims of the alleged offence.
The company pays restitution and fines.	A DPA may impose the requirement to pay to the prosecutor a financial penalty.
The company establishes or improves a corporate compliance program.	A DPA may impose the implementation of a compliance program or make changes to an existing compliance program.
The company establishes a compliance function.[2884]	A DPA may impose training for the company's employees.

Table 15 compares the terms found in US N/DPA, as discussed previously with the content of an UK DPA as set out in Schedule 17 of the Crime and Court Act.

Based on this comparison, it seems that the US N/DPAs include more specific binding content and requirements for the establishment of a compliance program and a corporate compliance function than the UK DPA, which merely recommends the implementation of a compliance program. Contrary to the DPAs in the US,

2882 *See e.g.* Djilani (2011), *supra* note 62 at 319; Lawrence D. Finder, Ryan D. McConnell & Scott L. Mitchell, *Betting the Corporation: Compliance or Defiance?*, 28 Corp. Counsel Rev. (2009).

2883 Crime and Courts Act 2013, *supra* note 2831 § 45, Schedule 17 para 5 (1) (2) (3) (a)-(g).

2884 *See also* A., I., 1.f, p. 210 - The seven minimum elements of a compliance program agreed in the examined US N/DPAs.

in the UK there is no requirement to establish a corporate compliance function. Apart from that, these agreements enable the government to improve corporate structures and behavior.[2885] One effect of these agreements is that the prosecutors are instructed to evaluate whether the company has adopted and implemented a compliance program.[2886] Furthermore, the US DPAs provide greater scope for the government to pursue individual wrongdoers.[2887]

The comparison shows that the number of prosecuted companies in the US is much larger than in the UK.[2888] According to English Company Law, companies should not be held criminally liable unless the entity, at its highest level of management, was responsible for the wrongdoing.[2889] As a result, the SFO prosecuted a vast majority of individuals for fraud and bribery.[2890] Nevertheless, with the English importation of American agreements (DPAs) between prosecuted companies and the government and the Guidance of the prosecutors like the DPP and SFO, the English Courts have begun to consider proactive and effective corporate compliance procedures within companies as a mitigating factor. When opening of an investigation, the prosecutors will take an effective compliance program into account against the prosecution.[2891]

In conclusion, the FCPA, the Bribery Act, and the prosecutors, including their DPAs, offer a powerful incentive for the companies affected to adopt an effective anti-bribery compliance program. Regardless of their characteristics and similarities, both Acts may receive wide consideration by compliance officers around the globe.

IV. The Concepts and Rules of English Employment Law

On the basis of the absence of the corporate compliance function under English Company and Bribery Law, this section provides a short overview of the main sources of English Employment Law in the UK, the key issues of the employment relationship, the nature of the employment contract, the duties of the employees and wrongful dismissal with respect to corporate officers, in particular the compliance officer. It also seeks to include and examine the relevant common law principles of binding precedents in terms of the duty of care and the possibility of protection against wrongful or unfair dismissal of the compliance officer. UK Employment Law covers the territory of England and Wales, Scotland, and Northern Ireland and has a number of specific institutions. For example, domestic courts, Employment Tribunals (ETs) and the Employment Appeal Tribunal (EAT)

2885 *See* Djilani (2011), *supra* note 62 at 319; *See also*, A., I., 1. p. 185.
2886 *Id.* at 320; *See also*, 1. p. 185.
2887 *Id.* at 320; *See also*, A., I., 1. p. 185.
2888 *See supra*, A., I., Table 5, p. 243.
2889 *See supra* A., II., 4., p. 343.
2890 *See supra* A., III., 2., Table 13, p. 367.
2891 *See supra* A., II., 5., p. 348.

are established to enforce employment rights or resolve employment disputes.[2892] The EATs are located in London and Edinburgh and hear appeals from the ETs.[2893] The ETs are staffed with one qualified lawyer and two laypersons.[2894] The EATs are staffed with judges of the high courts in England and Scotland.[2895] The lawyers and the judges must have experience in or an understanding of employment law.[2896]

Similar to the US, the common law and statutes are the most important primary sources of employment law in the UK.[2897] Nevertheless, the legal origins of employment law are based in the common law tradition.[2898] The common law and its rules with regard to formation, obligations, or termination govern the contract of employment between the employee and the employer.[2899] In addition, another important source of employment law is the legislation enacted by Parliament, particularly the employment protection legislation.[2900] The majority of UK employment protection legislation, for example the Working Time Regulations 1998, is derived from European Directives.[2901] The EU Directives provide employment rights directly into UK legislation and into UK courts.[2902] Thus, statutes regulate and control essential elements of the employment contract such as the wage-work bargain and the dismissal of employees.[2903] As such, the parties to the employment contract are not entirely free to negotiate the terms.[2904] Terms and conditions that are set down in collective agreements also create an employment agreement.[2905] However, in the UK, two-thirds of workplaces are not covered by such collective agreements.[2906] Therefore, collective agreements and collective employment law are not included in this examination.

Finally, under statutory authority it is permitted for a minister or statutory body to issue Codes of Practice in the context of employment

---

2892 *See* David A Cabrelli, Employment law 5 (4th ed. 2015).

2893 *Id.* at 5.

2894 *Id.* at 5.

2895 *Id.* at 5.

2896 *Id.* at 5.

2897 *See* David A. Cabrelli, Employment law in context: text and materials 24 (Second ed. 2016).

2898 *Id.* at 3.

2899 *Id.* at 24.

2900 *See e.g.* Employment Act 2008, c. 28 (2009); Employment Rights Act 1996, c.18 (1996); Equality Act 2010, c. 15 (2010); National Minimum Wage Act 1998, c. 39 (1998); The Working Time Regulations 1998, No. 1833 (SI 1998).

2901 Directive 2003/88/EC of the European Parliament and of the Council of 4 November 2003 concerning certain aspects of the organisation of working time, OJ L 299, pp. 9–19 (2003); Cabrelli (2016), *supra* note 2897 at 36.

2902 *See* Cabrelli (2015), *supra* note 2892 at 27.

2903 *See* Cabrelli (2015), *supra* note 2892 at 24.

2904 *See* David Lewis *&* Malcolm Sargeant, Employment Law: The Essentials 2 (13th ed. 2015).

2905 *Id.* at 13.

2906 *Id.* at 13.

relationships.[2907] These Codes serve to educate managers and workers to promote good employment relationships, include procedures, and respond to current developments in the field of employment law.[2908] The consequence of non-compliance with a Code of Practice will be that courts consider the non-adherence unfavorably in the claim.

1. The Nature of Employment Contracts

The contract of employment is shaped by a variety of features. According to *Cabrelli*, it is characterized by its personal relational, mutual, consensual, indefinite as well as authority and power relation features.[2909] Personal means, for example, that the death or incapacity of the employee leads to the automatic termination at common law.[2910] Typically, the employment contract is indefinite in duration. Additionally, the *"unrestricted reasonable notice rule"* has evolved.[2911] Therefore, the employer or the employee can terminate the employment contract on providing reasonable notice.[2912] This rule is contrary to the employment at- will doctrine in the US, which provides for lawful termination at any time, rather than with reasonable notice.[2913] Turning to the final feature of the employment contract, there is an asymmetrical authority power relationship.[2914] This relationship is based on the submission and subordination of the employee.[2915] In general, it is recognized that the employment contract has an interconnected nature involving unequal powers.

As regards the nature of the employment contract, the English Courts have considered the distinction between questions of fact and questions of law. Under common law, the rule that the construction of documents is a question of law was well established.[2916] However, there was also a contrary view in the old case of *Moore v. Garwood,* in which Lord Chief Baron stated:

2907 *See e.g.* CABRELLI (2015), *supra* note 2892 at 32; LEWIS AND SARGEANT (2015), *supra* note 2904 at 2.

2908 *See e.g.* CODE OF PRACTICE ON DISCIPLINARY AND GRIEVANCE PROCEDURE - ACAS CODE OF PRACTICE (2015), http://www.acas.org.uk/media/pdf/f/m/Acas-Code-of-Practice-1-on-disciplinary-and-grievance-procedures.pdf (last visited Dec 7, 2016); CABRELLI (2015), *supra* note 2892 at 32; LEWIS AND SARGEANT (2015), *supra* note 2904 at 2.

2909 *See* CABRELLI (2016), *supra* note 2897 at 146 Figure 5.1.

2910 *See e.g. Farrow v. Wilson* (1869) LR 4, CP 744, 766; *Ranger v. Brown* [1978] ICR 603, 605; *See in:* CABRELLI (2016), *supra* note 2897 at 146.

2911 *See* CABRELLI (2015), *supra* note 2892 at 147.

2912 *Id.* at 147.

2913 *See*, A., II., III., pp. 354 et seq.

2914 *See* CABRELLI (2015), *supra* note 2892 at 148.

2915 *Id.* at 149.

2916 *See in: Carmichael and Another v. National Power Plc* [1999] UKHL 47; [1999] 1 WLR 2042; [1999] 4 All ER 897 (18th November, 1999), Lord Hoffmann said that *"It was this rule upon which the majority in the Court of Appeal relied as entitling them to say that the construction of the exchange of letters between the C.E.G.B. and the*

> the nature of the contract into which the parties had entered was rather a question of fact than of law, because it did not consist of one distinct contract between the parties, but of a series of acts and things done, from which the jury were to determine what was the real intention and meaning of the parties when they entered into the mutual relation in which they stood.[2917]

Although the majority in the Court of Appeal thought that the industrial tribunal should have decided this question as a matter of law because the exchange of letters constituted an offer and acceptance, the courts additionally apply a test of whether there is a *"mutuality of obligation"* between the employer and employee.[2918] The next section examines which tests the English Courts and Tribunals will apply in order to determine when an individual has employee status.

2. The "mixed or multiple" Test for Establishing a Contract of Employment

English Courts and Tribunals apply the *"mixed or multiple"* test to determine when an individual is an employee, which comprises at least three criteria.[2919] The reason for this is that, under common law, four tests have been established in key cases for ensuring whether an individual works as an employee: (1) the integration test, (2) the economic reality test, (3) the mutuality of obligation test, and (4) the control test.[2920] For example, in *Ready Mixed Concrete (South East) Ltd v Minister of Pensions and National Insurance*, the judge considered what is meant by a *"contract of service"* by applying the control test.[2921] The judge concluded that three conditions must be fulfilled in order for a *"contract of service"* to exist.

> (i) The servant agrees that, in consideration of a wage or other remuneration, he will provide his own work and skill in the performance of some service for his master.
> (ii) He agrees, expressly or impliedly, that in the performance of that service he will be subject to the other's control in a sufficient degree to make that other master.

---

respondents, together with any terms which could be implied be law into the contract which they created, was a question of law."

2917 *Moore v. Garwood* (1849) 4 Exch. 681, 684–685 (1849); *See* in: *Carmichael and Another v. National Power Plc* [1999] UKHL 47; [1999] 1 WLR 2042; [1999] 4 All ER 897 (18th November, 1999).

2918 *Carmichael and Another v. National Power Plc* [1999] UKHL 47; [1999] 1 WLR 2042; [1999] 4 All ER 897, *supra* note 2916 *See* Lord Hoffmann.

2919 *See* Cabrelli (2015), *supra* note 2892 at 31.

2920 *See Id.* at 7 for (1) *Stevenson, Jordan and Harrison Ltd v. MacDonald and Evans* [1952] 1 TLR 101, (2) *Market Investigations Ltd v. Minister of Social Security* [1969] 2 QB 173; (3) *Carmichael and Another v. National Power Plc* [1999] UKHL 47; [1999] 1 WLR 2042; [1999] 4 All ER 897, *supra* note 2916; (4) *Ready Mixed Concrete (South East) Ltd v. Minister of Pensions and National Insurance* [1967] EWHC QB 3, (1967).

2921 *Ready Mixed Concrete (South East) Ltd v. Minister of Pensions and National Insurance* [1967] EWHC QB 3, *supra* note 2920.

(iii) The other provisions of the contract are consistent with its being a contract of service.[2922]

The control test includes two important features: first, the employer has a sufficient degree of control and, second, the individual is required to provide the work on his own.[2923] In addition, the English Courts and Tribunals apply the following three criteria as the basic components of the employment contract: (1) control, (2) mutuality of obligation, and (3) a degree of personal service.[2924] These three criteria are cumulative. If any one of these criteria is absent, the individual will not be considered an employee.[2925]

3. The Content of Employment Contracts

This section focuses on the content of the employment contract and explores the various terms of contracts. Like any other contract, a contract of employment is subject to the general principles of law.[2926] The contracting parties can freely negotiate the terms and conditions under the current statutes and the common law.[2927] The employment contract may be verbal or in writing.[2928]

In the UK, the sources of employment contracts are individual express terms, imposed terms, common law implied terms, work rules, workforce agreements, collective agreements, and statutes.[2929] The most important sources are the written or oral express terms, the imposed and the implied terms, which will be explained briefly. Firstly, express terms are explicitly provided for the contract and are binding.[2930] They may also differ from the description in a job offer.[2931] Express terms can be set down in writing, agreed orally, or established by conduct and take precedence over all other sources of contractual terms.[2932] If an express term establishes an obligation, any breach thereof may lead to an action in damages.[2933]

2922 *Id.* at 515–516.

2923 Degree of control *Troutbeck SA v. White & Anor* [2013] EWCA Civ 1171, (2013); *See in:* Lewis and Sargeant (2015), *supra* note 2904 at 47.

2924 *See* Cabrelli (2015), *supra* note 2892 at 32.

2925 *Id.* at 32.

2926 *See* Lewis and Sargeant (2015), *supra* note 2904 at 13.

2927 *See e.g.* Damages for breach of contract in: *Commerzbank AG v. Keen* [2006] EWCA Civ 1536, (2006); *See* in: Lewis and Sargeant (2015), *supra* note 2904 at 13.

2928 *See* Lewis and Sargeant (2015), *supra* note 2904 at 13.

2929 *Id.* at 15. Figure 2.1.

2930 *Id.* at 15.

2931 *Id.* at 15.

2932 *See* Cabrelli (2015), *supra* note 2892 at 151; Lewis and Sargeant (2015), *supra* note 2904 at 15.

2933 *See* Cabrelli (2015), *supra* note 2892 at 151.

According to Part I of the Employment Rights Act 1996 (ERA), the employer must provide for the employee *"a written statement of particulars of employment."*[2934] Under Section 1, this statement *"shall be given not later than two months after the beginning of the employment."*[2935] The employer's duty is to provide the employee a document in the form of a statement, a document in writing in the form of a contract of employment or letter of engagement where the particulars are contained as essential elements of the contract in accordance with Section 1 (3) and (4) of the ERA.[2936] These provisions of the ERA were implemented in EU Directive 91/533/EC.[2937] Thus, over time, both EU and domestic legislation have introduced terms directly into contracts.[2938] Such terms are often referred to as imposed terms. They include, for example, restrictions on a contract of employment such as the maximum weekly working hours.[2939]

Thirdly, under common law, implied terms *in fact* and implied terms *in law* are recognized.[2940] An implied term in fact applies only to the contract between the employer and employee.[2941] In the event that there is a gap in the employment contract, the court can imply a term to give efficacy to the contract.[2942] Hence, it is suggested that the contracting parties explicitly agreed to and approved this term.[2943] In contrast, the implied term in law applies to all contracts of a particular type *e.g.* a contract of employment.[2944] The courts consider the implied term as a *"necessary incident"* of the employment relationship.[2945] Therefore, this term is recognized and established as an implied term in law and will be imported into every employment contract.[2946] These terms in law comprise *inter alia* (1) the duties

2934 Employment Rights Act 1996, *supra* note 2900 § 1(1).
2935 *Id.*§ 1(2).
2936 *Id.*§ 7(A).
2937 Council Directive 91/533/EEC of 14 October 1991 on an employer's obligation to inform employees of the conditions applicable to the contract or employment relationship, L 288/32 (1991) Art. 2 and 3.
2938 *See e.g.* Restrictions under Equality Act 2010, *supra* note 2900 § 66; National Minimum Wage Act 1998, *supra* note 2900, Cabrelli (2015), *supra* note 2892 at 165; Lewis and Sargeant (2015), *supra* note 2904 at 23.
2939 *See e.g.* Restrictions under Equality Act 2010, *supra* note 2900 § 66; National Minimum Wage Act 1998, *supra* note 2900 § 17 (1); The Working Time Regulations 1998, *supra* note 2900 § 4 (1); *See in:* Cabrelli (2016), *supra* note 2897 at 166; Lewis and Sargeant (2015), *supra* note 2904 at 23.
2940 *See* Cabrelli (2015), *supra* note 2892 at 166.
2941 *Id.* at 167.
2942 *See* Lewis and Sargeant (2015), *supra* note 2904 at 23.
2943 *See* Cabrelli (2015), *supra* note 2892 at 167.
2944 *Id.* at 167.
2945 *Romford Ice & Cold Storage Co v. Lister* [1956] UKHL 6, (1956); *See* in: Cabrelli (2015), *supra* note 2892 at 167.
2946 *See* Cabrelli (2015), *supra* note 2892 at 167.

of the employer *e.g.* duty to provide work,[2947] pay wages,[2948] (2) the obligations of the employee *e.g.* duty to work and comply with instructions,[2949] and (3) the duty of care, loyalty, fidelity and confidence.[2950] They are binding at a high level of generality.[2951] The majority of these terms are long established common law principles.[2952] For example, the duty of care arises from the performance of the employee's work.[2953] An employee is required to perform his work in a competent manner.[2954] If an employee is in breach of this duty, the employer is entitled to recover damages.[2955] On the basis of the scope of responsibilities and tasks incumbent upon the compliance officer within a company, the duty of care could be liable to be important for the performance of his work. However, a review of the English literature and the English legal framework (*e.g.* Company Law, the Bribery Act and Employment Law) did not reveal any special duty of care of the compliance officers.[2956] In addition, an examination of the English court cases relating to breach of the duty of care did not reveal any cases involving corporate compliance officers.[2957] For this reason, it is necessary to examine whether there are enhanced special regulatory duties for compliance officers in the financial services sector, to search for examples of a duty of care imposed on internal control personnel in banks and investment firms.[2958] Therefore, the next section will explore whether the compliance officer owes a duty of care under the regulatory framework within banks and investment firms and its impact on this function.

2947 *See e.g. Collier v. Sunday Referee Publishing Co Ltd* [1940] 2 KB 647 [1940] 4 All ER 234; *Exception in: William Hill Organisation Ltd v. Tucker* [1998] EWCA Civ 615, 18 (1998).

2948 *See e.g. Driver v. Air India Ltd.* [2011] EWCA Civ 830, 36 (2011) "*The employer has to pay a reasonable sum.*"

2949 *See e.g. Robertson v. Newcastle Breweries Ltd* [2000] EAT 1373_99_1804, 6 (2000) The Court held that "*at common law all employees are under a duty to work honestly, faithfully and loyally for their employer.*"

2950 *See e.g. HM Attorney General v. Blake* [1997] EWCA Civ 3008 (16th December, 1997), (1997); *See* in: Cabrelli (2015), *supra* note 2892 at 178–216; Lewis and Sargeant (2015), *supra* note 2904 at 29–41.

2951 *See* Cabrelli (2015), *supra* note 2892 at 177.

2952 *See* Lewis and Sargeant (2015), *supra* note 2904 at 27.

2953 *See* Cabrelli (2015), *supra* note 2892 at 40.

2954 *Id.* at 40.

2955 *See e.g. Lister v. Romford Ice and Cold Storage* [1957] AC 555; *See in:* Cabrelli (2016), *supra* note 2897 at 40.

2956 *See supra*, A., pp. 315 et seq.

2957 By examining the case law in the UK Employment Appeal Tribunal (UKEAT) with the key words *"duty of care"* and *"compliance officer"* on the case database BAILII from 2010 to 2016 in England and Wales no case has been found.

2958 *See* Chiu (2015), *supra* note 2320 at 270.

a. The Reasonable Duty of Care Imposed on Control Functions

In the wake of the financial crisis of 2008 and 2009, a new statutory and regulatory framework aimed at strengthening individual accountability was established in the UK financial services sector. Compliance has been an important issue since the first Financial Services Act of 1986 in the UK.[2959] The current Financial Services (Banking Reform) Act 2013 requires significant changes to the FSMA 2000.[2960] These changes include *e.g.* the introduction of retail ring-fencing requirements for banks and a new conduct framework for senior managers within banks.[2961]

Furthermore, there are a number of regulatory bodies in the UK, which control the financial services activities of firms and individuals.[2962] One of them is the FSA, which was splitted into two regulatory bodies, the Financial Conduct Authority (FCA)[2963] and the Prudential Regulation Authority (PRA)[2964] in 2013.[2965] Since 2013, the FCA has pursued the following three objectives, (1) the protection of consumers, (2) enhancing the integrity of the UK financial system, and (3) the maintenance of competitive markets and the promotion of effective competition.[2966] In the UK, an individual or a firm has to submit an application for authorization to the regulator in order to carry out any regulated activity.[2967] Since 2000, a regime of internal *"control function"* has been in place under Section 59 of the FSMA 2000, as specified in rules such as a Code of Practice for Approved Persons (APER).[2968]

2959 Financial Services Act 1986 (Repealed), *supra* note 525. This Act was repealed by the FSMA 2000 in 2001.

2960 Financial Services (Banking Reform) Act 2013, c. 33 (2013). This Act will come into force on various dates until 2019.

2961 *Id.*§§ 1 to 6, §§ 19 to 20.

2962 *See* Lee Werrell, Compliance Managers Guidebook *&* Reference 12 (2. ed. 2014).

2963 Since 2013 the FCA, The Financial Conduct Authority, *supra* note 939, formerly the FSA *See* The Financial Services Authority, *supra* note 783. The FCA is responsible for the conduct supervision of financial services firms, which are not supervised by the PRA.

2964 *"The Prudential Regulation Authority (PRA) was created as a part of the Bank of England by the Financial Services Act (2012) and is responsible for the prudential regulation and supervision of around 1,700 banks, building societies, credit unions, insurers and major investment firms." See* Prudential Regulation Authority | Bank of England, http://www.bankofengland.co.uk/pra/Pages/default.aspx (last visited Dec 19, 2016).

2965 *See* Werrell (2014), *supra* note 2962 at 13.

2966 FCA, About Us FCA (2016), https://www.fca.org.uk/about (last visited Sep 6, 2016).

2967 Financial Services and Markets Act (2000), *supra* note 785 Part IV §§ 40 to 55 - Permission to carry on one or more regulated activities.

2968 *Re a Company* [1980] Ch 138, [1980] 2 WLR 241, *supra* note 2548 - Seite 2 a manager with supervisory control. Control functions are specific functions of internal control departments, *e.g.* compliance, legal or risk management within banks and

The APER takes the form of guidance containing, among other things, seven Statements of Principle for approved persons.[2969] Principle 2 and 6 state:

> An approved person must act with due skill, care and diligence in carrying out his accountable functions.[2970]
>
> An approved person performing an accountable higher management function must exercise due skill, care and diligence in managing the business of the firm for which they are responsible in their accountable function.[2971]

In the opinion of the FCA, the approved person does not comply with Principle 2 if he fails *e.g.* to inform a customer; or his firm about the risks of an investment, or provides inaccurate or inadequate information.[2972] Principle 6 means at first that an approved person performing a higher manager function needs to inform himself about the affairs of the business for which he has responsibility.[2973] Furthermore, Principle 6 refers to behavior such as permitting transactions without a sufficient understanding of the risks, inadequately monitoring highly profitable transactions, or accepting implausible or unsatisfactory explanations from subordinates.[2974] By delegating the authority to an individual, the approved person has to ensure that the other person has the necessary capacity, competence, knowledge, seniority, or skill.[2975]

Additionally, the amendments of the FSMA 2000 as set out in Part Four of the Financial Services Act 2013, define, for example, the senior management function as a person who is *"responsible for managing one or more aspects of the 'authorised person's' affairs."*[2976] Specifically, the Consultation Paper of the FCA and the PRA qualifies the key persons or the senior management functions as the chief executive officer, the chief risk officer, the head of the internal audit

investment firms. *See also* FINANCIAL SERVICES AND MARKETS ACT (2000), *supra* note 785 § 59 (3); FCA, STATEMENTS OF PRINCIPLE AND CODE OF PRACTICE FOR APPROVED PERSONS (APER) (2016), https://www.handbook.fca.org.uk/handbook/APER.pdf (last visited Dec 18, 2016) Rule 1.1A.2.

2969 FCA, *supra* note 2968 APER 2.1A.3 R The Statements of Principle are issued under; FINANCIAL SERVICES AND MARKETS ACT (2000), *supra* note 785 § 64A (1) (a).

2970 FCA, *supra* note 2968 APER 2.1A.3.

2971 *Id.* APER 2.1A.3.

2972 *Id.* APER 4.2.4.

2973 *Id.* APER 4.6.3.

2974 *Id.* APER 4.6.4.

2975 *Id.* APER 4.6.5.

2976 FINANCIAL SERVICES (BANKING REFORM) ACT 2013, *supra* note 2960 § 19 inserts after Section 59 of FSMA 2000. *"An authorised person means a a person who has the permission to carry on one or more regulated activities and is authorised for the purposes of the FSMA 2000."* *See* FINANCIAL SERVICES AND MARKETS ACT (2000), *supra* note 785 § 31 (1) (2).

and the head of key business areas.[2977] The Paper defines these individuals as the key decision-makers within banks and investment firms who are approved by the FCA and, hence, are within the scope of and subject to enhanced accountability requirements.[2978] The English Courts also apply this meaning of the term approved person. For example, in *Willford, R v Financial Services Authority* the Lord Justice states that

> An approved person performing a significant influence function must exercise due skill, care and diligence in managing the business of the firm for which he is responsible in his controlled function.[2979]

In order to define the responsibilities of these senior management functions, the FCA includes in its rules of conduct, the oversight of compliance with conditions and time limits on approval for example.[2980] The Consultation Paper by the FCA and PRA organizes the current controlled functions in a new FCA senior management system.[2981] The former compliance oversight function (CF10) is now the compliance oversight function (SMF16).[2982] Therefore, the FCA also approves the compliance oversight function.[2983] Generally, the FCA determines that this function "*is a function of acting in the capacity of a director or senior manager.*"[2984]

Since 2004, EU legislation has required all financial institutes that conduct investment business to establish a permanent and effective compliance function.[2985] However, the FCA applied this requirement to all regulated firms, or authorized persons, including banking and credit institutions.[2986] Hence, the conduct rules of both regulators also refer to the compliance officer. The rules require that the

---

2977 PRA and FCA, Strengthening accountability in banking: a new regulatory framework for individuals 14 (2014), http://www.bankofengland.co.uk/pra/Documents/publications/cp/2014/cp1414.pdf (last visited Dec 18, 2016) para 2.11.

2978 *Id.* at 25, para 2.57.

2979 *Willford, R (On the Application Of) v. Financial Services Authority* [2013] EWCA Civ 677, 2 (2013).

2980 PRA and FCA, *supra* note 2977 para 4.5.16, Annex C.

2981 *Id.* at 59. para 8.5, Figure 11.

2982 *Id.* at 59. para 8.5, Figure 11. The Abbreviation CF means *"control function"* and the abbreviation SMF means senior management function.

2983 *Id.* at 26, para 2.60, Figure 6.

2984 PRA and FCA, *supra* note 2977 para 10C.6.1, Annex C.

2985 Directive 2004/39/EC of the European Parliament and of the Council on markets in financial instruments amending Council Directives 85/611/EEC and 93/6/EEC and Directive 2000/12/EC (MIFID 2004), *supra* note 432; *See also* ESMA, Consultation paper | Guidelines on certain aspects of the MiFID compliance function requirements (2011), https://www.esma.europa.eu/sites/default/files/library/2015/11/2011_446.pdf (last visited Dec 7, 2016).

2986 *See* Chiu (2015), *supra* note 2320 at 84; PRA and FCA, *supra* note 2977 para 6.1.4-C, Annex C.

compliance officer has to *"act with due skill, care and diligence."*[2987] In essence, this means that it is important that the compliance officer sufficiently understands the risks of the business activities.[2988] He has to inform himself in order to obtain the necessary expertise of the firms' business.[2989] As important as a manager, he has to ensure that the business of the firm is controlled effectively and complies with the relevant requirements and standards of the regulatory system.[2990] Otherwise, the FCA can take disciplinary actions against senior managers of banks and investment firms and has the power to impose penalties on authorized persons.[2991] In order to examine the reasons behind and the frequency of the imposition of penalties, the next section presents the FCA actions against compliance officers in the course of the last 14 years.

b. Actions against Compliance Officers between 2002 and 2016

While the actions available to the FCA are wide-ranging, they are not court actions. Under the Financial Services and Markets Act 2000 (FSMA), the FCA has an extensive range of disciplinary, criminal, and civil powers to take action against firms and individuals who fail to meet the FCA standards.[2992] This includes *e.g.* the withdrawal of a firm's authorization, the prohibition of an individual from operating in financial services or the imposition of financial penalties.[2993] For example, research on the website of the FCA revealed that the FSA imposed fines totaling £66,144,839 on 35 individuals and on 22 banks and investment firms in 2011.[2994] Among these actions, one compliance officer was fined.[2995]

Table 16 shows the number of actions by the FCA between 2002 and 2016 and the number of individuals and compliance officers involved.

2987 *Id.* at 42, para 5.20, Figure 7.

2988 PRA and FCA, *supra* note 2977 para 4.1.4, Annex A.

2989 *Id.* para 4.1.4, Annex A.

2990 *Id.* para 4.1.8 (1) (a) (b), Annex A.

2991 *Id.* para 6.2.4, Annex C.

2992 *See* FCA, ENFORCEMENT INFORMATION GUIDE, https://www.fca.org.uk/publication/documents/enforcement-information-guide.pdf (last visited Dec 12, 2016). For instance, under Section 352 of the FSMA 2000 *"A person who discloses information in contravention of section 348 or 350(5) is guilty of an offence." See* FINANCIAL SERVICES AND MARKETS ACT (2000), *supra* note 785 § 352. The FCA can also use its statutory powers in criminal proceedings with regard to market abuse.

2993 FCA, *supra* note 2968.

2994 FINANCIAL SERVICES AND MARKETS ACT (2000), *supra* note 785 Schedule 1, Part III Penalties and Fees; FINANCIAL SERVICES (BANKING REFORM) ACT 2013, *supra* note 2960 §§ 73 (1), 139 (1) to (8); *See also* FCA, ENFORCEMENT FCA (2016), https://www.fca.org.uk/about/enforcement (last visited Dec 16, 2016).

2995 *FSA v.* Individual one, Action (2011); FSA, *supra* note 783.

Table 16 *The Actions by the FCA between 2002 and 2016*

Year	Actions	Firms	Individuals	CO	Indiv. Perc.
2002	9	9	0	0	0.00 %
2003	17	14	3	0	17.65 %
2004	32	22	10	0	43.78 %
2005	20	17	3	0	15.00 %
2006	27	23	4	0	14.81 %
2007	23	21	2	0	8.70 %
2008	52	35	17	0	32.69 %
2009	42	30	12	0	28.57 %
2010	80	34	46	0	57.50 %
2011	57	22	35	1	61.40 %
2012	53	25	28	2	52.83 %
2013	61	37	24	2	39.34 %
2014	40	26	14	1	35.00 %
2015	40	18	22	3	55.00 %
2016	23	9	14	0	60.87 %
Average	**38**	**23**	**16**	**1**	**34.88 %**
Median	**40**	**22**	**14**	**0**	**35.00 %**

The table clearly shows increased enforcement of actions after the financial crisis in 2008 and 2009.[2996] Just as the number of FCA actions has increased, since 2010, the number of actions against individuals is generally higher than the number of actions against firms.[2997] Nine of these individuals could be clearly identified as compliance officers.[2998] However, it could be that another approved person performed the compliance oversight (CF10) function and works as a compliance officer, but was not identified through the search on the website.

Having examined the final notices of the actions by the FCA against the nine compliance officers, it should be noted that they all ended with a financial penalty and with prohibition from performing any significant influence function in

2996 *See* Table 16 - The Actions by the FCA between 2002 and 2016, *Id.*
2997 *See* Table 16 - The Actions by the FCA between 2002 and 2016, *Id.*
2998 *See* Table 16 - The Actions by the FCA between 2002 and 2016, *Id.*

Table 17 *Word Frequency of the nine FCA Actions against Compliance Officers*

Word	Length	Count	Weighted Percentage (%)
authority	9	601	1.61
compliance	10	435	1.17
financial	9	403	1.08
person	6	303	0.81
penalty	7	271	0.73
relevant	8	247	0.66
approved	8	221	0.59
function	8	198	0.53
principle	9	169	0.45
conduct	7	158	0.42

relation to any regulated activity carried on by any authorized person.[2999] The word frequency analysis of the nine actions revealed that the words "*authority*",[3000] "*compliance*" and "*penalty*" were used most frequently.[3001]

In seven actions against compliance officers, the FCA states that the compliance officer *"failed to act with due skill, care and diligence in carrying out his CF10 controlled function, in his role as the approved person responsible for compliance oversight."*[3002]

The FCA sets out the reasons for the actions as follows: During the investigations, the FCA has examined the business conduct of the compliance officers and has accused them of the breach of Statements of Principle 2 or 6.[3003] This means, specifically, that the approved person has "*to take any steps to identify and address the risk, and recognise clear warning signs of market abuse.*"[3004] Furthermore, the compliance officers have failed to adequately keep records for investor certification, adequate oversight of investor certification, or failed to provide clear information

2999 *See e.g. FCA v.* Individual two, Action (2013); *FCA v.* Individual three, (2015); *FCA v.* Individual four, (2015); *FCA v.* Individual five, Action (2013); *FCA v.* Individual six, (2015).

3000 The term "*authority*" means the UK regulator previously known as the Financial Services Authority and renamed on 1 April 2013 as the Financial Conduct Authority.

3001 *See e.g.* Table 17, *Id.*

3002 *See e.g. FSA v.* Individual seven, Action (2012) para 4.1.

3003 FCA, *supra* note 2968 APER 2.1A.3. APER means the Statements of Principle and Code of Conduct for Approved Persons.

3004 *See e.g. FSA v.* Individual seven, *supra* note 3003 para 4.2., 4.6.

to investors.[3005] Therefore, in these actions, the FCA concluded that the compliance officers demonstrated a lack of competence and capability and are not fit and proper to perform any control function.[3006] In the view of the FCA, compliance oversight means that the compliance officer *"should be alert in order to protect both their firm and the integrity of the UK markets."*[3007]

According to Section 66 of the FSMA 2000, an approved person is guilty when he has failed to comply with a Statement of Principle.[3008] Under Section 69 of the FSMA 2000, the FCA must prepare and issue a statement of its policy in terms of its sanctions.[3009] Today, the authorities' policy and process in this regard is contained in the Enforcement Guide.[3010] Chapter 9 of this Guide provides the FCA's policy on prohibition and withdrawal of approval.[3011] In accordance with Section 56 of the FSMA 2000, the FCA can prohibit the individual from performing a specified function.[3012] In addition, under Section 63 of the Act, the FCA has the power to withdraw an approval if it considers that the approved person is not a fit and proper person to perform the function.[3013] Furthermore, the FCA also has the power to carry out an investigation in order to require and gather information.[3014] The investigation includes the requirement for firms and individuals to provide documents and reports to the FCA, or to attend interviews with the FCA and answer the questions.[3015]

An examination of the nine actions against the compliance officers by the FCA shows that six of them were prohibited from performing any controlled function in relation to any regulated activities carried on by any authorized persons.[3016] In two of the six actions, the FCA withdrew the approval given to the compliance officer to perform the controlled function.[3017] Furthermore, in all nine actions, the compliance officer was required to pay a financial penalty.[3018] Five compliance officers

---

3005 *See e.g. FCA v.* Individaul five, *supra* note 2999 para 4.8., 4.9., 4.12.

3006 *See e.g. Id.* para 5.8.

3007 *See e.g. FSA v.* Individual seven, *supra* note 3002 para 4.6.

3008 Financial Services and Markets Act (2000), *supra* note 785 § 66 (2) (a).

3009 *Id.*§ 69 (1).

3010 *See* FCA, The Enforcement Guide (2016), https://www.handbook.fca.org.uk/handbook/document/eg/EG_20160101.pdf (last visited Dec 15, 2016).

3011 *Id.* Chapter 9.

3012 Financial Services and Markets Act (2000), *supra* note 785 § 56 (2).

3013 *Id.*§ 63 (1).

3014 *Id.*§§ 165 to 169.

3015 FCA, *supra* note 3010.

3016 *FCA v.* Individual six, *supra* note 2999; *FSA v.* Individual one, *supra* note 2995; *FSA v.* Individual seven, *supra* note 3002; *FCA v.* Individual four, *supra* note 2999; *FCA v.* Individual five, *supra* note 2999; *FSA v.* Individual eight, Action (2011).

3017 *FCA v.* Individual five, *supra* note 2999; *FSA v.* Individual eight, *supra* note 3016.

3018 *See also FSA v.* Individual nine, (2011); *FCA v.* Individual two, *supra* note 2999; *FCA v.* Individual three, *supra* note 2999.

agreed to settle at an early stage of the investigation by the FCA and in return were granted a reduction.[3019]

In conclusion, the FCA has the power to take disciplinary action to fine, to suspend firms or individuals who have breached its and their requirements or to make a prohibition order. Therefore, it appears that under the regulatory framework in the financial services sector in the UK, the regulator determines whether an approved person has breached the duty of care and, hence, whether the individual is incapable of doing the job and of performing a control function. This matter is not decided by judges in the UK courts and Employment Tribunals. Therefore, it could be argued that the UK compliance officer remains an agent of regulation and the financial regulatory regime in the UK.

c. Specific Duties and Responsibilities of a Compliance Officer in the Regulatory Environment in the UK

By examining the legal regulatory framework and the reasons given in the notices by the FCA against compliance officers in the UK, it can be argued that filling the position of a skilled, high-quality compliance officer entails far-reaching duties and responsibilities:

(1) Dealing with increasing information published by regulators and exchanges, and the speed of regulatory changes,
(2) A thorough understanding of the legal environment including the regulatory impact on the firms and the Guidance,
(3) Compliance with Rules, Codes of Practice, and Statements of Principles by the regulators,
(4) To adequately inform oneself as an approved person about the affairs of the business for which he is responsible,
(5) To monitor and assess the adequacy of the firm's transactions including to supervise any agent,
(6) To recognise the signs of possible risk of market abuse and then to take appropriate steps to ensure no such abuse was taking place,
(7) To develop, implement and conduct a compliance monitoring plan,
(8) To clearly document the appropriate policies, procedures, and bulletins within the day-to-day work and to conduct file reviews and internal audits,
(9) To provide adequate, correct and consistent information to the senior management.[3020]

3019 *FCA v.* Individual six, *supra* note 2999; *FCA v.* Individual four, *supra* note 2999; *FCA v.* Individual five, *supra* note 2999; *FSA v.* Individual one, *supra* note 2995; *FCA v* Individual three, *supra* note 2999.

3020 This is a summarized overview of the Final Notices given by the FCA's actions against compliance officers – *See e.g. FSA v.* Individual seven, *supra* note 3002; *FSA v.* Individual eight, *supra* note 3016.

The evidence has shown that the scope of responsibilities of the compliance function in the regulatory environment is broad and serious. Therefore, the compliance officer should have sufficiently broad knowledge and professional experience and a high level of expertise.[3021] The Statements of Principle and the Code of Conduct for Approved Persons (APER) sets out the fundamental obligations of approved persons and, hence applies to the compliance officer.[3022] He could be guilty of misconduct for failing to comply with a Statement of Principle issued under Section 64 of the FSMA 2000.[3023] However, the APER 3.1.4G states that an approved person will only be in breach of a Statement of Principle when he is personally culpable.[3024] Additionally, the FCA points out that

> Personal culpability arises where an approved person's conduct was deliberate or where the approved person's standard of conduct was below that which would be reasonable in all circumstances.[3025]

In detail, the FCA will consider *"the context in which a course of conduct was undertaken, the circumstances of the individual case, the characteristics of the particular controlled function and the behavior expected in that function."*[3026]

In the course of investigation, the FCA examined the conduct of the compliance officers in the business. Specifically, they were in breach of the Statement of Principles 2 or 6, or failed to act with due skill, care and diligence, or failed to properly read a document, or failed to properly investigate and act on the information in order to prevent the misconduct of other employees. Hence, the FCA held them personally culpable in a situation in which their conduct was deliberate and, then, the FCA imposed a sanction.[3027] As a matter of fact, the FCA opined that a serious lack of competence in carrying out the compliance function would lead an individual to be banned from working in the financial service industry.[3028]

In conclusion, under the new senior management regime implemented by the FCA and PRA according to their rule-making activity to Section 64 of the FMSA 2000, the internal control functions and their conduct are subject to enhanced scrutiny. This approach could be seen critically since, apart from the regular jurisdiction, the regulators have established their own system in order to discipline

---

3021 ESMA, *supra* note 2985 para 34. IV.I. Effectiveness of the compliance function.
3022 *FSA v.* Individual one, supra note 2995 para 4.4.
3023 *FSA v.* Individual one, *supra* note 2995 para 4.3; FINANCIAL SERVICES AND MARKETS ACT (2000), *supra* note 785 §§ 64, 66 (2) (a).
3024 FCA, *supra* note 2968 APER 3.1.4G (1); *See* in: *FSA v.* Individual one, *supra* note 2995 para 4.6.
3025 FCA, *supra* note 2968 APER 3.1.4G (1); *See* in: *FSA v.* Individual one, *supra* note 2995 para 4.6.
3026 FCA, *supra* note 2968 APER 3.1.3G; *See* in: *FSA v.* Individual one, *supra* note 2995 para 4.8.
3027 *See e.g. FSA v.* Individual one, *supra* note 2995 Summary of reasons.
3028 *See* CHIU (2015), *supra* note 2320 at 275.

and sanction the conduct of approved persons. However, as previously discussed, the regulators' power is based on legislation. The basis for liability of compliance officers could arise from breaches of the Statements of Principle 2 or 6 of APER for failure to act with due skill, care and diligence. Finally, it can be argued that, contrary to the private sector, the compliance officer is covered by a specific duty of care in exercising and performing his job within the financial service sector.

4. Wrongful and Unfair Dismissal

After examining the specific duty of care in the regulated environment, this section will continue to examine whether the corporate compliance officer has the *"right not to be unfairly dismissed"* by the employer and whether he enjoys a protection against wrongful or unfair dismissal. As a result of legislation, other implied terms connected with unfair dismissal in the terms of breach or termination of the contract of employment have emerged.[3029] For this reason, this section will examine the concept of wrongful and unfair dismissal of an employee under common law and legislation. This concept is important to understanding the circumstances in which an employee is dismissed and when an employee like a corporate officer or compliance officer has the *"right not to be unfairly dismissed by the employer."*[3030]

The Employment Rights Act 1996 includes both notice and unjust dismissal provisions.[3031] According to Section 94, *"the employee has the right not to be unfairly dismissed by his employer."*[3032] The definition of what is a fair or unfair dismissal is a major issue in termination discussions.[3033] Generally, an unfair dismissal is defined as *"a dismissal of an employee which amounts to a repudiatory breach of contract on the part of the employer."*[3034] Hence, the individual who claims for unfair dismissal must be an employee and must have been employed for a period of no less than two years.[3035] In addition, the employer must provide a written explanation of the reason for the termination.[3036] These claims must be enforced in Employment Tribunals.[3037] The majority of cases involve an employee dismissed without notice.[3038]

Usually, in the event of breaches of a contract there is a claim. The vast majority of claims for wrongful dismissal are common law claims.[3039] The Judge explained the nature of such claims in *Cossington v. C2C Rail Ltd:*

3029 *See* Lewis and Sargeant (2015), *supra* note 2904 at 27.
3030 Employment Rights Act 1996, *supra* note 2900 § 94(1).
3031 *Id.* Part IX Termination of employment, §§ 86 to 93.
3032 *Id.*§ 94(1).
3033 *See* Estreicher and Hirsch (2013), *supra* note 2011 at 435.
3034 *See e.g.* Key definition in: Cabrelli (2015), *supra* note 2892 at 122.
3035 Employment Rights Act 1996, *supra* note 2900 § 92(3).
3036 *Id.*§ 92(4).
3037 *Id.*§ 93.
3038 *See* Cabrelli (2015), *supra* note 2892 at 122.
3039 *Id.* at 123.

> The wrongful dismissal claim is a claim for breach of contract by failing to give notice. The task of the Employment Judge in such a case is to decide whether the Claimant has committed a repudiatory breach of contract, often in employment terms called gross misconduct. For this purpose, he reaches his own findings and applies the law of contract to them. But the remedy is limited to an award of compensation for loss by reason of the failure to give notice.[3040]

The claim for wrongful dismissal is enforced in court and it is not necessary that the claimant is an employee.[3041] Nevertheless, this claim cannot be brought where an employee has a fixed-term contract.[3042] Unfair and wrongful dismissal should not be considered in isolation and instead operate in tandem.[3043] Under employment legislation, there are three types of remedies in the event that an employee was unfairly dismissed, (1) reinstatement, (2) re-engagement, or (3) compensation.[3044] In the case that an employee suffers monetary or non-monetary losses as a result of an unfair or wrongful dismissal, the employee can be compensated with payment in lieu of notice or for the legally entitled notice.[3045] The employee can also claim for contractual benefits such as *e.g.* pensions benefits, bonus payments or insurance payments to which he is entitled during the period of notice. In addition, the employee can claim for *stigma damages* if he is incapable of obtaining alternative employment.[3046] That means that in some cases the stigma of dismissal will render an employee effectively unemployable.[3047]

An examination of the employment cases between 2010 and 2016 for unfair dismissal in Employment Tribunals and the Employment Appeal Tribunal and for wrongful dismissal in domestic courts, found one case in which a compliance officer claimed for wrongful dismissal.[3048] This case will be discussed in the next section.

a. Unfair Dismissal of a Compliance Officer?

The defendant, a senior employee, was employed by an investment adviser (UK) Limited between 2008 and 2010 and performed her duties as the executive in overall charge of compliance in the investment group.[3049] The claimant is incorporated in

---

3040 *Cossington v. C2C Rail Ltd* [2013] UKEAT 0053_13_1209, 3 (2013).
3041 *See* Cabrelli (2015), *supra* note 2892 at 124 Figure 8.1.
3042 *Id.* at 124. Figure 8.1.
3043 *Id.* at 125.
3044 Employment Rights Act 1996, *supra* note 2900 §§ 114, 115 and 117.
3045 *See* Cabrelli (2015), *supra* note 2892 at 125.
3046 *Id.* at 125.
3047 *See e.g.* This issue is discussed in: *Mattu v The University Hospitals of Coventry and Warwickshire NHS Trust* [2012] EWCA Civ 641, 98 (2012).
3048 Neutral Citation Number: [2010] EWHC 3241 (QB), (2010).
3049 *Id.* at 3.

England and provides investment advice.[3050] Since 2009, the executive had suffered a number of health problems attributable to the high level of stress involved in her work-related tasks.[3051] She found it very difficult to deal with her huge responsibilities as a compliance officer and thus, wanted to find a new job.[3052] Over several months, she transferred a huge volume of confidential material to her private e-mail address when she felt that her relationship with her employer was in jeopardy.[3053] On 10 May, 2010 the compliance officer was informed that she was to be dismissed on the grounds of redundancy with three months' notice.[3054] Four days later, however, her transfer of material was discovered by the IT-department and, on this basis, she was dismissed without notice one month later.[3055] The compliance officer also claimed for unfair dismissal in the Employment Tribunal. She pointed out that she did not plan to use the confidential information for competitive purposes, but thought that this material could support her case in any future employment disputes with the investment firm.[3056] However, the judge did not uphold these arguments and held that she had breached her implied duty of fidelity, which is an *"implied term in a contract of employment that the employee will serve the employer with fidelity and in good faith."*[3057] The court concluded that her conduct was in breach of her contract of employment and she failed to recover salary pay and damages for wrongful dismissal.

Hence, the basis in this case was not a wrongful dismissal due to a mistake in the performance of her job responsibilities as a compliance officer, but a breach of contractual duty as an employee like every other employee. In conclusion, it seems that, to date, no corporate compliance officer has claimed for wrongful or unfair dismissal in the UK concerning his specific duties and responsibilities of his function.

b. The Duties and Responsibilities Placed on Corporate Compliance Officers

This section summarizes the special duties and responsibilities incumbent upon the corporate compliance officer under employment law. As has been shown the compliance officer, as an employee primarily, has the same duties as other employees. In the UK, there are different types of implied duties owed by an employee. As we have seen in the case outlined above, the duty of fidelity, loyalty, and confidentiality extends to not disclosing confidential information about the employer's

3050 *Id.* at 2.
3051 *Id.* at 4.
3052 *Id.* at 5.
3053 *Id.* at 8.
3054 *Id.* at 10.
3055 *Id.* at 12.
3056 *Id.* at 18.
3057 *Id.* at 15.

business.[3058] In this event, the employer can seek an injunction in order to prevent the disclosure of confidential information. However, the ERA 1996 covers *"protected disclosures"*, which defined in Sections 43C to 43H.[3059] These exemptions include, for example, disclosure to legal advisers or to prescribed persons, such as the FCA.[3060] In addition, the common law only recognizes this restriction as long as the non-disclosure is necessary to protect the interests of the employer.[3061]

Another duty that the corporate compliance officer should be aware of is the duty of care. An employee has to exercise and perform his job with a normal degree of skill and care.[3062] Nevertheless, the compliance officers may be subject to a higher degree to the requirement to perform their jobs competently and carefully. As has been noted in the examined final notices by the FCA, the regulator expected that the compliance officers should detect irregularities in e-mails and attached documents, telephone conversations or correspondence of employees.[3063] They should be aware of early warning signs or so-called "*red flags*".[3064] This is a higher standard of due skill and care.

It could be argued that, in practice, there is a gap between a compliance officer's assessment of the standard of due skill and care and the regulator's expectation. In the event that a compliance officer is in breach of this standard and rules of conduct by the regulator, they may be subject to personal liability within the regulated sector. The FCA did not answer the question as to how the compliance officer may exercise reasonable professional conduct. Hence, the compliance officers have to deal with this uncertainty. According to a 2013 study by PWC, which compared a sample of US and UK-based companies from three diverse industries – financial services, manufacturing and technology - the results have shown that less regulated industries have begun to adopt formal compliance structures from the financial sector.[3065] This means, specifically, the establishment of a compliance committee, a compliance program and the appointment of a standalone compliance officer in the private sector.[3066] Although no case concerning a breach of a corporate compliance officer's duty of care was found, this does not necessarily indicate that the higher standard of this duty could not also apply to corporate compliance officers.

3058 Neutral Citation Number: [2010] EWHC 3241 (QB), *supra* note 3048.

3059 Employment Rights Act 1996, *supra* note 2900 §§ 43C to 43H.

3060 *Id.* §§ 43D and 43F.

3061 *See* Cabrelli (2015), *supra* note 2892 at 49.

3062 *Id.* at 40.

3063 *FSA v.* Individual one, *supra* note 2995; *FSA v.* Individual eight, *supra* note 3016; *FSA v.* Individual seven, *supra* note 3002.

3064 *FSA v.* Individual seven, *supra* note 3002.

3065 PwC Study 2013, *supra* note 1623 at 8.

3066 PwC Study 2013 *Id.* at 8.

For example, a 2015 study by the UCL's Centre for Ethics and Law, which is based on interviews with 34 senior in-house lawyers and senior compliance staff in UK companies, examined the management of legal risk.[3067] This study also analyzes the responsibilities of the compliance officers as regards legal risk management. The interviewees identified a more systematic approach to their companies' risk processes:

(1) To conduct exception and error monitoring,
(2) To conduct audits *e.g.* of contract processes or sales, or a verification to test sales processes;
(3) Receive customer feedback,
(4) Review of risk assessments.[3068]

The interviewees described the compliance function as more procedural, risk and behavior-oriented than the legal function within companies.[3069] This approach saw compliance as a *"command-and-control model."*[3070] Under the focus of regulators and prosecutors, companies have to meet regulatory and legal requirements. The term *"command-and control model"* is defined as the *"direct regulation of an industry or activity by legislation that states what is permitted and what is illegal."*[3071] The term command means the standards imposed by a government agency that must be complied with; the term control means the sanctions against or prosecution of companies that may result from non-compliance.[3072] Under this model, the legal function provides legal advice whereas the compliance function developed the detailed systems for explaining, monitoring, and enforcing those requirements.[3073] However, the interviewees also saw the limits of the data gathered by means of such process.[3074] In addition, they observed challenges like having adequate time and resources, coping with being seen as a cost center for the business, as well as coping with changing business and regulatory environments.[3075]

As has been shown above, the function of corporate compliance officer does not comprise primary responsibility for establishing and maintaining a compliance program within UK companies outside the regulated sector. Compared to the US corporate compliance officer, the UK compliance officer is more engaged in assessing risks, gathering and evaluating data. Finally, although there is legislative

3067 Richard Moorhead & Steven Vaughan, Legal Risk: Definition, Management and Ethics 2 (2015).
3068 *Id.* at 15.
3069 *Id.* at 17.
3070 *Id.* at 18.
3071 P. McMagnus, *Environmental Regulation*, Elsevier Ltd. (2009).
3072 *See* Robert Baldwin, Martin Cave & Martin Lodge, Understanding regulation: theory, strategy, and practice 106 (2nd ed. 2012).
3073 Moorhead and Vaughan (2015), *supra* note 3067 at 18.
3074 *Id.* at 18.
3075 *Id.* at 19.

enforcement of directors' duties in the area of company and bribery law, no legal requirement for the appointment of a separate compliance function is found for UK companies in the private sector.

c. **Indemnity Agreements – Protection for Compliance Officers**

As outlined above, in the UK, the company directors, the senior management, the company secretary and the corporate compliance officers are also responsible for corporate compliance.[3076] The compliance officer usually has a contract of employment and is considered to be an employee. Therefore, he is subject to the same protection of employment rights as the other employees. However, as we have seen, compliance officers may also face personal regulatory action if they fail to meet their responsibilities and the higher degree of duty of care. This is why compliance officers ought to carefully consider their personal liability. The Solicitors Regulation Authority (SRA) recommends that compliance officers should conclude an indemnity agreement with their employers.[3077]

Specifically, at first, they should identify and document their role, their duties and confirmation that they can access relevant business information within the company.[3078] These clauses should be added to their contract of employment. Next, compliance officers should ensure that they have access to independent external legal advice for their personal use and should attempt to include an indemnity *"from the practice for liabilities arising from their role to the extent permissible by law."*[3079] In addition, compliance officers should take out professional indemnity insurance or other insurance products will to protect themselves against fines and penalties.[3080] However, compliance officers need to bear in mind that they will not receive "*an indemnity against liability resulting from their own unlawful conduct.*"[3081]

5. Comparison of Employment Rights under UK and US Employment Law

As stated previously, US employment law does not feature any form of protection against dismissal,[3082] although American common law is pervaded by federal employment protection law such as anti-discrimination legislation.[3083] There are

3076 *See supra* II., 3a.-c., pp. 254 et seq.
3077 SRA, Compliance officers - The Law Society Compliance officers (2016), https://www.lawsociety.org.uk/support-services/advice/practice-notes/compliance-officers/#co6 (last visited Nov 7, 2016).
3078 *Id.*
3079 *Id.*
3080 *Id.*
3081 *Id.*
3082 *See supra*, pp. 274 et seq.
3083 *See e.g.* Civil Rights Act 1964 (CRA), *supra* note 2001.

no dedicated employment courts or tribunals.[3084] Therefore, the timeline for litigating an employment-related claim may take as long as 613 days.[3085] Another characteristic of the American employment relationship is that a number of compliance officers do not have a written contract of employment. The basic principle under American common law in the area of labor law is the employment at- will doctrine.[3086] Every State in the US, except Montana, uses the employment at- will doctrine.[3087] Only a few states require any explanation on the termination of a contract of employment.[3088] In all other instances, the employer can terminate the contract of employment at any time without notice and cause.[3089] However, as shown above, there are also common law exceptions to the US at- will doctrine.

As regards the sources of employment law, it has been noted that UK common law is based on more than common law principle and domestic legislation. Employment rights also derive from EU law.[3090] Hence, in the UK, the employer is required to provide for the employee *"a written statement of particulars of employment."*[3091] Thus, the UK compliance officer will usually receive a written contract with legally stipulated terms. Under the Employment Rights Act 1996, the UK compliance officer, as an employee, has the right to claim for unfair dismissal when he has been employed for a period of not less than two years.[3092] This claim must be enforced in an Employment Tribunal.

In conclusion, the at- will doctrine under United States Employment Law differs significantly from the position of the compliance officer in the United Kingdom. It also reflects differences in employee protection against wrongful termination. It appears that the corporate compliance officer is more efficiently protected under employment rights in the UK than the US corporate compliance officer. However, it needs to be taken into account that the UK compliance officer in the financial services sector could be banned from performing the compliance oversight function by the UK regulator. In both the US and the UK, compliance officers may also face personal liability where they fail to meet their responsibilities and duties. They should therefore consider the recommendations of the prosecutors and their guidance in terms of their specific duties and responsibilities, which were set up throughout the financial service sector.

3084 *See* HAY (2011), *supra* note 87 at 243.
3085 *See* Estreicher and Hirsch (2013), *supra* note 2011 at 456.
3086 *See* HAY (2011), *supra* note 87 at 245.
3087 *See* Exception of Monatana: MONTANA CODE AN., MONTANA WRONGFUL DISCHARGE FROM EMPLOYMENT ACT (1987), *supra* note 2022 Title 39. Labor Ch. 641, (1987); *See* in: Estreicher and Hirsch (2013), *supra* note 2011 at 465.
3088 *See* Estreicher and Hirsch (2013), *supra* note 2011 at 479, Table 12.
3089 *See supra* A., II., III. 1, pp. 254 et seq.
3090 *See supra* IV., pp. 373 et seq.
3091 EMPLOYMENT RIGHTS ACT 1996, *supra* note 2900 § 1 (1).
3092 *Id.* § 92 (3).

B. The UK Code and the Need for Greater Corporate Governance

Having examined and compared the primary law, English Company Law, Bribery Law and Employment Law applicable to compliance it has been found that there is no requirement for companies to establish a corporate compliance officer. A corporate compliance structure would be desirable in the event of violation of the law. For this reason, the next part of this chapter deals with the soft law or secondary law, such as Codes and Rules relating to compliance and the compliance officer in the UK.

As previously discussed, the question that arose in the course of various corporate scandals and a series of financial market crises attributable to governance failures is how to provide an appropriate level of monitoring of management.[3093] There was a lack of shareholder and investor control over corporate affairs. Since 1990, the answer has been the enactment of new legislation and the corporate governance reform over the last few decades in both the US and the UK, with corporate governance being recognized as a mechanism that could prevent corporate failures.[3094] There is no single accepted definition of the meaning of corporate governance. A narrow UK definition of corporate governance can be found in the Cadbury Report (1992) as *"the system by which companies are directed and controlled."*[3095] For the purpose of the examination of the UK Code, it will be applied the following definition by *Solomon*:

> Corporate governance is the system of checks and balances, both internal and external to companies, which ensures that companies discharge their accountability to all their stakeholders and act in a socially responsible way in all areas of their business activity.[3096]

The reason for this is that this broader definition also describes the internal and external relationships of a company. Today, one of the trademarks of English corporate governance is *"a separation of ownership and control."*[3097] Therefore, nowadays, English Company Law and the corporate governance reform focus on increasing managerial accountability, especially for company directors and officers.[3098] As

---

3093 *See* N.V. Okoye, Behavioural Risks in Corporate Governance: Regulatory Intervention as a Risk Management Mechanism 1 (2015).

3094 *See e.g.* Davies (2000), *supra* note 2606 at 21; *See also* Corporate Governance Prabhakar, *supra* note 1525; The Cadbury Report (1992), *supra* note 796 para 1.9; Okoye (2015), *supra* note 3093 at 1.

3095 The Cadbury Report (1992), *supra* note 796 at 2.

3096 *See* J. Solomon, Corporate Governance and Accountability 14 (2nd ed. 2007).

3097 *See* B.R. Cheffins, *The Undermining of UK Corporate Governance(?)*, 33 Oxford Journal of Legal Studies 503–533, 503 (2013); B.R. Cheffins, Corporate Ownership and Control: British Business Transformed (2010).

3098 *See* Cheffins (2013), *supra* note 3097 at 503.

previously discussed, contrary to the mandatory provisions of the US SOX, the UK response to corporate governance failure has been the *"comply or explain"* approach.[3099] Until the publication of the Cadbury Report in 1992, the governance of companies was regulated by custom together with stock exchange requirements and some basic rules laid down by company law.[3100] In the EU Member States, ten codes on corporate governance were issued between 1991 to 1997.[3101] Six of them were issued in the UK *e.g.* the Cadbury Report (1992) and the Greenbury Report (1995) by committees, which developed corporate governance issues and mechanisms in order to increase its effectiveness.[3102]

Although the Cadbury Report of 1992, later the Combined Code and today the UK Corporate Governance Code influence the internal governance structure within companies, they are not legally binding.[3103] Nevertheless, the reports, which followed the financial crisis in 2008 and 2009, found that the behavior of company directors is not appropriate in the application of governance processes.[3104] The reason is that the directors failed to inform the shareholders sufficiently and the company risk management was not properly overseen, monitored, and reviewed by the board.[3105]

Pursuant to the Companies Act 2006, company directors are responsible for the management of the company's business, for which purpose they may exercise all the powers of the company.[3106] The first directors and the company secretary are appointed and their power is granted by the shareholders.[3107] Similar to US State Corporation Law, directors are permitted to delegate any of their duties, to management executives such as officers or a committee.[3108] However, this delegation

---

3099 *See supra* B., p. 101; A., I., p. 176.

3100 *See* Azizah Abdullah *&* Michael Page, Corporate governance and corporate performance: UK FTSE 350 companies VI (2009).

3101 *See* Weil, Gotshal *&* Manges LLP (2002), *supra* note 2355 at 8.

3102 *See e.g.* the Cadbury (1992), the Greenbury (1995), the Hampel (1998) and the Turnbull (1999 and 2005) committee and reports; *See in* Abdullah and Page (2009), *supra* note 3100 at 7 Table 2.1 - Development of UK Corporate Governance; Okoye (2015), *supra* note 3093 at 2.

3103 *See* The Cadbury Report (1992) , *supra* note 796; The UK Corporate Governance Code, *supra* note 468; Davies (2000), *supra* note 2606 at 22. *See also* chronologically A., I., pp. 176 et seq.

3104 *See* Okoye (2015), *supra* note 3093 at 2; David Walker, ICSA, Boardroom Behaviours 7 (2009) para 3.1.1 and 3.1.2.

3105 Walker and ICSA, *supra* note 3104 at 7 para 3.1.1.

3106 Companies Act 2006, *supra* note 532, § 20; Model Articles of Association for Private and Public Companies, Table A Schedule 1 (2014) Art. 3.

3107 Companies Act 2006, *supra* note 532, §§ 20, 156; Model Articles of Association for Private and Public Companies, *supra* note 3106 Art. 5; *See* in: Okoye (2015), *supra* note 3093 at 214.

3108 Companies Act 2006, *supra* note 532, § 20; Model Articles of Association for Private and Public Companies, *supra* note 3106 Art. 5.

cannot eliminate the director's primary responsibility for the company's management.[3109] All other corporate officers are required to act in accordance with instructions from the directors.[3110] English Company Law states that company directors are included in the group of company managers, who have duties in respect of the company.[3111]

Therefore, the next sections introduce the most important provisions of the UK Corporate Governance Code 2016 and the UK Listing Rules in terms of the main principles, structures, approaches and processes which are developed in order to establish effective behavior of the members of board and compliance with rules.

I. The UK Corporate Governance Code 2016

Generally, a code can be defined as a *"non-binding set of principles, standards or best practices, issued by a collective body and relating to the internal governance of corporations."*[3112] The UK Code was created to guide the board on an effective practice and it is part of a framework of best practice standards to improve high quality corporate governance.[3113] It was issued by committees organized by the government.[3114] It focuses on the principles of good governance, accountability, transparency, probity, and the relationship between the company and its shareholders.[3115] The UK Code contains main and supporting principles as well as provisions. The version of 2016 applies after June 2016 and to all companies with a listing of shares, regardless of where they are incorporated.[3116] The updated version of the UK Code was necessitated by changes from the implementation of the European Union's Audit Regulation and Directive in 2016.[3117] As a result,

---

3109 *See* Okoye (2015), *supra* note 3093 at 109.

3110 *Id.* at 109.

3111 Companies Act 2006, *supra* note 532 §§ 154 - 156, 171 - 177.

3112 *See e.g.* Andrew Keay, *Comply or explain in corporate governance codes: in need of greater regulatory oversight?: Comply or explain in corporate governance codes*, 34 Legal Studies 279–304, 279–280 (2014); Weil, Gotshal & Manges LLP (2002), *supra* note 2355 at 1.

3113 FRC, The UK Corporate Governance Code (2016), https://frc.org.uk/Our-Work/Publications/Corporate-Governance/Final-Draft-UK-Corporate-Governance-Code-2016.pdf, Preface para 1 [hereinafter The UK Corporate Governance Code (2016)].

3114 *Chronologically*, the Cadbury (1992), Greenbury (1995), Hampel (1998) and Turnbull (1999) Committees; *See e.g.* The Cadbury Report (1992), *supra* note 796.

3115 The UK Corporate Governance Code (2016), *supra* note 3113 at 5.para 5.

3116 *Id.* at 5. para 6.

3117 Directive 2014/56/EU of the European Parliament and of the Council amending Directive 2006/43/EC on statutory audits of annual accounts and consolidated accounts, L 158/196 (2014); Regulation (EU) No 537/2014 of the European Parliament and of the Council on specific requirements

e.g. provision C.3 of the Code was reviewed and amended in accordance with the European legislation.[3118]

1. The "Comply or Explain" Approach or Compliance Mechanism of the Code

In most instances, the concept of such a Code is the *"comply or explain"* approach.[3119] This comply or explain approach is referred to as the *"trademark"* or *"the heart of the voluntary corporate governance code"*.[3120] This flexible approach allows listed companies to choose either to comply with the principles of the Codes or to explain why they do not, which means companies have the choice to opt out of the recommendations of the Code.[3121] Therefore, listed companies need not implement the substantive Code provisions.[3122] However, the stock exchange listing requirements impose admission and disclosure standards for listed companies based on the degree to which they comply with Code recommendations.[3123] For example, listed companies on the London Stock Exchange (LSE) have to include in their annual financial reports a statement on how they have applied the main principles set out in the UK Code and, where they have not complied with the relevant provisions, they have to explain the reasons for non-compliance.[3124] Hence, the disclosure statement of the UK Code is strengthened.[3125] Finally, this disclosure requirement for listed companies could lead to pressure to comply with the provisions of the Code.[3126] In addition, where the LSE considers that a listed company has breached its obligations under the exchange standards and Listing Rules, the LSE may take disciplinary action against this company.[3127] Legal scholars are afraid that this pressure of compliance on companies could

---

REGARDING STATUTORY AUDIT OF PUBLIC-INTEREST ENTITIES AND REPEALING COMMISSION DECISION 2005/909/EC, L 158/77 (2014); THE UK CORPORATE GOVERNANCE CODE (2016), *supra* note 3113 Preface para 5.

3118 THE UK CORPORATE GOVERNANCE CODE (2016), *supra* note 3113 Preface para 5, Provision C.3.1–C.3.8.

3119 *See e.g.* Keay (2014), *supra* note 3112 at 280; WEIL, GOTSHAL *&* MANGES LLP (2002), *supra* note 2355 at 2.

3120 *See e.g.* Keay (2014), *supra* note 3112 at 279; THE UK CORPORATE GOVERNANCE CODE (2016), *supra* note 3113 para 1.

3121 *See e.g.* Arcot, Bruno, and Faure-Grimaud (2010), *supra* note 443 at 193; THE UK CORPORATE GOVERNANCE CODE (2016), *supra* note 3113 at 4 para 1.

3122 *See* WEIL, GOTSHAL *&* MANGES LLP (2002), *supra* note 2355 at 2.

3123 *Id.* at 2.; Admissions and Disclosure Standards LSE, *supra* note 2328 at 71 B8.

3124 Admissions and Disclosure Standards LSE, *supra* note 2328 at 71 B8, 32.3.1 and 32.3.2.

3125 *See* WEIL, GOTSHAL *&* MANGES LLP (2002), *supra* note 2355 at 2.

3126 *Id.* at 2.

3127 Admissions and Disclosure Standards LSE, *supra* note 2328 at 73 B10, 36.

lead to a *"compliance-driven box-ticking"* approach to monitoring.[3128] The Hampel Committee has already reviewed this risk to help prevent companies from pursuing a "*box-ticking*" approach.[3129]

In conclusion, the comply or explain approach of the UK Code encourages listed companies to comply with the Code in connection with the London Stock Exchange Standards and Listing Rules. This combination creates a voluntary mechanism and nature of the corporate governance principles and recommendations relating to disclosure requirements.[3130]

2. The Main Provisions of UK Codes as Regards Compliance

This section analyzes three of the eighteen provisions of the UK Code 2016 with respect to compliance. As already noted, the UK Code is based on principles and provisions. The principles comprise main and supporting principles, which are preceded by the provisions.[3131] The UK Code contains five main principles. These are: leadership, effectiveness, accountability, remuneration and the director-shareholder relationship, which is the heart of the Code.[3132] They are important for the board where they determine how the board should operate according to the Code.[3133]

At first, the provisions of the Code focus on the duties of the members of the board as a supervisory body that is distinct from senior management.[3134] Various corporate scandals led to the need for a distinction between the control and execution function within companies. Therefore, the UK Code emphasizes the composition of the board in order to establish the independence between the supervisory and managerial function.[3135] For example, Code provision A.3.1 states that

> A chief executive should not go on to be chairman of the same company.[3136]

Secondly, according to the UK Code, the effectiveness of a board is enhanced by its structure and procedures. Under the principle in Section B, the Code sets out the composition of the board.

> The board should include an appropriate combination of executive and non-executive directors.[3137]

3128 *See e.g.* Keay (2014), *supra* note 3112 at 289, 297.
3129 *See* Abdullah and Page (2009), *supra* note 3100 at 7 Table 2.1.
3130 *See e.g.* Okoye (2015), *supra* note 3093 at 162; Weil, Gotshal & Manges LLP (2002), *supra* note 2355 at 19 Table C.
3131 The UK Corporate Governance Code (2016), *supra* note 3113 at 4 para 2.
3132 The UK Corporate Governance Code (2016) *Id.* at 4. para 2.
3133 The UK Corporate Governance Code (2016) *Id.* at 4. para 2.
3134 *See* Weil, Gotshal & Manges LLP (2002), *supra* note 2355 at 77.
3135 *Id.* at 77.
3136 The UK Corporate Governance Code (2016), *supra* note 3113 at 8 A.3.1.
3137 The UK Corporate Governance Code (2016) *Id.* at 10. B.1.

However, a 2002 survey of FTSE chairmen found that the structure of the board and its independent members are of secondary importance to the effectiveness.[3138] In their view, one important issue is, for example the international experience of the members of the board.[3139] Today, the UK Code 2016 states that *"the board and its committees should have the appropriate balance of skills, experience, independence and knowledge."*[3140] The required board composition was already standard practice for larger companies with dominant shareholders listed on the London Stock Exchange.[3141] A study by *Abdullah & Page* shows the typical UK board structure of FTSE 350 non-financial companies in 2004, which comprises four executive directors and five non-executives of whom four were independent.[3142]

In addition, the Code sets out provisions that refer to disclosure obligations, such as B.1.1.

> The board should identify in the annual report each non-executive director it considers to be independent.[3143]

In detail, the Code includes specific requirements for disclosure in the annual report in order to comply with certain provisions, for example the names of the chairman, the deputy chairman, the chief executive, the senior independent director and the chairmen and members of the board committees and the names of the non-executive directors.[3144] This information should be made available through placing on the company's website.[3145]

Finally, the last provision that will be examined refers directly to the compliance duties of the board:

> The board should monitor the company's risk management and internal control systems and, at least annually, carry out a review of their effectiveness, and report on that review in the annual report. The monitoring and review should cover all material controls, including financial, operational and compliance controls.[3146]

3138 *See* Russell Reynolds Associates, What makes an effective UK Board? Views from FTSE Chairmen. (2002); See in: Abdullah and Page (2009), *supra* note 3100 at 13.

3139 *See* Russell Reynolds Associates, *supra* note 3138; *See* in: Abdullah and Page (2009), *supra* note 3100 at 13.

3140 The UK Corporate Governance Code (2016), *supra* note 3113 at 5.

3141 *See* Cheffins (2013), *supra* note 3097 at 522.

3142 FTSE 350 *See supra* note 847, p. 163; Abdullah and Page (2009), *supra* note 3100 at 8.

3143 The UK Corporate Governance Code (2016), *supra* note 3113 at 10 B.1.1.

3144 The UK Corporate Governance Code (2016) *Id.* at 28–29. *See e.g.* Schedule B - A.1.2., B.1.1, etc.

3145 The UK Corporate Governance Code (2016) *Id.* at 29.; *See e.g.* Card Factory, Board of Directors, http://www.cardfactoryinvestors.com/about-us/board-of-directors.aspx (last visited Nov 15, 2016).

3146 The UK Corporate Governance Code (2016), *supra* note 3113 C.2.3.

Therefore, the UK Code clearly points to the accountability of the board in terms of compliance. The board is responsible for determining and assessing the company's risks and should maintain the internal control systems.[3147]

It is clear from the foregoing that the main aim of the UK Code 2016 is to ensure that shareholders are empowered to make an informed evaluation of the company.[3148] The provisions of the UK Code support and benefit of shareholders, helping them, for example, to hold directors to account.[3149] Nevertheless, there has been more focus on the corporate structure and far less focus on the behavior of corporate directors or officers in the UK.[3150] The UK Code provides guidance in general terms and principles but cannot guarantee good corporate behavior of directors or officers.[3151] For this reason, it is essential to assess the capacity of directors because there is a lack of evaluation of the relationship between the personality and behavior of the directors.[3152]

In conclusion, it can be stated that the board has the power and the duty to monitor the management.[3153] In addition, the distinction between the executive directors and non-executive directors could be a distinction between the supervisory role and the management role within the board.[3154] Generally, non-executive directors are regarded as directors with no contract of employment. They should manage and judge independently the company and its affairs free from business considerations. Despite the fact that the UK Code does not include any provision referring to officers such as a compliance officer, it states clearly that the board is responsible for compliance controls.

3. The Effect of the UK Code on Compliance by FTSE 350 Companies

Following the examination of the goal, approach and main provisions in terms of compliance, this section reviews the impact of the UK Code regarding compliance by the largest listed companies in the UK. As already defined in a narrow sense, compliance refers to the duty to obey the rules or law. In a broader sense, it also includes the board of directors making decisions lawfully and acting in good faith.[3155] As has been noted, the structure of the senior or top management is not based on law.[3156] Similar to US Corporation Law, the location of power is laid down

---

3147 The UK Corporate Governance Code (2016) *Id.* at 17. Main Principle C.2.
3148 *See* Keay (2014), *supra* note 3112 at 279.
3149 Company Law Review Steering Group, *supra* note 2432 at 9 para 2.7.
3150 *See* Okoye (2015), *supra* note 3093 at 35.
3151 *Id.* at 35.
3152 The UK Corporate Governance Code (2016), *supra* note 3113 at 5; Okoye (2015), *supra* note 3093 at 41.
3153 *See* Mäntysaari (2006), *supra* note 2446 at 104
3154 *See* Davies (2000), *supra* note 2606 at 8.
3155 Company Law Review Steering Group, *supra* note 2432 at 29 para 3.40.
3156 *See* Mäntysaari (2006), *supra* note 2446 at 104.

in the articles of association.[3157] Hence, the companies can structure their management in different ways and have the freedom to make their own rules about their internal affairs.[3158] However, the UK Code recommends how they can govern the company in the best interests of shareholders and society. The board of directors should lead by example and ensure good standards of behavior throughout the company in order to prevent misconduct.[3159]

The UK Code aims to improve the long-term success of companies by putting in place an appropriate corporate governance structure.[3160] It has been established that, under the UK Code, there is increasing pressure for listed companies, like the FTSE 350, to separate the role of the chairman and the CEO, to structure the audit committee, to increase the number and role of non-executive directors (NEDs) and especially of independent NEDs in the UK.[3161] The Financial Reporting Council (FRC) states that 99 percent of the FTSE 350 companies and 99 percent of smaller companies are in compliance with Provision A.2.1 of the Code, 92 percent of the FTSE 350 companies and 88 percent of smaller companies are in compliance with Provision B.1.2 and 97 percent of the FTSE 350 companies and 94 percent of smaller companies meet the Provision C.3.1 requirement for the audit committee structure.[3162] In addition, listed companies or an issuer on the London Stock Exchange must be aware that there could be a binding force under stock exchange rules such as the UK Listing Rules.[3163] Hence, listed companies have learned that, today, non-compliance with the provisions of the Code is not sustainable and they should not underestimate the importance of the Corporate Governance Code quite apart from the hard or primary law such as company law or the law on bribery.[3164]

The current Grant Thornton 2016 Corporate Governance Review of FTSE 350 companies revealed that full compliance with the UK Code has risen at 62 percent.[3165]

3157 Companies Act 2006, *supra* note 532, § 18; *See* Mäntysaari (2006), *supra* note 2446 at 104.

3158 Companies Act 2006, *supra* note 532, Commentary on Section 18.

3159 The UK Corporate Governance Code (2016), *supra* note 3113 at 2 para 4.

3160 The UK Corporate Governance Code (2016) *Id.* at 2 Preface, para 1.

3161 The UK Corporate Governance Code (2016), *Id.* A.2.1, B.1.2, C.3.1; FTSE 350 London Stock Exchange, *supra* note 847.

3162 The FRC maintains codes and standards. *See* FRC, *supra* note 811; FRC, Developments in Corporate Governance and Stewardship 2015 5 (2016) Table - Compliance with selected provisions of the UK Corporate Governance Code.

3163 Admissions and Disclosure Standards LSE, *supra* note 2328 at 73 B.8 Corporate Governance para 32. The term issuer in the UK is defined as follows: *"Any company or other legal person or undertaking (including a public- sector issuer) any class of whose securities has been admitted, or is proposed to be, the subject of an application for admission to trading." See in: Id.* at 5.

3164 *See* Davies (2000), *supra* note 2606 at 23.

3165 Grant Thornton, Corporate Governance Review 2016 3 (2016), http://www.grantthornton.co.uk/globalassets/1.-member-firms/united-kingdom/pdf/

This Review comprised an analysis of the annual report with a sample of 308 of these companies.[3166] The fact is that, regardless of this success, a significant challenge remains in applying the provisions of the Code to larger companies. The greatest gap between compliance and non-compliance remains the independence of directors and chairs.[3167] The Review found that Code Provision B.1.2. has the greatest rate of non-compliance with 28.7 percent of FTSE 350.[3168] Only 7.8 percent of the FTSE 350 companies do not comply with the separation of the role of the chair and chief executive.[3169] Finally, only 19 percent of these companies provide good or detailed explanations of how they review the effectiveness of their internal controls regarding UK Code Provision C.2.3.[3170]

The Grant Thornton Review shows, on the one hand, that the UK Code improves transparency and the accountability of the boards of directors in particular regarding what information must be made available in- and outside the company.[3171] The UK Code and the Listing Rules have enforced compliance for listed companies through disclosure.[3172] However, it can hardly be said that corporate compliance has been strengthened given the non-conformity with provisions of the UK Code based on decisions of the company's shareholders. If the shareholders agree, the provision is ignored.[3173] In accordance with the Thornton Review, the board structure and composition remains the most important issue for non-compliance with the Code.[3174]

On the other hand, the UK Code 2016 and its predecessors have no statutory force. Listed companies are required by the Listing Rules to disclose in their annual report that they have governed the company in compliance with the provisions of the Code.[3175] In the event of non-conformity or non-compliance, shareholders can take appropriate actions against the company.[3176] Following the Grant Thornton Review and the studies by *Arcot et al.* and *Abdullah & Page*, it has been recognized

---

publication/2016/2016-corporate-governance-review.pdf (last visited Nov 20, 2016) [hereinafter GRANT THORNTON REVIEW 2016].

3166 GRANT THORNTON REVIEW 2016, *Id.* at 1.

3167 GRANT THORNTON REVIEW 2016, *Id.* at 3.

3168 GRANT THORNTON REVIEW 2016, *Id.* at 26. Table- Areas companies list as non-compliant.

3169 GRANT THORNTON REVIEW 2016, *Id.* at 26.; THE UK CORPORATE GOVERNANCE CODE (2016), *supra* note 3113 at 8 Provision A.2.1.

3170 GRANT THORNTON REVIEW 2016, *supra* note 3165 at 53; The UK Corporate Governance Code (2016), *supra* note 3113 at 17 Provision C.2.3.

3171 GRANT THORNTON REVIEW 2016, *supra* note 2983.

3172 *See infra* footnote 3178, p. 405 - The UK Listing Rules (DTR) and (LR).

3173 *See* OKOYE (2015), *supra* note 3093 at 83.

3174 *Id.* at 84.; THE GRANT THORNTON REVIEW 2016 , *supra* note 3165 at 26.

3175 COMPANY LAW REVIEW STEERING GROUP, *supra* note 2432 at 61 para 3.117.

3176 *Id.* at 61. para 3.117.

that since 1992, the main significance of the Code has been in developing an effective framework for compliance in the UK.[3177]

II. The UK Listing Rules

Corporate governance disclosure requirements are stipulated not only in the UK Code, but also in the FCA Disclosure and Transparency Rules (DTR), which set out certain mandatory provisions in the FCA Listing Rules (LR) and in the FCA Handbook, which includes the comply or explain requirement.[3178] The purpose of these requirements was to implement parts of the Accounting Directive.[3179] This Directive requires both credit institutions and investment firms to publish a corporate governance statement *"in order to strengthen legal compliance and corporate governance."*[3180] Nevertheless, DTR 7.2 also applies to issuers, which are listed on the LSE and which are companies within the meaning of Section 1(1) of the Companies Act 2006.[3181] As stated previously, pursuant to Section 1 of the CA 2006, a company is defined as a *"company formed and registered under this Act"*.[3182] DTR 7.2 states that an issuer *"must include a corporate governance statement in its directors' report."*[3183] However, there is an exemption to the DTR 7.2.8 AR for smaller and medium-sized companies as defined in the Companies Act 2006.[3184] The other issuers must include a corporate governance statement in their directors' report.[3185] This report must comprise the following information:

(1) the corporate governance code to which the issuer is subject;

3177 *See e.g.* Arcot, Bruno, and Faure-Grimaud (2010), *supra* note 443; ABDULLAH AND PAGE (2009), *supra* note 3100; GRANT THORNTON REVIEW 2016, *supra* note 3165.

3178 FCA, DISCLOSURE GUIDANCE AND TRANSPARENCY RULES SOURCEBOOK (DTR) (2016), https://www.handbook.fca.org.uk/handbook/DTR.pdf (last visited Nov 26, 2016) Sub-Ch. 7.1 and 7.2; LR 9.8.6 and 9.8.7 FCA, *supra* note 2390; See in: THE UK CORPORATE GOVERNANCE CODE (2016), *supra* note 3113 Schedule B.

3179 DTR 1B.1.4 FCA, *supra* note 3176; DIRECTIVE 2013/36/EU OF THE EUROPEAN PARLIAMENT AND OF THE COUNCIL (CRD IV DIRECTIVE), *supra* note 1053.

3180 DTR 1B.1.4 FCA, *supra* note 3176; DIRECTIVE 2013/36/EU OF THE EUROPEAN PARLIAMENT AND OF THE COUNCIL (CRD IV DIRECTIVE), *supra* note 1053 at (61).

3181 COMPANIES ACT 2006, *supra* note 532, § 1(1); DTR 1B.1.5 FCA, *supra* note 2990.

3182 COMPANIES ACT 2006, *supra* note 532, § 1(1).

3183 DTR 7.2.1 FCA, *supra* note 3176.

3184 DTR 1B.1.7R, 7.2.8AR *Id.*; COMPANIES ACT 2006, *supra* note 532, §§ 382 - 383, 465 - 466. According to the CA 2006 a small company has not more than £6.5 million turnover, not more than £3.26 million balance sheet total and not more than 50 employees. Generally, a medium-sized company has not more than £25.9 million turnover, not more than £12.9 million balance sheet total and not more than 250 employees.

3185 DTR 7.2.1 R FCA, *supra* note 3176.

(2) the corporate governance code which the issuer may have voluntarily decided to apply; and
(3) all relevant information about the corporate governance practices applied over and above the requirements of national law.[3186]

In addition, the issuer must state where the code is publicly available, where it departs from that code and its reasons for doing so.[3187] The issuer also has to describe the main features of its internal control and risk management systems.[3188] Finally, the issuer has to state the composition and operation of its administrative, management and supervisory bodies and its committees.[3189]

The Listing Rules for the UK apply to issuers with a Premium listing of shares on the London Stock Exchange.[3190] The requirements for these companies are set forth in LR 9.8.6. Their annual report must include a statement on how they have applied the five main principles set out in the UK Code.[3191] This statement should enable the shareholders to evaluate how the issuer has applied the principles.[3192] Furthermore, the Premium listed company must state that it has complied with all relevant provisions set out in the UK Code.[3193] In the event that the issuer has not complied, it must disclose those provisions that it has not complied with and set out the reasons for non-compliance.[3194]

Overall, it has been noted that there are some overlaps between certain mandatory disclosures required under the DTR and those provisions under the UK Code 2016.[3195]

3186 DTR 7.2.2 R *Id.*
3187 DTR 7.2.3 R *Id.*
3188 DTR 7.2.5 R *Id.*
3189 DTR 7.2.7 R *Id.*
3190 *"The Premium segment is only open to equity shares issued by trading companies and closed and open-ended investment entities. Issuers with a Premium Listing are required to meet the UK's super-equivalent rules which are higher than the EU minimum requirements. As Premium Listed companies comply with the UK's highest standards of regulation and corporate governance, as a consequence they may enjoy a lower cost of capital through greater transparency and through building investor confidence." See* LSE, About the Main Market - London Stock Exchange, http://www.londonstockexchange.com/companies-and-advisors/main-market/main/market.htm (last visited Dec 1, 2016).
3191 The UK Corporate Governance Code (2016), *supra* note 3113 Main Principles, Schedule B.
3192 Handbook FCA, *supra* note 863 LR 9.8.6; *See in:* The UK Corporate Governance Code (2016), *supra* note 3113 Schedule B.
3193 Handbook FCA, *supra* note 863 LR 9.8.6; *See in:* The UK Corporate Governance Code (2016), *supra* note 3113 Schedule B.
3194 Handbook FCA, *supra* note 863 LR 9.8.6; *See in:* The UK Corporate Governance Code (2016), *supra* note 3113 Schedule B.
3195 *See e.g.* The UK Corporate Governance Code (2016), *supra* note 3113 Provision A.1.1, A.1.2; DTR 7.2.7 R FCA, *supra* note 3176.

Hence, compliance with certain provisions of the Code results in compliance with the relevant DTR.[3196] It has been recognized that the present UK Code and the Listing Rules enhanced through disclosure transparency as to how companies govern their structure with which individuals. Based on this information, it is possible to identify potential risks for certain behavior in corporate governance. It has been shown that company directors are the primary corporate managers and accountable for corporate performance. In conclusion, the evidence highlights that good corporate governance, both as principles and processes, can affect responsible corporate behavior and balance the interests of shareholders and internal stakeholders of the company.

III. Comparison between the US SOX and the UK Code

This section compares the mandatory approach of the SOX and the comply or explain approach of the UK Code by summarizing the most important findings in the foregoing chapter three and sections of the chapter four regarding the content of disclosure requirements and the impact thereof on corporate governance and compliance. Table 18 presents an overview of mandatory and voluntary requirements placed on listed companies on the US and UK Stock Exchanges with regard to corporate governance and compliance. Both the Act and the Code apply to listed companies and to issuers or public companies on the exchanges.

Although the SOX is primary or hard law and the UK Code secondary or soft law, the disclosure requirements incumbent upon companies are similar. While comparing the content of mandatory and voluntary requirements it could be argued that the SOX provisions are more detailed as regards to individual accountability and the enforcement thereof. Compared with the UK Code, the SOX requires additional professional responsibility: a duty of care. Non-compliance with the law may result in criminal penalties. Furthermore, by reviewing the mandatory requirements of the SOX, it could be assumed that board and director independence and better board governance will be positively associated with greater mandatory disclosure completeness and timeless.[3197] However, the empirical evidence identified in the studies, shows that this link is not so clear cut.[3198]

As mentioned previously, a trademark or hallmark of UK corporate governance has been *"a separation of ownership and control."*[3199] It includes *inter alia* the enhancement of managerial accountability, similar to the US.[3200] UK corporate governance also involves the company's risk management and monitoring of internal control systems

---

3196 The UK Corporate Governance Code (2016), *supra* note 3113 at 25 Schedule B.
3197 *See* Choudhary, Schloetzer, and Sturgess (2013), *supra* note 1568.
3198 *Id.*
3199 *See* Cheffins (2013), *supra* note 3097 at 503.
3200 *Id.* at 503.

Table 18 *Comparison between the Mandatory and Voluntary Requirements Placed on Issuers on the US and UK Stock Exchanges*

Subject	SOX 2002	UK Code 2016
Source	Federal Securities Law Primary Law	Code – Set of Principles Secondary Law
Regulator and its Rules	SEC - Mandatory SEC Disclosure Rules.	FCA - DTR and LR Admission and Disclosure Standards of the LSE
Stock Exchanges	NYSE, NASDAQ	LSE
Application	Extraterritorial, Global Impact	All companies with a premium listing of shares, regardless of where they are incorporated.
Definition of Issuer	A company that has registered securities on the U.S. Exchange (§ 2)	Any company or other legal person or undertaking any class of whose securities has been admitted, or is proposed to be, the subject of an application for admission to trading. (DTR p.5)
Disclosure of Accounting	Each financial report that contains financial statements, and that **is required** to be prepared in accordance with (or reconciled to) generally accepted accounting principles under this title **shall reflect** all material correcting adjustments. (§ 401)	The directors **should explain** in the annual report their responsibility for preparing the annual report and accounts. Provision C.1.1
Corporate Responsibility for financial Reports and Disclosure	Required Certification by CEOs and CFOs (§ 302)	The directors **should confirm** that they have carried out a robust assessment of the principal risks. Provision C.2.1
Individual Accountability	The financial statements of corporate officers **shall certify** that the periodic report containing the financial statement **fully complies** with the requirements. (§ 906)	The annual report **should identify** members of the board and board committees. Provision A.1.2
Auditor Independence	Establishment of a Public Company Accounting Oversight Board to oversee the audit of public companies, (§ 101)	Establishment of an Audit Committee of independent non-executive directors. Provision C.3.1.

Table 18 *Continued*

Subject	**SOX 2002**	**UK Code 2016**
Disclosure of Compliance	Mandatory (*See* Form 8-K and Form 10-K)	Statement of *"comply or explain"*concerning the relevant provisions of the Code.
Corporate Governance Structure	The responsibility of management for establishing and maintaining an adequate internal control structure. (§ 401 (1))	The board **should** monitor the company's risk management and internal control systems. Provision C.2.3
Specific Duties	Fiduciary Duty of Care, Professional Responsibility for Attorneys (§ 307 (1))	The board and its committees **should have** the appropriate balance of skills, experience, independence and knowledge. (Main Principle)
Penalties	Whoever knowingly alters or destroys any record or document **shall be fined** with imprisonment. (§§ 802, 807)	Shareholders **can bring** an action against the company in the event of non-conformity or non-compliance with the Code.

through rules.[3201] Such control can be described as a system of checks and balances that regulates the relationships both inside and outside the firm.

The US system has attempted to enhance disclosure requirements for companies through a statute and mandatory provisions, as opposed to the concept of comply or explain, which is at the core of the voluntary Code in the UK.[3202] This concept or approach means that, if a company does not comply with a certain provision, it has to clearly state this, along with an explanation of why it does not.[3203] These company statements are not assessed by regulators.[3204] The aim of the UK comply or explain approach is for the shareholders to evaluate the non-comply statements of the company and then decide whether they will take any action against the company.[3205] It can be argued that a high level of stakeholder engagement or stewardship by shareholders has developed a compliance culture within companies in the UK. In sum, the UK Code has focused more on the development of corporate governance structures and far less focus on the behavior of corporate directors or officers than the provisions of the SOX.

3201 The UK Corporate Governance Code (2016), *supra* note 3113 at 17 Provision C.2.3.
3202 *See* Keay (2014), *supra* note 3112 at 279.
3203 *Id.* at 279.
3204 *Id.* at 279.
3205 *Id.* at 279.

However, the comply or explain approach faces two major problems. On the one hand, the explanations concerning non-compliance by companies are very often brief and uninformative; on the other hand, the shareholders do not sufficiently pay attention that the board provides adequate explanations.[3206] For this reason, there are considerations in the UK as to whether the establishment of a regulator could ensure the veracity of the statements and the quality of the explanations provided by companies.[3207] At present, these problems remain unsolved and are a matter for future debate. As such, in conclusion, it is difficult to say which approach works better and both the mandatory and the voluntary approach have a part to play in the development of corporate governance and disclosure requirements.

Finally, it has explored that a corporate compliance function is not required neither under the SOX nor under the UK Code. Foremost, in both the US and UK, the accountability for compliance lies and remains with the management such as the CEO, CFO and board in the private sector. On the contrary, the findings have revealed that there are no common law principles or secondary law that the corporate officer has the same duties as directors or board in the UK. However, the huge UK legislation in the area of company law has enhanced the duties of directors and corporate officers in default over the years.

C. The Model of the Corporate Compliance Officer in the UK

Having examined the legal framework governing compliance in the UK in the foregoing two parts of this chapter, it has been noted that an appropriate degree of protection for investors alongside the strengthening of shareholders' rights have shaped the duties and responsibilities of company directors and officers, the corporate structure and the role of compliance within UK companies. This part now lays down the corner-stones for the model of the UK corporate compliance officer, as revealed in the examination of the primary and secondary legal framework, as well as the existing case law in the UK. First, it introduces the legal duties and responsibilities incumbent upon corporate compliance officers, before going on to point out the command and control model of this position.

I. Development of Responsibilities and Duties of the Compliance Officer

In the UK, unlike other professions, such as barristers, the post of a corporate compliance officer is not legally defined. UK Company Law, the Bribery Act and the UK

3206 *See e.g.* Arcot, Bruno, and Faure-Grimaud (2010), *supra* note 443 at 200; Keay (2014), *supra* note 3112 at 303.

3207 *See e.g.* Arcot, Bruno, and Faure-Grimaud (2010), *supra* note 443 at 200; Keay (2014), *supra* note 3112.

Code do not stipulate a standalone position of corporate compliance officer, while *e.g.* a director or a company secretary is required under company law. Within the private sector, the compliance duties and responsibilities are spread over several corporate positions. It could be argued that the responsibilities of the compliance officer are often delegated to the director or executive officer in the UK, and to the vice-president in the US.[3208] Nevertheless, contrary to the combined US legal and compliance function, UK companies more often favor a standalone compliance function.[3209] As we have seen, the members of the board, the directors and the company secretary are involved in compliance monitoring or compliance controls. The title of compliance officer is transferred from other regulated industries, such as the financial services sector, in which a control function is required under the regulatory senior management system. However, under primary and secondary law in the UK with the enforcement of prosecutors, the existence of a seriously proactive and effective corporate governance regime or adequate corporate procedures could serve as a basis for a defense against prosecution. However, the features and requirements of an effective corporate compliance program and procedures have not been defined neither by law nor by the courts.

Secondly, in the UK, the responsibilities and duties of compliance are often carried by directors or the company secretary within companies. Directors are appointed by the board. They hold an office, not an employment. Under English common law, it has been established that the company director owes a duty of skill and care relating to the company's business affairs. Traditionally, the standard applicable to this duty was fairly low. However, this standard has evolved with the development of company law so that now, pursuant to Section 174 of the CA 2006, the company director owes a *"duty to exercise reasonable care, skill and diligence"*.[3210] This means the care, skill, and diligence that would be expected from a reasonably diligent person, exercising the performance of the daily business with general directors' knowledge, skill and experience.[3211] Therefore, this duty was codified in the law with a higher standard. In practice, the reasonable duty of care and skill includes an objective assessment of a director's conduct. Additionally, in the event that they delegate their powers to a manager, executive officer or the company secretary, the director is under a duty to supervise the delegated function since the director is not discharged of these delegated functions.

Thirdly, in accordance with the UK Code, the board of FTSE 350 companies should monitor the company's risk management and internal control systems.[3212] Thus, the board's monitoring duty also applies to compliance controls.[3213] The

---

3208 PWC Study 2013, *supra* note 1623 at 18.
3209 PWC Study 2013 *Id.* at 16.
3210 Companies Act 2006, *supra* note 532 § 174.
3211 *Id.*§ 174 (2) (a)(b).
3212 The UK Corporate Governance Code (2016), *supra* note 3113 at 17 Provision C.2.3.
3213 The UK Corporate Governance Code (2016) *Id.* at 17. Provision C.2.3.

board and its committees should consist of an appropriate combination of executive and non-executive directors.[3214] Overall, in large companies, the company director should monitor the company's risk management, internal control systems and compliance controls. This means that the company director is primarily responsible for implementing and managing the corporate compliance program or adequate corporate procedures for the company. This also includes a duty to monitor the company's activities and to investigate possible misconduct. In the event of delegating these responsibilities, the director has a duty to supervise.

Fourthly, under company law in the UK, the company secretary has a specific position with extensive responsibilities in public companies. The company secretary's responsibilities include ensuring good information flow within the board and its committees and advising the board, through the chairman, on all governance matters.[3215] Thus, the Code affords the secretary a key governance role. In addition, the secretary shares legal responsibilities with the directors for certain tasks *e.g.* filing documents required by the Companies Act. In listed companies, the company secretary has to ensure compliance with all rules concerning the listing of the shares, as well as compliance with company law and the company's articles. Therefore, in listed companies, the company secretary performs important tasks and responsibilities with respect to compliance.

Finally, under employment law, an employee is required to exercise and perform his job with a normal degree of skill and care. In the event that a company has a compliance officer position, then he is employed by the company. Therefore, he has the same duties and rights as other employees under UK employment law. Nevertheless, corporate compliance officers should be aware of their duties of care, since it has been shown that compliance officers may be subject to a higher degree to the requirement to perform their jobs competently and carefully such as in the financial services sector. In addition, they should also bear in mind that the prosecutor, the SFO, and the English Courts will apply the identification principle in the event of contravention of law when they are acting with directing mind and will within companies.

In conclusion, the post of corporate compliance officer comes with far-reaching responsibilities. The compliance officer needs to consider how compliance should be run within his specific company. Thus, compliance officers need a wide range of specific attributes. They need to be assertive, communicative, meticulous, diplomatic and credible. Their post also encompasses the preparation of a compliance charter, which includes, for example, a definition of compliance risks, the scope and limitation of compliance responsibilities, a definition of exclusions such as legal compliance, financial reporting, a definition of the powers of oversight, and dealing with the prosecutor. Thus, compliance officers can mark their boundaries and define their role and responsibilities in order to ensure that the board and

3214 The UK Corporate Governance Code (2016) *Id.* at 10. Provision B.1.1.
3215 The UK Corporate Governance Code (2016) *Id.* at 13. Provision B.5.

senior management are aware of the nature of the compliance activities. This is a key for the self-defense of compliance officers in the event of legal action.

II. The UK Command-and-Control Model of Compliance

As discussed in this chapter, in the UK, the term compliance is often described as adherence to statutes, rules and codes as well as identifying, assessing, and managing risk.[3216] The evidence has highlighted that subsequent regulation has increased the importance and authority of the compliance function, specifically within the financial service sector.[3217] This process not only includes listing the relevant legislation and rules, but extends to identifying the risks involved in the relevant business processes within the company operates.

In the UK, the position of compliance is viewed as a control function with a procedural approach.[3218] This approach is described as the *"command-and-control model"*.[3219] Risk controls can be imposed by external regulators or executed by the company itself.[3220] Within companies, risk controls can be operated by managers or officers.[3221] Therefore, the corporate compliance function should be seen as an improvement of the risk coordination, and quality of risk documents alongside the development of an effective compliance program.[3222] Additionally, the enforcement of compliance under company law, bribery law and corporate rules has also strengthened the need for a compliance position in the private sector. In addition, the compliance officer has had to develop a detailed system for explaining or embedding legal requirements, monitoring and enforcing them.[3223] Thus, the compliance position is considered to improve the risk coordination and quality of risk documents and is said to help in the development of a proactive compliance program through effective process design.[3224] A proactive and effective compliance program plays an important role in the event that a company faces prosecutions for non-compliant behavior. As the first UK DPA has shown, the program can provide scope for negotiation with prosecutors with the aim of reducing any penalties imposed.[3225]

3216 *See e.g.* Adams (1994), *supra* note 549 at 282; Moorhead and Vaughan (2015), *supra* note 3067 at 18.
3217 *See supra* IV., 3.a., p. 377.
3218 *See* Moorhead and Vaughan (2015), *supra* note 3067 at 18.
3219 *Id.* at 18. *See also* IV., 4.b., p. 393.
3220 *See* Robert Baldwin, Bridget Hutter & Henry Rothstein, Risk Regulation, Management and Compliance 2 (2011). *See also supra* A., p. 315.
3221 *Id.* at 23. para 2.5.1.
3222 *See* Moorhead and Vaughan (2015), *supra* note 3067 at 18.
3223 *Id.* at 18.
3224 *Id.* at 18.
3225 DPA | Standard Bank Plc DPA | SFO v Standard Bank PLC (now known as ICBC Standard Bank Plc), *supra* note 2830.

In conclusion, the reasonable duty of skill and care together with professional responsibilities and liability provide considerable incentives for the compliance officer to improve the quality of UK corporate governance. Through the efforts of the UK legislator, prosecutors, and regulators, compliance responsibilities and compliance officers have stepped out of the shadows to become an important part of business practice. Driven by the regulatory command-and-control model, compliance officers play a key role in managing and controlling business risks and in ensuring that the company and its employees adhere to the law and regulations and have in place an effective compliance program for its defence. However, the command-and-control model cannot guarantee full compliance with the law and relevant rules, but it can reduce business risk and financial penalties for companies.

The German Legal Framework of Compliance

Abstract
The following chapter provides a general overview of the German legal framework for compliance and the function of the compliance officer, as well as the German relevant case-law. As previously examined, the term corporate compliance officer is not defined under German Company Law. Nevertheless, the legal framework also has an effect on the position of the compliance officer. In the following, the most important provisions of primary and secondary German law, such as company law, criminal and employment law, as they apply to compliance and the compliance officer within companies will be analyzed. For this purpose, the most significant provisions of the German Stock Corporation Act, the Act of Regulatory Offences, the new draft of a corporate criminal law, the German Employment Law, and German Corporate Governance Code will be examined in detail. Finally, this chapter will present the dynamic model of the German corporate compliance officer.

A. The Importance of the Legal Framework for German Compliance

As we have seen, the legal roots of corporate compliance originated at the beginning of the 19th century from several business sectors in the US.[3226] In Germany, both terms - compliance and corporate governance - originating from the Anglo-American legal terminology, were adopted into German law.[3227] The American literature often describes compliance as *"adherence with all the laws, regulations, rules, and policies governing an organization."*[3228] Similar to the American scholars, legal German scholars view the narrow definition of compliance as *"organized legal conformity"* of the company.[3229] Other legal scholars, meanwhile, define compliance as *"the conformity of conduct and premise"*.[3230] Based on this, the term compliance means adherence to the law, which constitutes its legal basis.[3231]

3226 *See supra* A., I., p. 115.

3227 *See supra* A., I., p. 115, *See also* Corporate Compliance: Handbuch der Haftungsvermeidung im Unternehmen, 2 (Christoph E. Hauschka, Klaus Moosmayer, & Thomas Lösler eds., 3., ed. 2016) § 1.

3228 *See supra* A., I., pp. 115 et seq., *See also supra* footnote 663, p. 123.

3229 *See* Bürkle, *supra* note 971 at 2 § 1.

3230 *See* Rotsch (2015), *supra* note 1070 at 7 § 1.

3231 Corporate Compliance, *supra* note 3227 at 28 § 1.

On account of corporates misconduct and its effects, it is necessary to have a monitoring or control system to help corporations to avoid these legal risks.[3232] Hence, compliance constitutes a tool within this corporate monitoring system.[3233] The entire system is described as corporate governance and represents the regulatory framework for the management and monitoring of corporations.[3234] The entirety of these corporate measures intended to ensure the lawful conduct of corporations, of their management and employees, are referred to as corporate compliance. Hence, this term describes corporate strategies designed to prevent violations of law and policies by means of organizational measures.[3235] As such, corporate compliance is also an interaction between internal policies, legislative activities and current case -law.[3236]

Although the term compliance is not derived from the German terminology, the German Corporate Governance Code (DCGK) qualifies compliance with a similar legal definition:[3237]

> 4.1.3 The management board ensures that all provisions of the law and the enterprise's internal policies are abided by and works to achieve their compliance by group companies (compliance).[3238]

Thus, compliance comprises a guarantee of the observance of legal requirements, corporate policies and codes within companies, as well all activities capable of identifying and monitoring business risks.[3239] However, other legal scholars argue that this description is not a legal definition, since compliance is not a legal term such as Section 25a of the German Banking Act (KWG).[3240] One reason for this is that the Codex-Commission does not have the authority to define legal terms.[3241]

The distinction between the meaning of corporate governance and compliance is viewed in prospect.[3242] While corporate governance is considered from the perspective of the regulator, compliance encompasses the view of the companies

---

3232 HANDBUCH WIRTSCHAFTSSTRAFRECHT, 47 (Hans Achenbach, Andreas Ransiek, & Katharina Beckemper eds., 3. ed. 2012); Rotsch (2015), *supra* note 1070 at 7 § 1.

3233 HANDBUCH WIRTSCHAFTSSTRAFRECHT, *supra* note 3232 at 47; Rotsch (2015), *supra* note 1070 at 7 § 1.

3234 HANDBUCH WIRTSCHAFTSSTRAFRECHT, *supra* note 3232 at 47; Rotsch (2015), *supra* note 1070 at 7 § 1.

3235 Hölters in: HÖLTERS | COMMENTARY ON THE AKTG, 91 (Hölters ed., 2 ed. 2014) § 93.

3236 *See* Peter Fissenewert in: COMPLIANCE KOMPAKT: BEST PRACTICE IM COMPLIANCE-MANAGEMENT, (Stefan Behringer ed., 3. ed. 2013).

3237 *See* Bürkle, supra note 971 at 2 and 3 § 1.

3238 THE GERMAN CODE 2015, *supra* note 947 at 6.

3239 CORPORATE COMPLIANCE, *supra* note 3227 at 4 § 1.

3240 DEUTSCHER CORPORATE GOVERNANCE KODEX: KODEX-KOMMENTAR, 815 (Thomas Kremer ed., 6. ed., 2016) para 4.1.3 [hereinafter DCGK COMMENTARY].

3241 DCGK COMMENTARY *Id.* at 815. para 4.1.3.

3242 CORPORATE COMPLIANCE, *supra* note 3227 at 4 § 1.

affected.[3243] In the US, corporate governance is seen as *"the important legal relationship that exists between shareholders, management, auditors, and the board of directors."*[3244] Under common law, corporate governance rules aim to increase shareholder value.[3245] As a result of a number of high-profile instances of serious fraud and corruption at German companies such as Siemens and VW, and misconduct of the management, corporate governance has also gained influence in Germany in the context of the discussion of *"shareholder value"*.[3246] Although similar to the UK, German corporate governance is guided by the comply and explain approach as set forth in the German Corporate Governance Code (DCGK) and the regulatory requirements are likely to become increasingly stringent.[3247]

In Germany, the legal framework applicable to compliance comprises certain provisions in various areas of law *e.g.* criminal law in Sections 266, 299 and 300 of the German Criminal Code, Sections 9, 30, 130 of the Act of Regulatory Offences, or company law in Sections 91 (2) and 93 (1) of the German Stock Corporation Act.[3248] As regards these provisions, one group of German legal scholars considers it to be the primary duty of the management board to establish a compliance organization and to liable vis-à-vis the members of the board within companies.[3249] Pursuant to Section 76 (1) of the German Stock Corporation Act, the management board has the power of oversight of the stock corporation.[3250] In Germany, the members of the management board are appointed by the supervisory board.[3251] The supervisory board is charged with monitoring the management board.[3252] Both the management board and the supervisory board have a duty of care towards their company.[3253] These provisions are referred to as a general clause with a dual function.[3254] On the one hand, the general clause includes a standard of care,

---

3243 *Id.* at 4.§ 1.

3244 *See supra* footnote 1483, p. 216.

3245 *See supra* A., I., 3. p. 324.

3246 CORPORATE COMPLIANCE, *supra* note 3227 at 6 § 1. *See also* A., I.,1.d, p. 203.

3247 THE GERMAN CODE 2015, *supra* note 947 at 2.

3248 AKTIENGESETZ (AKTG) | GERMAN STOCK CORPORATION ACT, *supra* note 976 § 91 (2); GESETZ ÜBER ORDNUNGSWIDRIGKEITEN (OWIG) | ACT ON REGULATORY OFFENCES, BGBl. I p. 602, (1987) §§ 9, 30, 130; STRAFGESETZBUCH (STGB) | GERMAN CRIMINAL CODE, *supra* note 965 § 266.

3249 Under German law there are two separate bodies that manage and supervise stock corporations: a board of executive directors and a supervisory board. For this reason the German board structure is named as a *"two-tier board structure." See e.g.* MOOSMAYER (2015), *supra* note 1062 at 10 B. I.; Schneider (2003), *supra* note 997 at 645; Schulz and Renz (2012), *supra* note 41 at 2512.

3250 AKTIENGESETZ (AKTG) | GERMAN STOCK CORPORATION ACT, *supra* note 976 § 76 (1).

3251 AKTIENGESETZ (AKTG) | GERMAN STOCK CORPORATION ACT, *supra* note 976 § 84 (1).

3252 *Id.*§ 111 (1).

3253 *Id.*§§ 93 (1) 1 and 116 (1) 1.

3254 UWE HÜFFER & JENS KOCH, AKTIENGESETZ: AKTG 3 a (12. ed. 2016) § 93.

while on the other hand, it encompasses additional obligations of the management board, insofar these duties are not required under the Stock Corporation Act.[3255] In addition, for the purposes of ensuring the legal duty of care, the German Corporate Control and Transparency Act (KonTraG) stipulates in Section 91 (2) of the Corporation Act that the management board must *e.g.* take appropriate and reasonable measures to implement, in particular, a monitoring system to identify business risks at an early stage.[3256]

However, other scholars critically argue that a legal duty on the part of the management to implement compliance procedures cannot be derived from these provisions.[3257] Nevertheless, over the years, the German courts have provided guidance in terms of the supervisory and organizational duty to monitor and control the board with regard to risk analyzes and the establishment of compliance procedures.[3258] In addition, as examined in the foregoing chapters, the legal framework of compliance for German companies is not limited to German legal requirements, but must also take account of the legal peculiarities worldwide. Thus, the global legal framework of compliance is also relevant to German companies.

To ensure the supervisory and organizational duty of the board to monitor and control compliance procedures across all corporate levels, German companies have in the course of the implementation of compliance procedures created the dedicated position of corporate compliance officer.[3259] The reason for this is that, granting these persons responsibility for compliance establishes a clear accountability vis-à-vis the company. However, such delegation is limited.[3260] In the event of a single delegation, the responsibility of the management board will remain.[3261] The following sections will examine this legal issue in detail.

3255 *See* Jürgen Van Kann, Vorstand der AG: Führungsaufgaben, Rechtspflichten und Corporate Governance 262 (2. ed. 2012) Buchta *See* in: Ch. 3, B.

3256 Gesetz zur Kontrolle und Transparenz im Unternehmensbereich (KonTraG) | German Corporate Control and Transparency Act, BGB I, 1998, 786 (1998); Aktiengesetz (AktG) | German Stock Corporation Act, *supra* note 976 § 91 (2).

3257 *See e.g.* Werner Beulke & Klaus Moosmayer, *Der Reformvorschlag des Bundesverbandes der Unternehmensjuristen zu den §§ OWIG § 30, OWIG § 130 OWiG– Plädoyer für ein modernes Unternehmenssanktionenrecht*, CCZ 146–152, 147 (2014); Corporate Compliance, *supra* note 3227 at 31 § 1.

3258 *See e.g.* OLG Stuttgart, 7.9.1976 - 3 Ss 526/76 - Überwachungspflicht des Betriebsinhabers, *supra* note 1065; OLG Hamm, 16.07.2003 - 4 Ss (OWi) 373/03 - wistra 2003, 469 - Organisationsverschulden des Betriebsinhabers, 469 (2003); LG München I, 10.12.2013 - 5 HK O 1387/10, NZG 2014, *supra* note 973.

3259 *See e.g.* Bürkle, *supra* note 971 at 6; Gross (2012), *supra* note 42 at 60; Corporate Compliance, *supra* note 3227 at 7 § 36.

3260 *See* Bürkle (2010), *supra* note 28 at 5; Wolf (2011), *supra* note 41 at 1356.

3261 Corporate Compliance, *supra* note 3227 at 60 § 59.

I. The Development of German Law with Respect to Compliance

At an early stage, the term *"honorable businessman"* described the historical model of the accountable way of doing business in Germany since 1517.[3262] The guidelines comprise honorable and proper performance of business activities.[3263] Therefore, they focus on business ethics within companies.[3264] The core elements of business ethics encompass *e.g.* responsibility for business and society and maintaining good faith.[3265] These guidelines are considered a voluntary personal commitment on the part of the honorable businessman.[3266] This model could be viewed as the first non-regulatory predecessor of compliance prior to the advent of the term compliance in Germany.

The initial point of the establishment of compliance measures refers to the entry into force of the German Corporate Control and Transparency Act (KonTraG) in German law in 1998.[3267] The purpose of this legislation was to prevent the weaknesses of business control, which resulted in numerous corporate scandals.[3268] This Act came in the wake of criticism from international investors of the absence of corporate governance standards in Germany.[3269] On the other hand, the aim of the KonTraG Act was to implement preventative procedures or appropriate measures designed to avoid liability of the management board, the supervisory board and the auditors.[3270] Thus, the main objective was the enhancement of German corporate governance through a monitoring system and the improvement of corporate communication, transparency and disclosure for shareholders and investors.[3271] The majority of reforms of the Act were implemented in the German Stock Corporation Act (AktG) and the German Commercial Code (HGB).[3272] Under the KonTraG, the duties of the management board and the supervisory board were

---

3262 VEEK e.V., UNSERE WERTE | VERSAMMLUNG EINES EHRBAREN KAUFMANNS ZU HAMBURG E.V., http://www.veek-hamburg.de/organisation/veek-leitbild/ (last visited Feb 7, 2017).

3263 *Id.*

3264 *Id.*

3265 *Id.*

3266 *Id.*

3267 *See* Peter Fissenewert in: COMPLIANCE KOMPAKT, *supra* note 3236.

3268 *See* Peter Fissenewert in: *Id.*

3269 WHISTLE BLOWING UND CONCERN-MANAGEMENT (2007), *supra* note 1179 at 51.

3270 *See* Peter Fissenewert in: COMPLIANCE KOMPAKT, *supra* note 3236.

3271 WHISTLE BLOWING UND CONCERN-MANAGEMENT (2007), *supra* note 1179 at 51.

3272 AKTIENGESETZ (AKTG) | GERMAN STOCK CORPORATION ACT, *supra* note 976 § 91 Subsection 2 was added; HANDELSGESETZBUCH (HGB) | GERMAN COMMERCIAL CODE, (1900) § 317; GESETZ ZUR KONTROLLE UND TRANSPARENZ IM UNTERNEHMENSBEREICH (KONTRAG) | GERMAN CORPORATE CONTROL AND TRANSPARENCY ACT, *supra*

extended and the duty of care clearly enshrined in law.[3273] However, the term compliance was not specifically used in German Company Law.

Only in the intervening period since 1999 have the terms compliance function and compliance officer gradually been incorporated into German law in certain provisions in the financial service sector.[3274] The initial point was the approved EC Investment Services Directive, in 1993, which required the UK approach of compliance investment regulations and procedures throughout the European Union applicable to companies listed on stock exchanges.[3275] Article 10 of the Directive stipulates that *e.g.*

> Each investment firm has sound administrative and accounting procedures, control and safeguard arrangements for electronic data processing, and adequate internal control mechanisms including, in particular, rules for personal transactions by its employees.[3276]

For this reason, the financial services sector required a supervisory and organizational obligation of adequate internal control mechanisms for credit institutions and investment firms.[3277] The judicial bodies in the EU Member States are at least to be authorized to monitor compliance.[3278] In 1994, these provisions were enshrined in German legislation in Sections 31, 33 of the German Securities Trading Act

---

note 3256; WHISTLE BLOWING UND CONCERN-MANAGEMENT (2007), *supra* note 1179 at 51.

3273 AKTIENGESETZ (AKTG) | GERMAN STOCK CORPORATION ACT, *supra* note 976 §§ 93, 116; GESETZ ZUR KONTROLLE UND TRANSPARENZ IM UNTERNEHMENSBEREICH (KONTRAG) | GERMAN CORPORATE CONTROL AND TRANSPARENCY ACT, *supra* note 3256; WHISTLE BLOWING UND CONCERN-MANAGEMENT (2007), *supra* note 1179 at 51.

3274 WERTPAPIERHANDELSGESETZ (WPHG) | GERMAN SECURITIES TRADING ACT, *supra* note 951 § 33 (1) 1. as amended on July 16, 2007; last amendment on January 3, 2017, § 34d as amended on November 6, 2012. WERTPAPIERDIENSTLEISTUNGS-VERHALTENS- UND ORGANISATIONSVERORDNUNG (WPDVEROV) | SECURITIES TRADING IMPLEMENTING PROVISION, *supra* note 1015 § 12 as amended on July 20, 2007, last amendment on November 26, 2015.

3275 COUNCIL DIRECTIVE 93/22/EEC OF 10 MAY 1993 ON INVESTMENT SERVICES IN THE SECURITIES FIELD, L 141, p. 0027-0046 (1993); CORPORATE COMPLIANCE, *supra* note 3227 at 10 § 48.

3276 COUNCIL DIRECTIVE 93/22/EEC OF 10 MAY 1993 ON INVESTMENT SERVICES IN THE SECURITIES FIELD, *supra* note 3275 Art. 10.

3277 *See* Braun in: KWG, CRR-VO: COMMENTARY ON THE GERMAN BANKING ACT, VO (EU) No. 575/2013 (CRR) AND IMPLEMENTING PROVISIONS, 9 (Karl-Heinz Boos, Reinfrid Fischer, & Hermann Schulte-Mattler eds., 5. ed. 2016) § 25a.

3278 COUNCIL DIRECTIVE 93/22/EEC OF 10 MAY 1993 ON INVESTMENT SERVICES IN THE SECURITIES FIELD, *supra* note 3275 Art. 10.

(WpHG).[3279] Although the Act did not use the term compliance, the investment services enterprises approved under the German Banking Act (KWG), were required to implement adequate internal control procedures.[3280] In accordance with the report of the financial committee of the German Bundestag concerning the German Securities Trading Act (WpHG), the mere establishment of these measures and procedures is not sufficient to ensure adherence to legal obligations of the investment services enterprises, and demands periodic review through internal control systems.[3281] In addition, the report outlines that the establishment and development of compliance departments within investment firms is the correct way of monitoring the investment business.[3282] Finally, since 1999, the term compliance has entered into German legal terminology.[3283] The Regulation Concretizing the Organizational Obligations of Investment Services Enterprises pursuant to Section 33 of the German Securities Trading Act (WpHG) describes the control department as a compliance function.[3284] The compliance function is responsible for periodic reporting on the adequacy and effectiveness of principles and preventative measures to avoid violations of the Act.[3285]

Thus, since the beginning of the century, the importance of compliance has been extended into the financial services sector.[3286] Pursuant to the Amendment of Section 25a of the German Banking Act (KWG) in 2002, the legislator required credit institutions and investment firms to manage, monitor and control risks through an adequate internal control system that is required to improve compliance with the law.[3287] A further key milestone for the development of the Banking

---

3279 Wertpapierhandelsgesetz (WpHG) | German Securities Trading Act, *supra* note 951 § 33 as amended on July 26, 1994.

3280 Gesetz über das Kreditwesen (KWG) | German Banking Act, *supra* note 1013 § 32 (1) ; Corporate Compliance, *supra* note 3227 at 11 § 48. § 1 (1) (1a) of the German Banking Act (KWG) defines investment services enterprises as credit institutions and financial services institutes. They have also to comply with organizational obligations pursuant to § 25a (1), (2) and § 25e of the German Banking Act (KWG). *See* Wertpapierhandelsgesetz (WpHG) | German Securities Trading Act, *supra* note 951 § 33 (1) 1.

3281 German BT-Drs. 12/7918, 105 (1994).

3282 *Id.* at 105.

3283 Corporate Compliance, *supra* note 3227 at 11 § 48.

3284 *Id.* at 11.§ 48; Regulation Concretizing the Organizational Obligations of Investment Services Enterprises pursuant to Section 33 of the Securities Trading Act (WpHG) of October 25, 1999 | Federal Gazette No. 2010 of November 6, 1999, 18453 (1999), repealed on November 1, 2007.

3285 Wertpapierdienstleistungs-Verhaltens- und Organisationsverordnung (WpDVerOV) | Securities Trading Implementing Provision, *supra* note 1015 § 12 (3) 1 No. 1; (4) 1 as amended on July 20, 2007.

3286 Corporate Compliance, *supra* note 3227 at 13 § 48.

3287 Directive 2002/87/EC of the European Parliament and of the Council of 16 December 2002 on the supplementary supervision of credit institutions,

Act was the consultation paper on the compliance function prepared by the Basel Committee on Banking Supervision in April 2005.[3288] This paper defines the compliance risk as follows:

> as the risk of legal or regulatory sanctions, material financial loss, or loss to reputation a bank may suffer as a result of its failure to comply with laws, regulations, rules, related self-regulatory organization standards, and codes of conduct applicable to its banking activities (together, "compliance laws, rules and standards").[3289]

The purpose of this paper was the global improvement of corporate governance within banking institutions.[3290] The Basel Committee provides a framework of principles for banks to manage their compliance risk more effectively as well as guidance on the role of the compliance officer.[3291] Finally, the German legislator enshrined the compliance function within banks and investment firms into law for the financial services sector. Since 2014, the internal controls system of investment firms is additionally required, to encompass a risk-control function and a compliance function.[3292] Furthermore, Section 25d of the German Banking Act (KWG) stipulates that the management of the investment firm has to monitor the compliance function.[3293] Thus, the management is in charge of legal organizational obligations within banks and investment firms. However, the specific design of these obligations is at the discretion of the management.[3294]

In conclusion, on account of the legal developments concerning compliance and the compliance function, German legislation in the financial service sector has increased over the last twenty years. Following this brief overview of the legal developments in the financial service sector, the next sections will explore in detail the development of German Company Law in terms of compliance and the enforcement of the duties of corporate management.

INSURANCE UNDERTAKINGS AND INVESTMENT FIRMS, L 035, p. 0001–0027; (2003) Art. 9; GERMAN BT-DRS. 15/3641, 48 (2004).

3288 The Basel Committee on Banking Supervision, *supra* note 793 at 7 para 3 and 6.

3289 *Id.* at 7. para 3.

3290 *Id.* at 7. para 6.

3291 The Basel Committee on Banking Supervision, *supra* note 793.

3292 DIRECTIVE 2013/36/EU OF THE EUROPEAN PARLIAMENT AND OF THE COUNCIL (CRD IV DIRECTIVE), *supra* note 1053 Art. 92; GESETZ ÜBER DAS KREDITWESEN (KWG) | GERMAN BANKING ACT, *supra* note 1013 §§ 25a as amended on August 28, 2013; 25c as amended on August 7, 2013.

3293 GESETZ ÜBER DAS KREDITWESEN (KWG) | GERMAN BANKING ACT, *supra* note 1013 § 25d as amended on August 28, 2013.

3294 Braun in: KWG, CRR-VO, *supra* note 3336 at 12 § 25a.

II. The Enforcement of Duties in the Area of Company Law

Other than the guidelines and the model of the honorable businessman in doing business and the legal requirements for banks and investment firms to operate in an increasingly regulated environment, there was no uniform standard of legal responsibility in the German private sector.[3295] Prior to the establishment of adequate internal control systems, guidance for the liability of managing directors took the form of the general duty of care.[3296] In the private sector, the standard of care pursuant to Section 43 (1) of the German Act on Limited Liability Companies (GmbHG) is the level of culpability triggered by a breach of duty as set forth in Subsections 2 and 3.[3297] The German standard of care and loyalty of the managing director comprises the care of a proper businessperson pursuant to Section 43 of the German Limited Liability Companies Act (GmbHG).[3298] In accordance with the prevailing view, this is the same standard as that set forth in Section 93 (1) of the Stock Corporation Act.[3299] Nevertheless, this standard is higher than the standard due care of a proper businessperson pursuant to Section 347 of the German Commercial Code (HGB).[3300] The managing director owes the care, which a proper businessperson, who holds a management position, must take regarding shareholders' asset interests.[3301] The basis of liability is the appointment for the

3295 *See* Peter Fissenewert in: COMPLIANCE KOMPAKT, *supra* note 3236.

3296 *See* Peter Fissenewert in: *Id.*; GESETZ BETREFFEND DIE GESELLSCHAFTEN MIT BESCHRÄNKTER HAFTUNG (GMBHG) | LIMITED LIABILITY COMPANIES ACT, RGBl., 477 (1892) § 43 (1) as amended on January 1, 1964. This Act applies to companies, which are accompanied by the word GmbH- Limited Liability Company. *Id.*§§ 1, 4.

3297 *See* Zöllner, Noack in: BAUMBACH, HUECK | COMMENTARY ON THE GMBHG, 20, 8 (Baumbach & Hueck eds., 21 ed. 2017) § 43; Haas, Ziemons MICHALSKI | COMMENTARY ON THE GMBHG, 38 (Michalski ed., 2 ed. 2010) § 43.

3298 GESETZ BETREFFEND DIE GESELLSCHAFTEN MIT BESCHRÄNKTER HAFTUNG (GMBHG) | LIMITED LIABILITY COMPANIES ACT, RGBl., 477 (1892), last amended on May 10, 2016, § 43 (1); *See* Zöllner, Noack in: BAUMBACH, HUECK | COMMENTARY ON THE GMBHG, *supra* note 3297 at 7 § 43.

3299 *See* Zöllner, Noack in: BAUMBACH, HUECK | COMMENTARY ON THE GMBHG, *supra* note 3297 at 7 § 43 (1); Haas, Ziemons in: MICHALSKI | COMMENTARY ON THE GMBHG, *supra* note 3297 at 189 § 43 (1); Koppensteiner, Gruber ROWEDDER, SCHMIDT-LEITHOFF | COMMENTARY ON THE GMBHG, 7 (Rowedder & Schmidt-Leithoff eds., 5 ed. 2013) § 43 (1); OLG Celle, 15.3.2000 - 9 U 209/99 - GF bei nicht (wirksam) entrichteter Stammeinlage, 1178–1179, 1179 (2000).

3300 *See* Altmeppen in: ROTH, ALTMEPPEN | COMMENTARY ON THE GMBHG, 3 (Roth & Altmeppen eds., 8 ed. 2015) § 43; BGH, 6.12.2001 - 1 StR 215/01 - Untreue durch Zuwendungen aus dem Vermögen einer Aktiengesellschaft, NJW 1585–1589, 1585 (2001).

3301 *See* Altmeppen in: ROTH, ALTMEPPEN | COMMENTARY ON THE GMBHG, *supra* note 3300 at 3 § 43.

office of managing director, but not the contract of employment.[3302] In addition, the duty of care of the members of the board of stock corporations is set forth in Section 93 (1) of the German Stock Corporation Act (AktG).[3303] This provision stipulates that the members of the board owe the duty of care of a proper and diligent manager when doing business.[3304] Nevertheless, this standard is not legally defined in detail,[3305] so that the literature and the courts are responsible for applying and interpreting precisely what the standard means.[3306]

However, in the area of corporate compliance, the German legislator has also followed the trend towards globalization.[3307] As has been seen, as a result of increasing numbers of large international corporations, the risk inherent in wrong corporate decisions has also grown more pronounced.[3308] As previously discussed, under the KonTraG, corporate compliance measures have been introduced into company law.[3309] The next section describes the effects and impacts of these compliance measures and procedures on stock corporations in accordance with the German Stock Corporation Act (AktG), their boards and directors, as well as the liability of the compliance officer.

1. Appropriate Measures for Risk Prevention Pursuant to Section 91 (2) AktG

As previously noted, the purpose of the KonTraG Act was to change the Stock Corporation Act, the Commercial Code and the law governing the auditors.[3310] According to the German Federal Government's reasons for the amendment bill, the main objectives were to enhance the activities of the supervisory board, to improve transparency, and to strengthen control of the annual general meeting.[3311] Just like in the US and in the UK, under the previous control system, weaknesses and misconduct by the board and supervisory board necessitated a reform of the Act.[3312] Furthermore, German stock corporations are also listed on international

3302 *See* Altmeppen in: Roth, Altmeppen | Commentary on the GmbHG, *supra* note 3300 at 2 § 43.
3303 Aktiengesetz (AktG) | German Stock Corporation Act, *supra* note 976 § 93 (1) 1 as amended on September 6, 1965.
3304 *See* Hölters in: Hölters | Commentary on the AktG, *supra* note 3235 at 2 § 93.
3305 *See* Hölters in: *Id.* at 2.§ 93.
3306 *See* Hölters in: *Id.* at 2.§ 93.
3307 *See* Peter Fissenewert in: Compliance kompakt, *supra* note 3236.
3308 *See* Peter Fissenewert in: *Id.*
3309 Gesetz zur Kontrolle und Transparenz im Unternehmensbereich (KonTraG) | German Corporate Control and Transparency Act, *supra* note 3256.
3310 German BT-Drs. 13/9712, (1998).
3311 *Id.*
3312 *Id.* at 11.

and national stock exchanges, such as the LSE, NYSE or the DAX.[3313] Thus, foreign investors have become more important.[3314] Therefore, German companies need to consider shareholder value.[3315] Enhanced communication with disclosure to investors are crucial.[3316]

Under the KonTraG, Section 91 (2) of the German Stock Corporation Act (AktG) stipulates that the board must implement appropriate measures, in particular a monitoring system, which includes elements of an internal preventative and controlling system.[3317] This provision highlights the management responsibility of the board pursuant to Section 76 of the Act in terms of early developments that could threaten the company.[3318] The amended Subsection 2 describes in concrete terms the duties of the members of the board to inform themselves of pending developments and to ensure the continued existence of the stock corporation.[3319] The fulfilment of this duty can be seen in context with Section 317 (4) of the German Commercial Code (HGB) and is also subject to review by an auditor.[3320] Subsection 2 focusses on two steps: First, the obligation of the board to implement appropriate measures to recognize, at an early stage, developments that could pose a threat to the continued existence of the company.[3321] And, secondly, the establishment of a monitoring system to control these measures.[3322]

3313 *Id.* at 11.

3314 *Id.* at 11.

3315 *Id.* at 11.

3316 *Id.* at 11.

3317 Aktiengesetz (AktG) | German Stock Corporation Act, *supra* note 976 § 91 (2) as amended on April 27, 1998.

3318 German BT-Drs. 13/9712, *supra* note 3310 at 15; Koch in: Hüffer, Koch | Commentary on the AktG, *supra* note 3254 at 4 § 91; Müller-Michaels in: Hölters | Commentary on the AktG, *supra* note 3235 at 4 § 91.

3319 *See* Grigoleit, Tomasic in: Grigoleit | Commentary on the AktG, 5 (Grigoleit ed., 1 ed. 2013) § 91.

3320 German BT-Drs. 13/9712, *supra* note 3310 at 15; Handelsgesetzbuch (HGB) | German Commercial Code, *supra* note 3331 § 317 (4) as amended on April 27, 1998; Grigoleit, Tomasic in: Grigoleit | Commentary on the AktG, *supra* note 3319 at 5 § 91; Müller-Michaels in: Hölters | Commentary on the AktG, *supra* note 3235 at 4 § 91.

3321 *See* Müller-Michaels in: Hölters | Commentary on the AktG, *supra* note 3235 at 5 § 91; Koch in: Hüffer, Koch | Commentary on the AktG, *supra* note 3254 at 6–7 § 91.

3322 *See* Müller-Michaels in: Hölters | Commentary on the AktG, *supra* note 3235 at 9 § 91; Koch Hüffer, Koch | Commentary on the AktG, *supra* note 3254 at 8–10 § 91.

a. The First Step - Appropriate Measures

First, the board has to identify, analyze, and evaluate potential business risks within the corporation.[3323] Based on this risk assessment, appropriate measures should then be derived.[3324] These measures are intended to recognize at an early stage any potentially dangerous developments within the corporation.[3325] The measures are considered appropriate if the members of the board are informed in sufficient time to ensure the continued existence of the corporation.[3326] However, the specific requirements of the board's obligation to provide an appropriate risk management system are qualified by the corporation's size, type of business, structure and access to the stock exchange.[3327] For this reason, the board can exercise discretion when considering the specifics of the corporation and any adverse effects on the corporation.[3328] However, this discretion is not explicitly enacted into law.[3329] Nevertheless, the obligation of the board to respond to the risks is implicit in Sections 76 and 93 of the German Stock Corporation Act (AktG).[3330]

Finally, in the view of the German government, the requirement of appropriate measures will not be enshrined in the Limited Liability Companies Act (GmbHG), but the reform of the German Stock Corporation Act (AktG) will also affect other business entities.[3331]

3323 *See* Dauner-Lieb in: HENSSLER, STROHN | COMMENTARY ON BUSINESS LAW, 7 (Henssler & Strohn eds., 3 ed. 2016) § 91; Müller-Michaels HÖLTERS | COMMENTARY ON THE AKTG, *supra* note 3235 at 6 § 91.

3324 *See* Müller-Michaels in: HÖLTERS | COMMENTARY ON THE AKTG, *supra* note 3235 at 6 § 91.

3325 *See* Müller-Michaels in: *Id.* at 6. § 91; Koch in: HÜFFER, KOCH | COMMENTARY ON THE AKTG, *supra* note 3254 at 6 § 91.

3326 GERMAN BT-DRS. 13/9712, *supra* note 3310 at 15; Dauner-Lieb in: HENSSLER, STROHN | COMMENTARY ON BUSINESS LAW, *supra* note 3323 at 8§ 91; Müller-Michaels in: HÖLTERS | COMMENTARY ON THE AKTG, *supra* note 3235 at 6 § 91; Koch in: HÜFFER, KOCH | COMMENTARY ON THE AKTG, *supra* note 3254 at 7 § 91.

3327 GERMAN BT-DRS. 13/9712, *supra* note 3310 at 15.

3328 *See* Grigoleit, Tomasic in: GRIGOLEIT | COMMENTARY ON THE AKTG, *supra* note 3319 at 7§ 91; Dauner-Lieb in: HENSSLER, STROHN | COMMENTARY ON BUSINESS LAW, *supra* note 3323 at 8§ 91; Müller-Michaels in: HÖLTERS | COMMENTARY ON THE AKTG, *supra* note 3235 at 6§ 91; Koch in: HÜFFER, KOCH | COMMENTARY ON THE AKTG, *supra* note 3254 at 7 § 91; Spindler in:MUNICH COMMENTARY ON THE AKTG, 2 28 (Wulf Goette & Mathias Habersack eds., 4 ed. 2014) § 91; Fleischer SPINDLER, STILZ | COMMENTARY ON THE AKTG, 1 33 (Spindler & Stilz eds., 3 ed. 2015)§ 91.

3329 GERMAN BT-DRS. 13/9712, *supra* note 3310 at 15.

3330 *See* Müller-Michaels in: HÖLTERS | COMMENTARY ON THE AKTG, *supra* note 3235 at 6 § 91.

3331 GERMAN BT-DRS. 13/9712, *supra* note 3310 at 15.

b. The Second Step – The Risk Monitoring System

The second step encompasses the implementation of a risk monitoring system to review the appropriate measures whether the authorized departments, such as controlling or internal audits, have forwarded the information on time.[3332] Specifically, there is a need to clearly define responsibilities, and a need for reasonable and timely reporting within corporations.[3333] Such interpretation of the provision is not evident but pursuant to reasons cited by the German Federal Government, the legislator considered a risk monitoring system pursuant to Section 76 of the Act necessary.[3334]

The extent of such a risk monitoring system has been the subject of controversial discussions between business administration and legal scholars.[3335] The prevailing view in the legal literature is that based on a narrow interpretation of such a risk monitoring system.[3336] This is based on the previous version of Section 93 (1) 3 of the German Stock Corporation Act (AktG) of 1996.[3337]

> The board is responsible for the implementation of a risk monitoring system, which shall review the appropriate measures.[3338]

Therefore, the will of the legislator indicates that the implementation of a system to recognize early risk developments shall be provided.[3339] Finally, the board can decide which risk monitoring system it shall implement, but there is no obligation

---

3332 *See* Müller-Michaels in: HÖLTERS | COMMENTARY ON THE AKTG, *supra* note 3235 at 9§ 91; Spindler in: MUNICH COMMENTARY ON THE AKTG, *supra* note 3328 at 29 § 91; Fleischer in: SPINDLER, STILZ | COMMENTARY ON THE AKTG, *supra* note 3328 at 34 § 91.

3333 *See* Müller-Michaels in: HÖLTERS | COMMENTARY ON THE AKTG, *supra* note 3235 at 9 § 91; Koch in: HÜFFER, KOCH | COMMENTARY ON THE AKTG, *supra* note 3254 at 10 § 91.

3334 GERMAN BT-DRS. 13/9712, *supra* note 3310 at 15; Müller-Michaels in: HÖLTERS | COMMENTARY ON THE AKTG, *supra* note 3235 at 9 § 91.

3335 *See* Müller-Michaels in: HÖLTERS | COMMENTARY ON THE AKTG, *supra* note 3235 at 6 § 91.

3336 *See* Spindler in: MUNICH COMMENTARY ON THE AKTG, *supra* note 3328 at 29 § 91; Fleischer in: SPINDLER, STILZ | COMMENTARY ON THE AKTG, *supra* note 3328 at 34 § 91.

3337 *See* Müller-Michaels in: HÖLTERS | COMMENTARY ON THE AKTG, *supra* note 3235 at 9 § 91; Koch in: HÜFFER, KOCH | COMMENTARY ON THE AKTG, *supra* note 3254 at 9 § 91; Spindler in: MUNICH COMMENTARY ON THE AKTG, *supra* note 3328 at 29 § 91; Fleischer in: SPINDLER, STILZ | COMMENTARY ON THE AKTG, *supra* note 3328 at 34 § 91; Referentenentwurf zur Änderung des Aktiengesetzes (KonTraG), ZIP 2129–2139, 2131 (1996).

3338 Referentenentwurf zur Änderung des Aktiengesetzes (KonTraG), *supra* note 3337 at 2131.

3339 *Id.* at 2131.

on the part of the board to implement an encompassing or specific risk monitoring system pursuant to Section 91 (2) of the Act.[3340] Thus, in the view of the majority of legal scholars, the subject of the monitoring system is adherence to the measures, which means internal control.[3341] In conclusion, the board can decide to implement an internal risk monitoring system and must consider the specific needs of the corporation when doing so. Under Section 91 (2) of the Act, an assessment of the effectiveness of this system is not necessary.

c. Compliance Organization in a Broader Sense

The German legislator also includes violations of legal requirements of the corporate management and employees as a development that poses a risk to the continued existence of the corporation.[3342] However, the compliance duty of the board of is not explicitly enshrined in the Stock Corporation Act.[3343] Nevertheless, the Munich Court concluded in a recent *Siemens* case that it remains to be seen whether this duty derives from Section 91 (2) or Sections 76 (1), 93 (1) of the Act.[3344] In that case, the Court determined that the overall responsibility of the board encompasses adherence to law and the establishment of an effective compliance system.[3345] In the wake of the case, a controversial debate has flared up surrounding compliance as a management issue and whether the board is under a duty to implement an overarching compliance organization.[3346] In contrast to the view of the Court, the majority of legal scholars oppose a general duty to implement a compliance organization and refer to the duty of care of the board pursuant to Sections 76

3340 *See* Müller-Michaels in: Hölters | Commentary on the AktG, *supra* note 3235 at 10 § 91; Dauner-Lieb in: Henssler, Strohn | Commentary on Business Law, *supra* note 3323 at 9 § 91; Koch in: Hüffer, Koch | Commentary on the AktG, *supra* note 3254 at 10 § 91; *See also*: German BT-Drs. 16/10067, Accounting Law Reform Act (BilMoG). 76 (2008); Handelsgesetzbuch (HGB) | German Commercial Code, *supra* note 3331 § 289 (5).

3341 *See* Koch in: Hüffer, Koch | Commentary on the AktG, *supra* note 3254 at 10 § 91. *See also supra* footnote 3340.

3342 German BT-Drs. 13/9712, *supra* note 3310 at 15.

3343 *See* Fleischer in: Spindler, Stilz | Commentary on the AktG, *supra* note 3328 at 49 § 91.

3344 LG München I, 10.12.2013 - 5 HK O 1387/10, NZG 2014, *supra* note 973 at 346; Fleischer in: Spindler, Stilz | Commentary on the AktG, *supra* note 3328 at 49 § 91.

3345 LG München I, 10.12.2013 - 5 HK O 1387/10, NZG 2014, *supra* note 973 at 346.

3346 *See e.g.* Hauschka, Galster, and Marschlich (2014), *supra* note 463 at 244; Heuking (2014), *supra* note 4 at 327; Florian Modlinger, Anke Egelhof & Felicitas Berger, *Die Rolle des Aufsichtsrats in der Compliance*, ZRFC 254–258, 254 (2014); Patrick Ulrich, *Einfluss des Aufsichtsrats auf das Compliance-Management*, ZRFC 7–13, 7–8 (2017).

(1) and 93 (1) of the Act.[3347] However, in recent years, a growing number of scholars have examined responsibility for compliance of the board within joint-stock corporations.[3348] Both views emphasize the discretion of the board when designing the appropriate measures of the compliance organization.[3349]

Furthermore, this section examines whether there are specific organizational requirements pursuant to other provisions. For example, the financial service sector requires for regulated banks, investment firms and insurance companies, detailed principles and mandatory organizational specifications for the implementation of a risk management system.[3350] The specific organizational requirements for credit institutions comprise *inter alia* the definition of strategies, the procedures for identification, the assessment and the monitoring of business risks, a risk control function and a compliance function.[3351] These provisions are the result of EU legislation in the form of several Directives such as the CRD IV Directive or the MiFID II Directive, which were implemented over the course of the last decade.[3352] These

---

3347 *See e.g.* Holger Fleischer, *Aktienrechtliche Compliance-Pflichten im Praxistest: Das Siemens/Neubürger-Urteil des LG München I*, 10.12.2013 - 5 HK O 1387/10, NZG 321–329, 322 (2014); Hölters in: HÖLTERS | COMMENTARY ON THE AKTG, *supra* note 3235 at 92 § 93; Koch in: HÜFFER, KOCH | COMMENTARY ON THE AKTG, *supra* note 3254 at 14 § 91; Spindler in: MUNICH COMMENTARY ON THE AKTG, *supra* note 3328 at 52 § 91; Fleischer in: SPINDLER, STILZ | COMMENTARY ON THE AKTG, *supra* note 3328 at 49 § 91.

3348 *See e.g.* Holger Fleischer, *Corporate Compliance im aktienrechtlichen Unternehmensverbund*, CCZ 1–6, 3 (2008); Fleischer (2014), *supra* note 3347 at 323; Jochen Reichert & Nicolas Ott, *Die Zuständigkeit von Vorstand und Aufsichtsrat zur Aufklärung von Non Compliance in der AG*, NZG 241–251, 242 (2014); Spindler in: MUNICH COMMENTARY ON THE AKTG, *supra* note 3328 at 52§ 91; Fleischer in: SPINDLER, STILZ | COMMENTARY ON THE AKTG, *supra* note 3328 at 47 § 91.

3349 *See* Fleischer in: SPINDLER, STILZ | COMMENTARY ON THE AKTG, *supra* note 3328 at 49 § 91.

3350 *See e.g.* GESETZ ÜBER DAS KREDITWESEN (KWG) | GERMAN BANKING ACT, *supra* note 1013 § 25 a (I) (3); VERSICHERUNGSAUFSICHTSGESETZ | INSURANCE SUPERVISION ACT (VAG), VAG RGBl. S. 139 (1901) as amended on July 26, 2016; BGBl. I 2016 p. 1824 § 29 (I); WERTPAPIERHANDELSGESETZ (WPHG) | GERMAN SECURITIES TRADING ACT, *supra* note 951 § 33 (I) 1.

3351 GESETZ ÜBER DAS KREDITWESEN (KWG) | GERMAN BANKING ACT, *supra* note 1013 § 25 a (I) (3) (c).

3352 *See e.g.* DIRECTIVE 2011/61/EU OF THE EUROPEAN PARLIAMENT AND OF THE COUNCIL ON ALTERNATIVE INVESTMENT FUND MANAGERS AND AMENDING DIRECTIVES 2003/41/EC AND 2009/65/EC AND REGULATIONS (EC) NO 1060/2009 AND (EU) NO 1095/201, *supra* note 465; DIRECTIVE 2013/36/EU OF THE EUROPEAN PARLIAMENT AND OF THE COUNCIL (CRD IV DIRECTIVE), *supra* note 1053; DIRECTIVE 2014/56/EU OF THE EUROPEAN PARLIAMENT AND OF THE COUNCIL AMENDING DIRECTIVE 2006/43/EC ON STATUTORY AUDITS OF ANNUAL ACCOUNTS AND CONSOLIDATED ACCOUNTS, *supra* note 3117.

Directives have increased the establishment of the compliance function within banks and investment firms. Under the EU legislation, a specific legal requirement of the board's responsibilities has been developed in Germany to the effect that credit institutions and investment firms are effectively managed.[3353] In this context, the various risks of certain businesses, their protection requirements for consumers and, thus, their higher organizational duties should be considered.[3354] For this reason, in the view of legal scholars, these specific requirements are not sufficient to interpret Section 91 (2) of the German Stock Corporation Act (AktG) in this way.[3355] As a result of the scholarly debate and legal requirements in the regulated sector, a duty of the board to implement a specific compliance organization comprising certain elements, such as a compliance function, appears not to be enshrined in Section 91 (2) of the German Stock Corporation Act (AktG). Nevertheless, the members of the board ought to consider the recent court decisions on this legal matter.

d. Penalties for Non-Compliance with Section § 91 (2) AktG

Irrespective of the scholarly debate, it has been recognized that the context of a corporate monitoring system entails simple requirements with clear responsibilities, and a close reporting system.[3356] In the event that such documentation is missing, this could render the discharge of the management board contestable.[3357] In 2007, the Munich I Regional Court stated that there is a legal duty of the board of a joint-stock company to document the monitoring system.[3358] Specifically, the Court pointed out that a monitoring system requires clearly-defined responsibilities, a timely reporting system, and documentation in order to inform the relevant

---

3353 *See e.g.* Gesetz über das Kreditwesen (KWG) | German Banking Act, *supra* note 1013 § 25 a (I); Versicherungsaufsichtsgesetz | Insurance Supervision Act (VAG), *supra* note 3350 §§ 24, 26, 29; Wertpapierhandelsgesetz (WpHG) | Securities Trading Act, *supra* note 951 § 33 (I).

3354 *See e.g.* Spindler in: Munich Commentary on the AktG, *supra* note 3328 at 38 § 91; Fleischer in: Spindler, Stilz | Commentary on the AktG, *supra* note 3328 at 43 § 91.

3355 *See e.g.* Fleischer in: Spindler, Stilz | Commentary on the AktG, *supra* note 3328 at 43 § 91; *OLG Celle, 28.5.2008 - 9 U 184/07 - Pflichtverletzung des Vorstandes wegen unvertretbarem Risiko*, NZG 2008, 669, 669 (2008).

3356 *See e.g.* Müller-Michaels in: Hölters | Commentary on the AktG, *supra* note 3235 at 9§ 91; Koch in: Hüffer, Koch | Commentary on the AktG, *supra* note 3254 at 10§ 91.

3357 LG München I, 5.4.2007 - 5 HK O 15964/06 - Hohes Anfechtungsrisiko für Entlastungsbeschlüsse bei fehlender Dokumentation, NZG 2008, 319 70–73, 319 (2007); Koch in: Hüffer, Koch | Commentary on the AktG, *supra* note 3254 at 10 § 91.

3358 LG München I, 5.4.2007 - 5 HK O 15964/06 - Hohes Anfechtungsrisiko für Entlastungsbeschlüsse bei fehlender Dokumentation, *supra* note 3357 at 319.

corporate functions of existing risks and to introduce appropriate measures to manage those risks.[3359] For this reason, the monitoring system has to document in order to communicate this system internally.[3360] The disclosure of organizational requirements will contribute to enhancing procedures within the monitoring system.[3361] Thus, the Court concluded that the documentation of the monitoring system applies to the key tasks of the management board pursuant to the Section 91 (2) of the Act.[3362] In conclusion, it follows that the scope of the management of the board includes *inter alia* two key tasks: the implementation of a risk monitoring system and responsibility for compliance.[3363] Therefore, the board has to decide upon the implementation of compliance procedures and supervise the effectiveness of that system.[3364]

In addition, Section 93 (2) 1 stipulates that all members of the board are jointly and severally liable in the event of a breach of their duties under Section 91 (2) of the German Stock Corporation Act (AktG).[3365] For instance, Section 91 (2) of the Act requires the implementation of measures that identify early risks of potentially dangerous developments in the corporation as a duty of the board according to civil law.[3366] Non-compliance with Section 91 (2) can be a major cause for termination without notice or dismissal of the members of the board.[3367]

Secondly, in the event that the board has not implemented any risk monitoring system or has introduced an inadequate system, the question that arises is whether

---

3359 *Id.* at 320.

3360 *Id.* at 320.

3361 *Id.* at 320.

3362 *Id.* at 320.

3363 AKTIENGESETZ (AKTG) | GERMAN STOCK CORPORATION ACT, *supra* note 976 §§ 76 (1), 91 (2); *See e.g.* Koch in: HÜFFER, KOCH | COMMENTARY ON THE AKTG, *supra* note 3254 at 12 § 76; Fleischer in: SPINDLER, STILZ | COMMENTARY ON THE AKTG, *supra* note 3328 at 63 § 91.

3364 *See e.g.* Fleischer (2014), *supra* note 3347 at 323; Fleischer in: SPINDLER, STILZ | COMMENTARY ON THE AKTG, *supra* note 3328 at 63 § 91.

3365 *See e.g.* Hans Schaefer & Diethelm Baumann, *Compliance-Organisation und Sanktionen bei Verstößen*, NJW 3601–3605, 3604 (2011); Müller-Michaels in: HÖLTERS | COMMENTARY ON THE AKTG, *supra* note 3235 at 12 § 91; Spindler in: MUNICH COMMENTARY ON THE AKTG, *supra* note 3328 at 69 § 91.

3366 *See e.g.* Richter Jan Helmrich, *Zur Strafbarkeit bei fehlenden oder unzureichenden Risikomanagementsystemen in Unternehmen am Beispiel der AG*, NZG 1252–1256, 1253 (2011).

3367 LG Berlin, 3.7.2002 - 2 O 358/01 - *Zulässige fristlose Kündigung eines Bankvorstands bei mangelhaftem Risikomanagement,* 969–972 (2002) was repealed from: KG, 27. 9. 2004 - 2 U 191/02 - *Formale Anforderungen an fristlose Kündigung des Bankvorstands,* 1165–1168 (2004); *See e.g.* Müller-Michaels in: HÖLTERS | COMMENTARY ON THE AKTG, *supra* note 3235 at 11§ 91; Spindler in: MUNICH COMMENTARY ON THE AKTG, *supra* note 3328 at 69 § 91.

the board will also be held criminally liable in the event of a breach of duty.[3368] Under the German Criminal Code, criminal liability of the members of the board could arise from infidelity in accordance with Section 266 or bankruptcy under Section 283.[3369]

However, the recent case law of the Federal Supreme Court (BGH) affirmed criminal liability under Section 266 of the German Criminal Code only in the case of a serious breach of duty.[3370] In addition, the Federal Constitutional Court (BVerfG) follows a narrow interpretation of the term serious breach.[3371] In its view, a serious breach arises if the board has not introduced any measures to identify early risks of dangerous developments of the corporation, or has not introduced an adequate risk monitoring system.[3372]

Thirdly, the members of the board, who through negligence or wilful intent, violate the duty of compliance could be criminally liable under Sections 9 and 130 of the Act on Regulatory Offences (OWiG).[3373] Section 130 of this Act requires prosecution of the owner of the company in the event of the failure to carry out their supervisory duty as an administrative offence.[3374] Additionally, Section 9 of this Act also extends this responsibility to apply to the members of the board.[3375] This offence can be punished with a fine of up to one million Euros.[3376] Nevertheless, the Act on Regulatory Offences (OWiG) requires only a minimum of the supervisory

---

3368 *See* Helmrich (2011), *supra* note 3366 at 1254.

3369 BGH, 29.8.2008 - 2 StR 587/07 - *Siemens Case, supra* note 958; Helmrich (2011), *supra* note 3366 at 1252; Müller-Michaels in: HÖLTERS | COMMENTARY ON THE AKTG, *supra* note 3235 at 11 § 91; Spindler in: MUNICH COMMENTARY ON THE AKTG, *supra* note 3328 at 72 § 91.

3370 *See e.g.* BGH, 15.11.2001 - 1 StR 185/01 - *Anhaltspunkte für strafbare Untreue eines Sparkassenvorstands bei Verletzung der nach KWG normierten Pflicht zum Verlangen nach Offenlegung der wirtschaftlichen Verhältnisse bei Kreditvergabe*, 172–179 (2001); BGH, 6.12.2001 - 1 StR 215/01 - *Untreue durch Zuwendungen aus dem Vermögen einer Aktiengesellschaft, supra* note 3300.

3371 BVerfG, 23.6.2010 - 2 BvR 2559/08 - *Verfassungsrechtliche Anforderungen an den strafrechtlichen Untreuetatbestand,* 1143–1156 (2010).

3372 *See* Helmrich (2011), *supra* note 3366 at 1254.

3373 GESETZ ÜBER ORDNUNGSWIDRIGKEITEN (OWIG) | ACT ON REGULATORY OFFENCES, *supra* note 3307 §§ 9, 130; *See e.g.* Uwe H. Schneider, *Compliance im Konzern*, NZG 1321–1326, 1322 (2009); Fleischer in: SPINDLER, STILZ | COMMENTARY ON THE AKTG, *supra* note 3328 at 75 § 91.

3374 GESETZ ÜBER ORDNUNGSWIDRIGKEITEN (OWIG) | ACT ON REGULATORY OFFENCES, *supra* note 3305§ 130 (1); *See e.g.* Schneider (2009), *supra* note 3373 at 1323; Fleischer in: SPINDLER, STILZ | COMMENTARY ON THE AKTG, *supra* note 3328 at 75 § 91.

3375 GESETZ ÜBER ORDNUNGSWIDRIGKEITEN (OWIG) | ACT ON REGULATORY OFFENCES, *supra* note 3305 § 9 (1) 1; Fleischer in: SPINDLER, STILZ | COMMENTARY ON THE AKTG, *supra* note 3328 at 75 § 91.

3376 GESETZ ÜBER ORDNUNGSWIDRIGKEITEN (OWIG) | ACT ON REGULATORY OFFENCES, *supra* note 3305 § 130 (3).

duty.[3377] However, criminal law and the case law, both of which also refer to the duty of compliance of the corporate management and the effects on the post of compliance officer, will be examined in the next part of this chapter.[3378]

2. The Delegation of Responsibility to the Compliance Function

As previously discussed, the scope of the management tasks of the board encompasses *inter alia* a duty of compliance, which includes compliance measures and a compliance organization pursuant to Sections 76 (1), 91 (2) and 93 (1) of the German Stock Corporation Act (AktG).[3379] In order to reduce the liability of the members of the board, compliance tasks have been transferred to subordinate employees, such as the compliance officer.[3380] When delegating compliance tasks, legal requirements must always be taken into account.[3381] At first, it will be necessary to examine the extent of the delegation of the compliance task. There is, however, a limitation of the transfer of the compliance tasks in the course of the management tasks of the board.[3382] Thus, compliance tasks encompass monitoring duties that cannot be delegated to subordinate employees.[3383] For this reason, the members of the board cannot transfer the duty of compliance in full to other persons.[3384] Hence, ultimate responsibility for compliance remains with the

---

3377 *See e.g.* Pelz in: CORPORATE COMPLIANCE, *supra* note 3227 at 37 § 5.

3378 *See infra* III., p. 437.

3379 *See also* LG München I, 10.12.2013 - 5 HK O 1387/10 - Pflichten des Vorstands einer AG, supra note 973; Bürkle (2010), *supra* note 28 at 5; Sünner (2014), *supra* note 44 at 91; Martin Schulz & Wirnt Galster, § 4. Aufgaben im Unternehmen, in DER COMPLIANCE OFFICER, 80, 82 (Jürgen Bürkle & Christoph E. Hauschka eds., 1. ed. 2015); Koch in: HÜFFER, KOCH | COMMENTARY ON THE AKTG, supra note 3254 at 11 § 91; Fleischer in: SPINDLER, STILZ | COMMENTARY ON THE AKTG, supra note 3328 at 63 § 91.

3380 *See e.g.* § 4 Aufgaben im Unternehmen, *supra* note 3380 at 82 at 23; Bürkle (2010), *supra* note 28 at 5; Lackhoff and Schulz (2010), *supra* note 458 at 84.

3381 *See e.g.* Hüffer in: HÜFFER, KOCH | COMMENTARY ON THE AKTG, *supra* note 3254 at 11–12 § 76; Fleischer in: SPINDLER, STILZ | COMMENTARY ON THE AKTG, *supra* note 3328 at 64–66 § 91; Ulrich Tödtmann & Marc Winstel, *§ 13 Compliance als Vorstandsaufgabe, in* ARBEITSHANDBUCH FÜR VORSTANDSMITGLIEDER, 55–58 (Dietmar Kubis, Johannes Semler, & Michael Arnold eds., 2. ed. 2015).

3382 *See e.g.* BERND SCHMIDT, JÜRGEN TAEGER & BENEDIKT BUCHNER, COMPLIANCE IN KAPITALGESELLSCHAFTEN 152 (1. ed. 2010); Schulz and Galster (2015) § 4 Aufgaben im Unternehmen, *supra* note 3379 at 82 at 23; Bürkle (2010), *supra* note 28 at 5; Lackhoff and Schulz (2010), *supra* note 458 at 84.

3383 *See e.g.* Gößwein and Hohmann (2011), *supra* note 41 at 965; Lackhoff and Schulz (2010), *supra* note 458 at 83; Wolf (2011), *supra* note 41 at 1356; Schulz and Galster (2015), § 4 Aufgaben im Unternehmen, *supra* note 3379 at 82 at 23.

3384 *See e.g.* Bürkle (2010), *supra* note 28 at 5; Lackhoff and Schulz (2010), *supra* note 458 at 83.

management board.[3385] Finally, the organizational and supervisory responsibilities remain with all members of the board.[3386]

Secondly, the board members should carefully consider the question of to whom they can actually transfer compliance tasks. The transfer requires a duty of care when choosing a well-qualified candidate as a compliance officer, for instance.[3387] In the event of delegation, the board has to take into account the requirements of due care in the selection procedure, instructions, and supervisory duties.[3388]

Thirdly, in practice, joint stock corporations often establish a compliance department within the board.[3389] When doing so, it should be taken into account that the members of the board can appoint a compliance officer, but only the supervisory board can establish a compliance department within the board.[3390]

In conclusion, it has been noted that the requirement of the appointment of a compliance officer is not enshrined in German Company Law. In the event of any delegation of compliance tasks, only appropriately qualified persons should be charged with these tasks. Furthermore, the delegation of compliance tasks from the board to an appropriate person is restricted. The board can transfer only certain controlling tasks to other persons. Even after delegation, the supervisory duty and the overall managing responsibility remain with the board.

a. The Scope of Compliance Tasks Derived from the Delegation

It follows from the foregoing explanations that the board can transfer compliance tasks to subordinated employees, such as compliance officers. In general, the

---

3385 *See e.g.* Tobias Brouwer, *§ 59 Compliance in Verbänden*, *in* CORPORATE COMPLIANCE: HANDBUCH DER HAFTUNGSVERMEIDUNG IM UNTERNEHMEN, 60 (Christoph E. Hauschka, Klaus Moosmayer, & Thomas Lösler eds., 3. ed. 2016); Schulz and Galster (2015), § 4 Aufgaben im Unternehmen, *supra* note 3379 at 83 at 23.

3386 LG München I, 10.12.2013 - 5 HK O 1387/10, NZG 2014, *supra* note 973 at 347; Fleischer (2014), *supra* note 3347 at 323; Hölters in: HÖLTERS | COMMENTARY ON THE AKTG, *supra* note 3235 at 97 § 93; Koch in: HÜFFER, KOCH | COMMENTARY ON THE AKTG, *supra* note 3254 at 12 § 76; Spindler in: MUNICH COMMENTARY ON THE AKTG, *supra* note 3328 at 68 § 91; Fleischer in: SPINDLER, STILZ | COMMENTARY ON THE AKTG, *supra* note 3328 at 64§ 91.

3387 *See e.g.* Gößwein and Hohmann (2011), *supra* note 41 at 965; Lackhoff and Schulz (2010), *supra* note 458 at 84; Schulz and Galster (2015), § 4 Aufgaben im Unternehmen, *supra* note 3379 at 83 at 24; Tödtmann and Winstel (2015) § 13 Compliance als Vorstandsaufgabe, *supra* note 3381 at 62.

3388 *See e.g.* SCHMIDT, TAEGER, AND BUCHNER, *supra* note 3383 at 152; Schulz and Galster (2015) § 4 Aufgaben im Unternehmen, *supra* note 3379 at 83 at 24; Tödtmann and Winstel (2015) § 13 Compliance als Vorstandsaufgabe, *supra* note 3381 at 56.

3389 *See e.g.* Tödtmann and Winstel (2015) § 13 Compliance als Vorstandsaufgabe, *supra* note 3381 at 53.

3390 *Id.* at 54.

compliance officer has to monitor the employees as to their adherence to the law and company rules and must inform the members of the board of any deviations and specific events.[3391] With the transfer of tasks, the compliance officer takes responsibility for the management of the compliance procedures within the corporation.[3392]

The compliance officer thus takes on a wide range of tasks.[3393] The scope of compliance tasks encompasses the identification, assessment, and analysis of legal and compliance risks.[3394] Subsequently, it is necessary to develop steps to reduce and avoid such risks.[3395] These results should be incorporated into a compliance concept, which comprises the compliance strategy, the enhancement of the corporate compliance culture, the development of a compliance policy, and also the further development of compliance measures.[3396] In addition, the compliance officer gives advice to employees and to the management board on how to apply rules and provisions and how to avoid business risks.[3397] In the capacity of an adviser, the compliance officer must also provide training for employees.[3398] In the course of the performance of compliance tasks, the compliance officer must develop a reporting system in order to periodically inform the members of the board of compliance issues.[3399] The function is referred to as a collection point of information.[3400] Although the supervisory duty remains with the board, certain control and monitoring tasks can be transferred to the compliance function.[3401] Within the scope of the monitoring tasks, the compliance officer has to uncover and report to the members of the board on any violations.[3402] However, the board is responsible for sanctioning any violations, as well as for the type and scope of the penalties to be imposed on the employee.[3403] Finally, all activities of the compliance officer should

3391 *See e.g.* Hölter in: HÖLTERS | COMMENTARY ON THE AKTG, *supra* note 3235 at 98 § 93.

3392 *See e.g.* Tödtmann and Winstel (2015), *supra* note 3381 at 59.

3393 *See e.g.* Schulz and Galster (2015) § 4 Aufgaben im Unternehmen, *supra* note 3379 at 84 at 26.

3394 *Id.* at 85. at 27.

3395 *Id.* at 85. at 27.

3396 *Id.* at 30–44.

3397 *See e.g.* Schulz and Renz (2012), *supra* note 41 at 2514; Schulz and Galster (2015) § 4 Aufgaben im Unternehmen, *supra* note 3379 at 46.

3398 *See e.g.* Schulz and Renz (2012), *supra* note 41 at 2514; Schulz and Galster (2015) § 4 Aufgaben im Unternehmen, *supra* note 3379 at 47–49.

3399 *See e.g.* Schulz and Galster (2015) § 4 Aufgaben im Unternehmen, *supra* note 3379 at 57.

3400 *See e.g.* Lackhoff and Schulz (2010), *supra* note 458 at 85; Schulz and Renz (2012), *supra* note 41 at 2514.

3401 *See e.g.* Schulz and Renz (2012), *supra* note 41 at 2514; Schulz and Galster (2015) § 4 Aufgaben im Unternehmen, *supra* note 3379 at 50.

3402 *See e.g.* Schulz and Galster (2015) § 4 Aufgaben im Unternehmen, *supra* note 3379 at 53.

3403 *Id.* at 55.

be properly documented in order to demonstrate the fulfilment of his duties, and on the other hand, to fulfil the burden of proof of the organizational duties of the board.[3404] This list shows the broad scope of the work of the compliance function across all lines of business. In conclusion, it has been recognized that a separate assignment profile of the compliance function has been established.[3405]

b. The Position of the German Compliance Officer

As we have seen, the compliance officer is appointed by the board and is responsible for the compliance organization.[3406] In this post, the compliance officer should for the most part work independently and without directions from the employer.[3407] The reason for this is to guarantee the efficiency of the compliance organization.[3408] In 2009, the Federal Supreme Court (BGH) pointed out that it is necessary to clearly govern the responsibilities and tasks of the compliance officer.[3409]

In practice, this means that the board needs to document the current status of the responsibilities and tasks of the compliance function.[3410] In addition, the board should require confirmation from the compliance officer that he has taken note of this current status.[3411] In order to strengthen the position of the compliance officer, the board should clearly state his reporting duties.[3412] The compliance officer should be required to assess and forward the relevant information to the board.[3413]

3404 *See e.g.* Schulz and Renz (2012), *supra* note 41 at 2515; Schulz and Galster (2015) § 4 Aufgaben im Unternehmen, *supra* note 3379 at 61.

3405 *See e.g.* Schulz and Renz (2012), *supra* note 41 at 2517.

3406 *See supra* II., .2., p. 433; *See also* Tödtmann and Winstel (2015) § 13 Compliance als Vorstandsaufgabe, *supra* note 3381 at 59.

3407 *See e.g.* Fecker and Kinzl (2010), *supra* note 455 at 16; Illing and Umnuß (2009), *supra* note 461 at 1; Steffen Krieger & Jens Günther, *Der Compliance-Officer*, ZRFC 149–154, 150 (2011); Meier (2011), *supra* note 30 at 781; Meier-Greve (2010), *supra* note 461 at 218; Schulz and Renz (2012), *supra* note 41 at 2513; Sünner (2014), *supra* note 44 at 91; Tödtmann and Winstel (2015) § 13 Compliance als Vorstandsaufgabe, *supra* note 3381 at 59.

3408 *See e.g.* Tödtmann and Winstel (2015) § 13 Compliance als Vorstandsaufgabe, *supra* note 3381 at 62.

3409 BGH, 17.7.2009 - 5 StR 394/08, BGHSt 54, 44; BGH NJW 2009, 3173, *supra* note 25 at 3174; *See e.g.* Lackhoff and Schulz (2010), *supra* note 458 at 88; Krieger and Günther (2010), *supra* note 30 at 370; Wolf (2011), *supra* note 41 at 1359; Tödtmann and Winstel (2015) § 13 Compliance als Vorstandsaufgabe, *supra* note 3381 at 60.

3410 *See e.g.* Tödtmann and Winstel (2015) § 13 Compliance als Vorstandsaufgabe, *supra* note 3381 at 61.

3411 *Id.* at 61.

3412 *See e.g.* Krieger and Günther (2011), *supra* note 3407 at 153; Tödtmann and Winstel (2015) § 13 Compliance als Vorstandsaufgabe, *supra* note 3381 at 63.

3413 *See e.g.* Krieger and Günther (2011), *supra* note 3407 at 153; Tödtmann and Winstel (2015) § 13 Compliance als Vorstandsaufgabe, *supra* note 3382 at 63.

However, as has been examined, the nature of the position of the compliance officer is not enshrined in German Corporation Law. As a consequence, this function is not comparable with the legal position of corporate officers such as those for water protection, data protection or immission controls within the private sector.[3414] Contrary to the compliance function, those positions and their tasks are clearly defined in law.[3415] Therefore, their scope and responsibilities are clearly stipulated in the law; for example the employment contracts of those specific corporate officers may only be terminated for good cause.[3416]

In conclusion, just like the reporting duties and lines, it is necessary to clearly define the hierarchy of the compliance officer within the corporation. In the literature, there is an academic discussion concerning a right – respectively, a duty - of escalation for the compliance officer to report directly to the supervisory board in the event that the management board is personally involved in compliance issues.[3417] Although this is an ongoing debate, one possible solution could be the specific definition of the reporting lines in the contract of employment or in the job description. The position of the compliance officer under employment law and criminal law will be explored in the following sections.[3418]

III. The Enforcement of Criminal Law with Respect to Compliance

In Germany, interest in the compliance officer function was sparked by the widely discussed Federal Supreme Court (BGH) decision on complicity in fraud caused by omission.[3419] However, the Court only incidentally gave a view on the criminal liability of the compliance officer.[3420] Since 2009, this decision has been variously discussed in the literature. In addition to the negative views, other scholars take the stance that the Court wanted to initiate a discussion on the position and liability

---

3414 *See e.g.* Giesen (2009), *supra* note 459 at 104; Meier (2011), *supra* note 30 at 780; Meier-Greve (2010), *supra* note 461 at 219; Wolf (2011), *supra* note 41 at 1359.

3415 BUNDESDATENSCHUTZGESETZ | FEDERAL DATA PROTECTION ACT (BDSG), BDSG BGBl. I, 201 (1978) § 4 (f) (g); BUNDES-IMMISSIONSSCHUTZGESETZ (BIMSCHG) | FEDERAL IMMISSION CONTROL ACT, *supra* note 1012 §§ 53.

3416 *See e.g.* BUNDESDATENSCHUTZGESETZ | FEDERAL DATA PROTECTION ACT (BDSG), *supra* note 3415 § 4 (f) (3).

3417 *See e.g.* Johannes Sebastian Blassl, *Vorstandsüberwachung auch durch die Compliance-Funktion*, ZRFC 205–211, 209 (2016); Bürkle (2010), *supra* note 28 at 9; Krieger and Günther (2011), *supra* note 3407 at 154; Lackhoff and Schulz (2010), *supra* note 458 at 87; Raus and Lützeler (2012), *supra* note 460.

3418 *See supra* III., p. 437.

3419 BGH, 17.7.2009 - 5 StR 394/08, BGHST 54, 44; BGH NJW 2009, 3173, *supra* note 25.

3420 *See* the *obiter dictum* on a compliance officers' "*duty as guarantor*" pursuant to Section 13 of the German Criminal Code (StGB) *Id.* at 3175.

of the compliance officer.[3421] Yet other scholars see this decision as a consistent enforcement in terms of the principles of risk monitoring and the principal's liability under criminal law.[3422]

As a result of this decision, the BGH referred to the personal criminal liability of the compliance officer with respect to his duty to avoid violations of the law that could arise in day-to-day business within corporations.[3423] Thus, the compliance officer faces the risk of being held criminally liable for offences committed by other employees or managers.[3424] For this reason, the next sections will explore the criminal law as it applies to infidelity, bribery and fraud in terms of compliance, which can apply to the members of the management board and the compliance officer. This examination encompasses the "*duty as guarantor*" and the criminal liability pursuant to this duty of the compliance officer, as well as liability for administrative offences.[3425]

1. The Criminal Offence of Infidelity

The compliance officer as an offender has been widely discussed only in the context of the BGH decision of 2009.[3426] However, according to the PwC 2015 Global CEO Survey, the corporate compliance officer also faces the challenge of being involved in investigations of compliance-related risks to the business *e.g.* fraud, bribery and corruption.[3427] For example, according to the EY Study in 2016, a high-profile case of fraud was committed at one in every seven German corporations.[3428] In addition, the Study Compliance Manager 2013 shows that one important area of activity of compliance departments is the prevention of fraud and corruption.[3429] In recent years, several well-known German corporations, such as Siemens AG

3421 *See e.g.* contray view Markus Rübenstahl, *Zur „regelmäßigen" Garantenstellung des Compliance Officers*, NEUE ZEITSCHRIFT FÜR GESELLSCHAFTSRECHT 1341–1344 (2009). Discussion on the subject *See e.g.* Blassl (2016), *supra* note 3417; Bürkle (2010), *supra* note 28; Campos Nave (2009), *supra* note 457; Fecker and Kinzl (2010), *supra* note 455; Illing and Umnuß (2009), *supra* note 461; Krieger and Günther (2010), *supra* note 30; Rieble (2010), *supra* note 458; Wybitul (2009), *supra* note 28.

3422 *See e.g.* Dann and Mengel (2010), *supra* note 30.

3423 *See e.g.* Jürgen Wessing & Matthias Dann, *§ 9 Compliance Officer und Strafrecht, in* DER COMPLIANCE OFFICER: EIN HANDBUCH IN EIGENER SACHE 191–240, 215 (Jürgen Bürkle & Christoph E. Hauschka eds., 1. ed. 2015) at 73.

3424 *Id.* at 215. at 73.

3425 GESETZ ÜBER ORDNUNGSWIDRIGKEITEN (OWIG) | ACT ON REGULATORY OFFENCES, *supra* note 3306 §§ 30, 130; STRAFGESETZBUCH (STGB) | GERMAN CRIMINAL CODE, *supra* note 965 §§ 13, 266.

3426 BGH, 17.7.2009 - 5 StR 394/08, BGHST 54, 44; BGH NJW 2009, 3173, *supra* note 25.

3427 PWC STUDY 2015, *supra* note 1771 at 16.

3428 *See* STEFAN HEISSNER, GLOBAL FRAUD SURVEY – FINDINGS IN GERMANY 7 (2016).

3429 STUDY COMPLIANCE MANAGER 2013, HERZOG AND STEPHAN (2013), *supra* note 476 at 190 fig. 5.01.

or Mannesmann have been involved in high-profile scandals where the courts also had to examine the serious misconduct of managers in terms of infidelity.[3430] Additionally, a recent KPMG Study states that the respondents named the offences fraud, infidelity, and corruption as the most frequently identified risks within companies.[3431] The significance of compliance has increased in the context of infidelity pursuant to Section 266 of the German Criminal Code (StGB), since the principles of proper corporate management include effective compliance measures.[3432] According to legal scholars, corporate management is in breach of its fiduciary duty when the members of the management board and the supervisory board have not established statutory compliance measures and this omission has resulted in a financial loss.[3433] Moreover, it should be noted that the compliance officer may have a fiduciary duty.[3434] This is the reason why this section examines the offence of infidelity as it relates to compliance.

Infidelity means the abuse of the disposal of assets belonging to third parties.[3435] The abuse is the discrepancy between the legal ability outwards and the legal permission inwards.[3436] As a result, the third party will suffer a serious disadvantage resulting from the causation of financial loss.[3437]

3430 *See e.g.* BGH, 21.12.2005 - 3 StR 470/04 -, BGHSt 50, 331–346 - Mannesmann/Vodafone, NStZ 2006, 214; BGH, 29.8.2008 - 2 StR 587/07, NStZ 2009, 95, supra note 958.

3431 In this Study 500 corporations were interviewed in terms of economic crime within companies. KPMG Study 2016; Tatort Deutschland - Wirtschaftskriminalität in Deutschland 2016, 10–11 (2016), https://assets.kpmg.com/content/dam/kpmg/pdf/2016/07/wirtschaftskriminalitaet-2016-2-KPMG.pdf (last visited Jan 4, 2017) fig. 2 and 3.

3432 *See e.g.* Waßmer in: Wirtschafts- und Steuerstrafrecht | Commentary on Economic and Tax Criminal Law, 143e (Graf, Jäger, & Wittig eds., 2. ed. 2017) § 266.

3433 Aktiengesetz (AktG) | German Stock Corporation Act, *supra* note 976 §§ 76, 93, 116; Blassl (2016), *supra* note 3417 at 208; Helmrich (2011), *supra* note 3366 at 1252; Modlinger, Egelhof, and Berger (2014), *supra* note 3346 at 256.

3434 BGH, 17.7.2009 - 5 StR 394/08, BGHSt 54, 44; BGH NJW 2009, 3173, *supra* note 25; Dann and Mengel (2010), *supra* note 30 at 3267; Wybitul (2009), *supra* note 28 at 2592; Waßmer in: Commentary on Economic and Tax Criminal Law, *supra* note 3432 at 49 § 266.

3435 Strafgesetzbuch (StGB) | German Criminal Code, *supra* note 965 § 266 (1).

3436 *See e.g.* Wittig in: Strafrecht | Beck Online Commentary on Criminal Law, 6 (v Heintschel-Heinegg ed., 33. ed. 2016) § 266.

3437 *See e.g.* Kindhäuser in: Strafrecht | Commentary on Criminal Law, 30 (Kindhäuser, Neumann, & Paeffgen eds., 4 ed. 2013) § 266. Kindhäuser in: *Id.* at 28 § 266.

The examination of the offence of infidelity follows a multistage structure. First, the object of the offence requires assets from third parties, such as items owned by another person or assets of a company.[3438] In this case, the offender is not the owner or holder of the assets.[3439] Secondly, in the view of the legal scholars and the courts, the offence requires a fiduciary duty between the offender and the trustor.[3440] The necessary authority and status as guarantor for asset management services is based on law, at the request of the public authorities or contractual agreement.[3441] Therefore, the authority is established by either public or civil law.[3442] Traditionally, the guarantor for asset management services encompasses *e.g.* the supervisory board or the managing director of a private limited company.[3443]

Thirdly, the actual crime, particularly the abuse and the breach of the fiduciary duty, will be examined.[3444] In practice, the question of when an action is qualified as an abuse is difficult to answer. For instance, the following BGH cases provide guidance as to the circumstances in which an abuse could occur: (a) the permission of appreciation bonus by the supervisory board of a joint-stock corporation[3445] or (b) the engagement of unqualified personnel for management positions.[3446]

3438 *See e.g.* Wittig in: *Id.* at 10. § 266; Kindhäuser in: *Id.* at 28 § 266.; Heger in: STRAFGESETZBUCH | COMMENTARY ON THE CRIMINAL LAW, 3 (Lackner & Kühl eds., 28 ed. 2014) § 266.

3439 *See e.g.* Wittig in: *Id.* at 10. § 266; Kindhäuser in: *Id.* at 30 § 266; Heger in: *Id.* at 3 § 266.

3440 BGH, 21.12.2005 - 3 StR 470/04 -, BGHSt 50, 331–346, NSTZ 2006, 214, *supra* note 3430 at 216; Wittig in: BECK ONLINE COMMENTARY ON CRIMINAL LAW, *supra* note 3436 at 12§ 266; Kindhäuser in: COMMENTARY ON CRIMINAL LAW, *supra* note 3437 at 33§ 266; Heger in: COMMENTARY ON THE CRIMINAL LAW, *supra* note 3439 at 8§ 266.

3441 *See e.g.* Wittig in: BECK ONLINE COMMENTARY ON CRIMINAL LAW, *supra* note 3436 at 8§ 266; Kindhäuser in: COMMENTARY ON CRIMINAL LAW, *supra* note 3437 at 37 § 266; Heger in: COMMENTARY ON THE CRIMINAL LAW, *supra* note 3438 at 5a § 266.

3442 *See e.g.* Wittig in: BECK ONLINE COMMENTARY ON CRIMINAL LAW, *supra* note 3436 at 8§ 266; Kindhäuser in: COMMENTARY ON CRIMINAL LAW, *supra* note 3496 at 37 § 266; Heger in: COMMENTARY ON THE CRIMINAL LAW, *supra* note 3438 at 5a § 266.

3443 *See e.g.* Kindhäuser in: COMMENTARY ON CRIMINAL LAW, *supra* note 3437 at 58 § 266; Wessing and Dann (2015) § 9 Compliance Officer und Strafrecht, *supra* note 3423 at 196 at 9.

3444 *See e.g.* Wittig in: BECK ONLINE COMMENTARY ON CRIMINAL LAW, *supra* note 3436 at 13–24 § 266; Kindhäuser in: COMMENTARY ON CRIMINAL LAW, *supra* note 3437 at 59–93 § 266; Heger in: COMMENTARY ON THE CRIMINAL LAW, *supra* note 3438 at 5–15 § 266.

3445 BGH, 21.12.2005 - 3 StR 470/04 -, BGHSt 50, 331–346, NStZ 2006, 214, *supra* note 3430 at 214.

3446 BGH, 26.04.2006 - 2 StR 515/05 - *Verurteilung eines Landrats wegen Untreue*, NStZ-RR 307 (2006).

Additionally, the breach of the fiduciary duty requires a disadvantage in terms of the asset interests of the trustor.[3447] Furthermore, the breach of the duty must be serious.[3448] However, the courts will balance the circumstances of seriousness in each individual case.[3449] Legal scholars have identified four key aspects of a serious breach of duty: (1) inadequacy in terms of the assets and earnings position of the corporation, (2) the violation of information duties, (3) the presence of inappropriate motives, and (4) overstepping the decision-making authority.[3450] Finally, the offence of infidelity requires at least conditional intent, but the courts apply stringent requirements for the offender's intent.[3451]

In a 2005 BGH case, for example, the court concluded that appreciation bonuses which are not provided for in the employment contract, which are not included as special remuneration, and which do not provide any benefits to the company could constitute a waste of corporate assets and, therefore, a breach of this duty.[3452] In this constellation, there is no discretion on the part of the supervisory board.[3453] Finally, the court stated that the members of the supervisory board recognized the futility of the appreciation bonus and, therefore, cannot cite the absence of intent.[3454] It is at this point that the compliance officer will come into focus. In such cases, it could be that he has a duty requiring action to reasonably inform the management board in order to prevent a violation of law.[3455] However, under German Law there is no general duty to notify specific criminal offences by employees or third parties to the competent authorities.[3456] This is contrary to US and UK Bribery Law,

---

3447 *See e.g.* Wittig in: BECK ONLINE COMMENTARY ON CRIMINAL LAW, *supra* note 3436 at 25 § 266; Kindhäuser in: COMMENTARY ON CRIMINAL LAW, *supra* note 3437 at 94 § 266; Heger in: COMMENTARY ON THE CRIMINAL LAW, *supra* note 3438 at 16 § 266.

3448 *See e.g.* Dierlamm in: MÜNCHNER KOMMENTAR ZUM STGB | MUNICH COMMENTARY ON THE STGB, 5 , 175 (Joecks & Miebach eds., 2. ed. 2014) § 266; Wessing and Dann, (2015) § 9 Compliance Officer und Strafrecht, *supra* note 3423 at 198 at 14.

3449 *See e.g.* The breach of duty must not be additional serious in: BGH, 21.12.2005 - 3 StR 470/04 -, BGHSt 50, 331–346, NStZ 2006, 214, *supra* note 3430 at 214.

3450 *See in detail:* Dierlamm: MÜNCHNER KOMMENTAR ZUM STGB | MUNICH COMMENTARY ON THE STGB, *supra* note 3448 at 176–180 § 266.

3451 *See e.g.* Wittig in: BECK ONLINE COMMENTARY ON CRIMINAL LAW, *supra* note 3436 at 47 § 266; Kindhäuser in: COMMENTARY ON CRIMINAL LAW, *supra* note 3437 at 122 § 266; Heger in: COMMENTARY ON THE CRIMINAL LAW, *supra* note 3438 at 19 § 266.

3452 BGH, 21.12.2005 - 3 StR 470/04 -, BGHSt 50, 331–346, NStZ 2006, 214, *supra* note 3430 at 217–218.

3453 *Id.* at 216.

3454 *Id.* at 221.

3455 *See e.g.* Wessing and Dann (2015) § 9 Compliance Officer und Strafrecht, *supra* note 3423 at 221 at 93.

3456 STRAFGESETZBUCH (STGB) | GERMAN CRIMINAL CODE, *supra* note 965 § 138 (1) (2); Bürkle (2010), *supra* note 28 at 10; Wessing and Dann (2015) § 9 Compliance Officer und Strafrecht, *supra* note 3423 at 222 at 98.

pursuant to which the compliance officer can have a duty to notify the relevant law enforcement agency.[3457] Nevertheless, in individual cases, as listed in accordance with Section 138 of the German Criminal Code (StGB), the compliance officer could be required to notify the relevant law enforcement agency about the suspicious facts and the internal investigation.[3458] This obligation to notify in order to prevent damages to the company could also arise from the compliance officer's employment obligations, as will be examined later in this chapter.[3459]

However, in 2005, the court did not ask, nor examine, whether there were compliance measures or whether the function of the compliance officer in the corporation with his duties to inform other authorities applied to decisions of the supervisory board to pay appreciation bonus to certain members of the board. However, in recent times, it could be argued that the courts are likely to examine more comprehensively the corporate structures with respect to effective compliance measures and will also consider the position of the corporate compliance officer with regard to criminal offences.

2. Bribery and Corruption in the Course of Business

As opposed to US and UK Law with the FCPA and the UKBA 2010, Germany has no separate bribery statute.[3460] Furthermore, the German legislator has not established any special regulatory body or law enforcement agency with respect to the prosecution of corporate bribery and fraud.[3461] In Germany, the public prosecutor will open an investigation when it receives knowledge of facts indicating the commission of a criminal offence.[3462] Unlike in the US and in the UK, bribery and corruption have not hitherto been in the public focus in Germany. The acceptance and granting of personal gifts and hospitalities or offering entertainment are part of daily business in several industries.[3463] On the other hand, over the years, the German legislator has amended the German Criminal Code, adding certain provisions with respect to bribery and corruption within *e.g.* the private sector, the health sector and civil service sector.[3464] This section will examine Section

3457 *See supra* Ch. 3 and 4.

3458 *See e.g.* Heuchemer in: Beck Online Commentary on Criminal Law, *supra* note 3436 at 4 § 138; Wessing and Dann (2015) § 9 Compliance Officer und Strafrecht, *supra* note 3423 at 222 at 98.

3459 *See infra* IV., p. 467.

3460 *See supra* A., I., 1.a-e, pp. 189 et seq.; A., III., 1. pp. 355 et seq.

3461 *Compare* DOJ, *supra* note 1209; SFO, *supra* note 2603.

3462 Strafprozessordnung (StPO) | German German Code of Criminal Procedure, (RGBl. p. 253) (1879) §§ 152 (1)(2), 155 (2).

3463 *See e.g.* Wessing and Dann (2015) § 9 Compliance Officer und Strafrecht, *supra* note 3423 at 200 at 19.

3464 Strafgesetzbuch (StGB) | German Criminal Code, *supra* note 965 §§ 299 as amended on November 20, 2015 (BGBl. I p. 2025), 299 (a), 299 (b), 300, 331, 332, 333, 334.

299 - bribery and corruption connected with commercial practice. Similar to the provisions of the UK Bribery Act, Section 299 of the German Criminal Code legally defines bribery as follows:

> Sec. 299 (1) Anyone will be punished with imprisonment for a term up to three years, or to a fine when any activity connected with a business and any activity performed in the course of a person's employment:
>
> > He or she requests, agrees to receive or accepts a financial or other advantage to another person within the purchase of the goods and/or the services and takes unfair advantage in terms of domestic and foreign competition...[3465]

That is to say, where the donors grant an advantage to another person (bribery, active)[3466] and the bribed person accepts an advantage from another person (corruption, passive).[3467] Just like under the Bribery Act, both bribery and corruption are criminal offences under the Criminal Code.

In 1997, Section 299 enacted the first statutory anti-corruption provision.[3468] The implementation of this provision into the German Criminal Code (StGB) was intended to increase public awareness of the harmfulness of bribery conduct and its adverse impacts on the economy, society and the environment.[3469] Since 2015, the criminal liability of this offence has been broadly extended as a result of the second anti-corruption statute and now also comprises bribery in the course of a person's employment.[3470] Specifically, the first subsection of Section 299 (corruption) describes a special crime that can be committed only by employees or authorized representatives of a company.[3471] The bribed person has a special relationship – a contractual relationship - with the company.[3472] In the *Siemens* case,

---

3465 *Compare Id.*§ 299 (1) (2); United Kingdom Bribery Act 2010, *supra* note 433 §§ 1, 2, 11.

3466 *Compare* Strafgesetzbuch (StGB) | German Criminal Code, *supra* note 965 § 299 (2) 1; United Kingdom Bribery Act 2010, *supra* note 433 § 1(2).

3467 *Compare* Strafgesetzbuch (StGB) | German Criminal Code, *supra* note 965 § 299 (1) 1; United Kingdom Bribery Act 2010, *supra* note 433 § 2(2).

3468 Statute against Corruption, BGBI. I, p. 2038 (1997); Momsen, Laudien Beck Online Commentary on Criminal Law, *supra* note 3436 at 1 § 299.

3469 Momsen, Laudien in: Beck Online Commentary on Criminal Law, *supra* note 3436 at 1§ 299.

3470 Statute against Corruption, BGBI. I, p. 2025 (2015); *See e.g.* Momsen, Laudien in: Beck Online Commentary on Criminal Law, *supra* note 3436 at 2 § 299.

3471 *See e.g.* Sahan in: Commentary on Economic and Tax Criminal Law, *supra* note 3432 at 6 § 299; Momsen, Laudien in: Beck Online Commentary on Criminal Law, *supra* note 3436 at 12§ 299; Heger in: Commentary on the Criminal Law, *supra* note 3438 at 2 § 299.

3472 *See e.g.* Sahan in: Commentary on Economic and Tax Criminal Law, *supra* note 3432 at 12§ 299.

the BGH concluded that the contractual relationship as an employee also includes members of the supervisory board.[3473] In conclusion, every person of an employment relationship or engaged to perform services for the company and bound by instructions could be a bribed person.[3474] Only the principal or the sole shareholder and manager of a company who are not under instructions could be excluded as offender under Section 299 (1) of the German Criminal Code (StGB).[3475] Therefore, the compliance officer must define and qualify every person connected with the company.

The result of the corruption is an advantage. The advantage in a broad sense is defined as each benefit or everything that improves the economic and legal situation of the beneficiary or bribed person.[3476] The advantage could take the form of material benefits, such as cash, additional incomes, interest-free loans or invitations to trips, and immaterial benefits such as the awarding of honorary offices,[3477] where the bribed person has no entitlement to this advantage.[3478]

Similar to the UKBA 2010, Section 299 requires all activities connected with a business or trade to be for business purposes.[3479] Accordingly, these are business dealings of a company.[3480] Therefore, private activities and activities by employees within public agencies are excluded.[3481] In addition, the awarding that provides an

3473 *See e.g.* BGH, 29. 8.2008 - 2 StR 587/07, NStZ 2009, 95, *supra* note 958 at 95; Dannecker in: COMMENTARY ON CRIMINAL LAW, *supra* note 3437 at 21 § 299.

3474 *See e.g.* Sahan in: COMMENTARY ON ECONOMIC AND TAX CRIMINAL LAW, *supra* note 3432 at 11 § 299.

3475 LG Frankfurt a. M., 22.4.2015 - 5/12 Qs 1/15 - Angestellter oder Beauftragter, 2015 NStZ-RR 215–216, 215 (2015); *See e.g.* Sahan in: COMMENTARY ON ECONOMIC AND TAX CRIMINAL LAW, *supra* note 3432 at 11 § 299.

3476 *See e.g.* Sahan in: COMMENTARY ON ECONOMIC AND TAX CRIMINAL LAW, *supra* note 3432 at 18 § 299; Momsen, Laudien in: BECK ONLINE COMMENTARY ON CRIMINAL LAW, *supra* note 3436 at 15 § 299; Dannecker in: COMMENTARY ON CRIMINAL LAW, *supra* note 3437 at 35 § 299.

3477 *See e.g.* Sahan in: COMMENTARY ON ECONOMIC AND TAX CRIMINAL LAW, *supra* note 3432 at 19–20 § 299; Momsen, Laudien in: BECK ONLINE COMMENTARY ON CRIMINAL LAW, *supra* note 3436 at 15 § 299; Dannecker in: COMMENTARY ON CRIMINAL LAW, *supra* note 3437 at 37–38 § 299.

3478 *See e.g.* Sahan in: COMMENTARY ON ECONOMIC AND TAX CRIMINAL LAW, *supra* note 3432 at 18§ 299.

3479 *Compare* STRAFGESETZBUCH (STGB) | GERMAN CRIMINAL CODE, *supra* note 965 § 299 (1), (2); UNITED KINGDOM BRIBERY ACT 2010, *supra* note 433 § 3 (7).

3480 *See e.g.* Sahan in: COMMENTARY ON ECONOMIC AND TAX CRIMINAL LAW, *supra* note 3432 at 17 § 299; Momsen, Laudien in: BECK ONLINE COMMENTARY ON CRIMINAL LAW, *supra* note 3436 at 18 § 299.

3481 *See e.g.* Sahan in: COMMENTARY ON ECONOMIC AND TAX CRIMINAL LAW, *supra* note 3432 at 17 § 299; Momsen, Laudien in: BECK ONLINE COMMENTARY ON CRIMINAL LAW, *supra* note 3436 at 18 § 299.

advantage must constitute preferential treatment within the context of trading competition.[3482]

Active bribery is qualified as offering, promising or giving an advantage to another person, to an employee or to an authorized party of a company in the course of business.[3483] The offender acts in the course of business trading.[3484] Finally, the offender intends the advantage to induce a person to perform improper activity. As is the case with infidelity, criminal liability requires intent on the part of the offender.[3485] Such intent is not excluded by the offender's "*best intentions*".[3486]

Most recently, on March 29, 2017, the German Federal Cabinet decided to establish a central federal competition database to be run by the Federal Cartel Office in order to combat bribery and corruption.[3487] This database will list all registered corporations that have committed offences such as corruption or money laundering.[3488] Through this public disclosure, the legislator will ensure that such corporations can win contracts from public contracting entities only when they comply with the law.[3489] Despite this draft bill, legal scholars have criticized that the idea is not a new one.[3490] De facto, there have already been such databases or information points in several federal states like Baden-Wurttemberg, Berlin or Hamburg. In the past, proposed bills to regulate a federal database failed.[3491] Moreover, under certain provisions of other statutes, such as the Act Against Restraints of Competition (GWB) and the Act on Regulatory Offences (OWiG), corporations could be excluded from the award of public service contracts.[3492] Notwithstanding the academic concern, in July, 2017 the bill passed the Bundestag

---

3482 *See e.g.* Sahan in: COMMENTARY ON ECONOMIC AND TAX CRIMINAL LAW, *supra* note 3432 at 31 § 299; Momsen, Laudien in: BECK ONLINE COMMENTARY ON CRIMINAL LAW, *supra* note 3436 at 14, 22 § 299.

3483 STRAFGESETZBUCH (STGB) | GERMAN CRIMINAL CODE, *supra* note 965 § 299 (2) 1.

3484 *See e.g.* Momsen, Laudien in: BECK ONLINE COMMENTARY ON CRIMINAL LAW, *supra* note 3436 at 29 § 299.

3485 *See e.g.*Sahan in: COMMENTARY ON ECONOMIC AND TAX CRIMINAL LAW, *supra* note 3432 at 57 § 299; Momsen, Laudien in: BECK ONLINE COMMENTARY ON CRIMINAL LAW, *supra* note 3436 at 33 § 299.

3486 BGH, 29. 8.2008 - 2 StR 587/07, NStZ 2009, 95, *supra* note 958 at 99.

3487 ENTWURF EINES GESETZES ZUR EINFÜHRUNG EINES WETTBEWERBSREGISTERS | A BILL FOR ESTABLISHING A COMPETITION DATABASE, 18 (2017).

3488 *Id.* at 17.

3489 *Id.* at 16.

3490 *See e.g.* Sascha Süße, *Bundesweites Wettbewerbsregister – kommt es diesmal?*, NEWSDIENST COMPLIANCE 71001.

3491 *Id.*

3492 GESETZ GEGEN WETTBEWERBSBESCHRÄNKUNGEN (GWB) | ACT AGAINST RESTRAINTS OF COMPETITION, BGBI. I, p. 1081 (1958) as amended on March 29, 2017, (BGBl.

and the Bundesrat and is enacted and in force.[3493] The purpose of this Act is to establish a central federal competition database by the Federal Cartel Office to protect the competition between companies in attaining public contracts.[3494] The law applies to individuals and legal entities. They have to registered if they have been convicted of *e.g.* fraud, bribery, tax violations or have violated Section 30, 130 of the Act on Regulatory Offence.[3495] The database will likely start working in 2020. Section 8 of the Act for establishing a competition database (WRegG) allows a self-cleaning of a registered company.[3496] The registration of the company has to discharged if it has proved evidence of implementing *e.g.* appropriate specific technical, organizational, and personnel measures in order to prevent further criminal offences and misconduct.[3497] These measures can also encompass a compliance system and a compliance officer.

This development is a result due to global enforcement trends to combat the financing of terrorism, pressure on the German legislator to act and on German companies to identify and mitigate bribery and corruption issues have increased. The recent activities of the German legislator show that legal enforcement to combat bribery and corruption is likely to increase significantly in future. For this reason, board members and compliance officers should be aware that law enforcement agencies, such as the Federal Bureau of Investigation, are focusing on these behaviors and will be keen to hold individuals accountable over the next few years.

3. Comparison between American and German Bribery Case Law

A search of German cases shows that over the course of the last ten years, the number of court cases involving bribery and corruption pursuant to Section 299 of the German Criminal Code (StGB) is fairly reasonable.[3498] In 23 cases, the courts imposed financial penalties for convictions of *e.g.* public officials, physicians, employees or members of the supervisory board for bribery or corruption.[3499] The highest profile case was the *Siemens* case decided in 2008.[3500] In October 2007, the

---

pp. 626, 642) §§ 123, 124; Gesetz über Ordnungswidrigkeiten (OWiG) | Act on Regulatory Offences, *supra* note 3306 §§ 30, 130.

3493 Wettbewerbsregistergesetz (WRegG) | Act for establishing a Competition Database, BGBI. I, p. 2739 (2017).

3494 *Id.* § 1.

3495 *Id.* § 2 (1) Nr. 1.-3.

3496 *Id.* § 8 (1).

3497 *Id.* § 8 (1); Gesetz gegen Wettbewerbsbeschränkungen (GWB) | Act Against Restraints of Competition, *supra* note 3492 § 125 (1) Nr. 3.

3498 These are the findings of the German case research regarding bribery in the beck-online database between 2004 and 2017.

3499 *See e.g.* BGH, 29.8.2008 - 2 StR 587/07, NStZ 2009, 95, *supra* note 958; LAG Rheinland-Pfalz, 26.02.2016 - Aktenzeichen 1 Sa 358/15, 2016 FD-ArbR 378175 (Ls.) (2016).

3500 BGH, 29.8.2008 - 2 StR 587/07, NStZ 2009, 95, *supra* note 958.

Munich Public Prosecutor brought an action against a member of the divisional management board of the Siemens' business division Power Generation, who was responsible for controlling, economics and auditing for the European region.[3501] This case was related to the action by the SEC against Siemens in the US.[3502]

Both the SEC and the BGH actions against Siemens AG will be compared in terms of their scope and results. According to the complaint, between 2001 and 2007, Siemens AG made thousands of separate payments to third parties in return for business around the world.[3503] Approximately, US$ 1.4 billion were used to bribe foreign government officials to obtain contracts in order *e.g.* to build metro transit lines in Venezuela or signaling devices in China.[3504] At that time, Siemens AG was listed on the NSYE as a foreign issuer and, as such, was required to adhere to US Securities Law and the FCPA.[3505] Therefore, by engaging in a widespread and systematic practice of paying bribes to foreign government officials in return for business, Siemens violated *inter alia* Section 30A of the Securities Exchange Act of 1934.[3506] In the US, the examination of this case revealed an inadequate system of internal corporate controls and misconduct by employees at all levels of Siemens AG and its former senior management.[3507] In the US, Siemens AG ultimately settled the case and agreed to pay a huge fine based on its failure to supervise its officers and employees for paying illegal or corrupt payments, such as kickbacks.[3508]

Simultaneously, in Germany, the Munich Public Prosecutor brought an action against a member of the divisional management board of the Siemens AG pursuant to Sections 266 and 299 of the German Criminal Code (StGB).[3509] The management board member was responsible for controlling, economics and auditing for the European region and, additionally, was responsible for the proper implementation of compliance policies.[3510] Under these policies, doing business by means of bribery or corruption is prohibited.[3511] Nevertheless, within the Siemens Power Generation business division, there was an established system for illegal payments.[3512] The manager was aware of that improper system, which included *e.g.* several slush

---

3501 BGH, 29.8.2008 - 2 StR 587/07, NStZ 2009, 95, *supra* note 958 at 96.
3502 *United States v Siemens AG* (2008), *supra* note 1380.
3503 *Id.*
3504 *Id.*
3505 *See supra* A., I., 1.d., p. 203.
3506 Foreign Corrupt Practices Act 1977 (FCPA), *supra* note 438, 15 USC. § 78dd-I. *United States v Siemens AG (2008), supra* note 1380. The system is explained in the German case: LG München I, 04.10.2007 - 5 Kls 563 Js EGMR Aktenzeichen 45994/07, 2008 Beck RS 1235 (2007).
3507 *United States v Siemens AG* (2008), *supra* note 1380.
3508 *Id.*
3509 BGH, 29.8.2008 - 2 StR 587/07, NStZ 2009, 95, *supra* note 958.
3510 *Id.* at 96.
3511 *Id.* at 96.
3512 *Id.* at 98.

funds used to pay bribes to third parties to secure orders and contracts.[3513] The court concluded that through the management of these slush funds, Siemens AG sustained a disadvantage pursuant to Section 266 (1) of the German Criminal Code (StGB).[3514] However, the BGH concluded that the manager had not committed the offence of bribery pursuant Section 299 (2) of the German Criminal Code (StGB), since illegal payments within foreign competition that have not disadvantaged domestic companies were not included in the applicable version of the German Criminal Code (StGB) on August 29, 2002.[3515]

As we have seen, the results of both actions against Siemens AG varied markedly. In the US, Siemens AG as a corporation has to plead guilty to violations of the internal controls, books and records of the FCPA.[3516] Pursuant to USSC § 8 C4.1, Siemens agreed, settled and paid a criminal fine in the amount of $448,500,000.[3517] In addition, Siemens AG had to agree that, in the event of the sale, merger or transfer of its business operations, it shall include in any such contract a provision binding the purchaser(s) in full to the obligations agreed in the plea agreement.[3518] Furthermore, all Siemens AG officers, directors, employees, agents and consultants are required to cooperate fully with the US authorities and law enforcement agencies in any investigation or prosecution.[3519] Moreover, Siemens and its subsidiaries have to implement an effective system of corporate governance under corporate monitoring by a lawyer over the course of four years and are required to maintain a compliance program that includes, at a minimum, the basic components set forth in Attachment 1.[3520] Finally, Siemens AG was required to waive knowingly and voluntarily its right to appeal the conviction in this case.[3521] For this reason, since 2008, Siemens has undergone a full corporate reorganization of its governance structure, officers, directors, and members of the management board were replaced and a new compliance structure and compliance officers with relevant responsibilities have been established.[3522]

3513 *Id.* at 98.
3514 *Id.* at 98.
3515 *Id.* at 99.
3516 Foreign Corrupt Practices Act 1977 (FCPA), *supra* note 438, 15 USC 78m(b)(2)(A), 78m(b)(2)(B), 78m(b)(5) and 78 ff(a); United States v. Siemens Aktiengesellschaft, Plea Agreement; DOJ and United States Attorney's Office, *supra* note 1404.
3517 United States v. Siemens Aktiengesellschaft, Plea Agreement, *supra* note 1404.
3518 *Id.*
3519 *Id.*
3520 *Id.*
3521 *Id.*
3522 *See* Moosmayer and Winter (2011), *supra* note 1408 at 1.

In Germany, the former members of the Siemens management board were accused of bribery, but settled out of court with an amount of up to 5 million Euros.[3523] As discussed previously, only one member, a former CFO did not settle and, five years later, was prosecuted for failure to implement effective compliance measures pursuant to Sections 76, 93 (1) (2) of the German Stock Corporation Act (AktG) in order to prevent the criminal offence of bribery. He was ordered to pay Siemens AG compensation of 15 million Euros in a civil case heard by Munich I Regional Court.[3524]

In conclusion, it can be stated that in the case of bribery in the US, the corporation will be prosecuted and can be held guilty pursuant to the provisions of the FCPA. The criminal fine is a high financial penalty payable to the DOJ and SEC. For this reason, the corporation will enter bankruptcy or be required to establish corporate reorganization enforced by the law enforcement agencies. In Germany, the public prosecutor or the corporation has to prosecute the individual responsible for the misconduct. These court proceedings are more lengthy and complex. The individual offender will not pay as high a fine as a corporation. Lastly, the German courts do not have the authority to require fundamental changes to the corporate structures, unlike the prosecutors in the US.

4. Duty as Guarantor of the Compliance Officer

The vast majority of criminal offences, such as theft or rape, are described in such a manner that they can be committed only by active doing.[3525] Only a handful of provisions of the German Criminal Code (StGB) stipulate genuine offences committed through inactivity.[3526] In the context of criminal offences committed by a compliance officer, this essentially means false offences committed due to inactivity pursuant to Section 13 (1) of the German Criminal Code (StGB).[3527] A false offence can occur in the event that the offender with a special status of obligation within a guarantor status, is required to prevent the success of the criminal offence committed by another person.[3528] In this context, the guarantor is required legally to ensure that the result is not achieved.[3529] In addition, specific attention

3523 Handelsblatt (2013), Ex-Siemens-Finanzchef soll Millionen zahlen, *supra* note 973.

3524 LG München I, 10.12.2013 - 5 HK O 1387/10, NZG 2014, *supra* note 973 at 346.

3525 *See* Wessing and Dann (2015) § 9 Compliance Officer und Strafrecht, *supra* note 3423 at 215 at 74.

3526 *See e.g.* Strafgesetzbuch (StGB) | German Criminal Code, *supra* note 965 § 323 c - Neglected Support.

3527 *See* Wessing and Dann (2015) § 9 Compliance Officer und Strafrecht, *supra* note 3424 at 215 at 74.

3528 *See* Merz in: Commentary on Economic and Tax Criminal Law, *supra* note 3432 at 24 § 13.

3529 Strafgesetzbuch (StGB) | German Criminal Code, *supra* note 965 § 13 (1).

is focused on the criminal liability of the guarantor in the course of the delegation of tasks.[3530]

The false offences committed by inactivity require two conditions: the violation and the guarantor status pursuant to Section 13 of the German Criminal Code (StGB).[3531] The case-law and literature describe the requirements of the duty as guarantor as the guarantor status.[3532] Here, the duty as guarantor means "*the legal obligation that the success will not occur.*"[3533] In detail, the guarantor status requires a specific status of duties, which are more stringent than for other individuals.[3534] This specific status can arise by virtue of statute, voluntary adoption, between immediate family members and on account of previous behavior.[3535] In addition, the Federal Court of Justice (BGH) has decided on the basis of the nature of the specific status of duties that may arise from the guarantor status.[3536] Within the corporation, the activities of the compliance officer involve particular risks and require comprehensive analysis of legal matters and complex situations.[3537] An effective protection against criminal activities involves control and precaution.[3538] Thus, the compliance officer first has to recognize the circumstances under which a violation of law occurs *e.g.* a criminal offence committed by employees or managers within the corporation and, secondly, must also recognize when he has a duty to act.[3539] In the case of doubt, the compliance officer should cooperate with the legal department.[3540] Otherwise, the compliance officer could be held criminally

---

3530 *See* Gerhard Dannecker, *§ 5 Strafrechtliche Verantwortung nach Delegation, in* Criminal Compliance: Handbuch, 21 (Katharina Beckemper & Thomas Rotsch eds., 1. ed. 2015).

3531 Strafgesetzbuch (StGB) | German Criminal Code, *supra* note 965 § 13 (1); *See* Wessing and Dann (2015) § 9 Compliance Officer und Strafrecht, *supra* note 3480 at 215 at 74.

3532 *See* Merz in: Commentary on Economic and Tax Criminal Law, *supra* note 3432 at 24 § 13.

3533 *See* Merz in: *Id.* at 24.§ 13.

3534 *See* Kühl in: Commentary on the Criminal Law, *supra* note 3438 at 7 § 13; Merz in: Commentary on Economic and Tax Criminal Law, *supra* note 3432 at 24 § 13.

3535 *See* Kühl in: Commentary on the Criminal Law, *supra* note 3438 at 8–11 § 13; Heuchemer in: Beck Online Commentary on Criminal Law, *supra* note 3436 at 38–59a § 13; Stree, Bosch in: Strafrecht | Commentary on Criminal Law, 17–42 (Adolf Schönke & Horst Schröder eds., 29 ed. 2014) § 13.

3536 *See e.g.* BGH, 31.1.2002 - 4 StR 289/01 - *Wuppertaler Schwebebahn,* NJW 1887–1889 (2002); BGH, 6.3.2008 - 4 StR 669/07 - *Werkstattleiters einer Transportbetonspedition,* NJW 1897–1899 (2008).

3537 *See* Dann and Mengel (2010), *supra* note 30 at 3265.

3538 *See* Wessing and Dann (2015) § 9 Compliance Officer und Strafrecht, *supra* note 3423 at 194 at 1.

3539 *Id.* at 194. at 1.

3540 *Id.* at 194. at 2.

liable due to inactivity pursuant to Section 13 (1) of the German Criminal Code (StGB).[3541] For this purpose, the next section provides the German BGH case law in terms of the guarantor status of the compliance officer.

a. The Criminal Case Law of the BGH with Respect to the Compliance Officer

The most notable and the most widely discussed decision of the BGH with respect to the compliance officer is the *obiter dictum* issued on July 17, 2009.[3542] While this concerned a decision on the criminal liability of the head of legal and internal control department at *Berliner Stadtreinigungsbetriebe*, a public agency, the Court also commented on the criminal liability of the compliance officer.[3543] In this case, the Court pointed out that the tasks of the compliance officer encompass the prevention of violations of the law, particularly the prevention of criminal offences within corporations.[3544] Furthermore, the Court stated that such agents regularly have a duty as guarantor pursuant to Section 13 (1) of the German Criminal Code (StGB) in order to prevent offences by employees and managers doing business on behalf of the corporation.[3545] The Court concluded that this is the necessary flipside in discharge of the compliance officer's duty adopted by the corporate management to prevent violations of law, particularly the prevention of criminal offences.[3546]

The BGH continued this line of case-law in its decision on the status of the entrepreneur[3547] or the executive officers on October 20, 2011.[3548] Nevertheless, in this case the Court also defines the limits of the duty as guarantor, as the Court has to examine the circumstances in each individual case.[3549] For instance, the duty as guarantor is limited to the prevention of corporate criminal offences.[3550] This duty does not comprise offences committed by employees only in addition to their work.[3551]

Finally, the Court qualified the context and scope of the duty as guarantor through the specific responsibilities transferred to the responsible officer.[3552] As

3541 Strafgesetzbuch (StGB) | German Criminal Code, *supra* note 965 § 13 (1).
3542 BGH, 17.7.2009 - 5 StR 394/08, BGHSt 54, 44; BGH NJW 2009, 3173, *supra* note 25.
3543 *Id.* at 3175. at 27.
3544 *Id.* at 3175. at 27.
3545 *Id.* at 3175. at 27.
3546 *Id.* at 3173. at 27.
3547 In this context, the term entrepreneur describes a person who is the owner of a company.
3548 BGH, 20.10.2011 - 4 StR 71/11 - *BGH: Garantenstellung des Geschäftsherrn, Betriebsbezogenheit einer Straftat*, 2012 NJW 157–160 (2011).
3549 *Id.* at 1238. at 13.
3550 *Id.* at 1238. at 13.
3551 *Id.* at 1238. at 13.
3552 *See* Stoffers in: BGH, 17.7.2009 - 5 StR 394/08,BGHSt 54, 44; BGH NJW 2009, 3173, *supra* note 25 at 3176 Comment on the decision.

a result, the objective of the assignment is decisive.[3553] Despite numerous critical voices among the legal scholars with respect to the liability of the principal, these two Federal Supreme Court decisions are in force.[3554] Summing up, the BGH has consistently applied the principles of liability of the principal. By contrast with the Delaware *Caremark* case, the German Federal Supreme Court applied the duty as guarantor to a corporate officer in a similar way to that in which the Delaware Court applied the compliance duty to the Caremark directors.[3555] In the event that the loss eventuated from a "*sustained or systematic failure*" or in the event of "*unconsidered inaction*" the US Delaware Court does not apply the business judgment rule to the corporate director.[3556] Notwithstanding this risk of liability, the compliance officer should be aware that he has options as to limit this liability. For this reason, the next section explores the scope and limitations of the liability of the principal.

b. The Scope and Limitations of the Liability of the Principal

As previously discussed, the management board has a duty of loyalty and must ensure the adherence to the law by employees and managers within and outside the company.[3557] This duty comprises the criminal liability of the principal, which requires the principal to prevent offences by subordinates.[3558] The employees are considered as a source of risk for the legal assets of the company.[3559] It follows that the principal is responsible for monitoring and supervising his subordinates through instructions and regular controls within the company.[3560] Since 2011, this legal concept has been incorporated into the BGH case law.[3561] Specifically, the issue that arises from this legal concept is the distribution of employee responsibility for criminal offences committed in the course of doing business within corporations.[3562] The findings have shown a new direction in German criminal case law.[3563] As a result, misconduct is not only

---

3553 *See* Stoffers in: *Id.* at 3176. Comment on the decision.

3554 *See* Stoffers in: *Id.* at 3176. Comment on the decision; Rübenstahl (2009), *supra* note 3421; Stree, Bosch in: COMMENTARY ON CRIMINAL LAW, *supra* note 3535 at 53 § 13.

3555 *Compare* Ch. 3, A., II, pp. 254 et seq., Ch. 5, III., 4., pp. 449 et seq.

3556 *Compare* Ch. 3, A., II, pp. 254 et seq., Ch. 5, III., 4., pp. 449 et seq.

3557 *See* Wessing and Dann (2015) § 9 Compliance Officer und Strafrecht, *supra* note 3423 at 217 at 80.

3558 *See* Waßmer in: COMMENTARY ON ECONOMIC AND TAX CRIMINAL LAW, *supra* note 3432 at 143c § 266.

3559 *See* Wessing and Dann (2015) § 9 Compliance Officer und Strafrecht, *supra* note 3423 at 217 at 80.

3560 COMMENTARY ON ECONOMIC AND TAX CRIMINAL LAW, *supra* note 3432 at 217 at 80.

3561 BGH, 20.10.2011 - 4 StR 71/11, NJW 2012, 1237, *supra* note 3548.

3562 *See* Jan Schlösser, *Die Anerkennung der Geschäftsherrenhaftung durch den BGH*, NEUE ZEITSCHRIFT FÜR WIRTSCHAFTS-, STEUER- UND UNTERNEHMENSSTRAFRECHT 281–286, 281 (2012).

3563 *Id.* at 281.

considered to be an offence committed by an individual, but rather in the course of the organizational context.[3564]

In the event of criminal offences committed by the company, it is first necessary to examine whether a duty as guarantor can apply. Next, the scope and limitations thereof can be determined.[3565] It has been recognized that two grounds can establish a guarantor status: (1) the right of employers to issue instructions, and (2) the company as a source of risk.[3566] As we have seen, before the transfer of compliance responsibility to the compliance officer, the principal or the board members were in charge of the supervisory duty or the duty of compliance and, therefore, the duty to prevent criminal offences by employees.[3567] However, a different situation arises in the course of the transfer of such duties to the compliance officer. Following the transfer of the supervisory duty to the compliance officer, the BGH takes into consideration the guarantor status of the compliance officer on the basis of the delegation of duties.[3568]

In addition to the academic discussion on the scope of the guarantor status of the compliance officer, several limitations have been established, such as: (1) the specific scope of duty transferred to the compliance officer, (2) under reservation of the necessity and the reasonableness of legal behavior, (3) adequate resources, (4) the separate authority, (5) the connection with the company, (6) the further delegation to subordinates, (7) the individual responsibility of the subordinates, (8) the specific job description contains such limitation of specific areas of law or tasks, and (9) protection through external experts.[3569] It can be noted that these nine aspects of limitations are wide-ranging. They range from employment law issues[3570] to criminal law[3571] and organizational subjects.[3572] Therefore, the compliance officer should proactively seek to limit the scope of his guarantor status.

3564 *Id.* at 281.

3565 *See* Michael Lindemann & Janita Sommer, *Die strafrechtliche Geschäftsherrenhaftung und ihre Bedeutung für den Bereich der Criminal Compliance*, JuS 1057–1062, 1058 (2015).

3566 *Id.* at 1058.; Wessing and Dann (2015) § 9 Compliance Officer und Strafrecht, *supra* note 3423 at 217 at 80.

3567 *See supra* II., 2., p. 433.

3568 *See* Stoffers in: BGH, 17.7.2009 - 5 StR 394/08, BGHSt 54, 44; BGH NJW 2009, 3173, *supra* note 25 at 3176; Wessing and Dann (2015) § 9 Compliance Officer und Strafrecht, *supra* note 3423 at 218 at 81.

3569 *See e.g.* Wessing and Dann (2015) § 9 Compliance Officer und Strafrecht, *supra* note 3423 at 218–220; Bürkle (2010), *supra* note 28; Campos Nave (2009), *supra* note 457; Dann and Mengel (2010), *supra* note 30; Fleischer (2014), *supra* note 3347; Rübenstahl (2009), *supra* note 3421; Wolf (2011), *supra* note 41; Wybitul (2009), *supra* note 28.

3570 *See aspects* (1), (4), (6), (7) and (8).

3571 *See aspects* (2) and (5).

3572 *See aspects* (3) and (9).

To conclude, under the criminal law aspect *e.g.* the reservation of necessity and the reasonableness of legal behavior provide limitations to the guarantor status.[3573] The factors considered in the context of reasonableness are the skills of the guarantor, the seriousness of the risk, and the significance of the legal asset.[3574] In the event that the conduct is unreasonable, liability will not apply.[3575] The court weighs the vulnerable interests of the guarantor against the success in the course of the individual case.[3576] For instance, when the defendant can prevent the risk through sufficient information to be given to members of the board, the court can conclude that such reporting constitutes reasonable conduct.[3577] For this reason, the compliance officer should be aware of his duty to provide relevant information to the appropriate corporate officers. Other cases require the taking of appropriate measures in order to prevent risks.[3578] In the context of the examination of the reasonableness of the conduct, the court will also refer to the manageable size of the working area.[3579] Therefore, the compliance officer can decide at its reasonable discretion. In addition, his activities and decisions are limited when the management does not provide adequate resources for the compliance function.[3580]

Another limitation of the guarantor status under criminal law could be the corrective to the offence in the context of the company. Generally, a guarantor is responsible for certain sources of risk situated within his own area of responsibility.[3581] As previously discussed, therefore, the guarantor status is derived from the position as principal or supervisor within the company.[3582] From these positions arise a supervisory duty to prevent risks, but only within the own area

3573 BGH, 16.07.1993 - 2 StR 294/93 - *Zumutbarkeit bei Erfolgsabwendungspflicht,* NStZ 29 (1993); BGH, 17.7.2009 - 5 StR 394/08, BGHSt 54, 44; BGH NJW 2009, 3173, *supra* note 25 at 3175; *See e.g.* Heuchemer in: BECK ONLINE COMMENTARY ON CRIMINAL LAW, *supra* note 3436 at 73 § 13; Wohlers, Gaede in: STRAFRECHT | COMMENTARY ON CRIMINAL LAW, 17–18 (Kindhäuser, Neumann, & Paeffgen eds., 4. ed. 2013) § 13; Kühl in: COMMENTARY ON THE CRIMINAL LAW, *supra* note 3438 at 5 § 13.

3574 *See* Heuchemer in: BECK ONLINE COMMENTARY ON CRIMINAL LAW, *supra* note 3436 at 73 § 13.

3575 *See* Heuchemer in: *Id.* at 73.§ 13.

3576 *See* Heuchemer in: *Id.* at 73.§ 13.

3577 BGH, 17.7.2009 - 5 StR 394/08, BGHSt 54, 44; BGH NJW 2009, 3173, *supra* note 25 at 3175 at [31] (3).

3578 BGH, 15.7.1986 - 4 StR 301/86 - *Garantenstellung eines Ordnungsamtsleiters,* NJW 199, 199 (1986); BGH, 6.7.1990 - 2 StR 549/89 - *Strafrechtliche Produkthaftung - Lederspray-Entscheidung,* NJW 2560–2569 (1990).

3579 BGH, 31.1.2002 - 4 StR 289/01, NJW 2002, 1887, *supra* note 3536 at 1888.

3580 *See e.g.* Bürkle (2010), *supra* note 28 at 7; Hauschka, Galster, and Marschlich (2014), *supra* note 463 at 244; Heuking (2014), *supra* note 4 at 330; Meier-Greve (2010), *supra* note 461 at 218; Sünner (2014), *supra* note 44 at 91, 93.

3581 *See* Heuchemer in: BECK ONLINE COMMENTARY ON CRIMINAL LAW, *supra* note 3436 at 60 § 13.

3582 *See* Heuchemer in: *Id.* at 65 a.§ 13.

of responsibility.[3583] In addition, the BGH stated that the area of responsibility of the compliance officer is the prevention of criminal offences by employees committed through the company.[3584] Later in 2011, the BGH specified in more detail the aspect that the offence requires a definite connection with business activity.[3585] For example, in the case of harassment in the workplace or injuries between employees, the connection could be weak.[3586] In practice, it can be difficult to clearly define offences committed by employees in connection with business activity.

In conclusion, it has been recognized in the German legal literature and BGH criminal case law that the status and duty of the guarantor can be limited under criminal law. As such, the scope of the guarantor status of the compliance officer cannot be overarching. In his capacity as supervisor, a status as guarantor can be established to prevent criminal offences committed by subordinates. Generally, however, this duty can also arise and be required for other corporate functions, such as the heads of departments, the regional managers or the authorized officers of companies. This means that, in Germany, the discussion of criminal liability with respect to the compliance officer appears excessive. It seems that the BGH *obiter dictum* merely referred to that fact since the post of corporate compliance officer function is relatively new.

c. Protection against Loss, Damages or Liability

Compared to the US and the UK, German law does not include indemnification clauses, which are contractual terms and expressly applicable to officers, directors, employees, consultants, professional advisers or agents.[3587] For example, in the US, a director may also apply for court-ordered indemnification or an advance for expenses payable to the court.[3588] An indemnity clause is a component of a contract that gives the party who is legally responsible for a loss under the law, the right to contractually shift that loss to another party.[3589] As a result, "*a party promises to reimburse another in relation to specified loss or damage or, in some cases, to absolve them of liability.*"[3590]

3583 *See* Stree, Bosch in: Commentary on Criminal Law, *supra* note 3435 at 43 § 13.

3584 BGH, 17.7.2009 - 5 StR 394/08, BGHSt 54, 44; BGH NJW 2009, 3173, *supra* note 25 at 3175.

3585 BGH, 20. 10. 2011 - 4 StR 71/11, NJW 2012, 1237, *supra* note 3546 at 1238.

3586 *Id.* at 1238.; *See* Contrary view Wessing and Dann (2015), § 9 Compliance Officer und Strafrecht, *supra* note 3423 at 219 at 88.

3587 *Compare* tit. 8 Delaware Code, *supra* note 24, § 145.

3588 *Compare* Chew, *supra* note 1799 at 235–236; tit. 8 Delaware Code, *supra* note 24 § 145 (e); Model Business Corporation Act, *supra* note 1805 § 8.51 (a).

3589 *See* Anna Wang, Indemnity Clauses: Understanding the Basics Shake by LegalShield, http://www.shakelaw.com/blog/indemnity-clauses-understanding-basics/ (last visited May 1, 2017).

3590 *See* Melanie Ashworth, Drafting and negotiating an indemnity clause LexisNexis Comet, http://blogs.lexisnexis.co.uk/comet/indemnity-checklist/ (last visited May 1, 2017).

Under common law, the parties should ensure that the indemnity clause includes a duty to mitigate losses and should survive the termination of the agreement.[3591] Hence, the compliance officer can negotiate an indemnity clause. Contrary to the common law, German civil law does not contain such limitation of liability clauses. However, in the event that the compliance officer is commissioned by the management board to perform compliance tasks, it should consider that the contract of employment of the compliance officer may include an individual indemnity clause or an insurance clause in favor of third parties.[3592] In practice, the corporation agrees to pay D&O insurance for members of its management and supervisory board. This insurance can serve as indemnification against or reimbursement for losses and damages in the event of civil and criminal actions brought against members of the management and supervisory board. It is important to consider whether the compliance officer is also covered and protected by such insurance coverage. However, wrongful, wilful actions are typically not covered under D&O insurance.

5. The Liability of the Compliance Officer Pursuant to Sections 9, 30, 130 OWiG

In recent years, Section 130 of the Act on Regulatory Offences (OWiG) has been in the focus of the academic legal debate on compliance.[3593] However, its roots, the sanctioning of the supervisory duty, originate from the 19th century.[3594] In general, Section 130 of this Act punished the owner of a business since he is responsible for the supervisory duty within the company.[3595] The company is considered to be an organizational entity with a work purpose by means of personnel, objective and immaterial resources.[3596] It is the owner who is actually responsible for the supervisory duty.[3597]

3591 *Id.*

3592 *See* Fabian and Mengel in: § 7. Arbeitsrechtliche Stellung und Haftung, *in* DER COMPLIANCE OFFICER: EIN HANDBUCH IN EIGENER SACHE, 175 (Jürgen Bürkle & Christoph E. Hauschka eds., 2015) at 46.

3593 *See* Beck in: BECK'SCHER ONLINE-KOMMENTAR OWIG | COMMENTARY ON THE ACT ON REGULATORY OFFENCES, 125 (Peter Graf ed., 14. ed. 2017) § 130.

3594 *See* Beck in: *Id.* at 1.§ 130; PREUSSISCHE GEWERBEORDNUNG (PRGWO), (1845)§ 188.

3595 *See* Beck in: BECK'SCHER ONLINE-KOMMENTAR OWIG | COMMENTARY ON THE ACT ON REGULATORY OFFENCES, *supra* note 3593 at 26, 34 § 130; Rogall in: KARLSRUHER KOMMENTAR ZUM OWIG | COMMENTARY ON THE ACT ON REGULATORY OFFENCES, 22 (Lothar Senge ed., 4. ed. 2014) § 130.

3596 *See* Beck in: BECK'SCHER ONLINE-KOMMENTAR OWIG | COMMENTARY ON THE ACT ON REGULATORY OFFENCES, *supra* note 3593 at 27 § 130.

3597 *See* Beck in: *Id.* at 34. § 130; Rogall in: KARLSRUHER KOMMENTAR ZUM OWIG | COMMENTARY ON THE ACT ON REGULATORY OFFENCES, *supra* note 3595 at 25 § 130; Wessing and Dann (2015) § 9 Compliance Officer und Strafrecht, *supra* note 3423 at 226 at 115.

In 1974, the sanctioning of the supervisory duty was enshrined into Section 130 of the Act on Regulatory Offences (OWiG).[3598] Since then, the scope of liability has continually expanded, for example to include negligent breach of duty.[3599] Moreover, today Section 130 also applies to Section 9 of the Act on Regulatory Offences (OWiG).[3600]

a. The Application of Section 9 to the Compliance Officer

Within the scope of organizational duties, the owner of a business can transfer the performance of the supervisory duty to another corporate officer, for instance to the compliance officer.[3601] Therefore, the compliance officer must particular consider Section 9 (2) 1 No. 2, which states that:

> Sec. 9 (2) If the owner of a business or someone otherwise so authorized
>
> 1. commissions a person to manage a business, in whole or in part, or
> 2. expressly commissions a person to perform on his own responsibility duties which are incumbent on the owner of the business,
>
> and if this person acts on the basis of this commission, then a statute pursuant to which special personal characteristics are the basis of sanctioning shall also be applicable to the person commissioned if these characteristics do not indeed pertain to him, but to the owner of the business.[3602]

German legal scholars argue that the key tasks of the compliance officer encompass the implementation and maintenance of corporate compliance measures and the appropriate responses to violations of the law.[3603] Based on the view taken by the legal scholars and based on the legal requirements that today corporate governance also comprises compliance as a genuine management task, the compliance

3598 *See* Beck in: BECK'SCHER ONLINE-KOMMENTAR OWIG | COMMENTARY ON THE ACT ON REGULATORY OFFENCES, *supra* note 3593 at 3 § 130.

3599 *See* Beck in: *Id.* at 3. § 130.

3600 *See* Beck in: *Id.* at 3. § 130.

3601 *See* Wessing and Dann (2015) § 9 Compliance Officer und Strafrecht, *supra* note 3423 at 227 at 116; Zimmermann (2011), *supra* note 28 at 635.

3602 GESETZ ÜBER ORDNUNGSWIDRIGKEITEN (OWIG) | ACT ON REGULATORY OFFENCES, *supra* note 3306 § 9 (2) 1 No. 2.

3603 *See e.g.* Dann and Mengel (2010), *supra* note 30 at 3265; Gößwein and Hohmann (2011), *supra* note 41 at 964; Heuking (2014), *supra* note 4 at 328–329; Krieger and Günther (2010), *supra* note 30 at 367; Lackhoff and Schulz (2010), *supra* note 458 at 85; Renz and Wybitul (2012), *supra* note 1074 at 2512; Wolf (2011), *supra* note 41 at 1356; Wessing and Dann (2015) § 9 Compliance Officer und Strafrecht, *supra* note 3423 at 227 at 116; Wessing and Dann in: § 4 Compliance, *in* MÜNCHENER ANWALTSHANDBUCH: VERTEIDIGUNG IN WIRTSCHAFTS- UND STEUERSTRAFSACHEN , 224 (Klaus Volk & Heiko Ahlbrecht eds., 2. ed. 2014).

officer can be charged with the supervisory duty pursuant to Section 9 (2) 1 No. 2 of the Act on Regulatory Offences (OWiG).[3604] The reasons are as follows: The purpose of the role as the owner of a business and the responsibility for compliance are two different things.[3605] There could be a conflict between the objective of sales and the compliance tasks. Furthermore, within day-to-day business, the corporate management does not have sufficient time or capacity to fulfill the responsibility of compliance.[3606]

However, Section 9 (2) 1 No. 2 of the Act on Regulatory Offences (OWiG) requires two conditions for the delegation of compliance tasks: first, an express commissioning of the compliance officer by the owner of a business to perform certain tasks and, second, on the basis of this commissioning, the compliance officer should independently handle the delegated tasks.[3607] The legal effectiveness is not a required condition.[3608] Therefore, the compliance officer can take appropriate measures as and when necessary.[3609]

Finally, in the event that the compliance officer can handle the delegated area of tasks independently pursuant to Section 9 (2) 1 No. 2 of the Act on Regulatory Offences (OWiG), the relevant offence under the Act on Regulatory Offences (OWiG) will apply to the compliance officer.[3610] Nevertheless, the liability of the commissioning body, the owner of a business, will remain simultaneously, since the delegation does not include the transfer of liability.[3611]

3604 Aktiengesetz (AktG) | German Stock Corporation Act, *supra* note 976 § 91 (2); Gesetz über Ordnungswidrigkeiten (OWiG) | Act on Regulatory Offences, *supra* note 3305 § 9 (2) 1 No. 2; *See e.g.* Bürkle (2010), *supra* note 28 at 5; Gößwein and Hohmann (2011), *supra* note 41 at 964; Krieger and Günther (2010), *supra* note 30 at 368; Lackhoff and Schulz (2010), *supra* note 458 at 85; Wolf (2011), *supra* note 41 at 1356; Wessing and Dann (2014) in: Münchener Anwaltshandbuch, *supra* note 3603 at 152.

3605 *See* Wessing and Dann (2014) in: Münchener Anwaltshandbuch, *supra* note 3603 at 150–151.

3606 *See* Wessing and Dann (2014) in: *Id.* at 150–151.

3607 *See e.g.* Valerius in: Beck'scher Online-Kommentar OWiG | Commentary on the Act on Regulatory Offences, *supra* note 3593 at 33 § 9; Rogall in: Karlsruher Kommentar zum OWiG | Commentary on the Act on Regulatory Offences, *supra* note 3595 at 79–81 § 9.

3608 *See* Rogall in: Karlsruher Kommentar zum OWiG | Commentary on the Act on Regulatory Offences, *supra* note 3595 at 81 § 9.

3609 *See* Wessing and Dann (2015) § 9 Compliance Officer und Strafrecht, *supra* note 3423 at 227 at 117.

3610 *See e.g.* Valerius in: Beck'scher Online-Kommentar OWiG | Commentary on the Act on Regulatory Offences, *supra* note 3593 at 54 § 9; Rogall in: Karlsruher Kommentar zum OWiG | Commentary on the Act on Regulatory Offences, *supra* note 3595 at 97 § 9.

3611 *See "shall also be applicable to the representative"* Gesetz über Ordnungswidrigkeiten (OWiG) | Act on Regulatory Offences, *supra* note

b. The Application of Section 130 to the Compliance Officer

In the event that the compliance officer does not implement and maintain appropriate measures to prevent criminal activities by employees and managers through willful intent and negligence, he may be guilty of an administrative offence pursuant to Section 130 of the Act within the scope of delegation.[3612] Although the company cannot be criminally liable under the principles of German criminal law,[3613] the provisions of administrative offence law, Sections 9, 30 and 130 of the Act on Regulatory Offences (OWiG) state that the company can be guilty of an administrative offence and can impose a regulatory fine.[3614] The significance of the company's liability has increased as a result of the amendment of the scope of the regulatory fine; in the case of an intentionally committed criminal offence, fines may be up to 10 million Euros.[3615]

There are three instances in which the compliance officer could act improperly with respect to preventing violations of the law. First, if a criminal offence has actually been committed within the company.[3616] Then, the criminal offence is committed by a person other than the compliance officer.[3617] Moreover, the offence must be a violation committed within the business context.[3618] In detail, this means the breach of duties incumbent upon the owner of a business, for instance the supervisory duty.[3619] Therefore, finally, the compliance officer can be guilty pursuant to Sections 9 (2) 1 No. 2 and 130 of the Act on Regulatory Offences (OWiG) in the event that he has breached his supervisory duty and, thus, he can face a regulatory fine up to 1 million Euros.[3620]

3305 § 9 (1); Rogall in: Karlsruher Kommentar zum OWiG | Commentary on the Act on Regulatory Offences, *supra* note 3595 at 98 § 9.

3612 *See e.g.* Schaefer and Baumann (2011), *supra* note 3365 at 3604; Wessing and Dann (2015) § 9 Compliance Officer und Strafrecht, *supra* note 3423 at 228 at 119.

3613 This principle is based on the personal responsibility of the individual. *See* Meyberg in: Beck'scher Online-Kommentar OWiG | Commentary on the Act on Regulatory Offences, *supra* note 3593 at 1 § 30.

3614 *See* Beck in: *Id.* at 126. § 130.

3615 Gesetz über Ordnungswidrigkeiten (OWiG) | Act on Regulatory Offences, *supra* note 3305 § 30 (2) No. 1 as amended on June 30, 2013; Eighth Statute of the Amendment of the Act Against Restraints of Competition, BGBI I, P. 1738, 1748 (2013).

3616 *See* Beck in: Beck'scher Online-Kommentar OWiG | Commentary on the Act on Regulatory Offences, *supra* note 3593 at 80 § 130.

3617 *See* Beck in: *Id.* at 80. § 130.

3618 *See* Beck in: *Id.* at 86. § 130.

3619 *See* Rogall in: Karlsruher Kommentar zum OWiG | Commentary on the Act on Regulatory Offences, *supra* note 3595 at 81 § 130.

3620 Gesetz über Ordnungswidrigkeiten (OWiG) | Act on Regulatory Offences, *supra* note 3248 §§ 9 (2) 1 No. 2, 130 (3) 1.

Legal scholars criticize that the management and supervisory board attempt to pass on their liability through the implementation of compliance measures and compliance departments.[3621] Discussions are currently underway on whether appropriate compliance measures could prevent violations across the board within a company.[3622] Nevertheless, it has been recognized that full compliance is not possible.[3623] Similarly, an examination of the case law with respect to regulatory offence law as regards the compliance officer did not turn up any cases at all. It is likely that, over time, the German case law will lay out the relevant supervisory duties in concrete terms.

c. The Drafts of a German Statute on Company Liability

As we have seen, contrary to the US and UK, to the present-day Germany still has no statute governing corporate liability. Due to international criticism of this German approach, the coalition agreement of the German Federal Government on December 17, 2013 provided for the examination of a statute governing company liability for multinational corporations by the government in order to combat crime across all areas of society.[3624] At that time, the federal state government of North Rhine-Westphalia (NRW) introduced a draft criminal code of organizations (VerbStrG).[3625] This draft defines the term organization as forms and structures which produce goods, services, education and research activities within the modern industrial and knowledge society.[3626] Therefore, this definition encompasses all companies, institutions and corporations of all sizes and in every legal form.

3621 *See* Göẞwein and Hohmann (2011), *supra* note 41 at 966; Beck in: BECK'SCHER ONLINE-KOMMENTAR OWIG | COMMENTARY ON THE ACT ON REGULATORY OFFENCES, *supra* note 3593 at 127 § 130.

3622 *See* Göẞwein and Hohmann (2011), *supra* note 41 at 966; Beck in: BECK'SCHER ONLINE-KOMMENTAR OWIG | COMMENTARY ON THE ACT ON REGULATORY OFFENCES, *supra* note 3593 at 127 § 130.

3623 *See* Göẞwein and Hohmann (2011), *supra* note 41 at 966; Beck in: BECK'SCHER ONLINE-KOMMENTAR OWIG | COMMENTARY ON THE ACT ON REGULATORY OFFENCES, *supra* note 3593 at 127 § 130.

3624 *See* Sascha Süße & Carolin Püschel, *Die Diskussion um die Einführung eines Unternehmensstrafrechts in Deutschland – Gesetzgebungsvorschlag des Bundesverbandes der Unternehmensjuristen*, NEWSDIENST COMPLIANCE 11002; German Federal Government, THE COALITION AGREEMENT OF THE GERMAN FEDERAL GOVERNMENT 145 (2013), http://www.bundesregierung.de/Content/DE/_Anlagen/2013/2013-12-17-koalitionsvertrag.pdf; (last visited Apr 15, 2017).

3625 *See* Sascha Süße & Schneider, *Entwurf eines Gesetzes zur Einführung der strafrechtlichen Verantwortlichkeit von Unternehmen und sonstigen Verbänden aus Nordrhein-Westfalen*, NEWSDIENST COMPLIANCE 71002; GESETZESENTWURF ZUM UNTERNEHMENSSTRAFRECHT - VERBANDSSTRAFGESETZBUCH (VERBSTRG-E) | DRAFT OF A CRIMINAL CODE OF ORGANIZATIONS, *supra* note 32.

3626 GESETZESENTWURF ZUM UNTERNEHMENSSTRAFRECHT - VERBANDSSTRAFGESETZBUCH (VERBSTRG-E) | DRAFT OF A CRIMINAL CODE OF ORGANIZATIONS, *supra* note 32 at 1.

This bill considers the most recent compliance developments over the last few years. The purpose of the draft is to strengthen small and medium-sized enterprises (SME) in particular in implementing internal control systems, such as compliance programs.[3627] The authors see a gap in corporate compliance measures in the Act on Regulatory Offence (OWiG).[3628] For this reason, the draft requires an approach of company liability similar that under Anglo-American Common Law.[3629] In the course of the last twenty years, the criminal liability of companies was introduced into law in the majority of the European countries *e.g.* Portugal (1984), Sweden (1986), Norway (1991), France (1994), Italy, (2001), Austria (2006), Romania (2006), Luxembourg (2010), and Spain (2010).[3630] Initial results are positive: For example, the annual report 2011 by the Institution of Law and Criminal Sociology in Vienna, a study of 528 criminal cases involving individuals and corporations from 2006 to 2010 found that the new Austrian statute on the responsibility of legal entities (VbVG) has changed and strengthened the structures to prevent violations of the law within large corporations in Austria.[3631]

Until today, in Germany there have been two drafts of a statute of company liability.[3632] However, thus far, neither has passed the hurdles of approval in both the German Bundestag and the Bundesrat. The German Draft of a Criminal Code of Organizations (VerbStrG-E) highlighted certain control functions within companies.[3633] In addition to the supervisory board, as the BGH has already held, there are other corporate positions within a company that are responsible for a defined and limited area of business, such as the data protection officer, the head of audit, the business director, or the compliance officer, all of whom also have a monitoring and supervisory function.[3634]

3627 *Id.* at 4.

3628 *Id.* at 2.

3629 *Id.* at 2.

3630 *Id.* at 26.

3631 IRKS, Jahresbericht 2010/2011 und Forschungsplan 2011 43 (2011), http://www.irks.at/assets/irks/Publikationen/Jahresberichte/IRKS_JB_2010-11.pdf (last visited Apr 15, 2017); Verbandsverantwortlichkeitsgesetz (VbVG) | Austrian Statute on Responsibility of Legal Entities, BGBl. I Nr. 151/2005 (2006).

3632 Gesetzesentwurf zum Unternehmensstrafrecht-Verbandsstrafgesetzbuch (VerbStrG-E) | Draft of a Criminal Code of Organizations, *supra* note 39; BUJ, Gesetzgebungsvorschlag für eine Änderung der §§ 30, 130 des Gesetz über Ordnungswidrigkeiten (OWiG) | A Draft of Amendment of the Sections 30, 130 on the Act of Regulatory Offences (2014).

3633 Gesetzesentwurf zum Unternehmensstrafrecht-Verbandsstrafgesetzbuch (VerbStrG-E) | Draft of a Criminal Code of Organizations, *supra* note 32 at 42.

3634 *See e.g.* BGH, 29. 8.2008 - 2 StR 587/07, NStZ 2009, 95, *supra* note 958; BGH, 17.7.2009 - 5 StR 394/08, BGHSt 54, 44; BGH NJW 2009, 3173, *supra* note 25.

However, as previously examined, the German Draft of a Criminal Code of Organizations (VerbStrG-E) stated that individual criminal liability is often limited contrary to the damages.[3635] For this reason, the legislation should strengthen the focus on company liability.[3636] According to the draft Sections 2 and 3 of the German Draft of a Criminal Code of Organizations (VerbStrG-E), organizations that commit a crime will be punished with sanctions pursuant to the German Criminal Code (StGB).[3637] The sanctions take the form of a fine, a caution, or a public announcement.[3638] In addition, disciplinary measures for the organization could involve the loss of subsidies, the loss of public orders, and the dissolution of the organization.[3639] Nevertheless, it is particularly interesting to note that Section 5 states that the court can prevent organizations from imposing sanctions in the event that they have implemented adequate organizational and personnel measures in order to avoid criminal offences in the future.[3640] Even subsequently implemented compliance measures should be considered when sentencing organizations.[3641] Thus, this provision of the draft and this proposed approach provide a similar wording and a similar approach to the US Sentencing Guidelines and the UK Bribery Act 2010.[3642] Like the requirements of the US and UK law enforcement agencies and prosecutors DOJ, SEC and SFO, the draft states that the prosecuted company should cooperate with the prosecutor and disclose and submit the evidence to the investigating authority.[3643] In this context, the courts can mitigate a sentence pursuant to Section 5 (2) of the German Draft of a Criminal Code of Organizations (VerbStrG-E).[3644] Finally, pursuant to the draft Section 8 (2) No. 3 of the German Draft of a Criminal Code of Organizations (VerbStrG-E), the court can mandate that the sentenced company implement compliance measures and to report thereon to the court.[3645] This provision is also similar to the US and UK

3635 GESETZESENTWURFZUMUNTERNEHMENSSTRAFRECHT-VERBANDSSTRAFGESETZBUCH (VERBSTRG-E) | DRAFT OF A CRIMINAL CODE OF ORGANIZATIONS, *supra* note 32 at 1.
3636 *Id.* at 2.
3637 *Id.* at 8 .§§ 2 (1), 3 (1).
3638 GESETZESENTWURFZUMUNTERNEHMENSSTRAFRECHT-VERBANDSSTRAFGESETZBUCH (VERBSTRG-E) | DRAFT OF A CRIMINAL CODE OF ORGANIZATIONS, *supra* note 39 § 4 (1).
3639 *Id.*§ 4 (2).
3640 *Id.*§ 5 (1).
3641 *Id.*§ 5 (1).
3642 *Compare with* US SENTENCING GUIDELINES USSC, *supra* note 667 § 8 B2.1 ; UNITED KINGDOM BRIBERY ACT 2010, *supra* note 433 § 7 (2).
3643 GESETZESENTWURFZUMUNTERNEHMENSSTRAFRECHT-VERBANDSSTRAFGESETZBUCH (VERBSTRG-E) | DRAFT OF A CRIMINAL CODE OF ORGANIZATIONS, *supra* note 32§ 5 (2).
3644 *Id.*§ 5 (2).
3645 *Id.*§ 8 (2) No. 3.

approach and terms set forth in the deferred prosecution agreements between the law enforcement agencies and companies.[3646]

It is clear from the foregoing that this draft has been adopted from the American and English approach with little adjustment to reflect existing German provisions. Legal academics criticize, for instance, that this draft violates the principle of liability, the principle of equality and the principle of ownership of an established business in accordance with German constitutional law.[3647] Furthermore, they argue that the obligation to implement a compliance program within all organizations is contrary to the principle of entrepreneurial freedom. Particularly, the paradigm shift between the principle of the presumption of innocence of the individual and the principle of the presumption of a source of danger in the individual continues to be viewed with skepticism.[3648]

For this reason, the German Federal Association of Corporate Counsels (BUJ) in collaboration with several legal scholars submitted a counterproposal in April 2014.[3649] This legislative proposal does not provide a separate statute governing company liability, but would amend Sections 30 (7) and (8) and 130 of the Act on Regulatory Offences (OWiG).[3650] For instance, with the new subsection 7, the authors of the proposal intend to introduce a mandatory mitigating factor for the company in the event that it has implemented adequate compliance measures.[3651] In addition, they provide an amended Section 130 that comprises the obligation of the owner of a business to implement adequate mandatory measures in order to prevent violations of law.[3652] Section 130 (1) will enumerate five elements of these adequate measures, which depend on the size and the risks of the business.[3653]

3646 *Compare with* DPA United States v Montana DOJ, *supra* note 1339; Crime and Courts Act 2013, *supra* note 2831 § 45, Schedule 17.

3647 *See e.g.* Grundgesetz (GG) | Basic Law for the Federal Republic of Germany, *supra* note 37 Art. 1, 3, 14, 20; Zur Frage der Verfassungswidrigkeit und der Folgen eines Strafrechts für Unternehmen: Rechtsgutachten zum Gesetzesantrag des Landes Nordrhein-Westfalen, 34 (2013).

3648 Zur Frage der Verfassungswidrigkeit und der Folgen eines Strafrechts für Unternehmen, *supra* note 3647 at 30.

3649 BUJ, Bundesverband der Unternehmensjuristen e.V. (BUJ) | German Federal Association of Corporate Counsels, http://www.buj.net/index.php/de/home-buj (last visited Apr 16, 2017); Gesetzgebungsvorschlag für eine Änderung der §§ 30, 130 des Ordnungswidrigkeitengesetzes (OWiG) | A Draft of Amendment of the Sections 30, 130 on the Act of Regulatory Offences, *supra* note 3679.

3650 Gesetzgebungsvorschlag für eine Änderung der §§ 30, 130 des Gesetz über Ordnungswidrigkeiten (OWiG) | A Draft of Amendment of the Sections 30, 130 on the Act of Regulatory Offences, *supra* note 3679 at 8, 18.

3651 *Id.* at 8. § 30 (7) in a new version.

3652 *Id.* at 9. § 130 (1) in a new version.

3653 *Id.* at 9. § 130 (1) in a new version.

Although this proposal does not provide a new statute, the amendments of the Act on Regulatory Offences (OWiG) are, again, similar to the US and UK approach. Particularly the draft amendment with the five elements of adequate measures is reminiscent of the UK government's recommended Guidance Principles on proportionate procedures to prevent bribery for organizations.[3654] However, the UK Principles are not prescriptive. They are intended to be flexible and allow a huge variety of proportionate procedures for all sizes of companies.[3655]

In conclusion, although the approach of the German Draft of a Criminal Code of Organizations (VerbStrG-E) and the legislative proposal of the BUJ differ considerably, both will induce organizations to implement adequate compliance measures as a mitigating factor. Nevertheless, the response to the question of which measures are adequate remains absent, as does the establishment of a corporate compliance officer function. With a view to an increasing trend towards extraterritorial law, such as the FCPA, SOX or the UKBA, it will be necessary for internationally operating companies to adjust their internal control measures.[3656] It has been noted that the drafts have reopened the debate on the legal requirement to implement corporate compliance measures, but on the other hand, considerable concerns remain about possible violations of the constitutional principles. It remains to be seen whether the traditional principle of the rule of law will change in Germany. Ultimately, the German legislator will have to decide on this legal matter.

6. Conclusion - Recommendations for Compliance Officers in Practice

The question that arises from the above is: How can the compliance officer recognize and reveal criminal misconduct by employees and managers within the company? The answer to this question could be important, since, as previously examined, outside the financial services sector there have not, hitherto, been any legal requirements for companies to implement compliance measures and a compliance function.[3657] On the other hand, due to international legal developments over the past twenty years, large German corporations operating internationally have implemented compliance structures, such as compliance programs and compliance departments.[3658] In addition to banks and insurance companies, other sectors, such as the automotive industry, technology industry, chemical industry or

3654 *Compare Id.* at 9. § 130 (1) in a new version; The Bribery Guidance, *supra* note 860 at 21, 22 The six principles.

3655 The Bribery Guidance, *supra* note 860 at 20 The six principles.

3656 *See* Süße and Püschel (2017), *supra* note 3624.

3657 *See supra* A., II., III. pp. 423 et seq.

3658 *See* A study by PWC and the Martin Luther University found that 74 percent of the surveyed German companies have implemented a compliance program in 2013. Economic Crime and Corporate Culture 2013, 25–26 (2013).

energy supply companies have established the position of a compliance officer.[3659] Corporations in these industries, with more than 2,000 employees, have commissioned a compliance officer.[3660]

A good corporate compliance culture and the implementation of an adequate compliance program may mitigate the risk of criminal liability of the compliance officer. Nevertheless, the compliance officer should take preventative measures to ensure the prevention of criminal offences within the company. To answer the crucial question as to what these preventative measures are, it has been recognized that companies need to structure their compliance functions strategically for success.[3661] Firstly, as we have seen, since compliance is a task of the management board, the compliance officer has been assigned to the high-level employees.[3662] According to the Study Compliance Manager 2013, 8.44 percent of compliance officers are members of the board; 38.89 percent of them are assigned to a staff position and 22.02 percent of compliance officers work under the executive level with responsibility for decentralized compliance departments.

Secondly, adequate resources are necessary to fulfill the scope of compliance tasks. The personnel and financial resources should be oriented towards the size, scope and risks of the company's business.[3663] The Study Compliance Manager 2013 affirmed this connection and found a correlation between the size of the company and the numbers of employees in the compliance department.[3664] Up to 2,000 employees, a compliance team of between two and six individuals on average are employed and up to 50,000 employees, 171 individuals on average are employed in the compliance department.[3665]

Thirdly, the basis of effective prevention is the management of control.[3666] However, this is not a unique procedure, but an ongoing process of identification, assessment, and monitoring of the business risks within the day-to-day business

---

3659 Study Compliance Manager 2013, Herzog and Stephan (2013), *supra* note 476 at 17 fig. 2.03.

3660 Economic Crime and Corporate Culture 2013, *supra* note 3658 at 25; Study Compliance Manager 2013, Herzog and Stephan (2013), *supra* note 476 at 19 fig. 2.05.

3661 *See* Schulz and Renz (2012), *supra* note 41.

3662 *Id.* at 2513.; Study Compliance Manager 2013, Herzog and Stephan (2013), *supra* note 476 at 135.

3663 *See* Schulz and Renz (2012), *supra* note 41 at 2515.

3664 Study Compliance Manager 2013, Herzog and Stephan (2013), *supra* note 476 at 143 fig. 4.06.

3665 Study Compliance Manager 2013, Herzog and Stephan (2013), *supra* note 476 at 143 fig. 4.06.

3666 *See e.g.* Schulz and Renz (2012), *supra* note 41 at 2512; Wybitul (2009), *supra* note 28 at 2590; Wessing and Dann (2015) § 9 Compliance Officer und Strafrecht, *supra* note 3423 at 230 at 129.

of the compliance officer.[3667] This process also depends on the size and structure of the company. The company should have a clear organizational structure, as well as clear responsibilities.[3668] The compliance officer must have direct access to the reporting of the other business units.[3669] In addition, the compliance officer has to carry out internal audits, conduct interviews with employees within certain business units, and to monitor business processes.[3670] Only then he can effectively monitor and supervise the business activities of other employees and managers.[3671]

Fourthly, the compliance officer should protect himself by means of comprehensive and careful written documentation of the established compliance measures and his work.[3672] A number of legal scholars have called for the implementation of a central database in order to record all violations of compliance.[3673] The compliance officer has to ensure complete documentation confirming the procedure and the further development of compliance measures and, in the event of an offence, to verify the circumstances, the assessment and the initial measures for the defense.[3674] In addition, as previously noted, it is important to document the responsibilities and reporting lines within the company.[3675] The compliance officer can discharge himself of liability when he can prove that he fulfilled his reporting and information duties, for example, but other corporate functions or the management remained inactive.[3676]

Finally, for his own protection, the compliance officer must ensure that the managers, employees, agents and business partners are provided with information, skills and training relevant to the compliance policies, measures and legal

3667 *See e.g* Renz and Wybitul (2012), *supra* note 1074 at VII; Schulz and Renz (2012), *supra* note 41 at 2513; Wessing and Dann (2015) § 9 Compliance Officer und Strafrecht, *supra* note 3423 at 230 at 129.

3668 *See e.g* Wybitul (2009), *supra* note 28 at 2592; Wessing and Dann (2015) § 9 Compliance Officer und Strafrecht, *supra* note 3423 at 231 at 129.

3669 § 36. Compliance-Beauftragten-System, in: CORPORATE COMPLIANCE: HANDBUCH DER HAFTUNGSVERMEIDUNG IM UNTERNEHMEN , 49 (Christoph E. Hauschka, Klaus Moosmayer, & Thomas Lösler eds., 3. ed. 2016).

3670 *See* Wessing and Dann (2015) § 9 Compliance Officer und Strafrecht, *supra* note 3423 at 231 at 131.

3671 *See* Wessing and Dann (2015) § 9 Compliance Officer und Strafrecht, *supra* note 3423 at 231 at 131.

3672 *See e.g* Fecker and Kinzl (2010), *supra* note 455 at 16–17; Sünner (2014), *supra* note 44 at 91; Wybitul (2009), *supra* note 28 at 2593; Zimmermann (2011), *supra* note 28 at 636; Critical view: Hauschka, *supra* note 4 at 170.

3673 *See* Wessing and Dann (2015) § 9 Compliance Officer und Strafrecht, *supra* note 3423 at 232 at 135.

3674 *See e.g* Dann and Mengel (2010), *supra* note 30 at 3268; Fecker and Kinzl (2010), *supra* note 455 at 16–17; Wybitul (2009), *supra* note 28 at 2593; Zimmermann (2011), *supra* note 28 at 636.

3675 *See e.g.* By means of a compliance charter: *See supra*, C., p. 412.

3676 *See e.g* Raus and Lützeler (2012), *supra* note 460 at 98–100; Wessing and Dann (2015) § 9 Compliance Officer und Strafrecht, *supra* note 3423 at 232 at 136.

requirements.[3677] The participation in these periodical and appropriate training sessions should be confirmed and also documented by the compliance officer.[3678] The aim of these training courses is to provide the managers, employees, agents and business partners with information about the compliance measures, policies and legal requirements to enable them to act accordingly when doing business.[3679] The compliance officer is responsible for the organization and supervision of the training, but the company is responsible for the individual structure of the training sessions.[3680] Furthermore, the compliance officer himself has to participate in periodic further training, to keep abreast with recent legal developments, to regularly examine current statutory developments and, based on this, to adapt training accordingly.[3681]

This list is only a small selection of preventative measures that the compliance officer should carry out. In fact, even with the performance of all preventative measures, it is excluded that the compliance officer could avoid all violations of the law by employees or managers.[3682] His activities can also be limited if he receives insufficient resources from the management.[3683] However, in conclusion, the compliance officer has to verifiably demonstrate that he has taken adequate preventative measures before and after the occurrence of a criminal offence.

IV. The Civil Liability of the Compliance Officer under German Employment Law

In addition to criminal liability, the compliance officer could also face civil liability under employment law. For this reason, the next sections outline the key aspects of the German Employment Law and the German court cases with respect to compliance and the compliance officer and the risks of his civil liability. An examination of German Employment Law and the employment case law is essential, since the majority of German compliance officers have a contract of employment. According to the 2013 PwC Study, the compliance departments of German companies with

3677 *See e.g* Illing and Umnuß (2009), *supra* note 461 at 4; Schulz and Renz (2012), *supra* note 41 at 2513; Sünner (2014), *supra* note 44 at 93; von Busekist and Hein (2013), *supra* note 1019 at 187–188.

3678 *See e.g* Heuking (2014), *supra* note 4 at 328; von Busekist and Hein (2013), *supra* note 1019 at 187–188.

3679 *See e.g* Schulz and Renz (2012), *supra* note 41 at 2513; Sünner (2014), *supra* note 44 at 93; Wessing and Dann (2015) § 9 Compliance Officer und Strafrecht, *supra* note 3423 at 231 at 133.

3680 *See e.g* Illing and Umnuß (2009), *supra* note 461 at 4; Wessing and Dann (2015) § 9 Compliance Officer und Strafrecht, *supra* note 3423 at 231 at 134.

3681 *See e.g* Bürkle (2010), *supra* note 28 at 8; Fecker and Kinzl (2010), *supra* note 455 at 17; Illing and Umnuß (2009), *supra* note 461 at 6.

3682 *See* Bürkle (2010), *supra* note 28 at 7.

3683 *Id.* at 7.

between 1,000 and 4,999 employees include an average of two full-time compliance jobs and three part-time jobs.[3684] The German compliance officer is subject to German Employment Law. Therefore, the most interesting key aspects, which will be examined in the following sections, are the position of the compliance officer under employment law, the scope of the compliance tasks and duties under employment law, the risks of civil liability and whether he enjoys protection against dismissal.

1. The Position of the Compliance Officer under Employment Law

In Germany, employment law is defined as a set of rules laid down in the contracts governing employment and other similar employment legal relationships.[3685] Individual employment law governs the relationship between the employer and the employee.[3686] Therefore, it applies to the employed compliance officer as well. The German individual employment law is divided into employment contractual law[3687] and employment protection law.[3688] As has been noted, similar to the US and UK Employment Law, there is no unique statute of employment law but rather a variety of special statutes. In addition to the legislation, the employment case law of the German Federal Labor Court (BAG) can contribute to further legal development.[3689] Just like UK employment law, the development of German employment law has been greatly influenced by EU law over the last twenty years.[3690] Important European Directives were implemented into German law, such as the General Act

---

3684 Economic Crime and Corporate Culture 2013, *supra* note 3658 at 29 fig. 16.

3685 *See* Wolfgang Hromadka, Frank Maschmann & Wolfgang Hromadka, Individual Employment Law 17 (6. ed. 2015) at 1; Rainer Wörlen & Axel Kokemoor, Employment Law 1 (11. ed. 2014) at 1.

3686 *See* Hromadka, Maschmann, and Hromadka (2015), *supra* note 3685 at 1 at 1; Wörlen and Kokemoor, *supra* note 3685 at 1 at 1.

3687 *See* Hromadka, Maschmann, and Hromadka (2015), *supra* note 3685 at 1 at 2; Wörlen and Kokemoor, *supra* note 3685 at 4 at 9; *See e.g.* Bürgerliches Gesetzbuch (BGB) | German Civil Code, *supra* note 102 §§ 611–630; Grundgesetz (GG) | Basic Law for the Federal Republic of Germany, *supra* note 37 Art. 1 (I), 2 (I), 3, 12; Handelsgesetzbuch (HGB) | German Commercial Code, *supra* note 3273 §§ 59.

3688 *See* Hromadka, Maschmann, and Hromadka (2015), *supra* note 3685 at 1 at 2; Wörlen and Kokemoor, *supra* note 3685 at 4 at 9; *See e.g.* Allgemeines Gleichbehandlungsgesetz (AGG) | General Act on Equal Treatment, *supra* note 252; Arbeitsschutzgesetz (ArbSchG) | Act on the Implementation of Measures of Occupational Safety and Health to Encourage Improvements in the Safety and Health Protection of Workers at Work, BGBl. I p. 1246 (1996).

3689 Arbeitsgerichtsgesetz (ArbGG) | Employment Court Act, *supra* note 445 § 45 (4).

3690 *See* Hromadka, Maschmann, and Hromadka (2015), *supra* note 3685 at 21–34; Wörlen and Kokemoor, *supra* note 3685 at 10–11.

on Equal Treatment (AGG) in 2006 and the Law of Proof of Substantial Conditions Applicable to the Employment Relationship in 1995 (NachwG).[3691]

In order to categorize the position of the compliance officer, it is necessary first to define his status within German Employment Law. As previously discussed, in practice and in the academic debate, the compliance officer is referred to as an employee.[3692] The term employee is defined in German law as:

> Generally, an employee is a person, who is obligated to perform paid work, bound by instructions, other-directed or dependently, for another person (employer) on the basis of a contract under civil law.[3693]

In accordance with the BAG case law, the way in which the person is integrated into the company's business will additionally be examined.[3694] In the event that, following an examination of the five aspects of the definition of employee, differentiation remains difficult, the BAG will review further aspects such as the kind of remuneration.[3695]

In comparison to employment law in the US and the UK, the status of the German compliance officer as an employee needs to be identified specifically. Similar to the US and the UK, the contracting parties can freely negotiate the terms and conditions under the current statutes and pursuant to the BAG case law. However, in Germany as in the UK, the employer must provide the employee with *"a written statement of particulars of employment"* within one month of commencing work.[3696]

3691 Council Directive 91/533/EEC of 14 October 1991 on an employer's obligation to inform employees of the conditions applicable to the contract or employment relationship, *supra* note 2937; Nachweisgesetz (NachwG) | Law of Proof of Substantial Conditions Applicable to the Employment Relationship, BGBl. I p. 946 (1995); Directive 2006/54/EC of the European Parliament and of the Council of 5 July 2006 on the implementation of the principle of equal opportunities and equal treatment of men and women in matters of employment and occupation (recast), OJ L 204 23–36 (2006); Allgemeines Gleichbehandlungsgesetz (AGG) | General Act on Equal Treatment, *supra* note 252.

3692 *See e.g.* Giesen (2009), *supra* note 459; Illing and Umnuß (2009), *supra* note 461; Rebecca Julia Koch, *Der Compliance-Officer und die D&O-Versicherung*, ZRFC 135–139 (2016); Raus and Lützeler (2012), *supra* note 460; Zimmermann (2011), *supra* note 28.

3693 *See* Weidenkaff in: Commentary on the German Civil Code, *supra* note 272 at 7 § 611. *See also established case law e.g.*: BAG, 15.02.2012 - 10 AZR 301/10 - *Arbeitnehmereigenschaft bei ergänzendem Aufbauunterricht in einer Justizvollzugsanstalt,* 2012 NZA 731 (2012); BAG, 17.04.2013 - 10 AZR 272/12 - *Arbeitnehmerstatus - Cutterin,* 2013 NZA 903 (2013). Since 2017 there is a legal definition of the term employment agreement – Bürgerliches Gesetzbuch (BGB) | German Civil Code, supra note 102 § 611 a.

3694 BAG, 17.04.2013 - 10 AZR 272/12 - Arbeitnehmerstatus - Cutterin, *supra* note 3693.

3695 *See* Wörlen and Kokemoor, *supra* note 3685 at 23 at 51.

3696 *Compare* Employment Rights Act 1996, *supra* note 2900 § 1 (1); Nachweisgesetz (NachwG) | Law of Proof of Substantial Conditions Applicable to the

According to Section 2 (1) No. 6 of the (NachwG) the contract of employment must encompass the structure and the amount of the remuneration.[3697] Furthermore, the compliance officer is well integrated in the compliance department or other departments within the company.[3698] However, in the event that the compliance officer is not bound by instructions of his supervisor or the members of the board within his professional area, it could be questionable that he is an employee.[3699] According to Section 106 of the German Industrial Code (GewO) and the BAG case law, the employer's right of instruction comprises the context, the implementation, the time, the duration and the location of the work performance.[3700] The BAG Court also stated that services of employees at a higher level are not always bound by professional instructions by the employer.[3701] This nature of work could comprise a high degree of design, individual initiative and professional independence.[3702] Therefore, legal scholars and the BAG take the view that a certain degree of professional independence of the compliance officer function is not contrary to the status of an employee.[3703] The personnel subordination as an employee results from the local and functional integration within the corporate organizational context.

As a result, the compliance officer is considered to be an employee with all the rights and duties that this entails.[3704] Specifically, the compliance officer owes a key statutory duty to the employer to perform his work.[3705] Similar to the US and UK, the main sub-duties under German Employment Law are the duty of loyalty and

---

EMPLOYMENT RELATIONSHIP, *supra* note 3691 § 2 (1); Preis in: § 2 Law of Proof of Substantial Conditions Applicable to the Employment Relationship, 51 *in* ERFURTER COMMENTARY ON THE EMPLOYMENT LAW, 5 (Preis, Müller-Glöge, & Schmidt eds., 17 ed. 2017) § 2. [hereinafter ErfK] However, the written form is not a constitutive formal requirement.

3697 NACHWEISGESETZ (NACHWG) | LAW OF PROOF OF SUBSTANTIAL CONDITIONS APPLICABLE TO THE EMPLOYMENT RELATIONSHIP, *supra* note 3691 § 2 (1) No. 6.

3698 STUDY COMPLIANCE MANAGER 2013, HERZOG AND STEPHAN (2013), *supra* note 476 at 137 fig. 4.02; ECONOMIC CRIME AND CORPORATE CULTURE 2013, *supra* note 3658 at 31 fig. 18.

3699 *See* Giesen (2009), *supra* note 459 at 105.

3700 GEWERBEORDNUNG (GEWO) | GERMAN INDUSTRIAL CODE, § 106 BGBl. I p. 3412 (2003)§ 106; BAG, 09.06.1993 - 5 AZR 123/92 - Arbeitsrechtlicher Status eines Fernsehmitarbeiters, 1994 NZA 169–171, 169 (1993).

3701 BAG NZA 1994, 169, *supra* note 3700 at 169.

3702 BAG, 13.11.1991 - 7 AZR 31/91 - Dozentin in Schulabschlußkursen, 1992 NZA 1125–1129, 1128 (1991); BAG NZA 1994, 169, *supra* note 3700 at 169.

3703 *See* Giesen (2009), *supra* note 459 at 105; Illing and Umnuß (2009), *supra* note 461 at 4; Fabian and Mengel (2015)in: § 7. Arbeitsrechtliche Stellung und Haftung, supra note 3592 at 158 at 5.

3704 *See e.g. The right auf contractual vacation entitlement and the duty of work:* Weidenkaff in: COMMENTARY ON THE GERMAN CIVIL CODE, *supra* note 272 at 24, 126 § 611.

3705 BÜRGERLICHES GESETZBUCH (BGB) | GERMAN CIVIL CODE, *supra* note 102 § 611 (1).

the duty of confidentiality.[3706] These duties apply to all internally employed compliance officers, as well as to the head of the compliance department, but not to an externally commissioned compliance officer.[3707] As such, the employer can determine and regulate the tasks and duties of the employed compliance officer and the delegation of compliance tasks in the contract of employment.

2. The Sources of the Compliance Duties of the Compliance Officer

As we have seen above, from the position as an employee follows the duty of work performance based on the contract of employment. In addition to this contractual duty, legal requirements, the employer's right to issue instructions and corporate policies can further specify the terms of the employment agreement of the compliance officer.[3708] The view of *Krieger & Günther* that the compliance officer is completely free from professional instructions by the employer cannot be accepted, since the tasks and duties of compliance are delegated by the members of the management board to the compliance officer.[3709] Therefore, these compliance duties transferred will remain alterable *(dispositive)*.[3710] However, there are no legal requirements as to the design of the contract of employment of the corporate compliance officer or of his area of activities.[3711]

In addition to the key duty of work, the compliance officer is responsible for a certain defined area of compliance responsibilities.[3712] What are the sources of these compliance duties? First, as explored above, the contract of employment and the employer's authority to issue directives can define certain areas of tasks and duties, as well as the specific compliance tasks and duties. Secondly, in addition to the employment contract, the BGH viewed the actual acceptance of the extent and context of such areas of compliance duties as a source.[3713] This source of duties

3706 *Id.* §§ 241 (2), 242.

3707 *See* Fabian and Mengel (2015) in: § 7. Arbeitsrechtliche Stellung und Haftung, *supra* note 3591 at 158 at 5.

3708 ARBEITSZEITGESETZ (ARBZG) | WORKING TIME ACT, § 3 ARBEITSZEITGESETZ BGBI. I, p. 1170, 1171 (1994); § 106 GEWO, *supra* note 3747.

3709 *See e.g.* Krieger and Günther (2010), *supra* note 30 at 370; Fabian, Mengel in: § 7. Arbeitsrechtliche Stellung und Haftung, *supra* note 3592 at 158 at 6.

3710 *See e.g.* Fabian and Mengel (2015)in: § 7. Arbeitsrechtliche Stellung und Haftung, *supra* note 3592 at 158 at 6.

3711 *See e.g.* Fabian and Mengel (2015)in: *Id.* at 158. at 6; GROSS (2012), *supra* note 42 at 69; See the exception in the financial service sector: WERTPAPIERHANDELSGESETZ (WPHG) | GERMAN SECURITIES TRADING ACT, *supra* note 951 § 33 (1) 1.

3712 *See e.g.* Campos Nave (2009), *supra* note 457 at 2059; Raus and Lützeler (2012), *supra* note 460 at 96; Wolf (2011), *supra* note 41 at 1360; Wybitul (2009), *supra* note 28 at 2592; § 7. Arbeitsrechtliche Stellung und Haftung, *supra* note 3591 at 157 at 2.

3713 BGH, 17.7.2009 - 5 StR 394/08, BGHST 54, 44; BGH NJW 2009, 3173, *supra* note 25 at 3174.

requires a commissioning of certain duties. As previously discussed, the delegation of duties by the employer to the employee is permitted.[3714] Nevertheless, compliance is a key managing task that applies to all members of the management board as a general responsibility.[3715] Since the corporate compliance officer is not legally assigned, he can be commissioned by the management board in order to perform certain compliance tasks within a specific relationship of trust.[3716] Although such delegation leads to a limitation of the compliance responsibility of the management board, ultimate responsibility for compliance remains with the management board, since it is a key task of the corporate management.[3717] This commissioning must include the purpose and the particular circumstances of the company.[3718] This is important for the activities of the corporate compliance officer in practice, as well as for his job description since there is no legally defined scope of tasks and duties.[3719]

Thirdly, a standardized job description could provide a defined scope of compliance tasks and duties. Despite the extensive German academic debate on the profession of the compliance officer and initial approaches of various professional associations to establish a recognized, clearly-defined job description and guidance on the officer's activities, to date this has not been implemented uniformly within the private sector.[3720] The compliance officer function is recognized as an element of the compliance system, but the requirements of the compliance measures give no indication of the tasks and duties involved in this position.[3721]

In conclusion, just as there are no standardized compliance measures, there is no standardized profession of the compliance officer. The sources of the compliance officer's duties are a specific description in the contract of employment, the

---

3714 *See supra* II., 2. p. 433; Pelz in: § 20. Personalorganisation und Arbeitsstrafrecht CORPORATE COMPLIANCE, *supra* note 3227 at 4.

3715 LG München I, 10.12.2013 - 5 HK O 1387/10, NZG 2014, *supra* note 973 at 348; Bürkle (2010), *supra* note 28 at 5.

3716 *See e.g.* Bürkle (2010), *supra* note 28 at 5; Fabian and Mengel (2015) in: § 7. Arbeitsrechtliche Stellung und Haftung, *supra* note 3592 at 159 at 8; BGH, 17.7.2009 - 5 StR 394/08, BGH, 17.7.2009 - 5 StR 394/08, BGHST 54, 44; BGH NJW 2009, 3173, *supra* note 25 at 3174.

3717 LG München I, 10.12.2013 - 5 HK O 1387/10, NZG 2014, *supra* note 973 at 348.

3718 BGH, 17.7.2009 - 5 StR 394/08, BGHST 54, 44; BGH NJW 2009, 3173, *supra* note 25 at 3174.

3719 *Id.* at 3174–3175.

3720 Profession of the Compliance Officer BDCO, *supra* note 496; Fecker and Kinzl (2010), *supra* note 455; Guidance on the Activities of the Compliance Officer, Hauschka, Galster, and Marschlich (2014), *supra* note 463; Schulz and Renz (2012), *supra* note 41; Sünner (2014), *supra* note 44.

3721 ECONOMIC CRIME AND CORPORATE CULTURE 2013, *supra* note 3658 at 57 fig. 33; *See e.g.* Fabian and Mengel (2015) in: § 7. Arbeitsrechtliche Stellung und Haftung, *supra* note 3592 at 159 at 7.

professional or organizational instructions issued by the employer or the specific tasks transferred from the management board to the compliance officer. Overall, the scope of the compliance duties of the compliance officer are not standardized, but alterable.

3. A Comparison of the Scope and the Importance of the Activities of the Compliance Officer in Practice and in the Literature

A comparison of the scope and the importance of the key activities of the compliance officer between the required key tasks and responsibilities in job offers and the articles written by legal scholars found certain similarities, but also major differences.[3722] For the purposes of this book, sixteen articles and sixteen job offers for corporate compliance officers were evaluated outside the regulated sectors, such as the financial service sector or the health sector.[3723] The job offers were published in online job markets in April 2017.[3724] At first, the key tasks and responsibilities were summarized and coded; then the number of mentions captured. *Table 19* shows the results of the key tasks and responsibilities for the compliance officers that are presented in the articles and job offers.[3725] *Chart 13*, below, shows the comparison and, in particular, the differences between the requirements placed by corporations on the position of the compliance officer and the key tasks and responsibilities described by legal scholars.[3726]

The findings revealed that the advisory function, the reporting duties, trainings and the implementation and maintenance of a compliance program are the most important tasks and responsibilities of the corporate compliance officers' function. Nevertheless, there are also differences in practice and literature. The major differences in terms of the importance between the key tasks in the literature and

---

3722 *See supra* Figure 13, p. 475.

3723 *The comparison included following articles*: *See e.g.* Fecker and Kinzl (2010), *supra* note 455; Gößwein and Hohmann (2011), *supra* note 41; Hauschka, Galster, and Marschlich (2014), *supra* note 463; Hemeling (2010), *supra* note 1024; Heuking (2014), *supra* note 4; Illing and Umnuß (2009), *supra* note 461; Krieger and Günther (2010), *supra* note 30; Krieger and Günther (2011), *supra* note 3407; Lackhoff and Schulz (2010), *supra* note 458; Meier (2011), *supra* note 30; Meier-Greve (2010), *supra* note 461; Raus and Lützeler (2012), *supra* note 460; Renz and Wybitul (2012), *supra* note 1074; Schulz and Renz (2012), *supra* note 41; Wolf (2011), *supra* note 41; Zimmermann (2011), *supra* note 28.

3724 Bundesagentur für Arbeit (BA), Job Market - Results 56 (2017), http://jobboerse.arbeitsagentur.de/vamJB/stellenangebote.html (last visited Apr 19, 2017); Stepstone, Your ReseArch of Compliance Officer revealed 738 results StepStone Deutschland GmbH (2017), https://www.stepstone.de/5/ergebnisliste.html (last visited Apr 19, 2017).

3725 *See supra* Table 19, p. 474.

3726 *See supra* Figure 13, p. 475.

Table 19 *Key Tasks and Responsibilities of the Compliance Officer*

Key Tasks of the German Compliance Officer	Numbers in German Journals	Numbers in German Job Offers
Access to relevant information	10	0
Activities within internal investigations	9	3
Advisory function	8	16
Compliance bylaws	1	0
Conducting internal audits/Due Diligence	4	7
Continuing education	2	0
Coordination of communication	0	1
Cooperation with other corporate departments	2	4
Development and implementation of a legal database	0	1
Documentation	4	0
Establishing of policies	2	5
Identification of compliance risks and risk assessment	3	5
Identification of any changes in the regulatory environment	0	3
Implementation and conducting of pre-employment-screenings	0	1
Implementation and maintain of a compliance program	5	9
Monitoring and supervising activities	8	4
Prevention of violations of the law	8	3
Professional independence	8	0
Reporting duties	18	5
Training	8	9

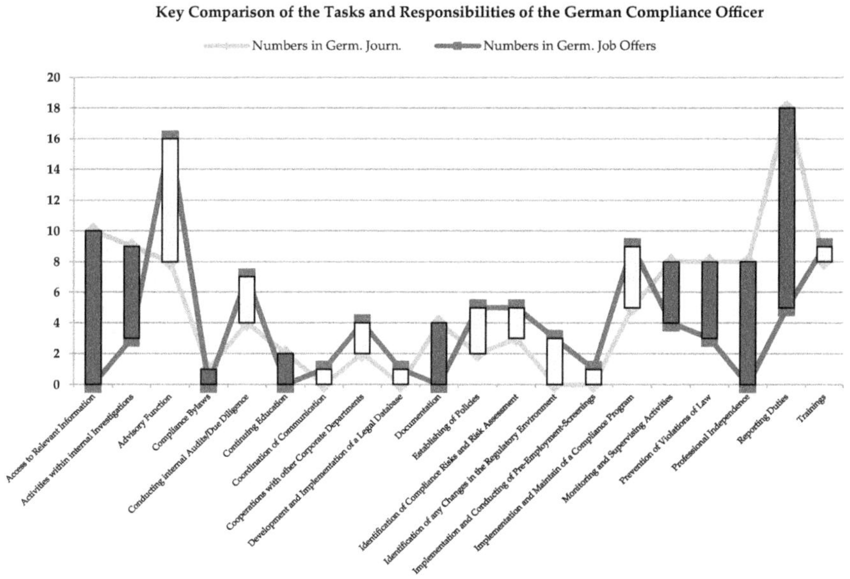

Figure 13 *Comparison of the Key Tasks and Responsibilities of the Compliance Officer as set forth in the Articles and Job Offers*

in practice concern the reporting duties, access to relevant information, the advisory function and professional independence.[3727]

In the job offers, corporations do not emphasize the professional independence of the compliance officer function, reporting duties in day-to-day business or access to relevant information.[3728] In corporations, the advisory function of the compliance officer, the conducting of internal audits, carrying out employee training and implementing and maintaining of a compliance program are afforded highest priority.[3729] Legal scholars consider access to relevant information, activities within internal investigations, monitoring and supervisory activities, the prevention of violations of the law, professional independence and reporting duties to be essential to the performance of the job of compliance officer.[3730] It is noteworthy that the coordination of communication within the corporation or the identification of any changes in the regulatory environment are not mentioned separately in the

3727 *See supra* Figure 13, *Id.*
3728 *See supra* Table 19, p. 474.
3729 *See supra* Table 19, p. 474.
3730 *See supra* Table 19, p. 474.

literature.[3731] The correct governance of communication should also be an important responsibility of the compliance officer in order to ensure that the relevant information reaches the right recipient at the right time. In the event of a crime, this could be vital for the compliance officer's release from liability.

In conclusion, this comparison has shown that the corporations give a clear picture of the priorities of required key tasks and responsibilities for the compliance officer. They emphasize the internal services that the compliance officer has to carry out for other departments, such as training, advice, internal audits, the risk assessment and the implementation of a compliance program as a key duty. In contrast, legal scholars focus mainly on reporting duties, access to relevant information and activities in internal investigations. Both corporations and legal scholars see the importance of the compliance officer as an advisory function. Finally, the scope and the importance of the tasks and responsibilities are broad and varied between literature and practice. The compliance officers should be aware off the wide-ranging responsibilities which occur in the course of their employment. In practice, the tasks and duties could be more far –reaching than described in the job-offers.

4. The Risks of Civil Liability of the Compliance Officer under Employment Law

Just like under common law, the general principle is that the party who holds duties could be liable under civil law. As previously examined, the compliance officer is considered to be an employee and, as a rule, receives a written contract of employment. His responsibilities could be derived from this contractual agreement, from employer's instructions or from the delegation of certain compliance tasks. The scope of his tasks and responsibilities is broad and varied. How could he be liable under civil law within the internal employment relationship? The examination of tortious liability of the compliance officer and claims for damages pursuant to Section 823 (1) and (2) of the German Civil Code (BGB) within the external relationship will be excluded in the course of this consideration of the civil liability.

Firstly, under German employment law, the compliance officer as employee is liable in the event that (a) he violates his contractual obligations, (b) the employer suffers a loss, and (c) there is a causal relationship between (a) and (b). Finally, (d) the employee is responsible for the violation.[3732] Generally, under German civil law, Section 280 (1) of the German Civil Code (BGB) is the basis for the claim based on breach of contractual duties.[3733] Conversely, in the event of the liability of an

3731 *See supra* Table 19, p.474.

3732 *See e.g.* Linck in: § 19 Employment Law-Manual, *in* Employment Law-Manual , 1 (Günter Schaub ed., 16. ed. 2015).

3733 *See* The claim for compensation due to breach of contractual duty: Bürgerliches Gesetzbuch (BGB) | German Civil Code, *supra* note 102 § 280 (1).

employee, the burden of proof pursuant to Section 619a of the German Civil Code (BGB), which overrules Section 280 (1) 2 of the German Civil Code (BGB) must be considered.[3734] In detail, that means the employer must provide evidence of the employee's culpability and breach of duty.[3735]

Secondly, over the years, the BAG has established principles on the limited liability of employees. Since the decision of principle of the Eighth Senate of the Federal Labor Court (BAG) on the removal of the requirement of high-risk work, these principles apply to all activities on the basis of an employment relationship within companies.[3736] The principle states that the amount of damage depends on the degree of liability.[3737] In the event of intent, the employee must bear the compensation costs, in the event of gross negligence, he usually has to bear the costs.[3738] In the case of moderate negligence, the court will consider the circumstances and calculates the compensation payable proportionate to the employer and to the employee.[3739] Where the employee is liable in the case of slight negligence, the employer has to bear the full amount of the damage.[3740] However, the BAG has not introduced maximum limits of liability. Nevertheless, thus far, in the event of gross negligence, the BAG has not yet decided that an employee has to pay compensation that is higher than his annual salary.[3741]

Thirdly, these principles on the limitation of liability also apply to the employed compliance officer, for example in the case that he performs his duties without the requisite care and diligence.[3742] The following examples could arise in day-to-day business practice: A compliance officer has an employment contract with the agreed term that he has to conduct periodic trainings for all employees on the corporate anti-corruption and/or anti-bribery policies. The compliance officer has received all relevant information about the specific business activities of the departments in the company, but failed to deliver training courses on the anti-corruption and/

3734 *Id.*§ 619 (a); *See e.g.* Weidenkaff in: COMMENTARY ON THE GERMAN CIVIL CODE, *supra* note 272 at 6 § 619a; Linck in: ArbR-HdB, *supra* note 3733 at 1.

3735 BÜRGERLICHES GESETZBUCH (BGB) | GERMAN CIVIL CODE, *supra* note 102 §§ 276, 619 (a); Weidenkaff in: COMMENTARY ON THE GERMAN CIVIL CODE, *supra* note 272 at 7 § 619(a).

3736 BAG GS, 27.09.1994 - GS 1/89 (A) - *Haftung des Arbeitnehmers - Abkehr von der gefahrgeneigten Arbeit*, 1994 NZA 1083–1086 (1994); *See e.g.* Preis in: ErfK, *supra* note 3696 at 10 § 619 (a) § 619a (BGB) Liability of the Employee.

3737 *See e.g.* Preis in: ErfK, *supra* note 3696 at 13 § 619 (a); Grüneberg in: COMMENTARY ON THE GERMAN CIVIL CODE, *supra* note 272 at 10 intent, 12 negligence § 276.

3738 BAG, 15.11.2012 - 8 AZR 705/11 - BGB § 611 Haftung des Arbeitnehmers No. 137, 137 AP AP BGB § 611 Haftung des Arbeitnehmers No. 137 (2012); *See e.g.* Preis in: ErfK, *supra* note 3737 at 13§ 619(a).

3739 BAG, 24.11.1987 - 8 AZR 524/82 - Haftung des Arbeitnehmers, 1988 NZA 579–584 (1987); *See e.g.* Preis in: ErfK, *supra* note 3696 at 13§ 619(a).

3740 *See* Preis in: ErfK, *supra* note 3696 at 13§ 619(a).

3741 *See* Preis in: *Id.* at 18. § 619(a).

3742 *See* Lackhoff and Schulz (2010), *supra* note 458 at 88.

or anti-bribery policies for sales employees; in this situation he could be liable in the event that a sales employee bribes a foreign public official in order to obtain or retain business in the conduct of business in the US under the FCPA. This may apply when the damage has been caused 'for' the company. Another case of the liability of the compliance officer could arise if the company was sentenced to a fine for the violation of the supervisory duty pursuant to Section 30, 130 of the Act on Regulatory Offences (OWiG).[3743] Under his contract of employment, the compliance officer was commissioned with the implementation of the adopted compliance measures from the management board. The compliance officer failed to establish these measures and thereby breached his contractual obligations.[3744] For this reason, it could be that the company attempts to impose compensation on the compliance officer.[3745] Lastly, the compliance officer's contract will be terminated for cause without notice.[3746] However, to date, there has not been any German landmark case in which a corporate compliance officer failed to perform his contractual obligations under German employment law.

In conclusion, civil liability within the internal employment relationship follows different principles from criminal liability. Pursuant to employment law, the compliance officer has limited civil liability, but he could face the risk of dismissal from employment.

5. The Compliance Officer's Protection against Dismissal

As previously discussed, the compliance officer is not legally assigned, unlike the data protection officer or the immission protection officer.[3747] Therefore, although he is also commissioned with certain tasks and should perform his compliance tasks without professional instructions from the employer, he has no specific statutory protection against dismissal in his position as corporate compliance officer. In Germany, the Protection against Unfair Dismissal Act (KSchG) applies to all employees, in companies with more than ten employees and an employment agreement lasting more than six months.[3748] The compliance officer does not occupy a special position, although he is responsible for confidential information and his

---

3743 Gesetz über Ordnungswidrigkeiten (OWiG) | Act on Regulatory Offences, *supra* note 3248 §§ 30, 130.

3744 Bürgerliches Gesetzbuch (BGB) | German Civil Code, *supra* note 102 §§ 276, 280 (1), 619a.

3745 It should be noted the BAG principles of the limited liability of employees.

3746 Bürgerliches Gesetzbuch (BGB) | German Civil Code, *supra* note 102 § 626 (1) (2).

3747 *See supra* II., 2., p. 433; *See e.g.* The ordinary termination of the employment contract is illegal. Bundesdatenschutzgesetz | Federal Data Protection Act (BDSG), *supra* note 3415 § 4 (f) (3).

3748 Kündigungsschutzgesetz (KSchG) | Employment Protection Law, § 1 Kündigungsschutzgesetz BGBl. I, p. 499 (1951) §§ 1 (1), 23 (1); *See e.g.* Vossen

relationship to the management board may be conflicted in the event of misconduct by the management.[3749] The compliance tasks and duties are thus caught in a conflict field between disclosure duties and the duty of loyalty.[3750] For this reason, a few legal scholars consider analogously applying these specific legal provisions to the commissioned compliance officer.[3751] However, there is no explicit legal requirement to implement a corporate compliance system and no statutory basis for the commissioning of a corporate compliance officer, meaning that there is also no legal basis for a specific protection against dismissal.[3752] Furthermore, as previously examined, within the financial services sector, the legislator has defined the compliance function for banks and investment service firms in Section 33 (1) 1 of the German Securities Trading Act (WpHG) and Section 12 (4) of the (WpDVerOV).[3753] Even these provisions show that the German legislator does not require a specific statutory specific protection against dismissal for the compliance officer.

Furthermore, the German Employment Courts do not see any need for such dismissal protection. In a case involving the termination of a compliance officer in 2010, the Berlin Employment Court did not hold that there was any specific protection against dismissal for compliance officers, but it examined the legitimacy of the termination for reasons of conduct under the Unfair Dismissal Act.[3754] The Court held that the contract of employment of a compliance officer, like other employees, could be terminated only in the event that the employee has culpably breached his contractual duties.[3755] Thus, the court does not see any need for a separate legal statutory protection against dismissal for the compliance officer.

---

in: § 1 Commentary on the Employment Protection Law, *in* KÜNDIGUNGSRECHT , 21 (Reiner Ascheid, Ulrich Preis, & Ingrid Schmidt eds., 5. ed. 2017) § 1.

3749 *See* Illing and Umnuß (2009), *supra* note 461 at 6.

3750 *See e.g.* Fecker and Kinzl (2010), *supra* note 455 at 19; Krieger and Günther (2010), *supra* note 30 at 152; Fabian and Mengel (2015) in: § 7. Arbeitsrechtliche Stellung und Haftung, *supra* note 3592 at 169 at 30.

3751 *See e.g.* Fecker and Kinzl (2010), *supra* note 455 at 19; Illing and Umnuß (2009), *supra* note 461 at 6; Meier (2011), *supra* note 30 at 781; *But critically*: Dann and Mengel (2010), *supra* note 30 at 3269.

3752 *See* Fabian and Mengel (2015) in: § 7. Arbeitsrechtliche Stellung und Haftung, *supra* note 3592 at 171 at 33.

3753 WERTPAPIERHANDELSGESETZ (WPHG) | GERMAN SECURITIES TRADING ACT, *supra* note 951 § 33 (1) 1; WERTPAPIERDIENSTLEISTUNGS-VERHALTENS- UND ORGANISATIONSVERORDNUNG (WPDVEROV) | SECURITIES TRADING IMPLEMENTING PROVISION, *supra* note 1015 § 12 (4); *See* Illing and Umnuß (2009), *supra* note 461 at 6.

3754 BÜRGERLICHES GESETZBUCH (BGB) | GERMAN CIVIL CODE, *supra* note 102 § 626; KÜNDIGUNGSSCHUTZGESETZ (KSCHG) | EMPLOYMENT PROTECTION LAW, *supra* note 3748 § 1; ArbG Berlin, 18.2.2010 - 38 Ca 12879/09 - Kündigung einer leitenden Compliance-Mitarbeiterin, 2010 CCZ 158–160 (2010).

3755 ArbG Berlin, 18.2.2010 - 38 Ca 12879/09 - Kündigung einer leitenden Compliance-Mitarbeiterin, *supra* note 3754 at 158.

In comparison with the US and the UK, the German compliance officer is protected under the Unfair Dismissal Act and has the right to review the legality of the termination in the employment courts.[3756] Contrary to the US common law at-will doctrine, Section 1 of the German Unfair Dismissal Act limits the employer's freedom to dismiss.[3757] An ordinary termination of the contract of employment will be possible only when there are reasons pursuant to Section 1 (2) of the Protection against Unfair Dismissal Act (KSchG).[3758] The German protection against unfair dismissal is based on the constitution, namely on the freedom of choice of workplace pursuant to Article 12 (1) of the Basic Law (GG).[3759] However, in practice, the real situation in terms of the law shows another picture. According to studies by the Max Planck Institute and by the Legal Faculty of the Martin-Luther-University Halle-Wittenberg, only 1.7 percent of plaintiffs return to their workplace after being involved in an action against dismissal.[3760] The majority of these cases have dissolved the work relationship in return for payment of compensation.[3761]

Finally, as we have seen, since the compliance officer enjoys general protection against dismissal pursuant to Sections 1 and 23 of the Protection against Unfair Dismissal Act (KSchG), there is no need for special legal provisions governing protection against dismissal for the commissioned compliance officer.[3762] Compliance officers occupy a specific qualified position of trust with the collaboration of the management, with a certain degree of flexibility in terms of their tasks.[3763] In conclusion, the right of the compliance officer to negotiate terms of contractually agreed protection against dismissal or individual indemnification clauses with his employer remains unaffected by the absence of a legally defined protection against dismissal.

6. Conclusion – The Relevant Content of the Contract of Employment

Having examined the civil liability of the employed compliance officer under German Employment Law, it is clear that, on the one hand, he faces the same liability as other employees in the event of a breach of his contractual duties. He is not afforded any exemption from ordinary dismissal, unlike the legally appointed

3756 *Compare* In Germany, the protection against dismissal is mandatory law: *See* Vossen in: Employment Protection Law, *supra* note 3749 at 5§ 1.

3757 *Compare supra* Ch. 3, A., II., III., pp. 254 et seq.; *See* Vossen in: *Id.* at 1.§ 1.

3758 *See* Vossen in: *Id.* at 1.§ 1.

3759 Grundgesetz (GG) | Basic Law for the Federal Republic of Germany, *supra* note 37 Art. 12 (1); Vossen in: Employment Protection Law, *supra* note 3749 at 2§ 1.

3760 *See* Vossen in: Employment Protection Law, *supra* note 3749 at 3§ 1.

3761 *See* Vossen in: *Id.* at 4.§ 1.

3762 Kündigungsschutzgesetz (KSchG) | Employment Protection Law, *supra* note 3748 § 1 (1), 23 (1); *See* Fabian and Mengel (2015) in: § 7. Arbeitsrechtliche Stellung und Haftung, *supra* note 3592 at 172 at 38.

3763 *See* Fabian and Mengel (2015) in: § 7. Arbeitsrechtliche Stellung und Haftung, *supra* note 3592 at 172 at 38.

data protection officer. The evidence presented has shown that there are no regulatory requirements governing the legal position of the corporate compliance officer in Germany. The provisions of the German Securities Trading Act (WpHG) and the (WpDVerOV), which require the assignment of the compliance officer function in banks and investment firms, were not adopted by the legislator into the private sector. They may merely serve as a measure of orientation for the corporate compliance officer function.

On the other hand, legal scholars have recognized that the contract of employment could govern the scope of tasks and liability regulation of the compliance officer and, additionally, that a clearly defined job description should be developed.[3764] In addition, the comparison of the scope and the importance of the activities and responsibilities of the compliance officer between practice and the literature has shown that the scope and importance of the tasks are comprehensive and varied. For this reason, it has been established that the contract of employment in particular should state clearly the tasks, the responsibilities, the powers and the possible protection of the compliance officer.[3765] Additionally, a clearly defined job description should be developed.[3766] The contract of the compliance officer can include *e.g.* the following subjects: (1) the professional independence of the employer in terms of monitoring the compliance measures, (2) his integration into the corporate structures and his powers relating to other departments or obtaining relevant reports and information, (3) his reporting lines and duties, (4) his further education, and (5) his resources.[3767]

A few scholars critically view clearly agreed tasks in the contract of employment of the compliance officer, since these terms are inflexible and could , in practice, be alterable by the employer.[3768] In addition, the case law of the BGH in terms of criminal liability should be considered as regards the status as guarantor in the event of a clearly agreed area of tasks and responsibilities specifically for the compliance officer as stipulated in his contract of employment.[3769] Through the definition in the employment contract, the breach of duties may be more precisely

3764 *See e.g.* Fecker and Kinzl (2010), *supra* note 455 at 20; Illing and Umnuß (2009), *supra* note 461 at 6; Meier (2011), *supra* note 30 at 782; Fabian and Mengel (2015) in: § 7. Arbeitsrechtliche Stellung und Haftung, *supra* note 3592 at 173 at 41.

3765 *See e.g.* Fecker and Kinzl (2010), *supra* note 455 at 20; Illing and Umnuß (2009), *supra* note 461 at 6; § 7. Arbeitsrechtliche Stellung und Haftung, *supra* note 3591 at 173 at 41.

3766 *See e.g.* Fecker and Kinzl (2010), *supra* note 455 at 20; Meier (2011), *supra* note 30 at 782.

3767 *See e.g.* Illing and Umnuß (2009), *supra* note 461 at 7–8; Meier (2011), *supra* note 30 at 782.

3768 Fabian and Mengel (2015) in: § 7. Arbeitsrechtliche Stellung und Haftung, *supra* note 3592 at 174 at 42.

3769 *See supra* III., 4.a., p. 451; *See* Fabian and Mengel (2015) in: *Id.* at 174. at 43.

evidenced. Therefore, in practice, the detailed and specific description should be balanced between the employer and the compliance officer.[3770]

Furthermore, it has been recognized that the scope of the compliance tasks depends on the size, the business sector or the nature and scope of the corporate business.[3771] It is therefore to be recommended that, similar to the IDW Auditing Standard, a typical area of compliance tasks should be summarized in general and described as follows: (1) the compliance culture, (2) the compliance objectives, (3) the risk analysis of the business, (4) the compliance program, (5) organizational compliance with the reporting, (6) compliance communication with training, and (7) compliance monitoring and compliance improvement with documentation.[3772]

In conclusion, from the above, the position and civil liability of the compliance officer under employment law is no different from other employees in Germany. Compared to the US and the UK, German law does not include any indemnification clauses expressly applicable to officers, directors, employees, and agents. However, German Employment Law comprises other protective measures. The Protection against Unfair Dismissal Act (KSchG) and the BAG principles set down in the case law on the limited liability of employees also apply to the employed compliance officer, provided he is not a senior executive. The compliance officer should therefore carefully negotiate his contract of employment with respect to his area of tasks and responsibilities and any possible exclusion of liabilty and ordinary termination for a certain period. Thus, a specific statutory regulation of this corporate position does not appear to be necessary at present.

B. The German Corporate Governance Code

Ever since the era of the major corporate failures in Germany and abroad, including in the US and in the UK, efforts have been made by governments and committees to improve corporate governance mechanisms in order to help prevent corporate failures. Therefore, this section will examine the provisions of German soft law applicable to compliance and the compliance officer. Since 1990, several codes, guidelines, principles, reports und statements have been established internationally, which comprise standards of good and responsible corporate governance.[3773] These efforts have also resulted in the introduction of principles of best practice

3770 *See* Fabian and Mengel (2015) in: *Id.* at 175. at 44.

3771 Berufsfeldstudie Compliance Manager 2013, *supra note* 465; *See supra* III., 5.c., p. 460.

3772 These are the basic elements of an appropriate compliance management system recommended by the Institute of Public Auditors (IDW) in Germany: *See* IDW, IDW Prüfungsstandard: Grundsätze ordnungsmässiger Prüfung von Compliance Management Systemen (IDW PS 980) 23 (2011); Fabian and Mengel (2015) in: § 7. Arbeitsrechtliche Stellung und Haftung, *supra* note 3592 at 175 at 45.

3773 *See e.g.* Belgium: Cardon Report (December 1998), The 2009 Belgian Code on Corporate Governance 12 March 2009, Brazil: Code of Best Practice of Corporate

in the UK and in Germany in the form of a Corporate Governance Code, which encompasses mechanisms geared towards increasing the effectiveness of corporate governance.[3774]

The Codes were issued by a committee or commission, best categorized as organized by government, with the objective of providing guidance for companies in general terms as to principles, structures and processes.[3775] Compared with the development of corporate governance codes in other countries, in Germany, the German Government Commission was charged by the German Federal Minister of Justice fairly late in the game, in September 2001.[3776] The first version of the German Code was published on February 26, 2002.[3777] Since 2009, the Commission has been required to publish the Code pursuant to Section 161 of the German Stock Corporation Act (AktG) in the official section of the electronic Federal Gazette.[3778]

Both the UK Code and the German Code define the term corporate governance similarly, as follows:

> Corporate governance is the system by which companies are directed and controlled.[3779]
> Corporate governance is the legal and effective regulatory framework for governing and monitoring of the company.[3780]

On the other hand, the term corporate governance code excludes statutes, regulations on corporate governance, and codes which are created by companies.[3781] The Corporate Governance Codes are intended to as soft law or secondary law, since they include

Governance (5th edition) 2016, France: Viénot I Report (July 1995), Code of Best Practice of Corporate Governance (5th edition) 2016, Italy: Preda Report (October 1999), Codice di autodisciplina ("Codice") 15 July 2015, Netherlands: Peters Report (June 1997), Spain: Olivencia Report (February 1998), Código de buen gobierno de las sociedades cotizadas February 2015, in: Comparative Study of Corporate Governance Weil, Gotshal & Manges LLP (2002), *supra* note 2355 at 14–15.; *See also* v. Werder in: Commentary on the DCGK (2016), *supra* note 1030 at 3.; European Corporate Governance Institute (ECGI), Index of all codes Corporate Governance Codes, Principles & Recommendations (2017), http://www.ecgi.org/codes/all_codes.php (last visited Apr 23, 2017).

3774 The German Code 2015, *supra* note 947; The UK Corporate Governance Code (2016), *supra* note 3113.

3775 *See* Okoye (2015), *supra* note 3093 at 83.

3776 The German Code 2015, The legislative Commission, *supra* note 1027.

3777 The German Code 2015, The legislative Commission, *supra* note 1027.

3778 Aktiengesetz (AktG) | German Stock Corporation Act, *supra* note 976 § 161 (1) 1; Bachmann in: Commentary on the DCGK (2016), *supra* note 1030 at 79.

3779 *See* The Cadbury Report (1992), *supra* note 796 para 2.5.

3780 *See* v. Werder in: Commentary on the DCGK (2016), *supra* note 1030 at 1.

3781 Comparative Study of Corporate Governance Weil, Gotshal & Manges LLP (2002), *supra* note 2355 at 11.

recommendations, which a company is not, however, always obliged to follow.[3782] The provisions of these Codes should supplement the companies' self-imposed rules with regulatory requirements.[3783] Nevertheless, these Codes do not have the status of primary law.

For this reason, both the UK Code and the German Code have been subject to criticism from the outset. In the UK, there is an academic debate on the effectiveness of corporate governance since legal scholars view the issue of compliance critically.[3784] In Germany, the legal policy debate concerning the Code revolves around the content and the work of the German Government Commission.[3785] Criticism has grown with the case law since the Munich District Court decided on the contestability of the management and supervisory board in the context of the non-compliance with their obligations pursuant to Section 161 of the German Stock Corporation Act (AktG).[3786] In 2011, the debate concerning the Code reached a temporary climax with the introduction of provisions on the increase of the percentage of women in the management and supervisory boards of German corporations.[3787] A few voices of scholars even demand the repeal of the German Code.[3788] However, in 2012, the Association of German Jurists decided to continue the regulatory framework of the German Code.[3789] Since then, the German Code has been periodically reviewed and developed further by the German Government Commission.[3790] The abolition of the Code appears unlikely due to international business practice.

The major objectives of the UK Code and the German Code are similar: first and foremost, to improve the quality of the board governance and, then, to improve the quality of governance-related information available to equity markets, shareholders and investors. In particular, one major aim of the German Government Commission of the 2015 Code is to explain the German dual system for foreign investors.[3791] In 2014, the Commission stated:

3782 *See* v. Werder in: Commentary on the DCGK (2016), *supra* note 1030 at 5.

3783 *See* v. Werder in: *Id.* at 5.

3784 *See supra* A., I., 3., p. 324; *See e.g.* Arcot, Bruno, and Faure-Grimaud (2010), *supra* note 443; The Grant Thornton Review 2016, *supra* note 3163; Okoye (2015), *supra* note 3093.

3785 *See* Bachmann in: Commentary on the DCGK (2016), *supra* note 1030 at 85.

3786 *See* Bachmann in: *Id.* at 85.; OLG München, 23.1.2008 - 7 U 3668/07 - *Folgen der Nichtabgabe einer Entsprechenserklärung nach § 161 AktG*, 2008 NZG 337–339 (2008) The case has not yet been settled.

3787 *See* Bachmann in: Commentary on the DCGK (2016), *supra* note 1030 at 85.

3788 *See* Bachmann in: *Id.* at 85.

3789 *See* Bachmann in: *Id.* at 86.

3790 *See* Bachmann in: *Id.* at 86

3791 Press Release dated on June 25, 2014 The German Government Commission, *supra* note 1027; *See* Bachmann in: Commentary on the DCGK (2016), *supra* note

> The German Corporate Governance Code is intended to make the rules applicable in Germany for company management and supervision transparent to national and international investors in order to strengthen trust in the management of German companies.[3792]

Secondly, the German Code 2015 applies to all listed companies that issue shares on the stock exchanges, and which are subject to the German Stock Corporation Act (AktG) including the KGaA[3793] and the European joint-stock company (SE).[3794] The declarations of the German companies listed on the DAX and MDAX are published on the website of the German Government Commission.[3795] Nevertheless, it is recommended that all companies comply with the Code.[3796]

Thirdly, the German Code 2015 aims to guide companies on the establishment of standards of corporate governance through the provision of concrete recommendations.[3797] The German Code 2015 comprises two components: on the one hand, the part of the applicable law and, on the other hand, international and nationally recognized standards, such as recommendations and suggestions for good corporate governance.[3798] The recommendations extend the parts of the Codes that describe the applicable law for the management and supervision of German listed companies, which refers mainly to the German Stock Corporation Act (AktG).[3799] The legal part of 91 described provisions has an informative nature for foreign investors, but the listed companies to which these provisions apply must also comply with them.[3800] The recommendations and suggestions do not have force of law and cannot guarantee effective board behavior.[3801] Therefore, as has been mentioned before, the German Code 2015 is not primary law.[3802]

1030 at 33. The code defines the dual system of German Stock Corporations as follows: "*The management board is responsible for managing the enterprise. The supervisory board appoints, supervises and advises the members of the management board and is directly involved in decisions of fundamental importance to the enterprise.*" *See* in: THE GERMAN CODE 2015, *supra* note 947 at 1 Foreword.

3792 PRESS RELEASE DATED ON JUNE 25, 2014 The German Government Commission, *supra* note 1027; *See* Bachmann in: Commentary on the DCGK (2016), *supra* note 1030 at 33.

3793 *See* KGaA's are defined as partnership limited by shares.

3794 *See* Lutter in: Commentary on the DCGK (2016), *supra* note 1030 at 1801.

3795 Declarations of Conformity pursuant to Section 161 (AktG) The German Government Commission, *supra* note 1027.

3796 THE GERMAN CODE 2015, *supra* note 947 at 2.

3797 *See* Bachmann in: Commentary on the DCGK (2016), *supra* note 1030 at 35.

3798 THE GERMAN CODE 2015 The German Government Commission, *supra* note 1027.

3799 *See* Bachmann in: Commentary on the DCGK (2016), *supra* note 1030 at 81; The German Code 2015 The German Government Commission, *supra* note 10276.

3800 *See* Bachmann in: Commentary on the DCGK (2016), *supra* note 1030 at 81; v. Werder *Id.* at 143.

3801 *See* Bachmann in: Commentary on the DCGK (2016), *supra* note 1030 at 39.

3802 *See* Bachmann in: *Id.* at 80.

However, it should be noted that, pursuant to Section 161 of the German Stock Corporation Act (AktG), the members of the management board and the supervisory board of listed corporations are required to declare annually:

> That the recommendations of the Government Commission on the German Corporate Governance Code published by the Federal Ministry of Justice in the official section of the electronic Federal Gazette have been and are being complied with or which of the Code's recommendations are not being applied. The declaration shall be made permanently accessible to stockholders."[3803]

The German Government Commission states on its website that:

> Through the declaration of conformity pursuant to § 161 (AktG) (German Stock Corporation Act), the Code has a legal basis. Accordingly, the recommendations and suggestions are not mandatory.[3804]

I. The "Comply or Explain" Approach of the German Code 2015

Similar to the UK Code, the German Corporate Governance Code also includes a voluntary disclosure comply or explain concept. The German Code 2015 governs this approach through recommendations and suggestions. These rules additionally amend the described legal provisions.[3805] The recommendations are described with the term *"shall"* and the suggestions with the term "*should*".[3806] Thus, in the first instance, the recommendations and suggestions are voluntary. However, non-compliance with the recommendations has to be explained and disclosed with the annual declaration of conformity comply or explain.[3807] Pursuant to Section 161 of the German Stock Corporation Act (AktG), the members of the management board and supervisory board of the listed company shall declare annually whether or not the company has complied with the recommendation.[3808] In the event that the company has not complied with the recommendations, it must explain the reasons for its non-compliance.[3809] This explanation of non-compliance with a

---

3803 Transparency and disclosure law The German Government Commission, *supra* note 1027, It entered into force on July 26, 2002 and was published in the Federal Gazette Part I No. 50 on July 29, 2002.

3804 The German Code 2015 The German Government Commission, *supra* note 1027.

3805 *See* v. Werder Commentary on the DCGK (2016), *supra* note 1030 at 144.

3806 The German Code 2015 The German Government Commission, *supra* note 1027; *See e.g.* The German Code 2015, *supra* note 947 at 4"*shall*" - para 2.3.2, "*should*" - para 2.3.3.

3807 The German Code 2015 The German Government Commission, *supra* note 1027.

3808 Aktiengesetz (AktG) | German Stock Corporation Act, *supra* note 976 § 161 (1); The German Code 2015 The German Government Commission, *supra* note 1027.

3809 Aktiengesetz (AktG) | German Stock Corporation Act, *supra* note 976 § 161 (1); The German Code 2015 The German Government Commission, *supra* note 1027.

recommendation has to be well justified.[3810] The justification has to be true.[3811] It has to be published jointly by the members of the management board and supervisory board on a permanent basis and annually in the current signed version.[3812] In addition, the company also must publish this declaration on its website.[3813] In the event that the members of the board do not provide such declaration, they will be in breach of their duties pursuant to Sections 93 (1) 1 and 116 1 of the German Stock Corporation Act (AktG) and will be liable to pay compensation.[3814] As a result, on the one hand, this approach is intended to enable companies to reflect specific business requirements and to act flexibly with greater self-regulation, but on the other hand, this kind of explanation for listed companies is not voluntary.[3815] Contrary to the recommendations, non-compliance with the suggestions does not need to be disclosed or explained.[3816]

Finally, just like under the UK Code 2016 in the context of UK exchange standards and Listing Rules, the disclosure requirement for German listed companies could lead to pressure to comply with the provisions of the Code. In conclusion, the comply or explain approach of the German Code 2015 encourages listed companies to comply with the Code in connection with Section 161 of the German Stock Corporation Act (AktG). This combination creates a voluntary mechanism of suggestions and recommendations relating to disclosure requirements.

II. The Main Provisions of the German Code with Respect to Compliance

The German Code 2015 contains three provisions[3817] with regard to compliance. As previously mentioned, the most relevant provision refers to the definition of compliance – *e.g.* adherence to the law - as the compliance task of the management board as follows:[3818]

3810 The German Code 2015, *supra* note 947 at 2; *See* v. Werder Commentary on the DCGK (2016), *supra* note 1030 at 148.

3811 *See* Lutter in: Commentary on the DCGK (2016), *supra* note 1030 at 1861.

3812 *See* v. Werder *Id.* at 151–153.

3813 Aktiengesetz (AktG) | German Stock Corporation Act, *supra* note 976 § 161 (2); The German Code 2015 The German Government Commission, *supra* note 1027.

3814 BGH, 7.12.2009 - II ZR 63/08 - Beschränkung der Revisionszulassung auf aktienrechtlichen Beschlussanfechtungsgrund, 2009 NZG 618–619, 9 (2009); *See* Lutter in: Commentary on the DCGK (2016), *supra* note 1030 at 1905.

3815 The German Code 2015, *supra* note 947 at 2; *See* v. Werder Commentary on the DCGK (2016), *supra* note 1030 at 146.

3816 The German Code 2015, *supra* note 947 at 2.

3817 *See* The German Code 2015 *Id.* at 4. para 3.4 Informing the supervisory board is the responsibility of the management board; *Id.* at 9. para 5.2.

3818 *See supra* footnote 1023; A., p. 416.

> 4.1.3 The management board ensures that all provisions of law and the enterprise's internal policies are abided by and works to achieve their compliance by group companies (compliance).[3819]

Section 4.1.3 thus points out that the management board is responsible for compliance, as derived from legal requirements of Section 130 of the Act on Regulatory Offences (OWiG), Section 13 of the German Criminal Code (StGB) or the duty of care in accordance with Sections 76 (1) and 93 (1) of the German Stock Corporation Act (AktG).[3820] Therefore, Section 4.1.3 emphasizes applicable law.[3821] However, para 4.1.3 does not include any legal definition of compliance, but merely a description of the term.[3822] The companies are not required to refer to Section 4.1.3 in the declaration pursuant to Section 161 of the German Stock Corporation Act (AktG).[3823] In addition, the definition of compliance and the Munich I Regional Court decision do not require the management board to prevent violations of the law in all cases.[3824] The Munich I Regional Court stated that, notwithstanding the term compliance, the management board has to ensure that the company and the employees comply with the legal requirements.[3825]

The problem is that the content of the compliance tasks is neither defined under the German Stock Corporation Act nor under Section 130 of the Act on Regulatory Offences (OWiG).[3826] Additionally, the German Code 2015 does not describe specific features, measures or tools in order to give the companies flexibility in the course of implementation.[3827] It has been recognized that there are no uniform compliance measures or procedures fit for all companies across the board.[3828] Although there is no uniform recognized compliance system, over the years, academics, business practice and court decisions have established standards relating to basic elements of an effective compliance organization.[3829] Based on these, an effective compliance

3819 The German Code 2015, *supra* note 947 at 6 para 4.1.3.
3820 *See supra* A., II., III. pp. 423 et seq.; *See* Bachmann in: Commentary on the DCGK (2016), *supra* note 1030 at 821–825.
3821 *See* Bachmann in: *Id.* at 811.
3822 *See* Bachmann in: *Id.* at 815.
3823 *See* Bachmann in: *Id.* at 811.
3824 *See* Bachmann in: *Id.* at 813.; LG München I, 10.12.2013 - 5 HK O 1387/10, NZG 2014, *supra* note 973.
3825 LG München I, 10.12.2013 - 5 HK O 1387/10, NZG 2014, *supra* note 973 at 345.
3826 *See* Bachmann in: Commentary on the DCGK (2016), *supra* note 1030 at 827.
3827 *See* Bachmann in: *Id.* at 827.
3828 *See* Bachmann in: *Id.* at 828.; The Bribery Guidance, *supra* note 860 at 21 Principle 1 - Proportionate procedures.
3829 *See e.g.* Corporate Compliance, *supra* note 3227; Bachmann in: Commentary on the DCGK (2016), *supra* note 1030 at 829; IDW Auditing Standard PS 980 IDW, *supra* note 3773; LG München I, 10.12.2013 - 5 HK O 1387/10, NZG 2014, *supra* note 973.

organization should include the following basic elements: (1) a legal and risk assessment, (2) the commitment of the management board, a mission statement, or tone from the top, (3) the management of information such as reporting lines, (4) training and advice, (5) documentation, and (6) monitoring and adherence.[3830] These elements could serve as a plan of measures and guidelines for companies.

In conclusion, on the one hand, the German Code 2015 emphasizes the compliance duty of the management board, while, on the other hand, this duty is subject to approval of necessity and reasonableness.[3831] Finally, the German Code 2015 has also recognized that the management board has broad discretion in the implementation of compliance measures.

III. Amendment to the German Code 2017 in order to Enhance Compliance

The amended version of the Code 2015 was published by the German Federal Law Gazette on April 24, 2017. On 7 February 2017, the German Government Commission decided on amendments to the German Code 2015 in order to enhance transparency as the basis for stakeholders to assess corporate governance and to concretize the compliance duties of the management board with regard to the compliance measures.[3832] At first, the Commission refers to the principle of an honorable businessperson in the context of the Preamble to the Code.[3833] Secondly, as a result of approximately 80 statements of national and international Code users, academics and advisers, one significant amendment is the enhancement of Section 4.1.3 in the German Code 2017 as follows:[3834]

> 4.1.3 The Management Board ensures that all provisions of law and the enterprise's internal policies are abided by and works to achieve their compliance by group companies (compliance). *Therefore, the Management Board provides for a proportionate Compliance Management System corresponding to the level of risk that the company is exposed to and shall publish the basic features of this system in the annual corporate governance report. Employees as well as third parties shall be given the opportunity of anonymously reporting misconduct within the company in a protected manner.*[3835]

3830 *Summarized by* Bachmann in: Commentary on the DCGK (2016), *supra* note 1030 at 830–836.

3831 *See e.g.* Fleischer in: SPINDLER, STILZ | COMMENTARY ON THE AKTG, *supra* note 3328 at 53 § 91; Bachmann in: Commentary on the DCGK (2016), *supra* note 1030 at 837.

3832 PRESS RELEASE ON FEBRUARY 14, 2017 The German Government Commission, *supra* note 1027.

3833 PRESS RELEASE ON FEBRUARY 14, 2017 *Id.*

3834 PRESS RELEASE ON FEBRUARY 14, 2017 *Id.*

3835 THE GERMAN CODE 2017 THE GERMAN CORPORATE GOVERNANCE CODE (DCGK), 6 (2002) para 4.1.3.

The companies *shall* publish the basic features of their compliance measures, which is described as compliance management system and the opportunity for employees to anonymously report misconduct.[3836] Therefore, it is a recommendation that the listed companies have to explain and disclose with the annual declaration of conformity pursuant to Section 161 (1) of the German Stock Corporation Act (AktG). In detail, the listed companies have to provide and publish their proportionate compliance measures in the Federal Gazette and on their websites for investors. The term proportionate is again reminiscent of the UK Bribery Guidance, which comprises the business risks of the company, and the nature, scale and complexity of the company's activities.[3837]

In their current declarations of conformity pertaining to the German Code pursuant to Section 161 of the German Stock Corporation Act (AktG) at the end of 2016, the companies simply state whether they have fulfilled the provisions of the Code.[3838] For example, Allianz SE stated on December 15, 2016 that the company complied with all recommendations of the German Code 2015 without further explanation.[3839] However, there is no transparency or disclosure for investors as to how Allianz SE fulfilled the requirements set forth in the recommendations. Nevertheless, additionally, by examining the annual report of Allianz SE, we see that the company has published the structure and the development of its compliance program, which also includes the structure of the central compliance function.[3840] In addition, the report states that Allianz SE has implemented interactive training programs around the world, as well as a code of conduct, an anti-corruption program, and "*a whistleblower system that allows employees to alert the relevant compliance department confidentially about irregularities.*"[3841]

Consequently, the amended German Code 2017 introduces the obligation for listed companies to disclose and provide proportionate compliance features and measures through the amended recommendation of Section 4.1.3 and disclosure in accordance with the German Stock Corporation Act (AktG).[3842] Thus, it is expected

---

3836 Press Release on February 14, 2017 The German Government Commission, *supra* note 1027.

3837 The Bribery Guidance, *supra* note 860 at 21 Principle 1.

3838 *See e.g.* Allianz SE, The management board & The supervisory board, German Corporate Governance Code at Allianz SE: Conformity with the Code Regulations in detail (2016), https://www.allianz.com/v_1481877271000/media/investor_relations/en/corporate_governance/declaration_of_conformity/161215-Synopsis-Allianz.pdf (last visited Apr 29, 2017).

3839 *See e.g.* Declaration of Conformity 2016 Id.

3840 *See e.g.* Allianz SE & The management board, Allianz Group Annual Report 2016 19 (2017), https://www.allianz.com/v_1489492630000/media/investor_relations/en/results/2016_fy/ar-2016-annual-report-allianz-group.pdf (last visited Apr 29, 2017).

3841 Allianz Group Annual Report 2016 *Id.* at 20.

3842 The German Code 2017, *supra* note 3835 at 6 para 4.1.3.

that the declarations of conformity pursuant to Section 4.1.3 will be extended in future. The objective is that investors, as well as the interested public, can assess the company's compliance efforts.[3843] Overall, the German Code 2017 requires that the listed company inform all shareholders and investors about the relevant facts with respect to compliance and financial aspects in the same and fair way.[3844]

IV. Conclusion – A Review of the UK and the German Code

This section has presented a conceptual framework for the German Code 2015 and 2017 in terms of corporate governance and compliance. As noted, the German Code and the UK Code apply to listed companies on the stock exchanges. Both the German and the UK Code provide provisions in terms of compliance as a task of the members of the board. The following section discusses the aims of the comply or explain approach. As we have seen, both Codes proceed on the basis of the comply or explain approach. In the UK, companies are required under the Listing Rules to disclose whether they have complied with the provisions of the UK Code. In Germany, companies are required to disclose whether they have complied with the provisions of the Code through the declaration of conformity pursuant to Section 161 (1) (2) of the German Stock Corporation Act (AktG). However, the monitoring of the explanation is different. In the UK, the investors assess these statements and the FRC will continue to monitor compliance with the provisions of the Code. In Germany, in 2017, the Code Commission takes the next step through statutory regulation in Section 161 (1) (2) of the German Stock Corporation Act (AktG) and the amended Section 4.1.3 in the 2017 Code to the effect that the companies have to state the basic features of their compliance measures, which can also include the compliance function. Thus, both the UK and the German Code encourage greater corporate governance disclosure by listed companies for shareholders and investors by indirectly taking into account the legal requirements for joint-stock corporations. However, the result of the comply or explain approach and the absence of any legal penalty mechanism in the Codes is that there is a considerable risk that certain provisions in the Codes may not be observed despite the explanation or declaration of conformity.

For this reason, academics have raised questions concerning the response to the provisions of the Codes and their actual implementation.[3845] Studies examining the effectiveness of the comply or explain approach found, for example, that only 62 percent of all FTSE 350 companies complied in full with the UK Code.[3846]

3843 Press Release on February 14, 2017 The German Government Commission, *supra* note 1027.

3844 The German Code 2017, *supra* note 3835 at 13 para 6.1–6.3; *See* v. Werder in: Commentary on the DCGK (2016), *supra* note 1030 at 1602–1612.

3845 *See* v. Werder in: Commentary on the DCGK (2016), *supra* note 1030 at 1929.

3846 The Grant Thornton Review 2016, *supra* note 3165 at 3.

The Corporate Governance Report 2015 shows a different picture.[3847] Based on 535 listed companies on the German stock exchanges, such as DAX, MDAX, TecDAX and SDAX, 109 listed companies were involved in the Corporate Governance Report 2015.[3848] One result of this Report was that 83.6 percent of these respondents comply with all of the recommendations in the German Code.[3849] Another result shows that the rate of compliance depends on the size of the company. The larger a company, the higher the probability that the company will comply with the recommendations of the Code.[3850]

Overall, it has been revealed that the acceptance of the comply or explain approach of the Codes as secondary law depends on the size of the company and the commitment governed by the provision. In conclusion, where the provision has been accompanied by higher legal obligations for companies, such as in the context of the German Corporation Law *e.g.* the German Stock Corporation Act (AktG), the rate of compliance will be higher. Finally, while the aim of corporate governance codes is to support companies in the form of guidance, in general terms, as to principles, structures and processes for reasonable corporate governance, is generally accepted, the effectiveness of the comply or explain approach remains questionable.

Thus, as has been shown, in response to high-profile criminal and bribery cases, increased regulatory pressure, the first court cases concerning compliance and a trend towards greater corporate governance with disclosure and transparency efforts in respect of shareholders and investors, companies listed on the stock exchanges are now required to consider adequate and proportionate compliance measures, which may also include a corporate compliance function. This development is similar to that in the US and the UK, the difference being that the enhanced implementation of the compliance officer took place a decade later in Germany. German companies have in the meantime developed a variety of organizational models for compliance measures and compliance departments based on the model of the US and the UK in accordance with the nature, size, and risk profile of their business.[3851] Within these compliance measures, it is favorable to establish a compliance function as a basic feature and to consider how the compliance officer communicates, interacts and collaborates with other business units. The role and

---

3847 *See* Axel v. Werder & Julia Turkali, *Corporate Governance Report 2015: Kodexakzeptanz und Kodexanwendung*, Der Betrieb 1357–1367 (2015) [hereinafter Corporate Governance Report 2015].

3848 Corporate Governance Report 2015 *Id.* at 1358.

3849 Corporate Governance Report 2015 *Id.* at 1359. Table 1.

3850 Corporate Governance Report 2015 *Id.* at 1359.

3851 *See e.g.* Cynthia A. Glassman, SEC Commissioner's Speech: Sarbanes-Oxley and the Idea of "Good" Governance (2002), https://www.sec.gov/news/speech/spch586.htm (last visited May 6, 2017); Study Compliance Mananger 2013 Herzog and Stephan (2013), *supra* note 476; Economic Crime and Corporate Culture 2013, *supra* note 3658.

responsibilities of the compliance function are not structured in the same way in all companies.[3852] Furthermore, the German corporate compliance officer is a young profession, which is still in the process of shaping its job tasks and responsibilities. As a result, it is challenging to present a model of the corporate compliance officer that fits all corporations. However, the much- discussed *obiter dictum* of the BGH has brought a major advance in the development of a more precise job profile in the literature, as well as in practice.[3853] Thus, new regulations in criminal law, guidance and recommendations in secondary law as well as the criminal case law concerning compliance breaches have led to the commissioning of corporate officers to support the management board in compliance matters.[3854]

C. The Model of the German Compliance Officer

This section now attempts to set out the corner-stones for a model of the German corporate compliance officer. First, it presents the findings from the development of the duties and responsibilities incumbent upon corporate compliance officers, before going on to describe the position and the integration within companies and the recommended standards for this profession using a dynamic model.

I. Development of Responsibilities and Duties of the Compliance Officer

First and foremost, corporate compliance and the compliance function have been enhanced and developed within listed companies in Germany over the course of the last ten years. In light of the examination this chapter, it is evident that German companies listed on stock exchanges are governed mainly by the provisions of the German Stock Corporation Act (AktG), the German Criminal Code (StGB), German Employment Law, the German Corporate Governance Code 2017, and German case- law, as well as by EU Directives and international law. It has been shown that this legal framework has had an increasingly large influence on day-to-day business within companies. Just as the legal framework has developed, corporate compliance and the compliance function have emerged, although there is no specific corporate law governing corporate compliance. In Germany, in the course of this development, there were many waves of corporate compliance issues in accordance with German Company Law, Criminal Law, the German Code 2017, and German case law concerning the extended compliance tasks and responsibilities of the management board. Considering Sections 91 (2),

3852 *See supra* A., IV., 3., p. 473.
3853 BGH, 17.7.2009 - 5 StR 394/08, BGHSt 54, 44; BGH NJW 2009, 3173, *supra* note 25.
3854 Aktiengesetz (AktG) | German Stock Corporation Act, *supra* note 976 § 91 (2); Strafgesetzbuch (StGB) | German Criminal Code, *supra* note 965 § 299 (1) (2); The German Code 2017, *supra* note 3835.

76 (1) of the German Stock Corporation Act (AktG) and the recent decisions of the Munich Courts, such as in the *Siemens* case, there is an overall responsibility for the management board to establish an effective monitoring system to prevent criminal conduct by the company.[3855] This key task of the management board encompasses the legal duty to document this system, to define clear responsibilities within this system, to specifically determine reporting lines within this system, to define appropriate measures, to implement these measures and to supervise their implementation.[3856] In order to limit their liability, the members of the management board can transfer certain compliance tasks to another corporate function without surrendering their ultimate supervisory responsibility.[3857] Hence, without explicit legal regulation relating to the commissioning of or the tasks of the compliance officer, this corporate position has evolved to take account of the competencies in the context of the tasks resulting from the response to the requirements of shareholders and investors. Furthermore, owing to the *obiter dictum* of the BGH and the subsequent academic focus on the liability of the compliance officer, the view of this profession has changed from that of a watchdog to an adviser to an active contributor within compliance measures. As previously examined, the scope of the compliance officer's tasks may be broad, but he should limit his own areas of responsibility.[3858] The compliance officer should be a central corporate interface for compliance with an involvement in reporting lines, access to information and cooperation with other business units. However, the priority of the compliance officer's tasks depends on the risk assessment of the corporate business. Thus, this position demands high-profile experts with excellent professional and interpersonal skills.

Secondly, the German debate on this corporate function has been limited and focused mainly on the compliance officer's liability. As a result, the academic discussion and perspective has been more limited than in the US.[3859] There is a need for a more comprehensive and forward-thinking consideration of the compliance officer function in the context of the specific circumstances of the company. The emphasis in the US and in the UK focused more on the integration of the compliance officer's function as a business partner; on his sufficient seniority, authority, time and adequate resources; on cooperation with other functions to ensure greater awareness of business risks; on the consideration of strategic and operational issues that affect the business the compliance officer serves, and on the further development of

3855 *See supra* A., II., pp. 415 et seq.

3856 *See supra* A., pp. 415 et seq.

3857 *See supra* A., II. 2. p. 433; *Compare* In the US, the *"CEO cannot delegate his or her ultimate responsibility, to fully carry out the mandate of Sarbanes-Oxley and the Commission's rules." See in:* SEC Commissioner's Speech, Glassman, *supra* note 3851.

3858 *See supra* A., IV.,3., p. 473.

3859 *See supra* A., III., IV. pp. 437 et seq.

this function.[3860] In Germany, the focus was on the area of responsibilities of this function and whether there is any protection against liability. Recently, the debate has shifted to the compliance officer as a recognized complex profession and as an executive manager, who is involved in the development of the compliance strategy and business processes.[3861] Since then, it has been recognized that the compliance officer has significant responsibility for preventing misconduct by managers and employees on the basis of adequate resources and powers.[3862] In order to properly fulfil this responsibility, the compliance officer should be aware of the extent of the tasks delegated from the management board. He should set his focus on a clear job description or a specified area of compliance tasks in the employment contract.[3863] Only in this way can he properly assess his risks and liability.

Thirdly, under German Employment Law the position of the corporate compliance officer was discussed in chapter five.[3864] We can state that, in Germany, the compliance officer as a rule is a full-time or part-time employee. As a result, he is first of all an ordinary employee under employment law, but relating to the compliance tasks transferred from the management board, it could be argued that he is an employee with a higher risk assumption than other ordinary employees. Thus, the compliance officer has a special position within companies. Additionally, it has been noted that, unlike other corporate functions, such as the data protection officer, the post of corporate compliance officer is not legally defined. For this reason, he does not enjoy any separate protection against dismissal. However, as an employee, he is covered under employment protection law.[3865] In addition, in recent years, in addition to directors or members of the boards, D&O insurance policies can also be taken out for additional groups of persons, such as employees with specific risk exposure.[3866] However, the conditions of insurance should be examined carefully to establish whether the policy covers financial losses from compliance risks.[3867] It is recommended that the function of the compliance officer should be

---

3860 *See e.g.* PwC Study 2015, *supra* note 1771 at 4; Trends in compliance organizational structures 3 (2016).

3861 *See e.g.* Study Compliance Manager 2013, *supra* note 502 at 1; Dann and Mengel (2010), *supra* note 30 at 3266; *See* Georg Gösswein, *Die Führungskräfte im Zentrum eines funktionierenden Compliance Management Systems*, CCZ 43–45 (2017); Moosmayer (2012), *supra* note 473 at 3015; Schulz and Renz (2012), *supra* note 41 at 2514; Schulz and Galster (2015), § 4 Aufgaben im Unternehmen, *supra* note 3379 at 88–90 at 36–40.

3862 *See supra* A., IV., 3. p. 473.

3863 *See supra* A., IV., 6. p. 480.

3864 *See generally* the discussions in A., IV., p. 467.

3865 *See supra* A., IV., 5., p. 478.

3866 *See* Koch in: § 14 Versicherungsschutz für Compliance Officer, *in* Der Compliance Officer: ein Handbuch in eigener Sache 343–364, 354 (Jürgen Bürkle & Christoph E. Hauschka eds., 1. ed. 2015) at 55.

3867 *See* Koch in: *Id.* at 353. at 52.

expressly included in the insured corporate persons.[3868] The requirements of the insurance cover for the compliance officer should be stipulated in the contract of employment.[3869]

In conclusion, in line with the increased importance of compliant behavior of companies, the management board is now more involved in compliance tasks and, thus, employees commissioned exclusively with compliance tasks have emerged. These employees *e.g.* compliance officers, have developed their own self-conception of compliance. Through the enhanced legal environment with respect to compliance and the statements of the courts concerning corporate practice, the compliance officer has evolved into an established position with a number of special characteristics. As we have seen, compliance measures need to be effective. For this reason, the compliance officer's work relies on cooperation and access to relevant information from other business units. Only with a well-founded understanding of the business can the compliance officer conduct a risk analysis and advise on the risks specific to the business.

In the meantime, professional associations and professional networks have been also established in Germany, such as the Compliance Network e.V. with experts groups, the German Federal Association of Compliance Officers (BDCO) and the Professional Association of Compliance Managers (BCM).[3870] Hence, the first attempts to develop guidelines for this profession are already underway.

II. The Model of the Corporate Compliance Officer in Germany

Owing to the importance of compliant behavior by companies and the specific characteristics of the compliance officer, the compliance function has a special significance within the organizational structure. Firstly, in practice, this function is often connected with the management board, for example as a staff function, which reports directly to the board.[3871] As confirmed by the Study Compliance Manager 2013, compliance is a high-level function.[3872] According to the findings of that study, approximately 8 percent of compliance is allocated to the management board, 39 percent is assigned as a staff function, 22 percent is integrated as decentralized compliance departments under the top level line, 10 percent is

---

3868 *See* Koch in: *Id.* at 355. at 55.

3869 *See* Koch in: *Id.* at 356. at 58.

3870 *See e.g.* BCM | Professional Association of Compliance Manager, https://www.bvdcm.de/ (last visited May 8, 2017); BDCO | German Federal Association of Compliance Officers, 3GRC, https://www.3grc.de/ (last visited May 8, 2017); Compliance Network e.V., http://www.netzwerk-compliance.de/netzwerk-compliance-ev.html (last visited May 8, 2017).

3871 *See* Moosmayer (2015), *supra* note 1062 at 107.

3872 Compliance Manager Study 2013 Herzog and Stephan (2013), *supra* note 476 at 135.

allocated to other business units on the same level and only 6 percent is integrated into other business units.[3873]

According to the findings, *Bürkle* presents an organizational model of the establishment of the compliance officer in the context of the commissioning by the management board within medium-sized companies, which is also applicable to small or large companies.[3874] He shows three corporate levels as components of a commissioned compliance system: (a) level 1: the management board, (b) level 2: the central commissioned compliance function and (c) level 3: the decentralized commissioned compliance function.[3875] According to this organizational model, the first level comprises the management board as the top corporate level responsible for the implementation of compliance measures, for example by means of a commissioned system.[3876] Thus, the board performs its legal duty or compliance task.[3877] Nevertheless, the board remains responsible for the supervision, monitoring and further development of this system.[3878] In addition, as previously examined, the board can exercise its duties within organizational powers of discretion.[3879] However, this discretion is limited by recognized standards or the recommendations of the German Code 2017.[3880] Since April 2017, the amended Code Section 4.1.3 has provided that the management board has to *"publish the basic features of the proportionate compliance management system in the annual corporate governance report."*[3881] Therefore, the German academic debate is set to continue on the questions of which are the basic features and what the term proportionate means? In the course of this debate, further standards for the board's discretion are likely to develop. The organizational model of a commissioned compliance system as put forward by *Bürkle* placed the centrally commissioned compliance officer on the second corporate level; his task is to act as an interface or a switching point with his reporting, advising, monitoring tasks and documentation duties.[3882] The third corporate level encompasses the decentralized compliance officers who are responsible within the relevant legal provisions and within cross-disciplinary areas such as data protection.[3883] For example, the head of this

---

3873 Compliance Manager Study 2013 *Id.* at 136. fig. 4.01.
3874 *See* Bürkle in: § 36. Compliance-Beauftragten-System, *supra* note 3669 at 7–9.
3875 *See* Bürkle in: *Id.* at 11–65.
3876 *See* Bürkle in: *Id.* at 11.
3877 Aktiengesetz (AktG) | German Stock Corporation Act, *supra* note 976 § 76 (1), 91 (2); The German Code 2017, *supra* note 3835 para 4.1.3.
3878 *See* Bürkle in: § 36. Compliance-Beauftragten-System, *supra* note 3669 at 11.
3879 *See* Bürkle in: *Id.* at 11.
3880 *See* Bürkle in: *Id.* at 18.; IDW, *supra* note 3773; The German Code 2017, *supra* note 3835 para 4.1.3.
3881 The German Code 2017, *supra* note 3835 para 4.1.3.
3882 *See* Bürkle in: § 36. Compliance-Beauftragten-System, *supra* note 3669 at 33–44.
3883 *See* Bürkle in: *Id.* at 58.

business department could be involved in compliance tasks.[3884] The main key tasks of these compliance officers include the risk analysis of the business by means of due diligence.[3885] Finally, in the context of this model, the commissioned compliance function can operate within cross-disciplinary areas, as well as in business departments.

This commissioned compliance system put forward by *Bürkle* can be summarized into two corporate tiers: (a) the top level – the management board, and (b) the corporate high level – the compliance department with a compliance officer. In practice, a compliance department is often commissioned by members of the management board to carry out the compliance tasks.[3886] The compliance department is headed by a chief compliance officer, who delegates certain compliance tasks to another compliance function, such as a compliance officer in other business units.[3887]

In conclusion, there are various different organizational models in corporate practice due to the organizational discretion of the management board and the specific needs of individual companies.[3888] The compliance organization chart below presents a dynamic model of the German corporate compliance officer that can be flexibly integrated into large or small-medium sized companies as the management board may be replaced through the principal, namely the owner of a company.

3884 *See* Bürkle in: *Id.* at 59–61.

3885 *See* Bürkle in: *Id.* at 62.

3886 *See e.g.* Schulz and Galster (2015), § 4 Aufgaben im Unternehmen, *supra* note 3379 at 2; Gross (2012), *supra* note 42 at 61; Moosmayer (2015), *supra* note 1062 at 106–107.

3887 *See* Schulz and Galster (2015), § 4 Aufgaben im Unternehmen, *supra* note 3379 at 2.

3888 *See e.g.* Schulz and Galster (2015) *Id.* at 2.; Bürkle in: § 36. Compliance-Beauftragten-System, *supra* note 3669; Moosmayer (2015), *supra* note 1062 at 106–107.

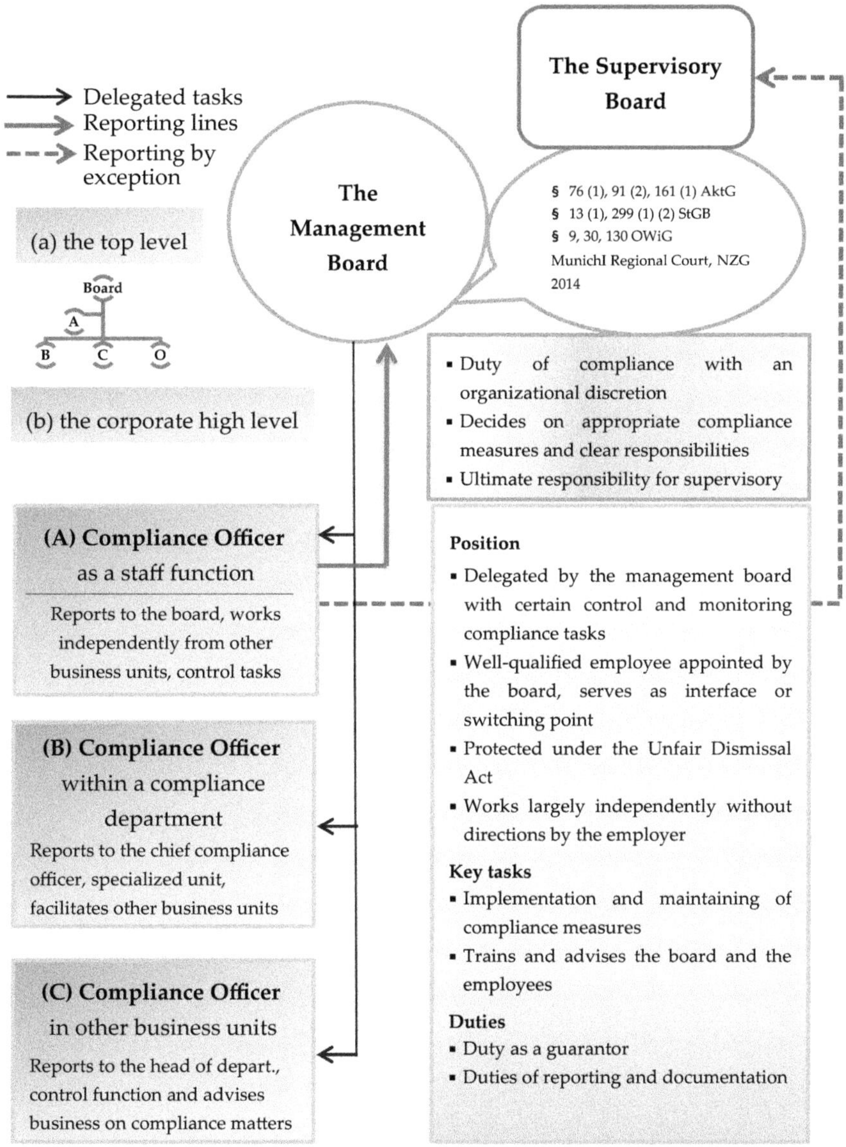

Figure 14 *Compliance Organization Chart – The Model of the German Compliance Officer*

The Model of the German Corporate Compliance Officer

Abstract
This chapter compares and summarizes the findings of the American, UK, and German corporate compliance officer under company, bribery, criminal, and employment law. This book has attempted to analyze the legal framework applicable to corporate compliance and the compliance function affording due consideration to the financial services sector in the case that relevant rules are absent. The knowledge of differences and similarities between the common law and civil law systems, the legal roots, and cultural background have contributed to a better understanding of the specific primary and secondary law concerning compliance and the corporate function that has developed in the US, the UK, and in Germany. The findings have shown that the emergence and the impact of the corporate compliance officer's function on compliant behavior of companies depends greatly on an enhanced legal environment. This book also examined the literature on corporate compliance, the role of the corporate compliance officer, the importance of the legal framework and the related case law; based on this, it framed three models of the corporate compliance officer in the US, UK and Germany. This last chapter will propose a dynamic model of the corporate compliance officer by identifying, evaluating and summarizing the special features of the three models presented in chapters three to five.

A. Comparison between the American, UK and German Legal Framework Pertaining to Compliance and the Corporate Compliance Officer

The overall findings of this book have provided consistent confirmation that recent legal developments have led to the strengthened emergence of the position of corporate compliance officer. Despite this fact, the post of corporate compliance officer is not enshrined in either American Corporation Law, or in UK, and German Company Law. In the course of this book, the results have demonstrated that the original sources of compliance originated from the financial-services sector in the context of the first UK Act in 1697 to limit the unfair practices of brokers and stock-jobbers. In response to the industrial revolution in the 19th century, preventative measures in the form of compliance measures gradually developed and were incorporated into UK Company Law. Furthermore, another source of compliance provisions was developed as a system of self-regulation within companies. This concept of compliance emerged in the private sector at the beginning of the 19th century as a key element of self-regulation within firms in America. In contrast to the development of compliance in the US and UK, the initial starting point for German compliance emerged late, as somewhat of an aside to the debate on corporate governance in the 1990s. Since then, a number of high-profile corporate scandals have focused attention on corporate compliance in Germany. In consequence, it can be argued that corporate compliance has no original source in Germany, and is instead a result of the globalization of economic transactions, growing economic pressure, and increasingly complex international legal norms and regulations, all of which have led to growing public awareness of compliant corporate behavior in Germany.

Following this, it is clear that the German compliance function was established comparatively late compared with American and UK corporate compliance officers. Financial services sector legislation first required the appointment of a compliance officer as a permanent and independent compliance function in 1994. The establishment of the post of corporate compliance officer came in the aftermath of a number of high-profile corporate scandals in the context of the enhancement of the regulatory reform of company law. Similar to the way the compliance officer's functions developed in Germany, in the UK, the compliance function originated from the Financial Services Act. However, the emergence of the compliance function in the English private sector has no legal origins. As a result of the bankruptcy of Maxwell Communication and its massive financial irregularities in 1991, the focus on corporate governance, reforms of English Company Law, and the growing influence of investors, in particular on listed firms, companies in the UK began to appoint key personnel or high-level personnel to perform a compliance function and oversee business risks. The very first ethics and compliance officers can be traced back to the Watergate scandal in the US. In the early days of this function, responsibility for compliance was incumbent upon legal departments, more recently, it has been recognized that an effective compliance officer works independently and as a separate function. While, even in the US, there are no legal requirements in primary law to establish a corporate function overall for concerning compliance, the American SEC and DOJ, for example, provide guidance on compliance functions within corporations in their Principles of Federal Prosecution of Business Organizations by means of DPAs. The following timeline outlines in chronological order the enhanced emergence of the compliance function within the legal framework:

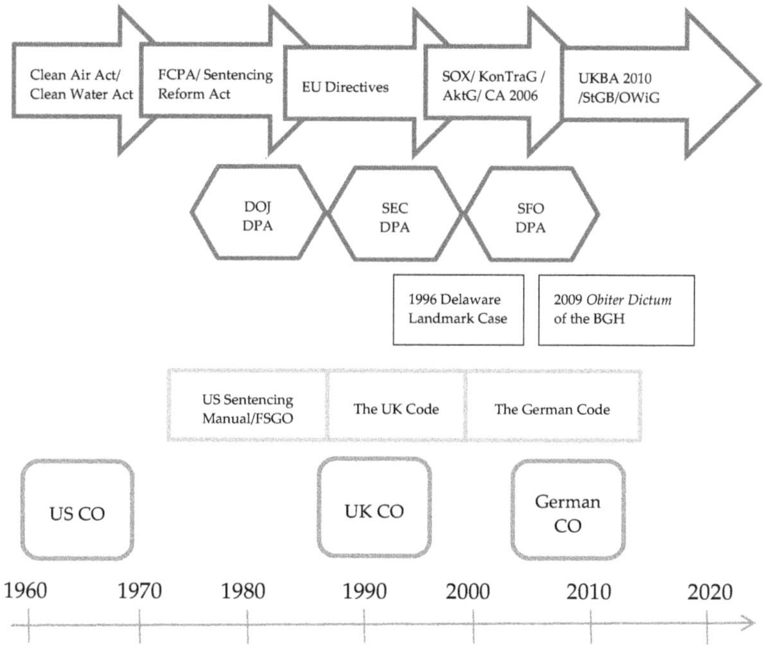

Figure 15 *Timeline of the Enhanced Emergence of the Compliance Officer*

This timeline illustrates that the emergence of the corporate compliance officer is connected to the subsequent enhanced regulatory framework, enhanced prosecution of corporate crimes, and greater focus by courts on compliance issues. Despite the absence of specific provisions governing the compliance officer in company law and bribery legislation in the US, UK and Germany, the findings of this book have demonstrated that, in order to ensure compliant behavior of companies, the regulatory framework has introduced more stringent requirements for companies, which have been reflected in the development of corporate compliance and the compliance function.

I. Comparison of the Duties of Compliance Officers under Company Law

This book has examined the duties of directors and compliance officers within listed companies under US, UK and German company law.[3889] One major

3889 *See generally* Ch. 3, A., I. p. 176, II., p. 254, B. p. 287; Ch. 4, A., II., p. 327; Ch. 5 A., II., p. 423.

difference lies in the structure of company law. American State Corporation Law is decentralized and has been significantly influenced by common law principles and the provisions governing the legal duties of directors and officers as enshrined in Delaware State Corporation Law. By contrast, UK and German Company Law takes the form of a uniform codified body of law that includes the duties of directors and officers, or the management and supervisory board. Secondly, as we have seen, board structures in the US and UK differ from the German board structure.[3890] The US and UK board structure is referred to as a one-tier or unitary board, while the German board comprises the members of both the management and the supervisory board and, hence, is referred to as the two-tier model.[3891] The one-tier board consists of a chief executive officer (CEO), a chairman, the executive directors, and the independent directors. Under Delaware Corporation Law, the shareholders have the right to elect the directors.[3892] A director is a natural person officially appointed in accordance with the company's articles or bylaws. The directors are responsible for governing and overseeing the business and affairs of the corporation.[3893] In Germany, the members of the management board are appointed by the supervisory board.[3894] The management board comprises executive directors, responsible *inter alia* for the objectives of the company and the implementation of appropriate compliance measures; the supervisory board consists of non-executive directors, whose tasks is to monitor the decisions of the management board.[3895]

The nature of the director's role is central to Corporation Law in the US and in the UK. Under common law, directors are considered to be fiduciaries, who owe certain duties to the company. These duties encompass three major fiduciary duties: (1) the duty of due care, (2) good faith, and (3) loyalty. Since 1996, it has been recognized that the landmark *Caremark* case developed a new duty of oversight or compliance duty for directors.[3896] In the UK and in Germany, the general duties of company directors or members of the management board are enshrined in law.[3897] Overall, the findings have shown that, over the last thirty years, the duties of directors have been enforced through case law in the US,

3890 *See supra* Ch. 3, A., II., p. 254, Ch. 4, B., I., p. 396, Ch. 5, A., footnote 3249, p. 417.
3891 *See supra* footnotes 1387, 1388, p. 204.
3892 *See supra* footnote 2094, p. 289; tit. 8 DELAWARE CODE, *supra* note 24 § 211 (b).
3893 *See supra* Ch. 3, B., p. 287; tit. 8 *Id.* § 141 (a).
3894 *See supra* Ch. 5, A., p. 415.
3895 *See supra* Ch. 5, A., p. 415; AKTIENGESETZ (AKTG) | GERMAN STOCK CORPORATION ACT, *supra* note 976 §§ 76 (1), 91 (2), 111 (1).
3896 *See supra* Ch. 3, A., II., a. i.-iii., p. 262. *In re Caremark International Inc. Derivative Litigation*, 698 A.2D 959 (DEL. CH. 1996), *supra* note 21.
3897 *Compare* Ch. 4, A., II., 2., p. 332; Ch. 5, A., II., p. 423; AKTIENGESETZ (AKTG) | GERMAN STOCK CORPORATION ACT, *supra* note 976 §§ 76 (1), 91 (2), 93 (1); COMPANIES ACT 2006, *supra* note 532 §§ 171–177.

through codification of common law and the inclusion of equitable principles in company law in the UK, and through the amendment of existing company law provisions in Germany.[3898]

Under both common law and civil law, directors are authorized to delegate certain tasks *e.g.* compliance tasks, to committees or corporate officers. The directors must exercise due care during the selection and transfer process.[3899] However, the ultimate responsibility and the task the board is required by statute or bylaws to perform, must remain with the members of the board.[3900] Nevertheless, in practice, responsibility for the company's compliant behavior is a comprehensive task. This is why executive directors attempt to share their responsibility for compliance by commissioning corporate officers. Corporate officers are appointed by the board of directors in accordance with the bylaws. The corporate officers include a president, vice-president, a secretary or a treasurer, as well as other officers. Thus, corporate officers also include the compliance officer. In the US, the courts tend to refer to key employees. US State Corporation Law does not make any clear distinction between the fiduciary duties of corporate directors and those of corporate officers. However, US case law clearly states that the "*fiduciary duties of officers are the same as those of directors.*"[3901] The UK legislator also applies the directors' duties to company officers.[3902] Hence, in general, the legal duties of directors also apply to corporate officers. In Germany, the duties of corporate officers are not stipulated in company law. The compliance officer is assigned duties by means of the delegation of tasks *e.g.* certain compliance tasks, by the management board. Thus, the compliance officer assumes a limited area of responsibility for the management of compliance procedures within the corporation.[3903] The following table provides a comparative overview of the duties of directors and compliance officers under company law in the US, UK and Germany:

3898 *Compare* Ch. 3, A., II., a. i.-iii., p. 262; Ch. 4, A., II., 2., p. 332; Ch. 5, A., II., p. 423; *In re Caremark International Inc. Derivative Litigation*, 698 A.2D 959 (DEL. CH. 1996), *supra* note 21; *Stone v. Ritter*, 911 A.2d 362 (Del. 2006), *supra* note 196; AKTIENGESETZ (AKTG) | GERMAN STOCK CORPORATION ACT, *supra* note 976 § 91 (2); COMPANIES ACT 2006, *supra* note 532 §§ 171–177.

3899 *See e.g.* tit. 8 DELAWARE CODE, *supra* note 24 § 141 (e).

3900 *Compare* Ch. 5; C., I., p. 493; *In re Walt Disney Co. Derivative Litig.*, (Del. Ch. 2004), *supra* note 1816; LG München I, 10.12.2013 - 5 HK O 1387/10, NZG 2014, *supra* note 973 at 347–348.

3901 *See supra* Ch. 3, A., II., c., p. 270.

3902 *See supra* Ch. 4, A., II., 3.a., p. 338.

3903 *See supra* Ch. 5, A., II., 2., p. 433.

Table 20 *Comparative Overview of the Duties of Compliance Officers under Company Law*

	US State Corporation Law, Case- Law	**UK Company Act 2006**	**German Stock Corporation Act (AktG)**
Structure of the Board	One-tier board	One-tier board	Two-tiers – the management board and the supervisory board
Members of the Board	Executive and independent directors	Executive and independent directors	Executive and non-executive directors
Duties of directors enshrined in law	Duties are conferred and provided in the certificate of incorporation, good faith requirement	General duties such as to act within powers, to exercise reasonable care, skill and diligence	To take appriopriate measures for risk prevention, duty of reasonable care of a diligent manager
Statutory provisions	Tit. 8 Delaware Code § 141 (a) (e)	CA 2006 Sections 171–177; Section 1121 (2)	AktG §§ 76 (1), 91 (2), 93 (1)
Common law principles and civil case law	Fiduciary duties owed to the corporation and its shareholders, (1) duty of good faith, (2) duty of loyalty, (3) duty of care, (4) duty of oversight	Fiduciary duties owed to the corporation and its shareholders, (1) duty of good faith, (2) duty of loyalty, (3) duty to act in accordance with the company's constitution	Ultimate responsibility for compliance *e.g.* the organizational and supervisory responsibilities of the management board
Cases	*Caremark, Stone v Ritter, Gantler v Stephen*	*Mothew v Bristol & West Building Society Respondent*	*LG München I, 10.12.2013 - 5 HK O 1387/10.*
Corporate Officers	Directors' duties also apply to officers and thus, to the compliance officer	Directors' duties also apply to officers and thus, to the compliance officer	The compliance officer is assigned a limited area of compliance responsibility through delegation.

In conclusion, it can be argued that English company law clearly stipulates that a corporate officer in default is considered to be and treated like a director for the purposes of the Companies Act. By contrast, US State Corporation Law does not clearly determine who is an officer and what his duties are. However, the case law has stated that the corporate officers owe the same duties to the company as the directors. In Germany, the officer's area of responsibility is limited through the scope of delegation by the members of the board and by the rules and principles set down in the case law. The officer's duties are not enshrined into law. It follows that the scope of the German compliance officer's responsibility is limited compared to the US and UK compliance officers, who have the same duties as directors. Overall, the legal framework of US, UK and German company law provides for the enforcement of compliance duties vis-à-vis directors and officers through a mixture of legislation, case law, and bylaws.

II. The Compliance Officer Compared under Bribery and Criminal Law

Taking account of the anti-corruption and criminal law as analyzed in chapters three to five, it can be argued that bribery legislation and provisions in criminal law have largely developed to protect investors in response to corporate bribery and misleading corporate disclosure. This book has identified continuous legal enforcement with a global impact regarding compliance at the beginning of the 19th century through the enhancement of the US Federal Law on bribery and fraud, in particular the FCPA legislation in 1977; a series of UK fraud and bribery legislation preceding the enactment of the UK Bribery Act in 2010; and certain provisions pertaining to bribery in German criminal law.[3904] While this book has presented only a small selection and excerpt of regulations and criminal statutes that are relevant to the corporate compliance officer, this section attempts to show the impact of this global regulatory framework on the position of compliance officer.

The first obvious difference between the US, UK and German bribery and criminal law is the control of the corporate adherence to the law by regulators or prosecutors in the US and in the UK. US regulators, like the DOJ and SEC, and UK law enforcement agencies such as the SFO and the financial regulator, FCA, which controls for bribery among the regulated institutions, have been developed as regulators and prosecutors in order to combat corporate bribery and fraud. For example, the SFO is authorized to bring actions against companies and individuals like compliance officers concerning fraudulent trading or bribery under the UKBA 2010. The authority of these regulators and prosecutors is far-reaching. Beyond the courtrooms, they are involved in rule-making, are authorized to bring enforcement actions against companies, executive directors or officers, to conduct corporate internal investigations, to compel disclosure of information and documents, and

3904 *See generally* Ch. 3, A., I., 1.- 4.; Ch. 4, A., III., 1.- 4.; Ch. 5. A., III., 1.- 6.

even to obtain evidence abroad, as well as to resolve cases through deferred prosecution agreements (DPAs) with the prosecuted company. In view of the regulator's activities in the context of DPAs concerning the implementation of compliance structures or a compliance function within the prosecuted company, it is clear that these have the power to alter corporate structures. Although such a regulator or prosecutor regime is absent from the private sector in Germany, German companies listed on the US and UK stock exchanges or trading in the UK are required to comply with certain provisions of the FCPA, SOX, and the UKBA. Chapters three to five revealed that German companies or officers were also prosecuted in the US and in the UK, prompting German companies to adapt their corporate structures. This evidence suggests that the enhanced emergence and the increase in numbers of corporate compliance officers were the result of the enforcement of bribery and criminal statutory regulations and requirements of the regulators and prosecutors.

The second distinct difference between the US, UK and German bribery and criminal law is its scope of application. The common law principles contain two kinds of corporate criminal liability, as discussed in chapters three and four:[3905] It is possible to prosecute (1) the company, and (2) the individual who committed an offence. In the first instance, a company is held liable for strict liability offences, vicarious liability, imposed by statutes in the areas of criminal law. Secondly, however, as regards serious offences the identification principle applies to the individual who was the *'directing mind and will'* of the company.[3906] Generally, this will be the senior officers of a company. However, over the years, these two common law principles have gradually altered. For example, several statutes governing business crime law, such as the Fraud Act 2006 or the UKBA 2010, provide an exception to the common law principles since the individual guilty of a bribery offence can be convicted separately without the company.[3907] In the US, the DOJ has recently shifted in a new direction and now refers to individual accountability in matters of corporate wrongdoing, because the threshold for prosecuting corporate criminal liability is higher than for prosecuting an individual.[3908] German bribery and criminal law generally applies to individuals with individuals who are held liable based on breaches of their legal duties.[3909] As examined in chapter five, under German Criminal Law the individual is even viewed as a guarantor in the event of any failure to act.[3910] Individuals convicted of bribery offences can be imprisoned or receive a fine. There is one exception: Under Section 30, 130 of the

3905 *See generally* Ch. 3, A. I., p. 176; Ch. 4., A., II., 4., p. 343.
3906 *See supra* Ch. 4, A., II., 4., p. 343.
3907 *See supra* Ch. 4, A., III., p. 353; FRAUD ACT 2006, c. 35 (2006) §§ 1, 2, 3, 4; THEFT ACT 1968, *supra* note 2867 §§ 17, 18, 19; UNITED KINGDOM BRIBERY ACT 2010, *supra* note 433 §§ 1, 2, 6, 11.
3908 *See supra* Ch. 3, A., I.e., p. 207.
3909 *See generally* Ch. 5, A., III., 4., p. 449.
3910 *See supra* Ch. 5, A., III., 4., p. 449.

Act on Regulatory Offences (OWiG), the owner of a company could be fined for intentional or negligent failure to carry out the supervisory measures required to prevent contraventions.[3911]

Another major difference between the US, UK and German bribery and criminal law lies in extra-territorial jurisdiction. Bribery law in the UK has a more wide-ranging scope than the FCPA since its extra-territorial jurisdiction for a commercial organization is clearly enshrined in the law.[3912] This legislation now covers every company that does business in the UK. Conversely, US extra-territorial jurisdiction is not explicitly enshrined in federal law and, thus, depends in particular on the wording of the legislative intent and the competence of the US Courts. In Germany, the principle of territoriality is recognized under criminal law.[3913] As a result, German criminal law will apply to all crimes committed by all individuals within the national territory, regardless of their citizenship. In contrast, its application to non-German companies is not explicitly defined, but Section 30 of the Act on Regulatory Offences (OWiG) could also apply to foreign companies in the event of the commission of a criminal offence.

The next difference lies in the structure of the US, UK and German bribery and criminal law. Compared with American and English bribery law, German bribery law appears small and insignificant. Unlike the US and the UK, Germany has no separate bribery statute, and currently governs this issue by means of amended provisions in the German Criminal Code and in the Act on Regulatory Offences.[3914] As mentioned previously, another inadequacy is the absence of German bribery guidelines for companies. For this reason, companies and the compliance officer in particular need, first and foremost, to refer to the court decisions that deal with compliance issues in individual cases. Consequently, it is difficult for the German compliance officer to assess which appropriate measure should be taken in order to prevent corporate misconduct. Despite this lean German bribery law, in an *obiter dictum, the* BGH considered the issue of when a corporate compliance officer faces criminal liability.[3915]

The possibilities for corporate defense also differ. In contrast to the FCPA and to German bribery law, the UKBA 2010 provides a defense pursuant to Section 7 for companies able to prove that they have in place an adequate procedure, such as a compliance program.[3916] This adequate procedure is described in the UK Bribery Guidance. As previously examined, similar to the FCPA Resource Guide, the UK Bribery Guidance contains helpful information and recommendations to companies in the form of six principles, including a commitment from the senior management, the risk assessment, a due diligence and communication and

3911 *See supra* Ch. 5, A., III., 5., p. 456.
3912 *See supra* Ch. 4, A., III., 1., p. 355.
3913 *Compare* STRAFGESETZBUCH (STGB) | GERMAN CRIMINAL CODE, *supra* note 965 § 3.
3914 *See generally* Ch. 5, A., III., pp. 437 et seq.
3915 *See supra* Ch. 5, A., III., 4.a., p. 451.
3916 *See supra* Ch. 4, A., III., 1., p. 355.

training, as well as other principles designed to prevent bribery.[3917] For example, the FCPA Resource Guide suggests the following measures: a clearly articulated policy against corruption, communicated by the management by means of a code of conduct and compliance policies and procedures; conducting a risk assessment of relevant business risks; carrying out training and continuing advice on anti-bribery regulations; implementing a compliance program with incentives and disciplinary measures; conducting third-party due diligence and payments; designing anti-bribery contract terms; and the ongoing monitoring and review of business risks.[3918] Therefore, in both the US and in the UK, companies are guided by recommendations relating to the relevant legislation and its application. Additionally, in the US, the FSGO, considered to be an advisory guideline system, requires that high-level personnel of the organization must ensure that the organization has an effective compliance program. By having an effective compliance program in place, companies may be able to mitigate criminal penalties in the event of prosecution for bribery or fraud. In line with this program, the FSGO require that *"specific individual(s) within the organization shall be delegated day-to-day operational responsibility for the compliance program."*[3919] This need demonstrates the importance of the compliance function and illustrates the key role played by the compliance officer, who is responsible for the implementation and maintenance of the compliance program and other preventative measures to ensure adherence with the law by managers and employees. The German counterpart is a provision in the German Stock Corporation Act (AktG). Section 91 (2) comprises the duty of the management board to implement appropriate measures regarding the early prevention of risks.[3920] However, Germany has no helpful guidance or advisory system on the implementation of appropriate measures in accordance with the legal requirements. The German legislator and legal scholars emphasize the size, nature, scale and complexity of the business risks subject to which a company operates.[3921]

The regulatory environment presented in this book has shown that new bribery and criminal laws place new legal responsibilities upon companies and their directors and officers. On the basis of the strong regulation and enforcement actions by regulators and prosecutors, companies are continuing to develop and expand their compliance procedures. In view of the legal requirements of the SOX, directors and officers should periodically review compliance policies and procedures; maintain disclosure controls and procedures, ensure internal control over financial reporting; file an annual report, increase the legal, accounting, financial and

3917 *See supra* Ch. 4, A., III., 1., p. 355.
3918 *See generally* Ch. 3, A., I., 1.a., p. 178; Ch. 4, A., III., 4., Table 14, p. 370.
3919 *See supra* Ch. 3, A., I., 3.b., p. 239.
3920 *See supra* Ch. 5, A., II., 1., p. 424.
3921 *See supra* Ch. 5, A., II., p. 423.

communication skills of the compliance officer; and oversee reporting deadlines.[3922] The compliance officer should provide information on compliance issues to the board via a clearly defined reporting line and maintain a good relationship with the regulators. Due to the required shift and enforced responsibilities of executive officers in accordance with the SOX, there ought to be a separation of the legal and compliance department within corporations.[3923]

Although the scope of application, the structure and the enforcement of US, UK, and German bribery and criminal law differ, the responsibilities and duties of the corporate compliance officers in all three systems are similar. The key compliance tasks and responsibilities first and foremost encompass, the assessment of business risks and, next, the implementation and maintenance of appropriate measures or proportionate procedures, such as a compliance program, commensurate to the bribery and business risks facing the company. Secondly, the tasks also encompass the provision of employee training and advice on these measures and procedures, as well as the periodic review and monitoring of those measures and procedures. Thirdly, under US and UK bribery law, the required compliance officer's due diligence analysis of third parties - such as contracting parties, agents and employees - plays a greater role than under German bribery and criminal law. There are also some differences as regards the scope of their tasks of the US, UK, and German compliance officers. In the US and in the UK, the compliance officer has to diplomatically deal with the regulator or prosecutor. The next major difference examined here is the limited area of responsibility of the German compliance officer. In practice, it could be that the German compliance officer is responsible only for a specific area of law. In contrast to this limited responsibility, the US or UK corporate compliance officer can have the same duties as the director. In detail, this means that the entire duty of oversight could apply to the compliance officer as an executive officer. However, an examination of the relevant case law with respect to the compliance officer in the US, UK, and in Germany, as discussed in chapters three to five, has revealed that despite the SEC actions against compliance officers in the financial services sector and the *obiter dictum* of the BGH, thus far, there has not been any case against a corporate compliance officer for breach of a legal duty under bribery and criminal law either in the US, in the UK or in Germany. As a result, it can be argued that even with the differences between the US, UK, and German bribery and criminal law and some differences in their scope of responsibilities, the key tasks and duties remain similar.

The chart presented at the end of this section provides an overview of the selected global regulatory influence on the corporate compliance officer's position and his responsibility under US, UK, and German bribery and criminal law as examined in this book The regulatory overview shown in this section applies to corporate compliance officers within companies that do business in the US,

3922 *See supra* Ch. 3, A., I., 2., p. 215.
3923 *See supra* Ch. 3, A., I., 2. e., p. 226.

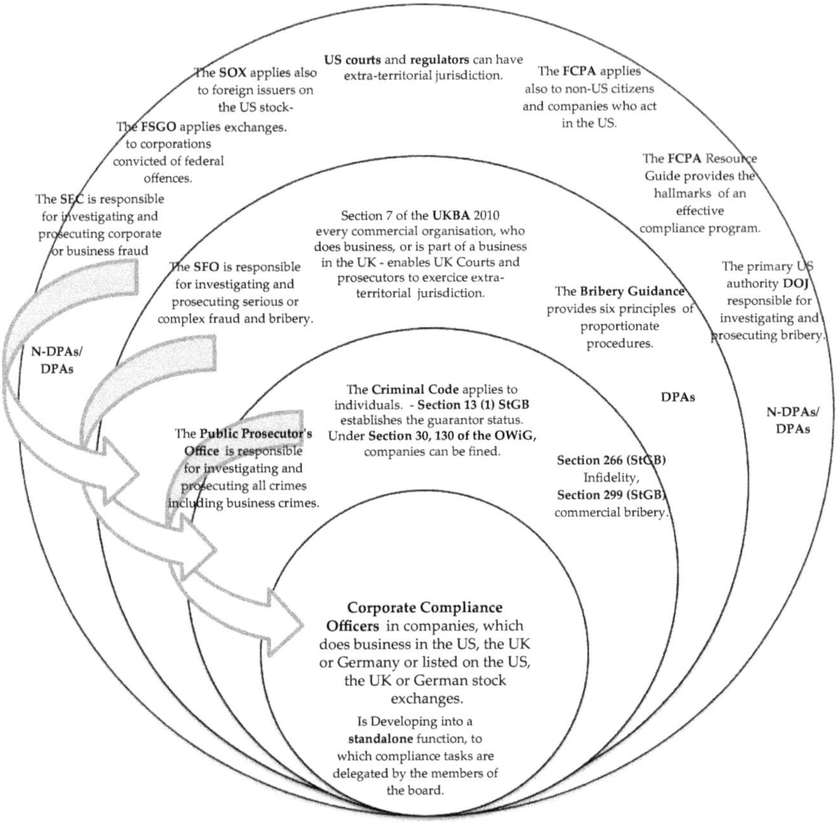

Figure 16 *The Compliance Officer Compared under US, UK, and German Bribery and Criminal Law*

the UK or in Germany, or are listed on the US, UK or German stock exchanges. In conclusion, the legal framework of bribery and criminal statutes or specific provisions thereof, the guidance on the law, the regulators, prosecutors and their actions against companies or individuals, agreements with prosecuted companies, as well as the case law demonstrate the importance of the function of the compliance officer in the US, UK, and Germany and illustrate the key role played by this position and its responsibility for the success or failure of corporate adherence to law when compliance tasks are delegated to it by the members of the board.

III. The Employment Status of the Compliance Officer compared

This section addresses whether those differences in the US, UK and German Individual Employment Law also reflect differences in compliance officers' protection against wrongful dismissal. In comprehensively analyzing the unfair dismissal regimes of the US, UK, and Germany in chapters three to five, this section summarizes the relevant provisions of employment legislation, the common law principles and concepts and the relevant cases, as well as the employment agreements applicable to the compliance officer.[3924] The employment status and the position of the compliance officer within companies are derived from these findings. The findings will be summarized as follows:

First of all, chapters three to five examined whether the compliance officer has an employment status. Whether an individual is considered an employee must be determined taking into account several characteristics developed by the courts since the term 'employee' has not always been clearly legally defined. One major difference between the US and the UK and German compliance officer is that in most cases the US written employment agreement is an exception for executive officers.[3925] In practice, it could be that the chief compliance officer is provided a written employment contract, but the vast majority of compliance officers do not receive any written agreement. In the US, under the Fair Labor Standards Act (FLSA) the term employee means any individual employed by an employer.[3926] The US Supreme Court has distinguished between employees and independent contractors and has determined that *"employees are those who as a matter of economic reality are dependent upon the business to which they render service."*[3927] Generally, in the US, the UK and in Germany, an employee is someone who performs services under an employment agreement, is bound by instructions under the supervision of the employer, and integrated within the company's organization.[3928] In 2017, the German legislator enshrined the German characteristics of an employment contract as set out by the BAG Court into the amended Section 611a of the German Civil Code (BGB).[3929] The UK and German Employment Courts and now the German Civil Code (BGB) state that the assessment of employment status is determined not by how the parties refer to the

3924 *See generally* Ch. 3, A., II.; Ch. 4, A., IV.; Ch. 5, A., IV.
3925 *See supra* Ch. 3., A., II., III., 2, pp. 254 et seq.
3926 Fair Labor Standards Act of 1938 (FSLA), *supra* note 2024 29 U.S.C. Chapter 8 (1938) § 203 (e) (1).
3927 *See e.g. Secretary of Labor United States Department of Labor v. Lauritzen,* F2d 1529 (1987).
3928 *Compare* Ch. 3, A., II., III., 1., pp. 255 et seq.; Ch. 4, A., IV., 1., 2., p.375; Ch. 5, A., IV., 1., p. 468.
3929 Bürgerliches Gesetzbuch (BGB) | German Civil Code, *supra* note 102 § 611 (a), amended on April 1, 2017.

relationship, but is instead a matter of fact. The English courts and Employment Tribunals have developed the "*mixed or multiple*" test to identify whether an individual is to be categorized as an employee.[3930] The key tests are the integration test, the economic reality test, the mutuality of obligation test and the control test.[3931] In contrast to the US, in the UK, and in Germany, the employer must provide for the employee *"a written statement of particulars of employment."*[3932] Thus, in the UK and in Germany an employee is an individual who enters into a contract of employment and his employment status is determined by the courts, taking into account certain characteristics. Only then the courts will apply to the individual the right to a statutory minimum notice period and protection against unfair dismissal, for instance. Therefore, the English and German compliance officer who is categorized as an employee is entitled to the full scope of statutory employment rights discussed and is protected against unfair dismissal as described in chapters four and five.

Secondly, as we have seen, there is a marked contrast between the unfair dismissal regimes of the United States on the one hand and the UK and Germany regimes on the other. An US constitutional, statutory, or ruling limiting the grounds for termination is absent in comparison to the UK Employment Rights Act 1996 and German Protection Against Unfair Dismissal Act.[3933] In the US, with the exception of Montana, the employment at-will doctrine has been established under common law as it is said to afford greater labor-market flexibility. Generally, the US Courts apply the employment at-will doctrine with some exceptions to improve the protection of the employee.[3934] However, the US Courts did not apply to other cases concerning a compliance officer the exception for the legal profession and this special relationship to a law firm, such as in the case *Wieder v. Skala.*[3935] Both *Sullivan v. Harnisch* and *Mayers v. Stone* have shown that there is no specific protection against dismissal for the compliance officer in the US. In contrast to the US legal framework, under EU Directives such as 91/533/EEC, 2003/88/EC or 2006/54/EC applicable to contractual obligations, UK and German Employment Law is governed mainly by EU Law with respect to the relationship between employers and their employees.[3936] Thus, as employees, compliance officers enjoy all the statutory protections applicable to them. For example, after a certain period of time of continuous employment, the employee is entitled to protection under the Employment Rights Act 1996 (ERA) or the

3930 *See generally* Ch. 4, A., IV., 2., p. 376.
3931 *See supra* Ch. 4, A., IV., 2., p. 376.
3932 *Compare* Ch. 4, A., IV., 1., 2., p. 375; Ch. 5, A., IV., 1., p. 468.
3933 *Compare* Ch. 3, A., II., III.; Ch. 4, A., IV.; Ch. 5, A., IV.
3934 *See supra* Ch. 3, A., II., III., 2.a., pp. 254 et seq.
3935 *See supra* Ch. 3, A., II., III., 2.a. and b., pp. 254 et seq.
3936 *Compare* Ch. 4, A., IV.; Ch. 5, A., IV.

Protection Against Unfair Dismissal Act (KSchG).[3937] Therefore, in contrast to the US common law doctrine, both the UK and Germany have a statutory protection against unfair dismissal, which includes the compliance officer as an employee under the conditions defined within the framework of the applicable law.[3938] However, specific protection against unfair dismissal for the compliance officer has been not recognized, despite the broad scope and sensitive nature of his tasks and duties. For this reason, the book has explored other solutions in response to an appropriate protection against unfair dismissal for the corporate compliance officer under common law, such as indemnification provisions and indemnification clauses.[3939]

Thirdly, due to the differences between protection against unfair dismissal in the US and that in the UK and in Germany, various different ways to protect employees from termination without cause and notice have developed in the US. The vast of majority of US corporate officers are at-will employees without a written employment contract and fall under the employment at-will doctrine.[3940] The US Courts can apply exceptions for various categories of cases. In addition, US Federal law, such as the Civil Right Acts or the National Labor Relations Act (NLRA) encompass a specific statutory discrimination protection for the employees.[3941] However, due to the absence of protection against unfair dismissal, the US compliance officer should negotiate the inclusion of exact grounds for termination, a termination period and indemnification terms in his employment agreement.[3942]

Finally, the duties of the compliance officer as an employee under US, UK, and German Employment Law should be compared. The duties of employees vary under US State Employment Law. In most cases, besides the key duty to perform the work, the duty of loyalty and the duty of confidentiality in respect of the employer have been recognized.[3943] In the event that an officer is appointed by the board, he furthermore has a duty to inform his principal under agency law.[3944] In the event of any breach of these duties, the employer can terminate the employment contract for cause, but the breach is not subject to damages. Generally, in the event of termination with cause, officers leave the

3937 *Compare* Ch. 4, A., IV.; Ch. 5, A., IV.

3938 *See supra* Ch. 4, A., IV. 4. p. 389 ;Ch. 5, A., IV.5. p. 478.

3939 *See supra* Ch. 3, A., II., p. 254 ; Ch. 4, A., IV. 4.c., p. 389.

3940 *See supra* Ch. 3, A., II., III., 2., p. 260.

3941 *See supra* Ch. 3, A., II., III., 1., p. 255.

3942 *See supra* Ch. 3, A., II., III., 2., p. 260.

3943 *See supra Mayers v. Stone Castle Partners, LLC, supra* note 2075.

3944 *See supra Smith v. Van Gorkom,* (Del. 1985), *supra* note 1838; American Law Institute, *supra* note 2087.

company without any severance compensation.[3945] Similar to the US, under UK Employment law, the implied duties owed by an employee include, *inter alia,* the duty of care, the duty of fidelity, the duty of loyalty and confidentiality towards the employer.[3946] In particular, for the compliance officer, the duty of care relates to the performance of his work. As we have seen, in the English financial services sector, the duty of reasonable care applies in enhanced form to control functions such as the compliance officer.[3947] If an employee is in breach of this duty, the employer is entitled to terminate the contract of employment and can recover damages.[3948] Overall, it appears that the duties of the UK employees are more extensive and any breach thereof is to a greater degree subject to legal action and investigations, particularly in the financial services sector, than is the case in the US and in Germany.[3949] By comparison with the duties owed by the employee in the American and English systems, the German employee has a similar duty of loyalty and confidentiality.[3950] Just like the US and UK employer, the German employer can terminate the employment contract and is entitled to recover limited damages from the employee in the event of the employee's breach of duties.[3951]

To conclude, the examination of the relevant statutory employment law, common law principles and court cases as discussed in chapters three to five has demonstrated that the compliance officer is an employee with employment status. In the UK and in Germany, this status comprises the statutory protection against unfair dismissal that applies to all employees who fall within the scope of the Employment Rights Act (ERA) and the Protection against Unfair Dismissal Act (KSchG). However, there is no specific statutory protection for the corporate compliance officer under US, UK, or German Employment Law.

3945 *See supra* Ch. 3, A., II., III., 2., pp. 254 et seq.
3946 *See supra* Ch. 4, A., IV., 3., p. 377.
3947 *See supra* Ch. 4, A., IV., 3.a., p. 380.
3948 *See supra* Ch. 4, A., IV., 4., p. 389.
3949 *See supra* Ch. 4, A., IV., 4.a., p. 390.
3950 *See supra* Ch. 5, A., IV., 1., p. 468.
3951 *See supra* Ch. 5, A., IV., 4,. p. 476.

Table 21 *The Employment Status of the Compliance Officer compared*

Concerning the CO	US Employment Law	UK Employment Law	German Employment Law
Relevant statutes	CRA, NLRA, FSLA,	ERA, EA	BGB, KSchG
Employee status	+	+	+
Written employment contract	-	+	+
Statutory protection against unfair dismissal	-	+	+
Common law principle	Employment at-will	-	-
Case law	No exception from the at will-doctrine	-	-
Specific statutory protection	-	-	-
Position under employment law	Corporate Officer, but not an executive officer	Company's Secretary	Corporate Officer, but not an senior executive officer
Relevant duties	Duty of loyalty and confidentiality	Duty of care, loyalty, fidelity and confidentiality	Duty of loyalty and confidentiality, in cases where the CO is delegated with compliance tasks – duty of care
Legal Consequences in the event of a breach of duties	Termination	Termination, damages	Termination, limited damages

IV. The Impact of Guidelines on Compliance Officers compared

This book has also discussed various approaches to existing corporate governance mechanisms by means of Codes or Principles in the UK, in Germany, and certain provisions of the SOX in the US.[3952] Corporate governance continues to have great significance in the context of the adoption of best practices within the framework of more stringent requirements of investors and shareholders vis-à-vis companies

3952 *See generally* Ch. 3, A., I., 2.; Ch. 4, B.; Ch. 5, B.

following high-profile scandals in the US, in the UK, and in Germany. Corporate governance provisions, code principles and recommendations govern companies with a listing of equity shares on the stock exchanges and set out best practices, for example regarding the roles of the board of directors, the board's composition and compensation, the responsibility of management, and the relationships with shareholders and investors.[3953] Here, the US SOX, federal law, takes a mandatory approach, while the UK and German Code employ the comply and explain approach to adhere to the principles or recommendations.[3954]

Regardless of these different approaches, the provisions, principles, and recommendations of all three aim toward a proactive and focused view of the members of the board to achieve the highest standards of management responsibility for compliance.[3955] In addition to the varying number of legal and regulatory requirements as set forth in primary law such as in the SOX, good governance practices, in the form of secondary or soft law, can be a flexible approach for the board and management to ensure corporate adherence with law. The overall goal is to establish more efficient corporate governance structures for effective decision-making by the members of the board, and their proper monitoring of compliance and performance of the company.[3956] Thus, a company can appropriately respond to changing circumstances and the enhanced legal framework in terms of required disclosure and transparency, and, in so doing, can provide value for shareholders and investors.

The UK Code, the German Code and the US SOX all provide the applicable responsibilities for the members of the board as regards compliance.[3957] The board is required to oversee the corporate compliance program. In addition, the board should ensure that the compliance procedure is implemented such that the board is informed at an early stage of any compliance issues that may arise. Only in this way can it be guaranteed that the compliance program will be effective.[3958] Beyond that, the German Code 2017 and amended provision 4.1.3 refer to management board responsibility for the provision of an appropriate compliance management system and for the publishing requirement concerning the basic features of this system in the annual corporate governance report.[3959] Hence, the recently amended German Code 2017 even requires the disclosure of the features of this system with the annual declaration of conformity pursuant to Section 161 (1) of the German

---

3953 *Compare* Ch. 3, A., I., 2.; Ch. 4, B.; Ch. 5, B.

3954 *See supra* in detail Ch. 5, B., IV., p. 491.

3955 *See supra* Ch. 3, A., I.,2., p. 215; Ch. 4, B., p. 396, Ch. 5, B., p. 482.

3956 *See generally* Ch. 3, A., I, 2., p. 215; Ch. 4, B., p. 396; Ch. 5, B., p. 482.

3957 *See* The German Code 2017, *supra* note 3835 para 4.13; The UK Corporate Governance Code (2016), *supra* note 3113 para C.2.3; Sarbanes-Oxley Act of 2002, *supra* note 47, § 302, 15 USC 7241 - Corporate responsibility for financial reports..

3958 *See supra* Ch. 3, A.,I., 2., p. 215; Ch. 5, B., p. 482.

3959 *See supra* Ch. 5, B., III, p. 489.

Stock Corporation Act (AktG). Thus, this recommendation is mandatory for all German corporations to which this Act applies.

However, neither the US SOX, the UK Code, nor the German Code refer explicitly to any principles, provisions or recommendations with respect to the corporate compliance officer and his responsibilities.[3960] This provides further evidence that the ultimate responsibility lies and remains with the members of the board. In essence, the board should take reasonable steps to develop, implement, maintain and oversee an effective legal compliance program, but in practice some of these tasks can be delegated to subordinates, such as a compliance officer. Ultimately, the Principles and Codes support the practical implementation of the compliance program within companies.

Furthermore, the US has established sentencing guidelines, such as the Federal Sentencing Guidelines for Organizations (FSGO), which create sentencing policies and practices for the federal criminal justice system.[3961] The FSGO apply to corporations that have committed a federal crime *e.g.* fraudulent misconduct pursuant to the SOX. These Guidelines recommend a range from a minimum to a maximum period of imprisonment or levels of fines for offences relating to the handling of compliance issues, the size of the corporation, its prior history regarding corporate misconduct, and timely reporting to the US authorities. For example, corporations can be afforded credit and can reduce criminal penalties if they are able to prove that they had established effective compliance procedures.[3962]

As a matter of fact, the US Supreme Court recognized the importance of these guidelines in the case *United States v. Booker*.[3963] The overall advantage for corporations of these guidelines is that they clearly describe seven minimum criteria for an effective compliance program. One important criteria set forth in the Guidelines is that *"specific individual(s) shall be delegated day-to-day responsibility and appropriate authority for the compliance and ethics program."*[3964] Therefore, this criterion refers to the transfer of the compliance tasks from the members of the board to *e.g.* the compliance officer. In addition, the amended FSGO added an eighth criteria concerning the periodic assessment of the compliance procedure. This serves to ensure that the compliance program continues to be effective.[3965] It has been recognized that the FSGO supported the creation of an entirely new job description: that of the corporate compliance officer through the assignment of compliance responsibilities. The guidelines led to a new focus on compliance structure, board oversight, and independent compliance reporting. The guidelines help to facilitate and enhance the role of the compliance

---

3960 *Compare* Ch. 3, A., I., 2.; Ch. 4, B.; Ch. 5, B.
3961 *See supra* Ch. 3., A., 3., p. 236.
3962 *See supra* Ch. 3., A., 3.a, p. 238.
3963 *See supra United States v. Booker, supra* note 1681.
3964 *See supra* Ch. 3., A., 3.a., p. 238.
3965 *See supra* Ch. 3., A., 3.b., p. 239.

officer, to integrate this function into the strategic corporate business and define his role more clearly.[3966] In addition, the organizational guidelines also influence sentencing practice, government enforcement, and finally corporate compliance structures.[3967]

To conclude, the overall system of guidance, guidelines, rulebooks, principles, and recommendations on the applicable law supports the refining and structuring of corporate compliance procedures within the framework of primary law. This system allows the companies flexibility in their implementation of compliance measures that fit the company's needs and circumstances, while the primary law stipulates requirements, prohibitions, and sanctions. By means of the guidelines, principles, and recommendations, reference was made to a new oversight duty of the members of the board with respect to the compliance program, which was first established in the *Caremark* decision in 1996. This duty comprises the identification, assessment, and management of all compliance risks, and ensuring that the company acts within the law. This system further refers to the practical handling of the oversight or compliance duty through *e.g.* the delegation of this duty to a specific individual, such as to a compliance officer. Due to the recommendation that the board should be informed as to compliance issues, the board has to consider appropriate reporting lines. Consequently, the system of guidance, guidelines, principles, and recommendations has contributed to the increasing numbers of compliance officers, to the establishment of a standalone compliance function, to the determination of reporting lines, and to a new job description.

B. The Findings of the American and English Corporate Compliance Officers' Model

Referring back to the major goal of this book, which was to establish a modern and dynamic role of the German corporate compliance officer, the selected relevant primary and secondary law concerning compliance and the corporate compliance officer in the US, the UK and in Germany have been examined. In addition, due to the absence of case law with respect to corporate compliance officers' liability, chapters three to five analyzed case law with respect to compliance officers' liability within the financial services sector and its findings, as well as the case law regarding compliance duties. By examining and analyzing the legal framework and compliance case law together, the findings have provided an overall picture of the role of the corporate compliance officer. This is why the third hypothesis cannot be confirmed in its entirety, because both the legal framework and the case law were helpful in achieving the goal of this book.

3966 *See supra* Ch. 3., A., 3.d., p. 247.
3967 *See supra* Ch. 3., A., 3.c., p. 242.

H3 It can be assumed that, due to the limited number of judicial decisions on the compliance officer's role in the common law system, it would be useful to analyze the legal framework pertaining to the corporate compliance officer.[3968]

Despite the differences between the American and English common law, there are similarities and shared characteristics such as the prevalence of case law and common law principles. Hence, this book has attempted to reflect the strengths of both the common law and civil law systems and has attempted to incorporate these. For this reason, chapter one presented a brief comparison of the common law and civil law systems, and in particular the fundamental differences between them. The conclusion was that, despite substantial differences, both legal systems have evolved, adapted, and converged over the course of time. The major differences can be seen to exist between the common law system in the US and Germany. On the basis of the impact of EU law on the English common law, English law appears more centralized, structured and consistent, similar to German law. Finally, chapter one set out the fundamental cornerstone of the analysis of the US, UK and German law with respect to compliance and the compliance officer.

In addition, chapter two outlined the legal roots and background of compliance and the compliance officer function to categorize the current situation in the US, the UK, and Germany. Generally, it is assumed that the roots of compliance originated in the US at the beginning of the 19th century, but it has been noted that the first attempt to achieve compliance was designed to limit the unfair practices of brokers and stock-jobbers in the UK in the 17th century. Hence, the earliest form of compliance and the compliance officer post were found in the financial services sector in the UK. It seems that the English concept of compliance comprises a narrow definition and takes place in a generally more ordered development than the US concept of compliance and its development. However, due to the huge increase in the establishment of companies, and in the growth of fraudulent actions by those companies at the beginning of the 19th century, the legal framework with respect to compliance has expanded considerably. As we have seen, American and English companies preferred formal rules and corporate norms. In contrast to the early development in the UK and US, it has been noted that compliance in Germany has no cultural background or specific legal origin. Apparently, the emergence of German compliance is connected with the global business of German corporations listed on US and UK stock exchanges. Thus, the term compliance and the compliance officer's function are relatively new in Germany compared with the UK and US.

Having compared the two legal systems and the historical classification of compliance, chapters three to five analyzed the legal framework in terms of compliance and before going on to reveal and illustrate the models of the US, UK and German corporate compliance officer. The three models introduced the responsibilities, the

---

3968 *See supra* Ch. 1, B., IV., p. 109.

legal duties, and liabilities incumbent upon corporate compliance officers.[3969] There followed a description of the role such as a high-level control, oversight, multifunctional in the US, a command and control function in the UK, and a control and monitoring function at a high corporate level in Germany.[3970] Hence, the common element of all three models is the description as a control function. This indicates that the compliance function emerged in the context of the enforcement of the legal environment, because legal requirements need controls for implementation. The enforcement of the legislation, the regulatory framework and case law, particularly in the areas of corporate law, bribery law and criminal law, as well as the continuous increase in the scope of the duties incumbent upon boards and directors, such as the creation of a new oversight duty, have led to the emergence of a established standalone compliance officer post through the delegation of compliance tasks by the members of the board to the compliance function. Due to the growing number of statutory provisions, companies are required to assign compliance tasks to an independent standalone compliance function with the authority necessary in order to fulfil the responsibilities and duties effectively. In line with this, the potential personal liability of the corporate compliance officer has also increased. Additionally, in the US and in the UK, the requirements and guidelines imposed by regulators and prosecutors have shaped a formal position of the compliance officer through a cooperative collaboration in the event of misconduct. Their agreements with the corporations that were prosecuted required the assignment to one corporate official of responsibility for oversight of compliance. Such officials shall have the authority and responsibility to implement and utilize monitoring and auditing systems and should report directly to the board. Only a standalone position of the compliance function will have clearly defined responsibilities. As we have seen, compliance tasks and responsibilities are wide-ranging and can be properly handled as separate function. Therefore, the findings of these three models have confirmed assumptions two, six and seven:

H2 It can be anticipated that the compliance officer emerged with enhanced legal requirements because the legal framework was able to establish a formal position of authority for the compliance officer at a high corporate level within companies.[3971]
H6 It can be suggested that, due to this multifunctional role, the function of the corporate compliance officer is unable to develop an independent standalone position, because the responsibilities are not clearly delimited and defined.[3972]
H7 It can be assumed that legislative regulation and a regulatory framework will be necessary to appoint an independent standalone compliance officer at a high-corporate level.[3973]

3969 *See generally* Ch. 3, B., p. 287, Ch. 4, C., p. 410, Ch. 5, C., p. 493.
3970 *See generally* Ch. 3, B., p. 287, Ch. 4, C., p. 410, Ch. 5, C., p. 493.
3971 *See supra* Ch. 1, B., IV., p. 109.
3972 *See supra* Ch. 1, B., IV., pp. 109 et seq.
3973 *See supra* Ch. 1, B., IV., pp. 109 et seq.

However, it would be necessary to establish whether an independent function can properly conduct the assessment of business risks. Nevertheless, the findings of the book have shown - and the proposed model of the German compliance officer recommended - that the compliance officer should have more business expertise in addition to his legal expertise by means of incorporating him into business units. This would enable the compliance officer to oversee and monitor the risks effectively while at the same time acting independently. This suggested model may be able to cope with the challenge of the fifth hypothesis:

> *H5 It can be assumed that the compliance officer is independent; he may not be sufficiently familiar with the risks of the business, because he is not involved enough in day-to-day business.*[3974]

In conclusion, the reasons for the emergence of the compliance function are a response to a series of high-profile scandals of corporate companies through the introduction of a criminal justice framework to deter and penalize organizational misconduct. Overall, the enhancement of legal requirements and an appropriate degree of protection for consumers and investors, alongside the strengthening of shareholders' rights, have influenced and adapted corporate structures in all three countries on a delayed basis and in various ways. The compliance responsibility has reached the highest levels within corporations and will be implemented by corporate officers such as compliance officers. Finally, due to the differing history and the evolving nature of compliance and as a result of different legal approaches, the role of the compliance officer is assessed, discussed and formed differently in the US, UK, and in Germany.

I. How are the Modern Role and Legal Position of the Compliance Officer Defined under the Common Law and in Practice?

The aim of this section is to highlight the key findings of chapters three and four with respect to the compliance officer under common law in order to present a model of their role and position. Corporate compliance officers are a group of corporate officers who are usually employed by companies under the employment law in the UK and under the employment at-will doctrine in the US. Generally, they are assigned partial compliance tasks and duties by the board of directors and act on behalf of the directors. As explored in chapters three and four, there is no statutory provision under corporate, criminal and bribery laws that clearly requires the designation of a compliance officer post or which stipulates in detail what the duties of the corporate compliance officer are in the private sector. Although their responsibilities are not legally defined such as for CEOs and CFOs

3974 *See supra* Ch. 1, B., IV., pp. 109 et seq.

under US State Corporation Law or the SOX in the US or for directors under company law in the UK, they must ensure that all corporate levels adhere to the rules, standards and the law. The findings in chapters three and four demonstrate that compliance tasks are complex and far-reaching, and that their scope has increased over the course of the last thirty years based on the enforcement of the directors' legal duties. In the meantime, the equitable and common law principles applicable to directors' duties, which govern the relationship between directors and shareholders, are for the most part enshrined into law. The companies' bylaws and the articles of association generally allow the delegation of directors' duties to senior executives. However, the ultimate responsibility remains with the directors.

In addition, the US and UK courts apply the same directors' duties, such as the duty of care and loyalty, to corporate officers. For this reason, the corporate compliance officer under common law takes up a difficult position between business and regulation. On the one hand, they have to understand the nature of the company's business, to identify, analyze and assess the business risk, and on the other hand, they sometimes have to restrict the business to ensure adherence the to law. Therefore, in the US, it has been recognized that a succinct explanation of their roles could be the dual-hatted position of the compliance officer.[3975] Since delegation is allowed, another specific feature of the compliance officer under common law is that the compliance duties and responsibilities were spread over several corporate positions. The titles varied from CEO to General Counsel in the US and from director to company secretary in the UK. Thus, the compliance officer position is also referred to as a multifunctional role. Another definition which describes the specific position within corporations could be that of an intermediary or gatekeeper role, first between the employees in the business units and the board of directors and second, between the corporation and the regulators or prosecutors.[3976] Hence, it is key that they act independently of the various interested parties.

In the UK, the title of compliance officer is transferred from other regulated industries, such as the financial services sector. As discussed in chapter four, this sector applies the control function regime. Consequently, in the UK, the corporate compliance officer's position is emphasized as a command and control model with a procedural approach.[3977] This model reflects that compliance and its function within companies is more self-determined and self-controlled. Compliance officers shape their business control of risks by means of guidance from the regulators and prosecutors.[3978] Hence, the compliance position

3975 *See supra* Ch. 3, B., p. 287.
3976 *See supra* Ch. 3, A., I., 2.e, p. 226.
3977 *See supra* Ch. 4, C., p. 410.
3978 *See supra* Ch. 4, C., p. 410.

is considered to improve risk coordination and the quality of risk documents. The difference is that the UK compliance officer more often has to deal with regulators and prosecutors, rulebooks and guidance even before an investigation is opened, while the US compliance officer has to deal with regulators in the event of an investigation. In this regulatory and risk-focused environment, the compliance officer needs a diverse set of skills *e.g.* a combination of communication and reporting skills, as well as business acumen in order to focus on specific risk areas of business. In particular, compliance personnel have to deal with various reporting lines inside and outside the company in order to keep the board of directors, the relevant committees, the business units affected by that risk area and the regulators duly informed. Due to the complex nature of compliance tasks, the traditional general counsel, company secretary or staff with legal expertise performing compliance tasks will gradually be replaced with standalone compliance experts, who have personal experience with regulatory compliance and a business background. The key task of compliance officers is the implementation of the requirements of legislators and regulators within companies. The compliance officer post is therefore categorized as a control function. As such, looking to the fourth hypothesis, the first assumption is confirmed:

> *H4 It can be assumed that the compliance officers' post is categorized as a control function in order to implement legal requirements. For this reason, this function is viewed as "corporate cop" or "watchdog" and does not obtain effective and relevant information of the business, because employees are wary of them.*[3979]

In practice, compliance officers should be integrated within the business units in order to identify business risks on-the-spot and periodically perform checks by means of unannounced surveys, audits and investigations to identify early risks and assess staff readiness. By understanding the business risks, they can identify where corrective actions are needed. Therefore, compliance officers should independently monitor and review business processes without specifically interfering with employees' work. In the event that they are authorized to do so and have access to relevant meetings and documents, they can obtain the effective and relevant information needed. Thus, the second assumption of the fourth hypothesis could not be confirmed.

By summarizing all of the results above, the model of the modern role and the legal position of the compliance officer in the US and UK can be illustrated as follows:

3979 *See supra* Ch. 1, B., IV., pp. 109 et seq.

Figure 17 - *The Model of the Modern Role and Legal Position of the US and UK Compliance Officer under Common Law*

This model, which summarizes the findings above, is applicable to public companies listed on the US and UK stock exchanges. As we have seen, under common law, the compliance officer function has evolved over recent years from a multifunctional role into a standalone independent corporate position as a control function in connection with the enhancement of the regulatory environment. In order to fulfill the compliance officer's tasks effectively and remain well-informed, this post should be integrated within business units and should work collaboratively with other functions and business units to establish effective compliance measures to prevent and detect criminal misconduct by employees. Nowadays, the chief compliance officer is also involved in strategic developments in the implementation of effective compliance structures.

Finally, it can be argued that the model of the modern US and UK compliance officer's role has changed and will continue to change from a multifunctional role to a standalone independent control and a gatekeeper function, responsible for implementing and monitoring the compliance measures in an effective manner, and on the other hand, for handling the coordination of compliance audit activities and communication of reporting results to all relevant parties.

II. Which Aspects are Transferable to the German Compliance Officer?

Having presented the model of the modern role and position of the corporate compliance officer under common law, this section will discuss which aspects could be adopted from this model to the German Compliance Officer. Although the differences between the common law and civil law show contrasting corporate board structures, contrasting handling of law by means of case law and the application to further cases versus the systematic codification of law, and the powers of regulators and prosecutors under common law, the German compliance officer's role and position appears not to be very different than the US and UK compliance officers' role within companies.

The analysis of the legal framework in the US and UK has revealed that over the course of the last few years, extensive criminal and bribery statutes have developed through which common law principles have been enshrined in legislation. The US and UK Courts have also applied these statutory provisions to corporate liability. Additionally, chapters three and four established that the common law principles and doctrines are applicable even under a non-regulated framework. On the other hand, in the civil law systems such as in Germany, the case law also plays a considerable role when interpreting and filling certain statutory provisions or gaps in the law. In addition, EU law has further influenced the convergence between the UK common law and the German civil law system. However, as previously examined, significant differences remain.[3980]

For this reason, it was useful to comprehensively examine the relevant hard and soft law in the US and the UK, as compliance and the compliance officer function originated from these countries. This book went beyond the text of the relevant statutes and cases by using information from principles and guidance, legal scholars and practitioners, studies, available data and the actual practice of compliance officers in these countries. The findings were presented in *figure 17*, in the section above.[3981] This allows for a consideration of which features could be applicable to the German compliance officer. In Germany, the legal scholars' attention was focused on the corporate compliance officer when the BGH issued its widely discussed *obiter dictum*.[3982] Since then, this function has come to the fore and a large-scale debate on the compliance officer's liability is underway. However, after examining the US and UK statutes and the case law, it has been revealed that this discussion appears more and more excessive. Under common law, the courts apply the same duties to a corporate officer as to the directors,

3980 *See supra* Ch. 1, pp. 53 et seq.
3981 *See supra* Figure 17, p. 526.
3982 *See supra* Ch. 5, A., III., 4.a., p. 451.

but the business judgment rule does not apply to an officer. Nevertheless, US State Corporation Law refers to possible indemnification, which implies reimbursement for the costs of litigation for directors and officers in the event they are held personally liable. Chapter five examined the situation that under German criminal law, the liability of the compliance officer can be limited, for example in accordance with his delegated area of responsibility. Additionally, the German compliance officer is protected under the Unfair Dismissal Act. In the US, the compliance officer seldom receives a written employment contract. In the majority of cases, he works under the employment at-will doctrine. In view of these findings, it is doubtful whether the enforcement of the legal duties of directors and officers under common law should be applied in the same way to the German compliance officer. This approach cannot be accepted because it has been recognized that the ultimate responsibility remains with the members of the board. However, due to the absence thus far of any case law holding a corporate compliance officer personally liable in the US, UK and Germany, it is difficult to argue which approach is better.

Therefore, the other features of the corporate compliance officer under common law should be considered. When taking into account two aspects of the modern role and position of the US and UK compliance officer, such as the development as a standalone and independent compliance function with business expertise, and the integration within business units, it can be noted that in practice, the German compliance officer embodies several of these features as we have seen in *figure 14*.[3983] The reason for this could be the late emergence of the German compliance officer compared to its US and UK counterparts. Thus, in practice, the Anglo-American approach to this function has already served in part as a model for German companies. These and further aspects of the compliance officers' model under common law will be examined with indications as to their effectiveness.

Firstly, both models of the compliance officer under common law and under civil law have shown that the post is integrated at the high corporate level in order to effectively deal with compliance issues.[3984] Many companies in the US, the UK and Germany, in the initial period, employed an officer with legal expertise and the authority to ensure compliance. These functions were referred to as a dual-hatted role. Over recent years, based on the enforcement of compliance duties, the increasing scope of the responsibilities, and the growing focus on business risk management, the compliance officers' function has been established and will develop as an independent standalone corporate function in order to perform the job effectively.

Secondly, the line of Delaware cases has developed a new duty of oversight under common law. Hence, the compliance officer is clearly defined as a control and oversight function. Although it has been illustrated that the German compliance officer is also assigned certain control and monitoring tasks by the members

---

3983 *See supra* Ch. 5, C., II., Figure 14, p. 499.
3984 *Compare* Ch. 5, C., II., Figure 14, p. 499; Ch. 6, B., II., Figure 17, p. 526.

of the board, this aspect could be emphasized and enhanced in practice. On the other hand, the continual expansion of the responsibility could lead to an increase of the degree of liability of the compliance officer. These should be carefully weighed against one another.

Thirdly, another aspect which should be considered is that the US and the UK understood original compliance and its background as a matter to be carried out *by* a company not *for* a company. Hence, compliance is performed by the company itself by means of self-regulation and has traditionally not been provided by an external source. However, over the last forty years, the legal framework for compliance has increased significantly, but the self-regulated thinking and handling of compliance issues and concerning the compliance function have remained. Thus, the compliance officer under common law plays a more proactive role in the implementation of corporate compliance structures. Recently, in the US and UK, the compliance function has been required to actively participate in the setting of corporate strategy to identify and manage compliance risks. Simultaneously compliance officers should be integrated within business units to better understand and to identify the business risks.[3985] Hence, the ideal model of the compliance officer under common law encompasses a proactive, well-integrated role within corporations. This aspect of the model can be transferred to the dynamic German compliance officers model. In Germany, the mindset is oriented more towards guidelines from outside. However, due to the absence of compliance guidance by the legislator or a regulator within the private sector, corporations and compliance officers should more actively shape compliance issues.

Fourthly, the next aspect refers to clearly required reporting lines. Under agency law, the employee as an agent has the duty to provide information to the principal on relevant facts, for example compliance issues. In addition, the legal framework, in the form for instance of the SOX, the FSGO, the US Principles, the DOJ and their DPAs, the UK Code 2015 and the enforcement of disclosure to investors and shareholders require an effective and periodic corporate reporting mechanism for the compliance program. Reports must be submitted to the board and to regulators, because the board has to review, report, and confirm aspects such as compliance controls in their annual report. For example, the FSGO has set standards for reporting by the high-level personnel. They should have direct access to the board. As PWC studies have shown, US and UK companies have enhanced their compliance risk reporting within the company based on legal requirements and risk assessment results in practice.[3986] Nevertheless, the corporation must also ensure an effective reporting line is in place outside the company with investigators or regulators. In the US, for example, the *Yates* Memo sets out the new approach that

3985 *See supra* Ch. 3, A., I., 3. d, p. 247; Ch. 4, C., I., p. 410.
3986 See PwC-Study 2014, *supra* note 8; PwC-Study 2015, *supra* note 1799.

the company must completely disclose to the DoJ all relevant facts about individual misconduct if they hope to be given credit in the event of investigation under the FSGO.[3987] Furthermore, in the context of its DPAs, the DOJ in some cases requires in the DPAs Attachment the establishment of a periodic reporting system between the compliance officer and the agency concerning suspected criminal conduct. The reporting requirements also include communications with regulators, which the English compliance officers usually carry out prior to the occurrence of corporate criminal conduct and before an investigation has been opened. Therefore, the compliance officer under common law plays a gatekeeper role inside and outside the company. This gatekeeper role of the corporate compliance officer is absent in Germany. The question of whether and how the company will inform the German Public Prosecutor's Office in the event of internal investigations or in the event of the filing of a criminal complaint against the company depends on the individual case. However, it is not a frequent practice and a matter of some controversy for the German company or the compliance officer to cooperate fully with the prosecutor before, at the commencement of and during the course of an investigation. There is no incentive like the mitigating system in the US. Nevertheless, the gatekeeper role could serve as a role model for the German compliance officer. In Germany, the extent and the recipient of the compliance officer's reporting and documentation duties are regulated by his contract of employment.[3988] As we have seen, the compliance officer is viewed as an interface or switching point within companies. However, it is suggested that additional incentives be provided to companies in Germany just like in the US and the UK, to enhance disclosure and cooperation with regulators or prosecutors in the event of corporate misconduct.

Therefore, fifth, another aspect comes to light, namely the absence of guidance from the German legislator with respect to the interpretation of the statutory regulation. It will be helpful for companies of all legal forms and sizes to obtain guidance and information by means of manuals, guidelines or rulebooks on the legal issues involved, *e.g.* including who and what is covered by the relevant statutes, the definitions of relevant legal terms, what is encompassed in certain terms and how preventative measures such as the compliance officers function should be designed. Hence, manuals, guidelines or rulebooks can provide valuable support in the implementation of corporate preventative measures and assist the German compliance officer's work.

Finally, the last aspect that will be highlighted is indemnification under common law. US State Corporation Law has adopted provisions on when the company has power or may indemnify its officers and directors *"against expenses including attorneys' fees, judgments, fines, and amounts paid in settlement"* to absorb the losses if they acted in good faith.[3989] In addition, under common law, there is a possibility

3987 *See supra* Ch. 3, A., I., 1.e., p. 207, *See supra* Memorandum for Assistant Attorney General Yates and DOJ, *supra* note 1282 at 3.

3988 *See supra* Ch. 5, A., IV., 6., p. 480.

3989 *See supra* Ch. 3, A. II., p. 254.

for the compliance officer to negotiate an indemnity clause in their employment contracts to the effect that one contractual party agrees to "*indemnify*" the other.[3990] These provisions and contract terms aim to protect the indemnified party against third-party claims. German law does not provide for any such statutory indemnification. In practice, it is not customary to include such indemnification clauses in employment contracts, but the compliance officer may be able to negotiate an individual protection from possible liability. This aspect seems to be appropriate to adopt into the German model of the compliance officer and into German law. Nevertheless, it should apply only to the members of the board and to high-level control functions, such as the chief compliance officer, who has overall responsibility for compliance in the event that he acted without willful intent or gross negligence.

In conclusion, despite the considerable similarities presented by the model of the compliance officer under both common law and civil law, there are several aspects that could also be tailored to the German compliance officer model. This section has examined six aspects with respect to the compliance officers' role within companies: (1) the development into an independent standalone function with business expertise, (2) the enhancement as a control and oversight function, (3) the shaping of a proactive role embedded in strategic thinking, (4) the development into a function with a gatekeeper role, (5) the development of guidance from the German legislator, which supports the compliance officer's work, and (6) the adoption of statutory indemnification provisions and indemnification clauses to protect the chief compliance officer in particular against high damages payments. While the adoption of certain elements of these is recommendable, the second aspect should be carefully considered in practice. The findings of this section will be shown below in the final presentation of the modern and dynamic role of the corporate compliance officer in Germany.

C. An Outlook - The Modern and Dynamic Model of the German Corporate Compliance Officer

This book has identified the modern and dynamic role of the establishment of a compliance function within American, British, and German private sector companies. The work can contribute to a better understanding and strengthening of the German compliance officer's position within companies by examining the compliance officer's role under common law. In the course of this book the legal framework, the case law, rules, principles, guidance relating to the law, the legal literature, views of legal scholars, available data from regulators and prosecutors, as well as bylaws were examined in order to present a modern and dynamic role of the German compliance officer with aspects derived from both the civil and the common law. The US and UK common law model has served as a role model because compliance and the compliance officer's function originated from the UK

3990 *See supra* Ch. 4, A., IV. 4.c., p. 394.

and the US. However, despite the historical development, legal roots and background under common law, it cannot be verified that the corporate compliance officer function is better defined and standardized in the common law than in the civil law system, due to the absence of any legal definition within the private sector. As we have seen, under common law, there are more guidelines on the establishment of this function. As such, the findings of this book have not confirmed the first hypothesis:

> *H1 Due to the legal framework the function of the compliance officer is better defined and standardized in the common law than in the civil law system on account of the specific historical and legal development.*[3991]

However, the book has recognized that, through the enforcement of the legal framework with respect to compliance, the corporate compliance officer's position and his duties have more clearly shaped his role in practice and this is taken into consideration in the development of the modern and dynamic model proposed. The modern and dynamic model of the corporate compliance officer provides suggestions on his role to be included in the risk business process, but the company is also permitted to develop its own model of this function to reflect the specific nature of the business, its size and its legal form.

In the first instance, this flexible model could apply to the two-tier system for German listed companies, which fall within the scope of the German Stock Corporation Act (AktG), such as the joint-stock company (AG) and the partnerships limited by shares (KGaA). Besides these two legal forms, this model may also be suited to companies with limited liability (GmbH) pursuant to the Limited Liability Companies Act (GmbHG) and to small-medium sized companies, which operate without a supervisory board, a management board and a compliance committee. For this purpose, therefore, it is suggested that the management board could be replaced by the managing director or the owner of the company. Based on the fact that the high corporate level may be absent in smaller companies, the senior executive level may be withdrawn in the model. By contrast, the aspects of the corporate compliance officer's post described may be suited to all sizes and legal forms of companies. This model, therefore, could be incorporated into all types of companies.

Finally, a key consideration in relation to the suggested model would be the development of the definition applicable to the German compliance officer's post. Having examined and analyzed the findings in chapters three to five and having summarizing the key aspects that could be adopted from the common law model to the German Compliance Officer, it can be concluded that the essential aspects of the compliance officer's post identified should be taken into account when defining the corporate compliance officer. The aspects to be included in the definition are: the embedding of this function within companies; the linkage between the compliance

3991 *See supra* Ch. 1, B., IV., pp. 109 et seq.

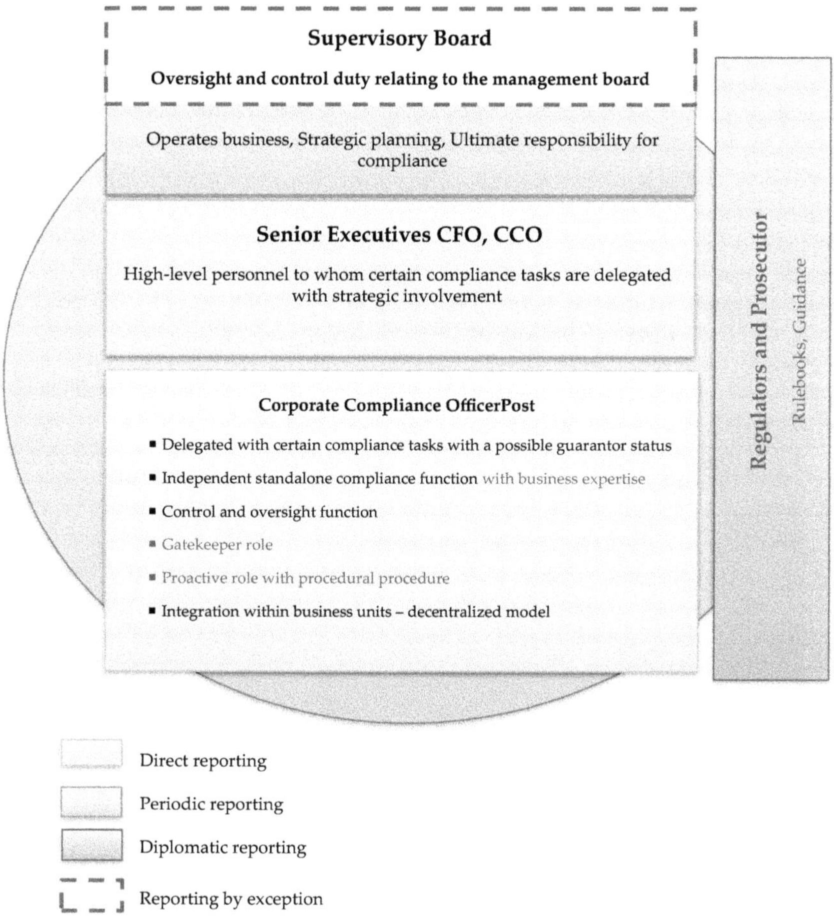

Figure 18 *The Modern and Dynamic Model of the German Compliance Officer*

tasks, the position and the status of the compliance officer; as well as corporate requirements for the compliance officer. Based on the knowledge that the key aspects of the definition of compliance officer in chapter two[3992] were expanded to include aspects of the common law model and the modern and dynamic model of the German Compliance Officer, presented in *figure 18* above,[3993] the general definition of the German Compliance Officer can be outlined as follows:

3992 *See supra* Ch. 2, C., III., p. 162.
3993 *See supra* Figure 18, *Id.*

The independent standalone ***German Corporate Compliance Officer*** *is an employee at a high corporate level to whom certain compliance tasks are delegated, with a possible status of a guarantor, who plays a proactive and gatekeeping role, is embedded in business units, is designated as a control and oversight function with business expertise and has direct access and periodic reporting duties to the management board or the managing director.*

In view of the modern and dynamic model of the German corporate compliance officer and the general definition of this post as developed in this book, and based on the knowledge derived from these, there follow some recommendations for future research. As the regulatory requirements of compliance processes continue to be enforced, it would be worthwhile examining the links between access by regulators and prosecutors to corporate data and individuals via the corporate compliance officer, his role within corporate investigations in the event of corporate misconduct by employees and the embedding of the compliance function and procedures into day-to-day business. This would provide a clearer and sharper picture of the compliance officer. It remains to be seen how this corporate function will develop in future: will it become an extended arm of the legislation or will it become a truly independent corporate function.

Bibliography

A Practitioner's Guide to the Financial Services Authority Listing Regime, 2012/2013, (25. ed. 2012).

Aaron D. Jones, *Corporate Officer Wrongdoing and the Fiduciary Duties of Corporate Officers under Delaware Law*, 44 American Business Law Journal 475–520 (2007).

Aileen Kavanagh, *A Hard Look at the Last Word*, Oxford Journal of Legal Studies 028 (2015).

Alastair Hudson, Understanding Company Law (2nd ed. 2013).

Albert L. Nagy & William J. Cenker, *Internal Audit Professionalism and Section 404 Compliance: The View of Chief Audit Executives from Northeast Ohio*, 11 International Journal of Auditing 41–49 (2007).

Alexander Baur & Phillip Maximilian Holle, *Ergänzungen und Anpassungen des Deutschen Corporate Governance Kodex 2017*, NZG 170–174 (2017).

Alexander Eufinger, *Zu den historischen Ursprüngen der Compliance*, CCZ 21–22 (2012).

Alexander G. Hughes, *Drawing Sensible Borders for the Definition of "Foreign Official" Under the FCPA*, 40 American Journal of Criminal Law 254–278 (2013).

Alexander Kern, *UK Corporate Governance and Banking Regulation: The Regulator's Role as Stakeholder*, 33 Stetson L. Rev. 991 (2003).

Alexander Richards, *Criminal liability of employees of financial intermediaries for money laundering: a British perspective*318–339 (1. ed. 2003).

Alisdair Gillespie, The English Legal System (5. ed. 2015).

American Bar Association Committee on Corporate Laws & American Bar Association Section of Business Law, 5. Corporate Director's Guidebook (2007).

American Bar Association Section of Antitrust Law, Antitrust Compliance: Perspectives and Resources for Corporate Counselors (2005).

Andrea Schneider, *Stellung des Compliance-Officers in Matrixorganisationen*, ZRFC 231–236 (2015).

Andreas Stephan, *Four key challenges to the successful criminalization of cartel laws*, 2 Journal of Antitrust Enforcement 333–362 (2014).

Andrew F. Tuch, *Multiple Gatekeepers*, 96 Virginia Law Review 1583–1672 (2010).

Andrew Keay, *Comply or explain in corporate governance codes: in need of greater regulatory oversight?: Comply or explain in corporate governance codes*, 34 Legal Studies 279–304 (2014).

Andrew Tylecote & Paulina Ramirez, *Corporate governance and innovation: The UK compared with the US and 'insider' economies*, 35 Research Policy 160–180 (2006).

Anja Schiemann, *Schiemann: Compliance-Verantwortliche unter Generalverdacht ?*, Neue Zeitschrift für Gesellschaftsrecht 657–659 (2014).

Annie Mills & Peter Haines, Essential strategies for financial services compliance (2nd ed. 2015).

Anthony Pirraglia, *A Tangled Web: Compliance Director Liability Under the Securities Laws*, 8 Fordham J. Corp. & Fin. L. 245–272 (2003).

Antoinette Dop, Introduction into legal English for Dutch law students (1. ed. 2009).

Aram Kaven-Moser, *Compliance bewegt ...*, ZRFC 37–38 (2017).

Aron Balas et al., *The Divergence of Legal Procedures*, National Bureau of Economic Research (2008).

Ashley Savage & Richard Hyde, *The response to whistleblowing by regulators: a practical perspective: The response to whistleblowing by regulators*, 35 Legal Studies 408–429 (2015).

Association of Corporate Counsel ACC, Compliance Program and Risk Assessment Benchmarking Survey 2005 (2005).

Axel v. Werder & Julia Turkali, *Corporate Governance Report 2015: Kodexakzeptanz und Kodexanwendung*, Der Betrieb 1357–1367 (2015).

Azizah Abdullah & Michael Page, Corporate governance and corporate performance: UK FTSE 350 companies (2009).

B. Sharon Byrd et al., Introduction to Anglo-American law & language: Einführung in die anglo-amerikanische Rechtssprache. Bd. 1: [...] (3. ed. 2011).

Beck'scher Online-Kommentar OWiG | Commentary on the Act on Regulatory Offences, (Peter Graf ed., 14. ed. 2017).

Beck'scher Online-Kommentar StPO | Commentary on the German Code of Criminal Procedure, (Graf ed., 27. ed. 2017).

Bernd Schmidt, Jürgen Taeger & Benedikt Buchner, Compliance in Kapitalgesellschaften (1. ed. 2010).

Bernd Schünemann, *Die aktuelle Forderung eines Verbandsstrafrechts – Ein kriminalpolitischer Zombie*, ZIS 1–18 (2014).

Bettina Lange, *Empirical compliance: A study of waste management regulation in the U.K. and German*, December, 1996.

Bettina Palazzo, *U.S.-American and German Business Ethics: An Intercultural Comparison*, 41 Journal of Business Ethics 195–216 (2002).

BJörn Siebler, Criminal-Compliance im interdisziplinären Kontext: Die Legitimierung von Compliance-Tätigkeiten und Massnahmen sowie deren Verwertbarkeit im deutschen Strafverfahren (1. ed. 2014).

Brandon L. Garrett, *Structural Reform Prosecution*, 93 Virginia Law Review 853–957 (2007).

Brenda E. Joyner & Dinah Payne, *Evolution and Implementation: A Study of Values, Business Ethics and Corporate Social Responsibility*, 41 Journal of Business Ethics 297–311 (2002).

Brian Horrigan, Corporate Social Responsibility in the 21st Century: Debates, Models and Practices Across Government, Law and Business (1. ed. 2010).

Brian R. Cheffins, Corporate Ownership and Control: British Business Transformed (2010).

Brian R. Cheffins, *The Undermining of UK Corporate Governance(?)*, 33 Oxford Journal of Legal Studies 503–533 (2013).

Brian Schwartz, Bobby Kipp & Andrea Falcione, Trends in compliance organizational structures (2016).

Brianna L. Gates, *The Enhanced SEC Enforcement Power Against Control Persons after Dodd-Frank: The Supreme Court Should Reject the "Culpable Participation" Requirement to Prevent SEC Forum Shopping*, 99 Iowa Law Review 393–414 (2013).

Bürgerliches Gesetzbuch: mit Nebengesetzen | Commentary on the German Civil Code, (Otto Palandt & Peter Bassenge eds., 75. ed. 2016).

Caleb Nelson, *The Legitimacy of (Some) Federal Common Law*, 101 Virginia Law Review 2–64 (2014).

Carol M. Bast & Margie Hawkins, Foundations of legal research and writing / Carol M. Bast, Margie Hawkins (5th ed. 2013).

Caroline Hunter et al., *Legal Compliance in Street-Level Bureaucracy: A Study of UK Housing Officers: A Study of UK Housing Officers*, 38 Law & Policy 81–95 (2016).

Center for Business Ethics, *Are Corporations Institutionalizing Ethics?*, 5 Journal of Business Ethics 85–91 (1986).

Center for Business Ethics, *Instilling Ethical Values in Large Corporations*, 11 Journal of Business Ethics 863–867 (1992).

Charles R. Hickson & John D. Turner, Partnerships (2005).

Charlie Weir & David Laing, *The Performance-Governance Relationship: The Effects of Cadbury Compliance on UK Quoted Companies*, 4 Journal of Management and Governance 265–281 (2000).

Chris Taylor, *The Evolution of Compliance*, 6 Journal of Investment Compliance 54–58 (2005).

Christian Becker & Thomas Rönnau, *Vorsatzvermeidung durch Unternehmensleiter bei betriebsbezogenen Straftaten*, NStZ 569–575 (2016).

Christian Glaser, *Der Dreiklang aus Governance, Risk und Compliance GRC bei Leasinggesellschaften*, ZRFC 56–61 (2015).

Christian Heuking, *Der Compliance Officer – Aufgaben und Anforderungen*, 65 Information - Wissenschaft & Praxis 327–330 (2014).

Christine Parker & Sharon Gilad, *Internal Corporate Compliance Management Systems: Structure, Culture and Agency*, *in* Explaining Compliance Business Responses to Regulation. 170–197 (1. ed. 2011).

Christine Parker, *Regulator-Required Corporate Compliance Program Audits*, 25 Law Policy 221–244 (2003).

Christine Parker, *The Ethics of Advising on Regulatory Compliance: Autonomy or Interdependence?*, 28 Journal of Business Ethics 339–351 (2000).

Christine Parker, The open corporation: effective self-regulation and democracy (1. ed. 2002).

Christoph E. Hauschka, *Compliance, Compliance-Manager, Compliance-Programme: Eine geeignete Reaktion auf gestiegene Haftungsrisiken für Unternehmen und Management?*, 2004 NJW 257–261 (2004).

Christoph E. Hauschka, Wirnt Galster & Annette Marschlich, *Leitlinien für die Tätigkeit in der Compliance-Funktion im Unternehmen (für Compliance Officer außerhalb regulierter Sektoren)*, 2014 CCZ 242–248 (2014).

Christoph E. Hauschka, *Zum Berufsbild des Compliance Officers*, 2014 CCZ 2014, 165 - beck-online 165–170 (2014).

Christoph Kämper, Die Aktionärsklage und die Kontrolle von Publikumsgesellschaften im deutsch-amerikanischen Vergleich (2008).

Christoph Van der Elst, The Risk Management Duties of the Board of Directors (2013).

Christopher D. H. Wilson, Ian David Williams & Simon Kemp, *An Evaluation of the Impact and Effectiveness of Environmental Legislation in Small and Medium-Sized Enterprises: Experiences from the UK: Evaluation of Impact + Effectiveness of Environ Legislation in SMEs*, 21 Business Strategy and the Environment 141–156 (2012).

Christopher D. H. Wilson, Ian David Williams & Simon Kemp, *Compliance with Producer Responsibility Legislation: Experiences from UK Small and Medium-sized Enterprises*, 20 Business Strategy and the Environment 310–330 (2011).

Cindy A. Schipani & George J. Siedel, *Legal Liability: The Board of Directors*, 1 Family Business Review 279–285 (1988).

Cindy R., Alexander et al., *Economic effects of SOX Section 404 compliance: A corporate insider perspective*, 56 Journal of Accounting and Economics 267–290 (2013).

Clearly Gottlieb, New York's Employment At-Will Doctrine Puts Private Company Compliance Personnel At Risk (2012).

Colette Panebianco, *The after-effect of Rule 203(b)(3)-2: what it means to take on the role of CCO to comply with the controversial measure*, 6 Journal of Investment Compliance 59–62 (2005).

COMMENTARY ON BUSINESS LAW, (Henssler & Strohn eds., 3. ed. 2016).

COMMENTARY ON THE AKTG, (Hölters ed., 2. ed. 2014).

COMMENTARY ON THE AKTG, (Uwe Hüffer & Jens Koch eds., 12. ed. 2016).

COMMENTARY ON THE AKTG, 1 (Spindler & Stilz eds., 3. ed. 2015).

Commentary on the German Banking Act, VO (EU) No. 575/2013 (CRR) and Implementing Provisions, (Karl-Heinz Boos, Reinfrid Fischer, & Hermann Schulte-Mattler eds., 5. ed. 2016).

COMMENTARY ON THE GMBHG, (Michalski ed., 2. ed. 2010).

COMMENTARY ON THE GMBHG, (Rowedder & Schmidt-Leithoff eds., 5. ed. 2013).

COMMENTARY ON THE GMBHG, 20 (Baumbach & Hueck eds., 21. ed. 2017).

Commission of the European Communities, Modernising Company Law and Enhancing Corporate Governance in the European Union - A Plan to Move Forward C5-0378-03 COM (2003) 284 final (2003).

Committee ABA Section of Business Law Corporate Compliance, *Corporate Compliance Survey*, 60 The Business Lawyer 1759–1798 (2005).

COMPANY LAW REVIEW STEERING GROUP, Modern Company Law for a Competitive Economy: Developing the Framework (2000).

COMPLIANCE IN HEALTH CARE, (R. Brian Haynes, D. Wayne Taylor, & David L Sackett eds., 1979).

COMPLIANCE KOMPAKT: BEST PRACTICE IM COMPLIANCE-MANAGEMENT, (Stefan Behringer ed., 3. ed. 2013).

Constance E Bagley, *What's Law Got to Do With It? Integrating Law and Strategy*, 47 American Business Law Journal 587–639 (2010).

CORNELIA INDERST, BRITTA BANNENBERG & SINA POPPE, Compliance (2. ed. 2013).

Corporate Compliance: Handbuch der Haftungsvermeidung im Unternehmen (Christoph E. Hauschka, Klaus Moosmayer, & Thomas Lösler eds., 3. ed. 2016).

Corporate Law and Governance Directorate & Department of Trade and Industry, Company Law Reform (2005).

CORPUS JURIS SECUNDUM (CJS), 15A (1964).

Court E. Golumbic & Jonathan P. Adams, *Dominant Influence Test: The FCPA's Instrumentality and Foreign Official Requirements and the Investment Activity of Sovereign Wealth Funds, The*, 39 Am. J. Crim. L. 1–51 (2011).

Craig Doidge, George Andrew Karolyi & Rene M. Stulz, Why Do Foreign Firms Leave U.S. Equity Markets? An Analysis of Deregistrations Under SEC Exchange Act Rule 12h-6 (2008).

Craig Mackenzie, *Boards, Incentives and Corporate Social Responsibility: the case for a change of emphasis*, 15 Corporate Governance: An International Review 935–943 (2007).

Cristie L. Ford & David Hess, *Can Corporate Monitorships Improve Corporate Compliance?*, 34 Journal of Corporation Law 679–737 (2009).

Cristie L. Ford, *New Governance, Compliance, and Principles-Based Securities Regulation*, 45 American Business Law Journal 1–60 (2008).

CSV Health, Corporate Social Responsibility Report (2014).

D. French, S.W. Mayson & C. Ryan, Mayson, French & Ryan on Company Law (32 ed. 2015).

Dan R. Dalton et al., *Meta-analytic reviews of board composition, leadership structure, and financial performance*, 19 Strategic Management Journal 269–290 (1998).

Daniel Geiger, *Nemo ultra posse obligatur - Zur strafrechtlichen Haftung von Compliance-Beauftragten ohne Disziplinargewalt*, CCZ 170–174 (2011).

Daniel Meier-Greve, *Zur Unabhängigkeit des sog. Compliance Officers*, 2010 CCZ 216–221 (2010).

Daniel Sandmann, *Die Compliance-Funktion unter Solvency II – Ein Überblick*, CCZ 70–77 (2015).

David A Cabrelli, Employment law (4th ed. 2015).

David A. Cabrelli, Employment law in context: text and materials (2nd ed. 2016).

David Block & Anne-Marie Gerstner, *One-Tier vs. Two-Tier Board Structure: A Comparison Between the United States and Germany*, Paper 1 Comparative Corporate Governance and Financial Regulation (2016).

David Brian Chandler, *Organizations and Ethics: Antecedents and Consequences of the Adoption and Implementation of the Ethics and Compliance Officer Position*, 2011.

David C. Fischer, *Responsibilities of principal executive officers under the Sarbanes-Oxley Act of 2002: A compliance checklist*, 5 Journal of Investment Compliance 97–105 (2004).

David Lewis & Malcolm Sargeant, Employment Law: The Essentials (13th ed. 2015).

David Vogel, *The Ethical Roots of Business Ethics*, 1 Business Ethics Quarterly 101 (1991).

David Yermack, *Higher market valuation of companies with a small board of directors*, 40 Journal of Financial Economics 185–211 (1996).

Deborah A. DeMott, *The Crucial but (Potentially) Precarious Position of the Chief Compliance Officer*, 8 BROOK. J. CORP. FIN. &COM. L. 56–79 (2013).

Department for Business and Innovation & Skills, Transparency & Trust: Enhancing the Transparency of UK Company Ownership and Increasing Trust in UK Business (2014).

Der Compliance Officer: ein Handbuch in eigener Sache (Jürgen Bürkle & Christoph E. Hauschka eds., 1. ed. 2015).

Deutscher Corporate Governance Kodex: Kodex-Kommentar, (Thomas Kremer ed., 6. ed. 2016).

Diana E. Murphy, *The Federal Sentencing Guidelines for Organizations: A Decade of Promoting Compliance and Ethics*, 87 Iowa Law Review 698–719 (2002).

Diana Illing & Karsten Umnuß, *Die arbeitsrechtliche Stellung des Compliance Managers – insbesondere Weisungsunterworfenheit und Reportingpflichten*, CCZ 1–8 (2009).

Dolores Freda, *'Law Reporting' in Europe in the Early-Modern Period: Two Experiences in Comparison*, 30 The Journal of Legal History 263–278 (2009).

DOMINIC CHAI ET AL., Corporate Governance, Legal Origin and the Persistence of Profits 37 (2015).

DOMINIC KÖSTNER, 70 Compliance-Richtlinien im Unternehmen: arbeits- und datenschutzrechtliche Implementierungsaspekte (1. ed. 2012).

Donald C. Langevoort, *Getting (Too) Comfortable: In-House Lawyers, Enterprise Risk and the Financial Crisis*, Wisconsin Law Review 495–519 (2011).

Donald C. Langevoort, *Monitoring: The Behavioral Economics of Corporate Compliance with Law*, 71 Colum. Bus. L. Rev (2002).

Dove Izraeli & Anat BarNir, *Promoting Ethics through Ethics Officers: A Proposed Profile and an Application*, 17 Journal of Business Ethics 1189–1196 (1998).

Duffy A. Morf, Michael G. Schumacher & Scott J. Vitell, *A Survey of Ethics Officers in Large Organizations*, 20 Journal of Business Ethics 265–271 (1999).

Eberhard Vetter, *Compliance im Unternehmen, in* Compliance in der Unternehmerpraxis: Grundlagen, Organisation und Umsetzung 1–18 (G. Wecker & B. Ohl eds., 3. ed. 2013).

Eckart Sünner, *Das Berufsbild des Compliance Officers*, 2014 CCZ 2014, 91 - beck-online 91–96 (2014).

Edward H. Freeman, *Regulatory Compliance and the Chief Compliance Officer*, 16 Information Systems Security 357–361 (2007).

Eilis Ferran, *The Break-up of the Financial Services Authority*, 31 Oxford Journal of Legal Studies 455–480 (2011).

Elisa Hoven, *Der nordrhein-westfälische Entwurf eines Verbandsstrafgesetzbuchs – Eine kritische Betrachtung von Begründungsmodell und Voraussetzungen der Straftatbestände*, ZIS 19–30 (2014).

Elisabeth Dedman, *An Investigation into the Determinants of UK Board Structure Before and After Cadbury*, 8 Corporate Governance 133–153 (2000).

Elisabeth Dedman, *The Cadbury Committee recommendations on corporate governance - a review of compliance and performance impacts*, 4 International Journal of Management Reviews 335–352 (2002).

Elizabeth E. Joh & Thomas Wuil Joo, *The Corporation as Snitch: The New DOJ Guidelines on Prosecuting White Collar Crime*, 101 Virginia Law Review 51–59 (2015).

Emily Harding, *The Proceduralization of Telecommunications Law: Adapting to Convergence*, 3 (1997).

Employment Law-Manual (Günter Schaub ed., 16. ed. 2015).

ERC, ECOA & SCCE, Leading Corporate Integrity: Defining the Role of the Chief Ethics &Compliance Officer (CECO) (2007).

Erfurter Commentary on the Employment Law (Preis, Müller-Glöge, & Schmidt eds., 17. ed. 2017).

ERNST & YOUNG, The UK Bribery Act: Developing an anti-corruption compliance framework 16 (2011).

ETHICS RESOURCE CENTER (ERC), The Federal Sentencing Guidelines for Organizations at twenty years a call to action for more effective promotion and recognition of effective compliance and ethics programs. (2012).

Financial Aspects of Corporate Governance - Cadbury Report 1992, (1992).

Florian Modlinger, Anke Egelhof & Felicitas Berger, *Die Rolle des Aufsichtsrats in der Compliance*, ZRFC 254–258 (2014).

Francesco Galietti, *Compliance in crossborder Corporate Groups*, July 14, 2015.

Frank C. Pierson, *The Education of American Businessmen: A Study of University-College Programs*, Business Administration 266–267 (1959).

Frank Maschmann, *Haftungsvermeidung durch Gesetzetreue - Compliance und Arbeitsrecht*, 15 *in* Corporate Compliance und Arbeitsrecht | Mannheimer Arbeitsrechtstag 2009 7–10 (Frank Maschmann ed., 1. ed. 2009).

Frederick G. Kempin, *The Corporate Officer And The Law Of Agency*, 1 American Business Law Journal 49–59 (2007).

G. Lamond, *Legal Sources, the Rule of Recognition, and Customary Law*, 59 The American Journal of Jurisprudence 25–48 (2014).

G. M. Razi, *Reflections on Equity in the Civil Law Systems*, 13 American University Law Review 24–45 (1964).

G. R. Sullivan, *The Attribution of Culpability to Limited Companies*, 55 The Cambridge Law Journal 515 (1996).

Gareth Adams, *What is Compliance?*, 2 Journal of Financial Regulation and Compliance 278–285 (1994).

Gary Hagland, *Effective Compliance v Regulatory Gestation*, 2 Journal of Financial Regulation and Compliance 11–21 (1993).

Gary R. Weaver, Linda Klebe Treviño & Philip L. Cochran, *Corporate Ethics Practices in the Mid-1990's: An Empirical Study of the Fortune 1000*, 18 Journal of Business Ethics 283–294 (1999).

GARY SLAPPER & DAVID KELLY, The English Legal System (18. ed. 2017).

Geoffrey P. Miller, *The Compliance Function: An Overview*, No. 14–36 NYU Law and Economics Research Paper (2014).

GEOFFREY P. MILLER, The Law of Governance, Risk Management, and Compliance (1. ed. 2014).

GEOFFREY SAMUEL, A Short Introduction to the Common Law (1. ed. 2013).

Georg Gößwein & Olaf Hohmann, *Modelle der Compliance-Organisation in Unternehmen - Wider den Chief Compliance Officer als "Überoberverantwortungs nehmer"*, 2011 Betriebs-Berater 963–967 (2011).

Georg Gösswein, *Die Führungskräfte im Zentrum eines funktionierenden Compliance Management Systems*, CCZ 43–45 (2017).

George J. Siedel, *Six Forces and the Legal Environment of Business: The Relative Value of Business Law among Business School Core Courses*, 37 American Business Law Journal (2000).

GEORGE MOUSOURAKIS, Roman Law and the Origins of the Civil Law Tradition (2015).

Georges Enderle, *FOCUS: A Comparison of Business Ethics in North America and Continental Europe*, 5 Business Ethics: A European Review 33–46 (1996).

Gerd Gerding, *United States of America, in* Directors' Personal Liability for Corporate Fault: A Comparative Analysis (1. ed. 2008).

Gerhard Dannecker, *§ 5 Strafrechtliche Verantwortung nach Delegation, in* Criminal Compliance: Handbuch (Katharina Beckemper & Thomas Rotsch eds., 1. ed. 2015).

Gernot Zimmermann, *Die straf- und zivilrechtliche Verantwortlichkeit des Compliance Officers*, 2011 BB 634–637 (2011).

Gideon Mark, *Private FCPA Enforcement: Private FCPA Enforcement*, 49 American Business Law Journal 419–506 (2012).

Giles Dixon, Georg Gößwein & Olaf Hohmann, *Gesetze zur Bekämpfung der Korruption im Vereinigten Königreich Großbritannien und Nordirland sowie in der Bundesrepublik Deutschland– Eine vergleichende Betrachtung der Rechtslage –*, Neue Zeitschrift für Wirtschafts-, Steuer- und Unternehmensstrafrecht 361–366.

Gordon McMurray, *Standards and Qualities expected of Compliance Staff*, 5 Journal of Financial Regulation and Compliance 59–61 (1997).

Gordon McMurray, *The Practical Compliance Officer: Technicality versus Commerciality*, 3 Journal of Financial Regulation and Compliance 141–146 (1995).

Great Britain et al., Any of our business? Human rights and the UK private sector: First report of session 2009–10. Vol. 2, Vol. 2, (2009).

Grigoleit | Commentary on the AktG, (Grigoleit ed., 1. ed. 2013).

H. Lowell Brown, *The Corporate Director's Compliance Oversight Responsibility in the Post Caremark Era*, 26 Delaware Journal of Corporate Law 1–145 (2001).

Handbuch Wirtschaftsstrafrecht, (Hans Achenbach, Andreas Ransiek, & Katharina Beckemper eds., 3. ed. 2012).

Hans Schaefer & Diethelm Baumann, *Compliance-Organisation und Sanktionen bei Verstößen*, NJW 3601–3605 (2011).

Hans-Georg Meier, *Der Arbeitsvertrag des Compliance-Beauftragten – Rechtliche Notwendigkeiten und Möglichkeiten*, 2011 NZA 779–782 (2011).

Hartmut Renz & Tim Wybitul, *Im Blickpunkt: Das Berufsbild des Compliance-Beauftragten Ein modernesVerständnis von Compliance*, BB (2012).

Hartmut Renz, *Chief-Compliance-Officer - Das Berufsbild im Jahr 2020 – Ein Zwischenstandsbericht*, ZRFC 38–43 (2014).

Heather E. Canary & Marianne M. Jennings, *Principles and Influence in Codes of Ethics: A Centering Resonance Analysis Comparing Pre- and Post-Sarbanes-Oxley Codes of Ethics*, 80 Journal of Business Ethics 263–278 (2008).

Heather Traeger & McAllister Jimbo, *Supervisory Liability: The SEC's Scrutiny and Support of Chief Compliance Officers: Part 1 of 2*, 21 The Investment Lawyer 12–21 (2014).

Heather Traeger, Kris Easter Guidroz & McAllister Jimbo, *Supervisory Liability: The SEC's Scrutiny and Support of Chief Compliance Officers: Part 1 of 2*, 21 The Investment Lawyer 25–33 (2014).

Henning Herzog & Gregor Stephan, Berufsfeldstudie Compliance Manager 2013: Vermessung eines Berufsstandes (Berufsverband der Compliance Manager (BCM) ed., 1. Aufl ed. 2013).

Henry Adobor, *Exploring the Role Performance of Corporate Ethics Officers*, 69 Journal of Business Ethics 57–75 (2006).

Hillary A. Sale, *Monitoring Caremark's Good Faith*, 32 Delaware Journal of Corporate Law 719–755 (2007).

Holger Fleischer, *Aktienrechtliche Compliance-Pflichten im Praxistest: Das Siemens/Neubürger-Urteil des LG München I*, NZG 321–329 (2014).

Holger Fleischer, *Corporate Compliance im aktienrechtlichen Unternehmensverbund*, CCZ 1–6 (2008).

House of Commons Library, How much legislation comes from Europe? (2010).

Hudson Hollister, *Shock Therapy' for Aktiengesellschaften: Can the Sarbanes-Oxley Certification Requirements Transform German Corporate Culture, Practice and Prospects?*, 25 Nw. J. Int'l L. & Bus 453 (2005).

Ian Ayres & John Braithwaite, Responsive regulation: transcending the deregulation debate (1995).

Ian B. Lee, *Corporate Criminal Responsibility as Team Member Responsibility*, 31 Oxford Journal of Legal Studies 755–781 (2011).

Int'l Business Publications USA, US Company Laws and Regulations Handbook Volume 2 Corporate Laws and Regulation in the Selected States of the US: Delaware Corporation (4. ed. 2009).

Iris H.-Y. Chiu, Regulating (From) the Inside: The Legal Framework for Internal Control in Banks and Financial Institutions (2015).

J. Kent & G.F. Comstock, Commentaries on American Law (3. ed. 1867).

J. Story, Commentaries on the Constitution of the United States: With a Preliminary Review of the Constitutional History of the Colonies and States, Before the Adoption of the Constitution (1833).

Jaclyn Jaeger, *The Real State of CCO Legal Liability*, 2015 Compliance Week 28–30 (2015).

James A. Fanto, *Surveillant and Counselor: A Reorientation in Compliance for Financial Firms*, Brooklyn Law School 1–65 (2013).

James Gobert, *Corporate criminality: four models of fault*, 14 Legal Studies 393–410 (1994).

James Gordley & A.T. von Mehren, An Introduction to the Comparative Study of Private Law: Readings, Cases, Materials (1. ed. 2009).

James Weber & Dana Fortun, *Ethics and Compliance Officer Profile: Survey, Comparison, and Recommendations*, 110 Business and Society Review 97–115 (2005).

James Weber & David M. Wasieleski, *Corporate Ethics and Compliance Programs: A Report, Analysis and Critique*, 112 Journal of Business Ethics 609–626 (2013).

Jan Christian Heller, Joseph E. Murphy & Mark E. Meaney, Guide to professional development in compliance (2001).

Jan Schlösser, *Die Anerkennung der Geschäftsherrenhaftung durch den BGH*, Neue Zeitschrift für Wirtschafts-, Steuer- und Unternehmensstrafrecht 281–286 (2012).

Jeffrey Coles, Naveen D. Daniel & Lalitha Naveen, *Boards: Does one size fit all*, 87 Journal of Financial Economics 329–356 (2008).

Jennifer Payne, *Legal Capital and Creditor Protection in UK Private Companies*, 5 European Company Law 220–228 (2008).

Jennifer Payne, Legal Capital in the UK Following the Companies Act 2006 (2008).

Jens Tiedemann, *Beginn und Hemmung der Kündigungserklärungsfrist für Ausspruch einer fristlosen Kündigung nach internen Ermittlungen durch Compliance-Abteilung der Konzernobergesellschaft*, jurisPR-Compl (2015).

Jerry Ellig & Hester Peirce, *SEC Regulatory Analysis: "A Long Way to Go and a Short Time to Get There"*, 8 BROOK. J. CORP. FIN. & COM. L. 361–437 (2014).

Jessica Erickson, *Corporate Governance in the Courtroom: An Empirical Analysis*, 51 William & Mary Law Review 1749 (2010).

Jessica Naima Djilani, *The British Importation of American Corporate Compliance*, 76 Brooklyn Law Rev. 303–341 (2011).

JILL SOLOMON, Corporate Governance and Accountability (2nd ed. 2007).

JOAN MACLEOD HEMINWAY, The Extraterritorial Application of U.S. Securities Fraud Prohibitions in an Increasingly Global Transactional World (2012).

Jochen Benz & Thomas Klindt, *Compliance 2020 – ein Blick in die Zukunft*, 49 BB 2977–2980 (2010).

Jochen Deister & Anton Geier, *Der UK Bribery Act 2010 und seine Auswirkungen auf deutsche Unternehmen*, CCZ 12–18 (2011).

JOCHEN GLÄSER & GRIT LAUDEL, Experteninterviews und qualitative Inhaltsanalyse: als Instrumente rekonstruierender Untersuchungen (2009).

Jochen Reichert & Nicolas Ott, *Die Zuständigkeit von Vorstand und Aufsichtsrat zur Aufklärung von Non Compliance in der AG*, NZG 241–251 (2014).

Johannes Sebastian Blassl, *Vorstandsüberwachung auch durch die Compliance-Funktion*, ZRFC 205–211 (2016).

John Armour et al., *Private Enforcement of Corporate Law: An Empirical Comparison of the United Kingdom and the United States: Private Enforcement of Corporate Law: United Kingdom vs. United States*, 6 Journal of Empirical Legal Studies 687–722 (2009).

JOHN C. COFFEE, Gatekeepers: The Professions and Corporate Governance (1. ed. 2006).

JOHN C. GRAY, The Nature and Sources of the Law (New ed. 2009).

JOHN H. MERRYMAN & R. PÉREZ-PERDOMO, The Civil Law Tradition: An Introduction to the Legal Systems of Europe and Latin America (3. ed. 2007).

John Runne, *The Confluence of Sullivan v. Harnisch & Dodd-Frank: Adapting New York's Common Law to Fill a Compliance Hole*, 79 Brooklyn Law Review (2014).

Jonathan Edwards & Simon Wolfe, *A compliance competence partnership approach model*, 14 Journal of Financial Regulation and Compliance 140–150 (2006).

Jonathan Edwards & Simon Wolfe, *Compliance: A review*, 13 Journal of Financial Regulation and Compliance 48–59 (2005).

Jonathan Edwards & Simon Wolfe, *The compliance function in banks*, 12 Journal of Financial Regulation and Compliance 216–224 (2004).

Jonathan Fisher, The law of investor protection (2nd ed. 2003).

Jonathan Shirley, *International Law and the Ramifications of the Sarbanes-Oxley Act of 2002*, 27 B.C. Int'l & Comp. L. Rev 501–528 (2004).

Jörg Fecker & Ulrich-Peter Kinzl, *Ausgestaltung der arbeitsrechtlichen Stellung des Compliance-Officers Schlussfolgerungen aus der BSR-Entscheidung des BGH*, CCZ 13–20 (2010).

Jörg Thierfelder, *Anforderungsprofil für Compliance Officer*, *in* Der Compliance Officer: ein Handbuch in eigener Sache § 2, 15–24 (Jürgen Bürkle & Christoph E. Hauschka eds., 1. ed. 2015).

José A. Campos Nave, *Strafbarkeit des Compliance Officer aufgrund einer aus dem Aufgabenbereich abgeleiteten Garantenstellung*, Betriebs-Berater 2059 (2009).

José A. Tabuena & Jennifer L. Smith, *The Chief Compliance Officer versus the General Counsel: Friends or Foes? Part II*, Journal of Health Care Compliance 13–18 (2006).

Joseph Chitty *&* H. G. Beale, Chitty on contracts. Vol. 1: General principles (31. ed. 2012).

Joseph D. Piotroski & Suraj Srinivasan, *Regulation and Bonding: The Sarbanes-Oxley Act and the Flow of International Listings*, 46 Journal of Accounting Research 383–425 (2008).

Joseph Dainow, *The Civil Law and the Common Law: Some Points of Comparison*, 15 The American Journal of Comparative Law 419–435 (1966).

Joseph E. Murphy, *The Compliance Officer: Delimiting the Domain*, *in* Guide to professional development in compliance 19–36 (2001).

Joseph Weber, *The New Ethics Enforcers - These corporate cops have unprecedented power to throw their weight around*, 4 Business Week 40–41 (2007).

Joshua Joseph, *Integrating Business Ethics and Compliance Programs: A Study of Ethics Officers in Leading Organizations*, 107 Business and Society Review 309–347 (2003).

Jürgen Bürkle, *Compliance als Aufgabe des Vorstands der AG – Die Sicht des LG München I*, CCZ 52–55 (2015).

Jürgen Bürkle, *Der Compliance Officer in regulierten Finanzsektoren*, *in* Der Compliance Officer: ein Handbuch in eigener Sache 315–342 (Jürgen Bürkle & Christoph E. Hauschka eds., 1. ed. 2015).

Jürgen Bürkle, *Grenzen der strafrechtlichen Garantenstellung des Compliance-Officers*, 2010 CCZ 4–12 (2010).

Jürgen Van Kann, Vorstand der AG: Führungsaufgaben, Rechtspflichten und Corporate Governance (2. ed. 2012).

Kalman J. Cohen & Richard M. Cyert, *Strategy: Formulation, Implementation, and Monitoring*, 46 The Journal of Business 349–367 (1973).

Kam C. Chan et al., *Compliance and determinants of US-listed foreign firms' 20-F filings under the new Securities and Exchange Commission accelerated deadline*, 23 Journal of Financial Regulation and Compliance 161–178 (2015).

KARLSRUHER KOMMENTAR ZUM OWIG | COMMENTARY ON THE ACT ON REGULATORY OFFENCES, (Lothar Senge ed., 4. ed. 2014).

Kathleen Mittelsdorf, *Zur Reichweite individueller strafrechtlicher Verantwortung im Unternehmen für Fehlverhalten von unterstellten Mitarbeitern*, ZIS 123–128 (2011).

Keith Stanton, *Comparative Law in the House of Lords and Supreme Court*, 42 Common Law World Review 269–296 (2013).

KLAUS J. HOPT, Comparative Company Law 37 (2006).

Klaus Lackhoff & Martin Schulz, *Das Unternehmen als Gefahrenquelle? Compliance-Risiken für Unternehmensleiter und Mitarbeiter*, CCZ 81–88 (2010).

Klaus Luig, *Die Anfänge der Wissenschaft vom deutschen Privatrecht*, Ius Commune I IUS COMMUNE 195–222 (1967).

KLAUS MOOSMAYER & JOSEF WINTER, The Siemens Compliance System: "Prevent – Detect – Respond and Continuous Improvement" (2011).

KLAUS MOOSMAYER, Compliance: Praxisleitfaden für Unternehmen (3. ed. 2015).

Klaus Moosmayer, *Modethema oder Pflichtprogramm guter Unternehmensführung? – Zehn Thesen zu Compliance*, 2012 NJW 3013–3017 (2012).

Kommentar zum Deutschen Corporate Governance Kodex: Kodex-Kommentar (Thomas Kremer et al., 6. ed. 2016).

KONRAD ZWEIGERT & HEIN KÖTZ, Einführung in die Rechtsvergleichung auf dem Gebiete des Privatrechts (3. ed. 1996).

Konstantin von Busekist & Oliver Hein, *Ein praktischer Compliance Standard in den USA? Eine Analyse von Prosecution Agreements mit dem Department of Justice*, CCZ 185–191 (2013).

Kündigungsrecht (Reiner Ascheid, Ulrich Preis, & Ingrid Schmidt eds., 5. ed. 2017).

L. C. B. Gower, *The English Private Company*, 18 Law and Contemporary Problems 535–545 (1953).

Lambertus Fuhrmann, *Internal Investigations: Was dürfen und müssen die Organe beim Verdacht von Compliance Verstößen tun?*, NZG 881–889 (2016).

LAW COMMISSION & SCOTTISH LAW COMMISSION, Company Directors: Regulating Conflicts of Interests and Formulating a Statement of Duties (1998).

Lawrence A. Cunningham, *The Sarbanes-Oxley Yawn: Heavy Rhetoric, Light Reform (And it Might Just Work)*, 36 University of Connecticut Law Review (2003).

Lawrence D. Finder, Ryan D. McConnell & Scott L. Mitchell, *Betting the Corporation: Compliance or Defiance?*, 28 Corp. Counsel Rev. (2009).

Lawrence J. Trautman & Kara Altenbaumer-Price, *The Foreign Corrupt Practices Act: Minefield for Directors*, 6 Virginia Law & Business Review (2011).

LEE WERRELL, Compliance Managers Guidebook & Reference (2. ed. 2014).

Linda Klebe Treviño et al., *Legitimating the legitimate: A grounded theory study of legitimacy work among Ethics and Compliance Officers*, 123 Organizational Behavior and Human Decision Processes 186–205 (2014).

Lori A. McMillan, *The Business Judgment Rule as an Immunity Doctrine*, 4 Wm. & Mary Bus. L. Rev . 521–574 (2013).

Lothar Bildat & Stefan Behringer, *Beruf mit Berufung: Eigenschaften, Kompetenzen, Probleme im Arbeitsalltag von Compliance-Managern*, ZRFC 278–286 (2016).

Lyman Johnson & David Millon, *Recalling Why Corporate Officers Are Fiduciaries*, 46 William & Mary Law Review 1597 (2005).

Lyman Johnson, *Corporate Officers and the Business Judgment Rule*, 60 Business Lawyer (2005).

Lynn S. Paine, *Managing for Organizational Integrity*, 72 Harvard Business Review 106–117 (1994).

M. Cruickshanks, *The Role of the Compliance Officer: The Influence of Culture and Company Constitution*, 1 Journal of Financial Regulation and Compliance 376–384 (1993).

MADS ANDENAS & DUNCAN FAIRGRIEVE, Courts and Comparative Law (1. ed. 2015).

MAGALI SARFATTI LARSON, The rise of professionalism: a sociological analysis (1. ed. 1977).

Mar Pérezts & Sébastien Picard, *Compliance or Comfort Zone? The Work of Embedded Ethics in Performing Regulation*, 131 Journal of Business Ethics 833–852 (2015).

MARC J. LANE, Representing Corporate Officers, Directors, Managers, and Trustees (2nd ed. 2010).

Marc Steffek, *Bundesgerichtshof verschärft strafrechtliche Verantwortung von Compliance-Officern - Das Urteil, der Hintergrund und die Auswirkungen*, ZRFC 249–251 (2009).

Marcus Kirsch, *Im Blickpunkt: Die Tätigkeitsschwerpunkte des Compliance-Officer*, 2011 BB V (2011).

Margot Cleveland et al., *Trends in the International Fight Against Bribery and Corruption*, 90 Journal of Business Ethics 199–244 (2009).

Maurice E. Stucke, *In Search of Effective Ethics & Compliance Programs* 77 (2014), http://www.ssrn.com/abstract=2366209 (last visited Feb 2, 2016).

MARIETTA AUER, Materialisierung, Flexibilisierung, Richterfreiheit: Generalklauseln im Spiegel der Antinomien des Privatrechtsdenkens (2005).

Mark E. Meaney, *Professional Ethical Development in Health Care Compliance, in* Guide to professional development in compliance (2001).

Mark Freeman, Robin Pearson & James Taylor, The Politics of Business: Joint Stock Company Constitutions in Britain, 1720–1844.

Mark S. Schwartz, Thomas W. Dunfee & Michael J. Kline, *Tone at the Top: An Ethics Code for Directors?*, 58 Journal of Business Ethics 79–100 (2005).

Markus Rübenstahl, *Zur „regelmäßigen" Garantenstellung des Compliance Officers*, NZG 1341–1344 (2009).

Martin Burgi, *Compliance im Staat – Staat und Compliance*, Corporate Compliance Zeitschrift 41–45 (2010).

Martin Petrin, *The Curious Case of Directors' and Officers' Liability for Supervision and Management: Exploring the Intersection of Corporate and Tort Law*, 59 American University Law Review 1161–1715 (2010).

Martin Schulz & Hartmut Renz, *Der erfolgreiche Compliance-Beauftragte - Leitlinien eines branchenübergreifenden Berufsbildes*, 2012 Betriebs-Berater 2511–2517 (2012).

Martin T. Biegelman & Daniel R. Biegelman, Foreign Corrupt Practices Act Compliance Guidebook: Protecting Your Organization from Bribery and Corruption (1. ed. 2010).

Martin Wolf, *Der Compliance-Officer - Garant, hoheitlich Beauftragter oder Berater im Unternehmensinteresse zwischen Zivil-, Straf- und Aufsichtsrecht?*, 2011 BB 1353–1360 (2011).

Massimo Belcredi & Guido Ferrarini, The European Corporate Governance Framework: Issues and Perspectives (2013).

Mathias M. Siems, *Legal Origins: Reconciling Law & Finance and Comparative Law*, 52 McGill Law Journal 55–81 (2007).

Matthew John Weait, *The Role of the Compliance Officer in Firms Carrying on Investment Business*, June, 2005.

Matthias Dann & Anja Mengel, *Tanz auf einem Pulverfass – oder: Wie gefährlich leben Compliance-Beauftragte?*, 2010 NJW 3265–3269 (2010).

Megan Barry, *Why Ethics & Compliance Programs can fail*, 23 Journal of Business Strategy 37–40 (2002).

Megan W. Shaner, *The (Un)Enforcement of Corporate Officers' Duties*, 48 UC Davis Law Review 271–336 (2014).

Melvin Eisenberg, *The Duty of Good Faith in Corporate Law*, 31 Delaware Journal of Corporate Law 1–75 (2006).

Michael Clarke, *What is Compliance? The Moral Dimension*, 3 Journal of Financial Regulation and Compliance 123–125 (1995).

Michael D. Greenberg, *Corporate culture and ethical leadership under the federal sentencing guidelines: what should boards, management and policymakers do now?* (2012).

Michael D. Greenberg, *Culture, compliance, and the C-suite: how executives, boards, and policymakers can better safeguard against misconduct at the top* (2013).

Michael D. Greenberg, *Directors as guardians of compliance and ethics within the corporate citadel: what the policy community should know* (Center for Corporate Ethics and Governance ed., 2010).

Michael D. Greenberg, *Perspectives of chief ethics and compliance officers on the detection and prevention of corporate misdeeds: what the policy community should know* (2009).

Michael D. Greenberg, *Transforming compliance: emerging paradigms for boards, management, compliance officers, and government* (Rand Corporation ed., 2014).

Michael J. Mumford, *Corporate Governance and Financial Distress: when structures have to change*, 11 Corporate Governance 52–64 (2003).

Michael Lindemann & Janita Sommer, *Die strafrechtliche Geschäftsherrenhaftung und ihre Bedeutung für den Bereich der Criminal Compliance*, JuS 1057–1062 (2015).

Michael Moran, Politics and Governance in the UK (2011).

Michael R. Rosella & Domenick Pugliese, *The Investment Company Chief Compliance Officer: Three years later – an Assessment of the Evolution of the Role of the CCO*, 7 Journal of Investment Compliance 16–22 (2006).

Michele Beardslee & DeStefano, *Creating a Culture of Compliance: Why Departmentalization May Not Be the Answer*, 10 Hastings Business Law Journal 71–182 (2013).

Mike Koehler, *Revisiting a Foreign Corrupt Practices Act Compliance Defense*, Wisconsin Law Review 609–659 (2012).

Miriam H. Baer, *Confronting the Two Faces of Corporate Fraud*, 66 Florida Law Review 87–156 (2014).

Miriam H. Baer, *Governing Corporate Compliance*, 50 B. C. L. Rev. 949–975 (2009).

Miriam H. Baer, *Organizational Liability and the Tension between Corporate and Criminal Law*, 19 Journal of Law and Policy 1–14 (2011).

Monika Roth, *Zur Haftung des Compliance-Officers - Ein weiterer Entscheid aus der Schweiz in Sachen Alstom S. A.*, ZRFC 132–136 (2014).

Muel Kaptein, *The Effectiveness of Ethics Programs: The Role of Scope, Composition, and Sequence*, 132 Journal of Business Ethics 415–431 (2015).

Münchener Anwaltshandbuch: Verteidigung in Wirtschafts- und Steuerstrafsachen (Klaus Volk & Heiko Ahlbrecht eds., 2. ed. 2014).

Münchener Kommentar zum Bürgerlichen Gesetzbuch, (Franz Jürgen Säcker & Roland Rixecker eds., 7. ed. 2015).

Münchner Kommentar zum StGB | Munich Commentary on the StGB, 5 (Joecks & Miebach eds., 2. ed. 2014).

Munich Commentary on the AktG, 2 (Wulf Goette & Mathias Habersack eds., 4. ed. 2014).

NACUA, *The Case for Compliance Programs: The Legal and Policy Mandates*14 (2011).

Nadja Fee Viola Groß, Chief Compliance Officer: Compliance-Funktionsträger im Spannungsverhältnis zwischen wirksamer Compliance und arbeitsrechtlicher / gesellschaftsrechtlicher Kompetenzordnung (1. ed. 2012).

Nadja Raus & Martin Lützeler, *Berichtspflicht des Compliance Officers – zwischen interner Eskalation und externer Anzeige*, 2012 CCZ 96–101 (2012).

Nancy Murphy & Mary Canales, *A critical analysis of compliance*, 8 Nursing Inquiry 173–181 (2001).

Ngozi V. Okoye, Behavioural Risks in Corporate Governance: Regulatory Intervention as a Risk Management Mechanism (2015).

Nicola Buffo & Bina Brünjes, *Gesucht wird ein Compliance-Officer – Ein 200.000 Euro-Beispiel aus der Praxis*, CCZ 108–112 (2008).

Nicole Dando et al., *The Evolving Responsibilities & Liabilities of Ethics Representatives: A practical guide*, *in* EBEF Paper One (2013).

Nigel G. Foster *&* Satish Sule, German legal system & laws (4. ed. 2010).

Norbert Nolte & Carsten Bormann, *Unzulässigkeit einer Durchsuchung von Privaträumen*, jurisPR-Compl (2014).

Oliver Hein, *Verbandsstrafgesetzbuch (VerbStrG-E) – Bietet der Entwurf Anreize zur Vermeidung von Wirtschaftskriminalität in Unternehmen?*, CCZ 75–81 (2014).

Pat K. Chew, Directors' and officers' liability (4. ed. 1993).

Patrick J. Gnazzo, *The Chief Ethics and Compliance Officer: A Test of Endurance*, 116 Business and Society Review 533–553 (2011).

Patrick Ulrich, *Einfluss des Aufsichtsrats auf das Compliance-Management*, ZRFC 7–13 (2017).

Paul E. McGreal, *Corporate Compliance Survey*, 67 The Business Lawyer 227–253 (2011).

Paul L. Davies, The Board of Directors: Composition, Structure, Duties and Powers (2000).

Paula Hannaford-Agor *&* Nicole L. Waters, Estimating the Cost of Civil Litigation (2013).

Pauline Ashall, *The New Settlement under the Financial Services Act 1986*, 1 Journal of Financial Regulation and Compliance 47–55 (1992).

Peter Fissenewert, *Compliance für den Mittelstand*, NZG 1009–1013 (2015).

Peter Fissenewert, *ISO 19600 Der neue Standard zur Zertifizierung von Compliance-Management-Systemen*, ZRFC 198–205 (2015).

Peter Hay, US-amerikanisches Recht: ein Studienbuch (5. ed. 2011).

Peter Hemeling, *Compliance im Erst- und Rückversicherungsunternehmen*, CCZ 21–25 (2010).

Peter Iliev, *The Effect of SOX Section 404: Costs, Earnings Quality, and Stock Prices*, 65 The Journal of Finance 1163–1196 (2010).

Peter L. Strauss, *Courts or Tribunals? Federal Courts and the Common Law*, 53 Alabama Law Review 891–925 (2002).

Petri Mäntysaari, Comparative Corporate Governance: Shareholders as a Rule-maker (1. ed. 2006).

Phil McMagnus, *Environmental Regulation*, Elsevier Ltd. (2009).

Pierre Teilhard de Chardin, The future of man (1. ed. 2004).

Prabirjit Sarkar, *Common Law vs. Civil Law: Which System Provides More Protection to Shareholders and Creditors and Promotes Financial Development*, 2 Journal of Advanced Research in Law and Economics 143–161 (2011).

Preeti Choudhary, Jason D. Schloetzer & Jason D. Sturgess, *Boards, Auditors, Attorneys and Compliance with Mandatory SEC Disclosure Rules*, 34 Managerial and Decision Economics 471–487 (2013).

R. H. Watzlaff, *The Bubble Act of 1720*, 7 Abacus 8–28 (1971).

Rafael La Porta, Florencio Lopez-de-Silanes & Andrei Shleifer, *The Economic Consequences of Legal Origins*, 46 Journal of Economic Literature 285–332 (2008).

Rainer Wörlen & Axel Kokemoor, Employment Law (11. ed. 2014).

Raluca Lupu, *Sources of Law - Judicial Precedent*, 5 Contemporary Readings in Law and Social Justice 375–381 (2013).

Raoul C. Van Caenegem, Judges, Legislators and Professors: Chapters in European Legal History (1. ed. 1993).

Rebecca Julia Koch, *Der Compliance-Officer und die D&O-Versicherung*, ZRFC 135–139 (2016).

Reinhard Zimmermann & Simon Whittaker, *Good faith in European contract law: surveying the legal landscape*, *in* Good faith in European contract law 7–62 (1. ed. 2000).

Reinier H. Kraakman, *Corporate Liability Strategies and the Costs of Legal Controls*, 93 The Yale Law Journal 857 (1984).

Richard A. Epstein, *In Defense of the Contract at Will*, 51 University of Chicago Law Review 947–982 (1984).

Richard Moorhead & Steven Vaughan, Legal Risk: Definition, Management and Ethics (2015).

Richter Jan Helmrich, *Zur Strafbarkeit bei fehlenden oder unzureichenden Risikomanagementsystemen in Unternehmen am Beispiel der AG*, NZG 1252–1256 (2011).

Rob Sobol, *Conversations at the top: the tone of the independent chief compliance officer*, 10 Journal of Investment Compliance 10–15 (2009).

Robert A. Kagan, Neil Gunningham & Dorothy Thornton, *Fear, Duty and Regulatory Compliance: Lessons from three research projects*, *in* Explaining Compliance Business Responses to Regulation. 37–58 (1. ed. 2011).

Robert Baldwin, Bridget Hutter & Henry Rothstein, Risk Regulation, Manangement and Compliance (2011).

Robert Baldwin, Martin Cave & Martin Lodge, Understanding regulation: theory, strategy, and practice (2nd ed. 2012).

Robert C. Bird & Stephen Kim Park, *The Domains of Corporate Counsel in an Era of Compliance: The Domains of Corporate Counsel in an Era of Compliance*, 53 American Business Law Journal 203–249 (2016).

Robert Rosen, Christine Parker & Vibeke Lehmann Nielsen, *The Framing Effects of Professionalism: Is There a Lawyer Cast of Mind? Lessons from Compliance Programs*, XL Fordham Urban Law Journal 297–367 (2013).

Robert Summers, *The General Duty of Good Faith – Its Recognition and Conceptualization*, 67 Cornell Law Review 810–840 (1982).

Robert W. Smith, *Corporate Ethics Officers And Government Ethics Administrators: Comparing Apples With Oranges or a Lesson to Be Learned?*, 34 Administration & Society 632–652 (2003).

Robyn Fairman & Charlotte Yapp, *Enforced Self-Regulation, Prescription, and Conceptions of Compliance within Small Businesses: The Impact of Enforcement*, 27 Law & Policy 491–519 (2005).

Roger Miles, *From compliance to coping: Experiences of Chief Risk Officers in UK banks 2007–2009*, July 4, 2012.

Ron Harris, Industrializing English law: entrepreneurship and business organization, 1720–1844 (2000).

Ron Harris, *The Bubble Act: Its Passage and Its Effects on Business Organization*, 54 The Journal of Economic History 610–627 (1994).

Roth, Altmeppen | Commentary on the GmbHG, (Roth & Altmeppen eds., 8. ed. 2015).

Rowan Bosworth-Davies, *An Analysis of Compliance Officer: Attitudes towards insider dealing*, 20 Crime Law Soc Change 339–357 (1993).

Rowan Bosworth-Davies, *Practical Training for Compliance Officers: An Assessment*, 1 Journal of Financial Regulation and Compliance 34–46 (1992).

Rowan Bosworth-Davies, *The SEC: An Examination of its Structures, Powers and Procedures*, 2 Journal of Financial Regulation and Compliance 31–41 (1993).

Rüdiger Werner, *Die Compliance-Aufgabe des Aufsichtsrats*, ZWH 449–456 (2014).

Russell Reynolds Associates, What makes an effective UK Board? Views from FTSE Chairmen. (2002).

Saleem Sheikh, A guide to the Companies Act 2006 (3. ed. 2008).

Sally Bernstein & Andrea Falcione, *Resilience | The CCO Star in 2025*, A journal of strategy and risk (2014).

Samantha Linsley, *SROs: A Compliance Officer's Perspective*, 1 Journal of Financial Regulation and Compliance 364–369 (1993).

Samuel Estreicher & Jeffrey M. Hirsch, *Comparative Wrongful Dismissal Law: Reassessing American Exceptionalism*, 92 North Carolina Law Review 343–480 (2013).

Samuel Richard, *To Bribe a Prince: Clarifying the Foreign Corrupt Practices Act Through Comparisons to the United Kingdom's Bribery Act of 2010*, 37 Boston College International and Comparative Law Review 419–450 (2014).

Sara Sun Beale, The Development and Evolution of the U.S. Law of Corporate Criminal Liability 32 (2014).

Sarah Worthington, *Reforming Directors' Duties*, 64 Modern Law Review 439–458 (2001).

Sascha Süße & Carolin Püschel, *Die Diskussion um die Einführung eines Unternehmensstrafrechts in Deutschland – Gesetzgebungsvorschlag des Bundesverbandes der Unternehmensjuristen*, Newsdienst Compliance 11002.

Sascha Süße & Schneider, *Entwurf eines Gesetzes zur Einführung der strafrechtlichen Verantwortlichkeit von Unternehmen und sonstigen Verbänden aus Nordrhein-Westfalen*, Newsdienst Compliance 71002.

Sascha Süße, *Bundesweites Wettbewerbsregister – kommt es diesmal?*, Newsdienst Compliance 71001.

Sascha Süße, *Der Compliance Officer im Fokus behördlicher Ermittlungen*, Newsdienst Compliance 71004.

Scott A. Roney & Patricia J. Harned, *Leading Corporate Integrity: Defining the Role of the Chief Ethics & Compliance Officer (CECO), in* Ethics Resource Center (ERC) (2007).

Securities Industry Association, Compliance & Legal Division, *The role of compliance*, 6 Journal of Investment Compliance 4–22 (2005).

Sharon Oded, *Inducing corporate compliance: A compound corporate liability regime*, 31 International Review of Law and Economics 272–283 (2011).

Sharon Ward, The changing face of compliance: managing regulatory risk (1. ed. 2015).

Shyamkrishna Balganesh & Gideon Parchomovsky, *Structure and Value in the Common Law*, 163 U. of Penn. Law. Rev. 1241–1310 (2015).

Sridhar Arcot, Valentina Bruno & Antoine Faure-Grimaud, *Corporate governance in the UK: Is the comply or explain approach working?*, 30 International Review of Law and Economics 193–201 (2010).

Stefan Behringer, *Aktuelle Entwicklungen der Regulierungen aus Sicht der Politik und der Unternehmenspraxis*, ZRFC 188–189 (2015).

Steffen Krieger & Jens Günther, *Der Compliance-Officer*, ZRFC 149–154 (2011).

Steffen Krieger & Jens Günther, *Die arbeitsrechtliche Stellung des Compliance Officers Gestaltung einer Compliance-Organisation unter Berücksichtigung der Vorgaben im BGH-Urteil vom 17. 7. 2009*, 2010 NZA 367–373 (2010).

Stephen Brammer & Andrew Millington, *The Development of Corporate Charitable Contributions in the UK: A Stakeholder Analysis*, 41 Journal of Management Studies 1411–1434 (2004).

Stephen R. Wilson et al., English legal system (1. ed. 2014).

Stewart J. Schwab & Randall S. Thomas, *What Do CEOs Bargain For? An Empirical Study of Key Legal Components of CEO Employment Contracts*, 63 Washington and Lee Law Review 231–270 (2006).

Strafgesetzbuch | Commentary on the Criminal Law, (Lackner & Kühl, 28. ed. 2014).

Strafrecht | Beck Online Commentary on Criminal Law, (v Heintschel-Heinegg ed., 33. ed. 2016).

Strafrecht | Commentary on Criminal Law, (Adolf Schönke & Horst Schröder eds., 29. ed. 2014).

Strafrecht | Commentary on Criminal Law, (Kindhäuser, Neumann, & Paeffgen eds., 4. ed. 2013).

Stuart H. Deming, The Foreign Corrupt Practices Act and the New International Norms (2nd ed. 2010).

Stuart Weinstein & Charles Wild, Legal Risk Management, Governance and Compliance: A Guide to Best Practice from Leading Experts (2013).

Susan Lorde Martin, *Compliance Officers: More Jobs, More Responsibility, More Liability*, 29 Notre Dame Journal of Law, Ethics & Public Policy 169 (2015).

T. Jean Engebretson & Heidi Hylton Meier, *The Perceived Effectiveness of the Officer Certification Requirement under Sarbanes-Oxley*, 15 International Journal of Auditing 176–190 (2011).

Tania Clench, Being Concerned in the Management of a Company–What Does it Mean? 29–31 (2012).

Tanina Rostain, *General Counsel in the Age of Compliance: Preliminary Findings and New Research Questions*, 21 Georgetown Journal of Legal Ethics 465–490 (2008).

The US justice system: an encyclopedia, (Steven Harmon Wilson ed., 2012).

THEODORE L. BANKS & FREDERICK Z. BANKS, Corporate legal compliance handbook (2nd ed. 2011).

Thomas M. Majewski, *Conflicts of Interest Chief Compliance Officers face in implementing Compliance Programs for Investment Funds and Investment Advisers*, 7 Journal of Investment Compliance 23–27 (2006).

Thomas Rotsch, *Compliance*, *in* Handbuch Wirtschaftsstrafrecht 45–78 (Hans Achenbach, Andreas Ransiek, & Katharina Beckemper eds., 3. ed. 2012).

Thomas Rotsch, *Grundfragen der Criminal Compliance*, *in* Criminal Compliance: Handbuch (Katharina Beckemper & Thomas Rotsch, 1. ed. 2015).

Tim Wybitul, *Strafbarkeitsrisiken für Compliance-Verantwortliche*, 2009 BB 2590–2593 (2009).

Tobias Brouwer, *§ 59 Compliance in Verbänden*, *in* Corporate Compliance: Handbuch der Haftungsvermeidung im Unternehmen (Christoph E. Hauschka, Klaus Moosmayer, & Thomas Lösler eds., 3. ed. 2016).

Tobias Nikoleyczik & Bernd Graßl, *Überarbeitung des Deutschen Corporate Governance Kodex (DCGK) – Die Änderungsvorschläge der Regierungskommission aus der Plenarsitzung vom 13.10.2016*, NZG 161–169.

Tom Giesen, *Die Haftung des Compliance-Officers gegenüber seinem Arbeitgeber – Haftungsprivilegierung bei innerbetrieblichem Schadensausgleich?*, CCZ 102–106 (2009).

Ton van Snellenberg & Rob van de Peppel, *Perspectives on compliance: non-compliance with environmental licences in the Netherlands*, 12 European Environment 131–148 (2002).

Ulf Klebeck & Peter Felix Zollinger, *Compliance-Funktion nach der AIFM-Richtlinie*, Betriebs-Berater 459–464 (2013).

Ulrich L. Göres, *Stellung des Compliance-Beauftragten*, ZRFC 178–184 (2011).

Ulrich Tödtmann & Marc Winstel, *§ 13 Compliance als Vorstandsaufgabe*, *in* Arbeitshandbuch für Vorstandsmitglieder (Dietmar Kubis, Johannes Semler, & Michael Arnold eds., 2. ed. 2015).

Uwe H. Schneider, *Compliance als Aufgabe der Unternehmensleitung*, ZIP 645–650 (2003).

Uwe H. Schneider, *Compliance im Konzern*, NZG 1321–1326 (2009).

Valentina Vadi, *Corporate Social Responsibility in the Twenty-First Century: Debates, Models and Practices across Government, Law and Business - By Bryan Horrigan: Book reviews*, 31 Legal Studies 667–670 (2011).

Vivienne O'Connor, *Common Law and Civil Law Traditions*, *in* PRACTITIONER'S GUIDE 1–35, 12 (2012), http://www.ssrn.com/abstract=2665675 (last visited Dec 20, 2014).

Virginia Bodolica & Martin Spraggon, *An Examination into the Disclosure, Structure, and Contents of Ethical Codes in Publicly Listed Acquiring Firms*, 126 Journal of Business Ethics 459–472 (2015).

Volker Rieble, *Zivilrechtliche Haftung der Compliance-Agenten*, CCZ 1–4 (2010).

W. Michael Hoffman & Mark Rowe, *The Ethics Officer as Agent of the Board: Leveraging Ethical Governance Capability in the Post-Enron Corporation*, 112 Business and Society Review 553–572 (2007).

W. Michael Hoffman, John D. Neill & O. Scott Stovall, *An Investigation of Ethics Officer Independence*, 78 Journal of Business Ethics 87–95 (2008).

Weil, Gotshal & Manges LLP, Comparative Study Of Corporate Governance Codes Relevant to the European Union And Its Member States (2002).

Wells, *Criminal Responsibility of Legal Persons in Common Law Jurisdictions, in* Paper prepared for Oecd Anti-Corruption Unit 10 (2000).

Werner Beulke & Klaus Moosmayer, *Der Reformvorschlag des Bundesverbandes der Unternehmensjuristen zu den §§ OWIG § 30, OWIG § 130 OWiG– Plädoyer für ein modernes Unternehmenssanktionenrecht –*, CCZ 146–152 (2014).

Whistle Blowing und Concern-Management: neue Herausforderungen für Unternehmer und ihre Prüfer, (Matthias Wolz ed., 1. ed. 2007).

Wilbur L. Fugate & Lee H. Simowitz, Foreign commerce and the antitrust laws (5th ed. 1996).

William H. Page & Seldon J. Childers, *Measuring Compliance with Compulsory Licensing Remedies in the American Microsoft Case*, 76 Antitrust Law Journal 239–269 (2009).

Wilma B. Liebman, Labor Law and the Trump Effect, 35. NZA 227–233 (2019).

Wirtschafts- und Steuerstrafrecht | Commentary on Economic and Tax Criminal Law, (Graf, Jäger, & Wittig eds., 2. ed. 2017).

Wolfgang Hromadka, Frank Maschmann & Wolfgang Hromadka, Individual Employment Law (6. ed. 2015).

Wulf A. Kaal & Timothy Lacine, *The Effect of Deferred and Non-Prosecution Agreements on Corporate Governance: Evidence from 1993–2013*, 70 The Business Lawyer 1–60 (2014).

Yael V. Hochberg, Paola Sapienza & Annette Vissing-Jørgensen, *A Lobbying Approach to Evaluating the Sarbanes-Oxley Act of 2002*, 47 Journal of Accounting Research 519–583 (2009).

Zachary S. Brez, Daniel O'Connor & Joseph G. Cleemann, Control Person Liability (2011).

Zack Harmon, *Confronting the New Challenges of FCPA Compliance: Recent Trends in FCPA Enforcement and Practical Guidance for Meeting These Challenges, in* Foreign Corrupt Practices Act compliance issues: leading lawyers on responding to recent FCPA enforcement actions, maintaining an effective compliance program and navigating risk in emerging markets. 62–63 (1. ed. 2010).

www.ingramcontent.com/pod-product-compliance
Ingram Content Group UK Ltd.
Pitfield, Milton Keynes, MK11 3LW, UK
UKHW021830100926
8556IPUK00004B/252

9 783631 798218